THE CAMBRIDGE HISTORY OF EGYPT

VOLUME 2

Modern Egypt, from 1517
to the end of
the twentieth century

⇥⇤

Volume 2 of THE CAMBRIDGE HISTORY OF EGYPT traces Egypt's modern history from the Ottoman conquest in 1517 to the end of the twentieth century. Scholars from the humanities and social sciences have been brought together to explore the political, social and economic history of Egypt under the Ottomans, through the British occupation to the post-independence era. The authors' conclusions not only reflect the work of traditional scholarship, but also indicate important recent advances in historical writing on modern Egypt which have been made possible as archival material becomes more accessible.

M. W. DALY is head of the Department of Humanities and Social Science at Kettering University, Michigan. He has worked extensively on the history of north-east Africa. His publications include *The Sirdar: Sir Reginald Wingate and the British Empire in the Middle East* (1997), *Imperial Sudan: the Anglo-Egyptian Condominium, 1934–1956* (1990), and *Empire on the Nile: the Anglo-Egyptian Sudan, 1898–1934* (1986).

THE CAMBRIDGE HISTORY OF EGYPT

General editor

M. W. DALY

Kettering University, Michigan

➤❮

THE CAMBRIDGE HISTORY OF EGYPT offers the first comprehensive English-language treatment of Egyptian history through thirteen centuries, from the Arab conquest to the end of the twentieth century. The two-volume survey, written by international experts, considers the political, socio-economic and cultural history of the world's oldest state, summarizing the debates and providing insight into current controversies. Implicit in the project is the need to treat Egypt's history as a continuum and at the heart of any regional comparisons. As Egypt reclaims a leading role in the Islamic, Arab and Afro-Asian worlds, the project stands as testimony to its complex and vibrant past. Its balanced and integrated coverage will make an ideal reference tool for students, scholars and general readers.

VOLUME I

Islamic Egypt, 640–1517

Edited by
CARL F. PETRY

VOLUME 2

*Modern Egypt, from 1517
to the end of
the twentieth century*

Edited by
M. W. DALY

THE CAMBRIDGE HISTORY OF EGYPT

VOLUME 2

Modern Egypt, from 1517 to the end of the twentieth century

EDITED BY
M. W. DALY

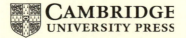

CAMBRIDGE
UNIVERSITY PRESS

PUBLISHED BY THE PRESS SYNDICATE OF THE UNIVERSITY OF CAMBRIDGE
The Pitt Building, Trumpington Street, Cambridge CB2 1RP, United Kingdom

CAMBRIDGE UNIVERSITY PRESS
The Edinburgh Building, Cambridge CB2 2RU, United Kingdom
http://www.cup.cam.ac.uk
40 West 20th Street, New York, NY 10011–4211, USA   http://www.cup.org
10 Stamford Road, Oakleigh, Melbourne 3166, Australia

First published 1998

Printed in Great Britain at the University Press, Cambridge

Typeset in Sabon 9.5/12pt   [CE]

A catalogue record for this book is available from the British Library

The Cambridge history of Egypt / general editor, M. W. Daly.
p.   cm.
Includes bibliographical references.
Contents: v. 1. Islamic Egypt, 640–1571 / edited by Carl F. Petry.
ISBN 0 521 47137 0 (hb)
1. Egypt – History.   I. Daly, M. W.   II. Pertry, Carl F., 1943–   .
DT94.C36   1998
962–dc21   98–16515   CIP

ISBN 0 521 47211 3 hardback

CONTENTS

✦✦

vii

Contents

CONTRIBUTORS

➤⬳

JOEL BEININ is Professor of Middle East History and Director of the Program in Modern Thought and Literature, Stanford University. His recent publications include *Was the Red Flag Flying There? Marxist Politics and the Arab–Israeli Conflict in Egypt and Israel, 1948–1965* (Berkeley, 1990), and *The Dispersion of Egyptian Jewry: Culture, Politics, and the Formation of a Modern Diaspora* (Berkeley, 1998).

SELMA BOTMAN is Vice President for Academic Affairs, University of Massachussetts. She is the author of *The Rise of Egyptian Communism* (Syracuse, 1988) and *From Independence to Revolution: Egypt, 1922–1952* (Syracuse, 1991).

DANIEL CRECELIUS is Professor of History at California State University, Los Angeles. His publications include *The Roots of Modern Egypt: A Study of the Regimes of Ali Bey al-Kabir and Muhammad Bey Abu al-Dhanab, 1760–1775* (Minneapolis and Chicago, 1981) and, as editor, *Eighteenth-century Egypt: The Arabic Manuscript Sources* (Claremont, 1990).

DARRELL DYKSTRA is Professor of History, Western Illinois University. Among his publications are "Pyramids, Prophets, and Progress: Ancient Egypt in the Writings of Ali Mubarak," *Journal of the American Oriental Society* 114 (1994) and "Joseph Hekekyan and the Egyptian School in Paris," *Armenian Review* 35 (1982).

KHALED FAHMY is Assistant Professor, Near East Studies Department, Princeton University. He is the author of *All the Pasha's Men: Mehmed Ali, his Army and the Making of Modern Egypt* (Cambridge, 1997) and, with Enid Hill and Ziad Baha Eldine, of *Re-introducing Capitalism in Egypt* (Cairo, 1998).

NELLY HANNA is Associate Professor in the Department of Arabic Studies, American University in Cairo. She is the author of *Making Big Money in 1600: The Life and Times of Isma'il Abu Taqiyya, Egyptian Merchant* (Syracuse, 1998) and *Habiter au Caire: La maison moyenne et ses habitants aux XVIIe et XVIIIe siècles* (Cairo, 1991) and has edited *The State and its Servants: Administration in Egypt from Ottoman Times to the Present* (Cairo, 1995).

HASSAN AHMED IBRAHIM is Head, Department of History and Civilization, International Islamic University, Malaysia. His publications include *The 1936 Anglo-Egyptian Treaty* (Khartoum, 1976), *Rihlat Muhammad Ali fil Sudan*, 2nd ed. (Khartoum, 1994), and many articles on the Sudan under Ottoman and British rule.

JANE HATHAWAY is Associate Professor of History, Ohio State University. Her publications include *The Politics of Households in Ottoman Egypt: The Rise of the Qazdaglis* (Cambridge, 1997).

F. ROBERT HUNTER is Professor of Middle Eastern History, Tulane University. His published works include *Egypt under the Khedives 1805–1879* (Pittsburgh, 1984).

DONALD MALCOLM REID is Professor of History, Georgia State University. He is the author of *Cairo University and the Making of Modern Egypt* (Cambridge, 1990) and *Lawyers and Politics in the Arab World, 1880–1960* (Minneapolis and Chicago, 1981).

ALAIN ROUSSILLON is director of research in the Centre national de la Recherche scientifique, Rabat.

PAUL STARKEY is Senior Lecturer in Arabic, University of Durham. His publications include *From the Ivory Tower: A Critical Study of Tawfiq al-Hakim* (London, 1987) and, as co-editor (with Julie Meisami), the *Encyclopaedia of Arabic Literature* (London, 1998).

EHUD TOLEDANO is Professor in the Department of Middle Eastern and African History, Tel Aviv University. Among other works he has written *State and Society in Mid-Nineteenth-Century Egypt* (Cambridge, 1990) and *The Ottoman Slave Trade and its Suppression, 1840–1890* (Princeton, 1982).

MICHAEL WINTER is Professor in the department of Middle Eastern and African History, Tel Aviv University.

PREFACE

✦

The Cambridge History of Egypt attempts to fill a gap in English-language treatment of Egyptian history since the Arab conquest. Given the long and continuing outside interest in Egypt, that such a treatment is overdue seems surprising; the very length of Egyptian history has inevitably led to its compartmentalization and to the increasing specialization of scholars interested in it. Essential, underlying continuities have sometimes therefore been obscured, while superficial points of demarcation have sometimes been exaggerated.

Advances in research in the last half-century amply justified the editors in undertaking this task. An explosion of interest in Egypt, the development of new disciplines and methods of academic research, and the increasing availability of Egyptian archival sources have led not only to important progress in the understanding of Egypt's past, but also to ever-increasing specialization in outlook, method, and, therefore, in the audiences to which historical writing has been addressed.

The Cambridge History is therefore an attempt to present a comprehensive survey for a general audience, to make use of recent advances in historical knowledge, and to synthesize from discrete sources – increasingly from fields beyond the traditional bounds of history – Egypt's political and cultural history since the coming of Islam.

This second volume of the *History* deals with "modern" Egypt, by which we mean Egypt since the Ottoman conquest in 1517 until the present day. The main object of this volume has been to bring together – from an increasingly wide spectrum of the humanities and social sciences – mainly younger scholars with an interest in the comprehensive, political, social and economic history of Egypt since the coming of the Ottomans. There have been particular needs to tie together periodical and monographic work on the earlier half of the period, before 1790, and to take account of new approaches from the social sciences; both political and socio-economic history, and indeed other fields have made increasingly important use of

xi

Egyptian archival sources, with consequences for both the focus and the results of historical research. Thus in terms of contributors, their backgrounds and research interests, their sources and their conclusions, this volume attempts not only to build upon the work of older scholarship but also to indicate present trends and future directions in historical writing on Egypt.

At various stages of this project the editor has had the generous assistance of William Murnane, Eberhard Kienle, Michaele Kennedy, and Marigold Acland and her colleagues at the Press, and the enthusiastic support and collaboration of Carl Petry.

M. W. DALY

NOTE ON TRANSLITERATION

><

The system of Arabic transliteration employed is that of the *International Journal of Middle East Studies*. Terms in other languages and styles have been rendered according to the usages of individual chapter contributors. In this connection, it should be noted that the Turkish name Mehmet ʿAli is rendered Muhammad ʿAli throughout, to conform to the standard transliteration.

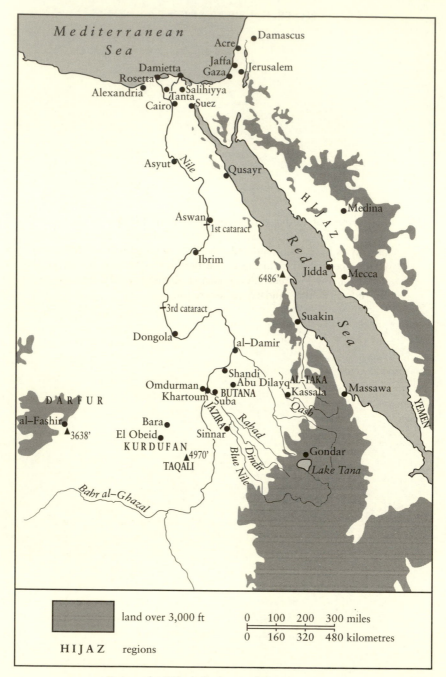

Egypt, the Nilotic Sudan, and the Hijaz

Ottoman Egypt, 1525–1609

MICHAEL WINTER

✦✦

The period 1525–1609 covers approximately the first third of the history of
Ottoman Egypt, and has distinct characteristics. It starts with the pacification of the country after the suppression of Ahmad Pasha al-Kha'in's revolt
and of the serious disturbances by Bedouin tribes that followed it, and the
promulgation of the code for the government of Egypt, *Qanun-name-i Misir*
by the grand vizier Ibrahim Pasha. Egypt remained tranquil and passive
under Ottoman rule that was firm and effective. Around the late 1580s,
however, the army became unruly owing to economic difficulties and in the
context of the general decline of the Ottoman empire. After that the viceroys
had increasing difficulty maintaining their rule. The whole period, which can
be described as the ascendancy of the viceroys (or pashas), ends in 1609 with
suppression of a serious soldiers' rebellion by a strong viceroy. New political
forces came to the fore, and the viceroys acted merely as formal representatives of the sultan.

The main sources

Historians attempting to describe the period face a dilemma of meager
source materials. Egypt during the Mamluk period is unusually rich in
historical sources – chronicles, biographical dictionaries, handbooks, and
the like. The last decades before the Ottoman occupation, the conquest
itself, and the next six years (until Dhu l-Hijja 928/November 1522) are
superbly covered by Ibn Iyas, one of the best representatives of the great
Egyptian historiographic tradition. 'Abd al-Samad al-Diyarbakri, an
Ottoman judge who came to Egypt with Salim's army, stayed there to serve
as a *qadi*. His chronicle is a translation into Turkish of Ibn Iyas's work, with
significant changes, and then a detailed continuation of the chronicle for a
period of two-and-a-half years (up to Shawwal 931/July 1525). Then the
narrative coverage stops abruptly, and it is not resumed before the first half
of the next century, and then by chronicles that, their importance notwith-

standing, fall below the quality of Mamluk historiography. This means that the greater part of the sixteenth century, the crucial period of transition, when the Ottoman regime was finally established in Egypt, is not covered by local contemporary chronicles.

One can only speculate about the reasons for this dramatic interruption of historical writing in Ottoman Egypt. The fact that Egypt was relegated from imperial to provincial status must be a part of the explanation. Cairo no longer had a sultan, but a viceroy whose term was renewed on an annual basis. The new rulers were complete strangers to Egypt and its culture, much more so than the Mamluks, who were at home in Egypt, did not have a home anywhere else, and were accustomed to local society. Many historians belonged to the *awlad al-nas* class; Ibn Iyas is a notable example. As historians, they were in an ideal position: they maintained close ties with the ruling military elite, and had good inside information about state affairs. On the other hand, they already were assimilated into the Egyptian people, completely identified with the Egyptians, and were immersed in the local society, language, and culture. The Ottoman occupation naturally changed all that.

Another possible explanation for the paucity of Egyptian historiography during those times is political. Sultan Sulayman's era (1520–66) was glorious and eventful, with many wars and victories, but Egypt remained in the empire's backwater. Its inhabitants did not witness the drama of the center. For a long time no extraordinary political events took place that would excite chroniclers' imagination or an impulse to record them. The times were relatively quiet, and Egypt enjoyed stable and orderly rule.

Indeed, in the early seventeenth century stormy developments took place in Egypt and are recorded in detail by Muhammad ibn Abi l-Surur al-Bakri al-Siddiqi, the most important Egyptian chronicler in the seventeenth century.[1] He was a member of an aristocratic Sufi family and had connections in government circles. Arabic and Turkish historical works that provide information about the early seventeenth century are also available.[2]

The scarcity of local contemporary chronicles in Egypt in the sixteenth century is somewhat compensated for by other sources. Qutb al-Din al-Nahrawali, a resident of Mecca of Indian descent, wrote an important chronicle mainly describing the Ottomans' exploits in Yemen. Yet the work includes information about Egyptian affairs, since Egypt was the strategic and logistic base for operations in the Red Sea region. A book by 'Abd al-Qadir al-Jaziri, who served for many years as secretary of the annual hajj

[1] On him, see Abdul Karim Rafeq, "Ibn Abi l-Surur and his Works," *Bulletin of the School of Oriental and African Studies*, 38/1 (1975), 24–31.

[2] For bibliographical surveys, see articles by P. M. Holt on Arabic sources and S. J. Shaw on Turkish sources in P. M. Holt (ed.), *Political and Social Change in Modern Egypt* (London, 1968).

caravan (he succeeded his father in that office), is an excellent source on the hajj. In addition, his book provides limited but interesting information about all the *umara' al-hajj*, commanders of the pilgrims' caravan, down to the year 957/1550.

The writings of 'Abd al-Wahhab al-Sha'rani (d. 1565), the most important Sufi of his time, throw light on the social and religious life of Egypt, although they are worthless for political history. There are also copious Hebrew sources, mainly the rabbinical responsa, which teach us a great deal about the Jewish community and the economy in general.

We have also a unique and fascinating description, in Turkish, of Cairo in 1599 by Mustafa 'Ali, a renowned Ottoman writer, intellectual, and traveler, whose account is too literary to be dependable but has many insightful and vivid observations on Egyptian society, including many important facts concerning the ruling class and the army.

The great advantage students of Ottoman history have over students of other pre-modern periods are the Ottoman archives. Yet, unfortunately, even the Ottoman archival sources concerning Egypt start to be abundant only toward the end of Sultan Sulayman's reign, leaving a gap of the crucial five decades following the conquest in 1517; several documents, mostly imperial decrees, provide some interesting information about earlier events. The best and richest corpus of documents for the period under study are the imperial decrees preserved in the Muhimme defterleri collection, located in the central Turkish archives of the Prime Minister's Bureau in Istanbul. One particularly valuable document from the Turkish archives is the detailed budget of Ottoman Egypt for 1005–06/1596–97, which has been published with an English translation.[3]

One kind of important archival source, available for many other Ottoman provinces, is missing. The Ottomans did not apply in Egypt the *timar* system, the typical fiscal and military organization of their territories. For the purpose of the *timar*, the Ottoman administration carried out detailed surveys of the provinces; these registers are gold mines of information for historians. The government's decision not to apply the system in Egypt, to avoid disrupting its time-honored and complex administrative and fiscal traditions, seems sound, but deprives historians of an extremely useful research tool.

Egypt as an Ottoman province

Egypt was the largest Ottoman province. It is hard to exaggerate its strategic and economic importance for the empire. True to their policy of pragmatism,

---

[3] Stanford J. Shaw, *The Budget of Ottoman Egypt, 1005–1006/1596–1597* (The Hague and Paris, 1968).

flexibility, and economy, the Ottomans clearly regarded Egypt as a special case. The *timar* system, which usually sealed the full integration of a province into the empire, was not applied to Egypt. The Ottomans must have understood that the prosperity of Egypt depended to a large extent on the complex and sensitive irrigation system of the water of the Nile. To ensure profits from agriculture, it made sense to refrain from interfering with local technical, administrative, and fiscal practices and traditions.

It should also be remembered that the *timar* was an administrative and fiscal system supporting a huge territorial army of cavalry, which would always be ready to be called up for campaigns. Considering the size of the country, Egypt's garrison was relatively small (about ten thousand men). Egypt was remote from the Ottoman center and from the main fronts in eastern Europe and Persia. Service in Egypt was usually considered by Ottoman soldiers as pleasant and tranquil compared with the rigors suffered in the heartland of the empire.[4] The tasks assigned to the army in Egypt were mostly defensive – garrisoning the capital, the provinces, and the ports, protecting the hajj caravan, and guarding ports along the pilgrims' route. Occasionally an Egyptian contingent was sent to join the main imperial army in Europe or on the Persian front, but these expeditionary forces were rare and small during the period in question. The Ottomans' efforts to pacify Yemen were an exception: many soldiers were sent from Egypt to fight the Yemeni tribesmen, but these units were reinforced by soldiers who were sent to Egypt especially for the purpose.

The value of Egypt to the empire was both strategic and economic. Egypt was an important base for operations in the Red Sea region, in Yemen, Ethiopia (Habesh), and the Hijaz. In the sixteenth century the port of Suez was expanded and included a considerable shipyard. In 1568 the Ottomans even attempted to construct a canal at the isthmus of Suez. The Mamluks had not been interested in having a navy, mainly because of a cultural bias against seafaring, but also because they did not think they needed it. Then the Portuguese surprised them and others by finding the sea route to India and disrupting the Indian spice trade through the Middle East. Consequently, the Mamluks turned for help to the Ottomans. After the annexation of Egypt, responsibility to resist the Portuguese passed to the Ottomans. The Portuguese were consolidating their base in India, attacking Muslim navigation in the Indian Ocean and penetrating the Red Sea, thereby threatening Islam's holiest places. The Ottomans were better prepared to face the challenge, since they had wide naval experience, rich resources, and, unlike the Mamluks, an offensive strategy. Nevertheless, the Ottomans were not successful in defeating the Portuguese convincingly. In 1538 they sent their

---

[4] See M. Winter, "Ali Efendi's 'Anatolian Campaign Book': A Defense of the Egyptian Army in the Seventeenth Century," *Turcica*, 15 (1983), 267–309.

navy to India under the command of Sulayman Pasha, viceroy of Egypt. En route, Sulayman captured Aden from an Arab ruler. In India the local Muslims betrayed him, and he was defeated by the Portuguese.

The Ottomans thereupon decided to consolidate control in the Red Sea. This strategy required establishment of bases in Yemen and Ethiopia. In Ethiopia, Imam Ahmad Gragn, a Muslim warrior for the faith, needed military aid. The Ottomans were busy fighting in Yemen against the Zaydi tribesmen, and their assistance was limited. The Christian Ethiopians, aided by a Portuguese force, put an end to Gragn's jihad (1543). Yet in 1555 the Ottomans from their base in Egypt established the Habesh Eyaleti, the province of Ethiopia, on the African Red Sea littoral and with its capital at Massawa. The man who acted for the Ottomans in Ethiopia, as previously in Nubia, was Özdemir Pasha, a former Circassian Mamluk and Ottoman governor of Yemen.[5]

Like conquerors before and after them, the Ottomans discovered that it was easier to invade Yemen than to control it. The Shi'i Zaydi imams revolted against the Ottomans and by 1567 the whole Yemen was lost except Zabid near the coast. It was during the reign of Sultan Salim II, Sulayman's son, that Yemen was reconquered (1569–70) by Sinan Pasha, viceroy of Egypt. Egypt's viceroys, and several of their ablest commanders, personally led the expeditions to Yemen, and Egyptian soldiers in large numbers were sent to conquer and hold this remote outpost of empire.

The acquisition of Egypt gave the Ottoman empire a huge economic and financial advantage. Revenues from land tax, urban taxes, and customs duties at sea and river ports financed the viceroy and his household, the army, and expenditures for operations overseas. In addition, the Egyptian treasury covered many expenditures of the annual hajj caravan, and supplied grain and financial support to inhabitants of the two holy cities in the Hijaz. Numerous religious and charitable projects in Egypt itself were supported by the treasury. The balance of Egypt's budget was sent each year as *irsaliyya Khazina* (Turkish *irsaliye-i hazine*; lit. remittance of the treasury) to Istanbul. The amount was fixed at 16 million *paras* a year after the conquest. At the end of the century, it rose to 20 million *paras*.[6] Egypt also provided the Ottoman center with various products and foodstuffs. Sugar, rice, lentils, and coffee were sent to the imperial kitchens and pantries. Egypt's viceroy was often ordered to send military supplies for the army and navy, such as gunpowder, twine, and cord.

It would be wrong to assume that this obvious exploitation of Egypt meant greater economic hardship than before the conquest. The country was

---

[5] On the Ottomans' policy in Ethiopia, see H. Erlich, *Ethiopia and the Middle East* (Boulder and London, 1994), 33–37.

[6] The *para* was the principal coin in circulation in Ottoman Egypt. Forty *paras* were equal to one gold coin.

now integrated in a vast empire enjoying a long period of prosperity and good government by the standards of the day. The economy of Egypt before the Ottoman conquest had been in a sorry state, and Ottoman rule brought prosperity and development, at least in the early period. Cairo benefited from commerce, stimulated by the annual pilgrimage to Mecca; Ottoman power and prestige made the pilgrimage safer and more orderly than before. Egyptian merchants (and the government) made profits from the international coffee trade, which began in the early sixteenth century and eventually took the place formerly occupied by the spice trade. Ottoman Cairo was the seat of a pasha and a center with a large number of soldiers and bureaucrats who consumed great quantities of luxury goods.[7]

The construction of magnificent monuments, such as mosques and mausoleums, for which the Mamluk sultanate was famous, ceased with the Ottoman occupation. The explanation for this is simple: Mamluk sultans and high-ranking amirs saw Egypt as their only home, where they planned to live, die, and be buried. They wished to immortalize themselves by building imperial mosques and tombs. The Ottoman viceroys' term of office in Egypt was temporary, often very short, and they expected to go back to the center; the pashas did not have the time, motivation, or the funds to undertake construction of monuments. Besides, the Ottoman sultan would not have allowed his viceroy to build an "imperial" mosque for himself. Nevertheless, there is evidence that the viceroys contributed a great deal to the economic and religious life of Egypt, and to Cairo in particular. They established many *waqf* foundations, and constructed mosques, shrines, and Sufi cloisters. One (Mustafa Pasha, 1560–63) built residences in Old Cairo and used revenues from the project for a *waqf* to finance charity. Al-Azhar was renovated. The treasury paid for soup kitchens for the poor and water supplies for pilgrims.

In contrast to Ibn Iyas's extreme hostility toward the Ottomans at the time of the occupation, the next generation of Egyptian writers, and Arab writers generally, viewed the Ottomans much more favorably. The historians and men of religion who have been mentioned above, such as al-Shaʿrani, al-Jaziri, al-Nahrawali, Ibn Abi l-Surur, and others, praise the Ottoman state, and especially its ruling dynasty, as impeccably Islamic. Sometimes flattery can explain these attitudes, but it cannot be the whole answer. There are indications that as the sixteenth century progressed, the empire was increasingly orthodox. There was a variety of reasons for this process, such as the empire's position between its adversaries, the Catholics in the west and the Shiʿis in the east. The Ottoman occupation of the Arab lands with their venerated traditions of Sunni religiosity and learning certainly played a

[7] A. Raymond, "The Ottoman Conquest and the Development of the Great Arab Towns," *International Journal of Turkish Studies*, 1/1 (1979–80), 84–101.

major role, although the impact of those conquests on Ottoman Islam still awaits a thorough study.

Naturally, the Ottomans and their subjects in Egypt (and elsewhere) became accustomed to each other. Their rulers accommodated their interests to local needs and sensibilities. They acted as patrons of Islam in many ways – taking care of the Hajj and the holy cities, supporting religious institutions, 'ulama', and Sufis, and emphasizing their adherence to the Shari'a. Yet all this did not preclude Egyptian–Turkish tensions and antipathies. Temperamental differences were too great to be overlooked, and stereotypes were created on both sides. Egyptians often saw the Turks as bad Muslims and people of harsh character. Turks questioned the Egyptians' ability to rule and fight: they used pejorative terms, such as "fallahin," "*Tat*," or "*Miqlaji*," in referring to Egyptians, and considered them socially inferior.

Salim was the only Ottoman sultan to visit Egypt until the nineteenth century. Egyptians regarded his successors as distant, though generally benevolent, figures. Chroniclers noted their accession to the throne and their deaths, but little else. In Cairo, celebration of the birth of a sultan's son or an Ottoman victory in war was limited to decorating the shops and houses, and firing cannons.

It should be emphasized that before the end of the eighteenth century the Ottoman sultan did not claim the title of caliph, but by then political conditions had changed. When the empire was at its zenith in the sixteenth and seventeenth centuries, the sultanate was strong enough not to need the historically loaded title "caliph." Historians have shown that the claim that the last 'Abbasid caliph of Cairo transferred his "rights" to Salim I after the Ottoman conquest of Egypt was a myth created in the late eighteenth century. Some panegyrists call the Ottomans "the inheritors of royalty and the caliphate," but this was an honorary title devoid of political or religious significance.

The pashas

In Egypt, as in most Ottoman provinces, the governor or viceroy was the sultan's representative and was personally responsible for protecting the state's interests. He was the addressee of the sultan's edicts dispatched to the province about almost all matters. He was supreme commander of the army in Egypt with the rank of pasha; several pashas also held the rank of vizier. In the sixteenth and early seventeenth centuries the viceroy was called *Misir beylerbeyi* (or in some financial documents *mirmiran*, the Persian equivalent) in the official language. The viceroy carried out administrative work through the Diwan, or council of state, which convened four times a week and was modeled on the sultan's Diwan in Istanbul.

The viceroy's appointment was for one year, but it was usually renewed for another two or three years. It also happened that a pasha was recalled after only a few months in office. The typical incumbency during the period under study was two or three years. Exceptions were the long terms of the vizier Sulayman Pasha (1525–38 including an interval of less than two years, when he was sent on a naval expedition to the Indian Ocean), and his successor Da'ud Pasha, who died in office after eleven years (1538–49).

The majority of the viceroys are not identifiable by ethnicity: it seems that they were recruited and trained through the Ottoman *devshirme* system, i.e., they were military slaves born as Christians in the Balkans. Three viceroys are described as a Bosnian, an Albanian, and a Circassian. One (Muhammad Pasha, 1596–98) was called *sharif*, as if a descendant of the Prophet; what is certain is that he was a Muslim from birth.

Several viceroys arrived in Egypt directly from the sultan's household. In the sixteenth century no fewer than six pashas were given the title of *hadim* (Arabic: *khadim*), "servant," a euphemism for eunuch, i.e., they were eunuchs who started their careers in the sultan's household. Mustafa 'Ali, a well-known Ottoman historian, writer, and poet, who visited Egypt at the end of the sixteenth century, explains: "It was the custom at the time ... that the governorship of Egypt was given to persons of the eunuch class whenever it became vacant, because they are free of the care for wives and children, and all their possessions revert in the end to the sultan."[8] Five of those who came from the sultan's palace had been officials in charge of the sultan's finances (as *daftardar* or *khazindar*); they must have had the expertise to manage a big budget and had, of course, the sultan's trust. Two viceroys, Uveys Pasha (1587–91) and Ibrahim Pasha (1604) had been *qadis*, then *daftardars*. Two came from military service at the imperial court. The governorship of Egypt was given to several governors of lesser provinces as a promotion. Thus, viceroys of Egypt had previously been governors in Yemen (two viceroys), Erzerum, Diyarbakr, Baghdad, and Cyprus. One viceroy had previously held the lower rank of *sanjaq beyi*, and on his appointment to Egypt was promoted to *beylerbeyi*.

The career of Mustafa Pasha is an exceptional case of a man who rose from the humblest origins to become governor of Egypt from 1561 until 1565. After serving as a saddler for the army, he became rich by looting the treasury of Ahmad Pasha "the traitor." He managed to be appointed as *kashif* and later became *amir al-hajj*. As such he earned the nickname *al-nashshar*, "the sawyer," for executing bandits along the pilgrim route by sawing them in half. After serving as *amir al-hajj* for nine years from 938/ 1532, he was eventually made governor of Yemen and finally of Egypt itself.

The ruler's religious attitudes were crucial to his public image. Several pashas were known by epithets that indicated religious inclinations. *Khadim*

---

[8] *Mustafa Ali's Description of Cairo of 1599*, ed. A. Tietze (Vienna, 1975), 73.

Hafiz Muhammad Pasha (1591–95) knew the Qur'an by heart (as his epithet indicates) and read it every Friday. Iskander Pasha (appointed in 1568) was known as *al-Faqih*, "the jurisconsult." In the period under study, two pashas were known as "the Sufi": Sufi 'Ali Pasha (1563–65) reportedly wore only coarse woolen clothes and paid many visits to tombs of saints in the Qarafa (Cairo's famous cemetery). Ibrahim Pasha (who was killed in 1604 by rebellious soldiers) had been a Mevlevi dervish in Konya.

Most of the pashas were reportedly pious men who adhered to the Shari'a. However, there was an exception. Dugakin-Oglu Muhammad Pasha (1554–56) was described as a wanton man; he was recalled at Sultan Sulayman's order on charges of violating the Shari'a and was executed. There were a few pashas who cut the 'ulama''s pensions, according to Ibn Abi l-Surur, the historian who expresses the sentiments and interests of men of religion.

Chroniclers usually distinguish popular and good rulers from cruel and hated ones. Some were generous and benevolent, others selfish, oppressive, and rapacious. Some pashas failed to deal efficiently with gangs of criminals, others were notorious for the ease with which they put people to death for the slightest offense.

The Ottoman army in Egypt in the sixteenth century

The Ottoman garrison in Egypt consisted of seven corps (*ojaqs*). The Janissaries, an elite infantry corps, had as their main task guarding Cairo and the Citadel, hence their other title, Mustahfizan, "Guardians." This was the largest and most important unit. The 'Azab infantry corps was less important than the Janissaries regiment, and was smaller in number. They were also guards, but on a subordinate level to the Janissaries, and were stationed at the approaches to the Citadel and to the seaports of Egypt. The Mutafarriqa and the Chavush (pursuivants) were two small units of both infantry and cavalry, who served as the viceroy's guards. The Chavush corps was created in 1524 and the Mutafarriqa in 1554. These were elite corps whose members were ranked above regular soldiers, although they were not amirs. The authorities trusted them even as general discipline declined. Members of these corps were often appointed as provincial governors and financial agents for the treasury (*kashifs* and *amins*) and this increased their chances of promotion to the beylicate. Some added to their income by serving as directors or trustees of *waqf* foundations or by tax-farming. There were also three cavalry (*sipahi*) corps, the Gonulluyan ("volunteers"), and Tufenkjiyan (Riflemen). The *Qanun-name* makes it clear that the former were armed with javelins and bows and arrows, while the latter used handguns, as their name indicates. The fact that the Mamluks were organized as a separate regiment, given the name *Cherakise ojagi*, the Circassian corps, is stated in the *Qanun-name*. In addition, there were units of soldiers who manned the forts in Egypt and along the hajj route, corps of armorers (*jebejiyan*) and cannoneers (*topchiyan*).

The seven corps of which the army consisted remained the official framework of Egypt's military organization throughout the Ottoman period, although, as will be seen in the following chapters, their importance would undergo profound fluctuations, and finally decline.

A soldier's income consisted of basic pay, *ibtida* (lit. start) according to his regiment or rank, plus bonuses, *teraqqi* (lit. a raise). A soldier was entitled to additional pay if he went on a campaign or was especially recommended. Also, when a new pasha took up his appointment, the troops demanded, and usually received, a special payment. In 1606–07, when a pasha refused to give this money, the rebellious troops collapsed his tent over his head.

Soldiers' pay was calculated in *aqchas* on a daily basis, and usually ranged from about six to twelve, according to the corps. The highest paid were the small elite guards units of the Mutafarriqa and Chavush, then the cavalry – Gonullu, Tufenkji, and Circassians, in that order, and finally the Janissaries and the 'Azab. The latter two were large and strong; they were stationed in the capital, and had means – often illegal – of increasing their income. In addition to salaries, soldiers were entitled to grain rations from the imperial granaries in Cairo and fodder for their animals. Retired soldiers, soldiers' widows, and orphans were given pensions.

The viceroy and highest-ranking amirs received yearly salaries (*salyane*). The viceroy's salary in the sixteenth century was 2 million *osmanis*, which equaled 20 million *aqchas*. The viceroy was assisted by high-ranking amirs called bey, or variably *sanjaq beyi*, or in the terminology of the financial documents, *mirliva* (the Persian form) or *Muhafaza beyi*. Unlike the situation in other Ottoman provinces, where *sanjaq* (lit. a standard, flag) meant a district under the jurisdiction of a *sanjaq beyi*, in Egypt the term did not have a territorial connotation (since the *timar* system was not applied there). Beys were given various assignments, such as *daftardar* (financial superintendent), *amir al-hajj* (commander of the pilgrims' caravan), captains of Egypt's ports, governors of rural provinces, *sirdars* (commanders of task forces to fight Bedouin or to lead the Egyptian contingent to the European or Persian fronts), or *amir khazna* (commander of the guard that conveyed overland the annual tribute of Egypt to Istanbul).

Several beys could remain without a specific assignment, awaiting an appointment. Some had previously been commanders (*aghas*) of one of the seven corps, and were promoted to the beylicate.

The beys' annual salaries ranged from 200,000 *osmanis* (or 2 million *aqchas*), mostly given to those who did not have specific assignments in that fiscal year, up to more than 500,000 *osmanis*, usually paid to those who held responsible positions which required many expenses, such as the *daftardar*, *amir al-hajj*, or captains of the ports of Alexandria, Damietta, and Suez. The highest salaries were to beys fulfilling these positions or to former holders of such assignments, either to cover past expenses or as recognition of their status.

Mustafa 'Ali, who describes Egypt at about the same time, names thirty beys. He complains of deterioration in the background and qualifications of the beys. Instead of coming from the palace or imperial military establishment as they should have, they were upstarts in the service of rich Arabs or veterans of service in Yemen. A bey's commission or *sanjaq* was sometimes given to a pasha's son, a Meccan *sharif*, or even to members of the 'ulama' class. It is important to note that none of the beys in the sixteenth century was a Mamluk and that the beylicate at this time had nothing to do with the high amirate of the Mamluk sultanate.

It was the intention of the government that the number of the beys in Egypt should not exceed twelve, yet their number at the end of the century had more than tripled. The budget of 1596/97 shows that forty-one *sanjaq beyis* received salaries. In 1609, at the end of the period under study, when Muhammad Pasha reorganized the army after putting down a military mutiny, he dismissed all but twelve of the ablest beys, banishing the other seventeen to Istanbul. But this measure was abandoned, and the number of beys again reached forty by the mid-seventeenth century.

The survival of Mamluks under Ottoman rule

The survival of the Mamluks and their eventual resumption of prominence and power is the most obscure but intriguing question in Egyptian political and social history during the Ottoman period. One obstacle to tracing their history is the scarcity of source material dating to the first decades of Ottoman rule. Another lies in the fact that after the conquest Mamluks were no longer called by the Turkish names that had distinguished them from their Arabic-speaking subjects. Now they were a part of a larger military ruling elite that was Turcophone, and in addition used Islamic, that is Arabic, names: the sultans themselves had Arabic names. It was impossible, then, for the Mamluks to be given Turkish names.[9]

As has been mentioned, the Mamluks were organized in the Circassian *ojaq*. This particular corps, one of the three cavalry *ojaqs*, never assumed a significant role. There is evidence that there were also Mamluks in other corps. Mamluks are mentioned in the service of high-ranking officers and

---

[9] See D. Ayalon, "Studies in Al-Jabarti," *Journal of the Economic and Social History of the Orient*, 3, part 2 (August 1960), 152–58.

dignitaries from the *beylerbeyi* down, and they served within the regular units (apart from the Circassian regiment), and also as retainers of military grandees outside the official payroll. Al-Jaziri, the secretary of the hajj caravan, provides many details about forces accompanying the caravan. He speaks of Mamluks of *amir al-hajj* as distinct from soldiers belonging to the regular corps.

The chief keepers of Mamluk identity and traditions were not Mamluk soldiers serving in the *cherakise ojagi* or in other units or in other units or places, but ranking Circassian beys (*cherakise beyleri*). They appear in the sixteenth- and seventeenth-century sources – archival materials and chronicles alike – as an identifiable group, distinct from both common Circassians and beys, who are referred to as *sanjaq beyleri* or *muhafaza beyleri* (defender beys). This distinction between the two categories of beys gives a clue about the Mamluk phenomenon in Ottoman Egypt, since here alone we have a clearly recognizable group with Mamluk values and traditions. The Circassian beys were, of course, army commanders, who were sometimes specifically mentioned in imperial decrees calling upon Egypt to send a contingent to the sultan's campaigns.[10] In festive processions, the *cherakise beyleri* marched separately under their own flags.

It is important not to confuse the Circassian beys (i.e. Mamluk amirs) with the above-mentioned beys (called also *sanjaq beyi* or *muhafaza beyi*). The order of the addressees in imperial edicts reflects the hierarchy: *muhafaza beyleri, cherakise beyleri* (also: *umara-i cherakise*), Mutafarriqa, and Chavush. Another edict orders that only higher-ranking officers, namely Circassian beys, Mutafarriqa, and Chavush be given villages to administer for the treasury, but not the lower-ranking cavalry corps of the Gonulluyan, sipahis, and the cherakise (the last being Mamluks who had not reached the rank of bey). The Circassian beys, then, were among the elite cavalry officers above the Mutafarriqa and Chavush and well below the *sanjaq beyleri*. Among other things, the beys had the authority to impose the death sentence, which the Circassian beys did not have.[11]

The Circassian beys were particularly useful as *kashifs*. The *kashif* had the responsibility of ensuring that dams and canals were in good condition. (*Kashif* is a shortened form of *kashif al-jusur al-sultaniyya*, "supervisor of the imperial dams.") He had to protect his region against marauding Arab tribesmen. Sultan Salim appointed at least one Ottoman officer as *kashif*, but soon Mamluk amirs were reappointed to these positions. During serious Bedouin disturbances following the revolt of Ahmad Pasha al-Kha'in, the performance of Ottoman commanders against the rebels was disastrous.

[10] See, for example, Muhimme defteri, vol. 27, no. 282, p. 118, Shawwal 25, 982 (January 25, 1576); vol. 59, no. 34, p. 10, Rabi' 1, 5, 993 (March 7, 1585).

[11] Muhimme defteri, vol. 39, no. 418, p. 203, Muharram 10, 988 (February 26, 1580); vol. 24, no. 616, pp. 232–33, Muharram 26, 982 (May 18, 1547).

Obviously, the Mamluk amirs' experience and knowledge of the terrain made them indispensable for the Ottoman government.

While Cairo was guarded and policed by regular Ottoman troops, Mamluk amirs controlled much of the countryside in their capacity as *kashifs*. It is remarkable that Mustafa ʿAli, writing at the end of the century about the oppressive rule of the *kashifs* and *multazims* (tax-farmers), says that this was "according to the Circassian law" (*cherkes qanunu uzere*). This does not mean that every *kashif* was necessarily a Circassian (Mamluk), although many certainly were, but it does indicate that the provincial administrative system was still based on Mamluk methods and traditions.

The Mamluks' experience and background convinced the Ottomans that Circassian amirs were natural and even preferable candidates to serve as *umaraʾ al-hajj*. An *amir al-hajj* had to protect the caravan against Bedouin who often attacked and pillaged it, or to negotiate and induce them to cooperate with the hajj rather than endanger it. Al-Jaziri writes in detail about *umaraʾ al-hajj* during the first thirty-three years of Ottoman rule, and provides information about the men who were appointed. The list from 1517 until 1550, where al-Jaziri's book ends, names fifteen *umaraʾ al-hajj*, six of whom were Mamluk amirs; some held the post for several years. Janim al-Hamzawi, who has already been mentioned, held the post several times, as did his son Yusuf. Janim al-Hamzawi was not a Mamluk, but belonged to the *awlad al-nas* class. From al-Jaziri's description it is also clear that experience as a *kashif* was an important asset for a candidate for the office. Even a few non-Mamluks, who were named *umaraʾ al-hajj*, had been *kashifs* before.

Problems of discipline and tensions in the army

Among other subjects, the *Qanun-name-i Misir* draws guidelines for maintaining order and discipline in the army. The principles underlying the policy expounded in the document are familiar from other Ottoman provinces. While accepting local conditions, the central government was obviously determined to control even the smallest details. The promulgators of the code were also aware of some cases of officers and soldiers breaking the law and military discipline. Indeed, some transgressions observed at such an early stage of the occupation were to grow and eventually transform military society, with far-reaching consequences for Egyptian society as a whole.

The insistence in the *Qanun-name* on strict discipline is, of course, typical of military codes. What should be noted is that Istanbul did not leave any autonomy to the viceroy of Egypt; all appointments in the ranks were subject to approval. The central government feared that the force in a distant and wealthy province such as Egypt might increase in numbers beyond the limits set by the government. This would burden the treasury, and also allow undesirable elements to enter the army. These apprehensions were well founded.

There is sufficient evidence that Egypt was, indeed, considered a safe place to do military service, even a refuge for shirkers from the empire's constant wars. An imperial decree dated 1605 states openly that soldiers desiring to avoid a military campaign were acquiring an imperial edict (emr-i sherif) "by certain means" and then going to Egypt under the pretext of official business. The pasha of Egypt is ordered to ignore these ill-gotten edicts and send the men to the front.[12] Worse still, the phrasing of several of the sultan's edicts reveals that, contrary to Istanbul's almost absolute control over Egyptian affairs at the beginning of the occupation, by the late sixteenth century the Ottoman high command had lost confidence in its own orderliness and integrity. Edicts dated 1591 and 1595 inform the beylerbeyi of Egypt that certain individuals had obtained appointments in Egypt's administration through connections in Istanbul. The governor is ordered to ignore the decrees and appointments (berat), to appoint no one before a position is vacated (mahlul), and to rely on his own sound judgment so as not to overburden the treasury. At the same time, Istanbul admits that the situation in Egypt is extremely "disorderly and muddled," and tries to determine the exact number of soldiers, their salaries, and ranks.

The relatively good life in Egypt and its remoteness from Istanbul contributed to the growth of the Egyptian bureaucracy and army, which imperial edicts frequently criticize. One decree dated 1568 states that there were more Chavush and Mutafarriqa soldiers in Egypt than in Istanbul itself. It further adds that the numbers should not exceed those specified in the Qanun-name (where only forty Chavushes are allowed). In 1573 there were 450 Chavushes, although only 180 (and 180 Mutafarriqa) were allowed at the time. There were considerable increases in other units also: in 1565 there were 1,400 Janissaries instead of the 1,000 allowed, and 700 'Azab soldiers instead of 500.[13]

According to firmly held convictions (or prejudices) of the period, only certain races were fit for military service. By the standards of medieval and late medieval Islam, the best qualified to fight were the Turks. Of course, the definition of this term was loose. We have seen that Circassians were regarded by Arab historians during the Mamluk sultanate as Turks, or at least as a division of the Turkish race. Similarly, many Turkish-speaking Ottoman soldiers, most notably the Janissaries, were not Turks by birth but natives of the Balkans. Yet the policy of limiting military service to Rumlu, namely people from Turkish-speaking provinces of the empire, is reflected in

[12] Muhimme defteri, vol. 75, no. 199, p. 111, Shawwal 1013 (February–March 1604).
[13] Muhimme defteri, vol. 7, no. 1329, p. 459, Dhu l-Qa'da 1, 975 (April 28, 1568); vol. 5, no. 1146, p. 430, Sha'ban 14, 973 (March 6, 1566); vol. 23, no. 693, p. 313, Dhu l-Qa'da 23, 981 (March 16, 1573).

many imperial edicts and documents. The Ottomans, too, esteemed the warlike Circassians, whom they spared after the conquest and accepted into the army. Imperial edicts sent from Istanbul to Egypt mention *Rumlu* as qualified to serve in the army. Yet a revealing document, dated 1586, orders that "able soldiers from among the Turks and Circassians" (*yarar qul Rumlu ve Cherkes qulundan*) be sent to Yemen. However, the frequency of official references to the Turks is far greater than those to the Circassians, itself highly significant.[14]

While the Circassians were accepted, there was no ambiguity in official attitudes about the possibility the Arabs would enter the army. Whether "Arab" meant Bedouin or *awlad 'Arab*, people of Arab origin, Arabic-speaking people – the attitude was totally negative. Yet it was impossible in Egypt as in other Arab lands to prevent Arabic-speaking locals from enrolling in the Ottoman army. One important reason for this development was the need to send large numbers of soldiers to Yemen. Service in this remote and dangerous land was extremely unpopular; Ottoman soldiers from Istanbul, Syria, or Egypt abhorred serving there. From the numerous edicts concerning Yemeni affairs, it is clear that the Ottoman government did not have a true picture of the numbers of troops in Yemen. The Porte found it impossible to provide hard-pressed and beleaguered governors with sufficient reinforcements. A viceroy ordered to send 500 men could send only 220; in one year only 500 men went to Yemen instead of the 3,000 that had been called up. Istanbul took various measures to induce people to serve. Bonuses were promised and shirkers were threatened. Service in Yemen was performed on a rotation basis, usually for three years. Permission was given to recruit men from outside the regular army; soldiers' sons and brothers (*qul oglu ve qarindashi*) were enlisted if they were Turks. Slaves and retainers of grandees enlisted, tempted by the prospect of acceptance as regular soldiers.

Under these circumstances *awlad 'Arab*, including Egyptians and men from other Arab provinces of the empire, infiltrated the army. Moreover, some Arabs (i.e., native Egyptians) were buying Mamluks, a serious breach of social norms which would have been unimaginable during the Mamluk sultanate. Toward the end of the sixteenth century Egypt, like other Ottoman provinces, experienced severe economic crisis. Inflation hit soldiers' salaries, and as a result they rioted and revolted, trying to protect their privileges, and resorted to illegal means to increase their income.

Since the Ottoman conquest the army had been divided between "Ottomans" and "Egyptians," although that division assumed with time different names and shapes. An Egyptian territorial army with *esprit de corps* and interests of its own emerged. The term *Misir qullari*, "the soldiers of Egypt,"

[14] Muhimme defteri, vol. 60, nos. 595, 596, p. 254, Jumada I 8, 994 (April 27, 1586).

appears as early as 1568 in an official document dealing with clashes
between them and the *Qapu qullari*.[15] A seventeenth-century chronicle
describes *Qapu qullari* envy of what they considered the better salaries paid
the *Misir qullari*. The language of imperial decrees distinguishes between
stationary or permanent (*muqim*) soldiers and military units that are on the
move (*musafir*). It was the strategy of the Ottoman high command in
Istanbul to move military units around the empire. For example, when
troops from Egypt were ordered to go to Yemen to fight local rebels, soldiers
from Syria were sent to replace them in Egypt; Egyptian troops were
transferred to Syria to replace soldiers sent to the Persian front. Now, it is
noteworthy that even in the sixteenth century Egyptian soldiers serving in
Palestine were under the command of their own officers, and were responsible not to the *beylerbeyi* of Damascus under whose jurisdiction their
sanjaqs lay, but to the *beylerbeyi* of Egypt. As soon as their term in Palestine
was over, they were ordered to return to Egypt.[16]

It is important to emphasize that tensions between "Ottoman" and
"Egyptian" elements within the army were based on economic interests,
social background, and sometimes on different mentalities (i.e., the "Egyptians" being more religious than the "Ottomans"). Yet these were not
usually tensions between Arbas and Turks; soldiers on both sides were
predominantly Turkish speaking. Nor was this division political; both sides
were loyal to the sultan in Istanbul. A treatise in the mid-seventeenth century
praising the *Misir qullari* and attacking the *Qapu qullari* was written in
Turkish.[17]

The strict separation of the military class (*'askari*, or *'askeri* in the Ottoman
usage, including also the bureaucracy and other elements of the government)
from the subjects (*ra'aya*) was a fundamental principle of the Ottoman order.
It is also expressed in the *Qanum-name-i Misir*. The document prohibits
civilians from carrying, keeping, or manufacturing arms. The Ottomans
changed the status quo regarding production of gunpowder in the Sa'id
(Upper Egypt), the remote district under the jurisdiction of the Arab tribal
confederation of Banu 'Umar. It was ordered that the large cauldrons used
to manufacture gunpowder be transferred to Cairo.

It is interesting to note that the *Qanun-name* already mentions the illegal
practice of soldiers opening shops and participating in trade. As we know
from subsequent developments, this warning was of no avail, and by the
eighteenth century artisans and merchants, on one hand, and the military on
the other, had thoroughly interpenetrated. As early as 1578, an edict

[15] Muhimme defteri, vol. 7, no. 1329, Dhu l-Qa'da *awa'il*, 675 (April 28–May 7, 1568).
[16] M. Winter, "Military Connections between Egypt and Syria (Including Palestine) in the
Early Ottoman Period," in A. Cohen and G. Baer (eds.), *Egypt and Palestine: A
Millennium of Association, 868–1948* (Jerusalem, 1984), 139–49.
[17] Winter, "'Anatolian Campaign Book'."

registers a complaint against amirs and *aghas* (regimental commanders), whose trading in food and other provisions, and gaining of a monopoly on some articles, had led to a food shortage in Istanbul.

Military revolts

Riots and revolts among the soldiers in the late sixteenth and early seventeenth centuries had primarily economic origins, although there were also ethnic and racial motives. The first serious disturbances occurred during the incumbency of Uveys Pasha (1587–91). He found the treasury in deficit, and decided to cancel salaries of those soldiers who owned shops and businesses. The army responded by demanding the revocation of salaries from the *awlad 'Arab* (Arabic-speaking people). In August 1589 mutinous soldiers forced their way into the Diwan and attacked the pasha personally. They killed members of his retinue, and pillaged his private quarters. Then the rebels rioted in the city. Their rage was directed against Arabs, particularly *qadis* and bureaucrats employed by the treasury. They proclaimed that *awlad 'Arab* would not be allowed to keep white Mamluks. Christians and Jews were forbidden to have any slaves at all. Arabs were warned not to wear Turkish clothes. The viceroy ordered his *qadi* to draw up a document to satisfy the rebels. The chronicler Ibn Abi l-Surur writes that only natural death saved the pasha from murder by his soldiers.

The next revolt broke out during the term of Sharif Muhammad Pasha (1596–98). In February 1598, while the viceroy was in the country with several Bedouin chiefs, he was attacked and shot at by soldiers. There were casualties in the pasha's retinue, but he escaped during a sudden sandstorm. The rebels demanded the execution of several notables and army officers. Again, Arabs were their target; several *awlad 'Arab* wearing Turkish clothes were murdered. A chaotic situation developed; the law courts closed, the chief *qadi* escaped, and the rebels appointed *kashifs* without regard to the authorities.

In March 1601 soldiers again broke into the Diwan and killed several high officials; the main issue this time was the grain ration.

Lawlessness reached a peak during the incumbency of Ibrahim Pasha, the first viceroy to be murdered by mutinous soldiers and who became known as *al-Maqtul*, "the slain." He demonstrated his resolve to resist the army's unjustified demands, and paid with his life. The main issue was the *tulba*, an illegal levy imposed by the *sipahis* in rural areas on the pretext of facilitating police duties. The *sipahis* compelled the *kashifs* to provide them with vouchers authorizing collection of money from the villagers. The rebels' opportunity came in September 1604. When the pasha left the Citadel to open a dyke at Shubra on the outskirts of Cairo, they met at Qarafa cemetery and swore on saints' tombs to kill him. He was attacked with his guards in the company of several beys and officials. Fifteen cavalry soldiers (*sipahis*) murdered Ibrahim Pasha with their swords and placed his head and the heads of three of his Janissaries at the Zuwayla gate, where criminals' remains were usually displayed. The chief *qadi* became acting governor (*qa'im maqam*) until the arrival of a new viceroy.

The new pasha brought with him an edict to suppress the *tulba* and punish Ibrahim Pasha's killers. Soldiers and notables were convened in the Qara Maydan (Black Square) below the Citadel and made to pledge allegiance to the state. A few rebels were caught and executed, but the government's rule was not restored.

It required the strong personality of the vizier Muhammad Pasha (1607–11), later known as *Qul Qiran*, "the breaker of the [rebellious] soldiers," to suppress the rebellious *sipahis* and abolish the *tulba*. He came from the imperial palace, where he had been *silahdar*, one of the highest-ranking officers of the sultan's guard. Ibn Abi l-Surur al-Bakri al-Siddiqi, our principal source for these events, extols his personality and policies in superlative terms. From the moment he landed at Alexandria, Muhammad Pasha showed energy and a talent for gaining popularity. He made public visits to the tombs of Muslim saints there and demonstrated goodwill towards Sufis and 'ulama'. He inspected the Citadel built by Qaytbay, the great Mamluk sultan, and ordered repairs. Later he executed oppressive district governors and warned others on pain of death not to give *tulba* vouchers. He executed the aged *kashif* of Buhayra province for disobeying that order. (The *kashif's* explanation that the soldiers had toppled his tent over his head did not save him.) The *kashif* of Gharbiyya province suffered the same fate.

Muhammad Pasha publicly reminded all the soldiers to stop the practice of the *tulba*. What prompted a final showdown were several appointments he made to the position of *kashif*. The rebels, members of the three *sipahi* regiments, who were stationed in rural areas throughout lower Egypt, gathered in early Dhu l-Qada 1017/early February 1609, at Tanta in the Delta. They solemnly swore at the shrine of Sidi Ahmad al-Badawi, the renowned thirteenth-century Sufi shaykh, Egypt's most popular saint, that they would stand united and would not give up their right to collect the *tulba*. Ibn Abi l-Surur reports that they chose a sultan and a vizier and planned how to divide the country among themselves. They mustered their forces, which also included irregular soldiers. Then they started to pillage villages.

The pasha summoned the troops on whom he could rely. Those were mainly *sanjaq beyis* and members of the elite Mutafarriqa and Chavush corps, as well as urban Janissaries and 'Azab who had no part in the *tulba*. Cairo-based *sipahis* were also called up. Some of Muhammad Pasha's officers suggested negotiation, and a Turkish mufti, Muhammad Effendi, nicknamed Alti Parmaq, and a regimental officer were sent to the rebels' camp. The cleric delivered a speech calling on them to obey "those in authority," according to the famous Qur'anic injunction, but to no avail. In Cairo, the viceroy ordered all troops to assemble. Every absent member of the three *sipahi* corps was declared a rebel. The army was reinforced by Bedouin in large numbers, and was armed with heavy cannons and falconets (*darbzens*). This force set out north on 8 Dhu l-Hijja/March 15, 1609 to Raydaniyya, and then on to the Birkat al-Hajj (Pilgrims' Pond). The Bedouin were forbidden to mingle with the regular army; their task was to encircle and harass the enemy.

The confrontation took place at Khanqah, fifteen miles north of Cairo. When the rebels saw the strong force they faced, and the cannons, they lost their courage. Some tried to escape or fight, but were killed by the Arabs. Some drowned in the Birkat al-Hajj as they tried to flee. Others managed to infiltrate the pasha's army and join their units; these were later identified and beheaded. Although there was sporadic fighting, resistance collapsed without a real battle. The captives who were not regular soldiers were beheaded on the spot. Some regulars were also caught and executed; their number reached 250. The chief *qadi* interceded and saved 300 rebels from execution. Instead, they were sent to Suez and thence to Yemen. Once the revolt had been crushed, the people of Cairo were ordered to dig out a cubit's depth of earth in front of their houses and shops, to wipe out the rebels' footprints. The chronicler concludes: "That was in truth the second conquest of Egypt during the Ottoman government, God bless it."

Muhammad Pasha now went on with his initiatives to repair mosques and promote public works. He also attempted to reform the fiscal and military administration. The number of beys was reduced to twelve, in accordance with the intention of the government when the beylicate was created in Ottoman Egypt. He revised the lists of those entitled to pensions and allowances, thus saving about a hundred purses.[18] He reformed peasants' obligations to contribute labour and animals to public agricultural works, and exempted poor villages. After four years, the pasha was recalled to Istanbul; contrary to custom, he was not dismissed.

Suppression of the *tulba* revolt put an end to a series of military uprisings that had threatened Ottoman rule. The fact that the rebels had chosen a sultan seems to support the view that the revolt was a separatist movement resembling revolts of a century before. Yet evidence of political motivation is extremely flimsy – one sentence by the chronicler about the rebels' choosing a sultan and vizier from among themselves. While Ibn Abi l-Surur wholly identified himself with the Ottomans, probably echoes their propaganda, and was familiar with the minutest details of the uprising, he

---

[18] One purse, *kese*, equaled 25,000 *paras*.

does not give the name of the "sultan," if, that is, there really was one at all.[19]

It is important to try to understand the social and ethnic background of the revolt. Some suggest that it was a Mamluk movement, an assumption that, if proven, would support the theory of separatist rebellion. But it is impossible to prove that the rebels were exclusively or even predominantly Mamluks. All available sources, Arabic and Turkish alike, speak of a *sipahi* revolt, never of a Mamluk revolt. Now, it has already been explained that the Circassians were only one of the three *sipahi* (cavalry) corps, and by the early seventeenth century the Circassian character of the corps must have been greatly diluted. The viceroy won for his suppression of the uprising the epithet *Qul Qiran*, the breaker of the *quls*. As is well known, "*qul*" in Ottoman terminology means a slave, usually a military slave of the sultan. The Turkish sources sometimes refer to the rebels as *jundi*, a word which means soldier in Arabic but horseman in Ottoman Turkish and thus a synonym for *sipahi*. While it is therefore quite possible that Mamluks comprised a strong element in the movement, there is no evidence that either the rebels or the government defined it as a Mamluk, or even a pseudo-Mamluk, rebellion.

Ethnic definitions were much more on the minds of contemporary actors and observers than most other categories were; it is the *Turkishness* of the rebels that is mentioned. In his treatise on the revolt, Ibn Abi l-Surur quotes a poem denouncing the *Rum*, Turks, who oppressed the people of Egypt. Of all the distinguished 'ulama' of Cairo, it was Muhammad Effendi, known as Alti Parmaq, a Turkish preacher, who was sent to talk sense to the rebels. But these soldiers already had deep roots in Egypt, and were strongly attached to the land; before their most important decisions, they visited the tombs of Muslim saints in Cairo and, most emphatically, the shrine of Sidi Ahmad al-Badawi at Tanta – all symbols of Egyptian Islam.

Arab chiefs, the tribes, and the state

The term "Arab" in Arabic sources in the Middle Ages and the Ottoman period is used almost exclusively to denote Bedouin, not Arabic-speaking town dwellers. Yet caution is called for in applying the term "Bedouin" to Egypt's tribes. Many were not nomads; some were semi-nomads, others were settled agriculturalists, and differed very little from the fallahin. What characterized the Arabs were tribal organization and a claim to Arabian origin. Unlike the fallahin, who as a rule were unarmed, Arab tribesmen carried weapons, rode horses, and were reputed to have martial qualities.

[19] It is worth noting that no such sultan is mentioned in the detailed account of the revolt, which Ibn Abi l-Surur wrote as a separate treatise, or in the Turkish chronicles.

They were the only sector of civilian society permitted to ride horses. While some tribes or clans were notorious bandits and rebels, others were obedient and submissive, rendering vital services to the state, including military assistance; one family could even have both loyal and rebellious shaykhs. Moreover, the same tribe or leader could alternately support the government and oppose it, depending on circumstances.

It will be recalled that Arab tribes harassed the Ottoman army on its way to conquer Egypt and formed an important part of Sultan Tumanbay's forces, especially after the battle of Raydaniyya. On the other hand, Tumanbay was betrayed to the Ottomans by Arab shaykhs to whose residence he had escaped. Eventually the Mamluks took their revenge. After the Ottomans reappointed Mamluk amirs as district governors, the *kashif* of Gharbiyya province invited the two Arabs responsible for Tumanbay's betrayal to a party, and when they were drunk, a number of Circassian Mamluks fell upon and killed them. Another Arab shaykh was put to death by a Mamluk *kashif* by exactly the same ruse. The Arab shaykhs complained that the Mamluks were killing them for their loyalty to the state. Khayrbay, who was then governor of Egypt, ordered the Mamluks to leave the Arabs alone.

Some Arab tribes participated in the Mamluk revolts that broke out after Khayrbay's death. The fact that the Arabs continued to challenge the Ottoman state after the rebellion of Ahmad Pasha al-Kha'in has usually been overlooked by historians. Politically, their threat did not seem as serious as Ahmad Pasha's actions, but militarily the Bedouin nearly exhausted the Ottoman forces in Egypt. The Arabs euphorically declared their intention to capture Cairo and then the rest of the country. These were idle dreams; the Arab tribes did not stand a chance against the superior arms, better discipline, and vast resources of the state. The Arabs' fear of cannon fire is a recurring theme in the annals of Ottoman Egypt.

In an insightful passage, Mustafa 'Ali explains that the Arabs' weakness is their disunity. The tribes fight and quarrel among themselves, enabling the government to play one against another. An Ottoman force not larger than 10,000 men could control the land, despite the Arabs' numerical superiority.[20]

Official Ottoman documents refer to Arab tribesmen as the most serious threat to Egypt's internal security. They are mentioned as troublemakers and rebels, a permanent source of harassment to the villagers and the state, sometimes causing real damage to agriculture. Occasionally, they were bold enough to attack people in outlying quarters of the capital, such as Old Cairo and Bulaq. Army officers were rewarded with promotions or transfers for fighting them and beheading as many as possible. Da'ud Pasha, a viceroy

---

[20] *Mustafa Ali's Description of Cairo in 1599*, 57.

praised as a particularly benevolent and enlightened ruler (1538–49), suppressed a Bedouin revolt in the ever-problematic Sharqiyya province, killing many and driving well-known clans from the region. But the tribes could also direct their arms against anti-government rebels and rival tribes, as shown already in their contribution to suppressing the *sipahi* revolt in 1609.

The *Qanun-name-i Misir* devotes several paragraphs to the Arab shaykhs. Ottoman policy toward them was similar to that toward the Mamluks. Despite revolts, the government understood that they were indispensable for governing rural areas and so integrated them into the administrative structure according to principles that had been in force under Sultan Qaytbay. The regional Arab chief, *shaykh al-ʿArab*, is given the same functions and authority as a *kashif*. The code states clearly: "These Arab shaykhs are like *kashifs*."

The office of *shaykh al-ʿArab* was inherited from the Mamluk sultanate, and was vital for fiscal administration. First and foremost, the Arab shaykh was a tax-farmer (*multazim*), who collected the taxes in cash (in Upper Egypt, also in grain) from the province under his control. He was responsible for public safety, agriculture, and, most importantly, the irrigation system. The great similarity between the functions of a *shaykh al-ʿArab* and those of a *kashif* is illustrated by the fact that no *kashifs* are mentioned in provinces under the control of Arab shaykhs and vice versa. There were clashes of two or more Arab shaykhs, or between an Arab shaykh and a *kashif* of a neighboring province, but not between an Arab shaykh and a *kashif* within the same province.

Like other office-holders, an Arab shaykh received an imperial patent (*berat-i humayun*) and a robe of honor (*khilʿa*). He usually received appointment from the pasha after it had been approved by the sultan. In some cases, however, shaykhs went directly to the sultan's palace in Istanbul and obtained their patents. In some cases, appointment was left to the pasha, who was authorized to name one, two, or more candidates for office. In lower-level decisions related to a remote province such as Egypt, the sultan had to follow the advice of his local representatives. The pashas took advantage of this, and appointed whomever they pleased. A special strongly worded decree in 1574 reminded them that they must obtain the sultan's approval for each appointment.

There is little doubt that Arab shaykhs were among the richest people in Egypt. A patent for a tax-farm required a down payment of several hundred purses. Information scattered in the documents shows that some shaykhs possessed property worth between 50,000 and 250,000 gold pieces (*altuns*). Shaykhs owned villages (as *mulk*, privately held land), plantations, agricultural equipment, livestock, and slaves. Some shaykhs became wealthy by administering their provinces prudently. One shaykh in Upper Egypt was granted monopoly of the emerald mines as a tax-farm for fifteen purses annually. Nevertheless, shaykhs were constantly in debt to the treasury, compelling them to borrow money, mainly from wealthy merchants of Cairo. The debts of the shaykhs of Upper Egypt were particularly heavy, sometimes exceeding 150,000 *altuns* and hundreds of thousands of *ardabbs* of grain.

There is ample evidence that Arab shaykhs were as oppressive and exploitative as the *kashifs*. There are many instances of heavy taxes, embezzlement of public funds, and harsh treatment of villagers.

In Ottoman Egypt Arab shaykhs sometimes became commanders of Ottoman and Mamluk soldiers. While this did not happen often, the fact that it happened at all bears witness to the vitality of the Bedouin Arabs and to the Ottomans' flexibility. A few Arab shaykhs were given the rank of *sanjaq beyi*. Arab governors in Upper Egypt had fifty to sixty Janissaries under their command to assist them to collect taxes.

The highest position achieved by Arab shaykhs in the sixteenth century was that of ruler of Buhayra province. At least two shaykhs were made *umara' al-hajj*, one of the most prestigious and lucrative positions in Egypt. In the Mamluk sultanate, only the highest-ranking amirs (*amir mi'a muqaddam alf*) could aspire to the office, and certainly no Arab shaykh could have attained it. 'Isa ibn Isma'il ibn 'Amir, the shaykh of the 'Awna Arabs of the Buhayra, was *amir al-hajj* in 1555-56 and from 1562–63 to 1564–65. His son 'Umar was *amir al-hajj* in 1590–92 and again in 1593–94 and 1594–95.

The Arab shaykhs' oppressive rule, financial irresponsibility, and vicious internecine competition for appointments as *multazims* – which were always given out by auction to the highest bidders – induced the government to dispense with their services. It appears that what prompted the authorities to action was the disappointing performance of Banu 'Umar, the Arab rulers of Upper Egypt, a region which, owing to its remoteness and economic importance as Egypt's main granary, was particularly important but also subject to misrule.

In a letter to Istanbul in 1574, the viceroy complains about the Arab shaykhs. Since the Ottoman conquest of Egypt, the shaykhs had never complied with the terms of their tax-farms, and had often embezzled public money; they gave shelter to bandits and rebels instead of suppressing them. The viceroy asked permission to dismiss the shaykhs and to appoint in their place *sanjaq beyis*, whose annual salaries would be paid by the Egyptian treasury. Instead of the *iltizam* system (tax-farming), taxes would be collected by salaried government agents (*umana'*, sing. *amin*); the beys would maintain law and order, and have authority to impose death sentences (which the Arab shaykhs did not have). The beys would be given soldiers in sufficient numbers to keep the Bedouin in check. It was decreed that all Egyptian provinces, not just the Sa'id (Upper Egypt), be placed under *sanjaq beyis*. The only exception to the new arrangement was Buhayra province. As has been shown, the Arab shaykhs there had a special status as *umara' al-hajj* and *sirdars* (commanders of expeditionary forces), either because of their proven loyalty and efficiency, or the sensitive nature of a border region that no outsider could handle.[21]

The new policy appeared extremely successful at first. A *sanjaq beyi* named Sulayman was appointed to govern the Sa'id. He built a fort at Jirja, the center of the province, and suppressed a Bedouin uprising, beheading 150 Arabs. However, Sulayman himself was soon suspected of financial irregularities, and was promoted to pasha and appointed governor of Habesh, which was tantamount to exile. After that experiment, the authorities in Cairo came full circle to the policy of five or six years before and reappointed Arab shaykhs of the Banu 'Umar clan. These ruled the Sa'id until 1610, when an Ottoman amir was appointed. It is not known whether the decision to replace Arab shaykhs with *sanjaq beyis* in other provinces was implemented. It probably was not, and certainly not in full; there is evidence in the budget of 1596–97 of Bedouin Arabs holding fiscal positions.

Religion in Egypt in the sixteenth century

We have seen that after the Egyptians' initial negative response, the Ottomans were viewed much more favorably as Muslims. It is difficult to exaggerate the importance of this central theme. The new rulers of Egypt regarded themselves as representing a genuinely Islamic Sunni state; the viceroys demonstrated respect and support for Islamic institutions and notables. The Ottoman government acknowledged, after inspection, all *waqf* foundations that had been established before the conquest, including those by the Mamluk rulers. To act otherwise would have been, of course, contrary to Islamic law, but the Ottomans did win gratitude for it.

The Ottomans took over the administration of justice, restricting the higher echelons of the judiciary, the post of *qadi 'askar* in particular, to outsiders, Turkish-speaking *qadis*, who came to Egypt to serve for a limited period, like other members of the military–bureaucratic class. Yet, apart from that, the Ottomans did not infringe upon the religious or scholarly life of Egypt. Indeed, they limited their interference to material things, such as repairs of buildings and facilities, financial contributions, and the like. Al-Azhar, the great college-mosque, flourished under Ottoman rule, and there is no trace of evidence of any attempt on the part of the government to influence its religious, educational, or scholarly activity. The Hanafi

[21] Muhimme defteri, vol. 24, no. 663, p. 258, Muharram 26, 982 (May 18, 1574).

madhhab, the official legal school of the empire, did not receive preferential treatment. Likewise, Arabic-speaking sufis, who naturally were the majority among Egyptian mystics, were not treated differently from Turkish Sufis who lived in Egypt.

Like the decline in historiography in Egypt following the Ottoman conquest, Islamic scholarship in the sixteenth century clearly sank beneath its level of previous centuries. As Ibn Iyas did not have worthy successors in historiography, so Jalal al-Din al-Suyuti (d. 1505), the great Islamic scholar, had none who could remotely compare with his erudition and creativity. The general question of cultural stagnation and decline in Egypt (and beyond) during the period under study cannot be discussed here. It must be said, however, that if the Ottoman occupation contributed to the decline, this was an indirect and unintentional repercussion of conquest.

The outstanding Egyptian man of letters in the sixteenth century was 'Abd al-Wahhab al-Sha'rani, a Sufi (d. 1565). He was a sensitive social commentator and critic and a prolific writer on various religious subjects, including mysticism, *fiqh*, ethics, and the history of Sufism. Indeed, Sufism is one dimension of Egyptian Islam that flourished during the Ottoman period and with Ottoman favor. The Sufi orders (*tariqa*, pl. *turuq*) multiplied and their activities intensified: more *mawlids* (saints' days) were created and celebrated; more Sufi institutions, *zawiyas* and *tekkes*, were built, and many more 'ulama' were affiliated with Sufi orders and showed interest in Sufism.

While the flourishing of Egyptian Sufism is evident, it is hard to determine underlying reasons for it. Certainly the Ottomans' disposition did much to enhance Sufis' positions and status. The Turks had been converted to Islam not by orthodox theologians, but by dervishes. All versions of Sufism flourished in the Turkish regions – from the sophisticated monism of Muhyi al-Din ibn 'Arabi (d. 1240)[22] to the mystical poetry of Jalal al-Din Rumi (d. 1273) and the crude practices of simple *dedes* (Turkish Sufi shaykhs). Generally speaking, the Turks had a much stronger mystical bent than the Arabs. But Sufism had been firmly entrenched in Egypt before the Ottoman conquest, and been popular among common people and Mamluk rulers alike.

Another possible reason for the advance of Sufism under Ottoman rule is a certain lethargy of the 'ulama' in early Ottoman Egypt. The scholars and jurists of Islam continued, of course, to fulfill their accustomed roles in society, but they seem to have lost much of their élan. The demotion of Egypt from empire to province may have spread a malaise favorable to Sufism, which nurtures the interior life with an apolitical and otherworldly orientation. And Sufism not only offered solace to the miserable, but also

---

[22] Note the reverence shown to this great and controversial mystic by both Salim I and Sulayman. See M. Winter, *Society and Religion in Early Ottoman Egypt* (New Brunswick, 1982), 163–65.

provided them with food distributed during the *mawlid* celebrations (these greatly multiplied during the sixteenth century), and through various Sufi-related institutions.

While the impact of Ottoman 'ulama' on Egyptian religious and social life was negligible, Turkish Sufism had made headway even before the conquest, and greatly increased in influence after that. The Khalwatiyya order was the most important representative of Turkish Sufism at that time; the most prominent Khalwatis in late Mamluk and early Ottoman Egypt came from a Turkish-speaking milieu and were disciples of 'Umar Rusheni from Tabriz (d. 1487). One of the most outstanding Khalwatis was Ibrahim Gulshani (d. 1534), who escaped from Tabriz after the Safavid occupation. He became very popular with Ottoman troops in Egypt; they even quarreled among themselves for the water with which he washed his hands. Summoned to Istanbul, since the government was wary of his popularity, upon his return he had to retreat into complete seclusion. Two other Khalwatis, also former disciples of Rusheni, were Muhammad Damirdash al-Muhammadi (d. 1522 or 1523) and Shahin al-Jarkasi (d. 1547). Shahin, an ex-officer in the army of Sultan Qaytbay, became a hermit and lived for several decades on the Muqattam mountain, east of Cairo.

The central principle of the Khalwatiyya was the concept of the *khalwa*, solitary retreat, whence the order takes its name. The adherent of the *tariqa* was obliged to retreat for long periods to his cell for prayer and contemplation. The Khalwatiyya offered a well-developed mystical system and a course of study and spiritual progress in which ideas of Ibn 'Arabi played an important role. This kind of Sufism was alien to the version of al-Sha'rani, a genuine representative of the orthodox, moderate, Egyptian Sufism. Intense religious disputes and personal rivalries developed between the more orthodox and quiescent Sufism personified by al-Sha'rani and the more mystical and ecstatic version of the Khalwatiyya, of Karim al-Din Muhammad Ibn Ahmad al-Khalwati (d. 1578). Karim al-Din did not consider al-Sha'rani a true Sufi, while the latter regarded the Khalwati shaykh as a Muslim who did not know the basic religious ordinances. According to 'Abd al-Ra'uf al-Munawi (d. 1621), who continued al-Sha'rani's work as historian of Egyptian Sufism, Karim al-Din al-Khalwati became the undisputed leader of Sufism in Cairo after al-Sha'rani's death.

In time, and with the establishment of Turkish rule, the influence of the Khalwatiyya increased. Al-Munawi, al-Sha'rani's disciple, was much more involved with them than his master, and he provides more information than does al-Sha'rani about their development. Al-Munawi's Khalwati shaykh was a Turk named Muharram al-Rumi, who did not know Arabic. The popularity of the Khalwatis and the influence they wielded accounts for the fact that al-Sha'rani did not dare to criticize them openly.

As has been mentioned, the Ottoman authorities were supportive of

Sufism generally, but they paid special attention to Turkish Sufism in Egypt. Sulayman Pasha established in 1526 a *zawiya* and founded a *waqf* to finance it for a certain Hasan ibn Ilyas al-Rumi (the Turk) al-Istanbuli. The *zawiya*, which included a mosque, a small religious college (*madrasa*), and a grave-yard, was reserved for non-Arab Sufis. All functionaries, from the shaykh to the manual workers, had to be non-Arabs (*'Ajam*). A second institution was a *takiyya* (a Sufi convent) for the above-mentioned Shaykh Ibrahim Gulshani.[23]

The reason for the contrast between the rise of Turkish, or distinctly Ottoman, Sufism in the midst of Egyptian society, and the absence of a visible impact of Ottoman 'ulama' on the Egyptian 'ulama' lies in the differences between *'ilm* (Islamic scholarship) and Sufism. The 'ulama' were a rigidly conservative body. Despite the fact that in the sixteenth century the Egyptian 'ulama' class was not at its best, the 'ulama' were the guardians of the norms of Sunnism, and Cairo was one of the most venerated centers of Islamic learning, if not the greatest. It stands to reason that the Ottoman 'ulama' were awed by the strength and depth of the Islamic scholarly tradition of Egypt, al-Azhar in particular, their own achievements in the era of Sulayman Qanuni notwithstanding. On the other hand, Sufism was always much more heterogeneous and fluid; it existed on many social and intellectual levels, and was more open to outside influences.

It must not be concluded that Egyptian Sufism itself suffered from the foreign competition. On the contrary, as has been mentioned, Sufism as it developed in Egypt after the Ottoman conquest became richer and more multifaceted than before. Al-Sha'rani was initiated into no fewer than twenty-six *tariqas*. The period saw also the advent of an Egyptian Sufi aristocracy in the families of al-Bakri and al-Sadat al-Wafa'iyya. The Bakris were a family of *ashraf* who claimed descent from Abu Bakr al-Siddiq, the first caliph. The family moved from Upper Egypt to Cairo in the early fifteenth century, but its head was known as a legist, not a Sufi. In the early sixteenth century, the family gained control of Sufi *awqaf*, and enriched itself. Since then, until the twentieth century, the Bakris were a Sufi family order. The family also produced one of Ottoman Egypt's most important historians, Muhammad ibn Abi l-Surur al-Bakri al-Siddiqi, whose name has been mentioned several times.

By the end of the sixteenth century, when it became possible for rich 'ulama', Sufis, and other civilians to convert their wealth into tax-farms (*iltizams*), Taj al-'Arifin al-Bakri (d. 1594–95), the historian's paternal uncle, had an *iltizam* of fifty villagers, which yielded an annual harvest of

---

[23] See Leonor Fernandes, "Two Variations on the Same Theme: The *Zawiya* of Hasan al-Rumi and the *Takiyya* of Ibrahim al-Gulshani," *Annales Islamologiques*, 21 (1985), 95–111.

10,000 *qintars* of sugar and similar quantities of rice, sesame seed, and wheat. The Bakris had a luxurious palace at the fashionable Azbakiyya pond in Cairo, which became a meeting place for the social and political elite. They had a considerable library and a literary salon. They also had Mamluks, which was most unusual for civilians.

The Sadat al-Wafa'iyya were an aristocratic Sufi family that like the Bakris enjoyed official recognition and financial support. They were also of *sharifi* descent. Like the Bakris, the Wafa'is gained their wealth by trustee-ships of lucrative *awqaf* and by investing the capital thus acquired to obtain tax-farms. The two families competed with each other for the most prestigious positions in Sufi society, and each was in charge of the organiza-tion of major *mawlid* celebrations. In the following two centuries, both families' fortunes grew even greater.

The religious minorities (dhimmis): Christians and Jews

It is important to examine the situation of the religious minorities in early Ottoman Egypt not only for their own sake, but also because the condition of minorities is an indicator of the majority. By and large, the *dhimmis*, Christians and Jews, in sixteenth-century Egypt enjoyed a period of relative tranquillity and stability and, in some quarters, even prosperity. This situation reflects the generally good government of the Ottoman empire at its best, especially under Sultan Sulayman. There are indications that with the general decline at the end of the period studied here, the religious minorities also experienced worsening conditions.

The sources, both official documents and chronicles, more often than not mention the *dhimmis* in a negative context: for example, when Jewish or Christian officials are accused of fraudulent practices, or when they forget their proper, that is inferior, place in society, according to Islamic law or the opinion of the government or the Muslim majority. The information in the Muslim sources on the minorities is scanty and episodic. Given the unbalanced nature of these sources – biased reports by authors of literary sources, who were mostly 'ulama' or Sufis; official documents often issued only in times of trouble – the picture that emerges may be gloomier than it was in fact. The Hebrew sources, including chronicles and rabbinical responsa, are more reliable as a barometer for the mood of the Jews, and these indicate a high degree of security and trust in the government.

Information about the Jewish community in Ottoman Egypt is not abundant; even less is known about the much larger Christian community. The disproportionate attention the sources pay to Jews is perhaps owed to the high positions some Jews attained in Egypt's fiscal administration, their greater visibility owing to the fact that the Jews lived mostly in Cairo, Alexandria, and the larger towns, and their presumed wealth.

The Mamluks were new converts to Islam and as such inclined to religious fanaticism. Conversely, in the sixteenth century, the Ottomans were tolerant (by the standards of the times) and pragmatic, with a healthy economic mind. These characteristics were welcome to minorities, the Jews in particular. The position of Egypt, with its immense economic value and remoteness from the empire's battlefields, acted also in favor of the *dhimmis*, whose economic and financial capabilities were appreciated and put to use by the Ottoman government.

The Jewish chronicler Capsali regards the fall of the Mamluks and the Ottoman conquest almost as messianic events.[24] The Circassians are called "enemies to Jews," while the Ottoman sultans are "benevolent kings." Jewish historiography, both contemporary and modern, rightly praises the Ottomans for granting asylum to Jewish exiles from the Iberian peninsula.[25] Capsali relates a story that on the eve of the battle of Raydaniyya, in which the Mamluks lost their kingdom, the Jews of Cairo were attacked by the mob and threatened by the Mamluks for rejoicing at their impending downfall. The story is most probably untrue or at least inaccurate, but it reflects the sentiments of the Jews, who indeed welcomed Sultan Salim's victory.

After the conquest, Jews and Christians were among those the Ottomans deported to Istanbul. Although this was, of course, a harsh measure, it should be regarded as the Ottomans' acknowledgement of the minorities' special skills in finances and administration that were needed in the capital. Khayrbay, the first governor of Egypt, and later his successors, continued the Mamluks' policy of appointing Jews as directors of the mint and employing Jews and Christians to work there. These officials and Jewish money-changers (*sarrafs*) were sometimes accused of debasing the currency and several were executed on such charges.

Ottoman notions of justice were different from those with which the Egyptians were familiar. In one early case, a Jew sued an amir for a sum of money. When the amir refused to appear in court, the Turkish *qadi* sent a Janissary to fetch him, and put him in custody until he satisfied the Jew's demands.[26] Under the Mamluks, it would have been unthinkable for a Jew to sue an amir, let alone to win his suit. But the vulnerability of the Jewish community became apparent again when news of Sultan Salim's death reached Cairo. The Janissaries claimed that an old custom entitled them to ransack the Jewish quarter when the sultan died. Several amirs intervened,

---

[24] Writing 150 years later, the Hebrew chronicler Sambari describes the Ottoman conquest matter-of-factly without Capsali's enthusiasm.

[25] The similar policy toward them on the part of the Mamluk sultan Qaytbay is usually forgotten.

[26] Muhammad ibn Iyas, *Bada'i' al-zuhur fi waqa'i' al-duhur*, ed. Muhammad Mustafa, 5 (Cairo, 1961), 461.

but the Janissaries threatened to pillage the whole city until placated by a sum of money. Shortly afterwards, when the atmosphere became tense again, the Jews hid their valuables and fortified their quarter.

The most serious menace to the Jewish community came in 1524 during the rebellion of Ahmad Pasha "the Traitor." He put pressure on the Jews to provide him with money, threatening the community with dire consequences unless his exorbitant demands were met. When Ahmad's forces overran the Citadel, they killed the Janissaries, and also Jews who were there, probably in connection with their work at the financial bureaus. The collapse of Ahmad Pasha's revolt came as a huge relief to the Jews, who celebrated their deliverance as "the Egyptian Purim."

The Jews were always aware of their basic vulnerability as a small minority (numbering a few thousands), whose religion was despised, and who were thought to be rich. There were many poor Jews in Egypt, but several members of the community held high positions in Egypt's fiscal administration. These offices were extremely lucrative, and raised the envy and hatred of the Muslim majority. Christians were in a similar situation, in theory but not in fact. Legally, believers of both monotheistic religions were *dhimmis* and, from the point of view of the Shari'a law, should be treated on an equal footing. Yet in the period we are discussing, attitudes toward Jews were much more negative than those toward Christians. In spite of all that, the Jews in sixteenth-century Egypt lived in security and usually trusted the government to protect them. This is stated explicitly in a responsa of Rabbi David ben Shlomo ibn Abi Zimra ("Radbaz"), the greatest Jewish religious leader and scholar of the period, who wrote: "It is rare that Jews are murdered because everyone fears the government." The state protected minorities against mobs that had been incited by religious fanatics; al-Sha'rani warns against "taking the law into one's hand" and demolishing, or encouraging others to demolish, churches or synagogues, since the authorities punish severely those who do.

The Jews and Christians in Ottoman Egypt enjoyed autonomy in religious and community matters, according to established Islamic tradition. The Ottoman occupation ended the old institution of the Jewish nagidate, the office of the *nagid*, or chief of the Jewish community, an office considered a historical continuity of the exilarch (*resh galuta*) of Babylon. The *nagid* was elected by leaders of the community and appointed by the sultan. Reasons for the disappearance of the nagidate at the time of the Ottoman conquest are not clear. Yet the autonomy of the Jews, and the Christians, was not reduced. The *nagid* was a secular leader elected because of his wealth and high standing with the authorities. In religious and spiritual matters, he was assisted by a court of law, whose jurisdiction covered religious, family, and community matters and internal disputes. Cases involving Muslims, or where the state was involved, such as property transactions, had to be brought before a *qadi*. Although the Jewish community under Ottoman rule no longer had a *nagid*, it was represented before the government by an influential and wealthy man who held a high official position, such as the master of the mint.

Egyptian Jewry at this time consisted of several congregations separated by ethnicity, such as indigenous ("Arabized") Jews, and Sephardic exiles and their descendants. Sephardic refugees who had arrived in Egypt from the Iberian peninsula transformed the community beyond recognition, bringing much-needed religious scholarship, economic experience, and international connections. The above-mentioned Radbaz personified in his unusually long life (1479–1573) the fortunes and misfortunes of this generation. He was born in Spain, exiled to Morocco, moved to Safad in Palestine, but, owing to economic hardships there, emigrated to Egypt. He lived by trade, but spent most of his time serving his community as rabbi, judge, and religious authority. A contemporary biographer writes: "He ruled over Israel for forty years." Toward the end of his life, he decided to renounce his position and wealth in Egypt, and went to live in the land of Israel.

From the rabbinical responsa we learn that many Jews were artisans and small traders; those mentioned in imperial edicts were naturally rich and influential. One such was Shmuel Cohen (or Kahana), simultaneously director of the mint, currency inspector, *multazim* of the customs revenues of Alexandria and Damietta, and holder of the tax-farm of the special cucumber (*khiyar shanbar*, which was used as a laxative) and spices. Other Jews were customs officials at Suez and al-Tur on the coast of Sinai. Several documents contain complaints against Shmuel Cohen and less prominent Jews. In most cases, these are accusations of an economic nature but with religious motives. Cohen is accused of molesting Muslim women; customs officials at Suez are charged with deliberately delaying ships on their way to the hajj in Mecca. Jews in Alexandria, who were supposed to live in the citadel to keep it from falling to ruins and becoming a refuge for criminals, were guilty of leaving their assigned residences without permission, and in addition of building houses and latrines on holy Muslim tombs. Similarly, the Jewish director of the customs house of Alexandria was accused of using building materials that he had taken from houses belonging to the *waqf* and stones from dilapidated mosques. Monks of the monastery in Sinai protested against the presence of a Jewish family at al-Tur; the very presence of Jews desecrated Mt. Sinai, made holy by God's revelation to Moses. Imperial edicts that respond to these charges against the Jews always order that Jewish officials not be dismissed without an investigation, but that if guilty, they must be replaced by "religious and trustworthy Muslims." The only accusation against Christians was that they hurt Muslims' feelings by flaunting their religion.

Many Jews were involved in tax-farming. This indicates their economic and administrative skills, and also their considerable financial assets. There was a communal agreement that a Jew should not outbid another Jew on an *iltizam* after it had been made. Yet against the ideal of Jewish solidarity there was the principle of the free market and the law of the land (*dina demalkhuta*).

While Egyptian Jews in the sixteenth century did not suffer persecution, they certainly experienced discrimination. According to Islamic law and custom, *dhimmis* were treated with tolerance, but not as equals to Muslims. There is evidence that sometimes discrimination went beyond the requirements of the Shari'a. But there was no consistency in application of certain measures, as the case of male and female slaves in the possession of *dhimmis* demonstrates. The Shari'a does not forbid *dhimmis* to keep slaves, but it does not allow them to have Muslim slaves. This was reconfirmed by distinguished Muslim jurisconsults in Egypt during the period under study. But efforts were made by the ruler and segments of the Muslim population to deprive *dhimmis* of the right to own slaves, which was taken for granted for Muslims. The number of extant documents dealing with slaves owned by *dhimmis*, Jews in particular, is considerably greater than of those dealing with other matters. Edicts reiterate the suspicion that slaves might be Muslims or, even worse – that they were Muslims whom *dhimmi* owners had influenced to convert to Judaism. Repeatedly, decrees state that *dhimmis* should be forced to sell their slaves to Muslims, but also emphasize that no injustice must be done to the *dhimmis*, who should receive full market price for their slaves. Jewish and Christian officials in Cairo and the seaports were also accused of selling Muslim slaves to Europeans. Needless to say, this was strongly condemned.

Again, application of these principles was not consistent. Radbaz complains: "We are not permitted to buy female slaves, although the king's law does not forbid it [to us]." (Incidentally, Radbaz, following the Muslim example, ruled against Jews treating their female slaves as concubines.) At the end of the century, Rabbi Yaacob Castro, author of an important collection of responsa, writes: "The king's decree [for us not to own female slaves] applies only to Muslim women. As for Christian female slaves, the *qadi* himself writes for us the legal document [*hujja*] of sale."

Dhimmis were required to wear special items of dress, particularly headgear, to distinguish them from Muslims. While this ancient rule was in effect in Egypt, the laws concerning dress were neither unambiguous nor generally obeyed; that regulations about the *dhimmis'* clothes were repeated several times, with significant variations, is proof for that. By order of Khadim Hasan Pasha issued in 1580, Jews were to wear high conical red hats (*taratir*) and the Christians black hats (*baranit*, sing. *burneta* or *shapqa*), instead of the usual yellow turbans (for Jews) and blue ones (for Christians). A chronicler named al-Ghamri leaves no doubt that the pasha's aim was to humiliate the infidels, for which he is praised, although generally he was seen as a bad ruler. Another governor, Sharif Muhammad Pasha (1596–98), decreed a change in the color of the headgear the Jews had to wear – from red to black.[27] It is noteworthy that these regulations were made by viceroys in Egypt during the late sixteenth century, and not by the central government in Istanbul. It is possible that owing to the weakening position of the pashas, and to the soldiers' riots, the viceroys decided to humiliate religious minorities in order to gain popularity among the 'ulama' and the common people.

[27] For more details and references see M. Winter, *Egyptian Society under Ottoman Rule 1517–1798* (London and New York, 1992), chap. 8.

2

Egypt in the seventeenth century

JANE HATHAWAY

➤✦

Ottoman transformation and Egypt's changing role

The seventeenth century was an era of momentous change for all provinces of the Ottoman empire, as the empire came to the end of the phase of continuous territorial expansion that had stretched from the mid-fifteenth century through the late sixteenth century.[1] The end of this phase of expansion has until recently been construed as the onset of the Ottoman empire's decline.[2] A critical reexamination of the so-called decline paradigm, however, has led some historians of the Ottoman empire to abandon the notion of an imperial golden age under Sultan Sulayman I (1520–66), and to recast the course of Ottoman history in terms of a late sixteenth-century fiscal and military crisis followed by an adjustment of imperial priorities.[3]

The crisis of the late sixteenth century changed the character of Ottoman military manpower and land tenure. Confronted with massive inflation, thought to have resulted at least in part from an influx of Spanish American silver,[4] the imperial treasury debased the Ottoman silver currency (*aqcha*)

---

[1] For an overview, see, for example, Halil Inalcik, part 1 of Halil Inalcik (ed.) with Donald Quataert, *An Economic and Social History of the Ottoman Empire, 1300–1914* (Cambridge and New York, 1994), 11–22; Halil Inalcik, *The Ottoman Empire: The Classical Age, 1300–1600*, trans. Norman Itzkowitz and Colin Imber (London, 1973), 23–40.

[2] See, for example, Inalcik, part 1 of Inalcik (ed.) with Quataert, *Economic and Social History*, 22–25; Inalcik, *Classical Age*, 41–52; Bernard Lewis, *The Emergence of Modern Turkey*, 2nd ed. (London, Oxford, and New York, 1968), 21–39.

[3] See, for example, Suraiya Faroqhi, part 2 of Inalcik (ed.) with Quataert, *Economic and Social History*, 413–14, 468–70, 572–73; Leslie P. Peirce, *The Imperial Harem: Gender and Sovereignty in the Ottoman Empire* (New York and Oxford, 1993), 153–85; Douglas A. Howard, "Ottoman Historiography and the Literature of 'Decline' of the Sixteenth and Seventeenth Centuries," *Journal of Asian History*, 22 (1988), 52–77.

[4] Ömer Lutfi Barkan, "The Price Revolution of the Sixteenth Century: A Turning Point in the Economic History of the Near East," *International Journal of Middle East Studies*, 6 (1975), 3–28.

and delayed the imperial troops' salaries; consequently, soldiery revolts, in particular among the imperial Janissaries, became increasingly common. In the countryside, inflation combined with overpopulation to force land-holding cavalry officers and peasants off the land in what was dubbed the Great Flight.[5] This upheaval coincided with a series of costly wars against the Hapsburgs (1593–1606) that ended in stalemate.[6] To counter the Hapsburgs' firepower, the Ottomans had armed peasants with rifles; in consequence, firearms spread throughout the countryside,[7] enabling dis-possessed landholders to turn to brigandage and to offer their services as mercenaries. The resulting wave of lawlessness throughout Anatolia at the end of the sixteenth century has come to be known collectively as the *jalali* (*celali*) rebellions.[8]

In brief, the Ottoman empire responded to the crisis of the late sixteenth century by transforming itself from a military conquest state into a bureau-cratic state and bastion of Sunni Islam. In this regard, Ottoman control of Egypt and the Hijaz, though achieved during an era of unprecedented territorial expansion, contributed to the empire's new role by giving the Ottoman sultan responsibility for the well-being of the holy cities of Mecca and Medina. Changes in court routine played their part, as well. By the end of the sixteenth century, the Ottoman court had grown more sedentary, venturing less and less frequently outside the walls of Topkapi palace in Istanbul. The sultan's increasing sequestration gave other palace elements, notably palace women and eunuchs, and various ministers, or viziers, the opportunity to establish their own power bases, whether within the palace, elsewhere in the imperial capital, or in the Ottoman provinces. All these figures cultivated their own entourages, or households, which functioned as competing loci of political and economic influence.[9]

Ottoman military victories in the seventeenth century, particularly the

---

[5] M. A. Cook, *Population Pressure in Rural Anatolia, 1450–1600* (London, New York, and Oxford, 1972); Suraiya Faroqhi, with Leila Erder, "Population Rise and Fall in Anatolia, 1550–1620," *Middle Eastern Studies*, 15 (1979), 322–45; Faroqhi, part 2 of Inalcik (ed.) with Quataert, *Economic and Social History*, 433–41.

[6] The tortuous diplomacy is described by the Hapsburg ambassador Ogier Ghiselin de Busbecq in *The Turkish Letters of Ogier Ghiselin de Busbecq*, ed. and trans. E. S. Forster (Oxford and London, 1968), 64, 79, 214–18. See also Inalcik, *Classical Age*, 42–43.

[7] Halil Inalcik, "The Socio-Political Effects of the Diffusion of Fire-Arms in the Middle East," in V. J. Parry and Malcolm Yapp (eds.), *War, Technology and Society in the Middle East* (London, 1975); Halil Inalcik, "Military and Fiscal Transformation in the Ottoman Empire, 1600–1700," *Archivum Ottomanicum*, 6 (1980), 286–88.

[8] Mustafa Akdağ, *Celali isyanları (1550–1603)* (Ankara, 1963); Faroqhi, part 2 of Inalcik (ed.) with Quataert, *Economic and Social History*, 433–41; Suraiya Faroqhi, "Rural Society in Anatolia and the Balkans during the Sixteenth Century," parts 1 and 2, *Turcica*, 9 (1977), 161–96, and 11 (1979), 103–53; Inalcik, *Classical Age*, 50–51.

[9] Peirce, *The Imperial Harem*, 159–77; Metin Kunt, *The Sultan's Servants: The Transformation of Ottoman Provincial Government, 1550–1650* (New York, 1983), esp. chap. 5 and conclusion.

conquest of Crete in 1669 and Murad IV's recapture of Baghdad in 1638, served chiefly to reinforce the empire's authority in the eastern Mediterranean and to confirm its position of dominance vis-à-vis the Shi'ite Safavid empire in Iran. Ironically, however, Ottoman military victories and defeats alike dealt a blow to Egypt's strategic position in the Mediterranean and Red Sea. In 1636, the Zaydi Shi'ite imams, who had enjoyed a stronghold in northern Yemen since the fourteenth century, swept southward, routing the Ottoman forces from southern Yemen after some fifty years of intermittent warfare.[10] The Ottomans would not regain their foothold in Yemen until the mid-nineteenth century. Meanwhile, the weakening of Portugal's maritime prowess drastically reduced the Portuguese threat to Ottoman shipping in the Red Sea and Indian Ocean and thus the need for Egyptian expeditions against the Portuguese. In 1669, Ottoman forces finally took the Venetian fortress at Candia on Crete after a twenty-five-year siege. Egyptian contingents continued to perform mopping-up operations and garrison duty on Crete,[11] while coffee from the Yemeni port of Mocha revitalized commerce in the Red Sea and eastern Mediterranean.[12] Nonetheless, the disengagement of imperial armies from active combat in these theaters diminished Egypt's strategic importance in the region. Disengagement also deprived Egypt's military grandees of an outlet for their followers' military energies. The culmination of this trend came with the debacle at Vienna in 1683, when the armies of the Hapsburg empire and its allies broke the Ottoman siege of the city and swept through a swatch of Ottoman territory stretching through Hungary to Belgrade. This rout resulted in a mass redistribution of Ottoman soldiery, many of whom sought their fortunes in Egypt. Under these altered circumstances, Egypt's chief importance to the Ottoman empire during the seventeenth century shifted from that of a staging area and source of military manpower to that of leading supplier of revenue to the imperial treasury and equipper of the annual pilgrimage caravan to the holy cities of Mecca and Medina. The formation of Egypt's military elite and rivalries within that elite would henceforth hinge on these two issues.

The transformation of Egypt's military elite

The transformations afoot in the Ottoman capital and the Ottoman empire's heartland had a profound effect on Egypt's military society, whose demo-

---

[10] On the Zaydi imams, see Fuad Ishaq Khuri, *Imams and Emirs: State, Religion, and Sects in Islam* (London, 1990), 120; Paul Dresch, *Tribes, Government, and History in Yemen* (Oxford, 1989), 198–99.

[11] See, for example, Istanbul, Başbakanlık Osmanlı Arşivi, Mühimme defteri, vol. 99, no. 75 (A.H. 1101/C.E. 1689).

[12] André Raymond, *Le Caire des Janissaires: L'Apogée de la ville ottomane sous 'Abd al-Rahman Katkhuda* (Paris, 1995), 55–56.

graphic composition and political rivalries were already highly distinctive. After conquering Egypt, Sultan Salim I had incorporated those members of the Mamluk forces who professed loyalty to the Ottomans into the administrations of Egypt and Syria. Before he returned to Istanbul, moreover, he pardoned a number of defeated Mamluks and allowed them to remain in Egypt.[13] These rehabilitated Mamluk amirs continued to purchase military slaves, or *mamluks*, from the region of the Caucasus. Later in the sixteenth century, perhaps to prevent the undue influence of the rehabilitated Mamluks and their clients, the Ottoman government attempted to "Ottomanize" the rank of *sanjaq beyi* in Egypt by limiting it to officers of the Chavushan regiment and the recently introduced Mutafarriqa regiment, all of whom were recruited from the imperial palace.[14] Nonetheless, it seems likely that these Ottoman beys of Chavush and Mutafarriqa origin, like the former Mamluk amirs, purchased *mamluks* from the Caucasus for their retinues. Thus, by the 1630s, the Ottoman traveler Evliya Çelebi reports that there are many Circassians in Egypt.[15]

While Caucasian *mamluks* were evidently still flowing into Egypt, the province was receiving an influx of military and administrative personnel from the Ottoman empire's Anatolian and Balkan regions. Toward the beginning of the seventeenth century, fleeing *jalali* rebels and opportunistic mercenaries, as well as dispossessed peasants, migrated to Egypt. Many enrolled in the Egyptian garrison forces as a means of securing regular salaries while plying various petty trades on the side. Similar relocations continued throughout the century. In the early decades of the century, following the protracted wars against the Hapsburgs, Egypt, like other Ottoman provinces, absorbed a wave of demobilized imperial soldiery as *Qapu qullari*, or troops from the imperial capital, spread throughout the empire.[16] A number of Arabic and Turkish chronicles speak of a quintet of rowdy soldiers from the imperial capital who ran amok in Cairo during the 1660s. They were known as the *zurub*, an Arabicized plural of the Turkish word *zorba*, or "rebel."[17] Meanwhile, Turcophone bureaucrats of various

13 On the Ottoman conquest of Egypt and its effects, see Muhammad ibn Ahmad ibn Iyas, *An Account of the Ottoman Conquest of Egypt in the Year AH 922 (AD 1516)*, trans. W. H. Salmon (London, 1921); Ibn Iyas, *Journal d'un bourgeois du Caire*, trans. Gaston Wiet, 2 vols. (Paris, 1955); Jean-Louis Bacqué-Grammont, *Les Ottomans, les Safavides et leurs voisins* (Istanbul, 1987), 189–99, 206–07; P. M. Holt, *Egypt and the Fertile Crescent, 1516–1922: A Political History* (Ithaca, 1966), 33–45.

14 Mühimme defteri, vol. 6, no. 487 (A.H. 972/C.E. 1564); vol. 29, no. 9 (A.H. 984/C.E. 1576).

15 Evliya Çelebi, *Evliya Çelebi seyahatnamesi*, ed. Ahmed Cevdet, 10 vols. (Istanbul, 1888–1938), VII, 723.

16 Inalcik, "Military and Fiscal Transformation," 288–91; Inalcik, *Classical Age*, 51.

17 Anonymous, *Akhbar al-nuwwab min dawlat Al 'Uthman min hin istawla 'alayha al-sultan Salim Khan*, Istanbul, Topkapi Palace Library, MS Hazine 1623, fos. 29v ff.; Muhammad ibn Yusuf al-Hallaq, *Tarih-i Mısır-ı Kahire*, Istanbul University Library,

ethnic origins arrived in Cairo to staff the provincial administration, and the Ottoman governors transported their own sizable entourages to Cairo. Several seventeenth-century governors were dispatched to Egypt with large complements of imperial troops, numbering as many as 2,000, to perform specific missions.[18] These troops were a motley crew of Anatolian Turks; Balkan youths recruited through the *devshirme*, the classical Ottoman method of collecting non-Muslim boys from conquered territories; and various Turkic and Kurdish tribal levies.

These demographic changes occurred at a time when Egypt's system of land tenure and revenue allotment was undergoing a gradual yet profound transformation, again comparable to changes taking place in the Ottoman empire at large. The classical Ottoman *timar* system, whereby a cavalry officer was assigned the usufruct of a piece of land in exchange for raising a certain number of troops, had never been extended to Egypt. In the early years of Ottoman rule, taxes were collected directly by functionaries appointed from Istanbul, known as *amins*. By the seventeenth century, the system of *amins* was giving way to tax-farming, or *iltizam*, whereby officials and local notables bid at auction (*muzayada*) for the right to collect the taxes of a given subprovince, district, village, or urban property or enterprise. In this fashion, virtually every significant office, from customs director to the governor of Egypt, came to consist of a tax-farm.[19]

Tax-farming spread throughout the Ottoman empire and, indeed, has widely been interpreted as a sign of the empire's decline.[20] In Egypt, its effect, in addition to decentralizing tax collection and thereby increasing the power of local figures, was to blur the status barrier separating regimental officers from *sanjaq beyis*. Tax-farming deprived Egypt of the logical rank distinctions between soldiery and beys that had prevailed under the Mamluk

TY628, fos. 139–44; 'Abd al-Karim ibn 'Abd al-Rahman, *Tarih-i Mısır*, Istanbul, Süleymaniye Library, MS Hekimoğlu 'Ali Pasha 705, fos. 80v–84v; Ahmad Çelebi ibn 'Abd al-Ghani, *Awdah al-isharat fi man tawalla Misr al-Qahira min al-wuzara' wa al-bashat*, ed. A. A. 'Abd al-Rahim (Cairo, 1978), 162. *Akhbar al-nuwwab* refers to them as زرب and Ahmad Celebi as ظرب. All-Hallaq, however, uses no epithet while 'Abd al-Karim refers to the group as the *surbe* (flock of birds).

[18] Notably Qara Ibrahim Pasha, who arrived in Cairo in 1670 with 2,000 troops. See al-Hallaq, *Tarih-i Mısır-ı Kahire*, fos. 203v–205r; *Akhbar al-nuwwab*, fo. 34r; Ahmad Çelebi, *Awdah*, 171.

[19] On Ottoman adaptation of the Mamluk system, see "Mısır Kanunnamesi" in Ömer Lutfi Barkan, *Osmanlı imparatorluğunda zirai ekonominin hukuki ve mali esasları* (Istanbul, 1943), I, chap. 105; Stanford J. Shaw, *The Financial and Administrative Organization and Development of Ottoman Egypt, 1517–1798* (Princeton, 1962), 28 ff., 60–62; P. M. Holt, "The Beylicate in Egypt during the Seventeenth Century," *Bulletin of the School of Oriental and African Studies*, 24 (1961).

[20] See, for example, Halil Inalcik, "The Ottoman Decline and its Effects upon the Reaya," in Henrik Birnbaum and Speros Vryonis, Jr. (eds.), *Aspects of the Balkans, Continuity and Change: Contributions to the International Balkan Conference held at UCLA, October 23–28 1969* (The Hague, 1972), 341–42.

system of land tenure or that might have prevailed under the Ottoman *timar* system. Under the Mamluk system, a manumitted slave rose to the rank of cavalry commander and received a grant of usufruct (*iqta'*). Under the classical Ottoman system, a *sanjaq beyi* by definition held a collection of *timars* known as a *sanjaq*. A Janissary, being an infantryman, could not hold a cavalry-supporting assignment of usufruct but received a salary, in cash and provisions, from the imperial treasury.[21] With the introduction of tax-farming, however, the beys joined the soldiery as salaried functionaries. As their salaries grew increasingly uncertain toward the end of the sixteenth century, the Janissaries and the rest of the Ottoman soldiery had every incentive to enter the game of tax-farm acquisition, so that both beys and officers were now competing for tax-farms. The competition between beys and officers would become a recurring theme in the course of the seventeenth century and beyond.

By the early decades of the seventeenth century, a key feature of this competition was the struggle for the *ri'asa* (lit. "headship"), a phenomenon whose precise meaning has been the subject of some speculation. As depicted by P. M. Holt, the *ri'asa* seems a rather nebulous form of powerfulness.[22] The leading bey or officer assumed the *ri'asa*, as indicated in the chronicles by the phrase *intaha 'alayhi al-ri'asa* (lit. "the *ri'asa* ended on him").[23] As the balance of power in Egypt shifted, the holders of the *ri'asa* changed accordingly. Thus, early in the seventeenth century a group of soldiers held the *ri'asa*, while by the middle of the following century the Janissary officer Ibrahim Katkhuda al-Qazdagli shared it with the 'Azaban officer Ridwan Katkhuda al-Jalfi.[24] Notwithstanding, scrutiny of the chronicles suggests that the *ri'asa* was no abstraction but a collective headship that comprised specific high-ranking offices, with the revenues accruing to them. These offices appear to have been the commands of the seven regiments plus the key beylical posts of pilgrimage commander, *daftardar* (treasurer), and, by

---

[21] On the Mamluk land regime, see Hasanayn Rabie, "The Size and Value of the *Iqta'* in Egypt, 564–741/1169–1341," in Michael Cook (ed.), *Studies in the Economic History of the Middle East* (Oxford, 1970); A. N. Poliak, "Some Notes on the Feudal System of the Mamluks," *Journal of the Royal Asiatic Society* (1937), 97 ff. On Mamluk slave society, see David Ayalon, *L'esclavage du mamelouk* (Jerusalem, 1951); David Ayalon, "Studies on the Structure of the Mamluk Army," parts 1–3, *Bulletin of the School of Oriental and African Studies*, 15 (1953), 203–28, 448–76, and 16 (1954), 57–90. On the Ottoman *timar* system see, for example, Inalcik, part 1 of Inalcik (ed.) with Quataert, *Economic and Social History*, 114–17; Inalcik, *Classical Age*, 104–18.

[22] For example, Holt, *Egypt and the Fertile Crescent*, 90.

[23] See, for example, 'Abd al-Rahman al-Jabarti, *'Aja'ib al-athar fi al-tarajim wa'l-akhbar*, 7 vols. (Cairo, 1958–67), I, 234.

[24] Holt, *Egypt and the Fertile Crescent*, 90, 93. Al-Damurdashi at one point distinguishes between the *ri'asa* of the Janissaries and that of the 'Azaban; see Ahmad Katkhuda 'Azaban al-Damurdashi, *Al-Durra al-musana fi akhbar al-kinana*, British Museum, MS Or. 1073–74, p. 185. On Ibrahim and Ridwan, see al-Damurdashi, *Durra*, 560.

the mid-eighteenth century, *shaykh al-balad*, or headman, of Cairo. The reason that individuals, pairs, and groups of three are variously credited with holding the *ri'asa* is probably that the chief figures in the *ri'asa* varied according to the wealth and importance of the offices it comprised. Thus the connotation of *intaha 'alayhi al-ri'asa* is perhaps not that the person in question is the sole holder of the *ri'asa* but that he is the wealthiest and most powerful holder: the *ri'asa* literally culminates, or ends, in him.

By the end of the sixteenth century, beys appear to be taking an increasingly prominent role in Egypt's administration and, concomitantly, amassing considerable wealth. At roughly the same time, chronicles begin to report soldiery revolts after decades of apparent calm. These revolts may have been a provincial manifestation of the *jalali* rebellions, resulting in large part from the empire-wide military and fiscal crisis of the late sixteenth century. Yet they were also, no doubt, a partial consequence of the beys' growing influence in Egypt; as the beys promoted the interests of their own *mamluks* and followers in the Mutafarriqa and Chavushan regiments, opportunities for less well-connected soldiers dwindled. Most deeply affected were the three cavalry regiments, the Gonulluyan, Tufenkjiyan, and Jarakisa. Although these regiments were often called *sipahi* regiments after the timariot forces of the central provinces, they did not hold cavalry-supporting assignments of usufruct but relied on monthly salaries that were lower than those of any of the other regiments.[25] As tax-farming grew more prevalent, the treasury's ability to disburse salaries on time diminished; the soldiers of the cavalry regiments suffered accordingly and began to manifest their disaffection. A group of *sipahis* murdered the governor Ibrahim Pasha (1604–05), who had refused to pay them an accession fee. Matters came to a head in 1609, when rebellious troops from the *sipahi* regiments renounced their loyalty to the Ottoman empire and named their own sultan. The Ottoman governor Muhammad Pasha (1607–11) brutally crushed the rebellion in an action that the chronicler Ibn Abi al-Surur deems "the second Ottoman conquest of Egypt." The leaders of the defeated rebels were executed; the remainder were paraded through Cairo in chains, then exiled to Yemen. To underscore the utter opprobrium in which the Ottoman authorities held the rebels, the governor ordered every householder in Cairo to dig up a cubit of soil in front of his door so as to erase symbolically the very footprints of the traitors.[26] Muhammad Pasha's sobriquet was *Qul*

---

[25] On the *sipahi* regiments, see "Mısır Kanunnamesi," 355–57, 359; Shaw, *Financial and Administrative Organization*, 196–97.

[26] Shams al-Din Muhammad ibn Abi al-Surur al-Bakri al-Siddiqi, *Al-rawda al-zahiyya fi wulat Misr wa al-Qahira*, abridgement of *Al-Kawakib al-sa'ira fi akhbar Misr wa al-Qahira*, Cairo, Dar al-Kutub Manuscripts Division, Microfilm no. 1640, unpaginated, under the rubrics 'Ibrahim Pasha al-Maqtul" and "Muhammad Pasha Qul Qiran"; Holt, *Egypt and the Fertile Crescent*, 75–76.

Qiran, which has been erroneously translated as "the *mamluk* breaker."[27] *Qul* in Ottoman usage, however, typically refers to the imperial soldiery, above all the Janissaries.[28] Thus Muhammad Pasha's most noteworthy achievement would seem to have been breaking the volatile soldiery. He did, however, purge the ranks of the beylicate, replacing ten of thirteen beys. This sort of purge at the hands of the governor would become an established pattern in Ottoman Egyptian political culture.

Of equally great significance was the fact that Muhammad Pasha had quashed the soldiers' rebellion with the cooperation of the new group of beys, who thereby augmented their influence. In succeeding decades, the beys were unafraid to challenge the governor overtly for authority. In 1631, they summarily deposed the governor Musa Pasha after he had had one of their number assassinated.[29] Musa's dismissal established a pattern whereby the beys would depose any governor who did not serve their interests.

The competition between beys and officers in seventeenth-century Egypt is too easily interpreted as a confrontation between traditional Mamluk institutions and Ottoman innovations. Because the regiments were introduced by the Ottomans, they are perceived as the natural domain of traditional Ottoman recruits: Anatolian and Balkan mercenaries and, initially, *devshirme* recruits. The beylicate, in contrast, is regarded as the successor to the amirate of the Mamluk sultanate. Thus, Holt, in a seminal article, asserts that the post of *sanjaq beyi* in Ottoman Egypt was in fact a continuation of the Mamluk office of *amir mi'a*, which denoted an officer who held an *iqta'* that supported one hundred (*mi'a* in Arabic) horsemen. While acknowledging the transformation of Egypt's land-tenure system and the absorption of new elements into Egypt's military echelons, Holt supports his contention by drawing parallels between Mamluk- and Ottoman-era offices.[30]

By the same token, Holt and other scholars have assumed that the elite households that became prominent in Ottoman Egypt during the seventeenth century were modeled on the households of the Mamluk sultanate.[31] Yet the

---

27 Holt, *Egypt and the Fertile Crescent*, 74.
28 *Encyclopaedia of Islam*, 2nd ed., s.v. "Kul," by C. E. Bosworth; Inalcik, "Military and Fiscal Transformation," 283–84.
29 Ibn Abi al-Surur, *Al-rawda al-zahiyya*, under the rubric "Musa Pasha."
30 Holt, "Beylicate," 223.
31 See, for example, Holt, "Beylicate," 218, 223, 225; Holt, *Egypt and the Fertile Crescent*, 73, 85, 90–92; Shaw, *Financial and Administrative Organization*, 33, 37, 63, 186, 194; David Ayalon, "Studies in al-Jabarti I: Notes on the Transformation of Mamluk Society in Egypt under the Ottomans," parts 1–2, *Journal of the Economic and Social History of the Orient*, 3 (1960); Daniel Crecelius, *The Roots of Modern Egypt: A Study of the Regimes of 'Ali Bey al-Kabir and Muhammad Bey Abu al-Dhahab, 1760–1775* (Minneapolis and Chicago, 1980), 30–31; Michael Winter, "Turks, Arabs, and Mamluks in the Army of Ottoman Egypt," *Wiener Zeitschrift für die Kunde des Morgenlandes*, 72 (1980), 100, 120–22; Gabriel Piterberg, "The

decentralization of Ottoman political authority after the sixteenth century
had led to an empire-wide political culture based on households, up to and
including the household of the Ottoman sultan himself in the Topkapi
palace. Such households were not exclusively or even necessarily kinship
based but included members bound to each other by ties of patronage and
clientage. Egypt's households can be construed as a provincial variation on
this general trend, although they, like the seventeenth-century beylicate, no
doubt absorbed elements of the Mamluk sultanate's political culture while
drawing on the common tradition of statecraft of medieval and early
modern Turco-Iranian empires generally. In Egypt, beys, regimental officers,
and Ottoman officials alike cultivated households in order better to exploit
new sources of fiscal aggrandizement such as tax-farming and the Red Sea
coffee trade; given the uncertainty of salaries from the imperial treasury,
meanwhile, the military rank and file looked to the grandees for suste-
nance.[32]

The Fiqari and Qasimi factions

The middle years of the seventeenth century, roughly 1630–60, constituted
a period of beylical dominance in Ottoman Egypt, during which rival beys
competed for preponderant political and fiscal influence. This competition,
however, can be understood only in the context of the distinctive factional
politics that engulfed Egypt during this era of profound demographic and
fiscal change. Around 1630 or 1640, to judge from the accounts of
chroniclers, two political factions emerged and began to permeate Egyptian
society. These were the Fiqari (from Dhu'l-Fiqar) and Qasimi (from Qasim)
factions, which virtually divided Egyptian society between them from
roughly 1640 through 1730, encompassing not only the military echelons
but also Cairo's artisanal population and various Bedouin groups in the
Egyptian countryside.

The origins of these factions remain obscure. The origin myths of the
Fiqaris and Qasimis that the Arabic chronicles report assign a highly
archetypal character to the two factions. There appear to be two basic origin
traditions: one ascribing the emergence of the two factions to the Ottoman
conquest of Egypt, the other stressing the factions' alignment with two
Bedouin blocs: the Nisf Sa'd, allied with the Fiqaris, and the Nisf Haram,
allied with the Qasimis. The first tradition appears in its most detailed form
in the early eighteenth-century chronicle of Ahmad Çelebi, the second

Formation of an Ottoman Egyptian Elite in the Eighteenth Century," *International
Journal of Middle East Studies*, 22 (1990), 280.
[32] See Jane Hathaway, "The Military Household in Ottoman Egypt," *International
Journal of Middle East Studies*, 27 (1995), 39–52.

tradition in the slightly later chronicle of Ahmad Katkhuda ʿAzaban al-Damurdashi. Both traditions are presented in typically cleaned-up and articulate form by the early nineteenth-century chronicler ʿAbd al-Rahman al-Jabarti.

According to the first tradition, the factions arise during the Ottoman sultan Salim I's occupation of Cairo in 1517, after his defeat of the Mamluk sultanate. On arriving in Cairo, according to the tradition, Salim hears of an old Mamluk amir named Sudun, who has avoided the fighting by sequestering himself in his house with his two sons, Dhu'l-Fiqar and Qasim. These two sons are experts in the chivalric exercises known as *furusiyya*; hearing of their prowess, Salim orders them to demonstrate their skills before him. In the course of the display, a permanent rift opens between the two brothers. As al-Jabarti tells it, the Ottoman soldiery fight with Dhu'l-Fiqar while the "people of Egypt" fight with Qasim. Dhu'l-Fiqar's faction adopts the color white, Qasim's faction the color red.[33]

Since al-Jabarti goes on to explain that the two factions have predominated since 1640, historians have naturally searched assiduously for contemporary figures named Dhu'l-Fiqar and Qasim who could have served as eponymous founders of these two factions. Doris Behrens-Abouseif traces the eponyms to the seventeenth-century grandees Dhu'l-Fiqar Bey and Qasim Bey, each of whom held a number of high offices toward the middle of the century.[34] In presenting them, she more or less dismisses Holt's observation that the characters Dhu'l-Fiqar and Qasim of the origin myth seem almost allegorical figures, not unlike Avarice and Ambition.[35] Yet Holt perceived that this origin myth is too archetypal to attribute to two seventeenth-century beys, even if those two beys did in actual fact figure prominently in the efflorescence of the two factions.

In particular, the two seventeenth-century beys cannot account for the myth's stress on the Ottoman conquest. Holt notes that Salim I himself inspired a genre of heroic chronicles known as *Salimnames*, in which he typically appears as the savior of Circassian chivalry after the collapse of the Mamluk sultanate. This could explain the framing device of two champions testing their skills before Salim; such a device is common in the *furusiyya* literature produced during the later Mamluk sultanate. Behrens-Abouseif notes, in fact, that the contest between Dhu'l-Fiqar and Qasim was one of several that allegedly took place in Salim's presence after the Ottomans took

---

[33] Al-Jabarti, *ʿAjaʾib*, I, 70–71. In Ahmad Çelebi's account (*Awdah*, 283–84), the affiliations are reversed, and colors are not mentioned.

[34] Doris Behrens-Abouseif, *Egypt's Adjustment to Ottoman Rule: Institutions, Waqf, and Architecture in Cairo (Sixteenth and Seventeenth Centuries)* (Leiden, 1994), 118–22.

[35] P. M. Holt, "Al-Jabarti's Introduction to the History of Ottoman Egypt," *Bulletin of the School of Oriental and African Studies*, 25 (1962), 51.

Cairo.[36] Moreover, the name Sudun or Suduni was common to several late Mamluk *furusiyya* champions.[37]

This particular origin myth seems to graft late Mamluk *furusiyya* lore onto the story of the Ottoman conquest, so that the competing Ottoman and Mamluk forces are embodied in two *furusiyya* champions. Of particular note in this regard is the heraldic paraphernalia of the two factions, which may begin to offer a clue to their true origins. To quote al-Jabarti: "The way one faction (*fariq*) was distinguished from the other was that when they rode in processions, the Fiqaris' flag was white, and their lances had a knob, while the Qasimis' flag was red, and their lances had a disk."[38] This seems to suggest that the Fiqari lance was the knob-headed *tug* of the Ottoman armies while the Qasimi lance was the Mamluk *'alam*, topped not by a knob but normally by an inscription worked in metal in the shape of a spade or disk. As for the banners, the Mamluk ones could have borne a number of symbols of office. The Ottoman ones, however, in all likelihood bore the image of the early Muslim caliph 'Ali ibn Abi Talib's (656–61) sword Dhu'l-Fiqar, which was commonly emblazoned on Ottoman battle standards, above all those of the Janissaries.[39] From all appearances, then, the two factions schematically represented Ottoman and non-Ottoman elements within Egypt's military population, as symbolized by specific Ottoman and Mamluk heraldic devices.

The origin myth transmitted by al-Damurdashi focuses on the two Bedouin factions, Sa'd and Haram, allied respectively with the Fiqaris and the Qasimis. By the late seventeenth century, according to his account, "the government of Egypt was in two factions (*farqayn*), Sa'd and Haram, Tubba'i and Kulaybi, [Husayni] and Yazidi; the Husayni's flag was white, and the Yazidi's flag was red," and he goes on to note the difference between their lances.[40] The allusions here are to much earlier Arab history, specifically to the late seventh-century conflict between the Umayyads under Yazid ibn Mu'awiyya and the party of 'Ali led by 'Ali's son Husayn, who was martyred by Yazid's army. "Tubba" was the title of the king of the ancient Yemeni kingdom of Himyar. "Kulaybi," meanwhile, may refer to the Kalb, a Yemeni tribal group who supported the Umayyad Marwan for caliph, or leader of the Muslim community, against Ibn al-Zubayr and the northern Arabs of Qays following the death of Yazid in 683. Alternatively, it could

---

[36] Behrens-Abouseif, *Egypt's Adjustment to Ottoman Rule*, 121–22.

[37] David Ayalon, "Furusiyya Exercises and Games in the Mamluk Sultanate," *Scripta Hierosolymitana*, 9 (1961), 31–62.

[38] Al-Jabarti, *'Aja'ib*, I, 71.

[39] Zdzislaw Zygulski, Jr., *Ottoman Art in the Service of the Empire* (New York, 1992), 45–51, 69ff.; Fevzi Kurtoğlu, *Türk Bayrağı ve Ay Yıldız* (Ankara, 1938), 74–77; Riza Nour, "L'histoire du croissant," *Revue de Turcologie*, 1 (1933), 117/346.

[40] Al-Damurdashi, *Durra*, 2.

refer to the Qaysi leader Kulayb. If the Fiqari–Qasimi rivalry contains an element of the ancient rivalry between northern, or Qaysi, and southern, or Yemeni, Arabs, this would explain the color dichotomy, for red is associated with Qays and white with Yemen.[41] In any case, an attempt would seem to be made in this origin tradition to link the tribal blocs, and by extension the Mamluks and Ottomans, to the party of 'Ali, on the one hand, and to the Umayyads, on the other. Which bloc conforms to which party is not entirely clear, however. On the one hand, the Ottomans could be linked to the Umayyads as an imperial power that allegedly usurped the caliphate and that was founded by a man named 'Uthman ('Osman). On the other hand, the Ottoman forces, above all the Janissaries, had a strong allegiance to 'Ali; hence the Dhu'l-Fiqar flag.

In any event, Sa'd and Haram can be identified as real Yemeni tribes. The fourteenth-century Moroccan traveler Ibn Battuta encountered the Bani Haram in a Yemeni town called Hali, which he claims was the seat of Yemen's ancient kings.[42] The Sa'd, meanwhile, would appear to come from the Hadhramawt.[43] To judge from a brief mention in the chronicle of Yusuf Effendi, the Haram were in Egypt before the Ottoman conquest; their most notable act was abandoning the last Mamluk sultan, Tumanbay, in the face of the Ottoman armies.[44] There is no evidence of the Sa'd in chronicles of Egypt before the seventeenth century, when the Fiqari and Qasimi factions are supposed to have come to the fore of Egyptian politics.

It is perhaps significant that the two factions came to prominence just after Ottoman armies had been expelled from Yemen by the Qasimi dynasty, a Zaydi dynasty that took its name from the ninth-century imam Qasim, a descendant of 'Ali's son Husayn. The Zaydis were strongest in mountainous northern Yemen, where the Himyarites and, presumably, the Haram originated, while the Ottoman stronghold had always been the south, including part of the Hadhramawt, ostensible home of the Sa'd. Perhaps Egypt's seventeenth-century factionalism was to some degree a playing out of the conflict in Yemen, which had been closely tied to Egypt until the Zaydi victory. Early Ottoman governors of Egypt were frequently sent to Egypt after serving in Yemen and vice versa, and troops from Egypt routinely went to Yemen to battle the Zaydis and to collect taxes. An intriguing footnote to this line of speculation is the appearance in al-

---

41 On the Qaysi–Yemeni rivalry see, for example, Ignaz Goldziher, *Muslim Studies*, ed. S. M. Stern, trans. C. R. Barber and S. M. Stern, 2 vols. (Albany, 1967), I, 65–97.

42 'Abdallah Muhammad b. Ibrahim b. Battuta, *Rihla Ibn Battuta*, introduction by Karam al-Bustani (Beirut, 1964), 246.

43 R. B. Serjeant, "The Coastal Population of Socotra," in Brian Doe (ed. and comp.), *Socotra: Island of Tranquility* (London, 1992), 162–63.

44 Yusuf Efendi, *Tarih-i Mısır*, Istanbul, Süleymaniye Library, MS Esad Efendi 2148, fo. 43v.

Damurdashi's chronicle of a group of Lower Egyptian Bedouin known as
Zayyidiyya – that is, Zaydis – who belong to the Nisf Haram.[45]

It seems possible that the Fiqari and Qasimi factions emerged in the
seventeenth century as a result of jockeying for position between Ottoman
and non-Ottoman elements in Egypt's military population at a time when
that population was becoming more and more diverse. The central government's attempt, late in the sixteenth century, to ottomanize the beylicate
even while the beys themselves were importing Caucasian *mamluk*s may
have prepared the ground for what appears to be a form of Circassian self-
assertion early in the seventeenth century. Particularly noticeable is a
resurgence of traditional Circassian Mamluk given names within the Qasimi
faction, in violation of Salim I's decree that Egyptian grandees take only
Arab Muslim names. During the 1640s, two Qasimi beys named Qansuh
and Mamay (or Memi) unsuccessfully challenged the Fiqaris for the posts of
pilgrimage commander and *daftardar*.[46] Later in the century, the Qasimi
chieftain Ridwan Bey Abu al-Shawarib ("mustachioed") named two of his
sons Azbak and Khushqadam, evoking the Mamluks of old in no uncertain
terms: Azbak was the general who led the Mamluk armies against the
Ottoman sultan Muhammad II during the 1450s; the Mamluk sultan
Khushqadam (1461–67) had been one of his patrons.[47] Yet taking Mamluk
names was by the seventeenth century apparently no more an act of rebellion
against the Ottoman sultan than was carrying the Mamluk standard.
Rather, evoking an idealized Mamluk sultanate through names and symbols
had evidently become an acceptable, or at least tolerable, feature of the
political discourse of seventeenth-century Ottoman Egypt. Indeed, Evliya
Çelebi's observation that the Circassian beys of Egypt turned their heads
away from the mausoleum of the collaborationist governor Khayrbay
(1517–22) but bowed their heads before the tomb of the last Mamluk
sultan, Tumanbay, might be interpreted in this same light.[48]

To this brand of Circassian self-assertion belongs the spurious genealogy
of one Ridwan Bey, whom Holt has identified as the Fiqari leader who
monopolized the post of pilgrimage commander during the 1630s and
1640s.[49] The genealogy traces Ridwan's lineage to the Mamluk sultan
Barquq (1382–99) and thence to the Prophet's clan of Quraysh. Holt

[45] Al-Damurdashi, *Durra*, 364.
[46] Al-Hallaq, *Tarih-i Mısır-ı Kahire*, fos. 143v–148r.
[47] On Azbak and Khushqadam Beys, see 'Abd al-Karim, *Tarih-i Mısır*, fos. 78v, 91v. On
    their Mamluk namesakes, see Carl Petry, *Twilight of Majesty: The Reigns of the
    Mamluk Sultans al-Ashraf Qaytbay and Qansuh al-Ghawri in Egypt* (Seattle and
    London, 1993), 47, 94–100.
[48] Evliya Çelebi, *Seyahatnamesi*, X, 581.
[49] P. M. Holt, "The Exalted Lineage of Ridwan Bey: Some Observations on a Seventeenth-
    century Mamluk Genealogy," *Bulletin of the School of Oriental and African Studies*, 22
    (1959), 224–27.

construes the genealogy as Ridwan Bey's attempt to forge a more legitimate pedigree than that of the Ottoman sultan and perhaps to justify a bid for autonomy. It seems likely, however, that the Ridwan Bey in question is not Ridwan Bey al-Fiqari but the Qasimi chieftain Ridwan Bey Abu al-Shawarib. One telling clue to this identification is the manuscript's revelation that Ridwan Bey has two sons named Azbak and Khushqadam, as did Abu al-Shawarib; Ridwan Bey al-Fiqari, in contrast, left no sons.[50] Furthermore, the work gives Ridwan Bey's title not as pilgrimage commander (*amir al-hajj*) but as "servant of the prophet's litter" (*khadim al-mahmil al-Muham-madi*), referring to the symbolic litter that was carried to Mecca from Egypt as part of the pilgrimage.[51] This title could be a virtual synonym for pilgrimage commander, as Holt asserts, but it could also be a calculated attempt to point up Ridwan's devotion to the pilgrimage and the holy places while avoiding the actual title of pilgrimage commander. The work as a whole is obsessed with the sacred mosque (*Bayt al-Haram*) in Mecca and goes to great lengths to demonstrate Ridwan Bey's descent from a long line of servants of the sacred mosque, going back ultimately to the Quraysh. This, then, would explain the Qurayshi genealogy, although it is important to note that the claim of Qurayshi descent did not originate with Ridwan Bey. Rather, it belonged to indigenous Circassian lore and was documented by the seventeenth-century Ottoman traveler Evliya Çelebi during his travels in Circassia.[52] Thus the genealogy seems designed to demonstrate that *this* Ridwan Bey deserves to be appointed pilgrimage commander by virtue of his Qurayshi-cum-Circassian heritage, undercutting the claims of non-Circassian, notably Ottoman, beys.

The truly novel element in this genealogy, however, is the purported link to the Mamluk sultan Barquq, the first of the Circassian, or Burji, Mamluk sultans, who held sway over Egypt from 1388 to 1517. In the context of Egyptian society alone, it would seem that Ridwan Bey was attempting to portray himself as heir to the Mamluk sultanate and therefore as an alternative to the Ottomans. Viewed in a broader context, however, Ridwan Bey's strategy gains greater subtlety. The tactic of invoking a past power was not uncommon among Ottoman provincial elites. In early seventeenth-century Basra, for example, the local Afrasiyab dynasty claimed descent from the Great Seljuks, who ruled in Iraq and parts of Iran from the mid-

---

[50] Anonymous, *Nisba sharifa wa risala munifa tashtamal ʿala dhikr nasab al-Jarakisa min Quraysh*, Princeton University Library, Garrett Manuscript Collection, MS 186H, fos. 19v–20r; Holt, "The Exalted Lineage of Ridwan Bey," 226. Holt examined manuscripts in the John Rylands Library, Manchester, England, and the British Museum.

[51] *Nisba sharifa*, fo. 2v.

[52] Evliya Çelebi, *Seyahatnamesi*, VII, 718ff. See also Schora-Bekmursin-Nogmow, *Die Sagen und Lieder des Tscherkessen-Volks* (Leipzig, 1866), 63ff.

eleventh through the early twelfth centuries.[53] Meanwhile, in the principalities of Moldovia and Wallachia, the Phanariot Greeks whom the Ottomans appointed governors in the eighteenth century posed as neo-Byzantines
to the extent of replicating Byzantine court ritual.[54] Yet neither of these
regional authorities contemplated rebellion against the Ottoman sultan;
rather, by invoking the pre-Ottoman rulers of the regions where they held
sway, they seem to have achieved the impression of having strong local roots
that did not depend on the Ottoman authority. This perceived local
authority complemented, rather than rivalled, the authority vested in them
by their allegiance to the Ottoman sultan.

During the first half of the seventeenth century the Fiqari–Qasimi
antagonism manifested itself primarily among the beys, centering particularly on control of the posts of *amir al-hajj* and *daftardar*. The Ottoman
government attempted to retain ultimate authority in the province by
dividing the posts between the two factions; a Fiqari pilgrimage commander
and a Qasimi *daftardar* appear to have been the ideal. How successful the
government was in achieving this ideal division is questionable, however;
each faction sought to monopolize both posts and the revenues accruing to
them. The Ottoman government could react only by shifting its support to
the opposing faction. In the wake of Musa Pasha's deposition in 1631, the
government threw its support to two Fiqari leaders, ʿAli Bey, the governor of
the Upper Egyptian superprovince of Jirja, and the remarkable pilgrimage
commander Ridwan Bey. Ridwan retained the post of pilgrimage commander for some twenty-five years, weathering the revolt of Qansuh and
Mamay Beys, and the efforts of Sultan Murad IV (1624–40) and various
governors to remove him from office.[55] During these years, he established
the Fiqari faction as a formidable power. His chief building projects remain
to attest to his wealth and influence. He founded the central market area
known as the Qasabat Ridwan, just outside the old Fatimid city of al-
Qahira, and took a leading role in the restoration of the Kaʿba after it had
collapsed during a flood in 1630.[56]

To counter the inordinate influence of Ridwan Bey and his Fiqari
successors, the central government shifted its support to the Qasimis, and in
particular to a new chieftain, Ahmad Bey Bushnaq ("Bosniak"). There is
some reason to believe that Ahmad Bey may have belonged to a group of
Bosnians injected into the Qasimi faction from the capital. Turkish chronicles

[53] Holt, *Egypt and the Fertile Crescent*, 134. Holt notes the similarity to Ridwan Bey.
[54] William H. McNeill, *Europe's Steppe Frontier, 1500–1800* (Chicago and London,
    1964), 107–10, 140–41, 173–76.
[55] Holt, "The Exalted Lineage of Ridwan Bey," 224–27; Holt, *Egypt and the Fertile
    Crescent*, 79–81.
[56] On Ridwan's role in the restoration of the Kaʿba, see Suraiya Faroqhi, *Pilgrims and
    Sultans: The Hajj under the Ottomans* (London and New York, 1994), 11, 115–19.

refer to Ahmad Bey Bushnaq, his brother Sha'ban, and his purported nephew Ibrahim Bey Abu Shanab ("mustachioed") as "Yeni Kapılı." This epithet most likely refers to the Yeni Kapi quarter on the Marmara coast of Istanbul, near where the palace of the sultan's mother stood.[57] Ridwan Bey's death in 1656 gave Ahmad Bey Bushnaq the opportunity to consolidate the Qasimis' power. Growing friction between the two factions erupted in a series of bloody battles throughout the Egyptian countryside during 1660 that culminated in a Qasimi massacre of defeated Fiqaris. Notwithstanding, the Ottoman court had grown alarmed by the beys' excesses and made haste to execute the victorious Ahmad Bey Bushnaq.[58] His purported nephew Ibrahim Bey Abu Shanab, however, remained a formidable power broker until his death during an epidemic in 1718.

Prominence of regimental officers in the late seventeenth century

In the wake of the torturous struggle among the beys and with the encouragement of the reforming grand viziers of the Köprülü family, regimental officers displaced beys at the forefront of Egyptian political and economic life late in the seventeenth century. While the beys' ranks had been decimated by the fighting, the soldiery's numbers had grown with fresh infusions of troops from the capital and uprooted mercenaries, particularly in the wake of the failed Ottoman siege of Vienna in 1683. A substantial proportion of these soldiers, to judge from salary registers of the period, were joining the households of officers, as well.[59]

The seventeenth century also witnessed a shift in the balance of power among the seven regiments. While the three cavalry corps remained the lowliest of the regiments, the relative wealth and influence of the other four regiments changed. As the military elite grew more localized and direct injections of palace personnel into the province waned, the Mutafarriqa corps, once the cream of the regiments and the channel of sultanic influence, dwindled in numbers and importance. By the end of the seventeenth century, its once-exclusive ranks were open to the clients of officers from other regiments.[60] Many of the privileged positions it had controlled, such as the

[57] Al-Hallaq, *Tarih-i Mısır-ı Kahire*, fos. 156r, 162v, 226r, 226v. "Yeni Kapili" can also refer to Bab al-Jadid in Cairo's Citadel; see al-Hallaq, *Tarih-i Mısır-ı Kahire*, fos. 159v, 320v; 'Abd al-Karim, *Tarih-i Mısır*, fo. 68v. However, none of the Arabic chronicles ever uses Bab al-Jadid as a *nisba*.

[58] Al-Hallaq, *Tarih-i Mısır-ı Kahire*, fos. 183v–185r; Ahmad Çelebi, *Awdah*, 58–59.

[59] This is evident from a salary register dated 1675–77: Istanbul, Başbakanlık Osmanlı Arşivi, Maliyeden Müdevver 4787.

[60] Maliyeden Müdevver 4787.

right to tax public spectacles,[61] had been usurped by the Janissary (Mustah-fizan) and ʿAzaban corps, which now emerged as Egypt's premier corps. Always the largest regiment, the Janissaries now took the Mutafarriqa's place as the wealthiest and most influential regiment.

The officers of the Janissary regiment were, in addition, expanding their sources of revenue during the seventeenth century. They farmed the taxes of the customs of Egypt's Red Sea and Mediterranean ports, which became extraordinarily lucrative during the seventeenth century with the intro-duction of coffee from Yemen and the resulting traffic in coffee beans across the Red Sea.[62] Many officers formed partnerships with the overseas mer-chants (tujjar) from a number of countries who handled trade in coffee and spices. The burgeoning coffee trade made it desirable for officers to acquire the tax-farms of the Egyptian villages that were endowed to the huge imperial pious foundations established to service the holy cities of Mecca and Medina. These foundations, known as Awqaf al-Haramayn, drew revenues from throughout the Ottoman empire and were overseen by the chief black eunuch of the imperial harem.[63] Villages endowed to the Awqaf produced the grain that accompanied the pilgrimage caravan to the Hijaz; although the grain was intended for the poor of the holy cities, a portion of it was traded in the Hijaz for coffee.[64] The tax-farms of a cluster of Awqaf villages in the Upper Egyptian subprovince of al-Bahnasa formed the basis of the fortune of one of late seventeenth-century Egypt's most influential grandees, the Fiqari chieftain and longtime commander of the Gonulluyan regiment Hasan Agha Bilifya, who took his sobriquet from the Awqaf village of Bilifya.[65]

By the end of the seventeenth century Egypt was, in actual fact, adminis-tered by a triumvirate consisting of Hasan Agha Bilifya, his son-in-law the longtime daftardar Ismaʿil Bey, and his client the Janissary katkhuda Mustafa al-Qazdagli. The Bilifya household achieved this degree of authority after weathering a muted challenge from the Fiqari grandee Ibrahim Bey ibn Dhu'l-Fiqar, son of Ismaʿil Bey's khushdash (mamluk of the

[61] On this right, see Shaw, Financial and Administrative Organization, 121, 194.
[62] Ralph S. Hattox, Coffee and Coffeehouses: The Origins of a Social Beverage in the Medieval Near East (Seattle and London, 1985), 11ff., 73–77; André Raymond, Artisans et commerçants au Caire au XVIIIᵉ siècle, 2 vols. (Damascus, 1973–74), I, 330–35.
[63] Shaw, Financial and Administrative Organization, 269–70; I. H. Uzunçarşılı, Mekke-i Mükerreme Emirleri (Ankara, 1972), 15.
[64] On this point, see Richard Pococke, A Description of the East and Some Other Countries, 2 vols. (London, 1743), I, 204; and Michel Tuchscherer, 'Le pèlerinage de l'émir Sulayman Gawiš al-Qazdugli, sirdar de la caravane de la Mekke en 1739," Annales Islamologiques, 24 (1988), 175.
[65] Jane Hathaway, "The Role of the Kızlar Ağası in Seventeenth–Eighteenth-century Egypt," Studia Islamica, 75 (1992), 153–54. In secondary sources, Hasan Agha's sobriquet is often erroneously rendered "Balfiyya."

same master) Dhu'l-Fiqar Bey, who attempted to realize a scheme of Fiqari aggrandizement. Ibn Dhu'l-Fiqar's challenge illustrates just how complex factional rivalries and the competition between beys and soldiers had become by the end of the century.

Ibrahim Bey ibn Dhu'l-Fiqar was appointed pilgrimage commander in 1691, replacing the powerful Qasimi chieftain Ibrahim Bey Abu Shanab; Hasan Agha's son-in-law Isma'il Bey, meanwhile, retained the post of *daftardar*. By allowing Fiqaris to hold both posts, the Ottoman government broke with its principle of dividing the positions between a Fiqari and a Qasimi. In pursuit of Fiqari supremacy, Ibn Dhu'l-Fiqar attempted to manipulate the Janissary corps, which until then had been controlled by Qasimis. He eliminated three Qasimi officers,[66] thus clearing the way for the return to the Janissary corps of the ambitious lower officer Kuchuk Muhammad Bashodabashi. Acting as an upstart Janissary "boss" antagonistic to the interests of the higher officers, Kuchuk Muhammad had been expelled from the regiment in 1680 and again in 1686.[67]

Kuchuk Muhammad is portrayed in Arabic chronicles and in secondary studies as a populist hero who defended the common soldiery and the populace at large against the abuses of the grandees, both officers and beys.[68] It is clear that the tales attesting to his heroism were generic stories that were also applied to other sympathetic figures of the era, such as the Ottoman governor Husayn Pasha.[69] In fact, Kuchuk Muhammad appears to have had a personal stake in the downfall of one of the Qasimi officers, the chief scribe Salim Effendi, to whom he owed 3,000 gold pieces (*sharifi altun*).[70] Notwithstanding, Salim Effendi may have been exactly the sort of extortionist higher officer whom popular lore praised Kuchuk Muhammad for opposing. Indeed, Mustafa Katkhuda al-Qazdagli, Kuchuk Muhammad's eventual archfoe, reportedly arranged Salim Effendi's expulsion from the Janissaries by accusing him of withholding money from the soldiers' salaries.[71]

---

[66] The Janissary *katkhuda* Khalil was assassinated while the *bash ikhtiyar* (head of the higher officers) Rajab Katkhuda and the chief scribe Salim Effendi were raised to the beylicate. Salim Effendi was eventually executed. See al-Damurdashi, *Durra*, 12–13; al-Jabarti, *'Aja'ib*, I, 230.

[67] On Kuchuk Muhammad's career, see al-Jabarti, *'Aja'ib*, I, 242–45; P. M. Holt, "The Career of Kuchuk Muhammad (1676–94)," *Bulletin of the School of Oriental and African Studies*, 26 (1963), 269–87.

[68] See, for example, al-Jabarti, *'Aja'ib*, I, 238, 241; Holt, "The Career of Kuchuk Muhammad," 285–87.

[69] Al-Hallaq, *Tarih-i Mısır-ı Kahire*, fo. 210r. See also Jane Hathaway, "Sultans, Pashas, Taqwims, and Muhimmes: A Reconsideration of Chronicle-Writing in Eighteenth-century Ottoman Egypt," in Daniel Crecelius (ed.), *Eighteenth Century Egypt: The Arabic Manuscript Sources* (Claremont, 1990), 65, n. 50.

[70] Mühimme defteri, vol. 108, no. 1315 (A.H. 1107/C.E. 1696). He was also in debt to two other Janissary officers and two customs officials.

[71] Al-Damurdashi, *Durra*, 14.

The officers' elimination, however, precipitated a higher-officer–lower-officer struggle between Mustafa Katkhuda and Kuchuk Muhammad. On recovering the status of Janissary "boss," Kuchuk Muhammad exiled Mustafa Katkhuda to the Hijaz. Only in 1694 did Hasan Agha Bilifya succeed in persuading Ibrahim Bey ibn Dhu'l-Fiqar to allow Mustafa Katkhuda to return to Cairo. Shortly after his return, Kuchuk Muhammad was assassinated by one of Mustafa Katkhuda's clients.[72] Ibrahim Bey ibn Dhu'l-Fiqar's flirtation with power ended not long afterward, when he colluded with the governor in an attempt to assassinate the Qasimi leader Ibrahim Bey Abu Shanab. The failure of the plot led to the appointment of a new governor favorable to Abu Shanab.[73] Ibn Dhu'l-Fiqar died shortly thereafter, in the plague of 1696.

A key feature of Ibn Dhu'l-Fiqar's scheme of aggrandizement concerned local supervision of the *Awqaf al-Haramayn*. Although the chief black eunuch of the imperial harem was superintendent (*nazir*) of the *Awqaf al-Haramayn*, so many Egyptian villages were endowed to the *Awqaf* that a superintendent on the spot, called either *nazir* or *mutawalli*, was selected from among Egypt's military elite.[74] While there seems initially to have been no stipulation as to the supervisors' ranks, beys dominated the posts until late in the seventeenth century. In 1670, however, a reform instituted by the governor Qara Ibrahim Pasha, the lieutenant of grand vizier Köprülü Fadil Ahmad Pasha, transferred supervision to specific officers of the Janissary and 'Azaban corps.[75] Shortly after being named pilgrimage commander in 1691, Ibn Dhu'l-Fiqar engineered the restoration of supervision to a group of almost exclusively Fiqari beys.[76] The timing of the beylical takeover makes one suspect that it was arranged by Ibn Dhu'l-Fiqar in an attempt to weaken the higher regimental officers. Such a strategy would have complemented his eliminating the Qasimi officers and championing Kuchuk Muhammad. It would also have put him at odds with Hasan Agha Bilifya, who was the foremost higher regimental officer.

Hasan Agha, for his part, took a much more eclectic, opportunistic approach to rank and factional loyalties than Ibn Dhu'l-Fiqar. In the wake

---

72 Al-Jabarti, *'Aja'ib*, I, 237. Al-Damurdashi (*Durra*, 20) has an ally of the dismissed Qasimis attempting to kill Kuchuk Muhammad earlier. Ahmad Çelebi (*Awdah*, 190) says merely that whoever killed Kuchuk Muhammad was not worth the price of a slipper on his foot.
73 Ahmad Çelebi, *Awdah*, 194–97; al-Hallaq, *Tarih-i Mısır-ı Kahire*, fo. 220r; 'Abd al-Karim, *Tarih-i Mısır*, fo. 99v; al-Damurdashi, *Durra*, 30.
74 Despite Stanford Shaw's rigorous terminological breakdown in *Financial and Administrative Organization*, 41–45, the titles seem to have been fairly fluid.
75 Al-Hallaq, *Tarih-i Mısır-ı Kahire*, fos. 204v–205r; *Akhbar al-nuwwab*, fo. 34r; Ahmad Çelebi, *Awdah*, 171.
76 Al-Hallaq, *Tarih-i Mısır-ı Kahire*, fo. 226v; *Akhbar al-nuwwab*, fo. 42v; Ahmad Çelebi, *Awdah*, 187; al-Jabarti, *'Aja'ib*, I, 75.

of Ibn Dhu'l-Fiqar's death, the Bilifya group did not choose to pursue his ruthlessly pro-Fiqari program. Al-Damurdashi stresses the care with which Hasan Agha maintained working relations with the Qasimis, in particular Ibrahim Bey Abu Shanab. After Hasan Agha's death in 1704, in fact, his son-in-law Isma'il Bey appears to have shared power with Abu Shanab.[77] Hasan Agha, along with Abu Shanab, appears committed to the balancing act between Fiqaris and Qasimis that the Ottoman government itself pursued. This commitment seems to have been common among the household leaders of the late seventeenth century. Ibrahim Bey ibn Dhu'l-Fiqar's scheme of Fiqari supremacy, however, threatened this balance of power.

The Bilifya household's most enduring legacy consisted in nurturing the Qazdagli household. Founded by Hasan Agha's client, the Janissary *katkhuda* Mustafa al-Qazdagli, the Qazdagli household would come to dominate Egypt for much of the eighteenth century. Mustafa al-Qazdagli was, according to al-Jabarti, *rumi al-jins* ("*Rumi* by ethnicity"), which in the Ottoman period typically connoted someone from western Anatolia or the eastern Balkans, particularly the vicinity of the imperial capital. Correspondingly, the sobriquet Qazdagli refers to someone from the vicinity of the Kazdağı, or Mount Ida, in western Anatolia.[78] Ottoman archival sources suggest that Mustafa Katkhuda was an Anatolian mercenary or *Qapu qulu* who migrated to Egypt early in the seventeenth century, and that he cultivated ties to the holy cities very early in his Egyptian career. An imperial order of 1753 refers to a "Qazdagli Mustafa of Egypt's *odabashis*" who was connected with the Basyatiyya Madrasa in Mecca a hundred *hijri* years earlier – around 1656.[79]

The influence of the chief black eunuch on Egyptian society

Underlying the struggle over supervision of the *Awqaf al-Haramayn* was the question of the Egyptian grandees' ties to the Ottoman chief black eunuch (*Aghat Dar al-Sa'ada, Darüssaade Ağa* or *Kızlar Ağası*), who was superintendent of all properties endowed to the *Awqaf* empire-wide. The post of chief harem eunuch was created under Sultan Murad III (1574–95) and fell exclusively to black Africans beginning in the late sixteenth century.[80] From 1644 deposed chief black eunuchs were routinely exiled to Egypt; hence

---

[77] Al-Damurdashi, *Durra*, 52; al-Jabarti, *'Aja'ib*, I, 237.

[78] There is at least one other mountain known as the Kazdağı near the town of Uşak, east of Izmir; see *Türk Ansiklopedisi*, s.v. "Uşak," by R. Izbirak. Mount Ida, however, is by far the best-known and most frequently encountered in atlases and geographical dictionaries.

[79] Mühimme-i Mısır, vol. 7, no. 82 (A.H. 1166/C.E. 1753).

[80] Mehmet Süreyya, *Sijill-i 'osmani*, 4 vols. (Istanbul, 1308 A.H.), IV, 724ff.; N. M. Penzer, *The Harem* (London, 1936, 1965), 161–67.

their influence in the province increased dramatically. Evidence points to
continuous interaction with Egypt throughout a eunuch's career. African
slaves arrived in Egypt with the annual caravans from the Sudan; certain of
them were castrated in Coptic villages in Upper Egypt, then sold in the slave
markets of Cairo, where they might be purchased for the household of the
Ottoman governor or those of the local grandees. Governors and eventually,
it appears, grandees regularly presented eunuchs as gifts to the imperial
palace.[81] Thus it cannot have been uncommon for African eunuchs newly
arrived in the imperial palace already to enjoy connections in Egypt.

While in office, the chief black eunuch paid close attention to affairs in
Egypt to ensure that revenues and grain owed to the *Awqaf al-Haramayn*
were delivered in a timely fashion. At the same time, the eunuch prepared
for his eventual exile in Egypt by amassing properties and founding his own
personal *waqfs* in Egypt. To serve both purposes, the eunuch employed
agents (*wakils*); one of these, Mustafa Bey Kizlar, served Yusuf Agha
(1671–86), al-Hajj Bashir Agha (1717–46), and possibly Nazir Agha
(1692–94).[82] An agent bearing the title *wakil dar al-saʿada* and dealing
chiefly with matters concerning the *Awqaf al-Haramayn* appears to have
been a permanent fixture in Cairo by the early eighteenth century.[83] In sum,
a continuous network of potential, acting, and exiled palace eunuchs and
their agents linked the imperial capital and its largest province.

In late seventeenth-century Cairo, the residences of exiled eunuchs seem
to have formed an identifiable cluster in the fashionable elite quarter
surrounding Birkat al-Fil.[84] A house might be handed down from one exiled
eunuch to another; thus, Yusuf Agha inherited the home of his patron, Tash
Yatur ʿAli Agha, who had been exiled to Egypt some years earlier.[85]

In effect, exiled eunuchs became localized grandees in Egypt; like other

---

[81] P. S. Girard, *Mémoire sur l'agriculture, l'industrie, et le commerce, Description de
l'Egypte*, 2nd ed. (1824), XVII, 278–96; H. A. R. Gibb and Harold Bowen, *Islamic
Society and the West*, 1 vol. in 2 parts (London, 1950), part 1, 305, n. 3.

[82] Mühimme defteri, vol. 99, no. 491 (A.H. 1101/C.E. 1690); al-Damurdashi, *Durra*, 293;
Mühimme-i Mısır, vol. 4, no. 8 (A.H. 1139/C.E. 1726–27); Hathaway, "The Role of the
Kızlar Ağası," 149; Mühimme-i Mısır, vol. 1, nos. 447 (A.H. 1128/C.E. 1716), 471 (A.H.
1129/C.E. 1717).

[83] Al-Damurdashi (*Durra*, 528–31) cites the *wakil dar al-saʿada* trying to persuade
Ibrahim Bey Qatamish to relinquish grain from villages endowed to the *Awqaf*. Two
firmans dated A.H 1160/C.E. 1747 (Topkapi Palace Archives, E5125/27 and 28) reveal
that this was al-Hajj Bashir Agha's agent ʿUthman Agha. The latter *firman* bears his
stamp on the reverse, with the date A.H. 1161/C.E. 1748. ʿUthman Agha also appears in
a number of imperial orders dealing with the disposal of Bashir Agha's estate; see
Mühimme-i Mısır, vol. 6, nos. 318, 319, 341, 342 (all A.H. 1159/C.E. 1746).

[84] Jane Hathaway, "The Wealth and Influence of an Exiled Ottoman Eunuch in Egypt:
The *Waqf* Inventory of ʿAbbas Agha," *Journal of the Economic and Social History of
the Orient*, 37 (1994), 305 and n. 54; Ahmad Çelebi, *Awdah*, 187.

[85] Al-Damurdashi, *Durra*, 322; al-Hallaq, *Tarih-i Mısır-ı Kahire*, fos. 219v, 220r, 222;
Akhbar al-nuwwab, fo. 40r; Ahmad Çelebi, *Awdah*, 181–82.

grandees, they amassed households, consisting of both clients from the imperial palace and coopted members of established local households. The exiled eunuch most prominent in the political culture of seventeenth-century Egypt was Yusuf Agha, who seems to have played a role in the Fiqari dominance of the 1680s and 1690s. His most visible client, the *wakil* Mustafa Bey Kizlar, was an ally of the Bilifya household.[86] Yusuf Agha seems, furthermore, to have promoted a series of Fiqari pilgrimage commanders for the superintendency of the Valide *waqf*, established by Rabiʻa Gulnush Amatullah, the mother of Ahmad III, in 1698.[87] Although the full extent of the chief black eunuchs' participation in Egypt's household politics is still unknown, their influence seems to have been pervasive. For this reason, the seventeenth-century polemicist Darwish ʻAbdallah asserts that "every one of these black traitors is connected to a bey of Egypt"; even as early as 1599, the Ottoman intellectual Mustafa ʻAli laments the black eunuchs' influence in Egypt.[88]

The eunuchs' ability to endow *waqfs* in Egypt appears to have had a profound effect on Egypt's economy. The personal *waqf* inventory of ʻAbbas Agha, who was exiled to Egypt in 1671, reveals that this eunuch patronized an extensive commerce in coffee and flax, not only within Cairo but throughout the Egyptian countryside. His patronage of a coffee complex in the Nile delta town of Minyat Zifta suggests that exiled eunuchs may have played a significant role in integrating the countryside into a regional economic network that, moreover, linked Upper and Lower Egypt.[89]

ʻAbbas Agha's *waqf* inventory includes a list of the books in his library. These comprise the works of Hanafi exegesis and Ottoman history that were central to a palace education,[90] yet they also include a number of obviously Sufi works, notably the works of the twelfth-century mystic Farid al-Din ʻAttar.[91] Given that two prominent chief black eunuchs of the eighteenth

---

[86] Al-Damurdashi describes an incident in which Hasan Agha Bilifya and his son-in-law Ismaʻil Bey interceded for Mustafa Bey with the governor Husayn Pasha and obtained the governorship of Jirja for Mustafa (*Durra*, 58–59).

[87] Topkapi Palace Archives, E33, is a series of accounts for the Valide *waqf* in which both Yusuf Agha himself and various Fiqari pilgrimage commanders appear at different times as *nazir* during the 1690s and early 1700s.

[88] Cengiz Orhonlu, "Derviş ʻAbdullah'ın Darüssaade Ağalari Hakkında bir Eseri: *Risale-i teberdariye fi ahval-i Darus-saʻade*," in *Ismail Hakkı Uzunçarşılı'ya Armağan* (Ankara, 1976), 248; Mustafa ʻAli, *Mustafa ʻAli's Description of Cairo of 1599*, ed. and trans. Andreas Tietze (Vienna, 1975), 81–83.

[89] Topkapi Palace Archives, D7657. For a detailed analysis of this inventory, see Hathaway, "Wealth and Influence."

[90] Barnette Miller, *The Palace School of Muhammad the Conqueror* (New York, 1951), 94ff.; Hathaway, "Wealth and Influence," 309–12.

[91] Specifically, the *Tadhkirat al-awliya*', a collection of Sufi saints' biographies, and *Mantiq al-tayr* (*The Parliament of the Birds*). See Hathaway, "Wealth and Influence," 300.

century are known to have been great bibliophiles,[92] we can probably conjecture that many exiled eunuchs brought their libraries with them to Egypt. In that case, they may well have been instrumental in literary exchanges between imperial center and province, and may therefore have played a critical role in transmitting the intellectual and spiritual culture of the Ottoman court to Egypt while bringing works produced in Egypt to the attention of the court.

Changes in Egypt's religious life

The suggestion that the seventeenth century could have been a period of increased intellectual integration between Istanbul and Cairo challenges the perception that Egypt was, at this very time, constructing a distinctly Egyptian intellectual and spiritual profile.[93] Key religious officials were still appointed from Istanbul, most notably the chief judge (*qadi 'askar*) and the head of the descendants of the Prophet (*naqib al-ashraf*),[94] and they, along with exiled palace eunuchs, the Ottoman governors, and sundry Ottoman administrative officials, no doubt played some role in importing the intellectual and religious attitudes of the Ottoman central lands to Egypt. The Hanafi legal school, to which the Ottoman court adhered, was the school followed by all religious officials appointed from Istanbul, as well as by Egypt's grandees. As a result, Hanafi religious officials constituted something of an elite in Egypt's legal culture, if not in Egypt's educational establishment.[95]

Far more pervasive among the Egyptian population at large were the Ottoman soldiery, who brought their own set of distinctive spiritual preferences to Egypt. In the years following the Ottoman conquest of Egypt, the Ottoman soldiery were staunch adherents of the various offshoots of the Khalwati Sufi order, itself imported to Egypt from Anatolia and Central Asia in the fifteenth century.[96] The 'Azab regiment had a strong attachment to the lodges (*tekkes* or *zawiyas*) of Shams al-Din Muhammad Damirdash and

---

[92] On al-Hajj Bashir Agha (1717–46), see Martin van Bruinessen and Hendrik Boeschoten (eds. and trans.), *Evliya Çelebi in Diyarbekir: The Relevant Section of the* Seyahatname (Leiden, 1988), 5; on Moralı Bashir Agha (1746–52), see Jean-Claude Flachat, *Observations sur le commerce et sur les arts d'une partie de l'Europe, de l'Asie, de l'Afrique, et même des Indes Orientales*, 2 vols. (Lyon, 1766), II, 128.

[93] Michael Winter, *Egyptian Society under Ottoman Rule, 1517–1798* (London and New York, 1992), 76–77, 198, 253–54.

[94] In the late eighteenth century this post was monopolized by the Bakris, a prominent Cairene family of descendants of the Prophet.

[95] Galal H. El-Nahal, *The Judicial Administration of Ottoman Egypt in the Seventeenth Century* (Minneapolis and Chicago, 1979), 16–17.

[96] B. G. Martin, "A Short History of the Khalwati Order of Dervishes," in Nikki R. Keddie (ed.), *Scholars, Saints and Sufis: Muslim Religious Institutions since 1500* (Berkeley, Los Angeles, and London, 1972), esp. 275–97; Ernst Bannerth, "La

Ibrahim Gulshani, two of the three Khalwati shaykhs who brought that order to Egypt.[97] By the late seventeenth century, however, the Khalwatis were under attack in the Ottoman central lands, owing to the influence of a stringently orthodox puritanical movement whose adherents were known as Kadizadelis.[98] The delayed influence of the Kadizadeli movement appears most forcefully in Egypt in the famous 1711 conflict at Bab Zuwayla between Cairene Sufis and Anatolian soldiers. The soldiers, tellingly, had been reading the *Risala* of the sixteenth-century preacher Birgeli Muhammad Effendi, the veritable *vade mecum* of the Kadizadeli movement.[99]

Egypt, like other outlying provinces, was not included in the hierarchy of Ottoman *madrasas* that employed Turcophone 'ulama' inscribed on a ranked roll.[100] Nonetheless, Egypt continued as a major center of Islamic education. Beginning in the seventeenth century, Cairo's ancient al-Azhar mosque-university in particular saw a massive influx of students from other Ottoman provinces, both Arab and non-Arab, as well as from such far-flung Muslim lands as India and Indonesia. No less significant was a migration of young men from villages in both Upper and Lower Egypt to al-Azhar for theological training, part of a broader trend of integration between the capital and the countryside, as well as between Upper and Lower Egypt, at work during the seventeenth century.[101] Perhaps as a partial result of this

Khalwatiyya en Egypte: Quelques aspects de la vie d'une confrérie," *Mélanges de l'Institut Dominicain des Etudes Orientales*, 8 (1964–66), 1–74.

[97] Al-Damurdashi, *Durra*, 146, 165; Martin, "Khalwati Order of Dervishes," 292–93, 296–97. Al-Damurdashi himself almost certainly takes his sobriquet from the Khalwati sub-order founded by Damirdash.

[98] Madeline C. Zilfi, *The Politics of Piety: The Ottoman Ulema in the Post-Classical Age, 1500–1800* (Minneapolis and Chicago, 1988), 129–81.

[99] Al-Hallaq, *Tarih-i Mısır-ı Kahire*, fos. 296r–301r; Ahmad Çelebi, *Awdah*, 251–55. See also Barbara Flemming, "Die Vorwahhabitische Fitna im osmanischen Kairo, 1711," in *Ismail Hakkı Uzunçarşılı'ya Armağan*; Rudolph Peters, "The Battered Dervishes of Bab Zuwayla: A Religious Riot in Eighteenth-century Cairo," in Nehemia Levtzion and John O. Voll (eds.), *Eighteenth-century Renewal and Reform in Islam* (Syracuse, 1987). Because Ahmad Çelebi denounces the soldiers as "that race of Turks who do not distinguish between *m* and *n*," this incident has been construed as a confrontation between illiterate Turks and Arab or Arabized Egyptian 'ulama'. However, Ahmad Çelebi is surely inveighing against the dialect of Turkish spoken by provincial, probably eastern, Anatolians (*Atrak*).

[100] Richard Repp, "Some Observations on the Development of the Ottoman Learned Hierarchy," in Keddie, *Scholars, Saints, and Sufis*; Inalcik, *Classical Age*, 167–72.

[101] Gabriel Baer, "Fellah and Townsman in Ottoman Egypt: A Study of Shirbini's *Hazz al-quhuf*," *Asian and African Studies*, 8 (1972), 221–56; S. D. Goitein, "Townsman and Fellah: A Geniza Text from the Seventeenth Century," *Asian and African Studies*, 8 (1972), 257–61. During the late Mamluk sultanate, in contrast, few Cairene 'ulama' were from Upper Egypt; see Carl Petry's series of articles on the geographical origins of fifteenth-century Cairene 'ulama' in the *Journal of the Economic and Social History of the Orient*, 21 (1978) and 23 (1980). On al-Azhar's student population, see J. Heyworth-Dunne, *An Introduction to the History of Education in Modern Egypt*

student migration, al-Azhar in the course of the seventeenth century eclipsed other prominent mosque-*madrasas* in Cairo as Egypt's premier theological institution.[102] Beginning around 1670, a rector (*shaykh al-Azhar*) was routinely selected from among al-Azhar's instructors. The origin and purpose of this office are still unclear, but its implementation may have stemmed in part from the university's growing size and stature. The first several *shuyukh al-Azhar* came from towns and villages in the Egyptian countryside; even more striking, until 1778 the rectors, as well as other prominent 'ulama' of al-Azhar, were adherents of the Maliki legal school, several from locales in Upper Egypt.[103] Al-Azhar served as a means of integrating the disparate Muslim populations who came to Cairo to pursue a religious livelihood. In this respect, the university performed a function similar to that of the military household.

Conclusion

In the course of the seventeenth century, Egypt underwent a series of demographic, fiscal, and military transformations. Many of these were part of broader trends at work throughout the Ottoman empire, as the empire's expansion slowed but as economic and military crises triggered migrations within it. The mobility of Ottoman military and administrative personnel served to integrate Egypt more closely with the empire as a whole, even as Ottoman rule became more decentralized. Toward the end of the century, however, Egypt felt the direct effect of the Köprülüs' attempts to reassert centralized authority. Egypt's educational and religious institutions, while retaining a separate status from those of the central Ottoman lands, were yet shaped by empire-wide trends even as a greater degree of integration within Egypt itself allowed them, arguably, to assume a distinctly Egyptian character. Egypt's military and administrative echelons, meanwhile, participated in the household political culture that characterized the post-sixteenth-century Ottoman empire. This household culture would broaden out, encompassing more and more elements of Egyptian society, in the following century.

(London, 1968), 25, 38–39; Bayard Dodge, *Al-Azhar: A Millennium of Muslim Learning*, memorial ed. (Washington, DC, 1974), 201–06.

[102] Winter, *Egyptian Society under Ottoman Rule*, 118–26.

[103] Ataf Lufti al-Sayyid Marsot, "The 'Ulama' of Cairo in the Eighteenth and Nineteenth Centuries," in Keddie, *Scholars, Saints, and Sufis*; Daniel Crecelius, "The Emergence of the Shaykh al-Azhar as the Pre-Eminent Religious Leader in Egypt," in Andrée Assabgui et al. (eds.), *Colloque international sur l'histoire du Caire* (Cairo, 1969), esp. 109–11; Winter, *Egyptian Society under Ottoman Rule*, 120–21. For the biographies of two prominent Maliki scholars from Upper Egypt, see al-Jabarti, *'Aja'ib*, III, 116–17, and IV, 28.

3

Egypt in the eighteenth century

DANIEL CRECELIUS

➤◄

General observations

Egypt continued its drift toward autonomy during the course of the eight-eenth century, moving at the same time from dominance by households to rule by individuals. As it emerged from the generally passive condition imposed on it by two centuries of Ottoman domination and freely developed closer links with Europe under the leadership of aggressive beys of a new and ambitious Mamluk household, Egypt assumed a central importance in European strategic planning that it has never lost.[1] Much of this importance rested on a unique geographic position, but Egypt sustained a vibrant economy of its own. It remained the richest and most important Ottoman province, for it distributed to various regions of the Ottoman empire (and increasingly, as the century wore on, to European states eager for its trade) agricultural bounty of such crops as rice, sugar, and wheat as well as a broad range of products, chiefly Yemeni coffee, from Africa, Asia, and the Red Sea region.

Despite the continuing tyranny of its military establishment, the seemingly incessant outbreaks of violence among competing military households, and frequent visits of plague and pestilence, Egypt's economy remained strong well into the century. During a lengthy period of political stability in mid-

---

[1] The Arabic manuscript sources for the history of Egypt in the eighteenth century are surveyed in Daniel Crecelius (ed.), *Eighteenth Century Egypt, The Arabic Manuscript Sources* (Claremont, 1990). The extensive documentation relating to *waqf* also forms an important source: see Daniel Crecelius, "The Organization of *Waqf* Documents in Cairo," *International Journal of Middle East Studies*, 2 (1971), 266–77, and *Fihris al-waqfiyyat al-mahfudha fi al-wizarat al-awqaf wa dar al-watha'iq al-qawmiyya al-ta'rikhiyya fi misr* (Cairo, 1992). On the important Turkish materials, see Stanford J. Shaw, "The Ottoman Archives as a Source for Egyptian History," *Journal of the American Oriental Society*, 83 (September–December 1963), 447–52, and Stanford J. Shaw, "Turkish source-materials for Egyptian History," in P. M. Holt (ed.), *Political and Social Change in Modern Egypt* (London, 1968), 28–48.

century the economy provided prosperity for the upper and middle classes, sustained a considerable population increase, and supported the physical expansion of Cairo and the port cities.

By the second half of the century, however, the long-term effects of Europe's economic expansion – the direct purchase of coffee, for instance, by the Europeans from the Yemen and their introduction into Middle Eastern markets of coffee and rice grown in the New World – began to have a debilitating impact on the Egyptian economy. This decline was greatly accelerated in the last three decades of the century by a series of natural disasters, the effects of which were exacerbated by the unrestrained tyranny of the ruling beys, whose short-sighted policies destroyed the prosperity created by their predecessors, ruined the merchant community, both foreign and domestic, left the countryside in chaos, and provoked two military expeditions (in 1786 and again in 1798) that undermined the very foundations of the system that had provided the political and military leadership of the province for centuries.

Declining influence of Ottoman officials

The Ottoman central government had already lost its ability to direct the affairs of Egypt in the seventeenth century as most of the leading positions within the administration and the garrison corps (ojaqat, sing. ojaq) had been taken by amirs. Its remaining representatives, such as the governor, the chief judge, or the exiled chief black eunuch (kizlar agha), could do little to halt the continuing penetration of the local households into the administration and the garrison corps, nor could they halt the redirection of Egypt's extensive revenues from imperial to local objectives.[2] Without the power any longer to control locally based military households, the central government in Istanbul resorted to other means to achieve its objectives in Egypt. Ottoman governors were frequently sent to Egypt with secret orders to bring down the local grandees who dominated the military and financial institutions of the province. Numerous examples exist of governors executing Egyptian leaders on secret orders, supporting the aspirations of weaker households against dominant ones, and giving consent for one household to eliminate another in return for hulwan, the fee paid by a new office-holder

---

[2] An outline of the political history of Egypt in the seventeenth and eighteenth centuries is P. M. Holt, *Egypt and the Fertile Crescent, 1516–1922* (London, 1966), and P. M. Holt, "The Pattern of Egyptian Political History from 1517–1798," in Holt (ed.), *Political and Social Change in Modern Egypt*, 79–90. The activities of the locally based Mamluk factions are central in Holt's work. More recently, Jane Hathaway has offered a new interpretation based on the household: "The Military Household in Ottoman Egypt," *International Journal of Middle East Studies*, 27, 1 (February 1995), 39–52.

when he assumed the position or tax-farm of a deceased or dismissed incumbent.

Early in the century the central government continued to support an equilibrium between the two main factions of Qasimi–Nisf Haram and Fiqari–Nisf Sa'd (see previous chapter), assigning the treasury to a bey of one faction and the leadership of the pilgrim caravan to Mecca and Medina (the *Haramayn*) to a bey of the other faction. Provincial governorships were likewise apportioned between the two factions. Egyptian beys were also responsible for commanding expeditions against the Bedouin, for leading the annual contingent of 2,000–3,000 troops that Egypt was obliged to send for participation in the empire's wars, and for escorting the annual *irsaliyya khazina* (remittance) to Istanbul.[3] So dominant had the beys become that they confined Egypt governors to the Citadel, deposed them without fear of retribution, continued to strip away the governor's prerogatives, and usurped from a succession of governors the tax-farms that had traditionally been assigned to them. Some governors were bankrupted by Egyptian service. When 'Ali Pasha ibn al-Hakim (1740–41) assumed the governorship in Cairo in 1740 after a particularly unstable period during which several predecessors had been involved in plots to assassinate Egyptian grandees, he assured the powerful beys and garrison officers that he would not interfere in their affairs. "I didn't come to provoke crises," he told them, "or to execute anyone. I only came to collect the taxes for the diwan, the *haramayn* and the imperial treasury the second of [the Coptic month of] Tut. I'll pay the monthly wages the third day and collect the grain for the imperial granary."[4]

In the second half of the century Mamluk leaders did not fear to assassinate governors or to refuse them entry into Cairo, but rather, as *qa'im maqam*, themselves assumed the executive powers of the absent governor. *Diwans*, or councils, were held in the palace of the leading amir in the city, not in the governor's compound in the Citadel. After the revolt of 'Ali Bey Bulut Kapan (1768–72) the English merchant George Baldwin noted that "the Basha is merely the representative of the Sovereign; the mere Pageant of Authority. His power extends to none of the executive functions of the state."[5]

---

3 The best description of the Ottoman financial administration in Egypt remains Stanford J. Shaw's *The Financial and Administrative Organization and Development of Ottoman Egypt, 1517–1798* (Princeton, 1962). See also Layla 'Abd al-Latif Ahmad, *al-Idara fi misr fi al-'asr al-'uthmani* (Cairo, 1987).

4 Ahmad Damurdashi Katkhuda 'Azaban, *al-Damurdashi's Chronicle of Egypt, 1688–1755*, trans. and annotated Daniel Crecelius and 'Abd al-Wahhab Bakr (Leiden, 1991), 339.

5 George Baldwin, secret memorial entitled "Speculation on the Situation and Resources of Egypt," India Office Archives (London), Factory Records, G/17/5 (Egypt and the Red Sea), 1773–85.

So dominant had local control of Egypt become by the 1720s that a new term appeared to designate the leading bey of the capital. The *ri'asa* (see previous chapter) now frequently devolved upon a single Mamluk bey who was recognized as *shaykh al-balad* (commander of the city).[6] This dignity, which carried no rank in the Ottoman bureaucracy or military administration, was originally opposed by the central government, but, because the government could not reverse the drift toward Egyptian autonomy, came to be used in official documents; imperial orders were frequently addressed to the governor, the chief judge, and the *shaykh al-balad*.

Loss of central control over the garrison corps

The central government's inability to block takeover of its administration by local households resulted from its loss of a loyal garrison. Preeminent power had passed from the Mutafarriqa corps, the small cadre of Ottoman troops attached to the governor's suite from which key officials of the Egyptian administration had previously been selected, to the Janissaries, and to a lesser degree to the ʿAzab corps, both of which had their barracks in the Citadel.[7]

Locally based household leaders had penetrated the highest ranks of these and other Ottoman corps and already by the early eighteenth century had filled virtually half the ranks with Mamluks from their own households. As this process continued, the corps were completely debilitated and made an adjunct to the beylicate. In 1786 Ghazi Hasan Pasha (see below) tried unsuccessfully to reconstitute them, but there is no evidence that the corps were part of the resistance to the French invasion in 1798.

Although each corps might still be headed by an *agha* (commander), effective command was in the hands of a locally appointed *katkhuda*, an officer appointed for one year, during which he was known as *katkhuda al-waqt*. These officers and their sub-commanders had previously derived profits from control of urban tax-farms, such as the customs houses of the ports and the two Nile quays at Bulaq and Old Cairo. Through supervision

---

[6] Although garrison officers of the chief Ottoman corps dominated the political life of Cairo in the first half of the century, they never carried the title of *shaykh al-balad*, which was claimed by the leading *sanjaq beyi* in the beylicate. Although the title seems to have first been claimed by Muhammad Çerkis Bey, it was not used exclusively, for we still find references in subsequent decades to the equivalent term *kabir al-qawm* or to a bey succeeding to the *ri'asa*. The title referred to the holder's preeminence among the beys resident in Cairo, for the government's power seldom extended to areas of the countryside.

[7] The Janissaries, the most powerful and dominant corps, had barracks in the vast flat area at the top of the Citadel; the ʿAzabs occupied a less advantageous area at the base of the Citadel facing Rumayla Square. The governor's quarters and meeting hall for the Diwan were also on the upper level of the Citadel near the main entrance to the Janissary compound.

of the Suez customs the Janissaries had become involved in the immensely lucrative coffee and spice trade of the Red Sea. As their power increased they competed with the beys for control of agricultural tax-farms. The two corps also derived large sums from the "protection" (*himaya*) they imposed on the artisanal and merchant groups of Cairo and the Bedouin of the provinces.[8] For a time, Janissaries even controlled the Cairo mint, which, as part of a dispute between them and the other six corps, was moved from their barracks to the courtyard of the Diwan in the Citadel in 1710.[9] Its financial strength made the Janissary corps the dominant power in Egypt; its senior officers played a leading role in the politics of the capital.

Local households

The two great combinations of households, the Fiqariyya and the Qasimiyya, which had dominated Egypt from the second half of the seventeenth century, were superseded by the mid-eighteenth century by a new combination of households, both of which had their origins in the late seventeenth–early eighteenth centuries as allies of the Fiqari household led by Hasan Agha Bilifya.[10] The lesser household, the Jalfiyya, was led by officers of the rank of *katkhuda* in the ʿAzab corps. The dominant household, the Qazdagliyya, traced its origins to Mustafa al-Qazdagli, who had become Janissary *katkhuda* and in the late seventeenth–early eighteenth century was a junior partner of the Fiqari leaders Hasan Agha Bilifya and his son-in-law Ismaʿil Bey *al-daftardar*. Following the collapse of the Fiqaris and Qasimis a number of Qazdagli leaders, while continuing to base their power in the Janissary corps, advanced increasing numbers of personal Mamluks to the rank of *sanjaq beyi*, a policy that had enormous consequences for the subsequent history of Egypt. In the second half of the eighteenth century these Mamluk beys enfeebled the Ottoman garrisons, took control of the financial administration of Egypt, and seized revenues assigned to the corps, the *Haramayn*, or to the sultan's use in Istanbul; at a time when other provincial leaders (such as Ahmad Pasha al-Jazzar in Palestine) were creating autonomous regimes and instituting new economic policies, the Mamluk beys plotted an autonomous foreign policy by means of which they once more tried to make Egypt a seat of empire.[11] In the late seventeenth and

---

[8] On this "protection tax" see André Raymond, *Artisans et commerçants au Caire au XVIIIᵉ siècle*, 2 vols. (Damascus, 1974), II, 688–92.

[9] *Al-Damurdashi's Chronicle of Egypt*, 141.

[10] The Arabic documentation allows no certainty for the pronunciation of the village whose tax-farm Hasan Agha controlled, but contemporary Egyptians render it "Balfiyya."

[11] An important new interpretation of this process is Jane Hathaway, *The Politics of Households in Ottoman Egypt: The Rise of the Qazdaglis* (Cambridge, 1997).

early eighteenth centuries Egyptian households founded by freeborn adventurers successfully combined Mamluk beys and freeborn Muslims holding key offices in the garrison corps, but the second half of the eighteenth century saw this system evolve into a powerful Mamluk regime in which freeborn members were excluded from leadership.

Important social groups of the eighteenth century

Some changes were not so dramatic, but were nevertheless significant. Egyptian society maintained its equilibrium as different social groups rose to prominence during the course of the eighteenth century. From the late seventeenth century a new wave of Anatolian Turks came to Egypt. These immigrants, particularly those from the Kazdag in western Anatolia, formed the backbone of the Qazdagli military household[12] or spread throughout Upper and Lower Egypt in search of trade. (They were particularly associated with the trade in tobacco, a fashionable product that reached Egypt from the growing fields in Asia Minor and northern Syria.[13]) This social element joined the sizable North African (Maghribi) population to comprise an important substratum of merchants and soldiers who were frequently recruited to serve Egypt's households.[14]

A lesser immigration of Circassians and Georgians continued to provide leadership for the Mamluk households, particularly for the Qazdagli households of the second half of the century. A third element, Russians captured during the Ottoman wars and sent into military slavery in Egypt, represented a distinct social group in the Mamluk ranks, particularly in the household of Ibrahim Bey, during the last decade of the century.

[12] Holt, for instance, suggests that the various households at the beginning of the eighteenth century were to some extent based on ethnic solidarity. The Fiqariyya were of Circassian origin; the Qasimiyya had a noticeable Bosnian connection; and the Qazdagliyya enrolled Anatolian Turks. See Holt, "The pattern of Egyptian Political History from 1517–1798."

[13] See, for instance, André Raymond, "Soldiers in Trade: The Case of Ottoman Cairo," *British Journal of Middle Eastern Studies*, 18 (1991), 16–37.

[14] North Africans (*Maghariba*) formed a cohesive social, economic, and political group in Egypt's main cities, Maghribi students had their own hostel (*riwaq*) at the collegiate-mosque of al-Azhar, and Maghribis formed a readily assembled mercenary contingent in military campaigns led by Mamluk beys or garrison officers. Many had been in Egypt so long as to form an indigenous element. Some Bedouin clans, for instance, such as the powerful Hawwara, were of North African origin. Some of the richest merchant families, such as the Shara'ibis who were deeply engaged in the coffee trade, were also of Maghribi origin. On this Maghribi community in Egypt see 'Abd al-Rahim 'Abd al-Rahman 'Abd al-Rahim, *al-Magharibi fi misr fi al-'asr al-'uthmani, 1517–1798* (Tunis, 1982), and the same author's collection of documents from Egypt's Shari'a courts relating to this community, *Watha'iq al-mahakim al-shar'iyya al-khassa bi al-maghariba* (Zaghouan, 1992). See also André Raymond, "Tunisiens et Maghrébins au Caire au XVIIIᵉ siècle," *Cahiers de Tunisie*, 26–27 (1959), 336–71.

Beginning in the 1720s and continuing throughout the rest of the century a migration of Melkite Christians from Syria, frequently called Greek Catholics in western studies because of their affiliation with the Church of Rome, settled in Egypt's major commercial centers, particularly the ports.[15] Within decades, these active merchant families, who worshipped in French churches in Egypt because they were not permitted to build their own, and who purposefully sought close affiliation with the French and their commerce, displaced the Jewish minority as customs officials in the ports. It was the Qazdagli amir ʿAli Bey Bulut Kapan who in 1768 began transferring the supervision of the customs houses from Jews to merchants of this Greek Catholic community.[16] Soon all customs houses were in Christian hands, under the general direction of Muhammad Bey Abu al-Dhahab's young and aggressive chief customs agent Antoine Qassis Pharaʿun. These Egyptian-based Syrian Christians, working with coreligionists along the Levant coast, challenged the French for control of the region's trade with Europe. They also played a major role in the attempt to open the Red Sea route, specifically the port of Suez, to European ships coming directly from India.

A large number of undisciplined Albanian troops were brought to Egypt by Ghazi Hasan Pasha, who led the Ottoman expeditionary force against the beys in 1786. The expedition's purpose was to destroy the Mamluk regime that had destabilized the economy, acted autonomously and withheld the annual revenues for the holy cities and Istanbul. Many of these troops remained behind when Hasan Pasha withdrew in 1787 to command Ottoman forces against the Russians.[17] New Albanian contingents, equally undisciplined, arrived in 1801 when the Ottomans attempted to coordinate military operations with the British to end the French occupation (1798–1801). The Mamluk system, weakened by decades of internal conflict and warfare, was reduced to between 2,000 and 3,000 men by the end of the French occupation and could not fight off so many enemies determined to annihilate it. So great was the confusion in the wake of the French withdrawal, as small groups of Mamluks, Ottomans, Albanians, and Bedouin terrorized the population in attempts to reestablish control, that in 1805 the

15 See Thomas Philipp, *The Syrians in Egypt, 1725–1975* (Wiesbaden, 1985); Albert Hourani, "The Syrians in Egypt in the eighteenth and nineteenth centuries," *Colloque international sur l'histoire du Caire* (DDR, 1969), 221–33; Daniel Crecelius, "An Attempt by the Greek Catholics to Control Egypt's Trade with Europe in the Second Half of the Eighteenth Century," in Abdeljelil Temimi (ed.), *La vie sociale dans les provinces arabes à l'époque ottomane*, 3 vols. (Zaghouan, 1988), III, 121–32.

16 See John Livingston, "Ali Bey al-Kabir and the Jews," *Middle Eastern Studies*, 7 (1975), 221–28; André Bittar, "Les juifs, les grecs-catholiques et la ferme des douanes en Egypte sous ʿAli Bey al-Kabir," *Annales islamologiques*, 27 (1993), 255–67.

17 Some of these Albanian adventurers attached themselves to local households and even rose to the rank of bey in the chaotic period between the French invasion and the appointment of Muhammad ʿAli as governor in 1805.

religious leaders of Cairo designated Muhammad 'Ali, an officer of one of
the Albanian units brought to Egypt by the Ottomans in 1801, as governor.
He seized the reins of power, eliminated both Mamluks and Albanians, and
created a dynasty in Egypt that survived until the mid-twentieth century.

The Bedouin

Spread across the Egyptian Delta and in all the provinces of Upper Egypt,
Bedouin were a constant irritation both to the authorities in the cities whose
caravans and trade had to pass through their territory, and to the farmers
who suffered their frequent predations. It was because of Bedouin control of
the area between Alexandria and Cairo, for instance, that travelers (and
their goods) proceeded from Alexandria along the coast, either by caravan
or by boat, to Rosetta, and thence up the Nile to Cairo, instead of taking the
shorter desert route. The merchants and authorities of Cairo had to arrange
for the immense seasonal trade unloaded at Suez to be carried, or guaranteed, by several Bedouin tribes inhabiting the region. These tribes migrated
over an area that included the pilgrim route along the Arabian coast, the
Sinai peninsula, Palestine, and Lower Egypt, and were difficult for the
authorities in Cairo to control. There are many examples from throughout
the century of Bedouin setting upon Cairenes just outside the capital; travel
to the pyramids (just seven kilometres from the Nile) was dangerous and
seldom undertaken. Likewise, the annual pilgrim caravan needed safe
passage through Bedouin territory or had to be well enough defended to
fend off Bedouin attack.

For much of the eighteenth century the Haba'iba, sedentary Bedouin
whose center was Dijwa in Daqahliyya province just north of Cairo,
controlled much of the Delta.[18] Because of their proximity to Cairo, the
Haba'iba were frequently drawn into the conflicts of the capital, as, for
instance, after 1711. Politically, they were Nisf Sa'd, while the dominant
clan of Upper Egypt was Nisf Haram (see previous chapter).

The most powerful confederation of Bedouin, also sedentary, was the
Hawwara, which dominated the entire area of Upper Egypt from its capital at
Farshut. Hawwara shaykhs maintained close relations with the authorities in
Cairo, purchased positions in the garrisons and accepted clientage, hence
protection, from garrison officers. Although the *sanjaq beyi* of Jirja was
ostensibly one of the most important provincial governors, responsible for the
entire area south of Jirja, his power was often circumscribed by the Hawwara
shaykh, who could even interfere in his selection. Relations between the
Hawwara shaykhs and the Janissary corps were particularly close.

---

[18] On the Haba'iba, see 'Abd al-Hamid Hamid Sulayman, "'Urban al-Haba'iba wa al-
    Mamalik al-Qasimiyya," *Majallat kulliyat al-adab*, Cairo University (April 1995).

For most of the century the Hawwara shaykhs maintained control of Upper Egypt (al-Saʿid), obtaining agricultural tax-farms, managing the Nile ships that carried grain to Cairo, and providing refuge for a continuous stream of dissident amirs fleeing the capital. If, as so often happened, these amirs were able to regain authority in Cairo, they were grateful to the Hawwara shaykhs who had offered them refuge; if circumstances did not permit return to Cairo they remained secure in Hawwara territory, inter-married, and were absorbed into Hawwara society. Shaykh Humam, who governed the Saʿid between 1740 and 1769, had over three hundred slave girls, black slaves, and even Mamluks of his own. He owned 12,000 oxen, in addition to herds of buffalo and cattle. In essence, he governed a principality beyond the control of authorities in Cairo.[19] Muhammad Bey Abu al-Dhahab was sent by ʿAli Bey to deal the Hawwara a severe blow in 1769 and, for the first time in the eighteenth century, Cairo was able temporarily to claim effective control of the Saʿid. Shaykh Humam died in December 1769 and his successors were unable to regain the power or prestige that Humam had enjoyed. Nevertheless, they reasserted some authority in the chaotic period that followed; the Saʿid, and other Bedouin territory in Egypt, would not be brought under Cairo's firm control until the early nineteenth century, when Muhammad ʿAli Pasha finally broke the power of the Bedouin and settled them permanently as fallahin.

Egypt's economic strength

Throughout the eighteenth century Egypt remained the richest province of the Ottoman empire. Its cornucopia of agricultural surpluses sustained not only its own population, but the inhabitants of Mecca and Medina; it sent quantities of rice, wheat, and sugar to Istanbul and rice, fruits, and wheat to ports of the eastern Mediterranean.[20] An extensive and complicated organization of officials was responsible for safely bringing vast amounts of wheat from Upper Egypt, storing it in government granaries, then dispersing it to the people, to the *Haramayn*, to Istanbul or to other Ottoman provinces.

[19] See Michael Winter, *Egyptian Society under Ottoman Rule: 1517–1798* (London and New York, 1992), 104–08.

[20] On Egypt's Mediterranean trade, see Paul Masson, *Histoire du commerce français dans le Levant au XVIIIᵉ Siècle*, 2 vols. (Paris, 1911); Raymond, *Artisans et commerçants*; Daniel Panzac, "Affréteurs ottomans et capitaines français à Alexandrie: la caravane maritime en Méditerranée au milieu du XVIIIᵉ siècle," *Revue de l'Occident Musulman et de la Méditerranée*, 34 (1982); Daniel Panzac, "International and Domestic Maritime Trade in the Ottoman Empire during the 18th Century," *International Journal of Middle East Studies*, 24 (1992), 189–206; Daniel Crecelius and Hamza ʿAbd al-ʿAziz Badr, "French Ships and their Cargoes Sailing between Damiette and Ottoman ports, 1777–1781," *Journal of the Economic and Social History of the Orient*, 37 (1994), 251–86.

By the second half of the century many products, particularly rice, were diverted from Ottoman ports to Europe. This growing trade with Europe, which the Syrian Christian and European merchants (Venetian, French, and English) resident in Egypt enthusiastically pursued, was encouraged by the Qazdagli amirs, but linked Egypt with an expanding European economy at a time when products introduced by European states, whether manufactured or agricultural, competed unevenly with Egyptian products. Along with trade came European political influence. Like the Qazdagli amirs of the second half of the eighteenth century, Muhammad 'Ali would endeavour enthusiastically to nurture this growing economic link and to benefit from expanding trade with Europe.

Egypt had a small manufacturing base in the Delta and exported cloth from its Mediterranean ports. It also shipped large quantities of its own agricultural products, but the single item that dominated Egypt's trade with the Ottoman empire and which brought the greatest wealth to the country, to the merchants handling the product, and to the *ojaq* officers and the *sanjaq beyis* who taxed it, was coffee, for which the inhabitants of the Ottoman empire, and particularly Istanbul, seemed to have an insatiable desire.

The Egyptian economy, particularly its export sector, remained vibrant and healthy well into the eighteenth century, but a noticeable decline in its trading position is observed in the second half of the century, by which time products grown in the New World, such as sugar, coffee, and rice, were competing successfully within the Ottoman market, even in Egypt.[21] Mamluk beys, accustomed to restricting themselves mainly to the affairs of Egypt, did not understand the complex combination of factors that were transforming European states into formidable competitors, whether in trade or in battle.

The emergence of an autonomous regime under Qazdagli leadership and the determination of these amirs to increase the customs revenues of Egypt by expanding trade with Europe, particularly through the Red Sea port of Suez, coincided with the global expansion of European power. Since their conquest of Egypt in 1517 the Ottomans had provided a shield against European penetration. The Ottomans had maintained a ban on European shipping north of Jidda since repelling the Portuguese from the Red Sea in the sixteenth century and had successfully restricted European contacts with Egypt through its Mediterranean ports. European merchants resident in Egypt's main ports or in Cairo were confined to their commercial residences (*khans*) and had few contacts with the native population. They bought and

---

[21] André Raymond, "L'impact de la pénétration européenne sur l'économie de l'Egypte au XVIIIᵉ siècle," *Annales islamologiques*, 18 (1982), 217–35. Raymond notes that these products of the western hemisphere were preferred even when they were inferior, as in the case of coffee, because of their lower price.

sold their goods wholesale through native middlemen, usually merchants from the local non-Muslim communities.

The willingness of the Qazdagli leaders to ignore Ottoman regulations and to welcome European ships coming directly from India to the port of Suez excited the commercial instincts of merchants from a wide spectrum of European states.[22] None worked so assiduously to obtain the support of his government as the English merchant and sometime vice-consul George Baldwin, who tried for several decades to convince his superiors in London of the commercial and strategic importance of Egypt. "She is the Magazine of all the trade of Yemen, the mart of all the coffee and rich gums of Yemen, the extrepot of all the interior parts of Africa, producing gums, gold dust, ivory, senna and drugs," he enthused, and then warned that "France in possession of Egypt would possess the Master Key to all the trading nations of the Earth."[23] At first the Europeans were much more interested in opening the Black Sea to their ships, but eventually England, France, Austria, Venice, and other European states showed appreciation of Egypt's strategic importance and of the profits to be made in Red Sea trade.[24]

At the same time European states tried to negotiate with the Ottoman central government for the right to bring ships to Suez, they were exasperated at the Ottomans' inability to protect their trade from the exactions made against it by semi-autonomous provincial rulers such as Ahmad Pasha al-Jazzar in Palestine or the Qazdagli amirs in Egypt.[25] By the 1790s the French merchant community, once flourishing in Egypt and along the Levant coast, had been greatly reduced in numbers and bankrupted by the exactions of these tyrants. The dispatch of Napoleon Bonaparte at the head of an expeditionary force to Egypt in 1798 was more the response of a French nation intent on retrieving its commercial and strategic position along the rich southeastern shores of the Mediterranean basin than an imperial thrust

[22] On European competition to open the Red Sea route, see François Charles-Roux, *Autour d'une Route. L'Angleterre, l'Isthme de Suez et l'Egypte au XVIIIe siècle* (Paris, 1922) and François Charles-Roux "France, Egypte et Mer Rouge, de 1715–1798," *Cahiers d'Histoire Egyptienne*, 3 (January 1951), 117–95.

[23] "Speculation on the Situation and Resources of Egypt," India Office Archives (London), Factory Records, G/17/5, pp. 2, 21. On Egypt's trade with Africa, see Terence Walz, *Trade between Egypt and Bilad as-Sudan, 1700–1820* (Cairo, 1978).

[24] On some of Baldwin's extraordinary activities, see Daniel Crecelius, "An Austrian Attempt to Develop the Red Sea Trade Route in the Late Eighteenth Century," *Middle Eastern Studies*, 30 (April 1994), 262–80.

[25] European attempts to open Suez were delayed until well into the nineteenth century by two events during the rule of the Qazdagli duumvirs Ibrahim and Murad. In 1779, just when the Europeans were gaining confidence in opening this route, the beys tricked a group of European merchants into unloading their cargoes for transport to Cairo. They then permitted the local Bedouin to seize the caravan; five of the group of European merchants accompanying the caravan were turned loose in the desert and died. Then in 1786–87 Ghazi Hasan Pasha's occupation of Egypt meant that the old Ottoman ban against European ships sailing north of Jidda could be enforced.

toward India. The occupation of Egypt by French forces from 1798 to 1801 focused the attention of an expanding European imperial system firmly on the autonomous Egyptian province, which after the French withdrawal fell to an aggressive, far-sighted Albanian adventurer who built on the political and economic foundations laid haphazardly by such eighteenth-century Mamluk amirs as 'Ali Bey and Muhammad Bey Abu al-Dhahab in Egypt, or Ahmad Pasha al-Jazzar in Palestine. Many of Muhammad 'Ali's "modernizing reforms," such as trade monopolies, were but rationalized continuations of changes these predecessors had initiated.

The crisis of 1711 and its consequences

In constructing his dominant household in the late seventeenth century, Hasan Agha Bilifya, the *agha* of the small Gönüllüyan regiment, successfully struck a balance among the households of his own Fiqari faction and those of the rival Qasimi households, and among the Ottoman garrison corps. He also maintained close relations with the representatives of the Ottoman central government, including the governor and the exiled chief black eunuch; it has been suggested that he himself had come out of the imperial palace milieu.[26] In combination with his son-in-law, Isma'il Bey the *daftardar* (the treasurer), and his client Mustafa al-Qazdagli, the *katkhuda* of the Janissary corps and progenitor of the Qazdagli household, he channeled the aspirations of such Fiqari leaders as Ibrahim Bey ibn Dhu'l-Fiqar and mediated the disputes of such garrison-based junior officers as Kuchuk Muhammad, who had tried to put an end to the system of protection taxes which benefited chiefly the senior officers of the corps.

Hasan Agha's death in 1704 provided the opportunity for the next generation of leaders. In 1708 the Fiqari amir Muhammad Bey al-Kabir (the elder) was angered by loss of the important and lucrative governorship of Jirja, from which the rich harvest of all Upper Egypt was controlled, to another Fiqari amir, Muhammad Bey al-Saghir (the younger) Qatamish, the Mamluk of Qaitas Bey. Support given to the elder Muhammad Bey by the powerful Ayyub Bey al-Fiqari split the Fiqari beylicate into two competing camps as the struggle for control of the governorship of Jirja continued. This rivalry, when merged with a simultaneous conflict within the Janissary corps between junior and senior officers, led to an explosion in 1711.[27]

[26] On Hasan Agha, see Jane Hathaway, "The Household of Hasan Aga Bilifya: An Assessment of Elite Politics in Seventeenth-Century Egypt," *Turcica*, 27 (1995), 135–51.

[27] The most comprehensive review of this crisis remains André Raymond, "Une 'révolution' au Caire sous les Mamelouks: La crise de 1123/1711," *Annales islamologiques*, 6 (1966), 95–120, a study based on a comparison of the contemporary Arabic manuscript histories.

In 1704 and again in 1707 a popular junior officer, Ifranj Ahmad, the *bashodabashi*[28] of the Janissary corps, provoked crises by challenging the existing political balance, particularly the dominance of the corps by such senior officers as Mustafa al-Qazdagli. Banished, but brought back to power in 1709 with the support of Ayyub Bey, Ifranj Ahmad in turn banished eight dissident members of his corps to villages controlled by Iwaz Bey, the Qasimi leader.[29] When the eight returned without permission in 1710 and enrolled in the rival 'Azab corps, which was controlled by the Qasimis, crisis escalated into civil war. A bloody conflict ensued from April to June 1711, with the two sides falling into place along all the traditional political fault lines in Ottoman Egypt.

On one side was Ifranj Ahmad, who dominated the Janissary corps from his base within the barracks at the top of the Citadel, supported by such powerful Fiqari beys as Ayyub Bey, Mustafa Bey, and Muhammad Bey al-Kabir. Ifranj Ahmad also secured the permission of the governor, who remained only an interested observer to the events that followed, to attack his enemies. The earliest fighting was confined to the corps, as all the other corps united to strip the Janissaries of their prerogatives, but as fighting in Cairo intensified, it drew in the beys, who had first tried to remain aloof from the struggle. Ultimately the Bedouin allies of the two warring sides also became involved. Muhammad Bey al-Kabir was called from Upper Egypt to Cairo with 6,000 Hawwara Bedouin, who were traditionally allied to the Janissary corps. Muhammad Bey's personal drive for power and the shocking participation of Hawwara forces in the street fighting in Cairo widened the split in Fiqari ranks. Fiqari beys such as Qaitas Bey, his Mamluk Muhammad Bey al-Saghir, and Husayn Bey Barim Dhayluh did not support the Janissary insurgents or the Fiqari beys around Ayyub Bey.

Arrayed against the Janissary–Fiqari–Hawwara forces were the other six Ottoman garrison units in Cairo. These corps, supported by the Qasimi beys and their own Bedouin allies, had long been jealous of the dominant position and wealth enjoyed by the Janissaries. Chief among the Qasimi leaders were Hasan al-Ikhmimi, whose position in Upper Egypt made him the natural rival of Muhammad Bey al-Kabir, and Iwaz Bey, the dominant Qasimi bey in Cairo. The 'Azab corps, the second most powerful but considerably less wealthy corps, led the fight against Ifranj Ahmad and the Fiqaris from its own barracks at the lower level of the Citadel, but the 'Azabs were ultimately aided by Iwaz Bey and other Qasimi amirs as the fighting spilled into many neighborhoods of the city and to the fields of Rawda Island.

The intense struggle in the streets of the capital finally claimed the life of

---

[28] Regiments were divided into *odas* (rooms), each of which was commanded by an *odabashi*. The *bashodabashi* was, as his title indicates, the chief of all the *odabashis*.

[29] Fiqari amirs had only recently gained control of the Janissary corps from the Qasimis.

Iwaz Bey on June 1; his death unnerved the Fiqari leaders, who fled to
Istanbul. The fighting ended in a complete victory for the 'Azab–Qasimi
forces. Ifranj Ahmad was killed on June 22, but the dissident Fiqari amir
Muhammad Bey al-Saghir Qatamish claimed the governorship of Jirja while
the dissident Fiqari leader Qaitas Bey imposed his authority on the leaderless
Qasimi beys until 1714, when he was surprised in a conference with the new
governor 'Abidin Pasha (1714–17) and executed on orders from Istanbul.[30]
Thereafter the Ottomans tried to restore a balance between the Qasimis and
Fiqaris by assigning, in the traditional way, the most important offices in the
administration to the leading beys of one or the other of the two rival
households. The political situation in Egypt remained in turmoil, however,
as the divided Fiqari and Qasimi households struggled for supremacy during
the next two decades. Although nine Qasimis were raised to the beylicate
after the execution of Qaitas Bey, their position was weakened by the death
of the powerful Qasimi leader Ibrahim Bey Abu Shanab in 1718 and by the
murder of their leader Isma'il Bey ibn Iwaz by the dissidents Dhu'l-Fiqar and
Çerkes Muhammad Bey in 1724 on the instigation of the governor,
Muhammad Pasha al-Nishanji (1721–25). 'Ali Pasha (1725–26), the next
governor, then secured the exile of Çerkes Muhammad Bey.

Another great explosion of violence claimed the lives of many amirs of
both households, both *ojaq* leaders and beys, in 1730. Although the Qasimis
avenged themselves with the murder of Dhu'l-Fiqar, they themselves suffered
a defeat in the fighting of that year from which they did not recover. Then,
in November 1736 the governor Bakir Pasha instigated a surprise assault
that claimed the lives of ten leading Fiqari amirs.[31] Nevertheless, the
governors were unable to act with the same audacity and success they had
recently demonstrated. Bakir Pasha (1735–37) was deposed in 1737 for
interfering in the affairs of the amirs and Sulayman Pasha (1739–40), who
had arrived in August 1739, was deposed in January 1740 for instigating the
assassination of 'Ali Katkhuda al-Jalfi. When the government ordered that
no tax-farms were to be assigned for the year 1152 AH/1739–40, the
garrison corps all protested.[32]

---

[30] *Al-Damurdashi's Chronicle of Egypt*, 192. See also Ahmad Shalabi (Çelebi) ibn 'Abd al-
Ghani, *Awdah al-isharat fi man tawalla misr al-qahira min al-wuzara' wa al-bashat*, ed.
and annotated 'Abd al-Rahim 'Abd al-Rahman 'Abd al-Rahim (Cairo, 1978), 271, who
dates Qaitas's execution to July 1715.

[31] The treachery, instigated by the Qasimi amir Salih Kashif against the Qatamish
household because the *shaykh al-balad* Muhammad Bey Qatamish had denied him
promotion to the sanjaqship, had been approved by the governor Bakir Pasha. See *Al-
Damurdashi's Chronicle of Egypt*, 310–11; Ahmad Shalabi, *Awdah al-Isharat*, 619.

[32] Sulayman Pasha ibn al-'Azm instigated a failed plot against the leading Qatamish beys
and their Qazdagli and Jalfi allies and was deposed. It was in this context that the new
governor, 'Ali Pasha ibn al-Hakim, promised the amirs in 1740 not to interfere in their
affairs. See *al-Damurdashi's Chronicle of Egypt*, 322–33.

Two opposing constants provide a secondary theme for this period. Whenever the opportunity arose, Ottoman governors, as we have seen, intervened in local affairs to execute, or to urge the assassination of, powerful household leaders, whether beys or *ojaq* officers. Despite the turmoil and political upheavals of the decades following the civil war of 1711, however, a succession of Qazdagli officers who controlled the Janissary corps continued to strengthen the foundations of their own household through control of an expanding range of revenues and the advancement of their own clients to positions within the garrison corps. When, therefore, the Fiqari and Qasimi households had finally exhausted themselves through strike and counter-strike, the Qazdagli leaders were in a position to claim the leadership of Egypt from the 1740s until the extirpation of the Mamluk system by Muhammad 'Ali Pasha in the early nineteenth century.

The rise of the Qazdagli household, 1730–1765

A succession of Qazdagli Janissary officers maintained control of the Janissary corps following the death of Mustafa Katkhuda, the founder of their household, in 1704. These were Hasan Katkhuda (d. 1715); 'Uthman Katkhuda, who emerged as one of the dominant amirs after 1724, but who fell victim to the ambush in 1736 in which ten leading amirs were killed; Sulayman Katkhuda al-Çukadar (d. 1739); 'Abdallah Katkhuda (d. 1743); Ibrahim Katkhuda, who dominated Egypt between 1747 and his death in 1754; and 'Abd al-Rahman Katkhuda (d. 1776). These household leaders derived enormous wealth from the Janissaries' control of the Alexandria customs, from exploitation of the Red Sea trade, from control of agricultural tax-farms (*iltizams*), from "protection rackets," and from their share, as Janissary *katkhudas*, of the partial estates of all the Janissaries and "protected" merchants who died in Egypt. Inheritance records show that this group of *katkhudas* controlled sizable agricultural tax-farms, owned and operated fleets of Nile boats to transport grain from Upper Egypt, and were deeply involved in the immensely lucrative coffee trade of the Red Sea, frequently operating ships that transported coffee to Suez in partnership with leading merchants. This succession of Qazdagli officers left enormous estates upon which rested the power of their household and the ability of their successors to dominate the politics of Egypt; to build large households of their own and to place their manumitted slaves within the beylicate and the *ojaq* corps; to endow Cairo with magnificent structures, both secular and religious; and to subsidize the religious and educational activities of the religious class.[33]

---

[33] On the economic activities of these Qazdagli officers, see André Raymond, *Le Caire des Janissaires: L'apogée de la ville ottomane sous 'Abd al-Rahman Katkhuda* (Paris, 1995),

The massacre of 1736 led to the emergence of a new generation of leaders. While the Qazdagli household remained firmly rooted in the Janissary corps, the remaining Fiqari leaders claimed positions in the beylicate. Although 'Abd al-Rahman, the freeborn son of Hasan Katkhuda, had the right to succeed to the leadership of the Qazdagli household, he tended to withdraw from the rough-and-tumble of politics, always deferring to other, more aggressive amirs.[34] He was perhaps too young to challenge the leadership of 'Uthman Katkhuda or even Sulayman Katkhuda al-Çukadar, but he was later dominated, even bullied, by Ibrahim, the *mamluk* of Sulayman Katkhuda al-Qazdagli, who made 'Abd al-Rahman the Janissary *katkhuda* for the first time in 1740, then exiled him to Mecca from 1747 to 1751; and by 'Ali Bey Bulut Kapan, who was designated *shaykh al-balad* through the support of 'Abd al-Rahman in 1760 and who then sent 'Abd al-Rahman into a second Meccan exile that lasted from 1765 until 1776.

Ibrahim Jawish, who survived a struggle with the powerful Fiqari amir 'Uthman Bey Dhu'l-Fiqar in 1743, did not himself become *katkhuda* of the corps until he weathered yet another plot in 1748 instigated by the governor, Raghib Muhammad Pasha, against the Qatamish beys who then dominated the beylicate. The Qatamish household was successfully broken up, but Raghib Muhammad Pasha, who had acted on secret orders from Istanbul, was deposed and the Dimyati household was banished. The new triumvirate that dominated Egypt during the middle years of the century, years of proverbial prosperity, was composed of Ibrahim Katkhuda, who controlled the Janissary corps, his ally Ridwan al-Jalfi, the *katkhuda* of the 'Azab corps, and the "elder statesman" of the Qazdagli household, 'Abd al-Rahman, whom Ibrahim Katkhuda had brought back from exile in 1751 and appointed Janissary *katkhuda* for an unusual two-year period.

Egypt remained stable during these middle years of the century under the guidance of this trio of garrison leaders. 'Abd al-Rahman, who eschewed direct involvement in politics, remained a figurehead for the Qazdagli

---

46–67. Hasan Katkhuda, for instance, left an estate of 3,508,903 *paras*. His *mamluk* 'Uthman Katkhuda left 21,537,176 *paras*. 'Uthman's *mamluk* Sulayman al-Çukadar Jawish left 6,893,195 *paras*. On Sulayman Jawish, see Michel Tuchscherer, 'Le pèlerinage de l'émir Sulayman Ğawis al-Qazdugli, Sirdar de la caravane de al Mekke en 1739," *Annales islamologiques*, 24 (1988).

[34] Perhaps it was his freeborn status that kept him from taking a central part in the struggles of the next three decades. On his career, see Raymond, *Le Caire des Janissaires*, 32–45. The justifiably famous history of Shaykh 'Abd al-Rahman ibn Hasan al-Jabarti is the major source for the second half of the eighteenth century. It has been published in several Arabic editions, and in Turkish, French, Russian, and, recently, English translations. References to al-Jabarti's history will be first to the well-known Arabic edition published by the Bulaq Press in 1888 and next to the new English translation. For an obituary of 'Abd al-Rahman Katkhuda, see *'Abd al-Rahman al-Jabarti's History of Egypt*, ed. and trans. Thomas Philipp and Moshe Perlmann, 4 vols. (Stuttgart, 1994), II, 5–8/II, 5–10.

officers and beys. He did not purchase many *mamluks* or promote his own *mamluks* to key positions within the administration or the beylicate. Instead, with the enormous wealth he had accumulated he undertook, beginning in 1744, the most extensive building program in Cairo's history.[35] Ridwan Katkhuda also remained a "silent partner" to Ibrahim Katkhuda and was likewise encouraged to devote himself to building impressive structures. From 1747 to 1754, the year of his death, Ibrahim Katkhuda was *de facto* ruler of Egypt. Ahmad al-Damurdashi remarks that "the leadership of Egypt devolved upon Ibrahim Katkhuda Qazdagli and Ridwan Katkhuda al-Jalfi. Everything first went to Ibrahim Katkhuda Qazdagli, whether the spice revenues, bribes, or the like, and then he gave one-third to Ridwan Katkhuda al-Jalfi."[36]

Although earlier in the century 'Uthman Katkhuda had appointed personal *mamluks* to the beylicate, Qazdagli power remained rooted in the Janissary corps; Ibrahim Katkhuda and Ridwan Katkhuda each appointed five of their personal *mamluks* to the beylicate.[37] Ibrahim Katkhuda died in November or December 1754, and Ridwan Katkhuda al-Jalfi was killed in a dispute with 'Abd al-Rahman Katkhuda six months later, finally leaving the latter in the position of leadership that his parentage and wealth seemingly warranted. True to character, however, he preferred to remain distant from politics; in 1760 he urged his household to accept the young and ambitious 'Ali Bey Bulut Kapan as *shaykh al-balad*. In his first drive for absolute power, 'Ali Bey turned on his benefactor in 1765 and ordered him into Meccan exile; 'Abd al-Rahman Katkhuda died only eleven days after his return to Cairo in 1776. Now the consequences of so many appointments to the beylicate by Ibrahim Katkhuda and Ridwan Katkhuda became apparent: henceforth the households would be rooted in the beylicate and the *ojaqs* would be reduced to adjunct status.

'Ali Bey Bulut Kapan changed the character of Mamluk politics and initiated policies that both moved Egypt toward autonomy and destroyed the stability and prosperity that Egypt had known under the leadership of

[35] On construction in general in Cairo during the Ottoman period, see Edmond Pauty, "L'architecture au Caire depuis la conquête ottomane," *Bulletin de l'Institut Français d'Archéologie Orientale du Caire*, 36 (1936), 1–69. On the numerous buildings of 'Abd al-Rahman Katkhuda see André Raymond, "Les constructions de l'émir 'Abd al-Rahman Katkhuda au Caire," *Annales islamologiques*, 11 (1972), 235–51.

[36] *Al-Damurdashi's Chronicle of Egypt*, 376.

[37] The five *mamluks* of Ibrahim Katkhuda whom he appointed to the beylicate were 'Uthman Bey Jirja, Husayn Bey, 'Ali Bey al-Ghazzawi, Husayn Bey, and 'Ali Bey Bulut Kapan. The six amirs, not all his personal *mamluks*, whom Ridwan Katkhuda named to the beylicate were Mustafa Bey, Isma'il Bey, the in-law of the rich Shara'ibi merchant family, Kuchuk Ahmad Bey, Ahmad Bey al-Khazindar, Muhammad Bey, and 'Ali Bey. See *al-Damurdashi's Chronicle of Egypt*, 381. Ultimately ten of Ibrahim Katkhuda's manumitted slaves attained the beylicate.

the *ojaq* officers Ibrahim Katkhuda, Ridwan Katkhuda, and 'Abd al-Rahman Katkhuda. The achievements of these *ojaq* leaders deserve review.

Egypt in the middle decades of the eighteenth century

Our understanding of the social, economic, and demographic history of Cairo, and by extension of Egypt, in the seventeenth and eighteenth centuries has been informed by numerous studies undertaken by André Raymond in the religious court records, particularly the inheritance inventories, of Ottoman Egypt. Raymond has demonstrated the continuing strength of the Egyptian economy well into the eighteenth century, and the existence of vast fortunes in families such as the Shara'ibis and Shuwaykhs and Janissary officers such as 'Uthman Katkhuda and Ibrahim Katkhuda, who managed the coffee trade.[38]

The period 1736–80 was particularly prosperous. Underlying this prosperity was the political, social, and economic stability that Egypt experienced under the Qazdagli garrison officers Ibrahim Katkhuda and 'Abd al-Rahman Katkhuda and the Qazdagli *shaykhs al-balad* 'Ali Bey Bulut Kapan and his *mamluk* Muhammad Bey Abu al-Dhahab. In addition to political stability, Egypt enjoyed during these middle years of the century freedom from the great plagues that would strike repeatedly in the last decades of the century; the country enjoyed a fiscal stability in the thirty years after 1741 that was unusual. Trade with Europe, particularly with France, continued to expand and tax-farmers enjoyed rising profits from agricultural *iltizams*. Coffee remained the most important item in Egypt's trade.[39]

In referring to the period of Ibrahim Katkhuda's dominance, the Egyptian historian 'Abd al-Rahman ibn Hasan al-Jabarti later noted that "Cairo was peaceful, free from strife and violence ... Cairo's beauties then were brilliant, its excellences apparent, vanquishing its rivals. The poor lived at ease. Both great and small lived in abundance."[40] Al-Jabarti offers a nostalgic look at the humane qualities of Egypt's political leadership at mid-century and at the social customs in both city and countryside that helped to support the weak and the poor. All this would change in the remaining years of the century.

Political stability and economic prosperity had observable effects upon

---

[38] The coffee trade reached its apogee in the period 1690–1750, when it accounted for one-third of Egypt's imports and one-fourth of its exports. On Egypt's Red Sea commerce and the dominant role played by coffee in this trade, see Raymond, *Artisans et commerçants*, I, 108–64.

[39] See Raymond, *Le Caire des Janissaires*, 46–67. Ibrahim Katkhuda, for instance, imposed taxes on coffee imported via the port of Jidda of 15.4 million *paras* in 1748, 19.8 million in 1949, and 14.6 in 1753. *Ibid.*, 64.

[40] *Al-Jabarti's History of Egypt*, I, 203, 331–32.

Egypt, and particularly upon its commercial centers. The population increased significantly during this period. Cairo's may have reached 300,000, but declined to 263,000 because of plagues, famines, and political crises in the last decades of the century. Men of great wealth endowed the capital with both secular and religious monuments such as palaces, warehouses, public fountains, bathhouses, schools, Sufi retreats, congregational mosques, and mausoleums. The years 1739–65, roughly coinciding with the active career of 'Abd al-Rahman Katkhuda, comprise one of the most active building periods in the history of Cairo. Between 1726 and 1775 twenty-six mosques and forty-one fountains were constructed; seventy-seven mosques and one hundred and eighteen fountains were erected during the whole 281 years of Ottoman rule in Cairo. The years 1726–75 saw rapid development of the western suburb, from the borders of Fatimid Cairo along the Nasiri canal to the western canal, as rich merchants and powerful amirs abandoned the crowded southern suburb around the Elephant's pond (Birkat al-Fil) in favor of the more open areas around the Azbakiyya pond (Birkat al-Azbakiyya).[41] None was as active in this process as 'Abd al-Rahman Katkhuda, whose enormous wealth and preference for construction over politics have left a monumental legacy in Cairo that delights visitors even today.[42]

Cairo was not alone in benefiting from this long period of peace, stability, and prosperity. Suez, a seasonal port without a secure water supply or permanent population, remained unaffected; Alexandria, also without a secure water supply and adjacent to open desert controlled by frequently hostile Bedouin, remained Egypt's chief Mediterranean port, but in the last decades of the century had certainly no more than 15,000 inhabitants. But the two upriver Mediterranean port cities of Rosetta (Rashid) and Damietta (Dimyat) both prospered. Both were surrounded by rich agricultural lands, and by gardens and orchards producing rice and fruits. A growing commerce supported an increase in population; both cities had a mixed population (roughly 20,000–30,000) of Turks, Syrian and North African Arabs, Albanians, and others that was larger than Alexandria's in the second half of the century. Both were endowed with markets, warehouses, collegiate-mosques, and public fountains that helped to sustain a pleasant lifestyle.[43] The troubles of the last decades of the century, however, reduced the

---

[41] Raymond, *Le Caire des Janissaires*, 87–98. See also Doris Behrens-Abouseif, *Azbakiyya and its Environs from Azbak to Ima'il, 1476–1879* (Cairo, 1985).

[42] See Raymond, "Les constructions de l'émir 'Abd al-Rahman Katkhuda," 235–51.

[43] On Rosetta, see the study published by a team of scholars from Cairo University and the French Institute, *Mudun misr dhat al-tabadul al-hidari: 'umran rashid*, 3 vols. (Cairo, 1994). On the middle-class lifestyle, see Nelly Hanna, *Habiter au Caire: Les maisons moyennes et ses habitants aux XVII*e *et XVIII*e *siècles* (Cairo, 1991).

populations of these two ports significantly, and left their agricultural surroundings and orchards in decline.

The second exile of ʿAbd al-Rahman Katkhuda by ʿAli Bey Bulut Kapan in 1765 was the end of an era, after which Egypt's political system underwent rapid change with the transfer of leadership to the beylicate; there were no builders or public benefactors to succeed him. The prosperity created by the garrison officers continued for a while under ʿAli Bey and his *mamluk* Muhammad Bey Abu al-Dhahab, but there was no continuation of the building program that adorned Cairo with so many religious monuments and public facilities. Muhammad Bey's mosque, erected in 1774 facing the main gate of al-Azhar, is the only great mosque built during the last thirty years of the century. Egypt changed dramatically under the next generation of leaders, whose constant quarrels and unrestrained tyranny, accentuated by repeated plagues, famine, and pestilence in the 1780s and 1790s, plunged Egypt into chaos. Al-Jabarti, who blamed ʿAbd al-Rahman Katkhuda for the Mamluks (particularly ʿAli Bey Bulut Kapan) whose rise to power he facilitated, nevertheless decried the end of an era, noting that "Nobody like him appeared after him."[44]

The resurgence of Egypt under ʿAli Bey Bulut Kapan and Muhammad Bey Abu al-Dhahab, 1768–1775

There is a clear distinction in the political character of the regimes of Ibrahim Katkhuda (1747–54) and his *mamluk* ʿAli Bey Bulut Kapan (1760–66; 1767–72). Ibrahim Katkhuda al-Qazdagli was the dominant amir of the middle years of the eighteenth century. His political influence was rooted in the Janissary corps which he controlled and the wide range of sources from which he drew his enormous wealth. But Ibrahim Katkhuda was content to rule through Ottoman institutions and within the parameters of Egypt's status as an Ottoman province. He undertook his obligations to the empire, received Ottoman officials, sent the required troops annually to fight in the empire's wars, dispatched the annual pilgrim caravans with money and foodstuffs for the inhabitants of the *Haramayn*, and sent the annual *irsaliyya* and supplies to Istanbul on time. He was content to enjoy his ambitions within the borders of Egypt.

By contrast, ʿAli Bey revolted against the empire by an unauthorized invasion of Palestine and Syria and by allying with Russia against the Ottoman empire. ʿAli Bey acted as an autonomous ruler in attempting to carry on direct foreign relations with European states. He minted an Egyptian coin with his own name cleverly inscribed on the obverse of the

---

[44] *Al-Jabarti's History of Egypt*, II, 8, 9.

sultan's *tughra*,[45] sent armies to conquer adjacent territory for the first time since the Ottoman conquest of Egypt in the sixteenth century, and willfully changed the rules governing the traditional economy of Egypt so as to derive ever greater profits to sustain his grandiose schemes. Egypt's eventual reemergence as an independent entity in the region owes much to 'Ali Bey's drive for autonomy between 1768 and 1772.[46]

We know very little of 'Ali Bey's activities as *shaykh al-balad* between 1760 and 1766. Following his expulsion of 'Abd al-Rahman Katkhuda in 1765 he himself was exiled in the following year, but once returned to power in 1767, 'Ali Bey unleashed an unrelenting campaign to eliminate his rivals within the garrison corps and the beylicate. Perceived enemies, but also allies such as Salih Bey and Ahmad Jazzar, were killed, driven into exile, or forced to accept banishment to Upper Egypt where the Hawwara absorbed many Mamluk dissidents. 'Ali Bey raised ten of his own *mamluks* to the beylicate, completing the Qazdagli triumph over rival Mamluk households.

'Ali Bey refused to tolerate an Ottoman governor in Egypt and, as *qaʾim maqam*, himself exercised the powers of the absent governor. All state offices, with the exception of the positions of chief *qadi* and exiled *kizlar agha*, were held by *mamluks* of his own household or by his clients. 'Ali Bey completed the emasculation of the garrison corps by substituting his own *mamluks* for the remaining regular troops he forced into retirement and by seizing the sources of their incomes. By 1768 he was ready to initiate the next phase of his scheme of personal aggrandizement.

'Ali Bey sent his *khushdash* Ismaʿil Bey to pacify the Bedouin of Lower Egypt in 1768 and dispatched his favorite and most trusted *mamluk*, Muhammad Bey Abu al-Dhahab, in 1769 to break the hold of the Hawwara over Upper Egypt, thus giving the government in Cairo, for the first time in centuries, effective control of the whole of Egypt. He was now in a position to tap enormous economic strength and to transform the relations between Egypt and the central government.

Al-Jabarti remarks that 'Ali Bey had read the history of the Mamluk sultanate destroyed by the Ottomans in 1516–17 and hints that he was interested in recreating it. 'Abbud Sabbagh, the historian of 'Ali Bey's Palestinian ally Shaykh Dhahir al-ʿUmar, also noted his conscious desire to recreate the Circassian state.[47] He surrounded himself with Christian

---

[45] See Samuel Lachman, "The Coins Struck by Ali Bey in Egypt," *The Numismatic Circular*, 83 (1975), 198–201, 336–38; and Husayn 'Abd al-Rahman, *al-Nuqad* (Cairo, 1939), 124 for photographs of this coin.

[46] For a lengthier review of this period, see Daniel Crecelius, *The Roots of Modern Egypt: A Study of the Regimes of 'Ali Bey al-Kabir and Muhammad Bey Abu al-Dhahab, 1760–1775* (Minneapolis and Chicago, 1981).

[47] *Ibid.*, 65; *al-Jabarti's History of Egypt*, I, 381, 638; 'Abbud Sabbagh, *al-Rawd al-zahir fi taʾrikh dhahir*, Bibliothèque Nationale, Paris, FA 4610, fo. 15.

advisors, all merchants, who urged an expansionist foreign policy upon him.[48] ʿAli Bey and his Qazdagli successors were completely seduced by the basic logic of the merchants' advice; the more trade that passed through Egyptian ports, the greater would be the taxes delivered to the regime. Trade with the Europeans was to be expanded in the Mediterranean ports, but the biggest profits were to be made by encouraging Europeans to bring the trade of India directly to Suez. ʿAli Bey completed the enfeeblement of the Janissary corps by taking the Alexandria, Rosetta, Damietta, and Suez customs for himself. He executed or dismissed Jewish merchants who had controlled the customs houses of the ports and transferred responsibility for their management to Syrian merchants of the Greek Catholic community, whose rise was now meteoric. He gave assurances to European merchants of his protection, and though he pressed them hard to help pay the enormous costs of his foreign wars, his policies were essentially beneficial to them. Their trade expanded and their profits rose, even as the extortions (*avanies*) increased.[49]

In 1769 a request from Istanbul for Egyptian aid to install a defeated claimant in Mecca reached ʿAli Bey, whose plans for the Red Sea had been taking shape for some years. With imperial sanction, he sent Muhammad Bey Abu al-Dhahab in May 1770 as *amir al-hajj* to install the Sharif ʿAbdallah as ruler of Mecca. On orders from ʿAli Bey, Muhammad Bey also announced to European merchants he found in Jidda that they could henceforth ignore Ottoman bans against their ships north of that port and bring their trade directly to Suez. By the time Muhammad Bey returned to Cairo in late 1770 ʿAli Bey had formulated his plans for the conquest of Syria, a campaign he coordinated in alliance with the Palestinian rebel Shaykh Dhahir al-ʿUmar, who controlled the Galilee. The Ottoman empire, then deeply engaged in a disastrous war with the Russians, could do little to thwart ʿAli Bey's plans.

ʿAli Bey opened his Syrian campaign in November 1770, but when the forces commanded by Ismaʿil Bey were held up, he ordered Muhammad Bey to lead another large army to Syria in April 1771. After Damascus surrendered to Muhammad Bey on June 8, 1771, ʿAli Bey ordered his commanders to consolidate their position and prepare for further conquests, but his plans collapsed with the stupefying news that his army had

---

[48] These were S. K. Lusignan, the Cypriot who had known ʿAli Bey in his youth, ʿAli Bey's Coptic secretary Muʿallim Rizq, and the Venetian merchant Carlo Rosetti. The first two were ruined by ʿAli Bey's flight from Egypt in 1772, but Rosetti remained for decades to play a major role in the evolving relations between Egypt and the European states.

[49] ʿAli Bey was not the first to extort money from the various communities in Egypt, Muslim as well as non-Muslim, but his excessive and repeated demands for ever greater sums set an example for his successors, whose insatiable appetite for these payments ultimately bankrupted the European commercial houses and helped to provoke the French invasion of 1798.

inexplicably abandoned Damascus only eight days after its surrender and was returning to Egypt in great haste. The consensus of modern historians is that Muhammad Bey had been bribed by the central government to bring his master down, but they have produced only circumstantial evidence for this contention. The contemporary historian al-Jabarti suggests only that "they became alienated from one another, and 'Ali Bey moved against Muhammad Bey."[50]

After a tense truce for six months between the infuriated 'Ali Bey and his brother-in-law Muhammad Bey, who refused to return to Syria, Muhammad Bey fled the capital for the safety of Upper Egypt, where he organized the remaining dissidents whom 'Ali Bey had rusticated among the Hawwara. When Isma'il Bey, who was sent at the head of an army to attack Muhammad Bey, instead submitted to his leadership, 'Ali Bey's fate was sealed. He fled Cairo in April 1772 and sought refuge with Dhahir al-'Umar in Palestine. A premature attempt to regain his position in Egypt cost 'Ali Bey his life, for he was wounded in a confrontation with Muhammad Bey at Salihiyya and died in Cairo on May 8, 1773.

In his struggle with his master, Muhammad Bey had argued that 'Ali Bey had placed Egypt in Christian hands and pursued policies detrimental to the empire. He had surrounded himself with Christian advisors, both Egyptian and foreign,[51] had welcomed a handful of European military advisors to strengthen his artillery corps, and had formed an alliance with the Czarist state in a war of destruction against the sultan's Islamic empire.[52] Although he made his submission to the sultan, received a governor, renounced the Russian alliance, and remitted payments owed to Istanbul and the *Haramayn* which 'Ali Bey had withheld, Muhammad Bey embraced most of his fallen master's other political objectives. He offered protection and encouragement to the Europeans to expand their trade in Egypt's Mediterranean ports, signed an agreement with the British East India Company to receive their ships at Suez,[53] continued his interest in Palestine/Syria, and main-

[50] *Al-Jabarti's History of Egypt*, I, 382.

[51] Al-Jabarti complained that "his Coptic secretary, Mu'allim Rizq, attained in 'Ali Bey's days a position no other Copt, as far as we know, had ever achieved. Mu'allim Ibrahim al-Jawhari followed in his footsteps and achieved high rank after him, in the days of Muhammad Bey and his successors." *Ibid.*, I, 381, 638.

[52] S. K. Lusignan, *A History of the Revolt of Aly Bey against the Ottoman Porte* (London, 1783), 146–47, reports Muhammad Bey's rallying speech against 'Ali Bey. The French consul D'Amirat also mentions that Muhammad Bey warned of the growing influence of Christians if 'Ali Bey made a successful return. See Archives Nationales (Paris), Affaires Etrangères, B1, 335 (Le Caire), May 5, 1773.

[53] On Muhammad Bey's treaty with Warren Hastings and other treaties signed by Ibrahim Bey and Murad Bey, see Daniel Crecelius, "Unratified Commercial Treaties between Egypt and England and France, 1773–1794," *Revue d'Histoire Maghrebine*, 12 (June 1985), 67–104. None of these treaties was accepted by the home governments, whose leaders did not want to hazard highly speculative and uncertain profits in Egypt against

tained complete control of Egypt. Muhammad Bey was actually named governor of Egypt with the rank of three horsetails and was assigned districts in southern Palestine, but died on campaign against Shaykh Dhahir at Acre on June 10, 1775, after a three-day illness, before the documents confirming these appointments reached him.[54]

The ambitious foreign campaigns of ʿAli Bey and Muhammad Bey could not have been undertaken without the vastly increased income these amirs derived from sources traditionally beyond the control of a single household. Their policies therefore mark the first attempt to restructure in a fundamentally new way the traditional equilibrium that had existed among socio-economic and political–military institutions in Ottoman Egypt and to create a strong centralized regime in complete control of the administrative and military institutions as well as the economy. These efforts presaged by almost half a century the emergence of a similar, but more successful, regime under Muhammad ʿAli Pasha. If they failed to achieve any of their bold foreign goals, ʿAli Bey and his successors had transformed relations with both the Ottoman central government and the European states and had laid out broad foreign objectives that were largely embraced by Muhammad ʿAli Pasha a few decades later. They regained for Egypt an international importance that it has not since surrendered. Their immediate successors had no such vision, confined their ambitions within the borders of Egypt, resorted to short-sighted and self-defeating policies, and imposed an unrestrained despotism that destroyed the economy and brought disaster to Egypt. Al-Jabarti, the moral beacon of the age, lamented that "after his death, [Muhammad Bey's *mamluks*] remained powerful, but their inclination was away from justice and towards the ways of folly. They, in turn, bought mamluks who were brought up in their ways and outdid their predecessors. They accustomed themselves to tyranny and thought it gain; they persevered in injustice and continued their oppression without interruption."[55]

Egypt's slide into chaos: 1775–1811

Egypt knew neither peace nor stability between the death of Muhammad Bey and the consolidation of power by Muhammad ʿAli in the early nineteenth century. The Qazdagli beylicate split into two factions, with the *mamluks* belonging to Muhammad Bey (al-Muhammadiyya) following either Ibrahim Bey or Murad Bey, while the others, having closer ties to ʿAli

---

the huge amount of trade they continued to carry on in other Ottoman ports. Moreover, the European leaders felt that the Qazdagli amirs could not be trusted to keep their word, as the attacks on the caravan in 1779 demonstrated.

[54] See Crecelius, *Roots of Modern Egypt*, 155–65.
[55] *Al-Jabarti's History of Egypt*, I, 420, 704.

Bey Bulut Kapan (al-ʿAliwiyya), or to the remnants of broken households, attached themselves to Ismaʿil Bey, ʿAli Bey's *khushdash*, or to Hasan Bey al-Jiddawi, one of ʿAli Bey's personal *mamluks*. Factional lines were not always rigid, and individual Mamluks frequently crossed from the ʿAliwiyya to the Muhammadiyya, or vice versa, as circumstances changed. Ibrahim Bey was recognized as *shaykh al-balad* on Muhammad Bey's death, Murad Bey took command of the pilgrimage, and Ismaʿil Bey remained in his palace, but almost immediately intrigues set the various households to fighting one another.

Ismaʿil Bey and his allies drove Ibrahim Bey and Murad Bey from Cairo in July 1777, but by March 1778 Ismaʿil Bey had to flee to Istanbul when his supporters abandoned him. Hasan Bey al-Jiddawi meanwhile found refuge along with other dissidents in Upper Egypt. For the next few years Ibrahim Bey and Murad Bey, each distrusting the other, maneuvered for advantage. In July 1780 they deposed one governor and in September 1783 deposed another. While Ibrahim held the customs houses of Suez and Alexandria, Murad claimed the provinces of Lower Egypt. Both sought to maximize their income by any means possible and in the process destroyed the bases of Egypt's wealth. Required payments, whether to the governor, to the central government, to the *Haramayn*, or to the religious students and the ʿulamaʾ, were frequently withheld or paid only in part. Payments to the tribes along the pilgrimage route were not made, with the result that the Bedouin attacked pilgrim caravans. In some years the pilgrims were unable to visit Medina, in others the caravans were attacked and many pilgrims lost their lives. Merchants, both local and European, suffered enormous losses when the Bedouin attacked their caravans and looted their goods.

Murad Bey made annual rounds through Lower Egypt, demanding extraordinary taxes from the already overtaxed farmers. Many fled the land or rebelled; Murad, whose activities could not be restrained by Ibrahim, leveled many villages as examples to others. For his part, Ibrahim Bey levied such heavy taxes on coffee and spices that the quantities of these products reaching Suez and Cairo declined, leading to a reduction in revenue.

Upper Egypt was again outside the control of the regime in Cairo and remained the refuge of dissident amirs who caused frequent food shortages in the capital by withholding the grain ships headed north. Ismaʿil Bey left Istanbul and found his way to Upper Egypt via Libya in early 1781, despite Murad Bey's attempt to block his passage. There in the Saʿid he joined Hasan Bey al-Jiddawi and other dissidents who claimed the taxes and products of the southern provinces.

In late 1783 and early 1784 Ibrahim Bey and Murad Bey had yet another falling-out, this time over Ibrahim Bey's willingness to return five dissident *khushdashes* to positions from which Murad Bey had dismissed them. Ibrahim Bey drove Murad Bey from Cairo and in January 1784 the two beys fired cannons at each other across the Nile, but to no effect. They made their peace in April, but in late 1784 Murad Bey entered Cairo and forced Ibrahim to flee. Murad deposed another governor in October 1784, by which time "the land [had] turned to waste, highway robbery flourished, marauders indulged in looting, security was non-existent, and the roads were impassable except with a protective escort, then at a dangerous risk. The peasants abandoned their villages because of a lack of irrigation and because of the oppression."[56] Plague, drought, pestilence, and famine struck Egypt during these years, making the life of the general population almost unbearable.

Another peace between Ibrahim Bey and Murad Bey was made in November 1784, then broken by Murad once again. A final peace was arranged in February 1785, by which time Murad Bey's depredations had left Alexandria's population isolated and demoralized. Murad's demands upon the French (and other) merchants had become so great that several French commercial houses had been bankrupted and many in their Cairo community had abandoned the city for the relative protection of Alexandria.[57] In early 1786 Murad Bey made another enormous demand upon them and, under the pretense that they had illegally rebuilt their churches in Alexandria, threatened to dismantle them if his demands were not met. When they resisted, he threatened to tear down their houses and execute them. When Murad Bey's agent tore down the walls of Terre Sainte, the community of foreign merchants appealed to the central government for succor, ominously stating that if the sultan's regime could not resolve their problem their own governments would intervene.

The Ottoman government, which had been contemplating an expedition for some years, was finally stung to action and sent forces, by land and sea, to destroy Ibrahim Bey and Murad Bey and their households.[58] But Ghazi Hasan Pasha, who landed with great ferocity and boldness in July 1786, succeeded only in driving the Muhammadiyya deep into Upper Egypt, where they now exchanged positions with the refugees from the various ʿAliwi

---

[56] *Ibid.*, II, 83, 139.

[57] On the French merchant community in Egypt, see R. Clément, *Les Français d'Egypte aux XVIIᵉ et XVIIIᵉ siècles* (Cairo, 1960).

[58] The Ottoman explanation for sending the expedition to Egypt in 1786 was given in a circular to the Hammam, Wafi Humam, and Hanadi Bedouin. In it the government accused Ibrahim and Murad of ruining Egypt's rich agriculture with their tyranny, of seizing the revenues of the *bayt al-mal* and the *awqaf* belonging to the sultans, of withholding the assigned monies and grains from the *Haramayn*, of seizing the properties of merchants and the stipends of orphans and the ʿulamaʾ, and of oppressing the *ojaq* troops and the tax-farmers, the poor and the unfortunate. A land force led by ʿAbdi Pasha and a sea force under the command of Ghazi Hasan Pasha had come to exterminate the *mamluks* of Muhammad Bey Abu al-Dhahab. See Başbakanlik Arşivi (Istanbul), Defter-i Muhimme-i Misir, 10 (1199–217), p. 53, item 107.

households. Unable to accomplish his goal of annihilation of the refugee amirs and under orders to return to Istanbul to accept the command of the war against the Russians, Ghazi Hasan Pasha had to compromise with Ibrahim and Murad. He originally assigned Qina to Ibrahim Bey and Isna to Murad Bey with the stipulation that they remain in those districts, but within a year the dissidents were in control of everything south of Jirja.[59] When Ghazi Hasan Pasha left Egypt in October 1787 he left Isma'il Bey, the *shaykh al-balad*, and Hasan Bey al-Jiddawi with sufficient troops to defend themselves against the Muhammadiyya amirs.

Plague and pestilence continued to strike Egypt during these years. Communication and the flow of agricultural products were disrupted by the division of the country into warring camps, leading to frequent shortages of food in the capital. Mercenaries from Albania and Rumelia flocked to Isma'il Bey, and the Bedouin continued to disrupt travel in the provinces. A great plague that entered the capital in early 1791 carried away virtually the entire regime in Cairo, including Isma'il Bey and most of his Mamluks. Ibrahim and Murad, who were pardoned by the sultan, entered Cairo without opposition in August 1791 and resumed their former activities with a vengeance,[60] withholding financial obligations to the empire, driving the Europeans into bankruptcy (and out of Cairo for a second time), and making demands on the various communities of Muslim merchants, guild members, ethnic communities, and farmers. The countryside, already battered by repeated plagues, droughts, a pestilence that carried off an enormous proportion of the animals, and a neglect that left its crucial irrigation system in disrepair, was now subjected to new demands for taxes as Ibrahim and Murad sought to recoup staggering losses. Lower Egypt in particular felt the wrath of the vengeful duumvirs, to the extent that villages were abandoned and the fields remained untilled. Rosetta and Damietta lost

---

[59] *Al-Jabarti's History of Egypt*, II, 146, 173, 240, 286.

[60] Ghazi Hasan Pasha had confiscated the personal belongings of the fugitive amirs, and acted with such ferocity toward the Mamluk grandees that, against all religious tradition, he sold their wives and concubines at auction, and extorted enormous sums from the personal wealth of Murad's famous wife Nafisa Hanim and Zulaykha Hanim, the daughter of Muhammad Bey Abu al-Dhahab and wife of Ibrahim Bey. It was reported that Zulaykha's jewels alone, which Ghazi Hasan Pasha seized and sent to Istanbul, were worth 7,000 purses, or 17,500,000 *paras*. Even Ibrahim Bey's son Marzuq and daughter 'Adila were sold at auction. See *al-Jabarti's History of Egypt*, II, 117–18, 193–95, 196, 317–21; Archives Nationales (Paris), Aff. Etr., B1, 113 (Alexandrie: 1783–87), fos. 239–41. During this period the central government attempted to claim the annual sums that Ibrahim Bey and Murad Bey had failed to send to Istanbul in the previous years. According to Shaw, *Organization*, 314, Isma'il Bey sent 83,000,000 *paras* as payments for *hulwan* and the *bayt al-mal* in 1787 and as part of their compromise with the central government in 1792 Ibrahim and Murad agreed to pay 235,000,000 *paras* for the same purposes.

half or more of their populations.[61] Alexandria was neglected and un-
defended; its water supply unsecured; Cairo's population was reduced by
almost 40,000. The tyranny of the Qazdagli amirs had ruined the richest
province of the eastern Mediterranean.

In 1795 the French sent a mission to Ibrahim and Murad, warning them
of the consequences of their attacks upon French merchants and trade, but
this threat, like the blusters of Ghazi Hasan Pasha, was dismissed by the
beys, who felt themselves safe from another expedition.

The French invasion

The wars of the French Revolution did much to disrupt French trade in the
Ottoman empire. French merchantmen were forced to remain idle for
months at a time in eastern ports. The attacks by the English and various
pirates upon French shipping, the refusal by local tyrants such as Ahmad
Pasha al-Jazzar in Palestine and Murad Bey and Ibrahim Bey in Egypt to
grant the European merchants the advantages of their capitulations, the
monopolies created by these tyrants, and their demands against European
merchants caused considerable losses in many ports and bankrupted French
commercial houses. French trade was in danger of elimination from regions
that had only recently produced substantial profits.

Continuing Russian military successes against the Ottoman empire
seemed to foreshadow imminent collapse of the Ottoman state and seizure
by the Russians of Istanbul itself and strategic ports along the northern rim
of the Mediterranean. Partly to secure its position along the Levant and
Egyptian coasts, to recoup losses, and to guarantee its trade, the Directory
sent Bonaparte to occupy Egypt and Palestine and destroy the local regimes
responsible for the losses suffered by the French since the deaths of 'Ali Bey
and Muhammad Bey Abu al-Dhahab in 1772 and 1775 respectively.[62]

---

[61] In 1777 two French sources estimated the population of Damietta at 20,000 to 30,000,
while Alexandria was said to have 20,000 inhabitants. But in 1795 the French traveler
Ollivier reported that Damietta was in ruins and that Rosetta had lost half its
inhabitants, more by people fleeing Murad Bey's exactions than by plague. See Quai
d'Orsay (Paris), Corr. Cons., Damietta (sans numéro), "Mémoire sur l'Echelle de
Damietta," fo. 19; Quai d'Orsay, Mémoires et Documents – Egypte, vol. I
(1778–1861), fo. 135. In 1777 Damietta exported 100,000 ardabs of rice, but during
the period 1791–98 it exported only 28,000 ardabs of rice annually on average. In a
French survey of 1800, twenty-seven villages in the vicinity of Damietta were found in
ruins and Damietta was reduced to approximately a thousand inhabitants. See Archives
de la Guerre (Vincennes), B6-53, fo. 214 (September 14, 1800).

[62] See Henry Laurens, Les origines intellectuelles de l'expédition d'Egypte: l'orientalisme
islamisant en France (1698–1798) (Istanbul and Paris, 1987); and Henry Laurens,
L'expédition d'Egypte, Bonaparte et l'Islam: Le choc des cultures (Paris, 1989).

4

Culture in Ottoman Egypt

NELLY HANNA

➤❮

States and elites

The culture of the Ottoman period has often been analyzed by using the same criteria applied to the periods before and after it, Mamluk Egypt (1250–1517) and the nineteenth century. This is problematic for two reasons, firstly because of the very different roles played by the state in relation to culture and learning and secondly because of the role of elites in providing models and patterns of culture. The influence of the ruling class in shaping culture can change between one period and another, and can be greater at certain times than at others. When the state is centralized, the ruling class is much more likely to play a dominant role than it is in a decentralized state. The cultural production is more likely to be polished and refined when ruling classes dominate the direction that it takes, and less so when their role is reduced. When the state is decentralized, as it was during the Ottoman period, and the structures at the top are weaker, the cultural forms and patterns from below are more likely to emerge. There-fore, rather than compare this period to those before or after it, we may approach it through the larger framework of its changing social and political structures.

In both Mamluk Egypt and Egypt under the rule of Muhammad ʿAli and his descendants (nineteenth century), the state was very centralized and played an active role in financing and shaping culture and in education. Likewise the ruling elites were actively involved in creating cultural models. In the nineteenth century, it was the elites who introduced western cultural models, in education as well as in housing styles, clothing, and so on. As for the Mamluk period, the sultans and their ruling amirs for over two centuries created the models and set the fashions, in the arts and in architecture. One has only to pay a visit to the Islamic Museum of Cairo and see the quality of glass, metalwork, carpets, and woodwork, to understand the role of elites, for whom these objects were produced, in setting up models. It would be hard to find equivalents, either in quality or artistic value, in the objects created in Ottoman Egypt.

Conditions were in some ways different in Ottoman Egypt. The role of the state and elites underwent an important change after the Ottoman conquest of 1517, resulting in a dislocation of some of its structures. Some of the change was a direct result of the integration of Egypt into a new political entity with its center, Istanbul, located at a certain distance. Egypt changed from being the center of an empire to a province, and Cairo became a provincial capital after having been an imperial capital. The complex bureaucratic structure that al-Qalqashandi described in the fifteenth century, with numerous *diwans* (government offices) and employees, was drastically reduced and simplified. The most important offices were in Istanbul, while in Egypt, as in other Ottoman provinces, a pasha sent from Istanbul on a short-term appointment presided over a much simplified bureaucracy.

Some of the changes during this period were also due to the fact that the policy of the Ottomans toward their provinces was one of restrained intervention in matters that were not of immediate interest to them. The Ottomans, for instance, did not have a policy of ottomanizing culture. They did not try to impose their language, and it never became the language of culture or learning; nor did they attempt to ottomanize the educational system. In Egypt, as elsewhere, indigenous populations maintained their own culture and way of life. Ottomanization was applied to the bureaucracy and to the judiciary in the sense that the systems set up in Egypt followed the same lines as in other provinces, with the bureaucracy headed by a pasha, a *qadi al-qudat* heading the judiciary, and a *daftardar* heading the financial bureau, all of whom were sent from Istanbul.

The Ottoman authorities nevertheless encouraged cultural expressions that enhanced the virtues of their rule, writings such as Mar'i ibn Yusuf al-Maqdisi's (d. 1623) *Qala'id al-'uqyan fi fada'il al-'uthman* and Muhammad al-Bakri's (d. 1598) *Nasrat ahl al-iman bi dawlat al-'uthman*, and Ahmad ibn Muhammad al-Hamawi's *Fada'il salatin bani 'uthman*, in praise of the Ottoman dynasty and state;[1] or writings praising the Hanafi *madhhab* to which the Ottomans adhered, like Muhammad ibn Yusuf's treatise on the virtues of Abu Hanifa, *'Uqud al-juman fi manaqib abi hanifa al-nu'man*, and Hajar al-Haytami's (d. 1567) *al-Khayrat al-hasan fi manaqib abi hasan al-nu'man*.[2] Several works of this kind were written, in Egypt and in Syria, especially during the first century of Ottoman rule. Subsequently, as the

---

[1] League of Arab States, *Catalogue of Microfilmed Manuscripts*, Institute of Arabic Manuscripts, vol. II, part IV, History (Cairo, 1970), 453; al-Muhibbi, *Khulasat al-athar*, 4 vols. (Cairo, 1248/1867), IV, 358–61; Ahmad ibn Muhammad al-Hamawi, *Fada'il salatin bani 'uthman*, ed. Muhsin Muhammad Hasan Salim (Cairo, 1993).

[2] Muhammad Sayyid Kilani, *al-Adab al-misri fi dhill al-hukm al-'uthmani 922–1220/ 1517–1805* (Cairo, 1984), 26.

power of the Ottoman state was overshadowed, this kind of praise in verse and prose was directed toward the powerful local amirs who held political power. The intrinsic value of many of these works is questionable.

The consequences of this situation were important as far as culture was concerned for a number of reasons. Some state projects were realized, but they were few in number when compared to other periods. In Cairo, as in other provincial cities, such as Damascus, Aleppo and Baghdad, construction projects were occasionally financed by the Ottoman sultans.[3] Their efforts were for obvious reasons concentrated in their own capital. The pashas who governed Egypt on behalf of the Ottoman sultan from their residence in the Citadel were involved in building programs, especially in Bulaq during the sixteenth century. The large-scale projects of Sulayman Pasha, in the 1530s, included a small mosque, a *hammam*, and several *wikalas*, while the monumental *wikalas*, the little mosque in Ottoman style, and the *hammam* that Sinan Pasha built are major landmarks in Bulaq.[4] They served more than one purpose, first by providing revenues to the owner, while at the same time increasing the commercial infrastructure of a river port with links to Anatolia, and second as visible pronouncements of Ottoman authority. Subsequently as the Ottoman pashas' political power became threatened, they lost their initiative in undertaking important projects such as these.[5] Moreover the style of these Ottoman buildings did not catch on, and their influence on the architecture of Cairo remained small; with the exception of the pencil-shaped minarets that became integrated into the local style, architecture, for the most part, followed the patterns set up during the Mamluk period or earlier.

Another consequence of the Ottoman conquest was that state-sponsored institutions created under the Mamluk sultans tended to become weaker, a tendency that had its beginnings in the late Mamluk period. Foremost among these was the *madrasa*, or institutions of higher education. In Egypt these had always flourished as a result of patronage by the rulers or ruling class. They supported numerous students and teachers financially. The situation of these institutions of higher education changed after 1517. Few new *madrasas* were built during the Ottoman period. With the exception of the al-Azhar, which grew and developed, many *madrasas* established in earlier centuries tended to shrink, to have looser functions, or to disappear. Some, for instance, became simple mosques or *takiyyas*; the living quarters intended for students were turned into apartments and let out to families. In some cases, the libraries of these colleges were dispersed or stolen. Some

[3] André Raymond, "L'architecture dans les pays arabes à l'époque ottomane," in Robert Mantran (ed.), *Histoire de l'empire ottoman* (Paris, 1989), 683–88.

[4] Nelly Hanna, *An Urban History of Bulaq in the Mamluk and Ottoman Periods* (Cairo, 1983), 47–53.

[5] *Encyclopedia of Islam*, 2nd ed., s.v. "Kahira," by Michael Rogers.

colleges, however, did continue to function as such, but their numbers considerably decreased.[6] The immediate reasons are unclear, but funds from the Mamluk *waqfs* (pious foundations) may have been dispersed; the fact that Istanbul was endowed with numerous sultanic foundations may have channeled some of the student population toward the capital of the empire; the fact that the bureaucracy in Cairo was much simplified under the Ottomans may have reduced the possibilities of employment of college graduates. Even al-Azhar, the only major institution of higher learning to undergo considerable development during the Ottoman period, had a degree of independence from state intervention. The state, for instance, did not have any say in the choice of its head, the *shaykh al-Azhar*, this being considered an internal matter. The person in this important position was chosen by the ʿulamaʾ themselves. Moreover, although the official *madhhab* of the Ottomans was the Hanafi, the *shaykh al-Azhar* was, throughout the Ottoman period, a Shafiʿi or a Maliki; al-Jabarti narrates the maneuver of shaykh ʿAbd al-Rahman al-ʿArishi (d. 1779), who was Hanafi, to gain political support from the amirs for his nomination as *shaykh al-Azhar*, an attempt strongly resisted by the Shafiʿis in al-Azhar, who argued that their institution had never been headed by a Hanafi before, and who finally managed to impose their own candidate, Shaykh al-ʿArusi.[7]

Other institutions sponsored by the state underwent a similar fate. The Sufi *khanqas*, like the *madrasas*, had flourished as a result of patronage by Mamluk sultans and ruling elites. These ceased to exist in the Ottoman period, and were replaced by much looser structures, the *takiyyas* and the *zawiyas*, usually created around an individual Sufi *shaykh* by his disciples.[8] The tendency to see institutionalized forms give way to looser structures or even to disappear entirely is manifest in one other body that had played an important role in the creation of Mamluk creature, the *diwan al-ʿamaʾir*, a bureau for construction work created by Sultan al-Nasir Muhammad ibn Qalawun (1303–41) to implement and supervise his extensive building program as well as the buildings of his amirs. This *diwan* continued to exist till the end of the Mamluk period. After the Ottoman conquest, this institution, which had brought together the best architects, workers, and artisans, and which must have provided a model for the building tastes and fashions of the time, ceased to exist. People would have to look elsewhere for their models.

The mutations that this period witnessed affected the way that the ruling

---

[6] J. Heyworth-Dunne, *An Introduction to the History of Education in Modern Egypt* (London, 1938), 15–19.

[7] *ʿAbd al-Rahman al-Jabarti's History of Egypt*, ed. and trans. Thomas Philipp and Moshe Perlmann, 3 vols. (Stuttgart, 1994), II, 83–84.

[8] L. Fernandes, "Some Aspects of the *Zawiya* in Egypt at the Eve of the Ottoman Conquest," *Annales Islamologiques*, 19 (1983), 4–17.

classes participated in culture in several ways. The weaker state participation in cultural projects meant that the ruling classes did not find clear-cut models to follow, unlike the ruling classes under the Mamluk sultanate who followed the models that were set up by the sultans and their entourages, and unlike those of the nineteenth century who were clearly inspired by European models. The ruling classes in Cairo during the Ottoman period were not primarily inspired by imperial models in Istanbul, the court of the Ottoman sultan being too distant. And the pasha's court did not offer significant models or have much bearing on elite culture; it was not the center of an imperial culture as the ruler's residence had been under the Mamluk sultans.

The kind of patronage provided by the ruling classes to cultural activities may have been affected by the channeling of funds, in the form of tribute, to Istanbul. The economic aspect of culture is a question that we do not know enough about at the present time, but which may have had an important bearing on cultural production, at least in the earlier part of the Ottoman period. The kind of patronage of art, culture, and education that the ruling classes, notably the high-ranking members of the militias and the Mamluk amirs, provided may well have been shaped by the fact that they were spending less money in these domains, at least during the sixteenth and seventeenth centuries, when the military groups had not yet fully consolidated their financial positions, and were not systematically spending as much money on cultural production as their counterparts of the fourteenth and fifteenth centuries. High-quality textiles, luxury products in metalwork and glass, and carpets had under Mamluk sultanate patronage become works of art. Expensive materials such as gold, silver, and marble may have become scarcer in the sixteenth to eighteenth centuries, and they tended to be used more sparingly. One rarely finds, for instance, the richly painted ceilings, generously ornamented with gold; and the brass or copper doors inlaid with fine silver or golden ornaments in works of this period. Likewise, the marble used as decorative material, to ornament a facade or the floor of a hall, was usually reused material cut up in small pieces, and therefore cheaper. These tendencies were more or less apparent before the arrival of the Ottomans, but were intensified subsequently.

The effects of such economic restraints are particularly evident in the domain of public construction, which required substantial funding. Architecture was the strongest point of Mamluk art, and served as an expression of the power of the patron. The ruling elites during the Ottoman period continued to be the main builders of public buildings; but rather than the monumental mausoleums and charitable foundations of the fourteenth and fifteenth centuries, the members of the ruling class of Ottoman Cairo concentrated their efforts on smaller public buildings. Most of them, for instance, satisfied themselves with tombs that were small unpretentious structures, often simple canopy tombs, no longer built in the conspicuous parts of the city but in the Imam al-Shafi'i cemetery.[9] Even as great a personage as 'Ali Bey al-Kabir had a tomb consisting of a small rectangular building surmounted by a dome-like structure, very modestly decorated, which can still be visited in the vicinity of al-Imam al-Shafi'i.[10] Many of their public buildings were either of a commercial nature or engendered revenues of some sort, *wikalas* or *suqs*, for instance, or apartment houses that were rented out. Their charitable or religious buildings were often mosques that were modest in size and decoration, and the small-scale *sabil-kuttabs*, public fountains built in numerous parts of the city, surmounted by elementary schools. As *waqfs*, or pious foundations, these provided free distribution of water to passers-by and funded the schoolboys and their teachers. More economic to run than the Mamluk *madrasas*, these *sabil-kuttabs* nevertheless served an important purpose in that they helped the ruling class to gain the support of the 'ulama' and to legitimize their rule, without necessarily undergoing a tremendous expense.

Later on, in the eighteenth century, the Ottoman governors lost some of their authority and local military groups more or less controlled the major financial resources, notably the tax-farms. This brought about an increase in public construction, like the mosque of 'Uthman Katkhuda with the numerous amenities around it, built along the banks of Birkat al-Azbakiyya in 1736;[11] the mosques, *zawiyas*, and *sabil-kuttabs* 'Abd al-Rahman Katkhuda built in various parts of the city, as well as the major repairs he made on the Maristan of Qalawun; and the mosque and *takiyya* Muhammad Abu al-Dhahab constructed next to al-Azhar. Nevertheless, economic restraints were created by the rivalries among the ruling clans in the eighteenth century and their constant in-fighting forced them to channel a portion of their budgets toward military expenditures, and the purchase of arms and of *mamluks*.

These changes in the forms of patronage did not mean that the ruling class refrained from trying to control society through culture, but that they redefined their own positions in relation to the changes taking place and used different tools. One trend that is very apparent in the eighteenth century was the development of various forms of cultural activities around individual households. In other words, the focal points for culture had moved from the courts of the rulers to a series of households of prominent amirs. These households became private political centers, around which amirs gathered their soldiers and their followers, and where they had their councils to discuss matters of state. They decided in their own houses such

[9] Rogers, "Kahira."

[10] *Index of Mohammedan Monuments*, no. 385, dated 1187/1773.

[11] Doris Behrens-Abouseif, *Azbakiyya and its Environs, from Azbak to Isma'il, 1476–1879* (Cairo, 1985), 55–58.

vital state matters as the removal of a governor, or the current price of the currency. The real center of power was, in other words, transferred from the pasha's headquarters in the Citadel to the private residences of the rival contenders for political power, that is the major clans of the Fiqariyya, the Qasimiyya, and later the Qazdagliyya.

The residences of the ruling amirs eventually became the buildings with which their power was associated; they were the buildings that, as the stature of the amirs increased, were embellished with numerous amenities and commodities, and new functions introduced to emphasize the stature of the owner. In their residences start to emerge functions associated with power, such as rooms called *diwans*, a word borrowed from the *diwan* or council the pasha held in the citadel; the *mahkama* such as that which 'Uthman Bey al-Qazdagli held in his house and which he presided over personally; and the prisons where the owner of the palace could throw his enemies.[12] This important change left its mark on culture. Households became centers for the amirs' cultural activities to support and enhance their social positions vis-à-vis the 'ulama' who legitimized their rule and, to a lesser extent, the populations they ruled.

The emphasis on private residences may have been a factor behind the more restricted interest in public construction. The architecture of power became associated with the palaces of the rival ruling amirs. Although some Mamluk households were very powerful, the fact that there were several centers of power, and that these centers moved from one household to another, as the rival households competed with each other, meant a diffusion of power that is characteristic of the late Ottoman period, a situation that had its parallels in cultural expression.

Historians who have approached the culture of the Ottoman period by an implicit or explicit comparison with that of the Mamluk sultanate have often found little more than negative features to emphasize. The few studies on the arts of the period have tended to stress the lesser quality of products such as metal bowls, textiles, rugs, and glasswork as compared to the Mamluk period.[13] This attitude has discouraged serious research on the cultural production of this period, its ceramics, its wooden and metal products, its textiles and rugs. Researchers who, in future, take an interest in these matters will have to start by asking for whom these products were intended, for ruling elites or, more likely, for members of the indigenous urban population. The answer may well explain why they are less luxurious. In reality, one cannot understand the fate of artistic products independently of the people for whom they were intended, their needs, and their financial

---

[12] Nelly Hanna, *Habiter au Caire au XVIIe et XVIIIe siècles* (Cairo, 1991), 74–75.

[13] The only book devoted to the arts of Ottoman Cairo is Rabi' Khalifa, *Funun al-qahira fil-'ahd al-'uthmani* (Cairo, 1984).

resources. Artistic production associated with the ruling class, which is the production that usually attracts attention, does not represent all the forms of expression, nor does it constitute all of culture. Because museums prefer elite products, we are less well informed about the products associated with other social groups. The study of architecture of the Ottoman period has fared somewhat better than that of the arts. A number of historians and architectural historians have formulated other approaches to the subject than the uncomplimentary comparison with Mamluk architecture and have looked at the architecture of the period on its own terms and for its own worth.[14]

Educational establishments, within and without

Changes affecting the top of the hierarchy had parallels in the educational establishment and on learning in general. In a period of decentralization and diffusion of power, al-Azhar appears to be an anomaly. It was so, since it came to dominate the scene, for reasons that are yet to be convincingly explained. Al-Azhar had by the Ottoman period become the focal point for intellectual life. The most eminent and productive scholars of the period, for instance Ibn Nujaym, al-Ramli, al-Ujhuri, al-Zurqani, al-Dardir, al-Khurashi, all of them authors of voluminous scholarly works, mainly in jurisprudence, were associated with it and helped to consolidate its position as a center of learning for the whole Islamic world. The constant movement of students from neighboring lands was an important factor in forging and maintaining a regional culture. The notice that al-Muhibbi includes in his biographical dictionary about Shaykh Shams al-Din Muhammad al-Babli (d. 1666) is by no means unique: the students he taught were from Cairo, from al-Sham, from Mecca, and from Medina. Likewise, Shaykh 'Abd al-'Aydarusi's itinerary along the major centers of learning indicates the ease with which scholars could travel and integrate into the learned circles of the time; he was born in Yemen, lived in Cairo for a while, lived briefly in Damascus, traveled to Istanbul, and died in Egypt.[15] Numerous are the students who came from Damascus, Jerusalem, and Aleppo, and stayed on to become themselves 'ulama' in al-Azhar.

There is some debate among historians about the value of many of these scholars' works, notably the many *hawashi* (colophones) and the *shuruh* (commentaries) that were written to explain earlier works. Some consider these to be repetitive and lacking in originality, while others have, not without contempt, called this the period of *hawashi* and *shuruh*.[16] The

---

[14] One of the first to do this was John A. Williams, "The Monuments of Ottoman Cairo," *Colloque international sur l'histoire du Caire* (Grafenhainichen, 1972), 453–63.

[15] al-Muhibbi, *Khulasat al-athar*, II, 328–29, IV, 39–42.

[16] Jurji Zidan, *Tarikh adab al-lugha al-'arabiyya*, 4 vols. (Dar al-Hilal, Cairo, n.d.), III, 291.

numerous *shuruh* were for long considered to reflect the absence of innovation and imagination of the period. Baber Johansen has demonstrated that
this is not the case, and that the *shuruh* and *hawashi* literature should simply
be considered as a format that allowed the author to elaborate his own
views, and that many new concepts were in fact expressed through these
commentaries. Johansen has opened the door to the reconsideration of many
scholarly works by showing how within the framework of traditional works,
legal doctrine was developed and new and radical ideas were being
formulated.[17] This makes sense since scholars in jurisprudence today still
consider works such as Ibn Nujaym's *al-Bahr al-ra'iq* and al-Khurashi's
Mukhtasar sidi khalil to be classics.

It is, however, important to make some distinctions at this point. At the
institutional level, al-Azhar dominated institutionalized education. But
decentralizing forces were at work at other levels. One can detect notably a
diffusion of knowledge among groups other than the religious scholars –
Sufi shaykhs, for instance, to whom the population more and more turned
for religious guidance. The scholars, in other words, cannot be said to have
had a complete monopoly on knowledge, since the kind of knowledge
associated with the 'ulama' was not the only kind of socially accepted
knowledge; other perfectly legitimate forms were acceptable, even to the
'ulama' class themselves. Furthermore, the scholars attached to al-Azhar, or
to one of the other educational institutions still functioning, did not confine
their activities to that institution, but operated on a wider basis, and forged
links with many social groups, a fact which had a bearing both on them and
on those with whom they interacted. It is at these levels that the diffusion
and decentralization of knowledge and learning operated rather than at the
institutional level.

It is only through an analysis of these levels that we can form a global
image of culture and learning that includes institutions but that does not
exclude non-institutionalized forms. Historians need to explain the situation
in its totality without simply rejecting certain domains of culture on the
basis that they are not serious or worthy of attention. Ottoman Cairo in fact
offers diverse forms of cultural expression flourishing independently of
institutions and scholarly elites. The study of education through the analysis
of educational institutions exclusively has often led to contradictions. Some
historians who have studied al-Azhar, for instance, believe that the range of
studies was limited and the outlook was narrow; that emphasis was on
memorization; that the curriculum had not changed or evolved over a long
time; and that the Islamic heritage was forgotten.[18] Yet they neither hesitate

---

[17] Baber Johansen, "Legal Literature and the Problem of Change: The Case of the Land
Rent," in Chibil Mallat (ed.), *Islam and Public Law* (London, 1993), 29–47.
[18] Gamal El-Din El-Shayyal, "Some Aspects of Intellectual and Social Life in Eighteenth-
century Egypt," in P. M. Holt (ed.), *Political and Social Change in Modern Egypt*

to admit that this institution was reputed all over the Islamic world, nor do they deny that some of the most prominent scholars of the period were associated with it. These contradictions are explained by isolating certain phenomena from their global context. Few scholars have tried to find explanations for the emergence of great writers, thinkers, and scholars such as al-Jabarti, Murtadi al-Zabidi, and Shaykh al-Damanhuri, among others. These are usually classified as exceptions, or as phenomena that one cannot explain, whereas in fact one needs to understand them as products of their age, and as part of the context in which they flourished, encompassing both its failings and its accomplishments. In his *Islamic Roots of Capitalism*, Peter Gran suggested that the eighteenth century witnessed an intellectual enlightening, and he studied the writers and thinkers in the light of what he considered were major transformations. More recently, André Raymond's book *Le Caire des Janissaires* talks about the eighteenth century as being a period of great prosperity. One could find a link between the economic conditions described by Raymond and the intellectual climate, a matter that still needs to be pursued by scholars.[19] Other historians have been trying to place al-Jabarti's chronicles in the context of the sources he made use of, therefore reducing the uniqueness of this *'Aja'ib al-athar*.[20] However, the general social and intellectual context of the work is still obscure.

One important factor in an analysis of the world of culture and those who participated in it is informal cultural and educational activities. The diffusion of learning took place through different channels and in different forms. It involved various social groups, including the 'ulama' and the ruling elites, in educational and cultural activities that were quite diverse in form and function, and which brought them in touch with other people who were neither parts of the educational establishment nor members of the ruling class. Central as al-Azhar was as the main educational institution of the period, it did not by any means monopolize all forms of intellectual or cultural activity, either of those who were attached to the institution or, more broadly, those who were not. One can, as a matter of fact, detect a number of channels through which learning could be obtained or spread independently of institutions.

The 'ulama' involved themselves in a variety of activities that were independent of the al-Azhar, but which at the same time widened the

---

(London, 1968), 118–19; J. Heyworth-Dunne, *An Introduction to the History of Education in Modern Egypt* (London, 1938), 1–2.

[19] Peter Gran, *Islamic Roots of Capitalism* (Austin, 1978); André Raymond, *Le Caire des Janissaires: L'apogée de la ville ottomane sous 'Abd al-Rahman Katkhuda* (Paris, 1995).

[20] Daniel Crecelius, "Ahmad Shalabi Ibn 'Abd al-Ghani and Ahmad Katkhuda 'Azaban al-Damurdashi: Two Sources for Al-Jabarti's *'Aja'ib Al-athar fi'l tarajim wa'l akhbar*," in D. Crecelius (ed.), *Eighteenth Century Egypt, The Arabic Manuscript Sources* (Claremont, 1990), 89–102.

horizons of the shaykhs and their followers with regard to subjects or approaches to knowledge that were not within the domains of this learned institution. One of the most revealing examples is that of Shaykh Hasan al-Jabarti, father of the historian 'Abd al-Rahman al-Jabarti. One of the great scholars of his time, Hasan al-Jabarti's interests were multiple, both as a religious scholar and as a scientist, and his writings prolific, a fact that is confirmed by the number of manuscripts, mostly unpublished, in the archives.[21] Much of his scholarly activity took place outside al-Azhar. His house was always full of students who not only came to discuss various subjects with him, but often came to live in his house so as to be able to talk to him and learn. In fact, the historian remembered one student, a great admirer of his father, who came to their house to live there for twenty years; when they moved to their Bulaq house he moved with them, and when they came back to the house in the center of Cairo, in the Sanadiqiyya quarter, he moved back with them. That approach to learning was apparently not an unusual one, except perhaps for the lengthy stay of this particular student. Al-Sayyid Murtada al-Zabidi (1732–91), lexicographer and author of the monumental *Taj al-'arus*, held sessions either in his own house or someone else's, including the Jabartis'. These were attended not only by students, but also by many others, including women, young boys, and young girls, the women listening from behind the curtains. Meetings and sessions of this kind, which were frequent, were open to people who were not necessarily attached to institutions.[22]

Some fields of knowledge, specifically the sciences, were much more developed outside institutions of learning. Astronomy seems to have been particularly in vogue in the eighteenth century, and a number of scientists devoted numerous works to it, like Ridwan Effendi al-Falaki (d. 1710), Shaykh Ramadan al-Khawanqi (d. 1745), and Jamal al-Din al-Kilarji (d. 1742), not to mention Hasan al-Jabarti.[23] They made instruments and carried out experiments in their houses. The limitations of having to undertake scientific experiments at home must have seriously curtailed their activity. Nevertheless, al-Jabarti does mention that a number of Frankish students had come especially to see his father's instruments and watch his experiments, which indicates the reputation he attained in his day. Moreover, we still have much to learn about medicine in the Ottoman period, which the voluminous number of unpublished medical manuscripts in the National Library can help to elucidate. The work of Da'ud al-Antaqi (d. 1599), *Tadhkarat uwla al-albab*, one of the few medical works that have

21 David King, *A Catalogue of the Scientific Manuscripts in the Egyptian National Library*, part 2 (Cairo, 1986), 132, 258, 316, 505, 571, 603, 763, 956, 969, 990.
22 *Al-Jabarti's History of Egypt*, II, 322–46.
23 *Ibid.*, I, 122, 265, 268–669, 644.

been published, needs to be put in a context with the intellectual climate of the period.[24]

Like many other shaykhs, Jabarti had an important private library at home. Students could borrow the books, a practice apparently quite common at the time. The case of Shaykh Hasan is well known because the historian dwells on it and gives lot of details regarding his life. However it is not unique, and numerous other biographies show both how widespread informal education and private libraries were. The records of inheritance registered in courts confirm the large number of private libraries, both among shaykhs and others, amirs, merchants, and occasionally tradesmen and artisans. The inheritance deeds recorded in the court where the division of property of deceased persons took place, the Qisma 'Askariya and Qisma 'Arabiyya, very often include detailed lists of these libraries; some were large, with hundreds of volumes, and others small, containing a dozen books or so. These constitute an untapped source for the cultural and intellectual history of the period.

What is most revealing is how widespread these libraries were, and how wide a subject matter they contained, from theological to legal works, literature and poetry, history, geography, medicine, and astrology. Even more significant is the fact that merchants, shaykhs, and amirs often allowed access to their libraries, allowing people to come into their houses to read and copy what they wanted, and sometimes even permitting the borrowing of books.[25] These private libraries were in fact more like public libraries. The significance of this trend is that it allowed people not necessarily attached to institutions the possibility of perusal of books, as it opened up possibilities for those who were attached to al-Azhar or elsewhere to read books that college libraries may not have had.

This kind of informal cultural and educational activity, independent of institutions, and centered around individual residences, is apparent among various social groups. We have some first-hand information from 'Abd al-Ghani al-Nabulsi who, in the course of his long travels from his home in Syria, to Egypt and to the Hijaz, came for a visit to Cairo where he was guest of Shaykh al-Bakri, head of the Sufi order, in his house in Azbakiyya. His smooth integration into the lifestyle of his host and his easy personal contacts with the people he met are indicative of the close cultural links between Egypt and Bilad al-Sham. During his weeks-long stay in Cairo he noted on a day-by-day basis the places he visited and the people he met. He spent the day roaming the city and visiting its landmarks. Almost every evening, either in the house of Shaykh al-Bakri or in another house, men

[24] Beirut, n.d.
[25] Nelly Hanna, "Cultural Life in Mamluk Households (Late Ottoman Period)," in Thomas Philipp and Ulrich Haarmann (eds.), *The Mamluks in Egyptian Politics and Society* (Cambridge, 1998).

would gather for a *majlis 'ilm*, a scholarly evening, or *majlis adab*, a literary evening. Poetry, often Sufi poetry, was recited, the guests improvising a poem in praise of Shaykh al-Bakri, or of Birkat al-Azbakiyya; *qasidas*, or poems, were analyzed and various subjects of scholarly concern discussed. These sessions were attended, according to al-Nabulsi, by numerous 'ulama', including Shaykh al-Azhar himself, as well as by students, and others not connected to institutions of education, *ahl al-adab*, including people coming from other parts of Egypt.[26]

The literary salon that al-Jabarti describes in relation to Ridwan Katkhuda al-Jalfi was probably similar in form except that it did not have the Sufi element that was so strong in the *majalis* at al-Bakri's house. Jalfi's house was a meeting-place for literary people, poets, and singers. He distributed prizes for the best performances. Such gatherings or *majalis* were frequent and widespread, their direction reflecting the interest of those who organized or attended. People read, composed, and often improvised verse and poetry, sometimes the panegyrics like those composed for Ridwan Katkhuda al-Jalfi by the poets who frequented his literary evenings, *al-Mudama al-urjuwaniya fi'l-mada'ih al-ridawaniyya* and *al-Fawa'ih al-jinaniya fi'l mada'ih al-ridawaniya*.[27] This type of gathering must have encouraged certain types of verse or prose, certainly those in praise of the host, topical in nature, but whose intrinsic worth was for the most part limited. People with special skills, however, were encouraged to exhibit their talents. The *majalis adab*, moreover, provided a forum for people involved in literary production, including some who traveled long distances in search of patrons and audiences. The biographical dictionaries of the period provide a large number of notices of poets (*sha'ir*), and literary men (*adib*), who roamed the region, traveling from one city or town to another, from Baghdad, to Yemen, to Aleppo, to Cairo, often in search of patrons, some more successfully than others. A poet such as Rajab ibn Hijazi al-Hariri was born in Damascus, lived in Hums, traveled to Egypt and Hijaz; another poet, Rawhi al-Baghdadi, left his town, traveled widely, and ended his days in Damascus.[28] These mobile artists who carried their art with them in their wanderings were an important factor in creating homogeneity of culture in the region.

In summary, then, the diverse forms and expressions of culture and learning were as much a product of the educational institutions as they were of the opening up to the outside, through informal channels that were numerous and diverse. The scholars of an institution such as al-Azhar were the most prominent thinkers and writers of their time, and yet their

---

[26] 'Abd al-Ghani Nabulsi, *al-Haqiqa wal-Majaz fi al-Rihla ila Bilad al-Sham wa Misr wal-Hijaz* (Cairo, 1986), 181, 184, 187, 202–05, 209.

[27] *Al-Jabarti's History of Egypt*, I, 314–15, 354–55.

[28] Al-Muhibbi, *Khulasat al-athar*, II, 160, 172.

intellectual contacts with the world outside al-Azhar were an important part
of their formation. Likewise, the situation gave the opportunity to many
people who were not attached to the world of scholarship to be in touch
with the learning of the period, even if this was to remain, for many of them,
a superficial contact. It was nevertheless an important contact in the sense
that the world of scholarship was not entirely isolated from its surroundings
and that it addressed not only the restricted circle within the institution but a
wider audience not necessarily attached to it.

The diffusion of learning and culture from below

Other factors shaping the direction that culture took during the Ottoman
period had their origins elsewhere, neither among elites nor among scholars,
but among the other strata of the urban society, the artisans and tradesmen,
for instance. Their role in shaping culture, too often neglected in historical
research, like that of the higher social strata, could change depending on the
conditions of the time, expanding or retracting according to circumstances,
and leaving their mark on different forms of expression. We are unfortunately not equally well informed about the many different kinds of cultural
production. Some, such as the written word, or the material products that
have survived, have left traces that are easier to identify and analyze; others,
such as music, song, or dance, are more difficult to deal with because no
concrete data have survived.

Analysis confirms what we already know – that popular culture was not
the realm of the popular classes alone, and that learned culture was not the
possession only of scholars and intellectuals. It indicates how different
groups made use of one or the other to fit their needs. "Learned" culture was
used by ordinary people, either educated or semi-educated, who, with the
spread of literacy, gave a direction to the written production. Much writing
was directed toward subjects that had popular appeal, and was presented in
a way that could be attractive to ordinary people. Analysis also shows the
way that features of popular culture penetrated learned culture. The style
and language of popular tales, notably, can be detected in learned forms of
writing, such as history, and in the development of linguistic studies that
stressed colloquial and dialect. Tastes were formed or developed by peculiar
circumstances sometimes, such as the emergence of the coffee-house in the
sixteenth century. The coffee-house played a role in the direction that
culture took, favoring certain types, helping in the development of others.

The diffusion of learning functioned at a powerful and influential level, as
the system of *kuttab* or elementary schools spread, reaching a broad base.
Many historians have taken it for granted that literacy was a development of
the modern period, and that before the nineteenth century, when the state
set up numerous schools, ordinary people did not have access to elementary

schooling. The data available indicates that this view is not correct, and that, in fact, many more people knew how to read and write beyond those who were attached to institutions of higher education. This was a development of vital importance because of the large number of people it affected, bringing about a rate of literacy that more than one European traveler noticed. Chabrol, who formed part of the team of experts accompanying Napoleon during his expedition and one of the contributors to the *Description de l'Egypte*, says that about one-third of the population of Cairo was literate, a relatively high figure. He does not specify which social strata they belonged to, but we can guess that the literate third of the population would include many artisans and shopkeepers, and that the other two-thirds of the population who were illiterate would belong to the poorest classes of the urban population, such as domestic servants, donkey and mule owners, carriers of goods of all kinds, and a multitude of other unskilled jobs. These strata, certainly very numerous, would not have benefited from the *kuttab* system, nor was the attainment of literacy within their means. Nevertheless, even excluding these strata, the portion of males who could read and write remained high and literacy was fairly widespread among the strata of tradesmen, shopkeepers, and artisans, who formed an important portion of the population.

Lane, in his *Manners and Customs*, confirms that most of the children of the higher and the middle classes as well as some of those of the lower orders were literate.[29] Lane notes actually that people who could read were very numerous, not only in Cairo, but in every large town and in large villages, the local mosque providing elementary education for children.[30] This is not surprising. As a matter of fact, we know that many of the students admitted to al-Azhar were of provincial origin and that their basic training was done before they came to Cairo. Shaykh Yusuf al-Shirbini, the author of *Hazz al-quhuf*, however, questions the quality of education that could be obtained in the villages and mentions, with irony and mockery, a *faqih* who misreads texts.[31]

The comments of Lane and Chabrol are corroborated by other indications. The number of elementary schools, called *kuttab* or *maktab*, run by pious foundations, where young children were taught basic education, were numerous in the city. A particular architectural form that they had makes them easily recognizable buildings, small structures built on two floors, the lower one being a *sabil* or public fountain, the upper one a school room which could have seated some ten, twenty or even sometimes thirty children. The same kind of *sabil-kuttab* had been constructed in many buildings of

---

[29] E. W. Lane, *Manners and Customs of Modern Egyptians* (London, 1836; repr. 1989), 66–67.
[30] *Ibid.*, 66.
[31] *Hazz al-quhuf* (Bulaq, 1274 H), 40.

Mamluk Cairo, and many of the large-scale building complexes of the fifteenth century had such structures attached to them. In the Ottoman period, their numbers multiplied and they were constructed independently of other buildings. There may have been up to three hundred of these in Cairo in 1798, according to the *Description de l'Egypte*. One can mathematically deduce that over a four-year period of education, 1,000–2,000 children would have finished schooling every year, and over a generation 30,000–60,000 people would have been to school. In addition to these elementary schools, some teaching of young boys took place in mosques, but for mosques offering such facilities no figures are available. Lastly, boys from more comfortable circles had private teaching, with *faqihs* coming to their houses to give them lessons.

Whatever reasons are forwarded to explain this phenomenon remain conjectural, and much more research is needed to elucidate its emergence. There must have been an economic factor behind the high rate of literacy, related to the condition of artisans and tradesmen. Their earnings must have been sufficient for their sons to spend three or four years in the *kuttab* or else the boys would have been sent out to earn a living at a young age. This is possible, since Egypt produced and exported products such as textiles and sugar in large quantities. Both these industries, for much of the Ottoman period, were doing very well and employed many artisans. Moreover, the fact that the ruling class were building more and more elementary schools and endowing them as pious foundations increased the educational facilities of the city. 'Abd al-Rahman Katkhuda, one of the great builders of the eighteenth century, was responsible for the construction of no fewer than eight elementary schools in Cairo; one of them is a major landmark of the city, the *sabil-kuttab* of Bayn al-Qasrayn.[32] André Raymond's work has shown that the eighteenth century experienced a steady increase in the construction of these buildings, considerably more than during the century before.[33]

One could also cite the courts as a factor in the spread of literacy. A comparison of the court records of the mid-sixteenth century with those of the mid-seventeenth century shows an amazing increase not only in the number of recorded cases but in the length of each case and the details provided, and in the variety of social groups who took their cases to court. The plaintiffs got copies of the deeds that we find recorded in the registers, to protect their rights in a claim or a dispute. The kinds of plaintiff that we find going to court – tradesmen, artisans, shopkeepers, skilled workers – the range of matters they took to court, the frequency of their contacts, and finally the fact that everything was done in writing may well have been an

[32] *Waqf 'Abdul Rahman Katkhuda*, no. 940, archives of the ministry of *waqfs*, Cairo, dated 1157 H and 1190 H, pp. 5, 41, 47, 63, 71, 85.
[33] André Raymond, "L'activité architecturale au Caire à l'époque ottomane (1517–1798)," *Annales islamologiques*, 25 (1990), 346–49.

enticement toward literacy, notably in a society where the court system was central in people's daily lives.[34]

Certainly, one could also argue that the Sufi movement was an important factor in spreading literacy. The role of Sufism in shaping culture and education in Ottoman Egypt was a vital, if little-known, force. The great development of popular Sufism and of numerous *turuq* is recognized by scholars, who now are beginning to place this in a social and cultural context. It is becoming apparent that the 'ulama' shared their position as providers of religious guidance to society with the growing number of Sufi shaykhs, whether these were associated with a *tariqa* or had a *zawiya* around which their disciples gathered. In other words, this indicates a clear diffusion of power from the 'ulama' class, a relatively restricted group, more or less homogeneous in their training, to a much larger group of Sufis, with much more diversity, since much of the group's approach was decided by the individual shaykh according to his own teachings. There were numerous such shaykhs, each of whom had his own disciples and whose teachings they followed; unlike the more formal institutions of learning, curriculums in Sufi circles were not set or uniform, but depended on the shaykh, his training, and on his personal leanings. The various Sufi groupings therefore offered a diverse picture. Moreover, the people who attended were not students whose careers would be in education and learning, but ordinary people who attached themselves to a shaykh of their liking for the spiritual guidance he could offer them. Some *zawiyas* were not averse to allowing women to participate in the lessons.[35] The teachings offered in these circles consequently reached a much broader stratum. The people living in the *zawiya* were of modest standing, and not graduates of al-Azhar or other institutions of higher learning. They probably formed part of the large body of people who had finished their formal learning at the elementary level.

Although some Sufis disdained books and discredited the erudition of jurists and commentators, other Sufis attached great importance to education and were often teachers and authors, and their *zawiyas* were schools. While the role of the shaykh in the guidance of his novices remained supreme, manuals for Sufis assumed a central position in Sufi education. Religious leaders such as Sha'rani enjoined their disciples to read and educate themselves. In his *zawiya* for instance, where some 200 Sufis lived, not counting the many daily visitors, Sha'rani boasted that Sufis read the Qur'an and Hadith night and day continuously.[36] Literacy, it seems, then,

---

[34] Nelly Hanna, "The Administration of Courts in Ottoman Cairo," in N. Hanna (ed.), *The State and its Servants, Administration in Egypt from Ottoman Times to the Present* (Cairo, 1995), 44–59.

[35] Muhammad Sabri Yusuf, *Dur al-mutasawifa fi tarikh misr fil 'asr al-'uthmani* (Cairo, 1994), 365.

[36] Tawfiq al-Tawil, *Al-Tasawwuf fi misr iban al-'asr al-'uthmani*, 2 vols. (Cairo, 1988), II,

was accorded a significant value. Often the *zawiyas* had their own libraries. People who were not attached to institutions of learning and who could not afford to buy books were thus provided with reading facilities. The profusion of Sufi writings and Sufi poetry, which formed the greatest portion of literary production of the period, must have reached many people, indicating a vital role for Sufism in the spread of learning.[37]

Some of ʿAbd al-Wahhab al-Shaʿrani's statements illustrate this tendency very well. His introduction to *Kashf al-ghumma ʿan jami ʿal-umma* explains the reasons he wrote the book, and who he expected his readership to be. He was, he says, approached by groups of workers and simple people who came to him to complain and express their chagrin and confusion. Whenever they performed one of the religious obligations or concluded a contract according to one *madhhab* or school of law, the jurists of another *madhhab* declared it null and void. In other words, with their level of education, the debates among the *fuqaha'* were beyond their comprehension, and they were eager to find a simpler way of understanding their religious duties. Shaʿrani satisfied their request by gathering in one book the basic principles of religion according to the four *madhhabs*.[38] This represented a trend, and many other shaykhs followed his example by writing tracts for their disciples – not highly intellectual or particularly innovative, but in a language that ordinary people could understand.

The consequences that the level of literacy, broadly spread among the urban population, engendered are complex and varied. With considerable numbers of artisans and tradesmen able to read and write, the bearing that this had on what was written and how it was written is a vital matter, worthy of more attention than it has so far received. It can, in fact, serve to explain many features of the Ottoman period that have so far been obscure or for which no satisfactory explanation has been given. The literate population formed a fairly wide readership whose tastes were taken into consideration, thus giving a certain direction to the written production. This trend can help to explain the volume and kind of writing produced during the age. As more and more things were put in writing, the quality of the manuscripts themselves declined. The annotations one often finds in the various catalogs of Arabic manuscripts written in this period refer to the poor quality of the calligraphy or paper. The frequently sloppy handwriting could mean that copyists were recruited from among people less well trained, or that they were less well paid; those copyists with beautiful handwriting sold manuscripts for higher prices to those who could afford

---

35–36; Michael Winter, "The Writings of Abd al-Wahhab Ash Shaʿrani: A Sufi Source for the Social and Intellectual Life of Sixteenth Century Egypt," Ph.D. thesis, University of California, 1972, 274, 277.

[37] Heyworth-Dunne, *History of Education*, 10.
[38] Winter, "The Writings of Abd al-Wahhab Ash Shaʿrani," 330–31.

them. The cheap paper of many manuscripts could likewise reveal the social strata that these works were destined for. In other words, the explanation for the handwriting and the paper could be economic.

The literature written during the Ottoman period included many works in popular fields such as the lives of saints and their virtues, embellished with miracles and wondrous stories. The period also produced numerous books on magic (*sihr*) and on talismans, subjects that seem to have been very popular among readers, as well as works on the occult sciences such as geomancy (*'ilm al-rimal*); divinations (*'ilm al-jafr*); magic squares (*'ilm al-awfaq*), and others.[39] The popularity of such works, which reflected the beliefs and superstitions of ordinary people, could also be considered an indication that the educational establishment was not imposing its standards effectively. The large number of literate persons also explains why there were so many works of vulgarization, summaries of larger works, that did not add anything very new to the state of knowledge, but tended to simplify and make them accessible to persons who were literate but whose education was limited. Many religious works were written, not to explain theological matters, but to set down the rules of conduct for a good Muslim, explaining concretely and in simple language the proper way to practice the various religious rituals, ablutions, prayer, and the pilgrimage. This kind of work had already gained some popularity before the Ottomans came to Egypt. In fact, Jean-Claude Garcin considers the numerous tracts written in the late Mamluk period, sometimes very short and concrete, and treating very diverse subject matter, such as those of al-Suyuti (d. 1505), as works of vulgarization.[40] With time, however, this kind of writing expanded and multiplied.

Another phenomenon that emerges as a consequence of the diffusion of learning concerns the category of people who created culture. One detects involvement of a different category of persons, notably artisans and tradesmen, in the creative process, a matter of great significance for which it would be interesting to look for parallels from other regions and periods. We have a number of chronicles of the seventeenth and eighteenth centuries written by historians, about whom little or nothing is known because they were not important enough to appear in the biographical dictionaries of the time – ʿAli al-Shadhili al-Farra, Yusuf al-Hallaq, Mustafa ibn Ibrahim al-Qinali al-Maddah, Muhammad al-Burulusi al-Saʿdi. The same applies to ʿAli ibn Jawhar al-Sukkari who wrote an itinerary of saints' tombs in Cairo and Shaykh Yusuf al-Shirbini, author of a satire on peasants. Whether ʿAli al-Farra was a seller of furs, Yusuf al-Hallaq a barber, ʿAli al-Sukkari a sugar

---

[39] Heyworth-Dunne, *History of Education*, 12.
[40] J.-C. Garcin, "Le Proche Orient à l'époque mamluke," in J.-C. Garcin (ed.) et al., *Etats, sociétés et cultures du monde Musulman médiéval Xe–XVe siècles* (Paris, 1995), I, 369.

producer, Ibrahim al-Maddah a poet by profession, or whether the names referred to their fathers' professions, can only be conjectured.[41] Raymond has suggested that ʿAli al-Shadhili al-Farra belonged to the artisan or tradesman group, meaning that he did not belong to either the category of historians associated with the ruling class or to that associated with scholars trained in al-Azhar. His point of view in the battles he described was that of the ordinary Cairene who sided with neither of the warring parties but had to endure, like so many others, the disastrous effects of conflicts that in no way concerned them.[42] The faulty language and grammatical errors in some of these works are indications that the writers are very unlikely to have received a college education, and were probably products of the *kuttab* system. Some "learned" cultural production was, in other words, created by people who did not form part of the educated elite.

The Ottoman period witnessed another significant phenomenon: much oral literature passed into writing. The development of the tales of al-Sayyid al-Badawi is typical. A recent study has shown that the first written biographies of this saint date from the fourteenth and fifteenth centuries, but consist of brief notices of a few lines. It is only in the mid-sixteenth to mid-seventeenth centuries that full biographies of al-Badawi appear. His three principle biographies, by ʿAbd al-Wahhab al-Shaʿrani, ʿAbd al-Samad, and ʿAli al-Halabi, are eighty years apart (1554, 1619, and 1633). Shaʿrani does not cite a written source for his work, but oral sources.[43] Other tales and romances from oral literature were put into writing. A considerable number of the manuscripts of *The Thousand and One Nights* that have survived until today were in fact written in the Ottoman period, both in Egypt and in Syria. Although the earliest extant manuscripts date from the Mamluk period, there was a proliferation of manuscripts subsequently, from the seventeenth, eighteenth, and early nineteenth centuries.[44] The most plausible explanation for this output is that people wanted not only to hear these tales narrated, but also to read them. This passage from the spoken to the written word implies a significant change in attitude, notably a more individual and personalized enjoyment of literature, a significant phenomenon in itself.

It is for the same reasons that so many works from prior periods, in

---

[41] André Raymond, "The Opuscule of Shaykh ʿAli al-Shadhili: A Source for the history of the 1711 Crisis in Cairo"; ʿAbd al-Rahim ʿAbd al-Rahman ʿAbd al-Rahim, "Yusuf al-Mallawani's *Tuhfat al-Ahbab* and Ahmad Shalabi ibn ʿAbd al-Ghani's *Awdah al-Isharat*"; Jane Hathaway, "Sultans, Pashas, *Taqwims* and *Muhimmes*: A Reconsideration of Chronicle Writing in Eighteenth Century Ottoman Egypt," all in Crecelius (ed.), *Eighteenth Century Egypt*, pp. 27–30, 39–44, and 52–58 respectively.
[42] Raymond, "The Opuscule," 27–35.
[43] Catherine Mayeur-Joouen, *Al-Sayyid al-Badawi, Un grand saint de l'Islam égyptien* (Cairo, 1994), 42.
[44] *The Arabian Nights*, trans. Husain Haddawy (London, 1990), xii–xiii; *The Thousand and One Nights*, ed. and trans. Muhsin Mahdi (Leiden, 1984), I, 25–34, II, 236–303.

diverse subjects, were copied, a trend for which no explanation has yet been offered other than the general lack of imagination and the absence of any spirit of innovation. The catalog of scientific manuscripts of the National Library in Cairo shows that an amazing portion of the manuscripts, composed at different times and places, including classic works by famous scientists of the past, exist in copies that date from the seventeenth and eighteenth centuries. The same is true of historical writing. The card catalog of the same library indicates that extant copies of many major Mamluk historians in Dar al-Kutub are also datable to the Ottoman period. The two dated copies of al-Maqrizi's *Khitat* date from 1569 and 1575; of the collection's nine dated copies of al-Suyuti's *Husn al-muhadara*, one is late sixteenth century, three date from the seventeenth century, two date from the eighteenth, and three from the nineteenth centuries. This cannot be accidental, but has to be seen in a context that gives it some meaning. If so many manuscripts were being copied, then they were in demand.

In summary then, the spread of literacy should be considered a major phenomenon because it affected what was being written and how it was written. A considerable portion of the written production was not primarily intended for people who were attached to institutions of higher education as students or teachers. The implications are far reaching, with regard to the process of education, its relation to institutionalized education, and to the way that the written production was affected by the broader spectrum of readers who were being addressed.

Other factors intervened in the cultural and artistic production of the Ottoman period. The coffee-house, significant for the development of some forms of expression, first appeared in the sixteenth century. By the beginning of the seventeenth century coffee-houses in Cairo numbered in the hundreds, and had spread to provincial towns. The figures for the end of the eighteenth century are 1,200 coffee-houses in Cairo, not counting those of Bulaq and Old Cairo.[45] This number is very high in relation to the population, estimated at between 260,000 and 350,000 at the time of the French expedition (1798), and even higher if one excludes the poor, unlikely to spend their time in coffee-houses, and women, who did not frequent them at all. In other words, this is a phenomenon of significance in the lives of an important sector of the urban population, the coffee-house being frequented by men of different socio-economic strata.

Its importance in the domain of culture was that the coffee-house became a center for various kinds of performance. Prior to its emergence, entertainers did not normally have a fixed place to practice their arts. Some

---

[45] Chabrol, "Essai sur les moeurs des habitants modernes de l'Egypte," *Description de l'Egypte, état moderne*, II/part 2, 438; Lane confirms the figure saying that there were over a thousand of them: *Manners and Customs*, 334.

entertainment took place in the street, where people would collect around dancers or singers and, at the end of the performance, pay them a tip. Some entertainment took place in private houses of the well-to-do, who on an occasion or a feast day had entertainers for guests or family. Many entertainers earned their living by moving from one *mawlid* to another, and from one town or village to another.

The emergence of the coffee-house introduced a new element. Entertainers came to exhibit their arts, encouraged by coffee-house owners eager to attract clients. This created a novel situation for entertainers in two ways. The coffee-house provided premises where hundreds of spectators were reached, and certain coffee-houses employed the narrators of tales and romances, musicians, players of *khiyal al-dhill* or puppet shows, and entertainers who put on burlesque farces, on a permanent basis; other coffee-houses provided them with regular access, so as to entertain their guests.[46] Certainly for artists or entertainers, this must have provided a degree of economic security that other mobile entertainers did not have, and allowed them to develop their art. The clientele of a particular coffee-house, moreover, was probably more difficult to please than the anonymous street spectator, an element that motivated poets or story-tellers to improve their performances or to be more original and inventive, so as not to bore the clients who watched with regularity. Clients would come to a particular coffee-house to watch those artists and entertainers who had made a reputation. When Jean Coppin traveled to Rosetta, for instance, he went to a coffee-house, not because of the coffee he was going to order, nor for the company, but because there was a puppet show (*karagoz*) that people had highly praised which he was eager to watch.[47] Artists or entertainers might also develop certain kinds of verse or prose that were in keeping with the taste and level of the audience and the informality of the premises.

As a result of this situation, the oral literature, or popular literature, of the period was developed. This is most apparent in the *siras* and romances, among others the *sira* of Abu Zaid al-Hilali, *The Thousand and One Nights*, the exploits of Genghis Khan, and the *sira* of Baybars. All these are part of an oral literature handed down from one generation to the next, whose sources go back to long before the Ottoman period. Lane writes extensively about the narrators of tales, stories, and romances exercising their profession in Cairo. Different troupes specialized in one of these tales or in another. In the course of the Ottoman period, this oral literature underwent a significant development. In his edition of *The Thousand and One Nights* Lane has

[46] These dramas were often improvised and no written record remains. Lane tells us of one play performed for Muhammad 'Ali in private, about a tax collector demanding payment from a poor peasant, and in the end accepting the services of the peasant's wife instead: *Manners and Customs*, 384–85.
[47] Jean Coppin, *Les voyages en Egypte de Jean Coppin 1638–1646* (Cairo, 1971), 32–33.

pointed out, on the basis of internal evidence, such as place names, currencies, and terms unknown before the sixteenth century, that a number of tales were created in Ottoman Cairo.[48]

The coffee-houses may have encouraged certain kinds of music, song, and dance, the puppet shows known as *khiyal al-dhill* or as *karagoz*, in other words, the multitude of popular forms of culture that had been developed over the centuries and to which each generation added or adapted to its own conditions, tastes, and needs.[49] Unfortunately, we know too little about the way many of them developed. One may however conjecture how the introduction of the coffee-house may have affected certain forms of expression. With regard to verse, for instance, the informality of the gathering encouraged a loose kind of verse where rhyme was not a primary concern, and where the poet could freely express himself without the restraints of form. This was in keeping with the trend for *irtijal* or improvisation for which the period is known.[50] The kind of client frequenting the coffee-house, together with its congenial atmosphere, moreover, was an encouragement to the use of colloquial in the verse or prose that narrators and poets presented.

The vitality of these art forms was such that we may in a number of ways trace their influence on other forms of expression. The conditions of the period, in fact, encouraged a trend whereby the tools, techniques, and attitudes of popular culture passed on to other kinds of writing. One can detect the style and language of oral tales, the use of colloquial, slang, or dialect to dramatize or to provoke humor, the open sexuality of burlesque farces, the building up of dramatic effect of the heroic romances, in literary forms that cannot be classified as popular literature, in which entertainment plays a more or less important part. These tools and techniques made this literature more accessible to larger segments of the population.

From the late Mamluk period, colloquial appeared in serious writing, and Ibn Iyas's chronicle written during the last years of Mamluk rule and the first of Ottoman rule uses direct speech intermingled with colloquial. The use of colloquial spread and developed, notably in historical writing, in the seventeenth and eighteenth centuries, in chronicles such as Ahmad Shalabi Abu al-Ghani's *Awdah al-isharat*, in the Damurdashi chronicles, and in the social satire on peasants, Yusuf al-Shirbini's *Hazz al-quhuf*, which used the dialect of peasants and imitated the way that Turks spoke by spelling out

---

[48] E. W. Lane, *The Thousand and One Nights*, 3 vols. (London, 1859), III, 216, no. 14.

[49] 'Abdul-Hamid Yunus, *Khiyal al-dhill* (Cairo, 1994), 44–48. The players of *khiyal al-dhill* of Cairo apparently participated in the wedding festivities in Istanbul for the daughter of the Ottoman sultan Ahmad in 1612, a clear recognition of their quality: see pp. 82–83.

[50] Muhammad Sayyid Kilani, *Al-Adab al-misri fi dhill al-hukm al-'uthmani 922–1220/ 1517–1805* (Cairo, 1984), 58.

incoherent sounds, as a way of making fun of them.[51] This aspect of the written language, the inclusion (or, for some, the intrusion) of a style that was not strictly speaking classic, and often not even correct grammatically, seems to have become fairly common in certain kinds of writing.

Inclusion of techniques of popular art and entertainment is evident in many ways. The open sexuality, for instance, repeatedly found in Yusuf al-Shirbini's work, was often used, seemingly, only to amuse, probably influenced by the oral literature and the burlesque farces which abounded in this kind of humour.[52] The combination of history and entertainment was noted by P. M. Holt in al-Ghamri's *Dhakhirat al-i'lam*, an unpublished chronicle of minor historical value, written in verse, which covers up to 1630; and by Jurji Zidan in al-Ishaqi's history *Lata'if akhbar al-awwal fiman tassaraf fi misr min arbab al-duwal*, a chronicle going up to 1623, which combined history and entertainment, intermeshing historical events with tales and stories that, in the words of Zidan, one would be ashamed to repeat.[53] In Mustafa ibn Ibrahim al-Qinali's *Majmu' latif*, a chronicle that goes up to the year 1739, the influence of the recitation of heroic tales is evident in the way the historian narrates events. He uses the methods of the story-teller to create dramatic effect and to build up tension, and applies such techniques as repetition of certain passages which in oral literature would have reminded the audience of a message that might be lost in the course of the narrative.[54] One consequence of this trend, as far as historical writing was concerned, was that while it became more accessible to ordinary people, some of it became more questionable as a reflection of historical realities it claimed to depict.

Transformations that the written language underwent can be linked to the development of a type of linguistic studies that focused on dialect, particularly evident in the seventeenth century. Studies of non-Arabic words used in Arabic had existed for a long time, interest probably dating from the time when many non-Arabs started using Arabic extensively, bringing with them words from their original languages. However, the late sixteenth and seventeenth centuries witnessed a resurgence of interest in the spoken language, both in Egypt and in Syria, and a number of works were written

---

[51] See al-Shirbini, *Hazz al-quhuf*, 20, for instance.
[52] See for instance *ibid.*, 9–10, 20.
[53] P. M. Holt, "Ottoman Egypt (1517–1798): An Account of Arabic Historical Sources," in P. M. Holt (ed.), *Political and Social Change in Modern Egypt* (London, 1968), 6; Zidan, *Tarikh adab*, III, 323.
[54] Madiha Doss, "Some Remarks on the Oral Factor in Arabic Linguistics," in *Dialectologia Arabica, A Collection of Articles in Honour of the Sixtieth Birthday of Professor Heikki Palva* (Helsinki, 1995), 49–61; Mahida Doss, "Military Chronicles of 17th century Egypt as an aspect of Popular Culture," paper presented to the Colloquium on Logos, Ethos and Mythos in the Middle East and North Africa, Budapest, September 18–22, 1995.

on the subject.[55] In other words, the Arabic used in Egypt during a particular period was considered to deserve scientific study. Among the scholars who produced important glossaries of colloquial Egyptian are Yusuf al-Maghrabi (d. 1610), Ahmad al-Khafaji (d. 1659), and Muhammad ibn abi l-Surur al-Bakri (d. 1676), who died within less than seventy years of each other. It is very significant that all three of them were closely linked to the establishment, and consequently familiar with the learned language. Al-Maghrabi was an Azharite and well connected to the religious and military elite of his time; al-Khafaji had studied in Istanbul and was sent to Egypt as *qadi al-qudat*; Muhammad ibn Abi l-Surur belonged to the famous Bakri family which headed the Sufi order. It is therefore quite revealing that these scholars interested themselves in the informal use of language rather than imposing formal usage.

The first of these chronologically is Yusuf al-Maghrabi's *Daf' al-isar*, for several reasons an important work.[56] One of its numerous merits is that al-Maghrabi explains the meanings of words in his glossary within a specific context, and he often specifies the social group it was used by, including words addressed to children below speaking age, such as *tata*, meaning walking; the words used by a donkey owner addressed to his donkey; or he compares a word or meaning as used in Egypt to the way it was used during his lifetime in Yemen or Mecca, by North African or Black African merchants, or the way that Turks used it. Moreover, even though al-Maghrabi constantly refers to the *Qamus*, meaning Firuzabadi, in order to find a link between the colloquial and the proper use of language, he indicates clearly that he finds the Arabic that Egyptians use to be quite proper.

Al-Maghrabi's work aroused the interest of his contemporaries. Muhammad ibn Abi l-Surur's work, *al-Qawl al-muqtadab fima wafaq lughat ahl misr min lughat al-'arab*, is in fact a glossary of colloquial Egyptian words for which he can provide an Arabic root.[57] His inspiration for this piece of work, as he says in his introduction, was Shaykh Yusuf al-Maghrabi's study. The works of al-Khafaji, who wrote *al-Shifa' al-ghalil fi-ma fi kalam al-'arab min dakhil*, can be put in the same context.[58] The importance of these studies of Egyptian dialect has not been sufficiently stressed by historians, nor has an explanation been offered for this resur-

---

55 Wajdi Rizq Ghali, *al-Mu'ajamat al-'arabiyya, biblighrafiyya shamila mashruha*, intro. Husayn Nassar (Cairo, 1971), 41–50; among the Syrian writers he mentions are Ibn Hanbal al-Hanafi (d. 1563), author of *Bahr al-'awwam fima asaba fihi al-'awam*: p. 41.

56 Yusuf al-Maghrabi, *Daf'al-isar'an kalam ahl misr*, ed. and intro. 'Abdul-Salam Ahmad Awwad (Moscow, 1968).

57 This important work was edited by al-Sayyid Ibrahim Salim, with an introduction by Ibrahim al-Ibiari (Cairo, 1962).

58 Al-Muhibbi, *Khulasat al-athar*, I, 331–43; *al-Adab al-misri*, 276–80.

gence of interest in the language as it was actually used. The links between this group of works and al-Sayyid Murtada al-Zabidi's *Taj al-ʿarus*, written at the end of the eighteenth century, specifically with regard to Zabidi's contextuality, are, moreover, yet to be elucidated.

By comparison to the Ottoman period, during which language was characterized by a strong element of colloquial and of dialect in certain kinds of writing, and by an emphasis on expression rather than on the correctness of the form, the nineteenth and twentieth centuries developed much more clear-cut criteria as to the proper way to use the language. Rules were elaborated in guide books showing the correct forms that should be followed. These criteria were set up from above, by those who held positions of power in the educational or other establishments. They were inspired not by the language that was used around them, but by their perception of the classical past.[59] From that perspective, it was easy to judge the kind of Arabic that was frequently written in the Ottoman period as being decadent or in decline.

Conclusion

The emphasis on using colloquial and on writing about it is but one manifestation of the larger picture. Through this, we may perceive the vitality and dynamism of a culture that was not directed by the establishment but that developed through its own impetus and its own informal structures. It was a culture less bound by rules imposed from above, one in which we find a looser kind of expression, and a freer use of forms. This implies a different set of criteria from those of refinement, correct use of language, originality, which in the Ottoman period did not have the same priority as they did in other periods. Culture was, in other words, created from below.

Seen from this perspective, the culture of the Ottoman period, with its failings and accomplishments, emerges as an interlude between the Mamluk period and the nineteenth century, an interlude that redefined the participation of the different social groups in the process of cultural expression and a period in which the needs and tastes of wider sectors of the population had a bearing on the way that culture developed and was expressed.

---

[59] Husayn al-Marsafi (d. 1890) is an excellent example of this trend, see Gilbert Delanoue, *Moralistes et politiques musulmans dans l'Egypte du XIXᵉ siècle (1798–1881)* (Cairo, 1982), 361–69.

5

The French occupation of Egypt, 1798–1801

DARRELL DYKSTRA

❖

Introduction

Of the span of Egypt's history since the arrival of Islam, no comparably brief period has received more scholarly and popular attention than the years 1798–1801, when the country was conquered and occupied by a French military expedition commanded by Napoleon Bonaparte.[1] Publication – for political, propagandistic, and scholarly motives – of materials pertaining to the expedition began early. Before the end of 1798 London publishers were selling collections of French despatches and correspondence intercepted in transit from Egypt to France.[2] At least one account of the military aspects of the expedition was in print before the French evacuated Egypt in 1801.[3] The first major intellectual product of the civilian intellectuals who accompanied the French army – Denon's *Voyage dans la basse et haute Egypte* – was in print in 1802, with English editions appearing the following year in London and New York.[4] The first edition of the vast *Description de l'Egypte* began to appear in 1810.[5]

---

[1] The basic bibliographic guides for the older literature are Henri Munier, *Tables de la Description de l'Egypte, suivies d'une bibliographie sur l'expédition française de Bonaparte* (Cairo, 1943), and Jean-Edouard Goby, "Contribution à l'inventaire des sources manuscrites et à l'étude bibliographique de l'histoire de l'expédition française en Egypte," *Bulletin de l'Institut d'Egypte*, 33 (1952), 305–22. A brief introduction to studies by Egyptian historians is M. M. el-Sorougy, "Egyptian Historiography of Napoleon Bonaparte in the Twentieth Century," *al-Majallah al-tarikhiyyah al-misriyya*, 20 (1973), 3–27. See also the extensive bibliography in the most recent scholarly treatment in French: Henry Laurens et al., *L'Expédition d'Egypte: 1798–1801* (Paris, 1989).

[2] *Copies of Original Letters from the Army of General Bonaparte in Egypt: Intercepted by the Fleet under the Command of Admiral Lord Nelson* (London, 1798).

[3] Louis-Alexandre Berthier, *Relation des campagnes du Général Bonaparte en Egypt et en Syrie* (Paris, 1800).

[4] Jean-Edouard Goby, "Les quarante éditions, traductions, et adaptations du 'Voyage dans la Basse et la Haute Egypte' de Vivant Denon," *Cahiers d'histoire égyptienne*, 4 (1952), 290–316.

[5] Commission des Monuments d'Egypte, *Description de l'Egypte*, 1st ed. (Paris, 1810–29).

Discourse in Arabic on the expedition also began early. 'Abd al-Rahman al-Jabarti composed his first narrative of events some seven months after the invasion, and a second account, dedicated to the Ottoman commander Yusuf Pasha, in December 1801; the latter had been translated into Turkish by 1810.[6] Another account in Arabic was written by Niqula al-Turk, who had been sent to Cairo by the Lebanese amir Bashir Shihab to report on the events of occupied Egypt.[7]

Many more memoirs, documents, and monographs have appeared, based mostly on western sources; only a few highlights can be touched on here. The "official" edition of Napoleon's correspondence, published during the Second Empire, includes nearly two thousand letters, edicts, and other documents from the Egyptian expedition.[8] These and other published and archival documents provided the basis for de la Jonquière's hugely detailed five-volume study of the military aspects.[9] Specialized monographs and articles on many aspects of the subject have been published, as have a number of single-volume narratives; of the latter, the most recent and extensive is that of Henry Laurens.[10] The immense *Description*, arguably the beginning of "scientific" publication on Egypt, continues to be mined, especially for the visual treasures of its hundreds of engravings and detailed maps, for scholarly publications and for "coffee-table" volumes that feed popular fascination with Egypt.[11] As for research in Arabic sources, al-Jabarti and Niqula al-Turk continue to receive and justify careful attention,[12] and there have been several publications of Arabic materials on the

---

[6] Shmuel Moreh, "Reputed Autographs of 'Abd al-Rahman al-Jabarti and Related Problems," *Bulletin of the School of Oriental and African Studies*, 28 (1965), 524–40, established the generally received sequence and dating of the composition of *Tarikh muddat al-faransis bi-misr* and *Mazhar al-taqdis bi-zawal dawlat al-faransis*. Moreh has also published the text and translation of the earlier narrative: *al-Jabarti's Chronicle of the First Seven Months of the French Occupation of Egypt, 15 June–December 1798* (Leiden, 1975). Al-Jabarti's third account of the French occupation is incorporated into his far more extensive chronicle, *'Aja'ib al-athar fi'l-tarajim wa'l-akhbar*.

[7] Afaf Lutfi al-Sayyid Marsot, "A Comparative Study of 'Abd al-Rahman al-Jabarti and Niqula al-Turk," in Daniel Crecelius (ed.), *Eighteenth-Century Egypt: The Arabic Manuscript Sources* (Claremont, 1990), 115–26.

[8] *Correspondance de Napoléon I: publiée par ordre de l'empereur Napoléon III*, 32 vols. (Paris, 1858–70), IV–V.

[9] Clément Etienne de La Jonquière, *L'Expédition d'Egypte*, 5 vols. (Paris, 1899–1907).

[10] In addition to Laurens, other narratives of note include Percival G. Elgood, *Bonaparte's Adventure in Egypt* (London, 1931); François Charles-Roux, *Bonaparte, gouverneur d'Egypte* (Paris, 1936), trans. E. W. Dickes as *Bonaparte: Governor of Egypt* (London, 1937); and J. Christopher Herold, *Bonaparte in Egypt* (New York, 1962).

[11] For examples, see Charles C. Gillespie and Michael Dewachter (eds.), *Monuments of Egypt. The Napoleonic Edition: The Complete Plates of Antiquity from the Napoleonic Description de l'Egypte* (Princeton, 1987); Robert Anderson and Ibrahim Fawzy (eds.), *Egypt in 1800: Scenes from Napoleon's Description de l'Egypte* (London, 1988); Fernand Beaucour et al., *The Discovery of Egypt*, trans. B. Ballard (Paris, 1990).

[12] See the published proceedings of an international conference on al-Jabarti held in 1974:

relations of other Arab societies (particularly those of Yemen and Libya[13]) with Egypt during the French occupation.

That brief moment in the continuum of Egyptian history has been valued differently by various historiographic traditions. Generations of western writers agreed with the expedition's commander in asserting that the French occupation was the great and necessary discontinuity in Egypt's history, the act of creative disruption that jolted Egypt out of centuries of somnolence. The west's traditional "orientalist" historiography has perceived Egypt to be fixed (and comprehensible) in static religious forms until prodded toward modernity.[14] The nationalist historiographies of both France and Britain regarded Egypt as a stage for heroes – Bonaparte, Kléber, Desaix, Nelson, Abercromby, Sidney Smith. Other interpreters agreed that the French occupation marked a discontinuity but saw it as damnably so. Egyptian and Arab nationalist historiographies have seen the occupation as the first great intrusion of western imperialism and have celebrated heroes of popular resistance.[15] To others, 1798 brought the first act of a prolonged and purposeful western violation of *Islamic* Egypt's cultural authenticity.

The orientalist image of an unchanging Islamic society being galvanized by western secular energies has lost its persuasive power, and only the staunchest Bonapartist would cling to the old orthodoxy, which may be paraphrased "without Bonaparte, modern Egypt is inconceivable." Does that mean that the years of the French constituted nothing more than a minor interruption, a mere wavelet on the surface of deep continuities? It is worthwhile to review the course of events, to consider the significance for Egypt of a period when it came to be central to the strategic concerns of outside powers – when it came indeed to be a theater of other peoples' war – and to look again at the major interpretive questions, particularly in the light of recent scholarship.

Ahmad 'Izzat 'Abd al-Karim (ed.), *'Abd al-rahman al-jabarti: dirasat wa buhuth* (Cairo, 1976), and relevant articles in Crecelius (ed.), *Arabic Manuscript Sources*. The first English translation of *'Aja'ib al-athar* has recently been published: *'Abd al-Rahman al-Jabarti's History of Egypt*, ed. and trans. Thomas Philipp and Moshe Perlmann, 4 vols. (Stuttgart, 1994).

13 *Nusus yamaniyah 'an al-hamlah al-faransiya ala misr: nusus mukhtarah min al-makhtutah al-yamaniyah* (Sana'a 1975); Muhammad 'Abd al-Karim Wafi, *Yusuf basha al-qaramanli wa'l-hamlah al-faransiya ala misr* (Tripoli, 1984).

14 The orientalist argument was not restricted to western writers; see for example Anouar Louca, "La renaissance égyptienne et les limites de l'œuvre de Bonaparte," *Cahiers d'histoire égyptienne*, 7 (1955), 1–20.

15 For example: Muhammad Qindil al-Baqli, *Abtal al-muqawamah al-sha'abiyah li-l'hamla al-faransiya fi misr* (Heroes of the Popular Resistance to the French Campaign against Egypt) (Cairo, n.d.); 'Abd al-Aziz al-Shinawi, *'Umar makram: batal al-muqawamah al-sha'biyyah* ('Umar Makram, Hero of the Popular Resistance) (Cairo, 1967); 'Abd al-'Aziz Hafiz Dunya, *al-Shahid muhammad kurayyim* (The Martyr Muhammad Kurayyim) (Cairo, n.d.); Muhammad Faraj, *al-Nidal al-sha'bi didd al-hamla al-faransiyya* (The Popular Struggle against the French Campaign) (Cairo, 1963).

Origins of the French expedition

The idea of a French military assault on Egypt had an extensive pedigree,[16] and in 1797–98 was brought forward in the context of revolutionary France's war against Britain. Soon after becoming foreign minister in July 1797, Talleyrand presented several memoirs advocating an Egyptian campaign as part of a forward colonial policy. Bonaparte in August 1797 urged the Directory to capitalize on the seizure of the Ionian Islands by extending French activities against the Ottoman empire, including the eventual capture of Egypt.[17] Early the next year the idea of a direct invasion of Britain was set aside (in no small part because of Bonaparte's own negative appraisal of the possibilities) in favor of seizing Egypt to threaten an essential component of British economic power, its trade with India, and to compel Britain to divert resources that would otherwise be used to support its continental allies. The Directory made its decision at the beginning of March 1798, and communicated its instructions to Bonaparte on April 12, 1798.[18]

In the most recent contribution to the study of the origins of the expedition, it has been argued that the specific decision to invade Egypt must be seen in a broader context of a developing "conceptual preparedness" in France during the eighteenth century. Central to that preparedness was the articulation of the difference between the Ottoman empire and Europe not so much in terms of the old religious ideology but in terms of the relative dynamism of distinctive civilizations: the Ottoman empire increasingly was seen as declining and therefore vulnerable, while Europe and especially France was seen as expansive and successful. That contrast dovetailed with the perception that the territory of the Ottoman empire would be a valuable alternative to the Americas as a field for French expansion. Another element in the mix by the last decade of the century was extension of the vocabulary of liberation, as justification for aggressive French action abroad.[19]

It has been suggested that the decision was taken primarily for material rather than strictly strategic motives.[20] Certainly, Europeans were not averse

[16] The classic studies are those of François Charles-Roux: *Les origines de l'expédition de l'Egypte*, 2nd ed. (Paris, 1910); "Le projet français de conquête de l'Egypte sous le règne de Louis XVI," *Mémoires de l'Institut d'Egypte*, 14 (Cairo, 1929); "France, Egypte et Mer Rouge de 1715 à 1798," *Cahiers d'histoire égyptienne*, 3 (1951), 117–95.

[17] Alain Silvera, "Bonaparte and Talleyrand: The Origins of the French Expedition to Egypt in 1798," *American Journal of Arabic Studies*, 3 (1975), 1–13.

[18] Text of the instructions in J. C. Hurewitz (ed.), *The Middle East and North Africa in World Politics, A Documentary Record*, 2nd ed., 2 vols. (New Haven, 1975), I, 115–16.

[19] Henry Laurens, *Les origines intellectuelles de l'expédition d'Egypte: l'orientalisme islamisant en France (1698–1798)* (Istanbul and Paris, 1987). See also Virginia Aksan, "Choiseul-Gouffier at the Porte, 1784–1792," *Studies in Ottoman Diplomatic History*, 4 (1990), 27–34.

[20] Peter Gran, "Late 18th–early 19th century Egypt: Merchant Capitalism or Modern Capitalism?" *L'Egypte au XIXᵉ siècle* (Paris, 1982), 267–81.

to using state power to further mercantile interests; certainly too, members of the French commercial community in Egypt had actively urged a French invasion. But such advocacy did not necessarily produce results. In previous decades, French (and British) commercial interests, eager to increase and monopolize trade with and across Egypt, had taken the lead in negotiating commercial treaties with the Mamluk beys which would provide preferential commercial treatment. Without fail, however, those agreements had been repudiated by authorities in Paris and London, who were reluctant to endorse actions that, however profitable they might be to some interests, would enhance the Mamluk side in the delicate balance of forces between Istanbul and its provinces, and thereby serve to damage what Britain and France regarded as more important relations with the Ottoman empire.[21]

Intentions, expectations, preparations

Having decided to invade Egypt, the French prepared to implement the decision. A force of 36,000, consisting mainly of veteran units from both the German theater and from Bonaparte's Italian campaign of 1796–97, was hastily assembled at Toulon and several subsidiary ports. A large fleet was assigned to accompany the transport vessels. In addition to the military personnel Bonaparte assembled a cadre of civilian experts – engineers, surveyors, translators, scientists – the "savants" whose involvement would attract much subsequent attention.

The nature and dimensions of those preparations cast light on France's expectations and also on its intentions. After all, the nature of what France intended was even more consequential for Egypt than the simple decision to invade. Was Egypt valued in and of itself, or as a way station toward broader territorial or other diplomatic, political and strategic goals, or as a prize to be traded for commensurate gains elsewhere? Above all, did France intend its stay in Egypt to be permanent?

Dictating his reminiscences of the Egyptian expedition during his St. Helena exile, Bonaparte recalled being guided by a formula expressed by Volney, whose book of travels in Egypt and Syria had been published in 1787: if France were to venture into Egypt, France must be prepared to fight three wars – against Britain, the Ottoman empire, and "the Muslims."[22]

---

[21] See, for example, Daniel Crecelius, "Unratified Commercial Treaties between Egypt and England and France, 1773–1794," *Revue d'histoire maghrebine*, 12 (1985), 67–104; Moustapha Fahmy, "La première convention commercial franco-égyptienne au XVIIIᵉ siècle (10 janvier 1785)," *Cahiers d'histoire égyptienne*, 7 (1955), 21–34; David Kimche, "The Opening of the Red Sea to European Ships in the Late Eighteenth Century," *Middle Eastern Studies*, 8 (1972), 63–71.

[22] The passage is cited by Edward Said, *Orientalism* (New York, 1979), 81–82.

French preparations can be seen as efforts to prevail in each of these three planes of confrontation.

Although there had been no British naval presence in the Mediterranean since France's alliance with Spain in 1796, the French did not take for granted the Mediterranean crossing; a significant portion of France's available naval strength was committed to accompany the vessels transporting the troops to Egypt. Since France already possessed the Ionian Islands, and would soon possess Malta (whose conquest was the first aggressive act in the French plan of action), it was assumed that the French fleet would be able to cope with anything the British might be willing to send into the Mediterranean, both in delivering the expedition to Egypt and in maintaining open sea lanes for future communication and reinforcement.

With regard to the Ottomans, with whom France had a long history of diplomatic alignment, the French had to deal with the implications of their provocative policy. Even if Ottoman authority in Egypt had become nominal, Egypt was still an important province. Bonaparte persuaded himself that Istanbul, frustrated over the continuing fractiousness and quasi-autonomy of Egypt's Mamluk beys, would not be upset by a French invasion. His thinking may well have been influenced by French understandings of the expeditionary force the Ottoman empire itself had sent to Egypt in 1786–87 to reassert more direct control over the province. Bonaparte may have believed that the Ottoman authorities really would be persuaded by the language of the proclamation he prepared for circulation in Arabic and Turkish upon his entry into Alexandria: "The French have shown at all times that they are the particular friends of His Majesty the Ottoman Sultan (may God perpetuate his rule) and the enemies of his enemies."[23] The French, the argument ran, were entering Egypt as friends of the sultan and as adversaries solely of the Mamluks, who themselves were so clearly the sultan's enemies. The French certainly calculated further that the Ottoman empire would not risk its traditional friendship with France, particularly since it now had to be more concerned about its traditional adversaries, Austria and Russia.

An assumption underlying French expectations and preparations was that the Egyptian population could be meaningfully differentiated into two distinct groups, the Mamluk ruling elite and the populace at large. Military resistance could be expected only from the former, and Napoleon fully expected his large and experienced expeditionary force to overwhelm the Mamluks.

To the Egyptian populace at large, the French prepared to present two arguments. The first asserted that the French purpose was to cleanse Egypt of a regime that had brought only oppression, tyranny, exploitation, and

[23] Laurens et al., *L'Expédition*, 66–76.

misrule to the Egyptian people; the French would bring a revolution for those who were unable to do so for themselves, but who would certainly welcome France's action as liberation. The second, collateral, argument was that the French were *not* hostile to Islam, presumably the primary loyalty of the Egyptian people. Again to quote from Napoleon's first proclamation: "Peoples of Egypt, you will be told that I have come to destroy your religion ... Do not believe it! ... I worship God more than the Mamluks do, and ... I respect His prophet Mohammed and the admirable Koran ... Tell the people that the French also are true Muslims." The proclamation closes with these words: "All Egyptians shall render thanks to God for the destruction of the Mamluks, saying in a loud voice, 'May God preserve the glory of the Ottoman Sultan! May God preserve the glory of the French army! May God curse the Mamluks and bestow happiness on the Egyptian nation!'"[24]

The inclusion of the savants in the expedition suggests a wish to bring civilian expertise – the self-conscious expertise of the Enlightenment – to bear on the pragmatic problems that would face an army of occupation: to communicate, to administer, to adjudicate, to tax. That does not exclude a second goal of cultural trophy-hunting. In Italy Bonaparte had made use of civilian expertise both to help administer and reorganize the country and to identify cultural treasures to be sent to Paris; given Europe's legacy of curiosity about Egypt, especially its ancient history, he certainly intended to pursue the intellectual possession of his new conquest.

In sum, the sheer size of the expeditionary force, the size of the war fleet sent to accompany it, and the inclusion of civilian savants all suggest that the French intent was to conquer, to crush all organized military forces that might resist, to occupy and administer the entire country, not just a strategic port or two, and to do so in such a way that Egypt would generate the revenues necessary to finance its own occupation. Possession of Egypt would presumably constitute a significant blow against Britain, whether or not Bonaparte intended to use Egypt as a base for further campaigning directly against British interests in India; but everything suggests that the French intended to reap benefit from *keeping* Egypt.

Shattered expectations

Napoleon's immediate expectations concerning the crossing of the Mediterranean were borne out, although not without incident. Responding to intelligence reports of the massing of French forces at Toulon, the British government in April had ordered a naval force into the Mediterranean.[25]

---

[24] *Ibid.*, 75–76; see al-Jabarti's acerbic analysis of this proclamation in Moreh (ed.), *al-Jabarti's Chronicle*; see also Marsden Jones, "The First French Proclamation and al-Jabarti," in 'Abd al-Karim (ed.), *al-Jabarti*, 29–44.

[25] For a discussion of the disagreements among British ministries concerning naval strategy

Nelson's force arrived off Toulon a day too late to challenge the departure of the main French convoy, and was then scattered by a storm and delayed in its further pursuit by some two weeks. On June 9 the French fleet reached Malta, whose "defenders" capitulated within forty-eight hours; leaving behind a garrison of 3,000 but taking along the contents of Malta's treasury, the fleet set sail again on June 19. On June 22 Bonaparte for the first time officially informed his army that their destination was Egypt. During the night of June 22–23, the French and British fleets literally crossed paths between Sicily and the Morea, missing each other in the dark by no more than an hour or two. There was another near miss a week later: Nelson reached Alexandria on June 28, found no news of the French, and sailed away to the north on June 29; later the same day the French fleet arrived off Alexandria.

The good fortune of the French would not last. After covering the landing of the French forces at Marabut, west of Alexandria, the French admiral moved his main fighting vessels to anchorage in Abuqir bay, east of the port. Nelson spent much of July searching the eastern Mediterranean before learning of the French landing in Egypt. Returning to Egyptian waters, he found and destroyed the French fleet at Abuqir. Thenceforth the French expeditionary force in Egypt was cut off from France, as Nelson left a portion of his fleet to blockade the Egyptian coast. No reinforcements would come from France; communication between Paris and Egypt would be extremely difficult.[26]

In London there was sharp difference of opinion about what to do about the French expedition. To Lord Grenville, head of the Foreign Department, whose priorities were centered on nurturing a coalition to defeat the French in Europe, the removal to a distant theater of a large and experienced French army under a gifted and ambitious commander was most welcome. To Henry Dundas, head of both the War Department and the Board of Control for India, that presence comprised so real a threat to India – and India was so valuable a part of Britain's empire – that decisive counter-measures should be taken. The result of their divergent readings of the situation was that only relatively small steps were taken, and not always in a coordinated way.

---

at this juncture, see Edward Ingram, "The Failure of British Sea Power in the War of the Second Coalition, 1798–1801," in Edward Ingram, *In Defence of British India: Great Britain in the Middle East, 1774–1842* (London, 1984), 67–77.

[26] Alfred Boulay de la Meurthe, *Le Directoire et l'expédition d'Egypte: étude sur les tentatives du Directoire pour communiquer avec Bonaparte* (Paris, 1885). According to this meticulous effort to catalog the fate of all attempts at communication, only three of the six despatches sent by the Directory, and only one of substance, ever reached Napoleon. That one, dated November 4, 1798 but not received until the end of March, informed him that the situation in Europe and the Mediterranean would make it impossible to send reinforcements.

One series of steps came out of Dundas's insistence on insulating India. As early as June 1798, before knowing the ultimate destination of the French fleet, the British ordered a fleet under Admiral Blankett to proceed from England around the Cape to the Red Sea, to be in position to block any possible French move by sea against India. In November Dundas ordered the governor of Bombay to send troops to occupy the island of Perim in the Bab al-Mandab; a garrison at Perim, it was believed, would anchor a blockade of the Red Sea and might serve as a base from which to mount an expedition against the French in Egypt. A force numbering some 1,000 troops left Bombay in early April and reached Perim – the first Middle Eastern territory occupied by Britain – a month later. Fearing a French effort to cross by land to the Persian Gulf, Dundas established a British resident of the East India Company at Baghdad.

Another series of steps was designed to bring Britain and the Ottoman empire into closer cooperation. By late July the ranking British diplomat in Istanbul, Spencer Smith, was holding lengthy discussions with the head of the Ottoman office of foreign affairs concerning terms of a possible alliance against the French. In September the Admiralty agreed to send Captain Sir Sidney Smith to join his brother in seeking an Ottoman alliance and to cooperate with the Ottoman fleet in the eastern Mediterranean. The British government also resolved to send a small military mission under General Koehler to assist in training units of the Ottoman army. In November 1798 the foreign department named the earl of Elgin to serve as ambassador to Istanbul, the first British ambassador there to be appointed and paid by the Crown rather than the Levant Company.[27]

Although these British initiatives were hardly well coordinated, they were successful at least to this degree: rather than tolerating the French presence, the Ottomans formally aligned themselves with both Britain and Russia. By late 1797 the Ottoman regime had begun to demonstrate concern about French intentions, both because the seizure of the Ionian Islands made the French territorial neighbors of the empire and because revolutionary thinking seemed to resonate among some of the empire's subject populations. To counteract the latter and to rally support among Muslims, the Ottomans launched their own counterrevolutionary propaganda.[28] The seizure of Egypt precipitated not acquiescence but, early in September 1798,

---

[27] Shafik Ghorbal, *Beginnings of the Egyptian Question and the Rise of Mehemet-Ali* (London, 1928), 53–69. The most extensive studies of British decision making at this stage are by Edward Ingram, each published in several installments in *Middle Eastern Studies*: "A Preview of the Great Game in Asia," four parts, 1973–74; and "From Trade to Empire in the Near East," three parts, 1978.

[28] See, for example, Richard Clogg, "The 'Dhidhaskalia Patriki' (1798): an Orthodox Reaction to French Revolutionary Propaganda," *Middle Eastern Studies*, 5 (1969), 87–115.

a decision in favor of war. By the beginning of 1799, a formal tripartite alliance linked the Ottomans with Britain and Russia in the War of the Second Coalition, and the Ottomans were beginning to assemble forces for offensive action against the French.[29]

With regard to the population of Egypt, at least the broad strokes of French preparations for invasion were apparently accurate. (The details were noticeably less well targeted: the French land forces suffered from heavy uniforms, utterly inadequate provision of fresh water, and other shortcomings.) There was virtually no military resistance to the landing of the French ground forces on the beaches of Marabut west of Alexandria, and that port's defenses were quickly overwhelmed. The size, arms, training, discipline, and organization of the French land forces were indeed sufficient to handle the military resistance mustered by the Mamluk elite, in an initial battle at Shubrakhit and then the larger battle at Imbaba across from Cairo, the so-called "battle of the Pyramids."

French responses to new realities

As of July 24, 1798 the French were in occupation of Cairo as well as Alexandria and Rosetta. Conquest had been apparently swift and complete. But the realities facing the French differed from what had been anticipated. The destruction of the fleet at Abuqir meant isolation from France and from any hope of reinforcement. The presence of an Anglo-Ottoman blockading fleet also meant sharp reduction in trade through Egypt's Mediterranean ports, and a concomitant loss of customs revenue. The Ottoman declaration of war imposed a need to devote manpower and treasure to further campaigning. Perhaps most important, in Egypt the French were hardly hailed as liberators.

The Mamluks, though routed in the set battles, were not annihilated. Ibrahim Bey led one group to safety in Palestine, while a larger body led by Murad Bey retreated to Upper Egypt. For nearly ten months, Murad and his Mamluks – reinforced by significant numbers of volunteers crossing from the Hijaz[30] – roamed up and down Upper Egypt, staying just ahead of a pursuit force commanded by General Desaix. Even after May 1799, when the French were able to occupy and close the Red Sea port of Qusayr and

---

[29] On the larger context of the activities of the Second Coalition, see Norman E. Saul, *Russia and the Mediterranean, 1797–1807* (Chicago, 1970), and Stanford J. Shaw, *Between Old and New: The Ottoman Empire under Sultan Selim III, 1789–1807* (Cambridge, MA, 1971).

[30] On the general situation of the Hijaz during the French occupation, see articles by Mordechai Abir: "Relations between the Government of India and the Shariff of Mecca during the French Invasion of Egypt, 1798–1801," *Journal of the Royal Asiatic Society* (1965), 33–42; and "The Arab Rebellion of Amir Ghalib of Mecca (1788–1813)," *Middle Eastern Studies*, 7 (1971), 186–200.

interdict the flow of Hijazi volunteers, Murad was able to move with relative impunity about Upper Egypt. The continued activity of a portion of the old military elite represented a steady drain on French military manpower and treasure, reduced the normal flow of food to the urban centers of Lower Egypt, and kept a significant portion of the country out of the reach of French taxation.

In Lower Egypt, France's military control was more effective but still far from unchallenged. Within weeks of the occupation of Alexandria, the head of the local administration, Muhammad al-Kurayyim, was at odds with the French commander, Kleber; Bonaparte had Kurayyim executed (as a "traitor") on September 6. In October, a major rising against the French erupted among the population of Cairo. Some 2,000–3,000 Egyptians and 300 French were dead at the end of two days of insurrection and the harsh French reconquest of the streets. The French had discovered that their propaganda – if they had ever taken it seriously – about coming to Egypt as "friends of Islam" and as "liberators from Mamluk tyranny" was a delusion, and that vigilance and repression would be necessary to maintain control of the cities. To enhance urban security, the occupiers began to disarm the population and to dismantle the old wooden gates that stood at the entry to most urban quarters and neighborhoods, to allow greater freedom of movement by troops. Acts of violent opposition occurred outside the cities as well; as part of the paraphernalia of control and administration, garrisons were posted in major towns of the Delta, while mobile columns patrolled the countryside between fortified positions in an attempt to extend French authority.

It may well have been Bonaparte's ultimate purpose to introduce fundamental restructuring in Egyptian economic and social affairs. It was certainly his intent to control and administer Egypt's revenues in such a way that the Egyptian economy would cover the substantial costs of the country's own occupation. But the immediate and continuing need to ensure internal security and the continuation and expansion of war in the eastern Mediterranean pushed the French into hasty and self-contradictory administrative decisions, especially in fiscal affairs.

Several fiscal measures were introduced almost immediately.[31] Merchandise on enemy vessels in Egyptian ports was confiscated. Contributions in the form of forced loans were extracted, such as a levy of 300,000 francs from the merchants of Alexandria, and other levies on the merchants and artisans of Cairo.

Perhaps the most far reaching (at least in its implications) of the early

---

[31] The most extensive analysis of fiscal matters is that of M. Chevalier, "La politique financière de l'expédition d'Egypte, 1798–1801," *Cahiers d'histoire égyptienne*, 7 (1955), 165–85, 223–44; 8 (1956), 47–68, 176–97, 213–40.

fiscal measures was confiscation of Mamluk properties. A number of extensive urban establishments maintained by leading Mamluks were taken over to house French officers and operations of the civilian savants. Other urban properties were restored to the use of the beys' wives on payment of stiff fines. Agricultural lands[32] held by Mamluks as *iltizams* were confiscated and categorized as "national domains," under the authority of the French financial director. (A *multazim* was in essence a tax-farmer, paying to the central treasury a specified amount in advance in exchange for the right to collect taxes and other fees from the villages of the cultivators – and to profit by keeping a significant share of the impositions on the fallahin.) The amount of property that thus came under French control was extensive: Chevalier estimates that as much as two-thirds of the cultivable property was held by Mamluk *multazims*.[33] Beyond removing the Mamluks, the French left intact the basic structure of taxes and the system (and veteran Coptic personnel) of tax collection. A simple edict of confiscation, taking the Mamluk *multazims* out of the system, did not automatically generate a stream of revenue. The way was open for new people to take over the functions of the displaced *multazims*, and some fallahin seem to have done so.[34] Apparently the *iltizams* were seen not as an attractively profitable venture but rather as an undesirable obligation, since the French wanted new *multazims* to pay all arrears. By February 1799 the French were trying by edict to get the *shaykhs al-balad* to take over the vacated *iltizams*, again with relatively little success.

Another early administrative innovation was the introduction in mid-September 1798 of a requirement that titles to property be registered with the government, within a month for Cairo and two months elsewhere. People who could not or did not properly register their properties risked having them confiscated. In a closely related measure, a month later Bonaparte issued an edict establishing a structure of taxes on urban buildings, something not regularly part of the previous tax system. It has been argued that these particular measures contributed significantly to

---

[32] Descriptions of the systems of land tenure and taxation can be found in these works: Stanford Shaw (ed. and trans.), *Ottoman Egypt in the Age of the French Revolution* (Cambridge, MA, 1964), esp. 122–24, 140–43; Kenneth Cuno, *The Pasha's Peasants: Land, Society, and Economy in Lower Egypt, 1740–1858* (Cambridge, 1992), 33–47; and two articles by ʿAbd al-Rahim A. ʿAbd al-Rahim: "Land Tenure in Egypt and its Social Effects on Egyptian Society: 1798–1813," in Tarif Khalidi (ed.), *Land Tenure and Social Transformation in the Middle East* (Beirut, 1984), 237–48; "The Documents of the Egypt Religious Courts (*al-mahakim al-sharʿiyya*) as a Source for the Study of Ottoman Provincial Administration in Egypt," *Journal of the Economic and Social History of the Orient*, 34 (1991), 88–97.

[33] Chevalier, "Politique financière," *Cahiers d'histoire égyptienne*, 8 (1956), 52.

[34] ʿAbd al-Rahim, "Land Tenure," 241.

turning the urban population from passive acquiescence to armed resistance later in October.[35]

A further aspect of French strategies of control involved what has been referred to as Napoleon's "Islamic policy."[36] This had been foreshadowed in the rhetorical assertion of the early proclamations that the French had come to Egypt as true friends of Islam. Another aspect was the early effort to associate Muslim leaders with the new regime, particularly in the *diwan* of Cairo and the larger general *diwan*, both established early in the occupation. Public ceremony was also affected, specifically by the French insistence that major Muslim occasions (such as the observance of the Prophet's birthday, *mawlid al-nabi* in August 1798, or the opening of the Khalij al-Masri[37]) be celebrated fully, and with the highly visible participation of French officials. To the apparent mystification of most Egyptians, French revolutionary ceremonials were also celebrated in high style. The response among leading 'ulama' varied. Some notables, such as 'Umar Makram, the *naqib al-ashraf*, fled to Palestine and refused to be lured back. 'Umar was replaced in the prestigious position of *naqib* by Shaykh Khalil al-Bakri, who would be a close associate of the French for the duration.[38] Other leading shaykhs accepted appointment to the new *diwans*. Bonaparte's purpose in establishing the *diwans* was to coopt leading local figures and use their prestige to promote popular acquiescence in the new regime's operations.[39]

The outburst of violence in October 1798 demonstrates the complex dynamics of the regime's Islamic policy. Although the rising was clearly a popular movement, it found particular focus and leadership at al-Azhar, among lower-ranking 'ulama' and students. That institution was hit hard – literally – as the French suppressed the rebellion. Following the rising, a

---

[35] Chevalier, "La Politique financière," *Cahiers d'histoire égyptienne*, 7 (1955), 239–44; Shaw, *Ottoman Egypt*, 161–63. See also Ibrahim el-Mouelhi, "Etude documentaire. L'Enregistrement de la propriété en Egypte durant l'occupation française (1798–1802)," *Bulletin de l'Institut d'Egypte*, 30 (1949), 197–228.

[36] This is discussed most thoroughly and most approvingly by Charles-Roux, *Bonaparte, gouverneur d'Egypte*.

[37] The Khalij al-Masri was the canal that was ceremoniously opened at the beginning of each year's flood season, to allow river water to fill several lakebeds in Cairo.

[38] John W. Livingston, "Shaykh Bakri and Bonaparte," *Studia Islamica*, 80 (1994), 125–43.

[39] On the "traditional" role of leading 'ulama' as intermediaries between the Ottoman and Mamluk regimes and the populace, see especially the articles by Afaf Lutfi al-Sayyid Marsot: "The Political and Economic Functions of the Ulama in the 18th Century," *Journal of the Economic and Social History of the Orient*, 16 (1973), 130–54; "The Role of the Ulama in Egypt during the Early 19th Century," in P. M. Holt (ed.), *Political and Social Change in Modern Egypt* (London, 1968), 264–81; and "The 'Ulama' of Cairo in the Eighteenth and Nineteenth Century," in Nikki Keddie (ed.), *Scholars, Saints and Sufis* (Berkeley, 1972), 149–65. See also Samir Girgis, *The Predominance of the Islamic Tradition of Leadership in Egypt during Bonaparte's Expedition* (Frankfurt, 1975).

number of 'ulama' were turned over to the French and put to death. Al-Jabarti's reaction to the affair reveals some of the tensions and complexities: he was critical of those who resorted to the chaos of violence and praised those among the 'ulama' who worked to restore social peace and order.[40] For the rest of the occupation, a number of leading 'ulama' pursued a comparable policy: fearful both of the anarchy of popular rebellion and of the violence that the French were clearly willing to use to suppress rebellion, they functioned as the kind of social intermediaries and controllers the French had in mind – collaborators, however reluctant. Were they persuaded by the French rhetoric of being friends of Islam, or virtual Muslims? Probably not; but that was not necessary in order to reach a decision in favor of pursuing social order.

French efforts to enforce order and find adequate financial resources were played out in the context of the imminent military and strategic challenge implicit in the British–Ottoman alliance. The first step in Ottoman military response was to order the pasha of Acre, Ahmad Pasha al-Jazzar, to attack the Egyptian frontier. While Jazzar engaged the French, the main Ottoman strategy would develop as a pincer movement on Egypt, with one army advancing from Syria through Palestine and across Sinai, while a second army would be ferried from its assembly point on Rhodes to the Egyptian coast under British naval protection. At least from November 1798 Bonaparte was primarily engaged in figuring how to counter those moves; his decision for a campaign in Palestine must be seen as a preemptive strike. He planned to advance rapidly, to take Acre and knock out Jazzar, block the army of Damascus, and then return to Egypt in time to deal with the army of Rhodes. He hoped, surely, that a swiftly administered setback would persuade the Ottoman regime to reverse itself and to abandon opposition to the French.

With a force of 13,000 Bonaparte left Katia, east of Damietta, on February 6, 1799. It took an unexpected eleven days to break Ottoman defenses at the fortified post of al-ʿArish. The French pressed on to Jaffa, which was taken under siege on March 3; following the surrender of the Ottoman garrison four days later, Bonaparte ordered that some 3,000 of the surrendering soldiers be killed, perhaps in an effort to intimidate other Ottoman forces in Palestine into submission.[41] By March 18 the French had reached Acre, where Jazzar's main force was in a well-fortified position, supported by a small British naval squadron. While maintaining the siege of Acre, Bonaparte diverted troops to the east to block the advance of Ottoman

---

[40] Laurens et al., *L'Expédition*, 143–55.
[41] *Ibid.*, 186–98. Bonaparte justified the massacre on two grounds: that some of the Ottoman troops at Jaffa had surrendered earlier at al-ʿArish, and had been released on stipulation that they participate in no further actions against the French; and that the French could not spare manpower and supplies to support prisoners.

troops, including the main part of the army of Damascus. Though the "battle of Mt. Tabor" was reckoned a French victory, Bonaparte failed to take Acre despite a number of efforts to storm the defenses. On May 20 the siege was lifted and the French began to retreat to Egypt. On June 14 Bonaparte staged a triumphal march into Cairo.

The Palestine campaign could be reckoned a triumph only in the minimal sense of temporarily impeding the preparations of one of the two Ottoman armies destined for Egypt. The second army, some 15,000 strong, landed at Abuqir bay in July 1799 but soon suffered a sharp defeat. Although the immediate Ottoman threat had been contained, Bonaparte by that point was thinking not so much about staying in Egypt as about returning to France.

After Napoleon

Would the historiography of the French occupation be less massive had the original command been given to a general other than Bonaparte? Almost certainly; Napoleon comes with heavy baggage. Surely the period following his departure would receive attention more in proportion to the timing involved: of the period of the French Napoleon was present for just under fourteen months; his successors, Kléber and Menou, held the command respectively for just under ten months and fourteen-and-a-half months.[42]

In August 1799 Bonaparte left Cairo ostensibly on an inspection tour of the Delta, and in secrecy left Egypt for France. Only a few knew his true intentions; even Kleber received his instructions after Napoleon's departure. His reasons for leaving were shaped by circumstances in France and Europe and by his own ambition. How if at all did his departure affect Egypt? Kléber (who is often treated with unalloyed admiration as a still-idealistic champion of the virtues of the Republic and a critic of the self-aggrandizement and ambition of his predecessor[43]) wanted nothing more than to negotiate the evacuation of the entire French garrison from Egypt on reasonably honorable terms.

The possibility of evacuation had already begun to occur to the French.[44] In Paris the Directory, responding to the summer's military setbacks, had concluded in early September 1799 that it would be necessary to evacuate

---

[42] Typically, La Jonquière's immense work – five volumes, nearly 3,500 pages – is devoted entirely to Bonaparte's fourteen months. Older works on the post-Napoleon period are few: F. Rousseau, *Kléber et Menou en Egypte depuis le départ de Bonaparte, août 1799–septembre 1801* (Paris, 1900) is primarily a collection of documents; Georges Rigault, *Le General Abdallah Menou et la dernière phase de l'expédition d'Egypte (1799–1801)* (Paris, 1911–12). Recently, Henry Laurens has published a selection of Kléber's papers: *Correspondance: Kléber en Egypte, 1798–1800: Kléber et Bonaparte, 1798–1799*, 2 vols. (Cairo, 1988).

[43] See Laurens (ed.), *Kléber en Egypte*, esp. v–viii, 1–101.

[44] Laurens et al., *L'Expédition*, 209–23.

the army from Egypt, although no such instructions would reach Kléber before (or after) Napoleon and his cohorts terminated the Directory. In his parting instructions, Bonaparte on his own authority instructed Kléber to try to negotiate the French evacuation – but only if no reinforcements had arrived by the following May, and if French losses to the plague exceeded 1,500 in a year. Rather than wait, in mid-September Kléber invited the Ottoman grand vizier to open negotiations, which eventually began late in December 1799. At first Kléber set a high price: France would evacuate Egypt and restore it to Ottoman sovereignty in exchange for a cease-fire, for a formal end to the Second Coalition, for the return of the Ionian Islands to France (the islands had been seized earlier by the Russian–Ottoman joint fleet), for the lifting of the blockade of Malta, and for the reestablishment of normal Franco–Ottoman relations. But as the talks continued, the grand vizier continued to move his army toward Egypt, and on December 29 the Ottomans took the frontier post at al-ʿArish.

Under those circumstances, compounded by instances of near-mutinous attitudes within the French army, Kléber determined there was no virtue in holding out for his original demands. The negotiators then concluded, on January 24, 1800, the Convention of al-ʿArish.[45] According to its terms, all French forces, with all arms and baggage, would evacuate Egypt, first redeploying in stages to Cairo and then, no more than forty to forty-five days after ratification of the convention, moving to the seaports; the Ottoman empire would provide additional ships as necessary to transport the army to France, and would pay the costs of maintenance of the French army during the time of redeployment and for the duration of the voyage; and the Ottoman empire along with its allies Britain and Russia would provide all necessary passports and safe conducts to the French forces. No more was said about the Ottomans withdrawing from their alliance or about Malta or the Ionian Islands.

Problems arose almost at once – not so much in Egypt, where the French began an orderly redeployment and allowed Ottoman forces to advance into Lower Egypt, but elsewhere. In Istanbul, the new British ambassador, Lord Elgin, argued against allowing a French evacuation, on the grounds that without the French in Egypt the Ottomans would soon fall away from the coalition. In London, discussions about the possibility of a negotiated settlement in Egypt had been going on since early autumn, and the argument that had come to prevail – at least for a time – was that the morale of the French in Egypt had deteriorated so badly that the advancing Ottomans

---

[45] *Ibid.*, 234–46; François Charles-Roux, "Une négociation pour l'évacuation de l'Egypte: La convention d'el-Arich (1800)," *Revue d'histoire diplomatique*, 37 (1923), 48–88, 304–47; text in Hurewitz (ed.), *The Middle East*, I, 142–45.

could and should settle the issue militarily; neither Britain nor its continental allies would welcome the return to France of an experienced army.

Although the British cabinet would in time reconsider, and would accept the terms of the convention (while criticizing Sidney Smith for exceeding his authority), events in the eastern Mediterranean rendered the reconsideration moot. Early in March, a letter from Lord Keith, the British naval commander in the Mediterranean, informed Kléber that Britain did not accept the terms of al-ʿArish and would instead treat French troops seized on the Mediterranean as prisoners of war. With the breakdown of diplomacy, initiative passed to the battlefield; at the battle of Heliopolis, northeast of Cairo, on March 20 the French devastated the Ottoman army.

During the aborted withdrawal of the French, the advance of the Ottoman army and the battle of Heliopolis, an insurrection had broken out in Cairo, more sweeping and substantial than that of October 1798, and armed opposition surfaced in the Delta. Having defeated the Ottomans, Kléber turned to what amounted to a "reconquest" of Cairo and Lower Egypt, an extended and destructive process. The French laid siege to Cairo for several weeks before a decisive assault led to the city's capitulation on April 21. Kléber then levied punitive fines on the city, including huge amounts on some leading ʿulamaʾ, and began to organize indigenous auxiliary forces. He also reached an agreement with Murad Bey, according to which the Mamluk leader would cooperate with the French effort to restore control in the Delta in exchange for recognition as the unchallenged power in Upper Egypt; the French thus had come to depend on the allegiance of one of the leading Mamluk beys whose oppressive exploitation of the Egyptian population had once served as justification for the French expedition.

Did these efforts mean that Kléber had set aside hopes of evacuation in favor now of a permanent French occupation? The ambiguity of Kléber's own intentions ended on June 14, 1800, when he was assassinated as he walked in the gardens at Azbakiyya. The succession as commander-in-chief of General Jacques Menou represented the ascendancy of the "colonialist" policy that sought to make the French occupation permanent. Menou's policy has sometimes been described as one seeking "fusion" or "assimilation" between French and Egyptian[46] (though certainly with unquestioned French dominance). To a degree he embodied the policy; he was the most senior Frenchman to convert to Islam, adding "Abdullah" to his name and marrying an Egyptian Muslim woman.[47] To prepare for systematic adminis-

---

[46] Laurens et al., *L'Expédition*, 288–97.

[47] ʿAli Bahgat, "Acte de mariage du General Abdallah Menou avec la dame Zobaidah," *Bulletin de l'Institut Egyptien*, 3rd series, 9 (1899), 221–35; ʿAli Baghat, "La Famille Musulmane du General Abdallah Menou," *Bulletin de l'Institut Egyptien*, 4th series, 1 (1900), 37–43.

trative reorganization, he commissioned Egyptian bureaucrats to report in detail on the workings of the taxation and judicial systems.[48] He established a cadastral commission, and embarked on the most sweeping change of the land-tax system during the occupation years, culminating in the replacement of the *iltizam* system by a direct tax on land.[49] His reorganization of justice included establishment of a *diwan* of 'ulama' (including al-Jabarti) for judicial purposes, indicative of a broader policy of seeking active collaboration with Egyptian notables, particularly among the high 'ulama'.

Further, Menou rejected Ottoman overtures to return to negotiations, insisting that the only thing to talk about was the exchange of prisoners. But as Menou acted in pursuit of his goal of colonial permanence, Egypt was becoming even more central to the broader war, and that would determine France's future in Egypt.

Part of that external context involved complex diplomatic and strategic calculations attending the disintegration of the Second Coalition from the winter of 1799/1800.[50] Russia had left the alliance before the end of 1799, and by early autumn 1800 had begun negotiations on an anti-British "League of Armed Neutrality," primarily of Baltic powers. In June French armies inflicted heavy defeats on Austria and imposed an armistice. By late August France proposed a naval armistice with Britain. The situation generated sharp and prolonged debates within the British cabinet, pitting those who emphasized Britain's commitment to its continental allies against those who thought it imperative to defend Britain's own global colonial interests. Dundas, still the strongest advocate of the colonial faction, feared that a naval armistice would allow France to reinforce its position in Egypt, and that it would be intolerable to allow France to keep such a strategically important site. At the beginning of October the cabinet finally decided in favor of a British military expedition to drive the French out of Egypt.

As early as May 1800 the British cabinet had ordered that an army of over 20,000, under General Abercromby, be sent to the Mediterranean, although

---

[48] The report by Husayn Effendi, an official of the treasury, was first published in Arabic by Shafiq Ghurbal, "Misr 'inda mafraq al-turuq (1798–1801)," *Bulletin of the Faculty of Arts, University of Cairo*, 4 (1936), 1–70, and later translated with copious notes by Shaw, *Ottoman Egypt*. A shorter report on the judicial system has been published by C. A. Bachatly, "L'Administration de la justice en Egypte à la veille des reformes de l'an IX, d'après un document arabe inédit," *Bulletin de l'Institut de l'Egypte*, 18 (1935), 1–18.

[49] Chevalier, "La politique financière," *Cahiers d'histoire égyptienne*, 8 (1956), 213–40.

[50] The following paragraphs are based especially on Edward Ingram, "The Geopolitics of the First British Expedition to Egypt," in four parts, *Middle Eastern Studies*, 30–31 (1994–95); Edward Ingram, "The Role of the Indian Army at the End of the Eighteenth Century," in Ingram, *In Defence of British India*, 48–66. The most recent military history is Piers Mackesy, *British Victory in Egypt, 1801: The End of Napoleon's Conquest* (London, 1995). For the European context, see Paul Schroeder, "The Collapse of the Second Coalition," *Journal of Modern History*, 59 (1987), 244–90.

it was uncertain what that army should seek to accomplish. An initial success came in September when the British seized Valetta, completing the ouster of French forces from Malta. A conspicuous failure followed: in early October Abercromby's army and Lord Keith's fleet failed miserably in an attempt to seize the Spanish naval base at Cadiz. Once the decision to invade Egypt was taken, Abercromby's force – the only substantial army Britain had available to use anywhere – was ordered to prepare to land on the Egyptian coast and seize Alexandria. A second part of the overall strategy would be a new Ottoman invasion overland from Syria, with a small British military mission accompanying the Ottomans; and the third part would be an attack from the Red Sea carried out by troops sent around the Cape from Britain to join a larger force from British India. Although the timetable broke down almost immediately, the basic outlines of the strategy would be carried out.

After several months of recuperation and retraining on the Anatolian coast, the British expeditionary force landed at Abuqir bay in March 1801. Menou's counter-attack along the narrow strip of land west of Abuqir, at the ancient site of Canopus, was unsuccessful in dislodging them (although casualties were high, including Abercromby, who died of his wounds a week after the battle). Menou then withdrew his forces into Alexandria. Leaving some forces to blockade the French in the port city, the British advanced toward Cairo. They were joined by an Ottoman force numbering 6,000–8,000 which had landed behind them at Abuqir bay, while the main Ottoman army under command of the grand vizier entered the Delta from Palestine. By the middle of June the two armies had reached and surrounded Cairo. The third prong of the British–Ottoman strategy was also in effect, though distantly, by then: British and Indian forces totaling some 5,000 landed at the Red Sea port of Qusayr in early June, and began to cross overland to the Nile. Though the force reached Cairo only after the French surrender and evacuation, their advance through Upper Egypt has been credited with dissuading Mamluks from continuing their active alliance with the French.[51]

The end came swiftly. In Cairo, the French forces under General Belliard surrendered on June 27, on terms similar to those of the Convention of al-ʿArish. By mid-July, Belliard's forces were en route to Rosetta, whence their evacuation was complete by the first week of August. Menou, surrounded in Alexandria, held out until the end of August before surrendering to the British; the remaining French forces too evacuated under terms similar to the al-ʿArish agreement.

---

[51] Laurens et al., *L'Expédition*, 317, where the strength of the Anglo/Indian force is put at 7,000.

After the French

The British expeditionary force would remain in occupation of Egypt for another two years. There is a pronounced contrast: unlike the French, the British displayed no intention of staying or of reshaping Egyptian institutions; the British had entered Egypt in conjunction with the Ottoman empire, and were committed to restoring Egypt to Ottoman sovereignty. The affairs of Egypt for the next few years would be determined by the broader diplomatic context, by British and Ottoman efforts to maintain a measure of control over Egypt, and above all by rivalries among a plethora of armed factions within Egypt.

The broader diplomatic context centered on the complete dissolution of the Second Coalition. In February 1801 France had imposed a harsh peace on Austria, in the treaty of Lunéville. Later that spring Britain and France began discussions which culminated in the signing on October 1 of the "preliminary peace of London," under which the French agreed to evacuate Egypt and to respect Ottoman territorial integrity. It is ironic that that peace was signed after the evacuation of Egypt had become a *fait accompli* but a day before news of it reached London.[52] The preliminary peace was the basis for the formal treaty of Amiens, signed in March 1802. The signatories agreed that the Ottoman empire and all its territories were to be restored to their pre-war status. England agreed to relinquish all its conquests save for Trinidad and Ceylon; Malta was to be restored to the sovereignty of the Knights; France recognized the independence of the Republic of the Ionian Islands. In June, a formal peace treaty was signed between France and the Ottoman empire, renewing all pre-war treaties and Capitulations.

But suspicions remained, and the peace did not last. Egypt would be a primary focal point of those suspicions. Although British troops completed their own evacuation of Egypt early in 1803, the British feared that France would attempt to return. Those fears were intensified with the publication of an edited report from Bonaparte's agent, Sebastiani, who had visited Egypt in September, suggesting that the French would be welcomed back into Egypt, and that a relatively small force would suffice for the reconquest. Relations disintegrated to the point that war resumed between Britain and France in May 1803.[53]

As these events unfolded in Europe, the occupying armies – British and Ottoman – did not by themselves fully control affairs in Egypt, and differed

[52] Charles John Fedorak, "The French Capitulation in Egypt and the Preliminary Anglo-French Treaty of Peace in October 1801: A Note," *International History Review*, 15 (1993), 525–34.
[53] Henry Laurens, "L'Egypte en 1802: un rapport inédit de Sebastiani," *Annales islamologiques*, 23 (1987), 99–116.

in their views concerning Egypt's future.[54] The Ottomans sought to reestablish direct authority, which in their eyes meant at least the dispossession and
exile of the leading Mamluk beys, if not their imprisonment or death.
Britain's primary concern was to determine which authority would best be
able to prevent a French return, once the British themselves had left. And the
British judgment, based in part on their reading of the performance of their
Ottoman ally during the final campaign, was that the remaining Mamluk
beys would be more effective in this task than the Ottomans. Shortly after
the French evacuation the British had compelled the Ottomans to grant
amnesty to the Mamluk leaders who had cooperated with the British against
the French, and in time the British actively sought to reinstate some form of
Mamluk household domination.

But the affairs of the next several years were shaped primarily by the
contention of several armed groups for control of Egypt. There were several
competing factions of Mamluks clustered around the leadership of Ibrahim
Bey, ʿUthman Bardisi Bey, Muhammad Alfi Bey, and Hasan Bey Jiddawi.
Other contenders were a succession of officially appointed Ottoman governors, Khusrav Pasha, ʿAli Pasha al-Jazaʾirli, and Khurshid Pasha. Contingents of Albanian troops originally sent by the Ottoman government were
actively involved under the command first of Tahir Bey and then of
Muhammad ʿAli. The players included, briefly, a contingent of Janissaries in
transit to Medina.

Since we know who would emerge the victor, it is tempting to see the
events of the period between late 1802 and 1805 as shaped by a single hand
– to see Muhammad ʿAli making a friendship here, discarding an ally there,
fighting sometimes, at others withdrawing from a battlefield, and always
maneuvering to the point where he alone could grasp and hold power. The
reality of the rivalries of those years is certainly more intricate and complex,
but need not be pursued in detail here. Two points seem significant. First,
the chaos of several years of armed contention coming on the heels of the
successive occupations brought significantly hard times to Egypt's population, particularly the urban masses of Cairo. Regular army troops, rarely
paid on time, frequently resorted to violence to force payment of their
arrears or to see to their material needs more directly. To try to raise money
to pay the troops, commanders often imposed heavy extraordinary levies on
one or more groups within the city. The movement of essential commodities

---

[54] On the rivalries and contentions of these years, see three articles by Karol Sorby,
published in *Asian and African Studies* (Bratislava): "The Struggle between Great
Britain and France to Influence the Character of Government in Egypt, 1801–1803," 22
(1986), 161–89; "Decline of Mamluks' Power in Egypt (1803–1804)," 23 (1988),
171–99; and "Egypt – The Last Phase of Political Anarchy, 1804–1805," 24 (1989),
151–77. See also Georges Douin, *L'Egypte de 1802 à 1804* (Cairo, 1925), and Georges
Douin and E. Fawtier-Jones (eds.), *L'Angleterre et l'Egypte, la politique mameluke,
1801–1803*, 3 vols. (Cairo, 1926), which are heavily documented.

from Upper Egypt to Cairo was frequently interrupted by factional block-ades. Second, the factional rivalries and popular misery seem to have carried forward and accentuated a level of popular opposition already evident with regard to the French. Several scholars have argued that, although both Britain and France in 1803–04 were angling to restore Mamluk authority in Egypt, social and political conditions in Egypt made a return to the structure that had prevailed prior to 1798 impossible. The predatory policies of the Mamluks were now openly opposed by the merchants and 'ulama' of Cairo, and also by the less privileged parts of the urban population. The urban uprisings of March 1804, which helped drive the Mamluks out of Cairo, and March 1805, which helped bring Muhammad 'Ali to power, were expressions of a politicized urban population.[55] Once in power, Muhammad 'Ali would pursue policies that would bring to an end that level of popular political activity.

Summary

Several points seem relevant to a summary assessment of the impact and significance of the years of the French.

First, in these years Egypt was dragged into a prominent position in the thinking of European diplomats and strategists. It is worth recapitulating the succession of invasions, to illustrate the perceived level of Egypt's impor-tance: the French invasion of July 1798 brought into Egypt some 35,000 soldiers and, after the disaster at Abuqir, perhaps 15,000 naval personnel; the first Ottoman army, entering in July 1799, brought perhaps 15,000; the second major Ottoman invading army may have numbered as many as 40,000 before its defeat at Heliopolis in March 1800; the British expedi-tionary force, landing at Abuqir in March 1801, numbered perhaps 22,000; the Red Sea contingent was at least 5,000; and the Ottoman forces arriving by land and sea that spring probably totaled 25,000–30,000. For genera-tions of European diplomats, Egypt would remain important; control of Egypt would not be the whole of the "Eastern Question," but it would be part of it, and that would affect Egypt's history on many future occasions.

Second, although the issue has not been systematically and analytically examined, the invasions and occupations seem to have contributed to, extended, and probably exacerbated an economic crisis that was already serious prior to the French arrival.[56] There are no estimates of the number of

---

[55] In addition to Sorby (see previous note), see especially André Raymond, "Quartiers et mouvements populaires au Caire au XVIIIᵉ siècle," in Holt (ed.), *Political and Social Change*, 104–16, and Afaf Lutfi al-Sayyid Marsot, *Egypt in the Reign of Muhammad Ali* (Cambridge, 1984), 36–59.

[56] André Raymond, "The Economic Crisis of Egypt in the 18th century," in A. L. Udovitch (ed.), *The Islamic Middle East 700–1900* (Princeton, 1981), 687–705; André

casualties incurred by the civilian population during Egypt's years as war zone and occupied territory. Nor has the impact of disease – so often aggravated by military movements – upon the Egyptian population been quantified, although there are any number of references to outbreaks of plague.

Nor has the impact of these years upon the economy of Egypt been directly examined, although some observations seem reasonable. Merchants involved in the Mediterranean coastal trade certainly suffered heavily from the blockades and embargoes of commerce; certainly those involved in the transit of goods between the Mediterranean and the Red Sea also suffered. Merchants trading between Egypt's Red Sea ports of Suez and Qusayr and the Hijaz and Yemen may have fared better, at least during the periods when British fleets were not present. The overland "commerce" in pilgrims seems to have continued – the French allowed and even patronized the annual hajj traffic, as part of the effort to appear as supporters of Islam. Within Egypt, people in a position to sell commodities and services to the occupying army may have profited from the presence of such a large new entity, unrooted in the local economy. But there is a very narrow line between an army that pays and an army that takes, and it is likely that in the aggregate, especially given the chronic fiscal problems of the French regime, depredation and confiscation were more prevalent than compensation. It is at least apparent that the years of foreign occupation saw no improvement in an economy that had been in a state of crisis through the last two decades of the eighteenth century.[57]

What of longer-scale economic changes? Here it seems evident that the French made little difference in basic patterns of production, exchange, and consumption. Surely in time those patterns would change, even drastically, but such changes would not be evident for decades, when they would emerge out of later initiatives by the new state of Muhammad 'Ali. The French did move in the direction of significant change in land tenure and taxation, with the elimination of the *iltizam* system and its replacement by a direct tax, but following evacuation there were efforts to reestablish the *iltizam* system including dominance by the Mamluks; permanent change here too would come only under Muhammad 'Ali.

Third, the experiences of these years had some significant social effects. A phenomenon common to episodes of occupation is the issue of collaboration. To a degree this may have been perceived in Egypt in majority–minority terms, that is, some may have seen the French as extending preference and privilege to non-Muslims. The French did rely on the existing tax-

Raymond, "L'impact de la pénétration européenne sur l'économie de l'Egypte au XVIIIᵉ siècle," *Annales islamologiques*, 18 (1982), 217–35.
[57] Raymond, "Economic Crisis."

collection bureaucracy, staffed primarily by Copts, though this was hardly
an innovation. Some non-Muslims became notorious as French agents, such
as the Greek Barthelmy, so active and intrusive in enforcing urban security,
or the Copt Mu'allam Ya'qub, commander of the so-called "Coptic legion,"
one of the auxiliary military units formed late in the occupation. But
members of other auxiliary units and other collaborators were clearly
Muslim, including a number of young Mamluks who found it easy to serve
new masters and even to accompany them to France.[58] And of course the
French had been able to associate a number of 'ulama' with their rule, as
members of the *diwans* and in other capacities. Some people feared the
consequences of having been too close; it has been suggested that al-Jabarti
prepared his second account of the French occupation soon after evacuation
and dedicated it to the Ottoman grand vizier in order to ward off suspicion
for his own involvement in Menou's judicial *diwan* – although the case has
also been made that his purpose was to articulate the genuine distaste with
which thoughtful Egyptians had viewed the occupation.[59] Some certainly
did suffer retribution; Shaykh al-Bakri was treated very roughly by the
urban mob during the great uprising of 1800, and after the French left his
daughter was turned over to the Ottoman authorities, condemned for
consorting openly with the French, and put to death.[60] But although there
were individual cases of condemnation, retribution, or flight, there does not
seem to have been a permanent revision of majority–minority perceptions.

Certainly the most significant socio-political consequence of these years
concerned the fate of the Mamluk ruling elite. The Mamluk regime was
already beginning to face a population discontented by economic crisis and
factional violence in the ten or fifteen years preceding 1798. There was,
ironically, a germ of truth in the French assumption of a growing gap
between rulers and ruled – the flaw of course was the conclusion that
Egyptians would welcome the French as allies against unpopular rulers. But
the French invasion and its sequels surely hastened the demise of the
Mamluk elite. In part it was a matter of numbers; wartime deaths from
battle and plague reduced the number of Mamluk fighters from 10,000 to
12,000 to perhaps 1,200 by 1802.[61] The Mamluks were disconnected from
both their sources of wealth in Egypt and from their traditional recruiting
grounds, and were exposed as ineffective in most of the set battles. (So were
the Ottoman armies; the repeated failures against French armies would
contribute to the developing assumptions underlying the "new order"

[58] Gabriel Guemard, "Les auxiliaires de l'armée de Bonaparte en Egypte (1798–1801),"
    Bulletin de l'Institut d'Egypte, 9 (1927), 1–17.
[59] Moreh, "Reputed Autographs"; Marsot, "Comparative Study of al-Jabarti and Niqula
    al-Turk."
[60] Livingston, "Shaykh Bakri," 139–43.
[61] Marsot, *Muhammad Ali*, 38.

regimes of which Muhammad 'Ali's would be a striking example.) After the French and British evacuations, the Mamluk households might have regenerated themselves in relatively short order, if they had been left unchallenged and in full possession again of the *iltizams*. But it was no longer just a question of recruits and resources; above all, the old ruling order seems to have irretrievably squandered whatever legitimacy it once possessed, through its ineffective performance against the French and through the destructiveness of its rivalries both before and after the occupation.

There is a related issue. Despite the undeniable formation of links, in previous generations, among families of leading 'ulama', merchants, and Mamluks,[62] there is no evidence, especially in the 1802–05 period, of a popular rallying to the cause of the Mamluks. That is, there was little functional sentiment of "Egyptianness" as distinct from the Ottoman connection. Some scholarly attention has been given to a so-called "project for Egyptian independence" addressed in 1801 to the French and British governments. That proposal, however, originated with the collaborator Mu'allam Ya'qub and with an adventurer who had joined the expedition following the French conquest of Malta, and was drafted on board a ship carrying evacuees back to France. One can hardly conclude that the proposal reflected any discernible sector of Egyptian opinion.[63]

A fourth area of significance involves the issue of cultural and intellectual impact, where the traditional western interpretations have made the most sweeping claims. A distinction may be helpful. There is no doubt that the French occupation, particularly through the subsequent publication of the memoirs and engravings of the savants, had an immense impact on what Europeans knew about Egypt[64] – but that impact was upon Europe, not Egypt. This is not irrelevant; the ideas and images of an Egypt so thoroughly and authoritatively "described" would shape European thinking about Egypt for generations. But that is distinct from the impact that European culture may have had on Egyptians during the French occupation. Al-Jabarti is virtually the only source on the Egyptian side. His account of his visits to the French Institute and his observations on the intellectual activities of the

62 See, for example, André Raymond, "La Fortune des Gabarti et leurs liens avec la caste dominante et les milieux commerçants," in 'Abd al-Karim (ed.), *al-Jabarti*, 73–83; and "Le Caire: Economie et société urbaines à la fin du XVIIIe siècle," in *L'Egypte au XIXe siècle*, 121–39; also Michael Winter, "Turks, Arabs, and Mamluks in the Army of Ottoman Egypt," *Wiener Zeitschrift für die Kunde des Morgenlandes*, 72 (1980), 97–122.

63 George A. Haddad, "A Project for the Independence of Egypt, 1801," *Journal of the American Oriental Society*, 90 (1970), 169–83.

64 Charles C. Gillespie, "Scientific Aspects of the French Egyptian Expedition 1798–1801," *Proceedings of the American Philosophical Society*, 133 (1989), 447–74; Michael Albin, "Napoleon's *Description de l'Egypte*: Problems of Corporate Authorship," *Publishing History*, 8 (1980), 65–85.

savants are cautious but in some respects positive; his reaction to French political concepts, as reflected in his analysis of the proclamations, is dismissive, and colored always by his sense of the French as either infidel or godless.[65] But the contact was too brief, and inescapably embedded in the matrix of invasion, conquest, and occupation. The primary and enduring dialogue between Egypt and Europe would come later, beginning especially with the establishment of a new network of relations between Muhammad 'Ali's state structure and the European world. To the long drama of cultural interaction and change that would take place the French occupation was only a prologue – noisy, dramatic, colorful, brutal, and short.

[65] Thomas Philipp, "The French and the French Revolution in the Works of al-Jabarti," in Crecelius (ed.), *Arabic Manuscript Sources*, 127–40; substantially different views reflecting the old interpretive orthodoxy are given by Henri Pérès, "L'Institut d'Egypte et l'œuvre de Bonaparte jugés par deux historiens arabes contemporains," *Arabica*, 4 (1957), 113–30, and Ismail K. Poonawala, "The Evolution of al-Gabarti's [*sic*] Historical Thinking as Reflected in the *Muzhir* and the *'Aja'ib*," *Arabica*, 15 (1968), 270–88.

6

The era of Muhammad 'Ali Pasha, 1805–1848*

KHALED FAHMY

>‹

The period of Muhammad 'Ali's reign, which started in 1805 when he was appointed by the Ottoman sultan as *wali* of Egypt and ended in 1848 with his deposition as a result of mental illness, offers one of the most interesting epochs of modern Egyptian history. During this period Egypt, while still forming a part of the Ottoman empire, assumed an increasingly independent stance, and was finally granted as a hereditary domain to Muhammad 'Ali by the sultan 'Abd al-Majid in 1841. The Pasha, as Muhammad 'Ali came to be known in Egypt (or the Viceroy, as he was commonly known to Europeans), managed in a long and effective reign to bring to an end Mamluk power in Egypt and to create in its stead a loyal elite composed of members of his own family, of friends and acquaintances from his home town of Kavalla, and of members of the expanding bureaucracy that he founded in Egypt. Moved by a desire to turn his tenure as governor into a more secure and permanent position, Muhammad 'Ali undertook various radical measures that changed Egypt's position within the Ottoman empire, strengthened its economic ties with Europe at the expense of older links with other provinces of the empire, and radically changed its social and cultural map. Most significantly, by creating a massive naval and military force, the Pasha was able to expand Cairo's control not only over the entire province of Egypt, but also much beyond the traditional borders of the province to include the Sudan, Crete, the Morea, the Hijaz, Yemen, Syria, and even parts of Anatolia, the heartland of the Ottoman empire. In short, Muhammad 'Ali had succeeded in reaping the considerable potential wealth of Egypt, in organizing its internal administration, and then in using this accumulated wealth and better organization to transform Cairo and its environs from a mere provincial capital within the Ottoman empire into the center of an expansive "empire" ruled by the Pasha and his elite. Not for nothing has

* Regarding transliteration of Turkish names, see Note on transliteration, p. xiii.

the beginning of "modern" Egyptian history been taken to coincide with the inauguration of the Pasha's reign, and has he been called the "founder of Modern Egypt."[1]

Rise and consolidation of power, 1801–13

The period that followed the French evacuation of Egypt in 1801 witnessed a complete breakdown of law and order. Men accused of collaborating with the occupation force and women suspected of consorting with French soldiers were lynched. The multiplicity of military forces in the provinces and the absence of effective control by the governor in Cairo allowed soldiers of various factions to disobey orders with impunity. In the cities soldiers forced merchants to lend them money, bought goods with counterfeit coins, attacked merchants, artisans, and their customers, and harassed women, children, and old men. The situation in the countryside was not much better, if not considerably worse. Peasants were repeatedly attacked by soldiers who had not been paid for months and who descended on villages to demand their delayed salaries; rural trade was badly affected when Nile boats were seized by warring factions. The situation was worsened when the Bedouin took sides with one or another warring faction.[2]

These conditions of insecurity reflected the precarious political situation in Egypt in the aftermath of the French occupation. This occupation, although brief, had seriously weakened the power of the Mamluks in a manner that led to a power vacuum after the departure of the French army. Napoleon had inflicted heavy defeats on the two leaders of the Mamluk warriors on the eve of the French occupation, Murad Bey and Ibrahim Bey, the former in the battle of Imbaba (commonly known as the battle of the Pyramids) outside Cairo on July 21, 1798, after which he fled to Upper Egypt, and the latter at Salihiyya in the east of the Delta on August 11, forcing him to flee to Syria. Determined to circumvent the power of the Mamluks altogether the French had excluded them from the various *diwans* formed to help rule the country and to which they appointed only members of the 'ulama'. Furthermore, the French army had relentlessly pursued both Murad Bey in Upper Egypt and Ibrahim Bey in Syria, but had stopped short of dealing a death blow to either amir.

This failure was not from lack of determination but because of the activities of another European power that would come to play an increas-

---

[1] Henry Dodwell, *The Founder of Modern Egypt* (Cambridge, 1931); Guy Fargette, *Mehemet Ali: Le fondateur de l'Egypte moderne* (Paris, 1996).

[2] See 'Abd al-Rahman al-Jabarti, *'Aja'ib al-athar fi'l-tarajim wa'l-akhbar*, 4 vols. (Cairo, 1880), III, 189ff., esp. 192–93 for attacks on "collaborators," 190 for soldiers engaging in trade, 199 for soldiers' attacks on markets, and 237 for breakdown in security in the countryside.

ingly important role in Egypt: Great Britain. While Napoleon was driving
Murad out of the Saʿid, news arrived of the disastrous loss of his fleet in
Abuqir bay to the east of Alexandria at the hands of Nelson (August 1,
1798). This forced him to rush north, thus giving Murad much-needed time
to regroup his forces. The following spring Napoleon decided to deal with
the threat in Syria of Ibrahim Bey, who had been given refuge by Ahmad
Pasha al-Jazzar of Acre. At the head of the *armée d'orient* he marched into
Syria before they could muster their forces or receive further assistance from
Istanbul. Again the British inadvertently came to the assistance of the
Mamluks when Sir Sydney Smith managed to capture Napoleon's siege
artillery, forcing the French to lift the siege of the formidable fortress of Acre
in the spring of 1799. Thus at two crucial moments when the very existence
of the Mamluk duumvirs was threatened, British intervention saved them,
while frustrating French designs for establishing a permanent foothold in the
eastern Mediterranean.

If the British were unintentionally kind to the Mamluks and their leaders,
the plague, which took a heavy toll in the French camp at Acre and proved
equally effective in forcing Napoleon to lift the siege of the city, was not:
Murad Bey succumbed to it in 1801. After departure of the French from
Egypt in 1801 his rival, Ibrahim Bey, now old, weak, and defeated, returned
from Syria but was so feeble that leadership of the Mamluks was usurped by
two amirs from Murad's household, ʿUthman Bardisi Bey and Muhammad
Alfi Bey. Instead of collaborating to repair the damage caused by the French,
they continued the rivalry of their predecessors; the severe blow the
Mamluks suffered during the brief French occupation went unmended
owing to the continued divisiveness of their new leaders, their lack of
insight, and their tragic failure to learn from past mistakes.

With the French gone, the situation was opportune for the Ottoman
sultan to fill the vacuum, reestablish effective control in Egypt, and deal
decisively with the remaining Mamluk menace. Even before the French
occupation the authorities in Istanbul had considered a military expedition
to Egypt to snatch the province from the Mamluks and bring it back within
the Ottoman fold. One such expedition was dispatched in 1785 but was
soon recalled owing to the Ottomans' own military weakness. After the
French conquest of Egypt, however, the situation was so alarming that the
sultan dispatched troops to Egypt with the explicit mission not only of
evicting the French but also of ending the Mamluk menace. With these
objectives the grand vizier, Yusuf Ziya Pasha, at the head of 7,000 troops,
left Syria and arrived in Cairo in June 1801.

Notwithstanding the fact that the Mamluks' position was now weaker
than ever, three factors prevented the sultan from accomplishing his aims.
The first was the British, who once again came to the assistance of the
Mamluks – literally saving their lives more than once after their leaders had

been rounded up by the Ottoman troops and put on ships for Istanbul to meet their fate.[3] The second factor was the Janissary troops the grand vizier had with him, which the British described as a "medieval horde" completely lacking in discipline, training, or even cleanliness; it soon became obvious that Ottoman troops would not be effective in reestablishing Istanbul's control.[4] The third, and most important factor, however, that hindered the Ottomans was the force they sent by sea to Alexandria to assist the grand vizier and the British in their joint efforts against the French. Paradoxically this was a well-trained body of troops commanded by Kuchuk Husayn Pasha, grand admiral of the Ottoman navy since 1792, when the sultan had appointed him because of his commitment to naval and military reform. He and his deputy and protégé, Muhammad Khusrav Pasha, had a force of some 4,000 troops, 1,200 of them trained and disciplined along modern lines and with German officers.[5] These were some of the earliest of the famous *al-nizam al-jadid* (Turkish *nizam-i cedid*) recently formed by Sultan Salim, which would later prove decisive in the history of the sultan and his empire.[6]

In spite of these obvious advantages, this force too was unable to reestablish the sultan's authority in Egypt, for together with its disciplined, well-trained troops it included a small Albanian contingent known throughout the empire for their fierce, rebellious behavior. It was this small force that Muhammad 'Ali, initially its second-in-command, used to establish his own control at the expense of the Ottoman sultan and which enabled him to usher in an increasingly independent rule that lasted for over forty years.

That this was possible owed less to Muhammad 'Ali's shrewdness than to the political and military situation in Egypt in the wake of the French evacuation in the summer of 1801. The Mamluks were exhausted after three years of harassment by the French and denial of access to their prized lands in the provinces (especially in the Delta) and their homes, families, and treasure in Cairo. The British, with the strongest naval force in the eastern Mediterranean, although crucially important in evicting the French from Egypt, were not prepared to occupy the province without the consent of the

---

[3] See *ibid.*, III, 201–02 (for events of Jumadi al-Thani 1216), and William Wittman, *Travels in Turkey, Asia-Minor, Syria, and Egypt, 1801* (London, 1803), 381, 383.

[4] For a description of the force see Piers Macksey, *British Victory in Egypt, 1801: The End of Napoleon's Conquest* (London and New York, 1995), 21–22, 24–26, 178–79; Wittman, *Travels*, 230–37.

[5] Macksey, *British Victory*, 155; Thomas Walsh, *Journal of the Late Campaign in Egypt* (London, 1803), 108, 111.

[6] Stanford J. Shaw, *Between Old and New: The Ottoman Empire under Sultan Selim III, 1789–1807* (Cambridge, MA, 1971), 135. For a contemporary description of the troops see Mustafa Rashid Celebi Efendi, "An explanation of the Nizam-y-Gedid," in William Wilkinson, *An Account of the Principalities of Wallachia and Moldavia* (London, 1820), 251–52.

Ottoman sultan; by the treaty of Amiens (March 1802) the British acknowledged the sultan's sovereignty over Egypt, and accordingly evacuated their troops from Egypt in the following year. The struggle for power was, therefore, practically limited to the Mamluks, who were desperate to restore their privileged position, the Albanian forces who, while small in number, were effective fighters, and who, more importantly, were famous for independence and insubordination,[7] and finally the Ottoman Janissary and *nizami* forces under the command of the grand vizier.

Shortly after the departure of the French the grand vizier returned to Istanbul, to be followed by the grand admiral, leaving Khusrav as the senior Ottoman official in Egypt. The sultan was quick to appoint him as *wali* in recognition of his efforts in fighting the French. As champion of military reform Khusrav set out to train some Mamluk soldiers along French lines after enlisting in his service French officers who had stayed behind when their army had left Egypt. He also raised a Sudanese regiment and trained it in the French style, even tailoring for them "tight" French uniforms, made it a private escort guard for himself, and appointed an officer to "teach them the positions of the French."[8] He did not have enough time to see the result of his military experiment, for soon afterward (April 1803) the Albanian troops, living up to their rowdy and rebellious reputation, mutinied over delayed pay. Khusrav, unable to control the situation in Cairo, fled to Damietta leaving it to the head of the Albanian troops, a certain Tahir Pasha, to deal with the insurrection.

Matters continued to deteriorate, however, and in the event Tahir himself was assassinated, leaving Muhammad ʿAli as commander of the Albanian force. Rather than rush to Khusrav's rescue he, now in charge of the most powerful military force in Egypt, realized that there was a golden opportunity to fill the fateful vacuum of power himself; he forged a coalition between his Albanian troops and the Mamluks under Bardisi Bey to fetch Khusrav from Damietta as a prisoner and then to deport him to Istanbul. The Porte quickly appointed another *wali* who was uninformed about the situation in Egypt and who was eventually put to death in 1804 by the same coalition of Mamluks and Albanians. Muhammad ʿAli then turned against the Mamluks, playing on their age-old divisiveness and the rivalry between Alfi Bey and Bardisi Bey. In doing so he was assisted by the leading ʿulamaʾ, merchants, and notables (*ashraf*) of Cairo who had been complaining of the high taxes the Mamluks were levying to pay their soldiers and placate the Albanian troops. In the meantime (1804–05) the Porte appointed yet another *wali*, Khurshid, who, while determined to rule and return some law

---

[7] For this reputation among contemporary military observers see Wittman, *Travels*, 237–39.
[8] Al-Jabarti, *ʿAjaʾib*, III, 222 (events of Muharram 1217).

and order to Cairo, eventually proved himself so hateful to the Cairene population as well as to the Mamluks and Albanian troops that he practically lost control of the city to Muhammad 'Ali. The notables and 'ulama' finally threw their weight behind Muhammad 'Ali, proclaiming him *wali* and imploring him not to raise taxes. When news of this reached Istanbul the Porte realized that Muhammad 'Ali was in control in Cairo, and the sultan finally acquiesced in his appointment as *wali* of Egypt in July 1805.

In this manner Muhammad 'Ali found himself at the age of thirty-five in control of Egypt, one of the wealthiest provinces of the Ottoman empire. He knew, however, how precarious his position was. For one thing his appointment had been forced on Salim, and he was wary that the sultan might try to depose him at the first opportunity. This concern haunted Muhammad 'Ali throughout his long career, and Egypt's history in the first half of the nineteenth century was considerably shaped by his attempt to make his tenure more secure and permanent. Second, the Albanian troops that brought him to power and continued to form the military base of his strength were unreliable: the soldiers were rebellious and untrustworthy and could turn against him as they had against their former commander. Third, the Mamluks had still not been dealt a death blow; they posed a serious threat to public security in the countryside and to Muhammad 'Ali's safety. Fourth, he in fact controlled no more than Cairo itself, which had witnessed a "revolutionary moment" as a result of a coalition of 'ulama', artisans, and *ashraf* that had brought him to power and forced the sultan to bend, but which could prove dangerous if it were not defused quickly.

The first thing he did after his appointment as governor was to calm the situation in Cairo. He thus broke the revolutionary coalition that had brought him to power and ordered the merchants to reopen their shops, much to the delight of the Cairenes who were tired after months of disruption in the city. Through a series of maneuvers he then undermined the leadership of the *ashraf* represented in the person of 'Umar Makram who had been instrumental in the crucial months of 1805. He used the same tactics of forging alliances and breaking them with the Mamluks, although their final hour had not yet come.

The most important threat, however, came from Istanbul and from the sultan's grudging acceptance of Muhammad 'Ali as *wali* of Egypt. Anxious to remove him, Salim ordered Muhammad 'Ali to dispatch a force to deal with the rising power of the Wahhabis in Arabia. Immediately after the Wahhabis had captured the holy cities of Mecca (1803) and Medina (1804) and disrupted the annual pilgrimage (thus delivering a severe blow to his reputation as Defender of the Two Holy Shrines) Salim told his governors in Syria, Egypt, and Iraq to deal with this menace, but none of them had the will or the means to undertake the required military expedition against them. After the appointment of Muhammad 'Ali as governor of Egypt Salim repeated the order in the hope that Muhammad 'Ali would get entangled in a military campaign that would weaken him and help in dislodging him from Egypt. The Pasha was aware of the Porte's motives and was reluctant to meet the sultan's request, arguing that his military forces were not ready and that he was busy fighting the Mamluks.[9]

Only a year after instating him in Egypt the sultan attempted to remove Muhammad 'Ali from Egypt in a more direct manner. This time he was tempted with another province, Salonika. In June 1806 Musa Pasha, *wali* of Salonika, was in fact sent to Egypt to fulfill the sultanic edict of trading places with Muhammad 'Ali. On his arrival, however, Musa found that Muhammad 'Ali had much stronger support than the sultan had thought and the Ottoman commanders sent with him were convinced that the force at their disposal was inadequate to dislodge Muhammad 'Ali from his important province.[10]

The following year, 1807, proved crucial in entrenching Muhammad 'Ali in Egypt. The year opened with the death of Alfi Bey on January 29, soon after that of the other leader of the Mamluks, Bardisi Bey, who had died on November 12, 1806. The Mamluk factions were thus deprived of leadership and left vulnerable to Muhammad 'Ali's intrigues. In March the Pasha managed to overcome another hurdle. The British, in their continuing war with Napoleonic France, feared that the French were contemplating reoccupying Egypt; a British force landed at Alexandria and, finding it devoid of grain, proceeded to Rosetta which was reputed to have large granaries. Although Muhammad 'Ali was fighting the Mamluks in Upper Egypt, the British still failed to capture Rosetta and later agreed to evacuate the country. In May Sultan Salim was himself deposed after failing to curb the power of the Janissaries in Istanbul, and his successor, Sultan Mahmud II, found himself with little room for maneuver. Muhammad 'Ali was therefore spared further requests to take action in Arabia.

To secure his position further in Egypt Muhammad 'Ali invited his family and friends to Egypt to take up residence. First to arrive were members of his immediate family, who were given posts; his son Ibrahim, then only sixteen years old, was immediately made governor of the Citadel in Cairo. This set a trend that was soon characteristic of the Pasha's long reign: members of his immediate family, relatives from his home town of Kavalla, and close and trusted friends were given important positions in the administration that he started to build.

---

[9] J. B. Kelly, *Britain and the Persian Gulf, 1795–1880* (Oxford, 1968), 105; Shaw, *Between Old and New*, 296–98.

[10] Al-Jabarti, *'Aja'ib*, IV, 9–20 (events of Rabi' al-Thani 1221); Georges Douin (ed.), *L'Angleterre et l'Egypte* (Cairo, 1928–30, II, *La politique mameluke, 1803–1807* (1930), 275, 291, 295; Shaw, *Between Old and New*, 290–91.

After taking this step toward creating a loyal elite, Muhammad 'Ali started to spread his control over wider areas of Egypt. The British evacuation of Alexandria (September 1807) after their abortive attempt to establish a foothold there gave the Pasha the chance to occupy that city and replace the Ottoman governor with a friend, Boghus Yusufian, who would later become the Pasha's adviser on foreign and commercial affairs. This was followed by small campaigns in the Delta to evict the Mamluks and push them to Upper Egypt. Throughout the following two years the Mamluks were practically given the Sa'id to govern in exchange for remitting its taxes to Muhammad 'Ali. Finally, in 1810, after dividing their ranks and after they failed to pay overdue taxes, he marched southward and snatched from them one after another of the Sa'idi provinces; by the end of the year he had taken control of all Egypt. The Mamluk leaders found no option but to accept the Pasha's invitation to reside in Cairo, where by offering them some of their former palaces to live in he kept them under his watchful eye.

Having strengthened his position against potential enemies the Pasha tried to conciliate the sultan in Istanbul. Besides continuing the age-old traditions of minting only Ottoman coins in Egypt, using the sultan's name in Friday prayers, and sending the annual tribute required of him, the Pasha did his best to show the new sultan that he was indeed the humble servant that a *wali* of an Ottoman province was expected to be. Thus he dispatched the much-delayed force to Arabia, a step he took as much to send his quarrelsome troops away from Egypt as to enhance his position in the empire by showing the sultan that he, unlike other *walis*, could be relied upon. In March 1811 he held a big ceremony at his residence in the Citadel to announce the official start of the campaign. At this ceremony, to which were invited members of the 'ulama', dignitaries, and above all, the Mamluk chieftains, it was announced that his son Tusun had been named by the sultan as leader of the campaign and would be given the title pasha of Jidda.

That day, March 1, 1811, proved to be the last of Mamluk power in Egypt, for the Pasha seized the opportunity of their grand and festive assemblage to deal a final death blow to them. On their way up to the Citadel in their colorful embroidered caftans they were trapped in a narrow alley where the Pasha's troops opened fire from every side. Over four hundred and fifty amirs were killed in this single incident, which was followed by a ferocious campaign against those who had succeeded in escaping. The Pasha's Albanian troops were unleashed against the Mamluks' houses in Cairo, plundering their property and raping the women. In the end, about a thousand Mamluk amirs and soldiers died in Cairo alone during the few days that followed the massacre in the Citadel.[11] A year later a military expedition under Ibrahim Pasha was dispatched to Upper Egypt

---

[11] Al-Jabarti, *'Aja'ib*, IV, 127–32 (events of Safar 1226).

against the Mamluks who had succeeded in evading the massacre in Cairo; another thousand were said to have been killed.[12] This was no small feat, for in this infamous massacre and its aftermath Muhammad ʿAli accomplished what the Ottoman sultans had been trying to do for centuries without much success – the end of the Mamluk presence in Egypt.

Equally important in strengthening his position in Egypt during this initial stage of Muhammad ʿAli's rule was the commercial opportunity afforded by the departure of the British from Alexandria. Given the havoc caused by the Napoleonic wars in Europe British forces in Malta and Spain needed grain, which was in short supply in Europe. The Pasha stepped in swiftly and supplied them with food collected in the Delta. Having established control over Alexandria, Muhammad ʿAli imposed a monopoly over the export of grain and reaped considerable profit.[13] This would prove to be an important and essential characteristic of his regime: establishing his control over the production of agricultural commodities and over their internal as well as external trade. For the time being, though, he proceeded slowly and cautiously, governed as ever by the prospect of lucrative trade with Europe; his previous residence in Albania and earlier vocation there as a merchant made him keenly aware that prospects were even brighter as a result of the continuing Napoleonic wars.

Muhammad ʿAli's next step was to control the agricultural system with the intention of maximizing profits from it. The fact that the land-tenure system, the system of collecting taxes from the countryside, and the manner of running the entire agricultural economy were inefficient and corrupt was realized by the French as soon as they landed in Egypt. Napoleon convened a *diwan* to discuss the issue; high on the agenda was the question of whether to replace the existing tax-farming system, the *iltizam*, with a system of direct taxation. The *multazims*, tax-farmers, it was believed, were inefficient, seldom having precise information about the lands from which they were to collect taxes, and were also corrupt, often pocketing more money (*faʾidh*) from their *iltizams* than they actually remitted to the *wali* in Cairo. In addition, and in compensation for their services, they were given land free of taxes (*aradi al-usya*). The *diwan* that Napoleon convened recommended abolition of the *iltizam* system and registration of the names of actual landowners. These recommendations would be repeated two years later, after Napoleon's departure, by General Menou, who envisaged an increase in revenue by replacing all land taxes with a single tax, the rate of which would very according to the quality of land. Menou also recommended imposing a tax on the *usya* land held previously by *multazims*, taxing *waqf*

---

[12] Public Record Office, London: FO 24/4, letter to Misset, May 6, 1813, quoted in Dodwell, *The Founder*, 35–36.

[13] Kenneth M. Cuno, *The Pasha's Peasants: Land, Society, and Economy in Lower Egypt, 1740–1858* (Cambridge, 1992), 104.

and *rizqa* lands that had been endowed for religious purposes, and allowing the fallahin, who up to that time had only usufruct over lands they tilled, to acquire them as private property.[14]

The French, however, had no chance to put these recommendations into practice. Following his assumption of power in Egypt, Muhammad 'Ali started to implement them in small steps. (The one recommendation he was adamant in opposing, however, was that of legally recognizing the fallahin's land [their *athar* as it was called] as private property. If he had believed that private ownership of land would not harm the "state" and its interests, he told a French visitor in 1833, he would have respected it as much as he respected private rights in urban property.)[15] In 1806 the Pasha started his gradual march toward establishing absolute control over the countryside by ordering the *multazims* to remit to him half of the *fa'idh* that they were collecting. The following year he canceled the tax exemptions of village shaykhs, the *masmuh al-mashayikh*, and in September of the same year inaugurated what would later prove to be a ferocious attack on the power and privileges of the religious shaykhs by canceling their exemption as *multazims* from half the *fa'idh*. Later, in 1808, when there were low floods and many villages proved incapable of paying taxes, he snatched some 160 villages from their *multazims*. These were allocated to members of his family and the gradually expanding elite, who were ordered to make sure that the normal level of cultivation was maintained despite the low Nile. In 1809 he started targeting *rizqa* lands, that is tax-free lands that were endowed for religious purposes, mostly for the upkeep of mosques and *madrasas*. In June he ordered all beneficiaries of *rizqas* as well as holders of *usya* land to present title deeds within forty days – those who failed to do so had their lands confiscated. These repeated attacks on the privileges of religious men triggered their revolt in July 1809, under 'Umar Makram, the *naqib al-ashraf*, who had been instrumental in bringing Muhammad 'Ali to power four years earlier. After repeated gatherings, petitions, and demonstrations, the revolt failed and Makram was exiled to Damietta. He would not be allowed to return to Cairo until ten years later, when his popularity and influence with the population were all but forgotten. Leaderless and hopelessly divided over their stance toward the Pasha, the 'ulama' were incapable of stopping Muhammad 'Ali from imposing taxes on land they held as *multazims*.

Having curtailed the economic power of the 'ulama' Muhammad 'Ali then turned against the Mamluks and confiscated their wealth. Following the massacre of March 1811 it was only natural for the Pasha to expropriate all

---

[14] Helen B. Rivlin, *The Agricultural Policy of Muhammad Ali in Egypt* (Cambridge, MA, 1961), 42–46.

[15] Georges Douin (ed.), *La mission du Baron de Boislecomte, L'Egypte et la Syrie en 1833* (Cairo, 1927), 80.

the *iltizams* the Mamluks had held. When Ibrahim was sent at the head of a military force to expel them from the Sa'id in the following summer he cleared the countryside and took the opportunity to seize all *rizqa* lands in Upper Egypt, triggering yet another series of complaints by the 'ulama' that went completely unheeded by him and his father. By 1811 Muhammad 'Ali had finally succeeded in establishing himself as uncontested ruler of Egypt, not only by getting rid of his political rivals, but also by extending his control over the actual cultivators of land, the main producers of wealth, and by getting rid of the various intermediaries who stood between the state and the *fallah*, be they Mamluk amirs, *multazims*, village shaykhs or religious scholars. This allowed the Pasha to amass a considerable fortune; between 1805 and 1812 Muhammad 'Ali increased his annual revenue nearly threefold[16] – the five-year period 1806–11 was also one of highly profitable trade with Europe.

This favorable situation altered after 1812 when, following Napoleon's disastrous Russian campaign and the opening of the Black Sea, resumption of British trade lowered demand for Egyptian grain. At the same time the military expedition he had sent to Arabia soon sucked him into a quagmire that put considerable strain on his finances, from which the indecisive leadership of Tusun did not help to extricate him.

Faced by these pressures on his finances, the Pasha felt the need to raise more revenue from the countryside and in 1813 he ordered a general survey of agricultural land throughout Egypt. This survey, begun in the spring of 1813 in Middle and Upper Egypt and completed in May 1814 in Lower Egypt, was extremely detailed and thorough, and proved to be instrumental in increasing the Pasha's revenue. With this cadaster in hand the Pasha and his officials succeeded in capturing more land from the *multazims* and reclassifying much of their *usya* land as *miri*, that is taxable land, by seizing land for which *multazims* could not produce title deeds, and by using a smaller measuring unit than was usual. And while the distinction between *rizqa* and *miri* lands was maintained, they were subjected to the same tax rate. In this manner the power of the *multazims* was even more severely curtailed and Muhammad 'Ali managed to extend control over the country-side, to raise revenue by subjecting hitherto tax-free lands to taxes, and to interfere as never before in the actual process of agricultural production.

The effect of all these policies, which were dictated above all by the Pasha's determination to entrench himself more securely in Egypt, was deeply felt by villagers and town dwellers alike. The fallahin's lives were gradually en-croached upon by the new bureaucracy that the Pasha was founding in Cairo and with which he intended to replace the old *multazims*. Armed with the new cadaster, his officials assessed higher and higher taxes, while at the same

[16] *Ibid.,* 125.

time paying little attention to the peasants' grievances or financial difficulties. The fallahin also suffered from the monopolies the Pasha introduced and from the more frequent demands of corvée that the Pasha's agricultural projects required. Reflecting the fallahin's realization that they were no longer controlled by the *multazims* but that Muhammad 'Ali now controlled their lives and livelihood was their response to some old *multazims*' demands by saying, "Your days are finished and we have become the Pasha's peasants."[17]

Townspeople also suffered heavily from the Pasha's policies in the first phase of his long reign. Specifically, urban notables, be they 'ulama', *ashraf*, or leading merchants, found their positions undermined by the Pasha's economic moves. The 'ulama', whose livelihood rested on their ability to extract a surplus in the form of fees for supervising *waqf* lands, or retaining a *fa'idh* from their *iltizams*, were hit hard by the Pasha's new system of direct taxation and his control of *waqfs*. The *ashraf*, for their part, were severely affected by the loss of their leader, 'Umar Makram, and found themselves defenseless in dealing with the Pasha's officials. Finally, the urban merchants were affected by the Pasha's new arrangements, chief among which was expansion of monopolies to include more and more commodities.

Preparing for military expansion, 1813–29

Having taken effective control of the entire province of Egypt and inaugurated the process of replacing the old Mamluk military oligarchy with trusted retainers, Muhammad 'Ali was still bothered by the unresolved tension between him and his sovereign. The campaign that he launched against the Wahhabis to restore the authority of the sultan in the Hijaz came to no rapid conclusion, and after initial successes it became clear that Tusun's command was costing the campaign dearly; after capturing Mecca and Medina (January–February 1813) his army soon suffered serious setbacks. This prompted Muhammad 'Ali to go to the Hijaz in person (August 1813) and eventually to appoint his eldest son, Ibrahim, as commander there. Nevertheless, and despite these problems, the Pasha believed that capturing the two holy cities provided enough evidence of his effort in defending the sultan's authority against the "infidel" Wahhabis. He thus sent one of his *mamluks*, a certain Latif Agha, to Istanbul to present the keys of both cities to the sultan as a sign of obedience and submission. During his stay in Istanbul, however, Latif Agha was given the title of pasha and encouraged to rebel against his master in Egypt. On his return to Cairo rumors circulated that he had come back with a *firman* to depose Muhammad 'Ali and replace him as *wali* of Egypt. Although the Pasha, in Arabia, was informed of the conspiracy in time, he could not rush back

---

[17] Al-Jabarti, *'Aja'ib*, IV, 207, quoted in Cuno, *The Pasha's Peasants*, 5.

owing to pressing military matters there, and it was left to his trusted deputy, Muhammad Lazughlu, to take personal revenge against Latif and have him beheaded at the foot of the Citadel.[18]

Although the Pasha succeeded in surviving this "palace coup," he knew only too well that his position in Egypt was still insecure in spite of already impressive accomplishments. Crucially lacking was a body of troops reliable and disciplined enough to confront any serious military threat from the sultan in case the latter tried to take Egypt from him. After receiving the alarming news of Napoleon's return from exile in Elba and the possibility of renewed conflict in Europe, Muhammad 'Ali hurried back to Egypt. There his hold on the Albanian troops was precarious, for besides their rowdy nature they had been hard hit by his recent reforms in the agricultural sector; a large number had acquired *iltizams*, and Ibrahim's attacks on the privileges of the *multazims* had severely affected them. Matters were made worse when a number of these Albanians came back with him from Arabia and, finding their *iltizams* practically unprofitable, started asking for long-delayed arrears in their pay. Soon after his own return to Egypt (June 1815), therefore, the Pasha decided to impose order on the troops by force, and "to put their pay and expenses under an organized principle ('*rabita ve nizam*')."[19] Influenced by Khusrav's earlier experiment in attempting to introduce the *nizam al-jadid* in Egypt, the Pasha thought he could now have his much-needed military force: he gathered his Albanian soldiers in Maydan al-Rumayla at the foot of the Citadel for target practice, and for over three hours the soldiers fired their guns in "successive volleys making a thundery noise like the French." The following day it was rumored that the Pasha wanted to have a count of the soldiers and "to train them according to *al-nizam al-jadid*, copying the positions of the French. He wanted them to put on tight clothes and to change their appearance."[20]

The attempt failed miserably, for the soldiers reluctantly complied with the Pasha's orders on the first day only to conspire to kill him on the following night. The Pasha was informed of the plot in time to escape assassination. When they knew that their conspiracy was foiled, the rebels went on a rampage in the streets of Cairo, looting and damaging a considerable amount of property. Muhammad 'Ali was able to pacify the merchants and the populace only by returning the stolen property or compensating them for the damages.[21]

---

[18] Al-Jabarti, '*Aja'ib*, IV, 181–83 (events of Dhu al-Hijja 1228); Sir John G. Wilkinson, *Modern Egypt and Thebes*, 2 vols. (London, 1843), II, 534. Cf. 'Abd al-Rahman al-Rafi'i, *Asr Muhammad 'Ali* (Cairo, 1989), 138–40.

[19] Dar al-Watha'iq al-Qawmiyya, Cairo (hereafter DWQ), Bahr Barra 4/149, 30 Ramadan 1230/September 5, 1815.

[20] Al-Jabarti, '*Aja'ib*, IV, 222 (events of Sha'ban 1230).

[21] DWQ, Dhawat 1/76, 1 Ramadan 1230/August 7, 1815; al-Jabarti, '*Aja'ib*, IV, 223–25;

Although the Pasha managed to meet this further challenge to his authority, he became more than ever aware of his need for a reliable, well-trained body of troops. For the time being, though, he turned his attention toward more reforms in the agricultural sector and initiated an ambitious and partly successful public-works program. This involved mainly irrigation projects such as digging new canals that together more than doubled the length of irrigation canals in Egypt,[22] cleaning these and other canals regularly from the alluvial mud that deposited as a result of the annual floods, and increasing the depth of canals in such a way as to allow the waters of the Nile to irrigate lands not adjacent to the river in times of low water. That in turn allowed perennial irrigation of huge tracts of land, especially in Lower Egypt where, eventually, the basin systems of irrigation all but disappeared. All in all, and as a result of these efforts, the area of cultivated land increased between 1813 and the 1830s by around 18 percent;[23] the area of cropped land was increased considerably by converting more land to perennial irrigation and planting more than one crop each year.[24]

Chief among these grand schemes was the re-digging of the ancient canal that linked Alexandria to the Nile, a project the Pasha started in April 1817 and that was eventually called Mahmudiyya, in honor of Sultan Mahmud II. Work lasted for three years (it was finished in early 1820) and provided Alexandria with a regular supply of fresh water, improved communication with the hinterland, and allowed reclamation of thousands of faddans along the canal's banks. The ambitious project involved coercing thousands of men and women from all the provinces of Lower Egypt to work on it. During the month of March 1819 alone the number of laborers was said to have been as high as 300,000. Upon completion the canal was 72 kilometers long and had cost 35,000 purses (around 7.5m francs).[25]

The Mahmudiyya canal exemplifies the degree to which the Pasha had managed to secure control of Egypt and testifies to his ability to undertake infrastructural projects on a scale that none of the Ottoman governors before him had managed to achieve. The project also shows the price paid by the Egyptian population (in this case mostly peasants from Lower Egypt) in fulfilling the Pasha's grand schemes; some contemporary reports put the casualty figures as high as 100,000! Most of the men, women, and children

---

Felix Mengin, *Histoire de l'Egypte sous le gouvernement de Mohammed-Aly*, 2 vols. (Paris, 1823), II, 49–50; J. J. Halls, *The Life and Correspondence of Henry Salt*, 2 vols. (London, 1834), I, 445.

[22] It is estimated that 686 of the 1,200 miles of canals in Egypt during Muhammad 'Ali's reign were created through his initiatives (Rivlin, *The Agricultural Policy*, 248).

[23] Cuno, *The Pasha's Peasants*, 115.

[24] Rivlin, *The Agricultural Policy*, 270.

[25] *Ibid.*, 216–21.

who perished in the corvée died as a result of the poor methods with which the canal was excavated.[26]

Meanwhile Ibrahim had managed to capture Darʿiyya, capital of the Wahhabis (September 1818), and as a further sign of loyalty to the sultan Muhammad ʿAli chose to send ʿAbdallah ibn Saʿud, the Saʿudi leader, to Istanbul (where he was beheaded) rather than have him punished in Cairo. After spreading his control to Arabia, albeit in the sultan's name, Muhammad ʿAli decided to expand southward, to the Sudan, where the sultan was known only by name. Although the Pasha told Istanbul that his aim was to capture the last of the Mamluk amirs who had taken refuge there, his letters to his son Ismaʿil Pasha, who headed the campaign, leave no doubt that his main object was to capture as many slaves as possible. He repeatedly wrote to Ismaʿil that he should not be distracted by raising taxes and searching for gold from this purpose there. "The value of slaves who prove to be suitable for our services," he wrote, "is more precious than jewels ... hence I am ordering you to collect 5,000 of these slaves."[27] With these men Muhammad ʿAli hoped to form a modern, disciplined army, the army he desperately needed to confront any possible threat to his position from Istanbul. We have already seen his attempt to train the Albanian troops along modern lines, and how this failed. Still uncomfortable with the idea of conscripting Egyptians, the Pasha resorted to the Sudanese to supply him with much-needed manpower.

In 1820 two expeditions were dispatched to Dongola and Kurdufan, one under Ismaʿil Pasha, the other under Muhammad ʿAli's son-in-law, Muhammad Bey the *daftardar*. The total force numbered 4,000 troops and was composed of a mosaic of ethnic and linguistic groups: Albanians, *mamluks*, Maghribis, and Egyptian Bedouin.[28] The expedition proved disastrous. For one thing it was dispatched without any accompanying medical services, and the troops soon fell victim to all kinds of diseases; in September 1821 alone, the number of dead reached 600, only to rise to 1,500 the following month. As a result the Albanian troops in Ismaʿil's company started to grumble and asked to be sent back to Egypt's more temperate climate. Moreover, Ismaʿil was inexperienced, indecisive, stubborn, and failed to inspire the troops, who deserted him in a steady stream. His brutality, rashness, and impetuous nature eventually cost him his own life. Moreover, owing to the haphazard way in which the campaign was conducted, there was a heavy toll on Sudanese civilians. The lack of effective means of transportation resulted in

26 See *ibid.*, 221, 353 n. 15; al-Jabarti, *ʿAjaʾib*, IV, 301–04; *Cf.* Cuno, *The Pasha's Peasants*, 122–22.

27 DWQ, s/1/50/2/340 on 19 Dhu al-Qiʿda/August 8, 1822. See also s/1/50/4/195 on 19 Muharram 1239/September 26, 1823.

28 See al-Rafiʿi's different estimate, *Asr Muhammad ʿAli*, 160.

the deaths of thousands of slaves before they even reached Egypt. Still more staggering is the fact that of 20,000 slaves who did in fact reach Aswan, by 1824 only 3,000 remained alive. The others perished "like sheep with the rot."[29]

Finally, having lost his own son in the campaign, and failed to raise the men required for his new army, Muhammad 'Ali realized that the Sudan campaign had been a complete failure. When he was informed that a large number of Turkish-speaking officers were about to desert the campaign and return en masse to Egypt he wrote to the governor of one of the Sa'idi provinces: "Since the Turks are members of our race and since they must be spared the trouble of being sent to remote and dangerous areas, it has become necessary to conscript around 4,000 men from Upper Egypt [to replace them]." These troops, he explained, would be drafted for three years, after which they would be given stamped certificates and allowed to return to their villages.[30]

This was the nucleus from which Muhammad 'Ali's army would expand in little over ten years to the impressive figure of 130,000 troops. For the time being, though, these first conscripts were sent to training-camps in Aswan and Farshut in Upper Egypt, where an officer corps was also being formed from *mamluks* belonging to the Pasha and to members of his family, chief among whom was his son Ibrahim. While the training of the soldiers was entrusted to the Pasha's loyal deputy and friend, Muhammad Lazughlu, the officers were trained by a group of French officers, many of whom had earlier served in Napoleon's army and needed employment after demobilization. Chief among these was a certain officer named Seves who claimed to have been a colonel in Napoleon's army and to have been present at Waterloo, and whom the French consul-general in Egypt, Drovetti, introduced to the Pasha. Seves would eventually convert to Islam, assume the Muslim name of Sulayman Agha and rise in the military hierarchy to acquire the title of pasha and be second only to Ibrahim Pasha. The French influence on the Pasha's new army may be further discerned in the arrival in 1825 of a French military mission to restructure the officer corps.

The Ottoman model was not far from the Pasha's mind, however, when he planned his new army. For soon after commanding Seves and Muhammad Lazuglu to attend to their business, he explicitly ordered Ibrahim Pasha to adopt the structure that Sultan Salim III had used in his own army more than twenty years earlier. "Although the plan that Sulayman Agha had put down is a wonderful one," he explained to his son, "it is similar to the one Napoleon had used to lead an army composed of several thousand

---

[29] Dodwell, *The Founder*, 64–65.
[30] DWQ, s/1/50/2/145 on 25 Jumadi al-Awwal 1237/February 18, 1822.

troops. Our army, however, is a new and much smaller one and we have only recently begun to create it."[31]

Both Muhammad 'Ali and Ibrahim had practical minds and they found no problem in adopting the Ottoman model to fit their new army while at the same time borrowing from the French the idea of conscripting and arming the peasants. Unlike the French army, however, Muhammad 'Ali's new army would be ethnically divided: while Arabic-speaking peasants formed the bulk of the soldiery and were gathered from the villages along the Nile by force, their commanders were Turkish speaking, and strict orders were issued to prevent Arabic-speaking peasants from rising beyond the rank of *yuzbashi* (captain). This ethnic and linguistic duality was characteristic of Muhammad 'Ali's reign: senior positions in the civilian bureaucracy as well as in the army were reserved for Turkish speakers, while lower ranks both in the military and civilian bureaucracies were filled by Arabic speakers, whose ethnicity and language guaranteed that they remained in the lower ranks.

This system had two aims. First, it was intended to attract men from all over the Ottoman world to come and serve Muhammad 'Ali and his expanding household. Through these positions and others in the rapidly expanding civilian bureaucracy a loyal elite was forming around the Pasha and his family. Second, the system aimed to deny the Arabic-speaking masses the leaders needed to challenge the Pasha's rule.

The need to keep the peasants, by far the overwhelming majority of the Arabic-speaking masses, in submission was crucial. In addition to the danger posed to agricultural production by moving thousands of men, conscripting the peasantry was an unprecedented step whose danger lay in arming them at the very time that resentment of the government's harsh policies was most acute. By the 1820s the Pasha had extended his monopolies to include most of the major staple foodstuffs and many other cash crops that the fallahin's livelihood depended on. As a result, the peasants were often forced to grow crops sold only to government warehouses and at prices fixed by the Pasha. They then had to buy back what they had grown themselves, and at prices considerably higher than the original sale prices. Violations of these rules were met with extreme severity. In addition, and in order to undertake his numerous and ambitious public works, the Pasha had wider recourse to corvée than had the *multazims* before him. Peasants were not only forced to work without pay on various public works for longer and longer periods every year, but they were also forced to do so on projects outside their villages and even outside their provinces. As if this were not enough, to finance his various projects the Pasha had increased land tax to the degree

---

[31] DWQ, s/1/50/2/209 on 18 Rajab 1237/April 11, 1822.

that it may safely be said that by the 1820s the countryside had reached the limit of its ability to meet the Pasha's insatiable needs.

As a result of deeply felt resentment of the Pasha and his policies the countryside would not withstand another burden. The decision to conscript the fallahin had repercussions that posed a serious threat to Muhammad 'Ali's authority. Immediately after conscription was introduced in Lower Egypt in 1823 a big revolt erupted in the province of Minuffiya in the Delta and the Pasha had to go there in person, guarded by his own palace troops and assisted by six field cannons, to subdue the revolt. The following year an even larger rebellion broke out in Upper Egypt and was soon joined by over 30,000 men and women. Looting, arson, and attacks on local officials were reported to the Pasha in Cairo who decided to deal with the rebellion by sending his new troops to quell the alarming revolt. This was a serious gamble indeed, for the troops were sent to the very provinces from which they themselves had been conscripted.

The gamble succeeded. One of the new regiments marched into the center of the revolt in Qina, and quelled the rising in two weeks, killing 4,000 people in the process. The new troops had two other chances to prove themselves to the Pasha. A contingent of 2,500 had been sent to the Hijaz to deal with renewed trouble there and managed to inflict a decisive defeat on a Wahhabi force ten times its size. A short while later, on March 24, 1824, a huge explosion in a powder magazine at the Citadel in Cairo killed over four thousand people. Rumors circulated that the explosion was the work of old Albanian troops disgruntled by the Pasha's creation of the new *nizami* troops. This incident posed a grave danger to the Pasha, whose position was compared to that of Sultan Salim when he had attempted to get rid of the Janissaries seventeen years earlier. A single battalion of the new troops, however, rushed to the scene and quickly brought the situation under control.

These repeated tests, successfully passed, delighted Muhammad 'Ali and set his bureaucratic machinery to conscript more and more fallahin. Waves of conscription followed each other in a swift, frenzied succession with no clear criteria to determine whom to conscript and whom to leave behind. In the absence of medical screening a large number of men who were rounded up had to be returned home after they were deemed unfit for military service.

By subjecting young, reluctant conscripts to strict military training, the Pasha managed finally to create a body of disciplined, reliable troops that he used to extend Cairo's control over the entire province of Egypt in a manner that had not been witnessed for centuries. Moreover, he used these troops to spread his influence over the Sudan in a way that the earlier expedition had failed to do; the Sudan became a colony. Muhammad 'Ali also employed them to establish a more permanent presence in Arabia and to extend his influence to the Yemen, where in 1819 he signed a treaty with the imam that ensured his effective control of the Red Sea.

From Istanbul, sultan Mahmud looked with envy and unease upon his *wali*'s accomplishments in Egypt. And while the Pasha tried to placate him by sending the annual tribute, by using his name in the Friday prayer, by minting coins bearing his name, and by naming the newly dug Mahmudiyya canal after him, the sultan was not fooled. For what Muhammad ʿAli had managed to do was to create within the Ottoman empire a vibrant alternative to Istanbul, the old capital that was stagnant with age-old traditions and political intrigues. Cairo still managed a far smaller proportion of the potential surplus of the Ottoman economy than Istanbul controlled, but it did so under Muhammad ʿAli in an increasingly effective way.

Most alarming for the sultan was the new army that his *wali* in Egypt had created, for this had been done while Mahmud still had his own hands tied by the Janissaries and while the empire was facing yet another military challenge from within. In 1821 a widespread revolt had broken out among the Greeks of the Morea. The revolt soon spread to the Aegean islands, and the European powers pressed the sultan to grant the Greeks their independence. The sultan rejected intervention in the internal affairs of his empire and determined to suppress the revolt. Khusrav Pasha, Muhammad ʿAli's old rival, was made grand admiral of the Ottoman navy and set about cutting the lines of communication of the Greek rebels. In desperation, and to divert the resources of his increasingly powerful *wali*, the sultan ordered Muhammad ʿAli to send troops to assist him in subduing the Greeks.

The Pasha received Mahmud's order with unease, for although he had earlier helped the sultan in Arabia it was obvious that the Greek conflict presented a much more complicated situation. Transporting the troops would require hiring or buying ships that would cost him dearly and put considerable strain on an already tight budget. In the event the Pasha acquired a fleet so large that he boasted that none had been seen like it in Muslim waters before. Another reason for the Pasha's apprehension was the realization that, unlike in the Arabian campaign, the European powers had high stakes in Greece, where they were using the sultan's Christian subjects to interfere in the empire's internal affairs.

In spite of his unease, Muhammad ʿAli had to comply with the sultan's order and only five months after receiving it he dispatched 17,000 newly trained and disciplined troops, with their food and equipment, on their first assignment. Heading the force was Ibrahim Pasha, who would prove himself as capable of leading modern troops as he had been eight years earlier in leading an Albanian and *mamluk* rabble in Arabia. Immediately after starting operations against the Greeks Ibrahim and his new regiments "caused as much alarm by defeating the Greeks as the Sultan had done by failing to do so,"[32] and his efforts were crowned in June 1827 when he took Athens. For some time, though, problems had mounted between Ibrahim and Khusrav, who was managing naval operations. Owing to the old rivalry between the two Ibrahim believed that Khusrav was not doing his best to assist his land operations. On his part Khusrav complained that Muhammad ʿAli was late in refitting and supplying the imperial fleet which had been sent to Alexandria for that purpose. Muhammad ʿAli would not tolerate such accusations and started, in turn, to ask for Khusrav's dismissal and for Ibrahim to be given a free hand in conducting the war. He threatened that unless Khusrav was dismissed he would order Ibrahim to withdraw and leave the incapable forces of the sultan to finish the war. Fifteen days after receiving this ultimatum the Porte acceded to Muhammad ʿAli's demands, and Khusrav was relieved of his post in February 1827.

During the previous year there had been serious signs that the more-or-less amicable relations between sultan and *wali* were nearing an end. When Mahmud succeeded in suppressing the Janissaries in June 1826 in what became known as the Auspicious Event, he summoned Muhammad ʿAli's agent in Istanbul, Muhammad Najib Effendi, and asked him to write to his lord in Cairo to request help in founding the sultan's new *nizami* army. He explained that it was because of Muhammad ʿAli, after all, "that we came to realize the importance of training the troops along modern lines."[33] Although the sultan gave Muhammad ʿAli credit for initiating such important reforms, the Pasha refused to help the sultan, but offered excuses: the officers in his army were better paid than their counterparts in the sultan's army, he said, and if some were sent to Istanbul the sultan's officers might get jealous and create serious friction.[34] The most he would do was send a letter to the grand vizier congratulating him on the bold move.[35]

Whether or not Muhammad ʿAli was already contemplating the likelihood of fighting the sultan's forces at some time in the future cannot be ascertained, although no evidence rules out this possibility. What is clear is that from this time onward a latent and mutual suspicion became more and more manifest. When the sultan appealed to his *wali* to help him face Russian military advances in Moldavia, the Caucasus, and eastern Anatolia, the Pasha refused unless the sultan granted him a governorship in Anatolia in return,[36] a request he well knew would not be granted.

What turned the Pasha so decisively against the sultan was the European

[32] H. W. V. Temperley, *England and the Near East: The Crimea* (London, 1964), 53.

[33] DWQ, Bahr Barra 10/123 on 25 Dhu al-Qiʿda 1241/July 2, 1826.

[34] Ahmed Lutfi Efendi, *Tarih-i Lutfi*, 8 vols. (Istanbul, 1873), I, 96.

[35] DWQ, s/1/50/6/402 on 16 Dhu al-Hijja 1241/July 22, 1826.

[36] Stanford J. Shaw and Ezel Shaw, *The History of the Ottoman Empire and Modern Turkey*, II: *Reform, Revolution and Republic, 1808–1975* (Cambridge, 1977), 31.

intervention which Muhammad ʿAli watched with increasing unease but Mahmud and his advisors characteristically dismissed as a bluff intended to intimidate them. When Ibrahim reported anxiety about the presence of a combined French–British–Russian fleet so close to the Egyptian–Turkish one in Navarino bay, the grand vizier urged him not to "take heed of the noise and clamour that the Europeans are making," and assured him that "victory does not depend on the number of ships but on the strength and conviction of men's hearts." He advised Ibrahim to ignore the feeble threats the European powers had issued to the "formidable Ottoman State."[37]

For their part, neither Muhammad ʿAli nor his son could dismiss the combined European fleet so easily. Before the fateful battle of Navarino (October 20, 1827) in which he lost his own beloved fleet, Muhammad ʿAli wrote to his agent in Istanbul a frank and rather desperate letter anticipating the disaster and saying that he was neither prepared nor willing to confront the European powers. He urged Najib Effendi to convince officials in Istanbul to accept in principle Greek independence and to seek Austrian mediation to achieve it. Convinced that the Europeans were not bluffing, he said:

We have to realize that we cannot stand in front of them, and the only possible outcome [if we do] will be sinking the entire fleet and causing the death of up to thirty or forty thousand men ... Taking the responsiblity of wasting [such numbers] is no easy task. I have, therefore, stopped sending letters to my son urging him to fight on. Wars are not won only by depending on God and trusting Him, but also by putting all possible human effort into it. [It is true, he added, that] God has ordered us in His Book to stand up to the enemy and to spare no effort in confronting him. This, however, necessitates a thorough knowledge of the art of war. Unfortunately, my dear friend, although we are men of war ... the Europeans are way ahead of us and have already put their theories of war into practice. [Then seeing that there was no way out but to grant the Greeks their independence, he added] Here I am at a loss: shall I grieve at the calamity of the Ottoman State or at my own lost effort. I am most sorrowful and anguished.[38]

On October 20, 1827, in less than three hours, the entire Ottoman fleet and most of the Egyptian one were either sunk or burnt in Navarino bay. This disaster, both Ibrahim and his father believed, was not the result of negligence or misconduct on their part but of the obstinate and arrogant refusal of the Porte to accept European mediation over Greek independence. Nor did this intransigent position change after Navarino: the Porte refused any suggestion by Ibrahim that he withdraw his troops to Egypt, and instead kept issuing unrealistic orders for campaigns against the Christian population and, if need be, to burn all villages on his way.[39] Muhammad ʿAli

[37] DWQ, Bahr Barra 12/15, on 6 Rabiʿ al-Thani 1243/October 28, 1827.
[38] DWQ, Bahr Barra 12/7, on 14 Rabiʿ al-Awwal 1243/October 6, 1827.
[39] DWQ, Bahr Barra 12/18, on 17 Rabiʿ al-Thani 1243/November 10, 1827.

refused these stubborn and unreasonable demands, and proceeded to sign a treaty with the Powers guaranteeing the safety of his son's withdrawal from the Greek mainland. To reward him for his considerable efforts in subduing the Greek revolt the sultan nonetheless gave Muhammad 'Ali the island of Crete to govern, a prize he considered unsatisfactory since it was already in his possession; Furthermore, Crete had been in a constant state of rebellion since the start of the Greek revolt. From this time onward Muhammad 'Ali resolved not to get involved in the sultan's adventures, and he set out to repair the damage he had suffered in this costly debacle.

The Greek campaign made obvious to the Pasha the serious deficiencies of his new troops. Although his soldiers were well trained and reliable, the same could not be said of their officers, many of whom had no previous military experience and had flocked to the Pasha's service for nothing more than the handsome pay he offered. In an attempt to improve the quality of his officers Muhammad 'Ali now accepted the advice of General Boyer (who had arrived in the country in 1824 at the head of a French military mission) and opened a staff college in October 1825 under another French officer, Jules Planat.[40] The lack of a well-trained cavalry had been immediately apparent to Ibrahim when he witnessed the superb performance of the French cavalry under General Maison in the Morea. After his return to Egypt he convinced his father to open a cavalry school and to create at once seven cavalry regiments. The Pasha set out with characteristic diligence to demand 2,500 horses from members of his household and his retainers; animals were imported from Syria or fetched from the Sudan. In due time the cavalry school was opened at Giza under yet another French officer, Noel Varin. To complement the work of this school a veterinary school and hospital were soon opened at Rosetta under Pierre Hamont.[41]

Most impressive, however, of the institutions the Pasha set out to create after the Greek debacle were the arsenal works of Alexandria and the new medical school at Abu Za'bal near Cairo. Following the destruction of his fleet at Navarino bay the Pasha was determined to acquire a new fleet, this time not by buying ships from foreigners but by building them in Egypt. With that purpose in mind he secured the services of a French engineer, de Cerisy, who started constructing an arsenal at Alexandria in June 1829. Besides building for the Pasha a magnificent fleet, the *liman* of Alexandria, as the arsenal came to be known, was also an infamous prison to which thousands of men and women were sent for hard labor. According to various decrees and laws of the Pasha, the *liman* was one of two places within his dominions designated as places of exile for serious and dangerous

---

[40] Planat published his impressions of the Pasha and his policies in a work considered a good source for the subject, *Histoire de la régénération de l'Egypte* (Paris, 1830).

[41] Hamont, unlike Planat, offers a very critical account of the Pasha's policies and of Clot's work especially: *L'Egypte sous Mehemet-Ali*, 2 vols. (Paris, 1843).

criminals, the second being Fazughli in the Sudan.[42] At one point the number of those interned in the *liman* was as high as six thousand.[43] So deep was the impression made by this prison that the word "*liman*," which in Turkish means nothing more than a port or harbor, came to be synonymous with "prison." It retains this meaning in Egyptian Arabic.[44]

The other important institution established in the wake of the Greek debacle was the Abu Za'bal hospital, founded in 1827. This was intended mainly to care for the needs of officers and soldiers of the nearby training-camp of Jihad Abad at Khanqah to the north of Cairo. The hospital was part of a large and ambitious project to meet the medical needs that had become apparent in the Sudan campaign and, to a lesser extent, in the Greek campaign. (Abu Za'bal was founded in the same year as another hospital, the Mahmudiyya in Alexandria, which was to treat sailors and marines as well as inmates of the *liman*.) Abu Za'bal, later famous as the Qasr al-Aini school after it moved to Cairo in 1837, was the first hospital to function also as a medical school. Its founder was a certain Dr. Clot from Marseilles, who had arrived in Egypt in 1825. Soon after his arrival he had convinced the Pasha of the need to train Arabic-speaking doctors if an indigenous medical profession was to be established, and students from al-Azhar were recruited to form the nucleus of a new medical corps. Clot set down a blueprint according to which students would be sent to the school for a period of five years, after which they would be given medical ranks and attached to military units under the supervision of European doctors. Infantry and cavalry regiments were each to have one European doctor assisted by two or three Egyptian *hakims*.[45]

These were not the only institutions that the Pasha founded to enhance his fighting capabilities and to improve his chances of winning a possible confrontation with the sultan. Numerous factories were built to turn out what were essentially war products: footwear, fezzes and uniforms for soldiers, sails for ships, guns and cannon. Other industrial institutions included sugar refineries, rice mills, tanneries, and indigo factories. Egypt being deficient in wood and coal, the main motive power for these establishments was supplied by oxen, mules, and other animals, and when these were in short supply by men, women, and children. These people were often

---

[42] See *Qanun al-filaha*, enacted in 1829, especially articles 18, 20, 27, and 56. The law is published in Filib Jallad (ed.), *Qamus al-idara wa'l-qada*, 4 vols. (Alexandria, 1890–92), III, 1323–29. See also Amin Sami, *Taqwim al-nil wa asr Muhammad 'Ali* (Cairo, 1928), II, 454, letter dated 12 Rajab 1251/November 2, 1835 concerning robbers and highwaymen.

[43] DWQ, Diwan Khidiwi 2/308, 6 Muharram 1251/May 14, 1835.

[44] *Liman* seems to have undergone a transitional meaning now lost, that of corvée or forced labor. See Wilkinson, *An Account*, I, 431.

[45] Clot refused to give his Arabic-speaking students the title "doctor." For a summary of this blueprint see Sami, *Taqwim*, II, 383–84.

dragged from their villages and tattooed on the arm with the factory's name, a practice that was also adopted in the navy to catch deserters. The managers of these establishments were initially mainly Europeans who, like the officers in the army, often lacked skill and experience and who flocked to Egypt seeking employment in the Pasha's expanding service. The lack of efficient motive power, the unskilled, coerced labor, and the inexperienced, often greedy managers hindered the Pasha's "industrial experiment." As a result, many institutions were brought to a standstill, leaving machines and equipment to rust and clog with dust and sand. Rather than closing them down, Muhammad 'Ali decided that the main reason they were not showing a profit was their expensive European managers, and in characteristic manner he set out to replace them with cheaper and more docile personnel. He sent hundreds of young men, "Arabs" as well as "Turks," on educational missions to Europe, mostly to France, to acquire the necessary skills to run these and other institutions.[46]

The considerable cost of these establishments was met mostly by siphoning off profits from the agricultural sector. Specifically, by abolishing the *iltizam* in the early years of his reign and by expanding monopolies to include most commodities produced in the countryside, the Pasha was able to increase his profits and then use them to invest. Most significant in this process was the introduction in 1821 of a new brand of cotton that soon became famous world-wide for its long staple, something that enhanced its competitiveness in European, and especially British, markets owing to its suitability for textile manufacturing. Immediately after its successful introduction, cultivation was expanded to cover huge tracts of land, especially in the Delta, which was practically turned into a huge cotton plantation. Sale of this most lucrative crop was monopolized by the Pasha, who used his considerable profits, which in good years contributed between one-fifth and one-quarter of all revenue, to finance his military and industrial enterprises.[47]

These projects were not made possible only by availability of new sources of income. Throughout this period, drawing from old Ottoman bureaucratic traditions as well as from the centralized French model, a more efficient system of administration was instituted with a clear chain of command, at the top of which was the Pasha himself. Mention has already been made of the abolition of the *iltizam* system whereby chaotic, arbitrary, and frequent tax levies were replaced by a more direct and efficient system of raising taxes

---

[46] For a biographical list of these students see Umar Tusun, *al-Ba'athat al-'ilmiyya fi ahd Muhammad 'Ali thumma fi ahdayy 'Abbas al-awwal wa Sa'id* (Alexandria, 1934).

[47] Roger Owen, *Cotton and the Egyptian economy, 1820–1914: A Study in Trade and Development* (Oxford, 1969), 40. *Cf.* Cuno, *The Pasha's Peasants*, 118, who states that profits from all monopolized goods, including cotton, contributed no more than 19–22 percent of total revenue.

from the countryside. A new structure of central as well as provincial government was also established. Accordingly, business in the central government bureaucracy was conducted on two levels, that of deliberative councils (*majalis*) and bureaucratic departments (*diwans*). These administrative bodies, however, had no independent authority; they were set up merely to give recommendations to the Pasha who reserved for himself the right to take final decisions. On the provincial level, the country was divided in 1826 into twenty-four departments (*qisms*), fourteen in Lower Egypt and ten in Upper Egypt. A rigid hierarchical structure was employed to clarify the duties and responsibilities of every official from the *mudir al-mudiriyya* (director of a province) to the *shaykh al-balad* (village headman).[48] Equally important, and in order to have tighter control over the fallahin, a large number of whom were deserting their villages in a desperate attempt to evade the Pasha's seemingly insatiable demands for army, navy, factories, and public works, a tight security system was instituted. This was carried out through new penal codes,[49] by tattooing workers and sailors, by spreading spies (*bassassin*) throughout the countryside and urban centers, and by introducing a sort of identity card (*tazkaras*) that men were required to carry, especially on visits to urban centers.[50]

The effect of the policies implemented in the second phase of Muhammad ʿAli's long career was deeply felt by the population of Egypt, and above all by the peasantry. In addition to the already heavy burden of corvée, higher taxes and the monopolies system, the creation of the new army subjected them to something close to universal conscription, a practice seen as a heavy tax exacted by an oppressive and alien regime. What made matters worse was that in spite of the Pasha's initial order limiting the conscription period to three years, and as a result of nearly unceasing war, these men were seldom released and, in practice, conscription seemed destined to last a lifetime until Ibrahim suggested in 1835 that it be limited to fifteen years.[51] Furthermore, the combination of conscription and corvée contributed significantly to the breakdown of families; women, like men, paid a high price for the Pasha's ambitious projects. Traditional family production came under severe pressure and many women had to accept employment under the increasingly harsh conditions of the Pasha's factories. A sign of the pressures put on women to provide for their families after the departure of

---

[48] Rivlin, *The Agricultural Policy*, 77, 87–88. See also *Qanun al-filaha* for an elaboration of these duties.

[49] *Qanun al-filaha* is the prime example of this new kind of legislation. For a comparison with penal legislation in the central lands of the empire see Gabriel Baer, "Tanzimat in Egypt," in Gabriel Baer, *Studies in the Social History of Modern Egypt* (Chicago, 1969), 109–32.

[50] DWQ, s/1/48/4/226 on 5 Rabiʿ al-Awwal 1249/July 23, 1833.

[51] DWQ, Sham 31/6 on 7 Muharram 1251/May 5, 1835.

the prime breadwinner was the number of women forced into prostitution, which spread alarmingly in the urban centers in the early 1830s. Worried about the spread of diseases, the authorities banned prostitution from urban centers in 1834.[52]

On the other hand, those fortunate students who were sent to government schools or those even more fortunate whom the Pasha sent to Europe found upon finishing their education that they had improved their lot considerably and joined the Pasha's various educational and medical establishments. Together these doctors, teachers, and engineers would form the nucleus of a professional elite, a new middle class that in due time would replace the 'ulama', *ashraf*, and urban merchants between the masses and their rulers.

The projects undertaken during the second phase of Muhammad 'Ali career allowed him to attract even more members of his family and friends to reside in Egypt and join his expanding service. Specifically the creation of his new professional army offered lucrative employment. Examples abound of such figures who together formed a loyal elite and whose fortunes were closely connected to the Pasha and his policies. Besides his three sons Ibrahim, Tusun, and Isma'il, all of whom had military positions, his grandson 'Abbas (Tusun's son) would be appointed first lieutenant, governor of Cairo, and then inspector general. His nephews Ahmad and Ibrahim Yakan, besides leading military campaigns (the first in Arabia, the second in the Yemen), were also assigned administrative tasks as provincial governors. Another nephew, Muhammad Sharif, held various important positions throughout his uncle's reign: these included governorship of the Sa'id, governorship of Syria (after it had fallen to his uncle's forces), and director of finances. Sons-in-law also occupied important positions: Muharram Bey (married to Tawhida) was appointed head of the navy, Yusuf Kamil (married to Zaynab) was director of the department of civil affairs and of the viceregal department, and Muhammad Bey the *daftardar* (married to Nazli) was appointed treasurer.

These and others not so intimately connected to the Pasha were new-comers to Egypt, spoke Turkish and knew little if any Arabic, and therefore had little connection to their new country. They were dependent on the Pasha for their livelihood and well-being and tried to appease him as best they could in order to enjoy the financial and social privileges that he bestowed on them. For his part, Muhammad 'Ali tried his best to strengthen his ties with these people and prevented them from acquiring land lest they forge links with Egyptian society. Through them he managed not only to create a reliable and trustworthy elite but also to organize the country in an absolute manner that concentrated all power in him and left key decisions in

---

[52] DWQ, s/2/32/5/72 on 18 Muharram 1250/May 28, 1834.

his hands. Through these tactics "a personally dependent elite helped make one-man rule possible."[53]

The final showdown: military expansion, 1829–41

Having consolidated his grip over Egypt and its inhabitants, increased its productivity, and completed his military preparations, the Pasha was ready for a final confrontation with the sultan, which was needed to transform his hard-won accomplishments into firm legal realities that would secure his tenure as governor of Egypt. For a while, though, Muhammad ʿAli flirted with the idea of using his newly structured military machine to expand westward. Throughout 1829 the French consul-general, Drovetti, suggested to the Pasha the annexation of Tripoli, Tunis, and Algiers. This, Drovetti believed (and it seems he was joined by Polignac, the French minister for foreign affairs), would allow the French to take revenge against the dey of Algiers (who had insulted the French consul there by striking him with a fly-whisk). The French were keen on expanding their influence in the Mediterranean but were apprehensive of the possible British reaction; it was thought that a force led by Muhammad ʿAli could avert confrontation with their old European adversary. In return, Drovetti promised the Pasha that France would supply men and ships to compensate for his lost fleet. In the event, however, the Pasha decided the idea was too risky and would distract him from his real objectives. For he clearly saw his proper course of action not in the west but to the east; it was in Syria, not the Barbary states, that Muhammad ʿAli's interests lay.

The reasons for Muhammad ʿAli's interest in Syria are varied, and may be traced to the beginning of his reign. As early as 1810 Muhammad ʿAli showed that he could influence affairs in Syria when he intervened with the Porte on behalf of the *wali* of Damascus, Yusuf Gench Pasha, whom the Porte had dismissed: as a result of his intercession Yusuf was pardoned, although he was not reinstated. In 1812 Muhammad ʿAli confided to the British consul his designs on the Levant. The following years, while his forces were facing difficulties in subduing the Wahhabis, he wrote to the grand vizier that his task would be made much easier if he was given the *wilayas* of Syria in addition to Egypt. In 1821 he again interfered in Syrian affairs when he pleaded with the Porte to pardon ʿAbdallah Pasha of Sidon (whom he would later fight and defeat): his mediation led to ʿAbdallah Pasha's reinstatement in his pashalik. Throughout the Greek war Muhammad ʿAli asked for Syria as compensation for his costly efforts in helping the sultan.

---

[53] F. Robert Hunter, *Egypt under the Khedives, 1805–1879: From Household Government to Bureaucracy* (Pittsburgh, 1984), 27.

This deep-seated interest in Syria had various causes. For one thing Syria was rich in wood, which was in short supply in Egypt and badly needed for Muhammad 'Ali's intended navy. Second, although Egypt was more populous than Syria, the Pasha's policies had put enormous strain on the Egyptian population and he was in clear need of an extra source of manpower. He may also have been interested in the tax potential of Syria, in acquiring the customs revenue of its important ports, and in using it as a captive market for his monopolies. Above all, if the sultan were to attempt to dislodge him from Egypt by force, Syria was the likely base from which such force would come; the Pasha needed a buffer area to separate Egypt from the central lands of the Ottoman empire. However, it was the Greek debacle that pushed the Pasha to an act of outright rebellion against the sultan; after exerting all his efforts for the sultan he had been rewarded with a small, rebellious island (Crete) and denied the province he had long coveted and had been requesting for years.

After dismissing the idea of collaborating with the French to capture the Barbary states, the Pasha set his war machine in motion for what was to prove his most daring and best-organized military adventure. Conscription was carried out at a rate that alarmed European observers and set them wondering about the Pasha's true intentions. The *liman* of Alexandria witnessed frenzied activity, and the military factories were geared to maximum production. Even the Friday holiday was canceled to meet the Pasha's targets. The army was scheduled to leave in the summer of 1831 but was delayed until the autumn owing to the appearance of cholera in Cairo; disease took a heavy toll on the civilian population, but Dr. Clot managed to limit its impact on the army. (He was rewarded with the title of bey.) Finally, on November 2, 1831, the crucial hour came. Using the pretext of some 6,000 peasants from the Delta who had fled to 'Abdallah Pasha to evade taxes and the corvée, Muhammad 'Ali ordered two expeditions, one by land and the other by sea, to move on Syria. The combined force totaled some 30,000 troops. Ibrahim Pasha landed at Jaffa and soon swept with this massive force through all the major towns of Syria, with the exception of the formidable fortress of Acre, which was besieged and captured only after six months of constant bombardment (May 27, 1832).

The Ottoman forces were no match for Ibrahim's disciplined army, and defeats followed in alarming and embarrassing succession. Ibrahim crossed the Taurus mountains and in July 1832 captured the strategic cities of Tarsus and Adana in southern Anatolia. Alarmed at this rapid and unprecedented advance, the sultan summoned yet another army under the grand vizier, Muhammad Rashid Pasha, a protégé of Khusrav, to save the empire. The two armies met on the plain north of Konya, in the heart of Anatolia, and Ibrahim inflicted a heavy defeat and captured the grand vizier. Finding the way to Istanbul wide open and with no major force left to oppose him, Ibrahim reached Kutahia, a day's march from the capital.

At this crucial hour Ibrahim Pasha pressed his father for permission to march into the capital of the empire and declare his independence. Muhammad ʿAli, however, was more cautious than his son and instructed him to halt his advance. The Pasha remained ambivalent about the hostilities he had initiated against the sultan, and he feared the reaction of the European powers to the break-up of the empire. In spite of undertaking a blatant act of aggression against the sultan, and even after the spectacular victories that his son had achieved, Muhammad ʿAli was still not willing to be declared a rebel. "Ottoman" in culture and sentiments, a native Turkish speaker, well-versed in the history of the empire and well-informed about events in the capital, the Pasha was at heart an Ottoman in an Ottoman world, a world he was endangering in a grave and unprecedented manner. Even after initiating hostilities against the Ottoman sultan, he could still not contemplate independence. When Halil Pasha, the commander of the Ottoman navy, arrived at Alexandria in January 1833 with peace offers from the sultan, Muhammad ʿAli did not raise the issue of independence. It was Ibrahim who repeatedly urged his father to ask for independence and assume the two crucial attributes of sovereignty: ordering his name to be used in Friday prayers and minting coins with his name on them. His father repeatedly replied that his "Muhammad ʿAli-ness" was enough of a title for him. Indeed, he wrote one letter after another to officials in Istanbul urging them to intercede on his behalf to ask the sultan's forgiveness *and* to be given legal title to the lands he had acquired by force.

The Pasha's hesitancy in negotiations was the result also of his unease about possible European reactions. After the sultan had lost his army and his grand vizier in the battle of Konya, he immediately sought British assistance, and specifically asked for a naval squadron to be sent to defend the capital. The British cabinet, however, was divided and turned down the sultan's plea, much to the chagrin of Palmerston, the foreign secretary. Having been denied British assistance, the sultan turned to the Russians, who were only too eager to send a naval force to Istanbul. They also sent an envoy to Muhammad ʿAli, General Mouarviev, who arrived at Alexandria only a week before Halil and delivered a strong verbal threat that Russia would oppose him by force if he persisted in his advance on Istanbul. The French, for their part, sent him messages of support in his struggle with the sultan. About the position of the one major power that mattered most and which he had tried hardest to appease and to win to his side, Britain, he was unsure. Although the British consul, John Barker, strongly opposed the Pasha's aggression, Muhammad ʿAli suspected that these remonstrations reflected the consul's own opinion and not that of Palmerston.

The result of European disunity, of the difference between Muhammad

'Ali and his son about the next move, and of the Pasha's own ambivalence about his rebellion was an inconclusive settlement that left no party completely satisfied. The "peace of Kutahia," reached in May 1833, retracted the sultan's earlier declaration of Muhammad 'Ali as a rebel and reinstated him in his *wilaya* of Egypt in addition to granting him the Hijaz and Crete. Ibrahim was named as *wali* of the Syrian *wilayas* of Acre, Damascus, Tripoli, and Aleppo. In addition Ibrahim was named as *muhassil*, that is tax-collector, of the province of Adana in southern Anatolia. Thus the Pasha managed to secure from the sultan official recognition of his new expanded power and dominions. But this recognition had to be renewed annually by the sultan, something that left the Pasha subject to the whims of the sultan and the intrigues of his courtiers, chief among whom was Khusrav Pasha, Muhammad 'Ali's old nemesis. In addition, the Pasha was to continue to pay an annual tribute to Istanbul, the size of which proved the subject of acrimonious debate for years to come. As a result, the settlement that ended the first round of direct military confrontation between Muhammad 'Ali and Mahmud was a compromise that left none of the principal parties satisfied: "The Sultan had suffered the vexation of a defeat by a contumacious pasha; the western powers were annoyed at the opening which Ibrahim's victories had offered to the Russians; while the Russians were disappointed at having been unable to entrench themselves more securely at Constantinople."[54]

After a year of military operations the Pasha regrouped and prepared for the second round which, given the inconclusive nature of the Kutahia settlement, was inevitable. First he set out to incorporate his much-coveted province, Syria, into his administration. This he found difficult to do, however, since the Syrians resisted his attempts to disarm them and when Ibrahim tried to conscript them a major revolt broke out that necessitated Muhammad 'Ali's presence to subdue it. Nevertheless, even after managing to quell the rebellion and extend his monopolies, and after he had begun to exploit Syria's considerable natural resources, the Pasha's administration there never managed to cover the cost of occupation.[55]

Back in Egypt, the Pasha issued more orders to raise men from the already exhausted and often underpopulated villages. More schools and factories were opened to meet the army's demands. New batches of students were sent to Europe to acquire the skills needed to run the Pasha's various institutions. One of the most impressive accomplishments of this third phase of the Pasha's reign was in the field of medical reform. Realizing that Egypt faced a shortage of manpower owing in part to a high infant mortality rate in turn caused by, among other things, a high incidence of smallpox among children and a high rate of stillbirths, Clot Bey suggested a wide-ranging

---

[54] Dodwell, *The Founder*, 122–23.
[55] See DWQ, s/5/47/2/220 on 19 Jumadi al-Thani 1255/August 31, 1839.

vaccination program to eradicate smallpox. In 1832 a school for midwives was opened in Cairo to create a female medical corps that would enable the authorities to vaccinate children at their homes. Moreover, it was realized that traditional midwives, the *dayat*, were not strict in reporting births, and Clot convinced the Pasha that these *dayat* used unscientific, superstitious techniques that led to high rates of stillbirths. In the wake of the heavy cholera epidemic of 1831 a board of health and a quarantine service were established, and following the plague of 1835 free clinics were opened in urban centers which had as one of their functions the conduct of postmortems to identify plague and suspicious cases. In 1837 a new hospital was established in Cairo which, unlike Qasr al-Aini, was exclusively for the civilian population. Named *al-isbitaliya al-mulkiyya*, the civilian hospital, it was located in the rich quarter of Azbakiyya and had a ward for the treatment of women. Most significantly, it also had a pediatric ward that administered smallpox vaccinations. Thousands of children were sent there for vaccination every month by the shaykhs of the quarters (*mashayikh al-harat*). In addition to these impressive accomplishments, the Abu Zaʿbal school managed in 1837, on the eve of moving to its new location at Qasr al-Aini, to train a total of 420 medical students, many of whom went to France to finish their medical training and came back to assume important positions in the expanding medical service.

Medical reform, therefore, seems to have been one of the most successful of the Pasha's policies and through it the authorities managed to control the devastating plague and cholera epidemics that had ravaged Egypt.[56] Even in this field, though, success was qualified. It was often reported, for example, that owing to time constraints, young doctors were discharged from medical school and sent to their posts, mostly military, before they had finished their proper courses of training. Moreover, while the Qasr al-Aini school was in itself a well-organized medical establishment, there were no preparatory schools founded to supply it with qualified students. Preparatory schools were in fact always founded after the advanced secondary schools, in a manner that reflected the Pasha's characteristic way of reacting to crises rather than following a well-thought-out plan. Nor were these medical institutions spared the usual problems of the Pasha's establishments: bad management, serious bureaucratic complications, constant fighting between Turkish-speaking officials and their European and Arabic-speaking subordinates, and a perpetual fear of the Pasha's wrath.

Educational reforms undertaken in the 1830s, like medical reforms, were directly or indirectly linked to military needs. While Muhammad ʿAli opposed the idea of education for its own sake, he was in desperate need of

---

[56] For a review of these reforms see LaVerne Kuhnke, *Lives at Risk: Public Health in Nineteenth-Century Egypt* (Berkeley, 1990).

trained personnel to run the various establishments being formed. The preparatory schools opened in Cairo and the provinces were aimed not at spreading primary education among the masses, but at feeding with literate students the secondary schools that had already been established. The textbooks required for these schools were printed at the Bulaq Press, which had been established in 1820. In its early years most of the press's output directly served the army, with more than half the books printed between 1820 and 1840 being military training manuals and compendia of laws.[57] Nevertheless, the Bulaq Press also published numerous medical and other scientific works, in addition to more general books translated from European languages. Presiding over this impressive work of translation was Rifaʿa Rafiʿ al-Tahtawi, who had been sent to France in 1826 as an imam on an educational mission and who later (1836) founded a school for translation and a bureau for translation (in 1841). Connected to these reforms was publication in 1828 of an official gazette, *al-Waqaʾiʿ al-Misriyya*, which, by carrying mainly news of the Pasha's administration and published in Turkish with an Arabic translation, was intended to impress a wider Ottoman readership with the Pasha's accomplishments and the superiority of his administration over that of the sultan in Istanbul.

The schools, like the hospitals, were not without their problems. In addition to the bureaucratic complications that plagued them, students seldom finished the required period of education and were often rushed to secondary institutions unprepared. Young boys were dragged to these new preparatory schools by Turkish-speaking officials in military uniforms who had been sent from Cairo to collect them, often against the wishes of parents who feared that their children were being drafted for the army. In general, little effort was ever made to convince the public, be they parents, village shaykhs, religious scholars, or community leaders, of the logic of the Pasha's new institutions; local opinion and regional sentiments were constantly dismissed as backward, superstitious, and as hampering "development" attempts by the authorities.

The projects put a heavy burden on the Pasha's finances, and by the mid-1830s it had become glaringly obvious that he had extended Egypt beyond its limits. The optimistic years of the preceding decade, which witnessed an all-time peak in revenue of 100m francs, gave way to more difficult times caused by a fall in the price of cotton, collapse in the administrative system, and by widespread opposition to his policies. Combined, these factors led to a 25 percent decline in revenue in 1833.[58] Rather than trim expenses, the Pasha decided to inaugurate yet another massive public works project, huge

---

[57] Jamal al-Din al-Shayyal, *Tarikh al-tarjama wa'l-haraka al-thaqafiyya fi asr Muhammad ʿAli* (Cairo, 1951), appendices 1, 2.

[58] Douin (ed.), *Boislecomte*, 125.

barrages at the apex of the Nile Delta to regulate the level of the water in the two branches of the Nile, which it was hoped would increase agricultural productivity in the Delta. Introduction of long-staple cotton and its widespread cultivation in Lower Egypt had necessitated new canals, the *sayfi* canals, deep enough to carry water in the summer months when the Nile was at its lowest levels. These canals had to be periodically cleared of the silt accumulating in them, a process that required more and more laborers at a time when the countryside's manpower had already been stretched beyond its limits. The solution, the Pasha was convinced, lay in accepting the old recommendation of the French engineers under Napoleon, of building a barrage at the point of bifurcation of the Nile north of Cairo to guarantee a steady flow of water regardless of the flood. The Pasha approved the findings of his French chief engineer, Linant, and ordered him to take the required stones from the masonry of the Pyramids, something Linant succeeded in avoiding. In the event, though, work on the project, which started in a confused manner in 1834, was called off two years later, resumed in 1847, and finally finished in 1861.

Rather than ease the Pasha's economic difficulties, this ambitious project added to them and by 1837 his financial situation was critical. Revenue had already reached an all-time low for the period four years earlier, in 1833, and a small increase in the price of cotton in 1834 helped to improve matters only slightly; Egypt was hard hit by the international economic crisis of 1836. Most importantly, though, the heavy conscription and increasing pauperization of the peasants seriously affected the agricultural sector which, between taxes and profits from the sale of monopolized goods, had contributed three-quarters of total revenue. Realizing that his system of controlling agricultural production had failed, a system that had been effectively based on turning the whole country into a huge government farm run by him and his cumbersome bureaucratic administration, Muhammad 'Ali started in 1837 to grant large parcels of land, *ib'adiyyat*, to members of his household and to Turkish-speaking officials in the army and civil administration. This marked a clear reversal of his previous policy of preventing Turkish-speaking immigrants "from becoming proprietors and creating for themselves a personal leverage over the population," as he himself had told a distinguished French visitor.[59] To retain some kind of control over these lands, the Pasha instituted administrative controls whereby the new landlords were forced to supply agricultural products at prices he set down. In other words, while 1837 witnessed an easing of control over land ownership, the same cannot be said regarding monopolies policy. In any case, the situation of the peasants did not improve, since the new landlords were less lenient regarding the collecting of taxes. And even

[59] *Ibid.*, 111.

this new policy did not improve the situation: in 1839 taxes were at least one year in arrears, and sometimes two and three years' taxes were owed.[60]

In addition to disaffection caused by the serious structural problems of his various projects, the Pasha and his administration faced deep resentment and opposition from the population at large. Most alarmingly, opposition was noticeable in the army where it often took the dramatic form of young men maiming themselves to avoid conscription. Equally serious was the steady wave of desertion which in the mid-1830s had reached the impressive figure of 60,000 – this in an army that the most exaggerated estimates put at slightly over twice this figure. In spite of all these problems Muhammad 'Ali refused to curtail his ambition; by 1838 he had started to voice to European consuls his desire to be recognized as an independent ruler and to cast off Ottoman authority altogether, something he knew must lead to a new military confrontation with the sultan. This alarmed the European powers: if Muhammad 'Ali were declared independent by Mahmud, then the sultan's empire itself would be gravely endangered. If the sick man of Europe were to be declared dead, an inter-European scramble would ensue for his possessions.

Alarmed at his rebellious *wali*'s increased military activity the sultan sent his foreign minister, Mustafa Rashid Pasha, to Britain to seek assistance in the event of a military confrontation with Muhammad 'Ali. Palmerston, once more foreign secretary, refused any military assistance unless the Pasha struck first or declared independence. The Porte's policy, therefore, lay in provoking Ibrahim's forces in Syria and in trying to provoke the Syrian population into outright rebellion against Muhammad 'Ali's rule.

In the event the Porte's policy failed and the Syrians proved too cowed by Ibrahim's iron fist to rise against their occupiers. On June 24, 1839 at Nezib, north of Aleppo, Ibrahim once again showed his military genius by inflicting a heavy defeat on the Ottoman army. Before news of this disaster had reached Istanbul, Mahmud II died, a bitter and defeated man. As if these calamities were not enough, the entire Ottoman fleet now sailed to Alexandria and defected to Muhammad 'Ali. This spectacle resulted from the Pasha's bribing of the Ottoman grand admiral, Ahmad Fawzi, who had feared that if his fleet remained at Istanbul the *sir'askar* (Turkish *serasker*, commander-in-chief of the Ottoman forces), Muhammad Khusrav, would have handed it over to the Russians.

In less than a month, therefore, the Ottomans had lost their army, navy, and sultan, and Muhammad 'Ali had emerged as the most powerful man in the empire. At his disposal was a huge army that had been successful in all its major battles, a combined Ottoman–Egyptian navy that stood a good chance of meeting a possible European threat, and a large number of

[60] Cuno, *The Pasha's Peasants*, 120.

retainers and "followers" in the capital of the empire itself who were ready to press his demands on the new sultan, ʿAbd al-Majid, a boy of sixteen. At the crucial moment, however, when Muhammad ʿAli awaited an invitation to Istanbul to accept magnanimously "peace offers" from his defeated sultan, he received instead an ultimatum from his bitter old rival, Khusrav Pasha, telling him to cede back the lands he had acquired by force. Khusrav spoke now in his new capacity as grand vizier, a position to which he had elevated himself after snatching the imperial seals during Mahmud's funeral and appointing himself *sadrazam*.

What saved the young sultan and his empire was not the grand vizier who, as effective as his dramatic gesture proved to be, would not have been able to withstand Muhammad ʿAli's formidable pressure, but the unified position that Europe, orchestrated by Britain, for the first time assumed in the confrontation between Muhammad ʿAli and the Porte. On July 27, 1839 representatives of the five European powers (Britain, France, Russia, Prussia, and Austria) handed the grand vizier a joint note asking him not to reach a final determination of the conflict "without their concurrence."[61] This gave Khusrav the breathing space he needed, and with a united Europe behind him he pressed Muhammad ʿAli to return the Ottoman fleet and hand back the lands he had acquired by force.

Coordinating this united European stance in the months to come would be Britain. Palmerston's hostility to Muhammad ʿAli had begun six years earlier when the Pasha's first Syrian war had forced Mahmud II to seek assistance from the Russians, thus giving them a golden opportunity to land their forces in Istanbul. As a further price for protection against Muhammad ʿAli the Russians had forced the sultan to sign the Hunkar Iskelesi treaty in July 1833, which had a secret clause allowing Russian ships, to the exclusion of all other foreign ships, to enter the Sea of Marmara. When Palmerston had learned of this treaty he was enraged not so much because of the secret clause but because of the stipulation that both signatories would consult before taking steps in foreign affairs. This meant, as far as Palmerston was concerned, that "the Russian Ambassador becomes the chief cabinet advisor to the Sultan." Palmerston's suspicion of Russian designs on the Ottoman empire was further fueled by the strong anti-Russian feelings in the British cabinet and among members of parliament and the public at large; above all it was fueled by the acrimoniously Russophobic reports of his ambassador in Istanbul, Ponsonby, who constantly warned against what he feared most and suspected strongly – an alliance between Russia and Muhammad ʿAli.

Palmerston was also fed regular reports from agents in India, the Persian

[61] For the text of this note and related documents see J. C. Hurewitz (ed.), *The Middle East and North Africa in World Politics: A Documentary Record*, 2nd ed., 2 vols., I, *European Expansion, 1535–1914* (New Haven, 1975), 268ff.

Gulf, and the Yemen, all warning against Muhammad 'Ali's expansion in Arabia. The British were eager to find safer and shorter routes to India now that steam navigation had proved technically and commercially feasible. By the 1830s it was hoped that naval communications with India, both for passengers and for mail, could exploit the new technology and use the Red Sea route. This required coaling stations along the route, but it soon became evident that Muhammad 'Ali had converted the Red Sea into an Egyptian lake. The other route to India considered for possible development in the mid-1830s was via the Euphrates. Here again Palmerston saw his efforts frustrated, this time by Ibrahim's troops, who did their best to thwart attempts to build two British steamships on the river.

Above all it was Muhammad 'Ali's military expansion and repeated confrontations with the sultan that alarmed Palmerston. For these, he believed, brought the Ottoman sultan and Russian czar closer to each other at the expense of the British empire in Asia. Trying to fathom the Pasha's intentions, Palmerston sent an emissary, John Bowring, to Egypt to report on the Pasha's policies and administration. From the report Bowring made after a year in Egypt, Palmerston deduced that it was the Pasha's monopolies policy that had allowed him to siphon off profits from the agricultural sector to build such a powerful military machine.[62] Palmerston was therefore determined to attack these monopolies at the base of Muhammad 'Ali's military might.

An opportunity arose when Mustafa Rashid, the Ottoman foreign minister, visited London in 1838 seeking Palmerston's promise of military assistance against Muhammad 'Ali. Although he failed in this respect, he agreed with Palmerston to strike at the Pasha's monopolies that threatened both empires' interests. The result was the 1838 Balta Liman treaty between the Porte and Britain, banning monopolies throughout the Ottoman empire. This naturally affected a considerable portion of the sultan's own revenues, but the Porte saw this as a fair price to pay to curtail the rebellious *wali*'s power. In the following year, 1839, at the height of the crisis between Muhammad 'Ali and the empire, Mustafa Rashid proved once again to be Palmerston's man in Istanbul. By drafting the Gulhane Edict and presenting it to the young sultan 'Abd al-Majid, Rashid showed that he was willing to introduce liberal principles of equality before the law, freedom of religious practice, and educational, legal, and economic reforms. These reforms, Palmerston believed, were necessary if ever the Ottoman empire was to protect its territorial integrity and face Russia's constant attempts to expand southward toward British possessions in India. In short, behind Palmerston's opposition to Muhammad 'Ali was not fear of the nascent power of

[62] Sir John Bowring, "Report on Egypt and Candia," *Parliamentary Papers: Reports from Commissioners*, 21 (1840), 44–45.

Egyptian industry or the closing off of Egypt's markets to British commodities, as some historians have argued.[63] Rather, Palmerston was convinced that the Pasha's policies endangered the Ottoman empire and threw it into the arms of Russia, the only European power that could directly threaten British possessions in Asia.

These were the reasons that informed Palmerston's policy toward Muhammad ʿAli in the crucial years 1839–41. As a result of British pressure, Muhammad ʿAli was forced to comply with the sultan's demands in spite of the latter's military defeat. After a year of tense deadlock over the "Egyptian question," while the Pasha refused to return the fleet or withdraw his troops and, on the other hand, the sultan refused to grant him independence, Palmerston intervened and called a conference in London in July 1840. The "Convention for the Pacification of the Levant" gave the Pasha an ultimatum to withdraw from Syria, Adana, Crete, and Arabia. When the Pasha still refused to comply, a British force landed at Beirut in September, defeated Ibrahim, and forced him to withdraw to Egypt. By December the Pasha had no choice but to accept the conditions of the British-led European coalition. On June 1, 1841 the sultan issued a *firman* naming Muhammad ʿAli governor of Egypt for life and granting his male descendants hereditary rights to office. In addition, the *firman* stipulated that the Pasha reduce his army to 18,000 troops in peacetime and, in a clear reference to the Balta Liman treaty of 1838, that "all the treaties concluded and to be concluded between my Sublime Porte and the friendly Powers shall be completely executed in the Province of Egypt likewise."

With this *firman* the most dramatic chapter in Muhammad ʿAli's career came to an end. Egyptian and French historians have for the most part argued that the *firman* frustrated "Egypt's" attempts to gain independence and prevented her from assuming a leading role in the eastern Mediterranean. The hostile policies of Britain, they argue, were dictated by its anxiety over the Pasha's increasingly independent role and his ambitious economic reforms which were closing off the Egyptian market to British goods by instituting a well-integrated import-substitution program. As attractive as this viewpoint is, it fails to account for the fact that the value of British exports had increased more than tenfold during Muhammad ʿAli's reign,[64] and that British merchants had already been treated in a privileged manner. Their constant complaint was not that their commodities could not be imported into the country, but that they were prevented from dealing directly with producers and consumers and had to conduct their commercial operations through the Pasha. Furthermore, this view ignores the fact that

---

[63] The most recent example of this attitude is Afaf Lutfi al-Sayyid Marsot, *Egypt in the reign of Muhammad Ali* (Cambridge, 1984).

[64] Roger Owen, *The Middle East in the World Economy, 1800–1914* (London, 1981), 85.

the Pasha's "industrial" experiment had fallen to ruins before the Anglo-Ottoman economic agreement of 1838 and not after it. An industrial experiment that was based on no more than seven or eight steam engines could not have been judged by the British government as a serious threat to the mighty industries of Manchester and Liverpool. Above all, though, this view overlooks the fact that Muhammad 'Ali's was not a "national" experiment at development or independence, but a reckless exercise by an ambitious governor of an Ottoman province to expand his control and make sure that his children would enjoy the benefits of his reforms. In this respect the 1841 *firman* does not so much show Britain's determined desire to frustrate "Egypt's" independence and development as it does the crowning success of the Pasha's long career. Through this *firman* Muhammad 'Ali was granted what he had always desired and what he had been fighting so long to achieve, the promise that Egypt and its inhabitants would be given to him and his descendants to govern.

Retrenchment and reprieve, 1841–48

The last period of the Pasha's reign saw him adjusting to the new political situation as defined in the 1841 *firman* and maximizing his profits from it. Having returned Syria, Crete, and Arabia to the sultan, and at the same time feeling finally secure in his position as *wali* after recognition as such by the European powers, he set out to improve his relations with the sultan. For his part, although the governorship of Egypt was no longer his to give to any of his pashas and retainers, the sultan realized that legally Egypt was still within the empire's fold. Above all, 'Abd al-Majid was pleased that the threat of dismemberment had been averted and he was keen to readmit Muhammad 'Ali into his imperial orbit. He bestowed numerous honors on his previous enemy and even invited him to Istanbul in 1846 to receive new titles and decorations.

Also improving were Muhammad 'Ali's relations with Britain. Having contained Muhammad 'Ali within Egypt the British government was interested in using the noticeable improvement in security that the Pasha's policies had effected in Egypt to improve its own communications with India. Although a rail link between Cairo and Suez was rejected, the Pasha allowed Britain to use the overland route from Alexandria to Suez. His dealings with European merchants were often antagonistic because of his desperate attempt to retain control over the countryside and their desire to bypass him altogether and deal directly with the Egyptian population.

During the last stage of his career Muhammad 'Ali's centralizing policies continued to be undermined. As we have seen, his "industrial" experiment had come to a virtual standstill in the mid-1830s even before the confrontation with Europe and the sultan in 1839. Likewise, his monopolies policy was gradually abandoned when he started granting large tracts of land to members of his family and the elite in 1837–38. After 1841 this tendency accelerated and he realized that he had to relinquish direct control over the production process to placate the rising Turkish-speaking elite he had transplanted to Egypt. Many saw no point in complying with the old Pasha's bureaucratic directives and became convinced that he had no means of stopping them from expropriating the agricultural surplus for their own benefit rather than channeling it to his coffers.

If the last period of the Pasha's rule witnessed a weakening of his control over the countryside and the firmer entrenchment of the Turkish-speaking elite, it also saw the rising middle classes secure for themselves a more stable position in Egyptian society. After demobilization of the army in 1841 hundreds, if not thousands, of senior and middle-ranking officers returned to Egypt and started seeking employment in the Pasha's civilian administration. Having been in close contact with their Arabic-speaking subordinates, most of them peasants from various parts of Egypt, they had come to understand local customs and realized that they had to acquire Arabic if they intended to stay in Egypt. Furthermore, the hundreds of doctors, engineers, and other professionals who had been educated in the Pasha's schools also carved out places for themselves, equipped as they were with nothing more than the educational training they had acquired. These, like demobilized officers, now sought employment in the civilian bureaucracy before being forced in a generation's time into private business. In this respect the Sudan, which had been granted to Muhammad 'Ali in the 1841 *firman*, offered some kind of employment opportunity, although service in Egypt proper was preferred.

As far as common Egyptians were concerned, the period 1841–48 saw recuperation from the heavy burden of Muhammad 'Ali's imperial projects. As such, this period properly belongs to what has been termed the "Middle decades of the nineteenth century,"[65] a period that also includes the reigns of 'Abbas (1849–54) and Sa'id (1854–63). These "middle decades" witnessed less aggressive taxation and fewer and lighter corvée burdens on the peasants. Although the new landlords set out to exploit peasants by forcing them to perform corvée labor on their *ib'adiyyat*, these corvée levies, by their very nature, were performed on the same plots of land and, unlike Muhammad 'Ali's earlier ones, seldom dispatched peasants to distant areas. The peasants also benefited from abolition of monopolies, although they soon found themselves vulnerable to fluctuations of the international market and the caprices of foreign merchants, money-lenders, and bankers. Above all, however, the peasants welcomed the end of conscription with no small degree of joy, and on returning from the different war fronts they rejoined

---

[65] Ehud Toledano, *State and Society in Mid-Nineteenth-Century Egypt* (Cambridge, 1990).

their long-lost families and reclaimed the lands they had been forced to abandon. This wrought havoc in the system of landholding and necessitated a new land law in 1847, one of whose main functions was to deal with this confusing situation.

Muhammad 'Ali's legacy

Muhammad 'Ali's long reign had an enormous impact on Egypt, on its position within the Ottoman empire, and its relations with Europe. The Pasha's policies emphasized to the British the importance of Egypt's position for their communications with India; increasing awareness of Egypt's strategic position contributed in no small degree to the British decision in 1882 to interfere militarily in Egypt, ushering in a period of occupation that lasted for seventy years.

Muhammad 'Ali's policies radically altered Egypt's position as a province of the Ottoman empire. The 1841 *firman* changed Egypt's legal and official relations with the Sublime Porte, but change came too on the economic and cultural fronts. The Pasha's reign witnessed developments that tied Egypt more firmly to the European world at the expense of its former connections with the Ottoman empire. The cultivation of cotton on a large scale effectively turned the Delta into a huge plantation that produced a crop predominantly destined for European markets. In this manner the Egyptian cultivator became well entrenched in the world market and found himself susceptible as never before to forces of the international economy. The monopolies that the Pasha instituted, furthermore, undermined the traditional urban merchants whose trade in coffee and spices had been primarily conducted within the Ottoman empire or with lands farther to the east. At the end of the Pasha's reign Europe, mainly Britain and France, were Egypt's main trading partners.

The configuration of Egypt's social structure was also completely changed during the Pasha's reign. Gone for good was the power of the Mamluk warlords who had controlled Egypt for centuries, and in their place were members of Muhammad 'Ali's family and numerous retainers. These hundreds and thousands of Turkish-speaking officials who flocked with their families to serve in his civilian and military bureaucracies formed a new ingredient in Egyptian society. After having been granted land in the mid-1830s they became permanent residents, started to learn Arabic and use it as their daily language, intermarried with Egyptians, and built palaces in Cairo and Alexandria rather than in Istanbul and Izmir. These formed the new landed aristocracy of Egypt, which was to play an increasingly important role in the decades to come. In opposition to this Ottoman-oriented elite, the hundreds of students whom the Pasha sent to Europe had a significant impact in reorienting Egyptian culture from the Ottoman empire with its

Islamic heritage to a more European, mostly French, model. The new cultural elite, backed, as it were, by the entrenched linkage of the Egyptian economy to the European market, was to decide Egypt's future orientation and lay the groundwork for a later cultural movement that would insist that Egypt had a Mediterranean identity, rather than an Oriental, Ottoman one.

Muhammad ʿAli's most lasting legacy, however, proved to be creation of a new kind of state in Egypt, a state that monopolized coercive power like contemporary European states and used this monopoly to spread Cairo's influence over distant areas of Egypt in an effective and permanent manner. Rather than limiting itself to traditional government duties of raising taxes, defending external borders against foreign encroachment, and keeping a certain degree of internal tranquillity, Muhammad ʿAli's government navigated waters seldom charted by any government before the nineteenth century. Chief among these tasks were new medical and educational concerns. Opening government schools, printing new kinds of books on a large scale, issuing a semi-regular newspaper, vaccinating young children, performing medical checkups on pupils, conducting regular cadasters and censuses, and above all conscripting thousands of young men into the Pasha's army – all these new policies altered the nature of the Egyptian state and changed people's relations with it.

The effect of the Pasha's policies, therefore, whether or not beneficial in the long term, were not always appreciated by average Egyptians, those masses of peasants and poor town dwellers along the Nile. The policies of conscription, corvée, increased taxation, monopolies, as well as the numerous "factories" and workshops into which they were pressed, made their lives miserable. They came to detest the authority of the Pasha and resist his regime as oppressive, intolerant, and inhumane. They realized that they had no place in the Pasha's dreams and aspirations except as a source of cheap and docile labor. In this manner Muhammad ʿAli was truly the founder of modern Egypt, an Egypt in which the Egyptians found themselves silenced, exiled, punished, and robbed of the fruits of their labor, an Egypt to be ruled as he had wished by his descendants for a hundred years after his death.

7

Egypt under the successors of Muhammad 'Ali

F. ROBERT HUNTER

>‹

The political history of Egypt between 1848 and 1879 is dominated by the buildup of the dynastic state and by European economic and political penetration leading to the establishment of foreign control.[1] These interacted with each other and provided the context for other important developments, such as the breakdown of viceregal autocracy. Power relations changed between the ruler and his elite, whose members were developing interests of their own, and between government and society. The central power became partially Egyptianized while subjecting the mass of society to greater regulation and control.[2]

The growth of the state was marked by consolidation of the Muhammad 'Ali family as an Egyptian dynasty, expansion of the administrative apparatus, and the appearance of a bureaucratic elite with a new indigenous component. Foreign penetration was expressed in appropriation by Europeans of part of Egypt's rural surplus, the self-assertion and intervention of foreign consulates, lending by European bankers, and the buildup of a huge debt owed entirely to foreigners. Beginning in 1875, these developments converged. An international control over Egyptian finances was established, creating a state within a state. The European powers and bondholders then destroyed the viceroy's autocratic powers while retaining the office and the dynasty. By 1879, Europe had taken over the state itself – the prize and object of power.

These developments were associated with three viceroys: 'Abbas (1848–54), whose reign was a time of paced and measured change; Sa'id

---

I wish to express appreciation to Donald M. Reid and Roger Owen for their helpful comments on this chapter.

[1] The state includes the ruler, his family, and the viceregal administrations; the bureaucratic apparatus; the military; the administrative elite; and all other persons employed by the government.

[2] The question of the limits of the government's ability to regulate and supervise is a matter that needs to be addressed by scholars.

(1854–63), who launched an active program of development; and Isma'il (1863–79), who accelerated economic changes begun earlier.[3] Envisioning an independent Egypt bound to the west culturally and economically, Isma'il embarked upon military campaigns in equatorial Africa and initiated reforms in education and other areas. Educational improvements under Isma'il were aimed primarily at providing trained cadres for the army and bureaucracy. "Reform" was thus subordinated to politics, and politics could not be separated from the state.

The viceroy possessed wide latitude in the governance of the country. His power was based upon a personally dependent elite of men bound to him through ties of clientage and common interest, and a set of ruling prerogatives derived from custom and Ottoman precedents. These enabled him to control the instruments of power – and army and the bureaucracy – and through them, the surplus of production. Legally the mere delegate of the Ottoman sultan, the viceroy could confiscate and reallocate land, appropriate peasant labor, appoint and dismiss officials, reward and punish at will. This system of personal government, created by Muhammad 'Ali, would be maintained intact until the late 1870s. If the viceroy's power was nearly absolute, he nonetheless operated within a context of Islamic norms and Ottoman and Egyptian legislation and practice. His power could also be tempered by outside intervention and mediation, and he ran the risk of provoking resistance if his measures or policies went too far.

Why did the state grow and change so rapidly, and how was its influence extended over the people and land of Egypt? Why did foreign economic and political penetration occur? How did the viceroys respond to the growing presence and power of Europe? The questions are complex because some causes were global while others derived from Egypt's particular situation.

Western expansion in Egypt occurred for the same reason that Europe was advancing elsewhere. Beginning in the late 1840s, European capitalist enterprise underwent a reorganization that greatly expanded its capacity and scope of influence. It passed rapidly from commercial exploitation in the age of the railway to finance capitalism, characterized by formation of huge syndicates and credit associations making their profits mostly from lending to foreign states. Backed by their national governments, European capitalist interests advanced on every continent.

Europe's material investment in Egypt was nearly all the result of foreign capitalist expansion. But British interests predominated. This was especially true of Egypt's foreign trade, the vast majority of which took place with Britain (France was a distant second). Domination of the Egyptian market dated to the 1840s, when extension of British industrial capacity had led to a search for raw materials and new markets in the Mediterranean. This drive

---

[3] Ibrahim Pasha ruled only a few months prior to his death in 1848.

brought Britain into competition with France, which sought to project its influence from bases in Algeria and Tunisia.

Britain also had a keen interest in the development of Egyptian communications and transportation – something that can be explained by the country's geographical location. Egypt was not only a rich and fertile agricultural land; it also lay astride the overland route between Europe and the east, the importance of which had greatly increased as a result of steam navigation and would increase still more with the advent of rail communications. Because of its Indian base, Britain had the greatest interest in the development and protection of this route, but since it was used by all European countries trading in Asia, other governments too began to display greater interest in Egypt.

"Europe," of course, was more than capitalism, material power, and strategic advantage. It was also a culture, a civilization. This too began to have an impact upon Egypt's rulers and their officials.

The other major cause of political change was the viceroys' own objectives and goals, which were threefold. The first was consolidation of family rule.[4] This derived from a sense of insecurity and a certain vanity, but also pride in the achievements of Muhammad 'Ali. The ruling family had achieved dynastic status quite recently, and Egypt's relationship with the Porte remained unclear. The imperial edict of 1841 granting hereditary governorship to Muhammad'Ali and his descendants had imposed restrictions (some of which were never implemented) that gave the sultan an opportunity to intervene in Egyptian affairs. Muhammad 'Ali's successors were constructing a monarchy; by the 1860s, they desired the formal recognition that would legitimize it.

The second viceregal objective was more money. Initially, this problem derived from the loss of revenue attendant upon the decline of the monopoly system, but it was accentuated by the decision to launch development schemes and other projects that cost more than the government could afford.

Finally, Muhammad 'Ali's successors were determined to maintain the political–administrative order bequeathed to them, which required a degree of European aid and support. The great dilemma faced by the viceroys stemmed from their need to rely upon Europe but also to resist it. Their struggle to maintain the country's development and overall direction while avoiding political dangers posed by growing foreign involvement is an important part of Egypt's political history. Various strategies were formulated and tried, from playing Britain and France against each other, to

---

[4] Most recently, in *State and Society in Mid-Nineteenth-century Egypt* (Cambridge, 1990), Ehud Toledano has called attention to this important development, which merits further study.

confining the most important projects to the government (thus contributing to the buildup of the state), but none succeeded in saving the country.

The reign of 'Abbas

Under 'Abbas, government did not revert to its pre-nineteenth-century condition. It remained centralized in the household of the ruler, whose officers formed the core of a foreign, Turkish-speaking elite of mostly military men bound to the viceroy through ties of clientage. Egypt's hierarchical bureaucracy and new conscript army were retained. While 'Abbas cut back in many important areas, including the army, he did not neglect the military establishment. A new military training school was established, which also provided education in technical subjects. If 'Abbas delivered the finishing stroke to most of Muhammad 'Ali's educational institutions, the school of engineering and the translation bureau remained in existence, and forty-one students were sent to Europe to study engineering, medicine, and other scientific subjects.[5]

The administration was also changing. Egypt's conciliar bodies were developing into effective legislative organs, and courts of first instance were established in the provinces to hear criminal and civil cases that had previously come under the authority of Shari'a courts. Executive departments also assumed greater responsibilities, and the creation of two new administrations – pious endowments and the railways – signaled the government's acquisition of still more functions. A glimmer of change was also visible in the social base of high administration with the appointment of a number of Egyptian technicians (mostly engineers) to important state posts. Promoted because of their knowledge of scientific subjects (acquired during studies in Europe), and 'Abbas's need for engineers as a result of the removal from government service of most of the Frenchmen employed by Muhammad 'Ali, these young Egyptians were a harbinger. Henceforth, Egypt's dwindling supply of *mamluks* (of whom some were in 'Abbas's personal service) and Turks – destined almost exclusively for government service – would be replenished not by free Turks and other recruits from abroad, as in the past, but by native Egyptians.

'Abbas also worked to strengthen dynastic power. The viceroy was interested in the land and people of Egypt. He sought to protect the country's antiquities, and even spoke Arabic.[6] During his rule, Egyptian cultivators were less liable for conscription for the army and public works

---

[5] James Heyworth-Dunne, *An Introduction to the History of Education in Modern Egypt* (London, 1938), 296–99, 301–07.

[6] The British consul, Walne, conversed with 'Abbas in Arabic. Helen Anne B. Rivlin, "The Railway Question in the Ottoman–Egyptian Crisis of 1850–1852," *Middle East Journal* 15/4 (1961), 386; Toledano, *State and Society*, 88–90.

than they had been under Muhammad 'Ali. But 'Abbas was also a military
man and an autocrat. Egyptians remained subject to an oppressive government and its agents, and corvée labor was supplied increasingly to the
estates of large landed proprietors – a development signaling a change in the
public nature of this institution.[7] To elevate the prince and distinguish him
and his family, 'Abbas built many imposing palaces, and organized an
ostentatious court with elaborate ritual – in sharp contrast to the simple
manner of Muhammad 'Ali, who sat crosslegged on his divan and welcomed
guests in austere chambers.

'Abbas initially desired closer relations with the Porte as a way of checking
European influence, but the Ottoman government embarked upon a policy
of reestablishing its authority. The issue was the Porte's wish to apply the
1851 Ottoman penal code to Egypt, and, in particular, its stipulation that
murderers should not be executed without the sultan's confirmation.
Muhammad 'Ali had exercised this prerogative, and 'Abbas rightly resisted
an attempt to reduce viceregal power. After a hard struggle, 'Abbas emerged
victorious. The viceroy's right to confirm death sentences (in certain cases)
was reestablished, and the Ottoman penal code itself was altered to meet
Egyptian conditions.[8] Later in his reign, 'Abbas took the offensive, requesting that the sultan award him the grandiose title of al-'Aziz, which had
designated certain of the country's rulers before the Ottoman conquest, and
authorize a change in the law of succession so that his son Ilhami could
succeed him.[9] Though neither request was granted, by the time of 'Abbas's
death, "Egypt's autonomous position [had become] an incontrovertible
political fact of life that no Ottoman administration would ever again
challenge."[10]

This victory, however, was not without a price. In order to achieve it,
'Abbas had had to rely upon the diplomatic support of Great Britain, and
had felt obliged to authorize construction of Egypt's first railway – a project
long promoted by Britain. The idea of a railway across Egypt was part of
British efforts to improve communications with India, and to facilitate
export and investment of national capital; the railway, as originally conceived, was to have been financed by British capitalists. It was also an aspect
of the keen rivalry between the British and French, who had developed the
competing idea of a ship canal across the isthmus of Suez. 'Abbas initially

---

[7] Toledano, *State and Society*, p. 191.

[8] 'Abbas received the right to confirm death sentences for seven years in certain cases. To
obtain this, he had to agree to increase the amount of yearly tribute paid by Egypt to the
Porte. Gabriel Baer, "Tanzimat in Egypt: The Penal Code," in Gabriel Baer, *Studies in
the Social History of Modern Egypt* (Chicago and London, 1969), 118–19.

[9] Bruce/Clarendon, no. 39, August 13, 1854 in FO 78/1036, Public Record Office,
London. On this title, see J. Deny, *Sommaire des archives turques du Caire* (Cairo,
1930), 76–77.

[10] Rivlin, "The Railway Question," 380.

opposed the railway, which he knew would increase foreign influence in Egyptian affairs. But once he realized the necessity of obtaining Great Power support in his struggle with the Ottomans, his strategy shifted. By relying solely upon Britain, he could reduce French influence in Egypt, which had grown during the 1840s. In 1851, 'Abbas told the British that he was prepared to authorize a railway between Cairo and Alexandria, on condition that it be financed and administered by the Egyptian government. (In this, 'Abbas must have had in mind the recent example of the transit service, which Muhammad 'Ali had taken out of the hands of a private British company and made into a government monopoly.) A contract was signed with the British rail magnate George Stephenson. As contractors, suppliers, and providers of technical expertise, British interests benefited greatly. The British government now had a lasting interest in the development of Egyptian rail traffic. The Egyptian government benefited too. Greatly extended in the years to come, Egypt's railway network became a major revenue provider.

The other main source of European pressure came as a result of 'Abbas's efforts to control the rural surplus. Midway through his reign, the gap between revenue and expenditures – always a problem – had begun to grow. This was caused mostly by pressures on the demand side (e.g., the cost of financing the railway project, and the need to send money and a military contingent to support the Ottomans in the Crimean war). At the same time, however, the ruler's control of agricultural surplus declined owing to the weakening of Muhammad 'Ali's monopoly system. Ties between European merchant houses and local traders (many of them from non-Muslim minorities), who became agents in the acquisition of wheat and cotton, alienated crops that had previously gone to the government. To combat this and maximize his own returns, 'Abbas had most taxes collected in kind, used his own purchasing agents, forbade sale of agricultural crops by cultivators in advance of the harvest, and prohibited grain exports. For some time, Britain had pressed Egypt to permit grain sales at public auction (thereby forcing prices down, to the benefit of British merchants). The Crimean war only made Britain's need for Egyptian grain greater, and a newly established entente with France (Britain's ally in the Crimean war) enabled joint pressure to be exerted. By 1854, the combined weight of Britain and France, and incessant pressure of the entire consular corps, was at last beginning to break down 'Abbas's prohibitions. Then on July 14, 1854, 'Abbas was murdered in a private dispute.

The 1854–75 period

These years were characterized by vast economic development, and Egypt's opening to European capital, technology, and enterprise. The dynastic state was consolidated, and a shift in the balance of power between the viceroy and the European community took place.

Breaking sharply with the conservative approach taken by 'Abbas, Sa'id and Isma'il became committed to an ambitious program of economic expansion, in which Europeans were to serve as junior partners. Soon after his accession, Sa'id put an end to the monopoly system by removing all restrictions upon the free movement of goods, and decreeing that taxes be collected in coin rather than kind (except for Upper Egypt). He also authorized a host of new development projects, including construction of a railway between Cairo and Suez.

More ambitious still, Isma'il accelerated trade and production for the market. The government drained and excavated irrigation canals, constructed bridges across the Nile, made numerous harbor improvements, and built 1,200 miles of railway and 9,500 miles of telegraph lines. The area under cultivation was expanded, agricultural output increased, and state revenues more than doubled.[11] For assistance, Sa'id and Isma'il called upon European capital and technical expertise. European private banks were established, foreigners were employed in the Egyptian administration (especially the railway department), and the number of European residents – immune from Egyptian laws and paying virtually no taxes – increased rapidly (more than 30,000 persons arrived each year between 1857 and 1861).[12] In the provinces, European merchants lent money to Egyptian cultivators in advance of the harvest, facilitating collection of taxes.

The main reason for this new course was financial, but other factors also played a role. Sa'id and Isma'il possessed a vision of Egypt much different from that of 'Abbas. Inspired by Muhammad 'Ali, they wished to reignite the country's development. Unlike 'Abbas, they had received a European education and spoke French. They felt comfortable with Europeans and had friendly feelings for them. Material circumstances were also important. At the time of his accession, Sa'id was faced with a shortage of funds and had a debt to pay, left to him by 'Abbas. He was also keenly aware of pressure developing to open up the country to foreigners. The crucial factor, however, was the huge European demand for Egyptian grain, at premium prices, as a result of the Crimean war. Profits from agricultural development and opening the country to Europeans would not only allow bills to be paid but also permit realization of other goals.

In 1863, when Isma'il came to power, Egypt was in the middle of a

---

[11] E. R. J. Owen, *The Middle East in the World Economy 1800–1914* (London and New York, 1981), 128–29. As Owen has cautioned, it was in Isma'il's interest to issue exaggerated figures in order to boost his own achievements.

[12] The influx of foreigners increased even more after the accession of Isma'il. David S. Landes, *Bankers and Pashas: International Finance and Economic Imperialism in Egypt* (Cambridge, MA, 1958), 87–88.

cotton-generated economic boom, owing to the American Civil War. The country was flush with money. The times did not call for retrenchment. Ismaʿil thus accelerated the development of Egypt's economy in expectation of greater revenues to finance even more ambitious plans, including independence from the Porte.

The viceroys, however, were under no illusion about the dangers that enhanced European influence could bring. Vain and imperious, they endeavored to maintain control in a variety of ways. They granted exclusive concessions to trusted European confidants, and created joint Egyptian–European development companies that involved foreigners known to them and chosen for their access to money markets. They also endeavored to confine projects to their government. The Cairo–Suez railway was financed mostly from revenues of the transit administration, and the vast infrastructure that emerged under Ismaʿil was administered almost entirely by the government. Whenever possible, the viceroys took advantage of Anglo-French rivalry, which had resumed following the accession of Saʿid (who favored French interests) and the end of the Crimean war.

Egypt's rulers, however, failed to control the Europeans. This was partly because of overambitious schemes that led to excessive reliance upon foreigners and to key blunders in relations with them. Of the latter, most costly was the concession awarded by Saʿid to Ferdinand de Lesseps for construction of a canal across the isthmus of Suez (Saʿid purchased 64,000 shares and made a verbal promise to accept all unsubscribed shares). Most importantly, the concessionnaires, contractors, and bankers exploited their position to create a vast field of opportunities for their own profit. The result was restriction of the ruler's freedom of action, and acceleration of Europe's penetration of the country.

The chief vehicles of this penetration were the consular offices of the European powers and foreign banking capital. The European consuls had formal political power and also wielded informal influence through contacts inside the administration. After 1854 their influence was broadened and deepened, partly because their governments intervened more in Egyptian affairs, but also because of the rapid growth of a large foreign colony, to whose interests the consuls and their governments had to be sensitive. The consuls extended their influence by abusing the legal authority vested in them by the Capitulations. Cases brought by Egyptian plaintiffs against Europeans, for example, were tried in consular courts in accordance with European laws rather than in local courts, as stipulated by the Capitulations.[13] Because of their maneuvers, consular jurisdiction over Egyptians was expanded, and Egyptian sovereignty over Europeans had to be aban-

---

[13] Nubar Nubarian, *Mémoires de Nubar Pacha* (Beirut, 1983), 324–25. The subject of the extension of the Capitulations awaits its historian.

doned. By supporting dubious or fraudulent claims for indemnification, the consuls facilitated abuse by foreigners of the concessions granted them by the viceroys, bringing huge losses to the Egyptian treasury. The consuls also came to exercise great influence through intermediaries within the government. These could be Europeans employed in the administration or in the viceroy's court, on whose behalf consuls intervened to secure redress of grievances, or viceregal subjects under formal European protection, whose interests they defended or advanced, or Egyptian officials close to a consul or supportive of the policy of a particular country, to whom patronage was extended. Threatening and cajoling, blustering and bullying, resorting even to gunboat diplomacy, the consuls demonstrated beyond any doubt their emergence as the new politicians of Egypt.

The second means of European penetration was financial. European capital had different manifestations, but its most pernicious form was banking capital, which led to buildup of a huge debt. The starting-point was the decision of Sa'id and Isma'il to use foreigners to help meet current expenditures, and the European money markets to help reduce their local debts and to finance development. By the mid-1850s, conditions for European profit taking had been established: banks, founded to promote trade and commerce but profiting more and more from speculation; the presence of Europeans whose success depended upon making loans to foreign states, and who were skillful in proposing new projects to spend money on; and the willingness of foreign governments to apply pressure to ensure that loans were raised from their nationals.

Initially, Europeans purchased treasury bonds issued by Sa'id (at the suggestion of Ferdinand de Lesseps) to meet the government's financial obligations. At first non-transferrable, these bonds were made negotiable, and renewed, at considerable profit to their holders.[14] This marked the origin of Egypt's floating debt. Second, private loans began to be made to the rulers by European bankers. In 1860, Sa'id took out a private foreign loan in the amount of 21 million francs, issued by French banking interests. Finally, there were public loans, arranged in Europe by contractors and offered by financial syndicates, in which market shares were sold to thousands of small investors. Issued in 1862 as a result of a floating debt swollen by continued sale of treasury bonds, Egypt's first public loan, contracted by Oppenheim & Nephew and sold mostly on the English market, returned to the Egyptian treasury an amount 35 percent less than its nominal value (£3,292,800).[15] The difference was taken by bankers, contractors, and their agents in fees and other charges.

The turning-point came in 1864, and was the result of two developments:

[14] Owen, *The Middle East*, 125.
[15] *Ibid.*, 126; Landes, *Bankers and Pashas*, 117.

the beginning of the end of the cotton boom, manifested in the decline of prices; and the award by Emperor Napoleon III of a huge indemnity (Fr.84,000,000) to be paid by the Egyptian government to the Suez Canal Company for return of privileges granted by Saʿid.[16] Ismaʿil thus was obliged to take out a new public loan, issued by Oppenheim. In return for a realized amount of £4,864,063 the Egyptian government committed itself to pay back £9,304,000.[17] The downward slide had begun. Over the next nine years, six more foreign loans were contracted on terms less and less favorable to Egypt, against which were mortgaged the revenues from the railways, the viceregal estates and other key resources.

For bankers, contractors, and bondholders who participated in these schemes, Egypt had indeed become a "klondike on the Nile."[18] Of the foreign loans issued between 1862 and 1873, £21,876,000, or 32 percent of their total nominal value, was siphoned off in fees, commissions, and hidden charges.[19] As for the total amount of money actually received by the Egyptian government (£46,621,000), the greater part was recycled to Europe in the payment of principal and interest charges (averaging almost 10 percent). But a significant portion of the loan money was also spent to develop the country's infrastructure.[20]

The 1854–75 period also saw the rapid growth of the Egyptian administration. This was spurred by the development of agriculture and the export sector generally, which increased the volume and flow of traffic throughout the country, propelling the extension of transport and communications. Another cause was the viceroys' determination to retain control over agricultural production (and with it, the land itself), and after 1864, their need for increased revenues. The Egyptian bureaucracy was thus extended further into the countryside.

Egypt's administration underwent major structural growth. This was reflected not only in the numerical increase of individual units, as, for example, the expansion of the governorates, or the establishment of new agricultural, administrative, and judicial bodies, but in the development of the bureaucracy as an institution. The central administration acquired greater control over the day-to-day activities of government, leaving the

---

[16] In granting the original concession, Saʿid gave the Suez Canal Company rights to land and corvée labor; Ismaʿil regarded this as a derogation of Egypt's sovereignty, and requested the mediation of the French emperor.

[17] F. Robert Hunter, *Egypt under the Khedives, 1805–1879: From Household Government to Modern Bureaucracy* (Pittsburgh, 1984), 39.

[18] The practice of issuing loans below par was common at the time. Individual bondholders, for example, were able to purchase a £5 bond for only £4. The phrase "klondike on the Nile," familiar to historians of modern Egypt, comes from a chapter title in Landes's book *Bankers and Pashas*.

[19] See table 19 in Owen, *The Middle East*, 127.

[20] *Ibid.*, 128–29.

viceregal household to deal increasingly with the ruler's personal needs.[21] A civil service, with ranks, salary laws, and a pension plan, also emerged. Egypt developed a distinctive set of administrative institutions, and became less Ottoman.

The bureaucratic apparatus was also the means for greater government control of society and its resources. In 'Abbas's time, penal and other legislation had been used to force some urban groups to give up part of their freedom.[22] After 1854, state influence was further extended. In the provinces, the number of government courts was increased. Administrative and agricultural councils were formed, and village courts established. These new bodies exercised a host of supervisory and regulatory functions, recording births and deaths, overseeing tax collection, inspecting charitable foundations, and so on.[23] New property laws enabled the government to impose new taxes, extend the area of cultivation, and resolve problems of land ownership. In 1867, as part of Isma'il's educational reform, the government assumed control over a large number of Islamic primary schools in the countryside, establishing rules that minutely regulated their activities, and administering the properties and monies bequeathed to them from charitable endowments. Through legislation and the administrative apparatus, the state thus extended its authority over the people of Egypt.

The appearance of a new bureaucratic elite was another important development. Inherited by Isma'il, this new elite of high office-holders was the product of a long evolution to which Muhammad 'Ali, 'Abbas, and Sa'id had contributed. No longer composed of the ruler's freed slaves, in-laws, and other relatives to the same degree as in the past, this was an elite of rank and position, with a decidedly administrative rather than military character.[24] Its members were differentiated mainly by ethnic affiliation and education (e.g., some had received a modern, scientific education in Europe or in Egypt during Muhammad 'Ali's time; others had not). This elite contained a much stronger indigenous component than had been true in 'Abbas's time, and included a small but growing number of European technicians, but the Turkish element – although rapidly declining in number – remained preponderant. Nonetheless, by intermarrying with Egyptians, and establishing landed and other ties with the country, Egypt's Turks were becoming assimilated in their adopted country. If Turkish officials still

---

[21] Hunter, *Egypt under the Khedives*, 63.

[22] The state, however, was also flexible, permitting wage adjustments, for example; and guild members and others received protection "in return for submission to government authority as enshrined in the laws of the viceroy." Toledano, *State and Society*, 230.

[23] Hunter, *Egypt under the Khedives*, 44–45.

[24] By mid-century, the armed forces had become assimilated in the administration, though this was perhaps less pronounced after Isma'il reorganized the army. Toledano, *State and Society*, 74.

regarded themselves as superior to the "natives," and even clashed with their Egyptian counterparts, they could no longer be called Ottomans.

By mid-century, Egypt's official class had evolved from servants of the ruler to men with interests of their own. What were they? As a group, Egypt's high-ranking officials supported policies designed to advance and protect their positions inside the government – something that may be described as deriving from a bureaucratic interest. These officials also had an interest in "reform." As a result of exposure to the ideas and material culture of the west, many officials were prepared to work for and support changes of a fundamental nature. Implicit in this orientation was the notion of "decline," the idea that Egypt had fallen behind and must somehow catch up with the rest of the world. Most reform-minded officials were committed to changes of a material nature, the adoption of new techniques and technology; a few were developing a new conception of Egypt along the lines of the French *patrie*. However, as Muslims, nearly all reformist officials rejected the idea of indiscriminate borrowing from the west. Some were also influenced by Islamic ideas, while others developed ideas derived from pharaonic models.[25] If the original stimulus to reform had come from contact with the west, Europe was by no means the sole or only model for change.

These officials also possessed an interest in land. By the 1860s, they and their families, along with the ruler and his, were the core element of Egypt's large landholding class. Their estates began to undergo great expansion and development, owing to the cotton boom, which made landholding a profitable investment. All high officials wished to promote and develop land. Because of the expanding need for labor and other services on their large estates, officials were also able to build up influence in certain localities. Large estates attracted people in search of work, markets for their goods, and other facilities. In addition, labor gangs and a captive peasant population of service tenants provided cheap labor and enabled owners to exploit and intervene in the lives of workers. The estates of Egypt's official class therefore became yet another way in which "government" entered more deeply into the life of rural society.

Possession of large estates by high-ranking officials also gave them an interest in cooperating with the viceroy – their chief patron. Much of the land owned by the elite originally had been awarded as gifts by the ruler, one of the many informal ways that viceroys sought to bind their men to them. The maintenance and development of a large estate likewise depended upon the ruler's continued favor and support. Hence the importance of high

---

[25] See, for example, Darrell Dykstra, "Pyramids, Prophets, and Progress: Ancient Egypt in the Writings of Ali Mubarak," *Journal of the American Oriental Society* 114/1 (1994), 54–65.

administrative position, and access to viceregal patronage. If the men of the new elite developed interests of their own, these coincided and overlapped with those of the viceroy.

The period 1854–75 also witnessed emergence of the Muhammad 'Ali family as an independent Egyptian dynasty. In his memoirs, Colonel Ahmad 'Urabi published a speech given by Sa'id to state dignitaries in which he spoke of himself as an Egyptian and expressed a determination to educate and elevate Egyptians in order to dispense with the need for foreigners who, he said, had ruled and enslaved the Egyptian people for centuries.[26] At this time, Sa'id was promoting Egyptians to administrative posts, but the reasons for this were far from sentimental. The need for more manpower, the numerical decline of the Turks, and the desire for administrators familiar with the people and resources of the countryside had made this essential. The Egyptians promoted were not peasants but members of the rural notability (e.g., village mayors and their families) whose rise had begun under Muhammad 'Ali when many had accumulated large estates and become more differentiated from peasant cultivators.

'Abbas had elevated a limited number of Egyptians to posts in the central administration, but Sa'id went much further. He promoted sons of notables to the rank of colonel in the army, and in 1856 he ordered that Egyptians be made subdistrict and district heads in all the provinces (Turks, though, continued to hold most of these posts).[27] A few Egyptians even became provincial governors. Isma'il went further still, promoting Egyptians to cabinet positions, elevating many prominent rural notables to provincial governorships, and associating the rural notability with his regime by creating the consultative chamber of delegates (*majlis shura al-nuwwab*). The rise of the indigenous notability not only moved the bureaucracy toward greater Egyptianization – by the 1870s, Arabic had triumphed over Turkish as the language of administration – but led also to the rise of new intermediaries in the provinces. With land and influence in their home districts, notable officials could use the patronage and authority of new posts to develop local power bases.

The ruling dynasty also implanted itself in Egypt by accumulating and developing landed estates, which by 1878 amounted to 917,046 faddans.[28] These vast, rich holdings were the result of the decision to increase government revenues by developing agriculture, and they were also linked to the ruler's efforts to retain control over cultivation by expanding private control of land. Egypt's viceregal estates propelled the construction and extension of irrigation canals and railways, but they were also a source of great upset to

[26] Ahmad 'Urabi, *Mudhakkirat al-thawra al-'urabiya* (Cairo, 1954?), part 1, 16.
[27] Amin Sami, *Taqwim al-nil wa asr muhammad 'ali* (Cairo, 1936), part 3, I, 189.
[28] Vivian/ Salisbury, no. 226, June 29, 1878 in FO 78/2855.

rural society. Especially in Isma'il's time, the buildup of viceregal estates was accompanied by seizure of thousands of faddans of ostensibly privately owned peasant property through assertion of the ruler's customary prerogative to confiscate and reallocate land. Viceregal properties were thus part of a restructuring of rural relations in which large estates grew at the expense of smaller peasant holdings, a class of landless laborers arose, and the labor force itself became concentrated more on large domains.

The amassing of royal estates had the effect of elevating the ruling family and distinguishing it from the mass of society. Sa'id and Isma'il continued the development begun under 'Abbas of an ostentatious courtly style, imitating the ruling houses of Europe. This was especially true of Isma'il, who built many imposing palaces and whose penchant for pageantry was inspired by the royalty of Europe.

On the external level, consolidation of the Muhammad 'Ali family as an Egyptian dynasty was manifested in *de facto* political independence from the Porte. Sa'id had aspired to greater independence; it was Isma'il who, after expending much effort and money, finally achieved it in the form of two Ottoman imperial edicts (in 1866 and 1867, ratified in 1872 and 1873). These *firmans* gave him the right to confer titles and increase the size of the army. The law of succession was changed so that the principle of seniority was replaced by primogeniture in Isma'il's own line, reducing intra-family conflict over this important question and ensuring the dynasty's future stability. Isma'il also obtained the right to raise loans on his own and to conclude treaties with other states, and he received the title of khedive, signifying lord or master, which gave him a status above that of other viceroys in the Ottoman empire. If Isma'il was still an Ottoman viceroy and Egypt a subject province, he and his country were independent in everything but name.

In a conversation with Isma'il, Nubar Pasha, the Armenian director of foreign affairs, remarked that Europe, not the Porte, posed the real threat to Egypt. If Isma'il wanted independence, Nubar said, he should try to bring European residents under a single Egyptian legal jurisdiction by offering the European powers a legal system independent of the executive and a new judiciary with a large European component.[29] The result, Nubar forecast, would be an end to the legal jurisdictions of the consulates and, with this, the problems costing Egypt so dearly. In 1867, Isma'il deputed Nubar to negotiate with the European governments – a diplomatic journey that took eight years to complete.

Nubar had been right. Egypt's mounting foreign debt was leading the country to bankruptcy and foreign control. After the final collapse of the cotton boom in 1866, the Egyptian government continued to issue treasury

---

[29] Nubarian, *Mémoires*, 268.

bonds, swelling the size of its floating debt. Public loans were taken out more and more in order to redeem short-term paper. A growing proportion of Egypt's revenues was devoted to debt repayment, leaving the government with less money for its own needs. In a desperate move to obtain more money, Isma'il in 1871 sanctioned the *muqabala* law by which land owners who paid an amount equal to six times their annual land tax would have future tax liabilities reduced by a half. Still the debt mounted, and Egypt's credit rating plummeted. In 1875, Nubar returned from Europe and announced triumphantly that the foreign powers had accepted the Egyptian proposal to set up mixed tribunals independent of the government's control. These new courts, with European and Egyptian judges, would administer justice in civil matters on the basis of the Napoleonic Code. Like so many of his "reforms," the mixed courts would disappoint Isma'il, for they were used by Europeans to pressure his government. But in 1875 his mind was on other things. A suspension of Egypt's debt payments to foreign creditors was inevitable. Disaster was looming.

The 1875–79 period

The period 1875–79 was marked by an unequal struggle between Europe and the ruler for control of Egypt's resources. Europe had previously appropriated a part of the rural surplus through loans, but Egypt's rulers had been able to maintain control of agricultural production through the buildup of large viceregal estates, expansion of the area under cultivation, and its more intensive use. Beginning in 1875, Europe used the debt crisis to destroy Isma'il's economic and political power and take over the state. This was accomplished by the creation of new institutions, run by foreigners, to administer revenues pledged to the payment of the debt; the confiscation of viceregal family properties; and the displacement of Isma'il from the center of administration. Forces hostile to Europe appeared, and these enabled Isma'il to make a valiant, but doomed, comeback. His deposition in June 1879 signaled the end of the autocratic power built up by his predecessors.

This was a sudden and stunning event. Despite Egypt's growing debt, Isma'il had been able to maintain a position of undisputed power through continued dependence of the elite upon him (achieved by means of a common economic interest and the exercise of informal prerogatives) and by his capacity to increase state revenues through development and in other ways. As late as 1876, Isma'il could order the murder of Isma'il Siddiq, the Egyptian minister of finance and most powerful official in the country; yet two years later, the autocratic power wielded by Muhammad 'Ali and his successors for three-quarters of a century was gone forever.

Europe's success was made possible by the cooperation of France and Britain (though not as equals), support from leading members of Isma'il's elite who defected to the European side, and the backing foreign bankers and bondholders received from their governments. If the driving force behind intervention came from financial interests, and if European political leaders found it convenient to equate the interests of thousands of small investors with those of the nation, the French and British governments also realized an opportunity to advance strategic interests.

In 1875, Isma'il's difficulties in meeting debt payments and the probability of an Egyptian default set in motion efforts by competing financial groups to consolidate Egypt's debt and control the final settlement. The contest was between the French, who owned most of the country's floating debt (a large part of which comprised notes and bonds issued by the khedive or the government departments) and the British, holders of the majority of the official debt, accumulated through public loans. Supported by their government, a group of French capitalists began pressing Isma'il to accept a scheme for international management and consolidation of the floating debt. Wishing to avoid foreign control entirely, Isma'il played upon Anglo-French rivalry by inviting the British government to send its own financial advisors to Cairo. Isma'il then sold Egypt's 176,000 shares (44 percent of the total capital) of the Suez Canal Company's stock to the British government, giving it a direct financial stake (along with its economic interest in trade and communications) in Egypt's fate. With its "investment" in Egypt far greater than France's, the British government would accept nothing less than predominant influence, and would work to defeat any settlement that put control of state revenues into the hands of the French.

In 1876, however, Isma'il was obliged to accept a French debt-settlement scheme that imposed upon Egypt an international body (*caisse de la dette*), composed of representatives of the bondholders. An entering wedge for the establishment of a state within a state, the *caisse* received control of revenues pledged to the payment of the coupon.

Because of British opposition to the French scheme – indeed, the London bankers were able to block its implementation – and because Isma'il himself had begun to promote the British approach of unifying all Egyptian debts, the French government eventually accepted a British proposal that the two countries develop a common Egyptian policy.[30] A plan for joint control was formulated, which deprived Isma'il of his remaining leverage. In 1876, Goschen and Joubert, representatives of the British and French bondholders respectively, produced a plan of debt consolidation that was much more favorable to British banking interests. Relying upon the support of their governments – Isma'il was threatened with the prospect of having claims brought against his government before the mixed courts – Goschen and

---

[30] J. Bouvier, "Les intérêts financiers et la question d'Egypte," *Revue Historique*, 224 (1960), 88, 92–96.

Joubert imposed a new "Dual Control" upon the khedive. The consolidated debt was funded at 7 percent. Two controllers, an Englishman and a Frenchman, with large staffs of foreign officials at high salaries, were appointed to supervise government revenues and expenditures. A commission was also set up, consisting of two Englishmen and one Frenchman, to manage the railways; and an Englishman was made director of customs. European control had now been established at the very heart of Egypt's administration.

The dismantling of Isma'il's personal power was the next step. The catalyst was the inability of the Dual Control to collect the amounts demanded. The Goschen–Joubert settlement had been based upon an exaggerated estimate of Egypt's revenues, for which Isma'il himself was to blame. The rate of interest was simply too great for the country to bear, but Egypt's creditors were unwilling to accept a reduction. To uncover new revenue sources and suggest needed reforms, a commission of inquiry, headed by an Englishman, was set up. Isma'il was charged with maladministraiton. Under great pressure, he was forced to surrender the unmortgaged portion (425,729 faddans) of his family's estates in return for a civil list. Isma'il was also separated from the cabinet by the creation (August 1878) of a new council of ministers, composed of a French minister of public works and an English minister of finance. This body administered Egypt virtually independently of the viceroy, who was denied the right to attend its sessions.

The success of this operation was made possible not only by Anglo-French pressure, but also by defection of three key reformist officials, who had longstanding ties with Europe and ideas that they hoped to realize by collaborating with the foreigners. One of these men, Nubar Pasha, became president of the council of ministers, where he formed an alliance with the English minister of finance, Rivers Wilson. This was a crucial development. For decades, the ruler's autocratic power had been maintained by dependence of the elite upon him, but that power had been undermined by Europe's penetration of the administration and direct intervention. Without support of persons inside the government, Europe would have had to impose its will by force of arms.

Still, Isma'il remained khedive. His signature was required before any decision of the council of ministers could become law, and ministers themselves served theoretically at his pleasure. In law, then, he retained his ruling prerogatives. Isma'il also enjoyed widespread personal authority in the country. These provided a starting-point for his return to the center of power, which was made possible by the continued loyalty of the vast majority of Egypt's high-ranking officials, and support of Egypt's wealthy rural notables in the *majlis shura al-nuwwab*. These men feared European proposals to increase their land taxes and repudiate the obligations they had gained by payment of the *muqabala*; and they saw their privileged position endangered by the appointment of large numbers of Europeans to government posts.

Ismaʿil could also take advantage of grievances against Europe in the countryside, where the European ministry's economy measures squeezed the population, and where European merchants increased the amounts lent to peasant cultivators against their properties and used the mixed courts to enforce their seizure of peasant lands. In the cities, the consuls continued to support European claims for indemnification despite creation of the mixed courts; a newly established press also became more critical of European control.

Ismaʿil and a handful of aides orchestrated opposition to the European ministry by taking advantage of the grievances of dismissed Egyptian army officers and by encouraging opposition from the chamber of delegates in the name of constitutionalism.[31] A national program was drawn up that called for replacement of the European ministry by an Egyptian ministry whose members would be appointed and confirmed by the khedive but responsible to the chamber; and full repayment by Egypt of its foreign debt at a reduced 5 percent rate of interest. On April 7, 1879, Ismaʿil acted. Claiming to respond to the dissatisfaction of the Egyptian people, he announced formation of a new "Egyptian" cabinet, one which in reality contained his most trusted Turkish aides and was therefore personally loyal to him.

Ismaʿil's return to the center of the political stage was brief. The true aim of the control – regular payment of the debt at 7 percent interest – had been challenged by the viceroy's insistence that foreign creditors accept a lower rate. This proved the signal for Ismaʿil's removal, a measure upon which the Europeans had already reached agreement.[32] Diplomatic maneuvers followed, and pressure was brought to bear upon the sultan. On June 26, 1879, Ismaʿil was deposed as viceroy, and succeeded by his weak and pliable son, Tawfiq. Foreign control was soon restored. Europe had established dominance over the state, with its hierarchical bureaucracy, semi-Egyptianized official class, and vast material infrastructure. And Egypt's relative political independence, for which more than one viceroy had fought and struggled, existed no more.

---

[31] Earlier, mostly nationalist, scholarship viewed the constitutionalist movement as having been indigenously inspired and imposed upon the viceroy, but this interpretation has been effectively demolished by Alexander Schölch (*Egypt for the Egyptians! The Sociopolitical Crisis in Egypt, 1878–1882* [London, 1981]).

[32] Goschen and Joubert had previously agreed that if Ismaʿil resisted the settlement, he should be removed from office and replaced by Tawfiq. Bouvier, "Les intérêts," 97, 100.

8

The Egyptian empire, 1805–1885

HASSAN AHMED IBRAHIM

>‹

Rising from obscurity to prominence in 1805, Muhammad ʿAli actively sought to carve out for himself an empire in the eastern Mediterranean. He might have planned to revitalize the Ottoman empire under his leadership, and may even have nursed the idea of replacing the sultan as Universal Caliph of Islam.[1] The Pasha's stormy expansionism on both sides of the Red Sea – in Arabia and the Sudan – and in Greece, North Africa, and above all in Syria, should be viewed within a grand design of independence and regional hegemony.[2] Since his other campaigns are dealt with elsewhere in this book (see chap. 6), we will concentrate here on the Pasha's adventures in the Arabian peninsula and his and his successors' drive into the interior of Africa.

Muhammad ʿAli's activities in Arabia

The Muwahidun movement – commonly known as the Wahhabis[3] – originated and developed in the remote plateau of Najd in central Arabia, outside the sphere of effective Ottoman power. Its founder, Shaykh Muhammad ibn ʿAbd al-Wahhab (1703–92), was a puritan and steadfastly fundamentalist *muslih* (reformer) of Islam. An *ʿalim* of the strict Hanbali *madhhab*, the shaykh "rebuked the errors and laxity of the times,"[4] and was in particular opposed to the European cultural invasion of *dar al-Islam*. He

---

[1] See Mehmet Maksudoglu, *Osmanli History* (Kuala Lumpur, forthcoming [1998]).

[2] *Encyclopaedia of Islam*, 2nd ed., "Muhammad Ali Pasha," by E. R. Toledano.

[3] Followers of Muhammad ibn ʿAbd al-Wahhab call themselves *muwahidun* (believers in the oneness of God: *daʿwat al-tawhid*). The term "Wahhabi" originated with opponents of the movement, who charged that it was a new form of Islam, and the name eventually gained wide acceptance. The movement is also sometimes called *al-Salafiyya*, those who follow the *salaf*, the great ancestors. Bernard Lewis, *The Middle East and the West* (London, 1968), 104.

[4] *The Cambridge History of Islam*, ed. Bernard Lewis, A. K. S. Lambton, and P. M. Holt (Cambridge, 1970), I, 380.

sought to eliminate the consequential *bi'da* (objectionable innovations) that had distorted Islam, and he dogmatically interpreted it in his *Kitab al-tawhid*. He recalled the Muslims to the pure and unadulterated faith and practices of the ideal state of the Prophet and the four Rightly Guided Caliphs of the seventh century. His world-view, overburdening Muslims with their past, was thus imitative, historical – and obsolete.[5]

Ibn 'Abd al-Wahhib branded all who disagreed with him as heretics and apostates, thereby justifying the use of force in imposing his austere doctrines and political will. Hence he declared a jihad – otherwise religiously impermissible – against all other Muslims, including the Ottoman sultan–caliph. The shaykh in fact considered the sultan the major source of evil and urged Muslims in Arabia and elsewhere to overthrow him. His other major target was Sufism, since its beliefs and practices transgressed, in his view, the all-important principle of *tawhid* (oneness of God), and were thus acts of *shirk* and *kufr*, polytheism and unbelief.

An alliance was established between the zealous shaykh and the warrior Muhammad ibn Sa'ud, ruler of a petty amirate around the town of Dar'iyya who, unlike some other tribal leaders, accepted the rigorous Wahhabi teachings. Armed with religious fervor and military skill, the Wahhibis waged aggressive campaigns that encroached upon the Ottoman domain. When the shaykh died in 1792, the house of Sa'ud established its domination, and the theological principles of the Wahhabis, over the whole of central Arabia. By the turn of the century, the first Sa'udi–Wahhabi state had been founded in Najd.

This state challenged the Ottoman sultanate at several levels. First and foremost was the military threat to provinces adjacent to Sa'udi-controlled territories, particularly in the Hijaz and Fertile Crescent. In 1802 the Wahhabis captured and pillaged Karbala', the burial place of the imam Husayn ibn 'Ali and a center of pilgrimage for all Shi'i Islam. Raids into the Iraqi provinces ensued in the following years. More serious were continuing Wahhabi attacks in the Hijaz, and the occupations in 1803 and 1805 respectively of Mecca and Medina themselves. Making matters worse, from 1807 Sa'ud ibn 'Abd al-'Aziz closed the Hijaz to Ottoman pilgrim caravans, thus insulting the Ottoman sultan and defying his claim to be Servitor of the Two Holy Sanctuaries.[6] Another dimension of the Wahhabi problem was its challenge to the whole Ottoman religious establishment with its hierarchy of 'ulama' and patronage of Sufi orders.

Britain, for its own reasons, shared the sultan's concern. Wahhabi expansion threatened two important international waterways – the Red Sea and the Persian Gulf – that were vital to British communications with the

[5] Abdul Hamid A. Abu Sulayman, *Crisis in the Muslim Mind* (Herndon, VA, 1993), 4–7.
[6] P. M. Holt, *Egypt and the Fertile Crescent 1516–1922*, 2nd ed. (London, 1980), 179.

east.[7] Though at odds with the Ottomans Muhammad ʿAli was himself also antagonistic to Wahhabi military and religious activities. The Wahhabi ideal of Islam, still uncorrupted by wealth, was in particular adamantly opposed to the Pasha's persistent and extensive modernizing experiments in Egypt.

To reassert his authority and restore his credibility in the eyes of the Muslims, Sultan Mahmud II (1808–39) was determined to break the power of the Wahhabis and expel them from the cradle of Islam. Conscious of his own weakness, the sultan called first upon the pashas of Baghdad and Damascus, but to no avail. His subsequent appointment of Muhammad ʿAli to organize an expedition against the Wahhabis was made in accordance with established precedent; since the extension of Ottoman suzerainty over the Arab lands, the affairs of the Hijaz had usually been overseen by the Ottoman governor of Egypt, as they had been by the Mamluk sultans.[8] This appointment may also have been a machiavellian stroke to exhaust the Pasha's resources and troops,[9] and thus prepare for the replacement of Muhammad ʿAli by another Ottoman nominee.

Muhammad ʿAli's favorable response to the sultan's command was essentially dictated by political expediency, not by loyalty or submission to his suzerain. The international situation was not conducive to any defiance; Britain and France were determined to maintain the territorial integrity of the Ottoman empire. The Pasha realized that it was in his interest not to upset the balance of power too drastically or too quickly. He temporarily concealed his ulterior motives and plans, and professed loyalty and obedience to his sovereign. He also calculated that quelling the Wahhabi revolt and winning control of the holy cities would give him immense prestige among his coreligionists, and hence enhance his chances for independence, and perhaps for the caliphate itself. He may also have seen in the engagement of his turbulent and insubordinate Albanian soldiers in faraway campaigns a chance to free himself from the threat they posed and to pursue his plans to create a loyal and disciplined army on western lines, the *nizam al-jadid*.

In 1811 the Pasha broke the power of the Mamluks by treacherously massacring their leaders in the Citadel in Cairo on the occasion of the investiture of his son Tusun as commander of the expeditionary force to the Hijaz. Tusun embarked at Suez, but his army, traveling overland, was ambushed by the Wahhabis; survivors, including some senior lieutenants, retreated. The Pasha took advantage of this disaster to execute disorderly Albanian officers and force others to retire. Tusun now organized another

---

[7] Sulayman M. al-Ghannam, *Qira'a jaddidah li siyyasat muhammad ʿali al-tawasuʿ aiyyah* (Jidda, 1980), 27–30.

[8] Holt, *Egypt and the Fertile Crescent*, 179.

[9] H. Dodwell, *The Founder of Modern Egypt* (Cambridge, 1931; repr. 1967), 43. Cf. Holt, *Egypt and the Fertile Crescent*, 179.

campaign and secured the support of the sharif of Mecca, Ghalib ibn Musa'd, and other tribal leaders. The Egyptian army took Medina, Mecca, and Jidda, and by 1813 most of the Hijaz had surrendered; prayers for the sultan were once again offered in the holy cities. The Pasha came in person to Mecca to perform the pilgrimage and give a helping hand to his son. He also replaced the wealthy sharif for alleged sympathy with the Wahhabis and sent him with three of his sons to detention in Cairo.

This strategy backfired by inciting a number of Arab tribes to revolt, and the Wahhabis began once more to gather in the desert. Reinforcements were summoned from Egypt, but this campaign, like its predecessor, opened with a disaster, after which ten senior officers fled. Nevertheless the Egyptian army regrouped under Muhammad 'Ali himself, and in 1814 decisively defeated the Wahhabi forces under Amir Faysal ibn Sa'ud. By mid-1814 Faysal was dead, and the Sa'udi front had collapsed. The Egyptian army had pressed southwards toward Yemen,[10] but the Pasha was obliged at a critical moment to return hurriedly to Egypt either because of a rumored conspiracy[11] or, more likely, owing to the tense atmosphere in Europe following Napoleon's escape from Elba. Tusun concluded in 1815 a truce with the new Sa'udi amir, 'Abdallah ibn Sa'ud, that in effect secured the status quo. The Wahhabis retained the Sa'udi homeland of Najd and some parts of the Hijaz, while the Egyptian forces controlled the holy cities and assured the safety of the pilgrimage.[12] Tusun appears to have accepted this arrangement because he feared overextension in Najd might cut him off from his supply base in the Hijaz. In any case he withdrew from Wahhabi territory, and on November 8, 1815 he returned to Egypt, where he was treated as a conquering hero although the war was not yet over. A few days later he contracted plague and died.

European affairs having been settled by the final defeat of Napoleon at Waterloo, in 1816 Muhammad 'Ali resumed the war in Arabia, where Tusun's withdrawal had encouraged Amir 'Abdallah to break the truce and start fighting again. Under the capable command of his ruthless eldest son, Ibrahim, the *wali*'s forces advanced steadily into Najd from their base at Medina. Within two years the Wahhabis' desert strongholds had fallen one after another, and in September 1818 the Sa'udi capital, Dar'iyya, was finally taken after a siege of six months and demolished. Ibrahim mercilessly executed Wahhabi 'ulama' after arguing with them over matters of doctrine.[13] Amir 'Abdallah was sent to Istanbul, where he was put to death. The sultan, guardedly pleased by the defeat of the Wahhabis, named Ibrahim a

[10] See above, p. 150.
[11] See chap. 6.
[12] Holt, *Egypt and the Fertile Crescent*, 180.
[13] Afaf Lutfi al-Sayyid Marsot, *Egypt in the Reign of Muhammad Ali* (Cambridge, 1984), 202.

three-tail pasha and appointed him governor of the Hijaz. With the awarding of this rank and title the sultan may have sought to sow seeds of dissension between father and son; Ibrahim remained loyal to his father.

Though defeated, the Wahhabis continued to resist. Ibrahim Pasha – called in Egyptian sources *qahir al-wahhabiyyin*[14] (annihilator of the Wahhabis) – failed to establish complete authority over their far-flung regions. In 1824 Najd was evacuated when Turki, son of ʿAbdallah ibn Saʿud, took power and founded the second Saʿudi–Wahhabi state which dominated the region until 1891. Muhammad ʿAli's protectorate over the Hijaz and the coastlands of Yemen lasted, however, until his general settlement with the Ottomans in 1840.

Yemen

Although Yemen had been under formal Ottoman suzerainty since early in the sixteenth century, successive imams of Sanaʿa remained virtually independent. By the turn of the nineteenth century, however, Yemen had been exposed to continual Wahhabi raids; the imam cautiously welcomed Muhammad ʿAli's initiative to stamp out the Wahhabis, though he suspected that the Pasha's eyes were set on his country. By 1813 the Egyptian army had pressed southwards, taken Qunfudha in Yemen, and controlled the southern region. In 1819 Muhammad ʿAli concluded a treaty with the imam that extended Egyptian influence down the Red Sea littoral to the Bab al-Mandab. The imam recovered in return extensive territories usurped by the Wahhabi sharif of Hudayyda, though he was obliged to pay tribute of 20,000 *bohars* of coffee. Muhammad ʿAli justified this tribute by alleging that former imams had been tributaries of the Porte through the pasha of Egypt, and secondly as a reward for restoration of nearly a whole province that the imam could not have reclaimed by his own efforts.[15]

Meanwhile the British East India Company looked with increasing suspicion on the Egyptian drive in Arabia. The company took advantage of an alleged insult to the British resident at Mocha to wage a naval and ground assault on the town in November 1820. The imam was compelled to sign a treaty on January 15, 1821 that established British influence in this chief Yemeni port, and gave Britain other important concessions. But Muhammad ʿAli was too preoccupied with other campaigns to pursue expansion in Yemen. He had to wait until a suitable opportunity arose.

While mired in his costly war in Syria, the Pasha was driven in 1832 to the Yemeni front by unforeseen developments in the Hijaz. These were related

---

[14] Abd al-Rahman al-Rafʿi, *Asr muhammad ʿali*, 4th ed. (Cairo, 1982), 164–65.
[15] Abdel Hamid al-Batrik, "Egyptian Yemeni relations 1819–1840," in P. M. Holt (ed.), *Political and Social Change in Modern Egypt* (London, 1968), 282.

to the mutiny at Jidda of some Albanian troops who had been encouraged and supported by the pasha of Baghdad. Their leader, Muhammad Agha, calculated on the eventual subjugation of his master by the Porte, and aspired to obtain the pashalik of Jidda for himself. He confiscated public property and Egyptian ships at Jidda, and planned an attack on Mecca. Defeated, he was forced to flee southwards into Yemen, where he captured several towns: Hudayyda, Zahid, Mocha, and in 1833 Aden itself. The rebels firmly established themselves in Yemen, with Mocha as their head-quarters, and seriously interrupted the Red Sea trade. This daring insurrection presented Muhammad 'Ali with the opportunity he had long wished for to invade Yemen.[16]

The death in 1832 of the ruler of Sana'a, the imam al-Mahdi, accelerated anarchy and civil war in Yemen. Commerce with Britain was largely suspended and all the coffee of Mocha was exported instead to the USA. In these circumstances Muhammad 'Ali erroneously calculated that Britain might not seriously object to his firm control of this strategic area in preference to the weak and unstable rule of the imam.

Without explicit British approval Muhammad 'Ali in 1833 sent an expedition to Mocha. Subsequently two campaigns began, one under Ahmad Yakan to Asir, and the other into Yemen under Ibrahim Yakan Pasha. The cream of Muhammad 'Ali's modern army defeated the rebels and forced them to flee. The Asir tribes were also compelled to withdraw from Mocha, and the Egyptian army and navy took most of the main towns and ports of Yemen. Ta'iz, the key to the capital (Sana'a), surrendered, and Egyptian forces reached Aden, though they withdrew after a few days. Preparations were made to capture Sana'a, where the imam had a reputation for dissoluteness and was expected to offer only token resistance. By 1838 Egypt had taken all the Arabian coast from Suez and Aqaba to Mocha.[17] With Egyptian influence spreading throughout Arabia, Muhammad 'Ali initiated plans to exploit the lucrative commercial resources of Yemen. He established a "coffee department" at Hudayyda, and planned to monopolize the coffee trade at Jidda.

Although the object of the Arabian wars was to break the power of the Wahhabis and restore the suzerainty of the Ottoman sultan, their practical result was to establish the power of the *wali* of Egypt on the east coast of the Red Sea. This threatened Britain's strategic and commercial interests. Despite Muhammad 'Ali's repeated denials of Egyptian antagonism to British interests, the British government had every reason to believe that his ambitions extended far beyond the peninsula. By the end of the 1830s the future of the region ceased to be decided by the viceroy of Egypt and was

---

[16] *Ibid.*, 284.
[17] *Ibid.*, 285.

instead determined by Britain. In 1839 the British occupied Aden and told the Pasha to evacuate Arabia. He played for time but was soon compelled to comply (in the 1840 treaty of London). Yemen was the first country to be evacuated, in May, whereupon it plunged into civil wars.

The Egyptian empire in Africa, 1805–85

Muhammad 'Ali's Arabian wars of 1813–18 were followed in 1820 by another campaign undertaken on his own initiative and account, and not that of his sovereign – although he subsequently got Ottoman recognition of his conquests. This was the campaign in Nubia, Sinnar, and Kurdufan that laid the foundation for what would be known as the "Egyptian" Sudan.

The term "Egyptian" in this context is somewhat misleading. For the Sudan was not conquered or ruled by Egyptians as we understand them today but by the Turkish-speaking elite that had dominated Egypt since medieval times. With few exceptions, true Egyptians – people of the lower Nile – were not given senior political or military posts in Egypt or the conquered Sudan. Hence the Sudanese and Europeans call the period 1821–85 in the Sudan the Turkiyya,[18] while others commonly use the clumsy neologism "Turco-Egyptian."

The strategy of Muhammad 'Ali's invasion of the Sudan has been the subject of much controversy among historians. According to many Egyptians, for whom writing is almost always an expression of patriotism, Muhammad 'Ali's primary object for what they call the *fath* ("opening up") was the welfare of the local people. The Pasha, they argue, so pitied the inhabitants of the deteriorating Funj sultanate (the Sudanese political entity best known to Egypt at this time) that he decided to step in to save them from misery and hardship, and subsequently to unite the Sudanese peoples with their brothers in Egypt in a strong state that would work for the welfare of both peoples.[19] Some Egyptian historians even claim that the Pasha undertook the *fath* "on the request of the Sudanese peoples themselves,"[20] as represented by some notables who urged it. Indeed a few Sudanese dignitaries did so, but their own motive was seemingly strictly personal and related to dynastic rivalries – they should not be assumed to have represented "the Sudan."

A prominent Egyptian historian, the late Muhammad Fu'ad Shukri, claimed that Muhammad 'Ali's conquest "firmly established Egypt's legal and historical rights" over the Sudan. The dissolution of the Funj sultanate

---

[18] Richard Hill, *Egypt in the Sudan* (London, 1959), 13.
[19] M. F. Shukri, *al-Hukm al-Misri fi'l sudan 1820–1885* (Cairo, 1948), 23.
[20] M. A. al-Jabri, *Fi sha'n allah* (Cairo, n.d.), 18.

made the Sudan, in his view, "a land without a sovereign,"[21] a no-man's land. Hence once the Pasha controlled it and established a government there, Egypt automatically became the indisputable sovereign by right of conquest.[22] One of Muhammad 'Ali's main reasons for visiting the Sudan in 1838–93 was to propagate this theory – the theory of "the vacuum" as he called it – and to use it to safeguard the unity of the Nile valley, that is to keep its two parts, Egypt and the Sudan, under one political system.[23]

This claim of Egyptian sovereignty over the Sudan was a major theme in Sudanese and Egyptian politics until at least the 1950s. Shukri seems to have been politically motivated to support the advocates of the unity of the Nile valley against those Sudanese who advocated an independent Sudan. It should also be added that the sultan of Sinnar, though a mere figurehead by 1820, remained until then the most important ruler in the country. Moreover, Egypt could not claim sovereignty over the Sudan by right of conquest, since the invasion was officially undertaken in the name of the Ottoman sultan, the territories acquired were formally annexed to his dominions, and Egypt itself continued to be an Ottoman province at least until 1914. In any case the Funj sultanate was not the Sudan as a whole, a territorial term still vague and ambiguous throughout the period of Cairo's rule.

The "welfare hypothesis" has similarly been challenged in recent studies.[24] These, based on archival data, demonstrate that the conquest was closely related to Muhammad 'Ali's grand design of autonomy and regional hegemony.[25] This in turn required a strong army and the wealth that the Pasha obviously looked for in the Sudan. Hence exploitation rather than welfare was the prime object of conquest.

Just before his invasion of the Sudan, Muhammad 'Ali embarked on the formation of a strong and docile army trained in the European manner and personally loyal to him. While at first ruling out for many reasons[26] the conscription of Egyptian fallahin, the Pasha planned to recruit twenty or thirty thousand Sudanese Africans for his *nizam al-jadid*. More Sudanese were also needed for his numerous agricultural and industrial enterprises in Egypt, and for sale too in the slave markets. The Pasha later constantly urged, and often scolded, his commanders in the Sudan to intensify their *ghazwas* – armed slave raids – and to send the greatest possible number of Africans to the training-camp at Aswan, sited for its remoteness from the noisy Delta towns and its proximity to the Sudanese slave reservoir. He

[21] M. F. Shukri, *Misr wa al-sayyadah ala al-sudan* (Cairo, 1946), 18.
[22] *Ibid.*, 38–39.
[23] M. F. Shukri, *Misr wa al-sudan* (Cairo, 1958), 13.
[24] See e.g. H. A. Ibrahim, *Muhammad 'ali fi'l sudan*, 2nd ed. (Khartoum, 1991); and B. K. Humaydah, *Malamih min ta'rikh al-sudan fi 'ad al-khidawi isma'il* (Khartoum, n.d.).
[25] See above, pp. 150–65.
[26] See chap. 6.

stressed in one directive that this was the most important reason for under-taking the "difficulties and expenditure" of the conquest, and described in another this inhuman practice as his "utmost desire irrespective of the means used to do it."[27]

Although hardly a year passed until 1838 without at least one *ghazwa* for blacks in the Nuba mountains and beyond Fazughli, the supply of slaves ran very short of demand. Muhammad 'Ali's optimistic hope of swelling the slave army of his dreams was based on no thorough survey of Sudanese potential. The Sudanese blacks, moreover, stubbornly resisted the *ghazwas*, some even committing suicide to avoid enslavement. Some of those captured were lost en route while others perished by the hundreds in the Egyptian climate and from diseases.[28] Faced with this failure, the Pasha finally began conscription of the Egyptian peasantry, and soon discovered that they made much better soldiers than anyone had expected.[29]

The few blacks recruited for the Egyptian army were unsuccessful in Egypt's adventures abroad. While Muhammad 'Ali employed them in his wars in Arabia and the Morea, the viceroy Muhammad Sa'id (1854–63), in response to a request by Napoleon III, in 1863 sent part of a Sudanese battalion to Mexico to take part in the French effort to suppress rebellion there.[30] Similarly the black recruits for military service in the Sudan itself were insubordinate and rebellious. Many military risings took place in the country, of which the most dangerous were in Wad Madani in 1844 and Kassala in 1865.[31]

Equally important was Muhammad 'Ali's desire to exploit Sudanese minerals, particularly gold. On his assumption of power in 1805 Egypt was one of the poorest Ottoman provinces, if not the very poorest. The Pasha anxiously looked for a source of revenue to achieve his expensive internal schemes and foreign adventures. Obsessed from early manhood to old age with the illusion of abundant gold in the Sudan, he made strenuous efforts to discover it, particularly in the Fazughli area and around Jabal Shaybun in the Nuba mountains. Apart from urging on his commanders the necessity of gold-prospecting, he occasionally sent mineralogists to the Sudan, for example the Austrian J. von Russeger and his own engineer, the Piedmontese Boreani. The disparity between the optimistic report of the former and the pessimistic one of the latter was intriguing enough to induce the Pasha to travel to Fazughli himself in 1838–39 – at the age of seventy – to supervise

---

[27] Quoted in Ibrahim, *Muhammad 'ali*, 25.
[28] Hill, *Egypt*, 25.
[29] *Ibid.*, 7.
[30] Richard Hill and Peter Hogg, *A Black Corps d'elite* (East Lansing, 1995); Umar Tusun, *Butalah al-urtah al-sudaniyyah al-misriyyah fi harb al-maksik* (Alexandria, 1933).
[31] For the Madani rising see Ibrahim, *Muhammad 'ali*, 93–94; for the Kassala rising see N. Shuqayr, *Gughrafiat wa ta'rikh al-Sudan*, 2nd ed. (Beirut, 1967).

mining activities. But his three-week stay was extremely disappointing.[32] Attempts to exploit the iron deposits of Kurdufan and the copper of Hufrat al-Nahhas in southern Dar Fur were also failures.[33] Government mining activities were expensive failures, costing a great deal and producing little.

The Egyptians were more successful in improving and exploiting the agriculture of the Sudan. They sent agricultural experts who improved irrigation, developed existing crops, planted new ones, and effectively combated plagues and pests, particularly locusts. Veterinary doctors were appointed to look after the animals, and experts were dispatched from Egypt to teach the preservation of hides and skins. After the many years of political disorder in the middle Nile that had almost stopped trade with Egypt, the conquest gave greater security to northern Sudanese and Egyptian traders, and made possible the eventual introduction of European commerce.[34]

Nevertheless, prosperity in agriculture and animal wealth were apparently not used to benefit the Sudanese. Instead, the government was concerned mainly with exporting wealth to Egypt. Muhammad 'Ali imposed a strict state monopoly on almost all of the country's products and exports. Consequently considerable quantities of Sudanese products – indigo, gum, ivory, and so forth – were exported to Egypt. Similarly, throughout the period of Egyptian rule the Sudan was Egypt's cheapest source of livestock. In spite of difficulties in moving them down the Nile, with raids by thieving nomads and a lack of organized feeding and watering arrangements, a steady flow of cattle arrived each year in Egypt. Animal products such as hides and hair were also sent.[35]

Besides the primary motive of exploitation, there were political considerations behind the conquest and administration of the Sudan. While presumably hoping to get rid in the Sudan campaigns of the rebellious Albanian soldiery that had brought him to power, Muhammad 'Ali was more concerned with the remnants of the Mamluks who, after the massacre and proscription in Egypt in 1811, had escaped southwards and established themselves at Old Dongola. Though remote and insignificant in number, the Mamluks' extraordinary vitality and tenacity caused anxiety to the Pasha. As early as 1812 he sent an embassy to the Funj sultan to expel them, but he was too weak to comply. The majority of the Mamluks finally surrendered to the invading army in 1820–21 and were allowed to return honorably to

---

[32] A report on this journey was supposedly published in the official gazette *Vagai i misriya*. Hill and Shukri place it as an appendix to issue 618 published in Alexandria on April 21, 1839. Attempts since 1965 to locate such an appendix have been unsuccessful. A copy found in 1977 in the Centre for Contemporary Egyptian Studies in Cairo has been published as *Rihlat muhammad 'ali ila al-sudan 15 October 1838–14 March 1839* (Khartoum, 1980; 2nd ed., 1991).

[33] Ibrahim, *Muhammad 'ali*, 129–32.

[34] Hill, *Egypt*, 49–57.

[35] Ibrahim, *Muhammad 'ali*, 135–54.

Egypt, though a few fugitives continued their flight, some toward Dar Fur, others toward Arabia, and vanished from history.[36]

Had not the Ottoman sultan insisted on an immediate Egyptian expedition to suppress the Wahhabis in Arabia,[37] the conquest of the Sudan might have been Muhammad ʿAli's first war after his expulsion of the British expedition of 1807.[38] The intelligence brought back by the embassy of 1812 that revealed the military weakness and fragmentation of the Funj sultanate encouraged the Pasha to go ahead with his plans to invade the Sudan. In 1819 he traveled to Nubia himself to supervise preparations for the expeditionary force that was sent under the command of his third son, Ismaʿil Kamil Pasha. Three ʿulamaʾ were attached to this expedition to urge the Sudanese Muslims to submit to the army of the representative of their caliph the Ottoman sultan. Apart from a brief resistance by the truculent Shaiqiya tribe,[39] the invaders advanced almost without opposition until June 1821 when they reached Sinnar, where Badi VI, the last Funj sultan, surrendered. Meanwhile another expeditionary force was sent in April 1821 under the command of the Pasha's son-in-law Muhammad Bey Khusrav, the *daftardar*, to conquer the remote sultanate of Dar Fur. This force struck across the desert to Kurdufan, a dependency of Dar Fur which was conquered after a couple of brutal engagements, in one of which its governor, the Maqdum Musallam, defiantly resisted the invaders and was killed in the fighting.[40] The ultimate objective of subjugating Dar Fur itself was, however, too risky to be accomplished, and thus was shelved for some fifty years; Dar Fur was annexed in 1874.[41]

The Sudanese had not paid regular taxes during the time of the Funj sultanate, and the burden of the government had been light, particularly on the poor. But in striving to mobilize and exploit Sudanese resources the Egyptian administration extended to the Sudan an oppressive and altogether unknown Egyptian system of taxation that disrupted the economic life of the country. What made matters worse was the brutal means used by the *bashbuzq* – irregular soldiers – and their frequent insistence that taxes should be paid in cash, though the use of coin was still restricted to merchants and townspeople.[42]

The reaction of the people was immediate and often violent. Some fled to Abyssinia while others rose in desperate tax revolts throughout the period of

[36] P. M. Holt and M. W. Daly, *A History of the Sudan*, 4th ed. (London, 1988), 47, 50–51.

[37] See above, pp. 144–45.

[38] A. al-Rafiʿi, *Taʾrikh al-haraka al-qawmiyyah wa tatwr nizam al-hukm fi misr*, III, ʿAsr muhammad ʿali (Cairo, 1930), 73.

[39] Ismaʿil recognized the value of the Shaiqiya and enlisted them as irregular cavalry.

[40] Musallam sent a defiant letter to the *daftardar*.

[41] See above, pp. 000–00.

[42] The Funj sultanate struck no coin, and most of its trade was by barter.

Egyptian rule. Perhaps the most violent of these was the widespread rebellion of 1822 in which Isma'il and his staff were burned alive by *mak* (chief) Nimr of the Ja'aliyyin tribe, and thousands of Sudanese fled to the Abyssinian borders.[43] That rising was soon crushed by the government's superior firearms and by the ruthless massacres of the *daftardar* who, on hearing of the assassination, rushed from Kurdufan to the Nile. Though a rising of despair, without united leadership, this revolt alerted Muhammad 'Ali to the necessity of conciliating the resentful Sudanese if the objectives of the conquest were to be actively pursued. Hence the Pasha's serious attempt to inaugurate after 1825 a policy of allaying the fear of the people and securing the collaboration of their leaders, notably Shaykh 'Abd al-Qadir wad al-Zayn (d. 1857), who progressively rose in rank to become the government's chief local advisor. The Pasha also started the practice, continued by his successors, of inviting Sudanese notables to visit him in Egypt.[44]

Despite Sudanese resistance, the Pasha continued his expansionist policy in Africa. His next major target was the eastern region where the Abyssinian marches gave a convenient refuge for malcontents from the Nile. When clemency failed to secure their return to the land of their fathers, the Pasha used force in the 1830s. There began in 1837 a series of raids and counter-raids across the borders that continued at intervals until 1889 when the Mahdist amir al-Zaki Tamal destroyed the Abyssinian army of King John IV at Qallabat.[45]

After Kanfu, the Abyssinian ruler of the frontier district of Kwara, had seemingly conspired with the Hadandawa tribes to invade the Egyptian Sudan, the battle of Wad Kaltabu, deep in Sudanese territory, in April 1837 ended in a heavy defeat for the Egyptians. Though the Abyssinians withdrew, the government was thoroughly alarmed lest the enemy annex the important frontier districts around Qallabat. Hence the governor-general, Khurshid Pasha (1826–38), got the approval of Muhammad 'Ali for a reprisal raid that was not, however, carried out because of a stern British warning against any attack on Christian Abyssinia. Khurshid's successor, Ahmad Pasha Abu Widan (1838–43), nevertheless annexed al-Taka province, the region of Khur al-Kash, and the Red Sea hills; Kassala developed as the chief administrative center. But the Hadandawa remained restive, and Ahmad Pasha al-Manikli, the new governor-general,[46] sent a punitive expedition that was carried out with such vigor (including the slaughter of

---

[43] Mekki Shibayka, *al-Sudan fi qarn* (Cairo, 1957), 33–35.

[44] Hill, *Egypt*, 46.

[45] See M. S. al-Qaddal, *al-Mahdiyya wa'l habasha* (Beirut, 1992), 141–44.

[46] Abu Widan was rumored to be plotting independence or conspiring with the Ottoman sultan for separation of the Sudan from Egypt; when Abu Widan died in October 1843 it was rumored that the Pasha had had him poisoned.

forty captured notables in Khartoum) that he won the slanderous nickname of *al-Jazzar* (the butcher).[47]

Extension of the Egyptian Sudan toward the Red Sea inevitably brought into prominence the question of future control of the important ports of Suakin and Massawa, then nominal dependencies of the Ottoman *wilaya* of the Hijaz. In 1843 Muhammad 'Ali raised the question of their status, and demanded that they should pay taxes to his Sudanese treasury. In 1846, however, Istanbul granted the ports to the Pasha on a lease, renewable annually, in return for an increase in tribute. But this lease was terminated in 1849 under British pressure, and another fifteen years passed before the ports were permanently annexed to the Egyptian Sudan in 1865.[48]

Exploration and control of the sources of the Nile is sometimes asserted to have been one of the main reasons for the conquest of the Sudan.[49] But this is far-fetched; Muhammad 'Ali exhibited interest in this geographical issue only some fifteen years after the conquest, and only in response to the growing desire of European learned societies to discover the sources of the White Nile. The Pasha seemingly expected abundant gold there as, in his own words, "the sources of the Nile should be on the same latitude as America."[50] Hence he sent the Egyptian Salim Qabudan on three famous journeys up the Nile in 1839–42.[51] Though the scientific and mining objectives were unrealized, these journeys opened the White Nile to navigation, gave great impetus to the lucrative trade in ivory and human beings, and accelerated Egyptian ventures in the interior of Africa during the era of Khedive Isma'il (1863–79).

The Egyptian drive to the interior of Africa, 1863–85

While neither of Muhammad 'Ali's two immediate successors ('Abbas and Sa'id, 1848–63) wished to emulate his foreign adventures, the ambitious and impatient modernizer Isma'il embarked on an aggressive expansionist policy in Africa. Suppression of slavery and the slave trade was the reason given by the khedive for this expansion. On his initiative Egypt and Britain concluded in 1877 an anti-slavery convention that promised to stop the slave trade immediately and to terminate the domestic slave trade (that is exchange of slaves between families) within twelve years.[52]

By 1869 Isma'il's campaign against slavery had been reasonably successful

---

[47] Holt and Daly, *A History*, 68.
[48] *Ibid.*, 67; Hill, *Egypt*, 83–84.
[49] Al-Rafi'i, *Asr muhammad 'ali*, 232.
[50] Quoted in Hill, *Egypt*, 32.
[51] For these journeys see Nasim Maqar, *al-Bikbashi al-masri salim qabudan wa al-kashf 'an Manabia al-nil al-abyad* (Cairo, n.d.).
[52] Cf. Humaydah, *Malamih*, 142–43.

in the upper Nile around Fashoda; the slavers remained dominant south of this district and in the Bahr al-Ghazal. He, however, continued his predecessors' policy of taxation and of discrimination against the already weakened European traders. By the end of the 1860s most of them had been forced to leave the Sudan, and trade was almost exclusively controlled by Egyptians, Turks, and northern Sudanese. These last, subsequently known as *al-jallaba*,[53] were originally employed by alien merchants but had gradually acquired responsibility and power of their own. They erected a series of *zara'ib* (sing. *zariba*, fenced enclosure) manned by armed retainers, which were used as bases for conducting forays into neighboring regions for ivory and slaves.[54]

Khedive Isma'il was particularly intrigued by expansion into the vast hinterland of the southern Sudan and toward the Great Lakes. His schemes to annex Equatoria were carried out by the freelance traveler Samuel Baker (in 1869–73) and the legendary Charles Gordon (in 1874–76 and 1877–79). Their terms of reference were to annex to Egypt the country south of the key station of Gondokoro, open the Great Lakes to navigation, and suppress the slave trade that had quickly eclipsed that in ivory. Lacking tact and statesmanship they, however, concentrated on crushing the slavers' power through a series of coercive measures, to the detriment of the khedive's other policies.

In spite of their advanced equipment Baker and Gordon were unable to extend Egyptian administration in Equatoria beyond a few scattered military posts. But their extensive use of violence destroyed the confidence of the southern peoples and provoked a wave of violent resistance. Rather than recognizing Egyptian sovereignty over his kingdom, as Gordon hoped, Mutesa, the king of Buganda, mobilized a powerful army against the invaders.[55] Added to this resistance were the hostility and intrigues of traders led by the Egyptian Muhammad Abu al-Su'ud, representing the firm of al-Aqqad; the formidable *sudd* barrier; and diseases that killed or invalided Baker's and Gordon's men. It should also be noted that slavery was a deeply rooted institution in African societies, and that its violent suppression disturbed their economies. While governor-general of the Sudan (1877–79) Gordon finally abandoned the Egyptian advance into the interior of Africa.

Gordon's successor as governor of Equatoria, the German doctor Eduard Schnitzer (1840–92), commonly known after his conversion to Islam as Emin Pasha,[56] inherited a weak and disorganized administration. This,

---

53 The Arabic word *jallaba* derives from the noun *jallab*, which in this context means "one who brings slaves."

54 R. O. Collins, *The Southern Sudan in Historical Perspective* (Tel Aviv, 1975), 18–19.

55 Richard Gray, *A History of the Southern Sudan 1839–1889* (London, 1961), 110–17.

56 See G. Schweitzer, *Emin Pasha, his Life and Work* (London, 1898); I. R. Smith, *The Emin Pasha Relief Expedition 1886–1890* (Oxford, 1972).

coupled with a mutiny in the ranks, led finally to his withdrawal during the Mahdiyya to the east coast. This disintegration of the Egyptian administration marked the *de facto* end of Egypt's rudimentary rule in Equatoria. By 1893 most of the region had been incorporated into the British protectorate of Uganda.

Meanwhile the Egyptian advance in the Bahr al-Ghazal was challenged by the powerful slave traders whose *zara'ib* were scattered throughout the region. They rallied behind the greatest of the region's traders, al-Zubayr Rahma Mansur,[57] a northern Sudanese who had come to the Bahr al-Ghazal in 1856 and within a decade had built a vast trading empire with its headquarters at Daym Zubayr. In 1872 he defeated a government expedition sent to annex Equatoria, and killed its leader, the Moroccan adventurer Muhammad al-Bilali (or Hilali). Confronted with this *fait accompli*, Khedive Isma'il officially recognized Zubayr as governor of the Bahr al-Ghazal. But Zubayr looked beyond the frontiers even of this vast province to Dar Fur, a largely untapped source of slaves. The Fur sultan Ibrahim mobilized his army and people, and put up a gallant resistance, but Zubayr's private and superior *bazinger* army defeated and killed the sultan at the battle of Manawashi in 1874.

The Egyptian government capitalized at once on Zubayr's conquest by rushing an expeditionary force from Kurdufan and formally annexing Dar Fur. Zubayr felt betrayed and went to Cairo to protest at what he considered an attempt by the governor-general in Khartoum, Isma'il Ayyub, to rob him of his rights of conquest. The khedive detained him in Cairo, and initiated policies to break up his power in the Bahr al-Ghazal. Nevertheless the slave dealers rallied to his son, Sulayman, and challenged the authority of the government to the extent of proclaiming an intention to march on Khartoum. They were defeated, and the governor of the province, Romolo Gessi, an Italian, executed Sulayman and his associates without a proper trial. The province, however, remained turbulent; Gessi himself left without authorization fifteen months after this incident and was tried in 1880 for abandoning his post. Another foreigner, the young British officer Frank Lupton, took over, but he lacked vision and ability to face the imminent threat of the Mahdist forces.

The Egyptian acquisition of Suakin and Massawa in 1865,[58] in return for increased tribute to the Porte and presents to the Ottoman ministers, opened a new phase in the relations of Egypt and Abyssinia. Khedive Isma'il, who gave substantial support to Britain against Abyssinia in 1867–68, expected British neutrality at least in his own contemplated war with Abyssinia. In 1871 he appointed an aggressive Swiss adventurer, J. A. W. Munzinger, as

[57] For Zubayr's own account of his career see Shuqayr, *Gughrafiat*, 568–99.
[58] See above, p. 210.

governor of Massawa, and subsequently extended his authority over the whole Red Sea and Somali coasts, including the sultanate of Harrar in eastern Abyssinia in 1875. After Munzinger died in 1875 in an ambush, the khedive continued his efforts to expand the Egyptian empire in East Africa. But the outcome was calamitous for Egypt and her army. Two expeditionary forces sent in 1875 and 1876 to invade Abyssinia underestimated the strength of an enemy fighting in his own country. They were overwhelmingly defeated after costing the depleted Egyptian treasury about 3 million pounds. The khedive had now no option but to negotiate a humiliating peace by which the Egyptian army withdrew from Abyssinia in disgrace.[59]

The outbreak of the Mahdist revolution in 1881 shook the very foundation of Egypt's rule in all its African dependencies, which by then comprised, in addition to the Sudan itself, the Eritrean and Somali districts. The most serious immediate consequence of the annihilation of the Egyptian army commanded by the British officer Hicks Pasha at Shaykan in November 1883, was the collapse of the Egyptian administration in the Bahr al-Ghazal and Dar Fur. The latter province had been ungovernable since its annexation in 1874, though its governor since 1881, Rudolf Slatin, publicly professed Islam in a vain attempt to secure the loyalty of the Muslim army and populace. By 1882 the unrest in Dar Fur had assumed a Mahdist complexion, and the Mahdi sent his cousin and a rebellious subordinate of Slatin, Muhammad Khalid Zuqul, to end Egyptian rule there. By December 1883 Slatin had submitted.[60] The provincial capital, al-Fashir, surrendered to the Ansar on January 15, 1884 after a week's siege. As for the Bahr al-Ghazal, it was already on the verge of anarchy when the Mahdi sent a certain merchant, Karamallah al-Kurkusawi, on a full-scale invasion of the province. Its governor, Lupton, who seems to have accepted Islam in terror, surrendered in 1884. His capitulation ended the brief Egyptian rule in the Bahr al-Ghazal.[61]

The Mahdi's next target was Khartoum, capital of the Egyptian Sudan, which was still in communication with Cairo by both the Nile and Suakin–Red Sea routes. Under the amir 'Uthman Diqna the Mahdists struck in 1884 in the strategic hinterland of Suakin. Within a few months they controlled the Suakin–Berber road and threatened Suakin itself, which remained in Egyptian hands only because of British military intervention to protect the Red Sea ports. Simultaneously Mahdist forces, under the command of Amir Muhammad al-Khayr, succeeded in cutting off the Nile

[59] For Egypt's expansion in East Africa see al-Rafi'i, *Asr isma'il*, 3rd ed., 2 vols. (Cairo, 1882), 136–52.
[60] For Slatin see Richard Hill, *Slatin Pasha* (London, 1965).
[61] For the collapse of Egyptian rule in Dar Fur and the Bahr al-Ghazal see P. M. Holt, *The Mahdist State in the Sudan*, 2nd ed. (Oxford, 1970), 73–80.

route; Khartoum was virtually cut off from Cairo. The Mahdi now left Kurdufan and placed the capital under close siege.

Egyptian rule in the Sudan was dominated during its last two years (1883–85) by British policy in Egypt. Britain had occupied Egypt in 1882, but regarded the revolt in the Sudan as outside its responsibilities – though Egypt was advised against large-scale operations to regain lost territory. Following the disaster of Shaykan, however, the British prevented despatch of the reorganized Egyptian army to suppress the rising, and ordered the Egyptian government to evacuate the Sudan. The premier, Muhammad Sharif, rejected this so-called "Granville doctrine"[62] and resigned in protest. He was succeeded by Nubar Pasha, who proceeded to implement the abandonment policy.

Thus there came about Gordon's third and tragic mission in the Sudan. It is not necessary to describe the train of events that led to this mission and the confusion that surrounded it, as these have been detailed in a flood of controversial literature the like of which the Sudan has never seen before or since.[63] It suffices to state here that Gordon totally underestimated the religious devotion, military strength, and political skill of the Mahdi, and that he abandoned the role to "report and advise" on the peaceful evacuation of the country, and assumed instead the authority to execute such a policy. A pious Christian, General Gordon seemed to have viewed the issue as a personal struggle between himself and the Mahdi, particularly when the latter strongly advised him in March 1884 to accept Islam and the Ansar uniform, the patched *jubba*. Hence Gordon openly spoke of the need "to smash up" the Mahdi, but the outcome was his beheading on January 26, 1885, and the loss of what remained of the Egyptian empire in Africa once and for all.

The Egypt legacy in Africa

The nineteenth-century Egyptian drive in Africa was largely unsuccessful in attaining its basic objectives, exploitation of African wealth, expansion of Egypt's dominions deep into the interior of Africa, and an immediate end to slavery and the slave trade. Egyptian rule, though not so disastrous as some critics have suggested, was oppressive, corrupt, and incompetent. Nevertheless Egypt left behind a legacy that cannot and should not be denied or ignored, particularly in that part of Africa that became known as the Sudan.[64]

It is generally agreed that modern Sudanese history starts with the

---

[62] See Afaf Lutfi al-Sayyid Marsat, *Egypt and Cromer* (London, 1968), 57.
[63] See Richard Hill, "The Gordon literature," *Durham University Journal*, see series, 16, 3 (1955), 97–101.
[64] See Nasim Maqqar, *Misr wa bina al-sudan al-hadith* (Cairo, 1993).

Egyptian campaigns of 1820–21. With the conquest of Sinnar and Kurdufan the nucleus of what is now the Republic of the Sudan was established. Egyptian control of the northern and central Sudan was rounded off in 1841 by the conquest of al-Taka, while Dar Fur, Equatoria, the Bahr al-Ghazal, and the Red Sea coast were all incorporated in the Sudan during the reign of Khedive Ismaʿil. On the eve of the Mahdiyya the Sudan had thus formed an immense block of territory extending from the second cataract to the equatorial lakes and from the Red Sea to the western marches of Dar Fur.[65]

Apart from politically uniting the Sudan within frontiers approximating those of the present republic, the Egyptian regime also started the process of modernization. The chief technological innovations introduced by the Egyptians were firearms, steamers, and the telegraph, which was extended to the Sudan during the reign of Khedive Ismaʿil. Their use played a vital part in Egypt's southward drive and was instrumental in the centralized administrative system established by the Egyptians in the nineteenth century and subsequently inherited by the Mahdists, the Condominium regime, and the independent Sudan. Egyptian centralism had gradually "imposed on the heterogeneous peoples of these diverse regions a greater uniformity than they had ever previously known,"[66] and Egypt's modernizing tendencies were continued by the Condominium administrators and dominated their administrative and educational systems.

The Egyptian opening of the south, the Nuba mountains, and Dar Fur offered new opportunities to the *jallaba*. While only a few of them had visited before the Egyptian conquest, many rushed in, particularly in the 1870s, after those regions became accessible from the north. The *jallaba* played an important part in extending the frontiers of Arabic and Islam in the south, Dar Fur, and the Nuba mountains. But the frequent resort to violence and a contemptuous attitude toward the African population succeeded, with other important factors,[67] in nurturing the distrust and fear that today dominates relations between the northern Sudan and those marginalized regions, particularly the south.

The religious life of the northern Sudanese people was also greatly affected by changes resulting from Egyptian rule. Though both the Egyptians and Sudanese had been loyal to Islam as such, there was a great gulf between the official Sunni Islam of the Egyptian administration and the Sufi Islam of the Sudanese that had developed since the Funj period. In the Sudan, as in Egypt, it was the policy of Muhammad ʿAli and his successors to establish a secular state in which Islamic institutions would have a minimal role, and mostly in personal matters. Consequently the Sufi Islam of the Sudan, which

[65] Besides the Sudan proper, the Egyptian Sudan included the Eritrean and Somali coasts.
[66] P. M. Holt, "The Islamization of the Nilotic Sudan," in Michael Brett (ed.), *Northern Africa: Islam and modernization* (London, 1973), 19.
[67] On this subject see M. O. Beshir, *The Southern Sudan* (London, 1975).

already had a profound grip on rulers and ruled, was bound to suffer severe blows. The Egyptian administration consistently underestimated the prestige of local religious leadership, which consisted of the hereditary *fakis* (teachers) of the Sufi orders. The Egyptians promoted orthodox Islam. By maintaining a hierarchy of 'ulama' and facilitating their education at al-Azhar, the Egyptian administration confronted the *fakis* with a rival group "more orthodox and alien in its outlook, and more directly dependent on the government." By the end of Egyptian rule, the prestige of traditional religious leaders had therefore "undergone considerable diminution." The essence of this policy that aimed at building up an orthodox Muslim establishment was subsequently adopted by the Condominium administrators to combat Mahdism and the Sufi orders which they regarded as "potential seed-beds of subversion and fanaticism."[68]

The process of modernization was accompanied and fostered by an increasing number of foreign residents and visitors,[69] both European and North American. While very few Europeans had visited the Sudan before 1820, the Egyptian conquest opened up the country to foreigners who came as travelers, traders, and missionaries, as well as technical experts and employees of the administration. Those employees, who were rapidly introduced into the service, particularly during the decade preceding the outbreak of the Mahdiyya, made an impact on Sudanese society both in the Arabized north and in other regions. Alien in language, customs, and religion, they created tension among the mass of the Sudanese people. Excessive use of Europeans in posts for which they were usually unsuited in fact provoked Sudanese resentment of foreigners to such an extent that xenophobia became general. Though employees of Muslim Egypt, these officials were, moreover, accused of serving Europe and Christianity rather than Egypt and Islam.[70] The Mahdi's declared intention of freeing the country from alien and Christian control therefore found ready support from the populace.

[68] Holt, "The islamization," 21.
[69] Rifaʿa Rafiʿa al-Tahtawi, one of the pillars of modernization in Egypt, spent a few unhappy years in Khartoum (1849–54), in virtual exile and without noticeable impact on the cause of modernization or education there.
[70] Mekki Shibayka, "The Expansionist Movement of Khedive Ismaʿil to the Lakes," in Y. F. Hasan (ed.), *Sudan in Africa* (Khartoum, 1971), 155.

9

The 'Urabi revolution and the British conquest, 1879–1882

DONALD MALCOLM REID

>‹

Introduction

Between September 1881 and September 1882 the 'Urabi revolution in Egypt tried to roll back Anglo-French financial and political predominance, the Turco-Circassian[1] monopoly on high military posts, and the authority of Khedive Tawfiq. Like Colonel Nasir, Colonel Ahmad 'Urabi gave his name to an upheaval that challenged the Muhammad 'Ali dynasty and European power. While Nasir's revolution was a qualified success, however, 'Urabi's failed, ending in outright British occupation and reducing the nominally restored khedive almost to a figurehead.

Egyptian partisans of Tawfiq and many westerners have dismissed the 'Urabi movement as a mere military revolt. It is called a revolution here to emphasize the movement's extensive civilian involvement and social depth. For some, a failed revolution is by definition only a rebellion or a revolt. But if we are to continue calling the failed upheavals of Europe in 1848 and Russia in 1905 revolutions, there is no reason to single out the 'Urabi movement for demotion to "revolt."

The military demonstration at 'Abdin palace on September 9, 1881 began

---

This chapter relies primarily on Alexander Schölch, *Egypt for the Egyptians! The Sociopolitical Crisis in Egypt 1878–1882* (London, 1981). The German original, *Ägypten den Ägyptern! Die politische und gesellschaftliche Krise der Jahre 1878–1882 in Ägypten* (Zurich, 1972), has fuller notes. The comparative approach of Juan R. I. Cole, *Colonialism and Revolution in the Middle East: Social and Cultural Origins of Egypt's 'Urabi Movement* (Princeton, 1993) yields additional insights. See also Michael Serge Horn, "The 'Urabi Revolution: Convergent Crises in Nineteenth-Century Egypt," Ph.D. thesis, Harvard University, 1973.

[1] "Turco-Circassian" rather than "Turkish" is used here to emphasize the Circassian origin of many of the Turkish-speaking elite. Ehud R. Toledano, *State and Society in Mid-Nineteenth-Century Egypt* (Cambridge, 1990), 77–82, prefers "Ottoman-Egyptians." Ibrahim Abu-Lughod, "The Transformation of the Egyptian Elite: Prelude to the 'Urabi Revolt," *The Middle East Journal*, 21 (1967), 325–44, emphasizes the assimilation of many "Turks."

the revolution, forcing the khedive to dismiss Mustafa Riyad's cabinet.[2] Wealthy landed notables from the previous *majlis shura al-nuwwab* (hereafter, the chamber) sanctioned the army's move in advance, and people from a range of social backgrounds quickly lent their support.

The slogan "Egypt for the Egyptians" underlines the proto-nationalist strand in the revolution. This was not conceived in narrow ethnic terms and coexisted easily with religio-political appeals to jihad and professions of loyalty to the Ottoman sultan–caliph (sultan 'Abd al-Hamid II did not denounce 'Urabi as a rebel until seven days before the fateful battle of Tall al-Kabir). Anti-"Turkish" comments were sometimes couched in "Arab" terms, but pan-Arabism was hardly on the horizon.

As the revolution unfolded in three stages between the Septembers of 1881 and 1882, several groups broke with the revolutionary coalition to stand with Tawfiq and the Europeans: Muhammad Sharif's clique of wealthy Turco-Circassian "constitutionalists," liberal Syrian Christian journalists, parliamentary deputies who were also great provincial landlords (such as Muhammad Sultan) or wealthy merchants, and some indigenous officials and 'ulama'. There is no prevailing consensus today on the socioeconomic dimensions of the minutely studied French Revolution. Generalizations on the 'Urabi revolution must be far more tentative, for socioeconomic archival research on it has a long way to go.[3]

Those who stayed with the 'Urabi revolution included a few Turco-Circassian officers and officials, indigenous Egyptian army officers, some provincial landlords and parliamentary deputies, and many indigenous officials, 'ulama', and village shaykhs or *'umdas*. The abundance of the very rich – Europeans, Turco-Circassians, indigenous landowners, and merchants – in Tawfiq's camp suggests a social edge to the revolution; so do middle- and lower-class participation in urban riots and occasional peasant seizures of estates. On the whole, however, widespread middle- and lower-class participation does not seem to have pointed toward a radical social revolution from below.

Over a century after the fact, historians still argue as to why Gladstone, the ostensibly anti-imperialist prime minister, occupied Egypt. Robinson and Gallagher's *Africa and the Victorians* (1961) thesis sparked a generation of

---

[2] Riyad Pasha. "Pasha," "bey," "effendi," and "shaykh" are often omitted here for reasons of economy, and "cabinet" stands for "council of ministers."

[3] Schölch, *Egypt*; Cole, *Colonialism*; and Horn, "'Urabi Revolution" make extensive use of the Egyptian National Archives. Arabic works based on archival research on the 'Urabi revolution include Abdel Moneim El Gameiy ('Abd al-Mun'im al-Jami'i), *al-Thawra al-'urabiyya: buhuth wa dirasat watha'iqiyya* (Cairo, 1982); Abdel Moneim El Gameiy (ed.), *al-Thawra al-'urabiyya fi da al-watha'iq al-misriyya* (Cairo, 1982); Latifa Muhammad Salim, *al-Quwwa al-ijtima'iyya fi al-thawra al-'urabiyya* (Cairo, 1981); and some of the studies in *Misr lil-misriyyin: mi'at amm 'ala al-thawra al-'urabiyyin* (Cairo, 1981).

debate and research. It emphasized political and strategic factors in this case of "informal empire" – a perceived collapse of law and order on the periphery, a proto-nationalist revolt, a threat to the Suez route to India, Anglo-French rivalry, and maneuvering by "men on the spot" in Egypt. Cain and Hopkins have recently returned to economic causes, stressing "gentlemanly" financial and commercial, rather than industrial, capitalism. The present chapter pays less attention to decision making in Whitehall, Westminster, the City of London, Calcutta, Paris, Istanbul, and Berlin than to the causes and course of the revolution in Egypt itself.[4]

Egypt at the end of Isma'il's reign[5]

In 1876 bankruptcy forced Khedive Isma'il to accept both a *caisse de la dette publique* (public debt commission) representing his European creditors, and British and French financial controllers (hence the Dual Control) in his government. Two years later he lost control of his family's estates and the cabinet itself when Boghos Nubar set up a European cabinet with an Englishman at finance and a Frenchman at public works. Beginning in 1876 the mixed courts provided yet another instrument by which Europeans were tightening their grip on Isma'il and Egypt.

The career of Evelyn Baring, the army officer from a famous banking family who later became Lord Cromer, tracked the progress of British domination. In 1877 he took a seat on the *caisse* as the representative of private British bondholders. In 1879 he moved inside Egypt's government as controller-general of revenues. Returning from India in 1883 to become consul-general, he set about making himself *de facto* ruler.[6]

The British never relaxed their wary eye on their French rivals in Egyptian affairs,[7] but by 1880 British economic interests clearly predominated. The British were taking 80 percent of Egypt's exports, supplying 44 percent of its imports,[8] and owned much of the public debt. De Lesseps and the French had built the Suez Canal over British objections, but 80 percent of its traffic

---

[4] Ronald Robinson and John Gallagher, *Africa and the Victorians* (London, 1961; 2nd ed., 1981); P. J. Cain and A. G. Hopkins, *British Imperialism: Innovation and Expansion, 1688–1914* (London, 1993). Robert T. Harrison's less reliable *Gladstone's Imperialism in Egypt: Techniques of Domination* (Westport, 1995) assigns Gladstone a more forceful and conscious role.

[5] F. Robert Hunter, *Egypt under the Khedives, 1805–1879: From Household Government to Modern Bureaucracy* (Pittsburgh, 1984).

[6] The earl of Cromer, *Modern Egypt*, 2 vols. (London, 1980); John Marlowe, *Cromer in Egypt* (New York, 1970).

[7] J. W. Parsons, "France and the Egyptian Question, 1875–1895," Ph.D. thesis, Cambridge University, 1976.

[8] A. G. Hopkins, "The Victorians and Africa: A Reconsideration of the Occupation of Egypt, 1882," *Journal of African History*, 27 (1986), 379.

was British and Disraeli had snatched up 44 percent of the Canal Company's shares from Isma'il in 1875.

With Egypt enmeshed in the European-dominated world market as an exporter of raw cotton and importer of manufactures, over 90,000 Europeans had settled there. The Capitulations backed by European power made it nearly impossible for Egyptians to compete in large-scale commerce, finance, and construction. In 1882 over a thousand Europeans clogged Egypt's upper bureaucracy, 2 percent of all officials but drawing 16 percent of the payroll.[9] The necessity of hiring numerous interpreters, mostly Syrian Christians, further strained the exhausted treasury.

Through corvée, taxes, and military conscription, the fallahin paid dearly for Isma'il's Sudanese empire, irrigation works, building projects, and financial mismanagement. The emerging class of large land owners, both Turco-Circassian and indigenous Egyptian, escaped with light taxes. From its founding in 1880 Crédit Mobilier financed mortgages to large land owners, while small farmers had to borrow from Greek money-lenders at usurious rates. Contrary to local custom and Islamic law, the mixed courts enabled creditors to dispossess fallahin who defaulted.

Indigenous army officers and their men had their own grievances. From 94,000 troops in 1874, with another 30,000 in the Sudan, Isma'il's army shrank under bankruptcy to 36,000 in early 1879, with plans to take it down to 18,000 or even 12,000. The retirement of 1,600 officers at half pay provoked them to demonstrate on February 18, 1879 for arrears, fair discharge procedures, and alternative employment. Nubar, the prime minister, and Wilson, the minister of finance, were assaulted. The quick release of arrested Circassian ringleaders was in glaring contrast to the disciplining of 'Urabi and two other indigenous officers who were probably innocent.[10] Isma'il, who had encouraged the demonstration, seized on it to dismiss Nubar's hated cabinet. Not since the early days of Muhammad 'Ali had the army so openly intervened in politics.

Since Britain and France persisted in their refusal to acquiesce in Isma'il's coup d'état, he had his Turco-Circassian loyalists draft, in the name of an Egyptian national party, a manifesto demanding cabinet responsibility to an elected chamber and a more lenient debt settlement. 'Urabi and other indigenous officers, officials, 'ulama', and parliamentary deputies were among the 329 who signed the manifesto.[11]

---

[9] Schölch, Egypt, 353–54 n.105.

[10] See 'Urabi's version in Wilfrid Scawen Blunt, Secret History of the English Occupation of Egypt (New York, 1922; repr. 1967), 368–69. The basic work on the army is Muhammad Mahmud al-Suruji, al-Jaysh al-misri fi al-qarn al-tasi' 'ashar (Cairo, 1976). The often-cited figure of 2,500 retirements is far too high; Horn, "'Urabi Revolution," 74–75, and Schölch, Egypt, 65.

[11] Schölch, Egypt, 89, 329–30 n.66.

Isma'il's first chamber of deputies dated to 1866. *Shaykhs al-balad* or *'umdas* – the indigenous landed elite of the provinces (fifty-eight of seventy-five deputies in 1866), along with a few wealthy merchants from the towns, dominated the chamber. The body was a powerless showpiece until the late 1870s, and even then its opposition targeted the Dual Control, not Isma'il. Egyptians also learned about constitutionalism from the Ottomans' parliamentary experiment of 1876–78.

In April 1879 Isma'il had Muhammad Sharif form a cabinet and draft an organic law for an elected chamber. The cabinet lived up to its "truly Egyptian" billing only in excluding Europeans; all the ministers were Turco-Circassians, not indigenous Egyptians. Britain and France might be liberal democracies at home but they would not hear of constitutionalism in Egypt. With a prod from Bismarck, Britain and France jointly compelled the sultan to depose Isma'il in favor of his son Tawfiq. Sharif was nimble enough to head up the first cabinet, again 100 percent Turco-Circassian, under Tawfiq. But Tawfiq had no use for the constitutionalism now associated with Sharif. He dismissed the chamber, dropped Sharif, and attempted personal rule. Britain and France rejected the last, so in September 1879 Tawfiq turned to the frankly autocratic Mustafa Riyad to form a government.

Incubating the revolution: Riyad and the Dual Control

Riyad had learned much as Nubar's minister of interior. Now, with Anglo-French backing through the reestablished Dual Control, Tawfiq's support, and the chamber out of the way, Riyad kept control for two full years. Although Baring and de Blignières (formerly Nubar's minister of public works), the financial controllers, were not voting members of the cabinet, they had the final say. They prepared the budget and were irremovable without their governments' consent. In 1880 Auckland Colvin, another stern Anglo-Indian, replaced Baring. In 1882 Colvin and Edward Malet the consul-general – "men on the spot" – would send home alarmist reports which maneuvered the British cabinet toward the invasion of Egypt.[12]

The Riyad cabinet made the law of liquidation of July 17, 1880 and related tax reforms its top priority. Interest on the unified debt was lowered from 6 percent to 4 percent, but even then debt service ate up half the country's annual revenue of £8.4 million. "Egypt is as closely bound as an Indian province,"[13] lamented E. Farman, the American consul-general.

The financial settlement stung big land owners, both Turco-Circassian

---

[12] Alexander Schölch, "The 'Men on the Spot' and the English Occupation of Egypt in 1882," *The Historical Journal*, 19 (1976), 773–85.

[13] United States National Archives, Department of State, RG59. Despatches from American Consuls in Cairo, 1864–1906. Microfilm T41, Roll 8. Farman to sec. of state, July 22, 1880.

and indigenous. Taxes shot up on hitherto privileged (*'ushriyya*) estates, the *muqabala* (advance tax payments in return for later low rates and full land title) was abolished with only token compensation for sums already paid, and private land owners lost the right to levy corvée. Indigenous provincial landlords missed the chamber, where they could have voiced their protests.

Under Riyad the Turco-Circassian element to which he himself belonged lost posts and power to Europeans and even to indigenous Egyptians. Turco-Circassians had never had a broad social base, and Isma'il's fall scattered his former clients. Turco-Circassians variously plotted to restore Isma'il, supported Tawfiq, schemed to enthrone Isma'il's uncle 'Abd al-Halim, bet on constitutionalism with Sharif, and defected like Riyad to the Europeans.

Sharif's faction resurfaced briefly in November 1879 in a manifesto of the "Egyptian national party" (or Helwan Society) and in May 1880 with a petition castigating Riyad for selling out to Europe and ignoring the interests of landlords. Many of the eighty-four signatures on the May petition were Turco-Circassian, though the organizer, Hasan Musa al-Aqqad (a merchant and agent of Halim), and some others were indigenous. Riyad came down hard, banishing al-Aqqad to the White Nile.[14]

An enlightened despot of sorts, Riyad abolished the poll tax and other regressive taxes, decreed fair land taxes, banned the kurbash (whip), abolished corvée on private estates, and ordered fair sharing of irrigation water. Though many of the decrees favoring the fallahin were not implemented, rural prosperity did return during 1880.

Benefiting from Riyad's appointments to official posts, the emerging indigenous intelligentsia did not complain about this autocracy. Educated at al-Azhar or the new state schools and sometimes also in Europe, these clerks, engineers, doctors, teachers, and journalists noticed that Riyad, in contrast to Sharif, had two Egyptians in his seven-man cabinet: 'Ali Mubarak, an engineer, and 'Ali Ibrahim, a physician. Riyad also named Egyptians to reform commissions on education and justice. Even 'Urabi, who overthrew Riyad, called him "the father of the Egyptians."[15]

During the 'Urabi revolution, this new intelligentsia also propelled the Arabic press into a major role in national politics for the first time. As Benedict Anderson has suggested for other parts of the world, nationalism, capitalism, and print serials here went hand in hand.[16] Egypt's official journal was first published in 1828, but (after a few earlier experiments) the private Arabic press began to thrive only in 1876–77 with encouragement

---

[14] Schölch, *Egypt*, 120–30, challenges accounts making 'Abduh, Nadim, Mahmud Sami al-Barudi, and Sultan major players in this episode.

[15] *Ibid.*, 119. For the paragraph generally, see 118–20.

[16] Benedict Anderson, *Imagined Communities: Reflections on the Origin and Spread of Nationalism*, 2nd ed. (London, 1991).

from Isma'il and Jamal al-Din al-Afghani, the charismatic revivalist Riyad brought to Egypt in 1871.[17]

Religious minorities supplied many of the pioneers of the private press. The Syrian Christian Taqla brothers' *al-Ahram*, staunchly francophile, first appeared in Alexandria in 1876. Jamal al-Din, of unacknowledged Shi'i Iranian origin, developed a web of freemasonic ties in Egypt. He encouraged his disciples Ya'qub Sanu', Adib Ishaq, and Salim al-Naqqash to seize the opportunity offered by the new print technology. Sanu' was an Egyptian–Italian Jew, Ishaq and Naqqash Syrian Christians. Isma'il quickly banned Sanu''s satirical *Abu naddara al-zaraqa* (1877), but it carried on from Paris. One cartoon showed the army preventing Riyad from handing over the keys of Egypt to the British. Sanu' claimed to have coined the slogan "Egypt for the Egyptians."[18]

Ishaq and Naqqash started the papers *Misr* (1877) and *al-Tijara* (1878), and Ishaq had a hand in the short-lived bilingual *Jeune Egypte/Misr al-fatah*. This "Young Egypt" circle, heavily Christian and Jewish, defined "Egyptian" broadly; Ottomans born or having resided in Egypt for three years, regardless of race or creed, and naturalized foreigners were included.[19] Mikha'il 'Abd al-Sayyid's *al-Watan* (1877) was both a national and a Coptic communal paper.

As for Muslim Egyptian journalists, Muhammad 'Abduh in 1880 was rusticating (exiled to his village as a disciple of the expelled Jamal al-Din) when Riyad made him editor of the official journal *al-Waqa'i' al-Misriyya* and director of Arabic publications. *Al-Waqai'* became livelier, and Riyad acquired an able defender. "I was not in favor of a revolution, and thought that it would be enough if we had a Constitution in five years time," recalled 'Abduh. "I disapproved of the overthrow of [Riyad]."[20] Not until after Riyad's fall did 'Abduh expound favorably on *shura* (consultation) as an Islamic form of constitutionalism.

Husayn al-Marsafi had commended 'Abduh to Riyad; both were Azharis who taught at Dar al-'Ulum teachers' college and advocated gradual reform. Marsafi's book *Eight Words* came out in October 1881, a month after Riyad's fall. It elaborated on ideas of nation (*umma*), fatherland (*watan*), government, justice, oppression, politics, freedom, and instruction; more

---

[17] William Phelps, "Political Journalism in the 'Urabi Revolt," Ph.D. thesis, University of Michigan, 1978; Ibrahim 'Abduh, *al-Ahram: tarikh wa fann 1875–1964* (Cairo, 1964); Ibrahim 'Abduh, *Tarikh al-sihafa al-misriyya 1798–1951* (Cairo, 1951); Sami 'Aziz, *al-Sihafa al-misriyya wa mawqifuha min al-ihtilal al-injlizi* (Cairo, 1968); Sami 'Abd al-'Aziz al-Kumi, *al-Sihafa al-islamiyya fi misr fi al-qarn al-tasi ashar* (Cairo, 1991); Cole, *Colonialism*, 110–32.

[18] Phelps, "Journalism," 168; Schölch, *Egypt*, 334–35 n.100.

[19] Raouf 'Abbas Hamed, "al-Mu'arada al-qawmiyya wa irhasat al-thawra," in *Misr lil-misriyyin*, 66.

[20] Blunt, *Secret History*, 379.

radical choices might have been *shura* and organic law (in relation to the chamber), revolution, tyranny, equality, and brotherhood.[21]

Riyad closed papers that challenged his rule or supported his rival Sharif, banning *Misr*, *Tijara*, and *Jeune Egypte/Misr al-fatah* late in 1879 and later shutting three European-language journals despite their claims of legal immunity. Ishaq fled to Paris and published *Misr al-qahira* for Sharif's faction; Naqqash brought out the more circumspect *al-Mahrusa* in Cairo.

The road to revolution: Qasr al-Nil to 'Abdin
(February 1–September 9, 1881)

Opposition journalists in exile were merely a minor nuisance, and Turco-Circassian and indigenous big land owners alone could not bring Riyad down as long as he kept European and khedival backing. But Riyad, lacking military expertise himself, made the fatal mistake of leaving military matters to Tawfiq and the Circassian minister of war, 'Uthman Rifqi.

The Egyptian/Turco-Circassian divide was eroding in the provinces and bureaucracy, where Arabic had officially replaced Turkish, indigenous Egyptians such as 'Ali Mubarak and Isma'il Siddiq had reached the top, and intermarriage was frequent. In the army, however, Turco-Circassians insisted on keeping Turkish as the official language, blocked fallah[22] officers from rising above colonel, and reinforced their ethnicity by marrying Circassian slave women from the palace.

'Urabi was born in 1841 in Hiryat Raznah, near Zagazig in the eastern Delta province of Sharqiyya. If his rural origin made him a typical Egyptian (only 13 percent of Egypt's 7,930,000 people lived in the twenty-three largest towns in 1882),[23] being the son of a village shaykh gave him a distinct advantage. 'Urabi inherited eight-and-a-half faddans from his father, a bit above the five faddans a fallah family needed to live comfortably. He studied at a local Qur'an school and with the village's Coptic *sarraf* (financial officer), then attended al-Azhar like many another *'umda*'s son. He dropped out and returned home after several years, however, well short of the rigorous course required of a senior *'alim*.

Muhammad Sa'id began drafting *'umdas*' sons in 1854 and promoting them into the officer corps; this opened a whole new world. 'Urabi landed

---

[21] Gilbert Delanoue, *Moralistes et politiques musulmans dans l'Egypte du XIXe siècle (1798–1882)*, 2 vols. (Cairo, 1982), II, 357–78; Timothy Mitchell, *Colonising Egypt* (Cambridge, 1988), 131–42, 202.

[22] "Fallah" could mean all ethnic Egyptians, all rural ones, or only ordinary peasants. Nathan J. Brown, *Peasant Politics in Modern Egypt: The Struggle against the State* (New Haven, 1990), 167.

[23] Gabriel Baer, *Studies in the Social History of Modern Egypt* (Chicago and London, 1969), 136.

first in the quartermaster corps but insisted on transferring to the regular infantry in quest of better opportunities. He was only twenty when he accompanied Saʿid to Medina as a lieutenant-colonel, but then Saʿid's premature death at forty-one deprived him, and all fallah officers, of an indispensable patron.[24]

Ismaʿil reverted to favoring Turco-Circassian officers, decreeing that sons of ʿumdas could buy their way out of the army.[25] ʿUrabi stayed on, but languished without promotion throughout Ismaʿil's reign. A quarrel with a Circassian superior even forced him out of the army for a time until his marriage to a Circassian from the palace facilitated his reinstatement.

The Abyssinian campaign (1875–76), in which the Egyptian army was routed at Qura, embittered ʿUrabi and a fellow fallah officer, ʿAli al-Rubi. Because of alleged inadequacies, ʿUrabi lost his duties in transport to a Circassian. The Circassian commanders Muhammad Ratib and ʿUthman Rifqi led the army to disaster, yet their careers prospered. "After this I thought much about politics,"[26] ʿUrabi later confided, just as Nassir decided in Palestine in 1948 that the first enemy was at home.

Upon his accession Tawfiq promoted ʿUrabi to colonel at last, but the minister of war, ʿUthman Rifqi – "a Turk of the old school, who hated the fellahin"[27] – soon shattered any resulting goodwill. In July 1880 a decree limited service in the ranks to four years, removing the ladder by which ʿUrabi and other Egyptian officers had reached the officer corps.

In January 1881, when colonels ʿUrabi, ʿAbd al-Al Hilmi, and ʿAli Fahmi got wind of plans to replace fallah with Circassian officers, they boldly petitioned for Rifqi's dismissal. Summoned to military headquarters at Qasr al-Hil on a transparent pretext, the three were arrested. Their court martial was already under way when their forewarned regiments burst in and rescued them. Tawfiq and Riyad capitulated, pardoned the rebels, and replaced Rifqi with Mahmud Sami al-Barudi. A Circassian later famed for his Arabic poetry, Mahmud Sami had deep Egyptian roots and sympathized with ʿUrabi.

Between February and September 1881, ʿUrabi quickly evolved from an obscure colonel into a national politician. He talked politics with ʿAbduh, accepted gifts of produce and horses from Muhammad Sultan's vast Minya estates, and met other provincial notables such as Hasan al-Shariʿi and Sulayman Abaza. The notables hailed the fellah officers as their "sons and

---

24 ʿUrabi's autobiographical accounts include *The Defense Statement of Ahmad ʿUrabi the Egyptian*, ed. and trans. Trevor Le Gassick (Cairo, 1982); *Mudhakkirat ʿurabi: kashf al-sirar an sirr al-asrar fi al-nahda al-misriyya al-mashhura bi-l-thawra al-ʿurabiyya*, 2 vols. (Cairo, 1953); and Blunt, *Secret History*, 367–75, 379–80.
25 Schölch, *Egypt*, 23.
26 Blunt, *Secret History*, 368.
27 *Ibid.*, 370.

brothers," and 'Urabi flattered the notables as "our fathers and our brothers, the heads of our families."[28] The officers not only came to see that a constitution might shield them from khedival reprisals but also began to present themselves as champions of the people. Even Tawfiq courted 'Ali Fahmi, commander of his palace guard: "You ... are three soldiers – with me you make four"[29] – an invitation to plot against Riyad. But 'Urabi was not yet sure of Fahmi, an Egyptian who moved in palace circles and had a Circassian wife. The French seizure of Tunis in May 1881 shocked the Egyptians, who realized that they might well be next. The fallah colonels discounted Tawfiq's protestations of friendship, and feared that the khedive's assassins might await them around every corner. In August, Tawfiq's brother-in-law Da'ud Yakan replaced Mahmud Sami as minister of war, a signal that a showdown was imminent.

The fallah colonels struck first, when the khedive tried to transfer 'Urabi's and 'Abd al-Al's regiments out of Cairo. 'Urabi announced that the army would present its demands before 'Abdin palace on September 9. The rank and file trusted their indigenous Egyptian colonels more than the aloof Turco-Circassian generals; even Fahmi's palace guards went over to 'Urabi. Colvin and Cookson, acting British consul – their French counterparts being abroad – showed where real authority lay by accompanying the shaken khedive to 'Abdin Square. 'Urabi demanded the dismissal of Riyad's cabinet, election of a new chamber, and the raising of the army to its legal limit of 18,000. Tawfiq had little choice; he dismissed Riyad (who took refuge in Europe) and sent for Sharif.

Sharif and the revolutionary coalition
(September 1881–February 1882)

Both prior coordination with Muhammad Sultan and 'Urabi's demand for an elected chamber show that the 'Abdin demonstration was more than an army revolt. It brought to the fore the alliance of indigenous officers and landed notables who would dominate the new chamber. The third part of the new coalition – Sharif's faction of Turco-Circassians – was more reluctant to join. Sharif refused to form a cabinet until Sultan and other notables plied him with civilian petitions for constitutional rule and until the army officers agreed to withdraw from politics and accept transfers out of Cairo.

Back as minister of war, Mahmud Sami rushed through the desired army reforms, then dispatched 'Urabi's regiment to Ras al-Wadi (Sharqiyya) and 'Abd al-Al's regiment (which was Sudanese) to Damietta. But to Sharif's

[28] Schölch, *Egypt*, 44; Urabi, *Defense*, 23.
[29] Blunt, *Secret History*, 111.

dismay, 'Urabi returned to the capital on various pretexts and conferred with notables, his future champion Wilfrid Blunt, and even Colvin. Promotion to undersecretary of war at the beginning of 1882 legitimized 'Urabi's return to Cairo.

Sharif's cabinet was again entirely Turco-Circassian.[30] Sultan was furious at being excluded, but becoming the first indigenous Egyptian to preside over the chamber mollified him. The appointment of 'Abdallah Fikri (an Azhar-educated official) and Sharif's journalist protégé Adib Ishaq (back from Paris to relaunch *Misr*) as secretaries to the chamber helped link its provincial notables to the Egyptian and Syrian intelligentsia.

The network of 'ulama' was vital in mobilizing popular support for 'Urabi. Colonels Rubi and 'Urabi had even studied at al-Azhar themselves. Like the army officers, the 'ulama' were hailed as "sons and brothers" of the provincial notables. In December 1881 thousands of Azhari shaykhs and students, and particularly the numerous Malikis and Shafi'is with their strong Egyptian roots, met to strip the Hanafi grand mufti Muhammad al-'Abbasi al-Mahdi of his post as *shaykh al-Azhar*. Associating Hanafis with Turks and khedival largesse, Egyptians feared that al-Mahdi was about to denounce 'Urabi and constitutionalism. In addition, Shafi'is and Malikis felt the pinch of reduced state funding for al-Azhar in the wake of the bankruptcy. The Azharis wanted the Maliki mufti Muhammad 'Ilish to succeed al-Mahdi, but settled for Muhammad al-Inbabi (a Shafi'i *'alim* and cloth merchant with Manchester ties) in order to avoid an open break with Tawfiq.[31]

While the editors of *al-Ahram*, *al-Watan*, and *Misr* hailed Sharif as a symbol of stability, the more populist 'Abdallah al-Nadim emerged as the leading journalist and orator of the revolution. Born a poor baker's son in Alexandria, Nadim dropped out of his studies at the Shaykh Ibrahim mosque to try his hand as a vagabond poet, telegraph operator, teacher, and journalist. After working in journalism on Salim al-Naqqash's *al-Mahrusa*, Nadim left to found the Islamic Benevolent Society and an associated school. In June 1881 he launched his satirical *al-Tankit wa al-tabkit* (Laughter and Tears), using colloquial dialogues like *Abu naddara* to broaden its appeal.

'Urabi suggested that Nadim change *Tankit*'s name to Voice of the Nation (*Lisan al-umma*), but it was Nadim's second paper, *al-Ta'if*, that became the voice of the 'Urabists. The populist editor blamed the chamber for representing only the rich, and denounced foreign usurers, liquor dealers, and cruel estate overseers. Sometimes Nadim's rhetoric carried him away: "With our cannon, we can reach Cyprus. And so can the cannon of the Sultan

---

[30] Muhammad Qadri did have an Egyptian mother, however, and had studied at al-Azhar as well as at state schools.

[31] On 'Ilish (Schölch, *Egypt*, 348 n.54, reads it 'Ullaish), Mahdi, and Inbabi, see Delanoue, *Moralistes*, 1; 129–67, 137, 168–84; Cole, *Colonialism*, 37–38, 104.

himself, fired from the Bosphorus. What will the enemy's fleet do between two fires?"[32]

Sharif the "constitutionalist" proved as hard on the press as Riyad. He banned *L'Egypte* for an inflammatory article calling Muhammad a false prophet, balancing this with suspensions of the ʿUrabist journals *al-Hijaz* and *al-Mufid*. Sharif also institutionalized censorship with the harsh press law of November 26, 1881. It required security deposits from presses and editors and elaborated a scale of offenses and penalties.

Sharif also revealed the limits of his constitutionalism by conducting elections under Ismaʿil's restrictive law of 1866 rather than the chamber's more liberal draft of 1879. Provincial landed notables again predominated in the new chamber, with a sprinkling of wealthy merchants. After a two-and-a-half year hiatus, the chamber convened at the end of December 1881.

The chamber was inclining toward Sharif's proposals for an "organic law" with little real parliamentary power when the delivery on January 8 of the Anglo-French "Joint Note" touched off an uproar. The note stressed the two powers' determination to uphold khedival authority. Gambetta's new ministry in France hoped a tough stance in Cairo would forestall resistance to French rule in Tunisia, and Charles Dilke, undersecretary at the Foreign Office, helped persuade Gladstone and the foreign secretary Granville.[33]

The note had precisely the opposite of its intended effect. It shocked Malet, laid bare Tawfiq's dependence on Europe, undercut Sharif, and drove the chamber and moderate intellectuals such as ʿAbduh to close ranks with the army. When the chamber insisted on its right to debate the half of the budget not pledged to the debt and Ottoman tribute, de Blignières suspected "a project not of a Parliament, but of a 'Convention.'"[34] Europeans in Egyptian service feared for their posts and comfortable salaries. The blunder of the Joint Note infuriated Sharif, but he nevertheless broke with the chamber to stand by Tawfiq, observing:

The Egyptians are children, and must be treated like children. I have offered them a Constitution which is good enough for them, and if they are not content with it they must do without one. It was I who created the National Party, and

---

[32] Jacques Berque, *Egypt: Imperialism and Revolution*, trans. Jean Stewart (New York, 1972), 118. On Nadim, see Abdel Moneim El Gameiy (Abd al-Munʿim al-Jamiʿi), *ʿAbdallah al-nadim wa dawruhu fi al-haraka al-siyasiyya wa al-ijtimaʾiyya* (Cairo, 1980); and Najib Tawfiq, *ʿAbdallah al-nadim: khatib al-thawra al-ʿurabiyya* (Cairo, 1970). *Al-Tankit wa al-tabkit* has been reissued (Cairo, 1994), intro. by Abd al-Munʿim al-Jamiʿi.

[33] M. E. Chamberlain, "Sir Charles Dilke and the British Intervention in Egypt, 1882: Decision Making in a Nineteenth-Century Cabinet," *British Journal of International Studies*, 2 (1976), 231–45.

[34] Blunt, *Secret History*, 147. On this chamber, see Ismaʿil Muhammad Zayn al-Din, "al-Thawra al-ʿUrabiyya," in *Misr lil-misriyyin*, 211–40. Deputies listed in ʿAbd al-Rahman al-Rafiʿi, *al-Thawra al-ʿurabiyya wa al-ihtilal al-injliz*, 3rd ed. (Cairo, 1966), 195–99.

they will find that they cannot get on without me. These peasants want guidance.[35]

The Mahmud Sami–'Urabi revolutionary cabinet
(February 4–June 11, 1882)

The revolution entered its second stage with Mahmud Sami's ensuing cabinet, which included 'Urabi as minister of war. "Egypt for the Egyptians" took a long stride forward, starting with the seven-man cabinet. Its only Turco-Circassians were Mahmud Sami and foreign minister Mustafa Fahmi, included for his French and his contacts with the consuls. Hasan al-Shari'i was a provincial notable from the chamber, 'Urabi and Mahmud Fahmi were fallah officers, 'Abdallah Fikri an Azhar-educated official, and 'Ali Sadiq a European-educated engineer.[36]

The Basic Law of February 7 affirmed the chamber's right to vote on bills submitted by the cabinet, discuss the half of the budget not encumbered by the foreign debt and Ottoman tribute, and to supervise all officials (even, in theory, the controllers). Buoyed by public support, assertive deputies dared to ask pointed questions of the ministers. Completing its three-month session amidst much acclaim, the chamber adjourned late in March.

Since the government insisted it would meet its international obligations and in practice hesitated to dismiss European officials, Egyptianization that spring came at the expense of Turco-Circassians and Syrian Christians. In the army, 'Urabi and four other fallah officers were promoted to brigadier general, with others moving up accordingly. Most of the Turco-Circassians were among the nearly six hundred officers forced to retire. The backlash came in April, in an aborted "Circassian plot" on the lives of the 'Urabist leaders. 'Uthman Rifqi was among the forty Turco-Circassians court-martialed and sentenced to loss of rank and banishment to the Sudan. But ethnicity was not destiny. The prime minister, the informant who betrayed the plot, the president of the court martial, two of seven new brigadier generals, and eighty-one still-active officers were Turco-Circassians.[37] The revolution's Islamic coloring increasingly unnerved Syrian Christians and Europeans. Egyptian territorial consciousness had been discernible in many of the names of earlier journals, whether run by Muslims (*al-Waqa'i' al-misriyya* – Egyptian Events, *Wadi al-nil* – the Nile Valley); Copts (*al-Watan* – The Fatherland); or Syrian Christians (*al-Ahram* – The Pyramids, *Misr* – Egypt, *Misr al-Qahira* – Cairo [or Egypt] Victorious, *al-Iskandariyya* –

---

[35] Blunt, *Secret History*, 149.
[36] 'Ali Sadiq's ethnicity is not certain, however. J. Heyworth-Dunne, *An Introduction to the History of Education in Modern Egypt* (London, 1938; repr. 1968), 262, n.92.
[37] Schölch, *Egypt*, 226–28.

Alexandria). But the names of the three new 'Urabist papers – *al-Ta'if*, *al-Hijaz*, and *Fustat* – had an Arab–Islamic ring.[38]

Most of Egypt's perhaps seven thousand Syrian Christians had arrived with the Europeans since mid-century. More at home in European languages and customs than most Egyptians, they snatched up jobs in the bureaucracy, business, journalism, and education. The Taqlas identified with France politically; others like Ishaq and Naqqash reached out to Muslims as fellow Ottomans or "Easterners," denounced European exploitation, and supported constitutionalism.

With Sharif's fall in February, however, Syrian Christian fellow travelers neared the end of the road. Ishaq's *Misr* lost out to Nadim's *al-Ta'if* in the chamber's favor, and Ishaq's promotion to bey fell through. He broke bitterly with his Muslim colleagues. The 'Urabist newspaper *al-Mufid* demanded the dismissal of all Syrian officials. The suspension of *al-Ahram* and *al-Mahrusa* in June swept the field clean of Syrian Christian journals. But *al-Ahram* would soon reopen in British-occupied Alexandria, Bashara Taqla would call to insult 'Urabi in his prison cell, and Ishaq would sing Tawfiq's praises in *al-I'tidal*.[39]

Before the Joint Note, Malet and Gladstone had leaned toward Wilfrid Blunt's belief that the 'Urabists expressed legitimate national feeling. After the installation of the Mahmud Sami/'Urabi cabinet, however, Malet's dispatches to London became as alarmist as Colvin's. As correspondent for the *Pall Mall Gazette* in addition to being controller, Colvin reinforced the British image of 'Urabi as a military dictator who threatened European lives and property. Gladstone could hardly forget that 37 percent of his personal portfolio was in Egyptian stock.[40] The whole delicate structure of Britain's financial and political supremacy in Egypt seemed at risk.[41]

The nationwide Egyptian census of May 3, 1882 suggests business as usual, but on May 2 Malet had already encouraged Tawfiq to provoke a showdown. The khedive commuted the "Circassian plot" sentences from exile in the Sudan to simple exile. Outraged, Mahmud Sami summoned the chamber into informal session. Tawfiq brushed aside mediation efforts by Muhammad Sultan, for he knew that British and French warships were on their way to Alexandria. On May 25 the British and French demanded that

---

[38] Misr al-Qahira, the name of the conquering Fatimids' new city of Cairo, did have Arabic-Islamic associations as well.

[39] 'Urabi, *Defense*, 48. Thomas Philipp, *The Syrians in Egypt, 1725–1975* (Stuttgart, 1985), 102–05; Phelps, "Journalism," 209–11.

[40] H. C. G. Matthew (ed.), *The Gladstone Diaries* (Oxford, 1990), X–XI, January 1881–December 1886, lxxii.

[41] In addition to already cited sources on British decision making, see John S. Galbraith and Afar Lutfi al-Sayid-Marsot, "The British Occupation of Egypt: Another View," *International Journal of Middle East Studies*, 9 (1978), 471–88.

the cabinet resign, 'Urabi go into exile, and colonels 'Ali Fahmi and 'Abd al-Al retire from Cairo.

The cabinet resigned in protest. Tawfiq tried unsuccessfully to seize direct control of the army, and notables and officers met at Muhammad Sultan's house on May 27 to seek a way out. Only five deputies favored 'Urabi's proposal to petition the Ottoman sultan to depose the khedive. The next day the notables persuaded Tawfiq that the only way to avert a collapse of law and order was to reinstate 'Urabi as minister of war.

The Alexandria riot to the fall of Cairo
(June 11–September 15, 1882)

The Alexandria riot, British bombardment, and the ensuing invasion propelled the revolution into its third stage, the final break with Tawfiq and war with Britain. No credible evidence supports the widespread charge that 'Urabi engineered the June 11 riot. Counter-charges that Tawfiq staged the riot – through the governor of Alexandria, 'Umar Lutfi, and the chief of police – to discredit 'Urabi are scarcely more credible. The riot probably ignited spontaneously in the tinderbox city of 232,000, where every fifth person was a European. Enriched by the booming import–export trade and shielded by the Capitulations, Europeans flaunted their wealth and privilege. Many of the Egyptian population – Nubian servants, donkey drivers, and dock-side porters were the largest indigenous occupational groups – served the mainly European rich. The old artisan and trade guilds were hard-pressed, with only a few indigenous traders finding ways to grow rich through the European-driven economic transformation.[42] The Russo-Ottoman war of 1877–78, in which Egypt fought, had exacerbated anti-European feelings, and the French conquest of Tunisia made the warships off Alexandria seem ominous indeed. The nervous Greek consul armed his compatriots, and the British consul, Cookson, armed the Maltese, who were British subjects.

The riot erupted one afternoon when bystanders joined a fracas between an Egyptian and a Maltese. Greeks and Maltese fired on the crowd from upper windows, and Egyptians attacked Europeans in the streets with clubs. Notified by telegraph in Cairo three hours later, 'Urabi ordered in the army to restore order. About fifty Europeans and perhaps two hundred and fifty Egyptians were dead. Cookson was among the wounded. A recent study challenges dismissals of the crowd as lower class, noting that guild leaders

---

[42] M. E. Chamberlain, "The Alexandria Massacre of 11 June 1882 and the British Occupation of Egypt," *Middle Eastern Studies*, 13 (1977), 14–39; Michael J. Reimer, "Colonial Bridgehead: Social and Spatial Change in Alexandria, 1850–1882," *International Journal of Middle Eastern Studies*, 20 (1988), 531–53.

and members were among those later arrested for rioting.[43] In the aftermath, Tawfiq fled Cairo for Ras al-Tin palace in Alexandria and the protection of British guns. Thousands of Europeans fled the interior, briefly producing a *de facto* Egyptianization of the bureaucracy and economy. Tawfiq had Isma'il Raghib form a compromise cabinet (five Egyptians and three Turco-Circassians), with 'Urabi staying on as minister of war.

'Urabi and the khedive had been vying for the sultan's ear ever since the demonstration at 'Abdin. A first Ottoman investigatory commission had come in October 1881 and another arrived just two days before the bombardment. 'Abd al-Hamid II hoped to ward off western conquest and regain a measure of Ottoman control. General Darwish headed the second commission, with Shaykh Ahmad Asad (an Arab) as special envoy to 'Urabi. In the wake of the bombardment Darwish and As'ad could accomplish nothing. The British convened a diplomatic conference in Istanbul and toyed with the idea of a tightly circumscribed Ottoman expedition to restore khedival power. The French government feared a precedent for Tunisia and would have none of it. By the time the sultan finally denounced 'Urabi as a rebel on September 2, the British invasion was fast rendering the issue of Ottoman intervention moot.[44]

Colvin, Malet, Dilke, and British cabinet hardliners such as Hartington, secretary of state for India, had set the stage for the bombardment, and Admiral Seymour used the pretext that Egyptian work on harbor forts threatened his ships. Having followed Britain's lead since the fall of the aggressive Gambetta early in 1882, the French premier Freycinet now withdrew the French fleet rather than join the bombardment. Seymour began the bombardment on July 11 and continued it the next day.

Tawfiq went through the charade of ordering the army to resist, but the forts soon fell silent. 'Urabi retreated inland, and Bedouin and others looted the burning city until British troops belatedly landed to restore order. A month earlier, Europeans had fled the interior and tens of thousands took ship abroad; now tens of thousands of Egyptians reversed the tide and fled inland. Their tales of horror contributed to attacks on Greeks in Tanta and other delta towns. Safe at Ras al-Tin in the shadow of the British fleet, Tawfiq ordered an end to all resistance. But 'Urabi dug in at Kafr al-Dawwar, on the strategic between-the-lakes isthmus that carried Alexandria's rail, fresh water (the Mahmudiyya canal), and telegraph links to Cairo. He ordered emergency preparations to resist invasion, a flat contradiction of Tawfiq's orders to cease resistance.

British warhawks soon brought Gladstone around to a full-scale invasion.

---

[43] Cole, *Colonialism*, 249–53.
[44] Selim Deringil, "The Ottoman Response to the Egyptian Crisis of 1881–82," *Middle Eastern Studies*, 24 (1988), 3–24.

Exaggerating the threat to the Suez Canal helped carry the Commons vote for military credits by a margin of 275 to 19. Freycinet's request for credits for a similar French force was defeated, bringing down his government. Fear of playing into Bismarck's hands by dispersing forces abroad outweighed France's anguish at seeing Britain triumph alone on the Nile.

In Cairo, no one thought of convoking the chamber. Some deputies had joined Tawfiq in Alexandria, and others had discretely retreated to their estates. ʿUrabi was with the army at Kafr al-Dawwar, the rest of the cabinet in Alexandria. Ministerial undersecretaries and army officers left in Cairo therefore convened an emergency administrative council (*al-majlis al-ʿurfi*), with the undersecretary of war, Yaʿqub Sami, in the chair. The *majlis ʿurfi* ran the day-to-day business of government and removed strong supporters of the khedive from provincial administration. This cautious body gave orders to ʿUrabi, not the other way around. Afraid of provoking Britain, the *majlis ʿurfi* initially refused his request to reinforce points near the canal. It also rejected ʿUrabi's call to send Cairo policemen to the front, fearing the social effects of replacing them with a popular guard at home.[45]

For the great decision of war or peace, the *majlis ʿurfi* deferred to two larger, *ad hoc* general assemblies (*jam ʿiyyat umumiyya*), which met on July 17 and 29. About seventy men participated in the first, and 250–400 in the second. Muhammad ʿAbduh acted as secretary, reading out contradictory orders from ʿUrabi and the khedive. At the first assembly, shaykhs ʿIlish and ʿIdwi denounced Tawfiq as a traitor and called for jihad. A speech in Turkish by one of the khedive's men provoked protests that Arabic was the proper language for the assembly. ʿAli Mubarak boldly defended Tawfiq, joined a mediatory mission to Alexandria, and defected to him. A few weeks later he was rewarded with a seat in the cabinet that Sharif assembled in British-occupied Alexandria; Mubarak became the first (and only) indigenous Egyptian to join a Sharif government.

The second assembly included the *majlis ʿurfi*, other officials and officers, three princes from rival lines of the khedival family, ʿulamaʾ, Christian clergymen and Jewish rabbis, guild leaders and other merchants, eight deputies from the chamber, provincial governors, and ʿumdas. The body nullified the khedive's dismissal of ʿUrabi and sanctioned disobedience to Tawfiq on the grounds that he was under British control and had violated Shariʿa and civil law. The *shaykh al-Azhar*, the grand *qadi* of Egypt, the Coptic patriarch, and other religious notables all signed the manifesto. But

[45] Schölch, *Egypt*, 292–93; ʿAli Barakat, *Tatawwur, al-milkiyya al-ziraʿiyya fi misr wa atharuh ala al-haraka al-siyasiyya (1813–1924)*, 415–16. Yaʿqub Sami's account is in A. M. Broadley, *How we Defended Arabi and his Friends* (London, 1884; repr. Cairo, 1980), 218–23.

the document is a poor litmus test of support for the revolution; many later claimed their signatures were coerced.[46]

'Urabi called for 25,000 new recruits, emergency rations and supplies, and labor levies to dig trenches. The intentions of the early contributors and volunteers are unclear, however, for Tawfiq did not anathematize 'Urabi as a rebel and criminal until August 7.[47] Even after that, notables and officials orchestrated the mobilization, making it difficult to sort out popular revolutionary enthusiasm from mere submission to extraordinary taxes, corvée, and conscription.[48] Strikes by Port Said coalheavers, mostly Upper Egyptian fallahin and Nubians, had both nationalist and class overtones.[49]

Tawfiq's party in Alexandria and the 'Urabists in Cairo did their best to exploit the new technology of the press, telegraph, and railroads in addition to traditional means of communication and transport. The *majlis 'urfi* decreed emergency censorship rules in the press law of July 22. Tawfiq sent ciphered telegrams to rally provincial support, so the 'Urabists cut the lines out of Alexandria and banned cipher except for military purposes. After the occupation, three journalists and five telegraphers were arrested in Cairo as suspected 'Urabists, emphasizing the importance of their role. The official who kept the trains running, to the benefit of the 'Urabists, was sharply questioned.[50]

Cairo banned the circulation of Alexandrian papers – the *Egyptian Gazette*, *al-Ahram*, and Shaykh Hamza Fathallah's *al-I'tidal*, with their respective British, pro-French, and khedival points of view. The French version of the official gazette (*Moniteur égyptienne*) was reconstituted in Alexandria to counter 'Urabi.[51] Muhammad 'Abduh's Arabic version from Cairo, *al-Waqa'i' al-Misriyya*, joined Nadim's *al-Ta'if* and other ephemeral papers in supporting the revolution.

If the signatures of July 29 are discounted, most of the high official 'ulama' either stood by Tawfiq or avoided identification as active 'Urabists. Most declined to sign a *fatwa* declaring Tawfiq's unfitness to rule.[52] The grand mufti al-Mahdi's loyalty to Tawfiq would be rewarded with restora-

---

[46] Lists in 'Abd al-Rahman al-Rafi'i, *Thawra 'urabiyya*, 390–94. See Cole, *Colonialism*, 245–47.

[47] Horn, "'Urabi Revolution," 291–92.

[48] Brown, *Peasant Politics*, 188–90, sees most peasant "contributions" as forced. Latifa, al-Quwwa, and 'Ali Shalabi, *al-Rif al-misri fi al-nisf al-thani min al-qarn al-tasi 'ashar* (Cairo, 1983), 430–42, assume voluntary peasant support.

[49] Zayn al-'Abdin Shams al-Din Najm, *Bur Sa'id: tarikhuha wa tatawwuruha mundhu nash'atiha 1859 hatta amm 1882* (Cairo, 1987), 385–417; D. A. Farnie, *East and West of Suez: The Suez Canal in History 1854–1956* (Oxford, 1969), 289, 297–99; Joel Beinin and Zachary Lockman, *Workers on the Nile: Nationalism, Communism, Islam, and the Egyptian Working Class, 1882–1954* (Princeton, 1987), 27–30.

[50] Cole, *Colonialism*, 241, 244, 317 n.45.

[51] John Ninet, *Lettres d'Egypte 1879–1882*, ed. Anouar Louca (Paris, 1979), 220 n.159.

[52] Schölch, *Egypt*, 247, 355–56 n.16.

tion as *shaykh al-Azhar*. Shaykh 'Abd al-Baqi al-Bakri (the supreme head of official Sufi orders) and the shaykh al-Sadat (a descendant of the Prophet Muhammad and influential Sufi leader) steered official Sufi orders clear of identification as 'Urabists.

The middle and lower 'ulama', many al-Azhar students, and some Sufi leaders of unofficial orders mobilized mass support for the revolution in Cairo and the provinces. Lawyers and students in state schools were too few for the vanguard role they would assume in 1919 and after.[53] The Ottoman commissioner, Darwish, made the mistake of rudely rebuffing 'Ilish, Idwi, and other 'ulama' who petitioned him in support of 'Urabi; a huge student demonstration protesting against the insult to their shaykhs forced Darwish to soften his approach and agree to receive 'Urabi.

As Maliki mufti and the favorite to replace al-Mahdi as *shaykh al-Azhar*, the aged 'Ilish was the leading *'alim* to champion the revolution. This was not incompatible with his reactionary theology. He had resisted Isma'il's and Jamal al-Din's reform efforts at al-Azhar and demanded reimposition of strong restrictions on non-Muslims, and just before the British took Cairo he ordered the removal (as unislamic) of the lion statues on the Qasr al-Nil bridge and the equestrian statue of Ibrahim. Like 'Ilish, 'Idwi was shaykh of an unofficial Shadhiliyya Sufi order and a die-hard supporter of 'Urabi. 'Idwi owned large estates in Middle Egypt, a reminder of the interlocking of landed and religious elites.[54] 'Abdallah al-Nadim belonged to an unofficial Sufi order; unofficial Khalwatiyya lodges in Upper Egypt backed 'Urabi as well.

Copts weathered the storms of 1881–82 reasonably well. The patriarch resented western missionary challenges, both Protestant and Catholic, to his authority over his flock. Coptic laymen resented Syrian Christian competition for financial and secretarial jobs. Copts could thus join their Muslim compatriots in defining "Egypt for the Egyptians" to exclude Syrians as well as westerners. Two Coptic deputies sat in the 1881–82 chamber, the future prime minister Butrus Ghali and another Coptic undersecretary were active in the *majlis 'urfi*, and Copts joined in the emergency general assemblies' debates.

Copts who had ventured into western religious, political, and economic orbits, however, were vulnerable to occasional Muslim attacks during the revolution. The Asyut merchant Wasif Khayat had trouble with the fallahin; he was both a money-lender and an American citizen. Mikha'il 'Abd al-

[53] Donald M. Reid, *Lawyers and Politics in the Arab World, 1880–1960* (Minneapolis, 1981).

[54] F. de Jong, "The Sufi Orders in Egypt during the 'Urabi Insurrection and the British Occupation (1882–1914): Some Societal Factors Generating Aloofness, Support, and Opposition," *Journal of the American Research Center in Egypt*, 21 (1984), 131–40. On Idwi, see Delanoue, *Moralistes*, I, 261–84, and Broadley, *Arabi*, 365–67.

Sayyid of *al-Watan* and the Muslim journalist Nadim did their best to dampen down religious tensions, and ʿUrabi and the *majlis ʿurfi* moved quickly to squelch attacks on Copts.[55] Copts in the emergency general assembly warned that a religious war against British invaders would exclude them, but that they could support a patriotic war if it had the sultan's sanction.[56]

On the military front, General Wolseley kept ʿUrabi guessing until too late whether he would strike through Kafr al-Dawwar, Damietta, or the canal. Abandoned by France, Ferdinand de Lesseps waged a one-man campaign from his Ismaʿiliyya villa to keep "his" canal free of war. He kept ʿUrabi from attempting to block the waterway until it was too late but could not stop the British, who seized Port Said and Suez, landed at Ismaʿiliyya, and struck out along the railroad and fresh-water canal for Tall al-Kabir and Cairo.[57]

Istanbul's Arabic newspaper *al-Jawaʾib* broke the news of the sultan's repudiation of ʿUrabi a week before Tall al-Kabir, undercutting the morale of the army. Muhammad Sultan, now Tawfiq's agent, softened up the Bedouin with gold, and Bedouin guides led the British on an all-night march to surprise ʿUrabi at dawn on September 13. ʿUrabi's best officers and men were unavailable and much of his force were scantily trained fallahin. Fifty-seven Britons and about two thousand Egyptians died in the battle. ʿUrabi fled by train to Cairo, hoping to continue the resistance, but the *majlis ʿurfi* insisted he surrender to prevent the sacking of the city. ʿUrabi signed a surrender statement to Tawfiq and turned himself in to the British. The rest of the army laid down its arms within the week.

The British disbanded the defeated army, restored Tawfiq, and jailed suspected ʿUrabists. Britain's ambassador to Istanbul, Lord Dufferin, arrived in November for five months to reorganize affairs. A lone indigenous Egyptian sat among the Turco-Circassian judges on the extraordinary tribunal that tried the leading ʿUrabists.[58] To the disgust of Tawfiq, many Turco-Circassians, and some Britons, the British spared ʿUrabi's life. Blunt financed A. M. Broadley's defense of the seven key prisoners: ʿUrabi, Mahmud Sami, Tulba Ismat, ʿAli Fahmi, Mahmud Fahmi, ʿAbd al-Al Hilmi, and Yaʿqub Sami.[59]

Embarrassingly, the charge of burning Alexandria could not be proved. The Gladstone cabinet acquiesced in a plea bargain: guilty to the charge of rebellion, death sentences, and immediate commutation to exile. The seven lost their ranks and property and were exiled to Ceylon. ʿUrabi, Mahmud

[55] Barakat, *Tatawwur* (Cairo, 1977), 221–22; ʿAli Barakat, "Mawqif min al-ajanib fi al-thawra al-ʿurabiyya," *Misr lil-misriyyin*, 368–71.
[56] Schölch, *Egypt*, 263–64.
[57] Charles Royle, *The Egyptian Campaigns, 1882 to 1885* (revised ed., London, 1990).
[58] Schölch, *Egypt*, 358.
[59] On the trial, see Broadley, *Arabi*.

Sami, Tulba Ismat, and 'Ali Fahmi lived to return home in 1900 and 1901. 'Urabi died in obscurity in 1911.

After lesser trials, one officer was hanged for complicity in the Alexandria riot, and several defendants were exiled to the Sudan. 'Abduh, 'Ilish's son 'Abd al-Rahman (his father having died in jail), Nadim, and thirty others were simply exiled for varying periods. Sixty-two other officials lost their jobs, and forty-four notables were put under surveillance on their estates; some were also fined. Another 250 army officers of the dissolved army were stripped of rank and pension rights.[60]

Early in 1883 Tawfiq amnestied suspects who had not yet been tried, and £4,000,000 in compensation for property losses, mostly European, was added to the public debt. 'Abduh's disciple Sa'd Zaghlul, the future national hero, was among those detained in mid-1883, but not convicted, for allegedly plotting revenge through a Patriotic Egyptian League.[61]

Conclusion

At the end, Tawfiq had the backing of most of the Turco-Circassian landed elite (including both Sharif's and Riyad's factions), most of the high 'ulama', and many former deputies – both rich provincial landlords (Sultan, Muhammad al-Shawaribi, Sulayman Abaza) and wealthy merchants ('Abd al-Salam al-Muwaylihi, 'Abdallah al-Siyufi). A number of indigenous officials, such as 'Ali Mubarak, supported Tawfiq, as did the Syrian Christians.

Indigenous army officers and common soldiers backed 'Urabi, as did many 'umdas and mid-level officials, 'ulama', and merchants.[62] A small minority of Turco-Circassian officers and officials (Mahmud Sami, Ya'qub Sami) stood by 'Urabi until Tall al-Kabir, and ten of eighty-three deputies from the chamber were punished as 'Urabists. Four were from Sharqiyya, showing home-region support for 'Urabi. 'Abduh, Nadim, and a third journalist were exiled.

Some of the richest indigenous land owners and merchants welcomed General Wolseley to Cairo with indecent haste. But there was also wealth, to a lesser extent, on 'Urabi's side. Five of the ten deputies punished owned over a thousand faddans,[63] and a large purchase early in 1882 put 'Urabi himself near that bracket. Despite talk of canceling usurious peasant debts to foreigners and an officer's telling peasants near Zagazig that the lands of the rich rightfully belonged to them, a convincing case has not yet been made for

---

[60] Rafi'i, *Thawra 'urabiyya*, 527–55; Broadley, *Arabi*; Schölch, *Egypt*, 301–03.

[61] On the League, see Zayn al-Din 'Abdin Shams al-Din Najm, *al-Jam'iyya al-wataniyya al-misriyya sanat 1883: jam 'iyyat al-intiqam* (Cairo, 1987).

[62] See Cole's analysis of the arrest lists after the British occupation, *Colonialism*, 242–65.

[63] Lawrence Mire, "The Social Origins of Liberal Political Thought in Egypt, 1879–1919," Ph.D. thesis, Princeton University, 1980, 95–96.

a social revolution from below. Shaykhs usually led peasant land seizures, and these were mostly directed against former royal estates and absentee partisans of the khedive.[64]

Access to royal favor may have counted as much as wealth in choosing sides. Among the Abazas in ʿUrabi's home province of Sharqiyya, Sulayman Abaza's branch had long benefited from royal largesse, and he backed the khedive. Ahmad Abaza, from a branch that had won few such favors, backed ʿUrabi.[65]

The elusive relation between Turco-Circassian and indigenous Egyptian identities needs further research. A thorough study of intermarriage would provide one key to the problem. Women's roles in the revolution have thus far only been noted in passing; several princesses related to Halim backed ʿUrabi, and women and girls joined in digging fortifications and in riots.

The British occupation intensified trends the revolution had tried to reverse: concentration of power in British hands, employment of European officials and Syrian Christian middlemen, and the priority given to the European debt. The accumulation of huge estates at the expense of the fallahin continued as well. The chamber of 1881–82 represented only the well-to-do, but it enjoyed far more legitimacy than its quasi-parliamentary successors under Cromer.

Turco-Circassians returning with Tawfiq in the baggage of the British army dominated the cabinets (admittedly largely powerless), for the next quarter of a century. The Sharif–Riyad–Nubar (Nubar was of course an Armenian Christian) trio and Mustafa Fahmi monopolized the prime ministry. During these years only three indigenous Muslims reached the cabinet.[66] Tawfiq rewarded Turco-Circassians with provincial governor-ships; in the army their rewards were more limited because of the influx of British officers to high positions.

The Muhammad ʿAli dynasty survived, at an ultimately fatal price in legitimacy and power. After the catastrophe of 1882, it remained for the revolutionaries of 1919 and 1952 to take up again the cause of "Egypt for the Egyptians." In the upheaval of 1919, British domination was too complete for a colonel to emerge as national champion as happened in 1882 and 1952. By 1952, however, Egypt had won enough autonomy to enable Nassir to step into a role considerably resembling ʿUrabi's. Sensing the kinship, Nassir sponsored a historiographical revolution which rapidly transformed ʿUrabi from the villain he had been, for the most part, under the monarchy into a nationalist and sometimes even a socialist hero.[67]

---

[64] Brown, *Peasant Politics*, 180–82, 190–93, 248 n.28.
[65] Mire, "Social Origins," 93–96, 99–100.
[66] Jeffrey Collins, *The Egyptian Elite under Cromer* (Berlin, 1984), 223, 362–63.
[67] Thomas Mayer, *The Changing Past: Egyptian Historiography of the Urabi Revolt, 1882–1983* (Gainesville, 1988).

10

The British occupation, 1882–1922

M. W. DALY

→←

The events of 1882 mark a watershed in the modern history of Egypt.[1] By defeating the Egyptian army and occupying the country, Britain brought a forceful conclusion to almost a century of Great Power rivalry and of increasing Egyptian independence. While Egypt remained a province of the Ottoman empire, and the dynasty founded by Muhammad 'Ali continued on the throne, the country now moved to an even further orbit of Ottoman influence, and its direction fell to a small number of Europeans backed by a British garrison. Whether the mistaken result of haste in the face of diplomatic protest, or the inevitable consequence of geo-political realities, Britain's promises soon to evacuate Egypt went unfulfilled, and there began a long new chapter in Egypt's foreign domination and Britain's global empire.

Early in the occupation it became clear that the problems that had precipitated intervention would not quickly be solved, however benign or uncertain were British intentions. The financial crisis that had led Isma'il inexorably into the web of European bondholders had worsened; the weakness of the Egyptian regime, exploited by 'Urabi and fully revealed at Tall al-Kabir, was only worsened by the obvious subordination of the new khedive, Muhammad Tawfiq, to the British; the insecurity of imperial communications that political and financial collapse had threatened was deepened, not corrected, by British intervention; rebellion in the Sudan threatened Egypt's entire African empire and even the security of her southern borders. To restore Egypt's finances would take years of painful and painstaking economizing; to restore authority to the Egyptian govern-

[1] For the entire period see John Marlowe, *Anglo-Egyptian Relations 1800–1953* (London, 1953); Robert L. Tignor, *Modernization and British Colonial Rule in Egypt, 1882–1914* (Princeton, 1966); P. J. Vatikiotis, *The Modern History of Egypt* (Baltimore and London, 1969); P. M. Holt (ed.), *Political and Social Change in Modern Egypt* (London, 1968); Gabriel Baer, *Studies in the Social History of Modern Egypt* (Chicago and London, 1969).

ment while maintaining British strategic objectives would require a constant balancing act. To do both in the face of European, especially French, hostility and Ottoman sniping necessitated a degree of resolve that in the event was provided by deft and stiff-necked management in Cairo and almost obsessive attention in London to the primacy of imperial communications.

In the historiography of the British occupation there is constant reference to "anomalies." Britain occupied the territory of a friendly power (the Ottoman empire) against its will; Britain only "advised" the government of that Ottoman province, but its advice had to be followed; Britain's representative operated until 1914 with the lowly title of agent and consul-general, yet in effect ruled the country. Improvisation is a hallmark of the occupation, as indeed it is of the British empire. But while this gave valuable scope for justifying and continuing Britain's predominant position, and was of practical use in the tactical solution of day-to-day problems, it also constrained British attempts at reform and bred frustration and cynicism in Egypt.

A British intention to end the occupation as soon as possible was itself instrumental in providing the foundations for a long stay. Only strong measures could begin the restoration of Egypt's political and financial stability, without which the British would not consider (nor could the European powers profess to expect) evacuation. Thus in the early months of occupation the British were able to act, in concert or unilaterally, in ways that both solidified the occupation and brought its end arguably closer. In December 1882 Sir Evelyn Wood was appointed to raise a new Egyptian army under British officers; the Dual Control, by which Britain and France had jointly supervised Egyptian revenues, was abolished. But more drastic steps, easily justifiable by appeals to good government, but which might have signaled British perfidy, were avoided: the khedival system was retained (together with the annual tribute to the Ottoman sultan), as was much of the international apparatus – the Capitulations, the *caisse de la dette*, the mixed courts – despite difficulties these would inevitably pose for British administration. "Internationalism," while therefore a brake on reform, was also, however, an excuse too often retailed for self-interested British inaction or for mistakes.

Efforts to create financial and political stability in Egypt are usually associated with the masterful Lord Cromer (Sir Evelyn Baring), agent and consul-general from 1883 to 1907.[2] His arrival in Egypt coincided with the imminent bankruptcy of Egypt; emergency measures were adopted, and by the London Convention of 1885 the European powers agreed to changes in

---

[2] For Cromer's period see Afaf Lutfi al-Sayyid Marsot, *Egypt and Cromer* (New York, 1969); Lord Cromer, *Modern Egypt*, 2 vols. (London, 1908); John Marlowe, *Cromer in Egypt* (London, 1970); Marquess of Zetland, *Lord Cromer* (London, 1932).

the law of liquidation to avert the crisis. There followed a long period of adjustment, during which sound accounting rather than financial wizardry was the order of the day. In political affairs Cromer worked through and with the khedival system: an Egyptian council of ministers remained responsible in theory to the khedive; in practice British advisors were appointed to the principal ministries, and British advice was expected to be followed. Muhammad Tawfiq, who owed his throne to the British, was pliant; successive prime ministers chafed at British interference which, owing to the primacy of finance, could be justified in every sphere. Nubar Pasha (prime minister 1884–88) survived a series of disagreements until forced to resign over British refusal to allow an Egyptian to head the national police. His successor, Riaz Pasha, likewise resigned in 1891 over Cromer's insistence on appointment of a British judicial advisor. While even these episodes were the last in series, they are symptomatic of the way in which British administrative control tightened during Cromer's long tenure; the claims of "efficiency" were paramount in a regime dedicated to, indeed justifying itself by, reform, but uneven intervention betrayed other or unconcerted motives, and with time an influx of British officials seemed increasingly to supplant rather than improve the Egyptian bureaucracy. Riaz was succeeded by Mustafa Fahmi Pasha, who served as prime minister almost continuously from 1891 to 1908.

The death of Muhammad Tawfiq in 1892 signaled an end to the era of British conquest and consolidation, and the beginning of a period of more intense Egyptian opposition to the British. This gradual change had social and generational as well as purely political aspects. The new khedive, Tawfiq's son 'Abbas Hilmi, was seventeen at his accession, and in inept early tests of strength was humiliated by Cromer. He remained thereafter disaffected, and a potential focal point for Egyptian opposition to the occupation. Notable leaders of that opposition included Mustafa Kamil who, through a circle of disciples, a newspaper (*al-Liwa*, founded in 1900), and his National Party, made common cause with the khedive; and Shaykh 'Ali Yusuf, whose *al-Mu'ayyad* newspaper hewed to an Islamist, anti-British line. They represent, in fact, a transitional phase in the development of modern Egyptian political consciousness, during which leadership passed from what can with some latitude be called Islamic reformers to those who, with rather less diffidence, may be termed secular politicians. This process, reminiscent of the changes in character and tone that the Egyptian socio-economic elite underwent during the reign of Muhammad 'Ali, would have important consequences for the Egyptian state, the independent identity of its people, and the directions in which its politics would develop in the twentieth century.[3]

---

[3] For the background and development of early party politics see Tignor, *Modernization*; Vatikiotis, *Modern Egypt*; Jacob Landau, *Parliaments and Parties in Egypt* (Tel Aviv,

Contemporary opponents and current critics of the British administration in Egypt have concentrated on its illiberality, its preoccupation with finance, the arrogance of Cromer, and what they see as the political and economic measures to which problems of the 1950s or 1990s may be traced; defenders have stressed the revival of the Egyptian economy, the establishment or reestablishment of law and order, administrative and legal reform, and the continuing distancing and finally separation of Egypt from the Ottoman empire. There is much even in the record of Cromer's long administration to support both schools. In general, however, it may be observed that Cromer himself was fortunate; the situation in Egypt upon his arrival could hardly have been worse, and the British government at home was willing to support strong corrective measures. Then too, the very certainties that informed the spectacular European assertion of global rule in the late nineteenth century had not yet given way to liberal self-doubt or engendered their own logical local opposition; to Cromer Egypt presented a financial and administrative problem, not a moral dilemma, while to Egyptian elite interests the British were hardly viewed as inimical.

As an estate manager there is little argument about Cromer's success. During his tenure the proportion of Egypt's budget devoted to servicing the debt was reduced by half; annual government revenue almost doubled, while taxes were progressively reduced; the value of imports rose fourfold. Huge sums were expended on irrigation and agriculture, and agricultural productivity (admittedly difficult to measure) increased. In an era and in a part of the world where government action was still largely limited to administration and defense, important if unspectacular reforms occurred in the areas of sanitation and health. The kurbash and corvée were abolished. The national police force was revamped, the corrupt provincial police abolished, and the new Egyptian army – after an uncertain start against the Mahdist Sudanese – proved itself; the Sudan was "reconquered," and a new Anglo-Egyptian Condominium restored the honor of Egyptian arms and preserved at least a nominal Egyptian role on the upper Nile. Few if any critics have argued that the fallahin were worse off in 1907 than they had been two decades earlier. Judged by the standards of an occupation limited by debt and by the domestic political system and international controls it inherited, the British regime under Cromer achieved important success.

This success was won at a cost in areas at least as essential as finance to the process of nation building; administrative reform by decree often proves easier to achieve than its authors expect, but it rarely leads to the social and political changes they purport to have in mind as inevitable long-term results

1953); Jacques Berque, *Egypt: Imperialism and Revolution*, trans. Jean Stewart (New York, 1972); Marius Deeb, *Party politics in Egypt*, 1979; and Albert Hourani, *Arabic Thought in the Liberal Age* (London, 1962).

of their reforms. Similarly the social policy that would logically complement a program of economic and administrative reform requires a degree of imagination and willingness to experiment that are foreign to the bureaucratic mentality. Notwithstanding contemporary limits to government provision of education, for example, Cromer's policy was notoriously disdainful of even secondary schooling; the frankly racist ideology Cromer propounded as justification for European rule dismissed higher education as not only dangerous but irrelevant for the proper development of subject peoples. But the lower levels of education were neglected too, and even technical schooling, arguably apolitical and essential for the future development of the Egyptian economy, received little attention. Likewise judicial reform was timid, and not only because of the continuing nuisance of the mixed courts.

The most glaring failure of the period was in the political sphere. While a good case could be made for retaining the constitutional forms of the khedivate, nothing was done to strengthen them and much was done to sap their authority. This resulted as much from routine administrative decisions, the creeping aggregation of powers by the ever-increasing number of British advisors and bureaucrats, as from deliberate policy. There was indeed no long-term policy of political reform, no strategy. Early recommendations for consultative institutions were shelved, neglected, or implemented in such diluted form as to excite no interest. Moreover the long and increasing dependence on European, mainly British, bureaucrats and experts created a new foreign interest-group, whose status and future were tied to indefinite continuation of the current regime. The need for political reform became disastrously clear at the end of Cromer's tenure, when the British administration was revealed to be dangerously out of touch.

The Dinshawai incident of 1906 was the most important milestone in Anglo-Egyptian relations between 1882 and 1914. What began as a minor fracas, and should have remained a routine police matter, ended as a two-headed icon of Egyptian nationalist mythology and British imperialism. After an affray between British officers and villagers at Dinshawai in the Delta one of the officers died; four villagers were subsequently executed after a trial before a special court, and others were sentenced to floggings and hard labor. The incident was seized upon by nationalists, to whom it epitomized the brutality and humiliation of British rule; British handling of the case was symptomatic of the regime's increasing aloofness and insensitivity, and indeed unarguably was inept. Cromer, who was in England at the time, resigned in poor health a few months later.

Egyptian mass reaction to the Dinshawai incident surprised the British, but it had been clear for some time – a generation after the outset of a "temporary" occupation – that political change was overdue. Cromer's successor, Sir Eldon Gorst, had as longtime Financial Adviser advocated reform, and backed by a Liberal government in London he embarked upon a program to promote self-governing institutions and conciliate the khedive.[4] In 1909 a new system of elected provincial councils was introduced; the powers of the legislative council, which under Cromer had been toothless, were enhanced; steps were taken to reduce the number of British officials; greater Egyptian interest and participation in the governing of the Sudan were encouraged. But Gorst's moderate reforms satisfied no one: discerning weakness and uncertainty, nationalists rejected them; personal relations between the consul-general and khedive were restored, but the airing of constitutional issues created a breach between the autocratic ʿAbbas Hilmi and liberal nationalists; and to the important foreign community, including especially British officials and businessmen, Gorst and his untidy reforms compared unfavorably to the magisterial Cromer. The luckless Gorst had also to contend with serious local effects of a European economic recession; Cromer's single-minded attention to agricultural development had left the country severely exposed to the fluctuations of the world cotton market, and Egyptian reception of political reform was inevitably colored by general dissatisfaction during hard times. Gorst, fatally ill, resigned in 1911, his tenure generally considered then and since a failure, remarkably even by those who sympathized with his views.

The appointment of Lord Kitchener as agent and consul-general was widely seen as a British attempt to turn back the clock.[5] To Europeans he was a no-nonsense Cromerian, to Egyptians the longtime (and hugely unpopular) *sirdar* (commander-in-chief) of the Egyptian army and conqueror of the Sudan. But in politics (as in battle) Kitchener rarely rushed in, guns blazing; while brooking no opposition, he was yet circumspect and shrewd, and whether or not he had any intellectual conception of administration or saw ultimate British purpose in Egypt beyond holding on to it, he was no reactionary. Like Cromer, Muhammad ʿAli, and indeed the pharaohs he paid special attention to irrigation and agriculture; the Aswan dam was heightened, and the fallahin were relieved of debt. Like Gorst, Kitchener inaugurated political reform; the organic law of 1913 created a legislative assembly with a greater proportion of elected members than the old council and with wider powers. Constitutional advance was halted by the outbreak of the First World War, but the reforms of Gorst and Kitchener – and the Egyptian social and economic impetus for and response to those reforms – had already stimulated the political development that would culminate in the crisis of 1918–19.

From modest beginnings as circles of students and personal admirers of one or another scholar or philosopher, Egyptian political parties had

---

[4] For Gorst's reforms see Peter Mellini, *Sir Eldon Gorst: The Overshadowed Proconsul* (Stanford, 1977).

[5] For Kitchener in Egypt see George Arthur, *Life of Lord Kitchener* (London, 1920); Philip Magnus, *Kitchener: Portrait of an Imperialist* (London, 1958).

emerged. Many factors contributed to this process: the shocking reality of (Christian) British occupation and rule; the concomitant and accelerating decline of the Ottoman empire (and other Muslim states); the influence of European political philosophy and the introduction of secular political institutions; effects of economic recovery and prosperity; and emergence of a younger generation of Egyptians, some of them lawyers, many with exposure to western secular education.[6] These and other developments, both domestic and foreign, tended to reorient Egyptian politics from a purely Islamic and philosophical bent toward the secular and practical arena of economics, administration, and international relations. While the political parties of the early twentieth century had roots extending to the beginning of the occupation and beyond, their formation owes much to the stifling atmosphere of the late Cromer years, to the shock of the Dinshawai incident, and to changes in the international sphere that made clear the terminal decline of the Ottoman empire and the ever-rising power of Europe. Thus although students of the great reforming shaykh Muhammad 'Abduh were prominent in all the new political parties, their very dispersal in this way reveals the changes that had occurred in Egypt and the world since his death in 1905.

In 1907 three parties were established. The anti-British National Party (*Hizb al-Watani*) of Mustafa Kamil only with difficulty survived his premature death in 1908; Ahmad Lutfi al-Sayyid's Umma Party advocated cooperation with the British until reforms necessary for social and educational development had prepared Egypt for independence; the Constitutional Reform Party of Shaykh 'Ali Yusuf took the part of the khedive. A number of smaller "parties" were likewise closely associated with one or another prominent politician or journal. Meanwhile the British only slowly and incompletely understood the changes in Egyptian political dynamics for which their own occupation was partly responsible. While the world war would curtail British reforms, it only further stimulated Egyptian political consciousness.

The anomalies of Egypt's juridical status, which had never been completely dormant, were suddenly revived with the advent of war in 1914.[7] Since Egypt was still legally a province of the Ottoman empire, her people were still Ottoman subjects; the sultan's shadowy claims to the caliphate had

---

[6] On the emergence and growth of political parties see Jamal Mohammed Ahmed, *The intellectual origins of Egyptian nationalism* (London, 1960); Hourani, *Arabic Thought*; Landau, *Parliaments and Parties*; and Elie Kedourie, *Afghani and Abduh* (London, 1966).

[7] For Egypt in the First World War see Mahmud Zayid, *Egypt's Struggle for Independence* (Beirut, 1965); Royal Institute of International Affairs, *Great Britain and Egypt 1914–1951* (London, 1952); Viscount Wavell, *Allenby in Egypt* (London, 1943); Marlowe, *Anglo-Egyptian Relations*.

struck a chord in occupied Egypt, as elsewhere in a Muslim world almost totally under European domination, and divided loyalties at least had to be expected. In August–October 1914, before the Ottomans entered the war, the British took urgent steps to buttress their position. A proclamation forbade intercourse with the enemy; censorship was imposed; the legislative assembly was prorogued; sale of Egypt's vital cotton crop was ensured. At the beginning of November martial law was declared. When the Ottoman empire entered the war on November 6 further steps were taken. As before, British annexation of Egypt was debated and rejected; in December a protectorate was declared. Khedive 'Abbas Hilmi was deposed, and his uncle, Husayn Kamil, was installed as sultan. Fearful that in Egypt (and indeed elsewhere in their colonial empire) Muslims would support the Ottoman sultan's call to jihad, the British promised to undertake the entire burden of Egypt's defense and depicted the protectorate as a step toward self-government. But the precise meaning of "protectorate" was in fact no more certain to the British than to the Egyptians; protectorate status was a wartime improvisation to cut Egypt adrift from the Ottoman empire without inciting Egyptians with the prospect of tightened British control.

Although distant from the trenches of the western front, Egypt and the Egyptians were caught up from beginning to end in the world war. The first British priority there was defending the Suez Canal against possible invasion from Palestine. Thus Egypt quickly became home base to large numbers of British and imperial troops; in 1915 first a Mediterranean expeditionary force, then an Egyptian expeditionary force were based there, and other forces followed, all of which had to be quartered and supplied. Civilian land and buildings were requisitioned. An Egyptian labour corps and camel transport corps were established; when voluntary labor and animal sales dried up, the British resorted to conscription and confiscation, which were moreover enforced harshly and with inadequate compensation. The British demand for cotton led to a decline in food production that in turn contributed to hardship for the urban masses in the form of inflated food prices.

These and other developments were symptomatic of and worsened by the distraction and incompetence of British administrators. That the British government in London, and indeed its representatives in Egypt, should have seen the titanic struggle with Germany as subordinating all other concerns was natural; that Egyptians and others did not share British singlemindedness is equally understandable. Short-handed and increasingly represented by inexperienced newcomers who were themselves absorbed by the war effort, the British turned a blind eye to abuses. Kitchener had been made secretary of state for war in August 1914, and his successor in Cairo (with the new title of high commissioner), Sir Henry McMahon, was without experience in Egypt; direction of affairs fell to the second tier of advisors who sometimes pursued unconcerted interests and were in any case stretched by the exigencies of the war. Although McMahon's successor in 1917, Sir Reginald Wingate, had long experience in Egypt and the Sudan, he too was yet unequipped personally and indeed legally to deal with the complex intramural British military situation and its effects on Egypt and the Egyptians.[8]

Thus even before the end of the war the future political status of Egypt had to be debated. The British proclamation of November 1914 had foreseen progress toward self-government, and Egypt's contribution to the war effort was substantial and continuous. Moreover British and French propaganda depicted a war between democracy and autocracy, law and barbarism, and Egyptians expected post-war measures consistent with wartime rhetoric. But the same factors that Egyptians enumerated as justifying and indeed leading to their independence the British saw as necessitating continued occupation. The war seemed to clarify the British empire's military and economic dependence on the land and sea routes passing through or near Egypt, while the expected dissolution of the Ottoman empire after the war would make Egypt the lodestar in any new Afro-Asian imperial constellation. While the war continued, however, the British refrained from constitutional change that might inflame Egyptian opinion; when Sultan Husayn Kamil died in 1917 he was succeeded by his brother Ahmad Fu'ad, and British debates about the future of Egypt (as indeed about the future of the Ottoman empire) never involved the subject peoples themselves. British commissions appointed in 1917 to suggest capitulatory and constitutional reforms indeed recommended changes that even before the war would have been unacceptable to Egyptian moderates.

Thus when the war ended two wholly incompatible sets of expectations were revealed. Egyptian nationalists, both by right and by virtue of Egypt's contribution to the war effort, and spurred on by the wartime promises of the Allies (including President Wilson's much-discussed Fourteen Points), looked forward naively at least to early self-government if not to immediate independence. The British government, grimly triumphant at great cost, and with global issues foremost, just as unrealistically presumed Egyptian acquiescence in a continued status of dependency, relieved perhaps by minor reforms implemented gradually and after long deliberation. Between these two extremes were the moderate Egyptian ministers, led by Husayn Rushdi Pasha, who had collaborated with the British throughout the war and needed something to show for it; the young new sultan, Ahmad Fu'ad, who had yet to prove himself; and the resident foreign community, who were suspicious of any reform that heralded a reduction in British authority.

[8] For Wingate's high commissionership see Janice Terry, *The Wafd 1919–1952* (London, 1982); and M. W. Daly, *The Sirdar* (Philadelphia, 1997).

It was in this context that a few Egyptian ex-ministers called on Wingate, the high commissioner, on November 13, 1918, two days after the European armistice, to demand the complete independence of Egypt. The delegation (Wafd) was led by Sa'd Pasha Zaghlul, a former minister of education and of justice who, as vice president of the new legislative assembly in 1913–14 had emerged as leader of the opposition to the pro-British government.[9] By presenting demands to the high commissioner so soon after the end of the war Zaghlul and his associates were not so much stealing a march as filling a vacuum. Rushdi Pasha and his ministers were tainted by a wartime collaboration with the British that had produced no evident progress toward Egyptian independence, and were more closely associated with Sultan Ahmad Fu'ad than with any of the nascent nationalist parties; the British had nothing to offer Rushdi. Those parties, moreover, were either so vehemently opposed to the British or so strongly identified with the palace as to preclude their credible leadership in dealing with the British. The members of Zaghlul's delegation, on the other hand, had both administrative and legislative experience, and a claim to represent the new class dominated by indigenous urban lawyers and cotton farmers rather than the old Turkish elite.

Wingate's actions on November 13, 1918, and his subsequent recommendations, were and still are heavily criticized. He could have declined to receive the delegation, which had no constitutional standing, and deferred instead to Rushdi and his ministers. But Wingate not only told Zaghlul he would refer the delegation's demands to the Foreign Office in London, but he also advised the Foreign Office to receive Zaghlul and his colleagues there. While thus clearly (and, crucially to his detractors, unwittingly) undercutting the Rushdi government Wingate may have intended either merely to exhibit British openness to the views of distinguished Egyptians, or more likely to coopt what he saw as the up-and-coming leadership of moderate nationalism. In any event the Foreign Office brusquely rejected his advice, and the train was set in motion – either by Wingate or the Foreign Office – that would lead to a violent outbreak in 1919.

While the British argued among themselves, Zaghlul and the Wafd organized the Egyptian masses behind their demand for independence. Rushdi resigned, was belatedly invited to London, then resigned again when London rejected his proposal that Zaghlul (and anyone else who wished) should be allowed to travel too; Rushdi could not afford to be seen as handpicked by the British to negotiate with them. Wingate was recalled for consultations. Within a few short weeks Wafdist agitation had so strength-

---

[9] For the Wafd see Terry, *The Wafd*; Afaf Lutfi al-Sayyid Marsot, *Egypt's Liberal Experiment, 1922–1936* (Berkeley, 1977); Elie Kedourie, "Sa'ad Zaghlul and the British," *St. Antony's Papers*, 11, *Middle Eastern Affairs*, 2 (Oxford, 1961).

ened Zaghlul's grip on public opinion that a new government could not be formed. In early March 1919 the British arrested Zaghlul and two associates and exiled them to Malta. Demonstrations immediately took place up and down the country, followed by riots, then looting and random violence, which included the murder of British soldiers; mass action involved people from all walks of life, urban workers and fallahin, members of ethnic and religious minorities, and even women, something unprecedented in Egypt. Martial law was reinforced, and General Allenby sent from England to supersede Wingate as high commissioner. Allenby, without an Egyptian government, ruled by decree, and order was not restored until early April when the British, having concluded that the Allies in Paris would in any case recognize their protectorate in Egypt, announced Zaghlul's release and freedom to travel to Europe to make his case.

The events of November 1918–April 1919 had shown that the protectorate had no support among Egyptians, and that at the very least the status of Egypt and of the British in Egypt must be substantially altered. While to Allenby this was as clear as it was to all sections of Egyptian opinion, the British government was unconvinced. The next two years were therefore characterized by acrimony and disorder, as the Wafd solidified its hold over Egyptian opinion, the British government tried to maintain a position unsupportable in the face of virtually unanimous Egyptian opposition, and Allenby acted in effect as intermediary, to whom maintenance of order and defense of British interests necessarily involved reasonable concessions to the Egyptians.

In the aftermath of the crisis Egypt did not return to normal. In Cairo a stable ministry proved impossible to form. British attempts to appear firm yet conciliatory were seen as repressive and dishonest. In Paris, meanwhile, Zaghlul moved from defeat to defeat; the Allies, including the United States, in which much sentimental hope had been placed by Egyptians, officially recognized the British protectorate. In London, in time-honored fashion, the government sought to temporize by appointing a committee. This, the Milner Mission, tellingly reached Egypt only in December 1919, by which time it had been thoroughly discredited by its announced terms of reference; the mission was to enquire about the causes of the recent disturbances and report on "the form of Constitution which, under the Protectorate," would "be best calculated to promote its [Egypt's] peace and prosperity, the progressive development of self-governing institutions, and the protection of foreign interests." Since emergence from "under the Protectorate" was the irreducible goal of Egyptian nationalism, the mission was boycotted by all but officials. Returning to London, Milner therefore welcomed an opportunity for talks with Zaghlul himself, who arrived in England in June 1920. A general agreement was reached by which the British declared themselves ready to replace the protectorate with a treaty recognizing Egyptian independence but stipulating a British military presence and other provisions. Zaghlul pressed for further concessions, and negotiations broke down; what critics then and since have seen as intransigence did in any event establish a baseline from which subsequent Anglo-Egyptian negotiations would proceed: the British had admitted willingness to abandon the protectorate and recognize Egyptian independence.

Having acknowledged that the protectorate must go, the British could hardly defend it. They therefore followed up the failed Milner–Zaghlul negotiations with an attempt to negotiate a treaty with the Egyptian government itself. The new prime minister, 'Adli Pasha Yakan, tried but failed to persuade Zaghlul to join a delegation to London for this purpose. That delegation was therefore hamstrung by Zaghlul's continuing mastery of Egyptian public opinion. Nothing short of total British evacuation from Egypt would now have defanged Zaghlul, and negotiations therefore broke down. 'Adli resigned, Zaghlul was placed under martial-law restrictions, then deported to the Seychelles.

While the trend of events seems in hindsight (and seemed to many at the time) to have pointed inevitably to abolition of the protectorate, the Foreign Office continued in 1921 to insist that in the absence of negotiated settlement the status of Egypt would remain as it was. Of this Allenby himself was forced to disabuse them. That the soldier on the spot recognized the impossibility of ruling Egypt by force, but that the politicians in London did not, is a remarkable feature of the crisis that had begun with Wingate's reception of the Wafd in November 1918. Now, having returned to London in early February 1922 for consultations, which took place against a backdrop of violent outbreaks in Egypt, Allenby, under threat of resignation, finally succeeded in wringing from the British cabinet agreement to a unilateral declaration of Egyptian independence.

This declaration (of February 18, 1922) abolished the protectorate, foresaw the immediate end of martial law, and "absolutely reserved to the discretion" of the British government four "matters": British imperial communications; the defense of Egypt; protection of foreign interests there; and "the Sudan." The Reserved Points, as they came to be called, clearly implied severe limitations to the independence thus proclaimed, and would form the basis for often-bitter Anglo-Egyptian relations for another thirty years. But the fact remains that a course had been set, away from colonial dependency – it had not been long since British officials had pressed for the annexation of Egypt – and toward "complete independence." Nor can it be denied that that course had been determined by the mobilization of Egyptian opinion by Sa'd Zaghlul. In Egypt, as elsewhere, British wartime promises of post-war political progress had proved impossible to withdraw. But another generation of Anglo-Egyptian tension would also reveal that even in 1922 those promises had not been fully kept.

While British involvement in Egypt's government would continue in one form or another until 1956, and at times (such as during the Second World War) would again resemble in all but name the hated protectorate, the events that culminated in the declaration of February 1922 mark more than an artificial and formal divide. For the Egyptians, Reserved Points notwithstanding, the 1922 declaration was a real achievement; while all the attributes of sovereignty would be won only after further protracted struggle, administrative control now passed largely to Egyptian hands. But that the subsequent development of constitutional government was severely hampered by continuing British involvement is undeniable; it can be argued that protectorate status had lent clarity and a degree of legitimacy to British action in Egypt that both occupation before the First World War and blatant interference after 1922 lacked. For the British the 1922 declaration marked a return to the preferred imperial methods of informal control, and away from the unavoidable responsibility that the protectorate had represented. The legality (however "anomalous") of unilateral action that the protectorate had allowed but which the war had discredited was exchanged in 1922 for a return to the freedom of action ironically made easier by occupation and "independence." That freedom of action knew no formal bounds, and would be limited largely by changing British notions of Egypt's geo-political importance, not by their effects, however disastrous, on Egyptian political development. Thus inherent in the logic of the occupation of 1882–1922, in the Reserved Points with which the period ended as much as in the bombardments with which it had begun, and indeed in the methods by which the British prolonged their control until the 1950s, was the idea that Egypt could not and would not be allowed to rule itself.

Social and economic change
in the "long nineteenth century"*

EHUD R. TOLEDANO

✥

Introduction

Unlike political events, social and economic processes are not amenable to periodization according to precise starting and ending-points. By their very nature, such processes do not begin at a certain moment in history, but rather mature over time; nor do they end abruptly, but rather tend to peter out gradually. Since the purpose of this chapter is to chart the main processes that took place in Egyptian society, we shall try to define a time frame that can accommodate within its loose boundaries the main social and economic developments. "The long nineteenth century" as conceived here spills over in both directions – it begins with the third quarter of the eighteenth century and ends in the first quarter of the twentieth: "just as the coming of the French in 1798 should not be thought of as a beginning, so the coming of the English in 1882 should not be thought of as an end."[1]

It has been argued that if we focus on both "continuity and rupture" it is quite obvious that the period of Muhammad ʿAli should be discussed in conjunction with the second half of the eighteenth century. But at the same time, the 1860s and 1870s were a period of intense change, which mark a rupture with the past:

The expansion of European commerce, leading to the inflow of European capital, the great changes in communications with the coming of the telegraph in the 1870s, the opening of new schools, the beginning of newspapers and periodicals in the 1870s, and behind them all the demographic changes ... all these are very important, and in some ways they can be regarded as opening a new period, and one that continues far beyond 1882.[2]

Thus we shall look at a number of social and economic processes as they

---

* Regarding transliteration of Turkish names, see Note on transliteration, p. xiii.
[1] Albert Hourani, "Conclusions," Groupe de recherches et d'études sur le Proche-Orient, *L'Egypte au XIXᵉ Siècle* (Paris, 1982), 333.
[2] *Ibid.*

developed during the "long nineteenth century" with special attention to the three decades from the 1850s to the 1880s as a period of meaningful and long-range changes. However, this continuity is not regarded as a static situation, but rather as a dynamic force and a major axis of human – here Egyptian – history. The reproduction of even the same social formations is, by itself, a process requiring a great deal of human and social energy, often incorporating relatively small and routinized change, which is distinguishable from Hourani's "ruptures." Recruitment and socialization, for example, may play an important role in reproducing a certain institution, such as the Ottoman–Egyptian elite household, but they are also the very practices through which changes were introduced into the household, that cumulatively transformed it over the century.

This chapter's approach in studying processes specifically does not trace "beginnings" nor seek "early signs" of things to come. Historical phenomena are best understood and most fruitfully investigated when they have attained a "critical mass," that is when they are clearly what they are. Therefore, we will not explore the origins of private land ownership in Egypt, for example, but look at what constituted private ownership in land at various points during the period under consideration and evaluate the significance of different stages in the development of private landholding. Similarly, we shall try to understand what the state meant and did within Egyptian society, not when aspects of the state began to emerge in Egypt.

The importance of the French occupation of Egypt in 1798 is therefore considerably reduced in this analysis. The brief and intriguing rule of the French in Egypt cannot be seen as having inaugurated the modern era in Egyptian history, because it triggered political, economic, and intellectual processes, under the impact of Europe, that had transformed the country. On the contrary, such a view belittles both the fact that Egypt continued to form part of the Ottoman empire, and the role of local traditions regarding religion, thought, culture, economics, and human relations.[3]

Demographic and social trends

We may begin by looking at some figures that stand out when we compare the early to the later parts of the period. Since there is no reliable information for the late eighteenth century, scholars have usually begun their work from the data provided by the French scientific delegation that came to Egypt with Napoleon's forces. The population of Egypt in 1800, according to Panzac, was 4.5 million, while at the end of the nineteenth century it stood at close to 10 million.[4] But the population growth rate was not the

[3] Robert Mantran, "Avant-propos," *L'Egypte au XIXe Siècle* (Paris, 1982), 9.
[4] Figures and analysis in this section are based on Daniel Panzac, "The Population of

same throughout the period, reflecting the impact of other socio-economic processes and the general state of the country. A low rate was detected in the first four decades of the century, with an increase of only 0.3–0.4 percent per annum between 1800 and 1830, and no growth at all between 1830 and 1840.

With the end of Muhammad 'Ali's years of war and aggressive reforms, a return to calm in the 1840s and the success of counter-epidemic measures produced a 1 percent annual growth rate between 1840 and 1848. By the end of his reign, plague and smallpox had almost disappeared due to quarantine measures and mass vaccination. However, cholera and other diseases (such as bilharzia) surfaced and caused great loss of life and debilitation. The middle decades (1840–60) witnessed a significant rise to a sustained annual growth rate of about 1.2–1.3 percent for the remainder of the nineteenth century, reflecting profound change in living conditions. In the final analysis, despite impressive successes in fighting smallpox and the plague, the demographic structures of the Egyptian population remained virtually unchanged: high levels of birth and mortality rates (especially infant mortality), and the same rate and age of marriage.[5]

Most of the population continued to be rural, eking a living out of the land. Urbanization, in general, did not become a major feature of nine-teenth-century Egypt, and the size of the urban population rose only from 8 percent in 1820 to less than 10 percent at the end of the century. However, that population was by then concentrated in two very large cities (Cairo with 570,000 and Alexandria with some 320,000, representing a 40 percent increase from 1850 to 1880), and some middle-size ones, as compared to the beginning of the century, when Cairo (with 260,000 inhabitants) was the only large city, while some 140,000 persons lived in small towns ranging from 6,000 to 20,000.[6]

There were relatively few foreign residents in Egypt at the beginning of our period, but by 1907 their number had dramatically surged to about 140,000. They flocked to the country from Europe and America in the wake of the cotton boom of the 1860s, further encouraged by the British occupation of 1882. They owned about 15 percent of the land and most of the trading and manufacturing companies.[7] The presence of such a large

Egypt in the Nineteenth Century," *Asian and African Studies*, 21/1 (March 1987), 11–32.

[5] *Ibid.*, 15–16, 19–20, 31–32. On public health and the fight against epidemics, see also LaVerne Kuhnke, *Lives at Risk: Public Health in Nineteenth-Century Egypt* (Berkeley, 1990).

[6] Panzac, "Population of Egypt," 28–31.

[7] E. R. J. Owen, *Cotton and the Egyptian Economy, 1820–1914: A Study in Trade and Development* (Oxford, 1969), 320–21.

foreign community and its important role in the socio-economic processes that impacted on Egypt will be discussed later.

What, then, were these processes? Although there are and have been disagreements among scholars with regard to the nature of the main social, political, and economic processes, these have tended to center around the question of hierarchy more than substance. Thus, for example, some historians have privileged economic processes over others, attributing to them greater importance than to, say, socio-cultural or "merely" political ones. It is not our purpose here to rank the various types of "continuities and ruptures" that characterize Egypt's history in the "long nineteenth century," but rather to mention and describe those major processes over which there is broad agreement in the literature.

There is hardly any doubt that such an analysis must include all of the following: the emergence of a strong and centralized state; the rise and transformation of various elites; Egypt's incorporation in the world economy and concomitant European penetration into the country; and changes in the relations between individual and society. These processes were closely interrelated, and we treat them separately only for analytic purposes; it is impossible fully to understand these phenomena without realizing that they evolved in a kind of "symbiotic relationship" to each other.

A similar approach has recently been expressed in describing the processes of transformation in the non-European world as

a type of capitalist development in which, in very general terms, expanding international trade, increasing agricultural specialization, and the beginning of modern industry act to dissolve the old solidarities and to replace them with others based on the emergence of the individual citizen as peasant, or farmer or worker, and so to the possibility of the formation of new forms of association based on class.

It was in these circumstances that the modern Middle Eastern state was created, and this calls for examination of the relations of state, nation, and religious community in terms of particular types of political and administrative forms.[8]

In adopting the approach to the history of Egypt in the nineteenth century suggested in this chapter, we avoid such metaphors and concepts as "the impact of the west" and "the European challenge and the Egyptian response." These are too one-directional and one-dimensional; we are dealing here with an *interactive* reality rather than a *reactive* one.

---

[8] E. R. J. Owen, *State, Power and Politics in the Making of the Modern Middle East* (London and New York, 1992), 5.

Hegemonic rule, dynastic order, and the emergence of a centralized state

A strong, centralized state in Egypt during most of the period discussed in this chapter is a very noticeable phenomenon, yet one that is not easily defined. It is difficult to conceptualize the state and its relation to society, as political theorists have pointed out. One scholar rightly contends that states are not single things, but rather "a bundle of structures, institutions, arenas, practices and claims," adding that these bundles should be examined in concrete historical situations. This he posits in opposition to the view of the state "as autonomous, that is, as something that simply acts upon society from a position quite outside it."[9]

The formalistic view that pits the state versus society, or civil society, as the case may be, is increasingly thought to misrepresent the actual relationship between the state and various groups – both powerful and powerless – in society. The main objection is to common formulations that describe the changes that occurred in nineteenth-century Egypt, for example, as "an ever greater centralization of power and government control *over* society," with the state assuming more and more functions so that "social groups became *subordinated* to the demands of the state"; the bureaucratic elite is then seen as "a bridge between government *and* society."[10] The distinction between "public" (state) and "private" (society) spheres is also criticized as artificial and resulting from the state's power to define and restrict, by coercion, "concepts of the person, the body, the family, gender," and to consign "all these to a voluntaristically-conceived sphere of the private."[11]

Rather than delve any further into this theoretical discussion, we shall simply look at the main manifestations of state power within society, emphasizing that they are not separate, autonomous entities, but rather symbolically existing ones, with boundaries that are hard to define and constantly shifting, being negotiated and redrawn. At the center of the state stood the house of Muhammad ʿAli, the source of its power and legitimacy. Beginning with the governor-general himself, hereditary rule in the Ottoman province of Egypt was extricated from the sultan and enshrined in a decree issued in 1841, as part of the settlement that ended a decade of bitter conflict between the governor and his sovereign. Muhammad ʿAli's heirs – ʿAbbas, Saʿid, and Ismaʿil – continued to resist the Ottomans' attempt to annul the decree of hereditary rule, and their efforts resulted in increased

---

[9] *Ibid.*

[10] F. Robert Hunter, *Egypt under the Khedives, 1805–1879: From Household Government to Modern Bureaucracy* (Pittsburgh, 1984), 230 (the italics are mine).

[11] Bernard S. Cohn and Nicholas B. Dirks, "Beyond the Fringe: The Nation State, Colonialism, and the Technologies of Power," *Journal of Historical Sociology*, 1/2 (June 1988), 227, quoting O'Hanlon, p.c.

autonomy.[12] Finally, after the demise of the Ottoman empire and under British domination, the khedivate – after a brief sultanate – became a monarchy, which lasted until 1952.

The broader context of these developments takes us back to the eighteenth century and the recent scholarly debate about the nature of the socio-political order in Egypt during the second phase of Ottoman rule. It has been common in the literature to present Egyptian society in the eighteenth century as made up of Mamluk beys, Ottoman *ojaq* (Turkish *ocak*) officers, merchants, 'ulama', artisans organized in guilds, and peasants. In the nineteenth century, the first two groups are supposed to have been replaced by an Ottoman–Egyptian dynasty and elite, and European resident communities; the other groups remain the same, with the changes at the top having had seemingly little impact upon them. Following recent developments in the study of Egyptian elites in both centuries, an alternative model has been suggested, which we shall adopt and explicate in the following pages.

The main processes that took place in Egypt from the seventeenth century onward were similar to those that occurred in the other Ottoman provinces of the Middle East and North Africa.[13] Rather briefly, these consisted in a dual adjustment process that emanated from the empire's need to cope with the changing world around it and adopt a policy of decentralization. The Ottoman military–administrative elites became localized, while the local elites gradually became ottomanized. These processes were both socio-political and socio-cultural. As a result, Ottoman-local elites emerged in this vast region, which were Ottoman in outlook and orientation, but very much embedded in the provincial setting and social networks. The process as a whole was inclusivist in nature, and it enabled longstanding local notable families to bond themselves to the empire and develop both a sense of belonging and loyalty to the house of Osman.

The central government in Istanbul allowed those Ottoman-local elites a large measure of autonomy in exchange for revenue and acceptance of Ottoman sovereign privileges, which meant, *inter alia*, that Ottoman administrative structure and traditions were to be preserved, and that appointments had to be confirmed by Istanbul. The latter ensured that the central government could meddle in local affairs and protect its vital strategic interest, as defined at any given moment. With the symbols of Ottoman sovereignty intact, the sultan's legitimizing power remained uncontested

---

[12] For the rise of dynastic order in Egypt, see Ehud R. Toledano, *State and Society in Mid-Nineteenth-century Egypt* (Cambridge, 1990), 50–67.

[13] For a fuller argument, see Ehud R. Toledano, "The Emergence of Ottoman-Local Elites (1700–1900): A Framework for Research," in Ilan Pappé and Moshe Ma'oz (eds.), *Middle Eastern Politics and Ideas, A History from Within* (London and New York, 1997), 145–62.

virtually until the demise of the empire; it was one of the most tangible assets the Ottomans held in the Middle East and North Africa.

The Ottoman government in Egypt was made up, as elsewhere, of a central administration located in the capital, Cairo, and a rural subprovincial structure (the beylicate), which appropriated the agricultural surplus and maintained law and order in the countryside. The localized garrison regiments came to be regarded as "Ottoman," while the beylicate was seen as "mamluk." In fact, both were part of the Ottoman administrative structure in Egypt, and both recruited and employed *mamluks* as well as men recruited in other ways. Mamluks and non-Mamluks crossed over from one branch to the other, established households (*kapi* in Turkish, *bayt* in Arabic), and kept varying numbers of retainers to protect and promote their interests. In other words, after the demise of the Mamluk sultanate in 1517, the *mamluk* track became just one of the methods of recruitment and socialization into the Ottoman–Egyptian elite. Thus, what is celebrated as a "Mamluk household" was actually an Ottoman provincial household, though it quite naturally possessed local characteristics (some even borrowed from Mamluk sultanate traditions), which made it an Ottoman–Egyptian household, rather than any other Ottoman household.[14]

The single most important factor in the process that altered the composition of the Ottoman–Egyptian elite in the first half of the nineteenth century, and significantly changed its nature, was the hegemonic standing that the household of Muhammad 'Ali achieved within the Ottoman–Egyptian elite by the year 1811. The concomitant elimination of other households as potentially destabilizing power bases also reduced the recruitment of retainers via the *mamluk* track, restricting it to the leading households of the ruler and his immediate family. In the second half of the nineteenth century, Ottoman–Egyptian elite households did not recruit *mamluks*, who became an exclusive symbol of rule. The rest of the century saw the process of elite formation develop under stable dynastic rule toward yet another "rupture" point, the opening up of the socio-political arena in the 1860s and 1870s, to be discussed further below.

The interpretation suggested here places the history of social forces and elite formation on one continuum from the Ottoman occupation in the sixteenth century to the rise of the Egyptian nation state in the twentieth century. Accordingly, the seventeenth century witnessed the emergence of an Ottoman–Egyptian elite that was gradually organizing itself around the grandee household, but it still lacked a coherent power center and no single household or faction managed to achieve hegemony. This initial period –

---

[14] This passage represents a new interpretation of the traditional view of the beylicate as a "neo-Mamluk" phenomenon; it draws on insights provided by Jane Hathaway, *The Politics of Households in Ottoman Egypt: The Rise of the Qazdaglis* (Cambridge, 1997), and on my own research.

we might wish to name it the first Ottoman period – ends with the rise of the Qazdagli household to a dominant position in the first part of the eighteenth century.

The second Ottoman period in Egyptian history is marked by the consolidation of central authority, which later is only temporarily interrupted: Qazdagli hegemony peaks under ʿAli Bey al-Kabir and Muhammad Abu al-Dhahab (1760–75); comes under domestic Ottoman (1785) and then French (1789) challenges, but manages to survive under the duumvirate of Murad and Ibrahim (1779–98); it is finally broken and replaced by the hegemony of the household of Muhammad ʿAli (from 1811 on), which becomes a dynamic rule; it is then challenged by the Ottomans and the French under Abbas (until 1852), then internally by the ʿUrabists (1880–82), and externally by the British (1882), but manages to survive into the present century under British rule.

During the first six years of his rule (1805–11), Muhammad ʿAli devoted a great deal of energy to the eradication of the various militias that still controlled pockets of resistance in the countryside. Once this was accomplished with much bloodshed, no armed force other than the province's army and police would operate in the province of Egypt for the entire period under discussion. Muhammad ʿAli suppressed any attempt by rural leaders and peasants to revolt, and a strict policy of law and order, especially along sensitive trade routes, was maintained by all the viceroys. When extra-legal forces tried to engage in subversive action, as when Sait plotted against ʿAbbas, the matter was treated very seriously and crushed right away. Irregular forces, mostly those under Bedouin shaykhs, were either incorporated into the army as whole units or used by the government for preventing lawlessness on the margins of the towns. A "gun-control" policy was introduced during the reign of ʿAbbas, but it was never fully successful.[15]

The mainstay of Egypt's dynastic order was a dependent and loyal ruling elite, made up of the senior office-holders in the province. Since we shall deal with this elite as a social force in the next section, let us stress here that what is often conceived as "the state" essentially consisted of the power that emanated from and was represented by the governor-general's household government. The state was practically embodied in the dynasty and the Ottoman–Egyptian elite.[16] To all other parts of Egyptian society, the state was what these people did and said, and it was symbolized by how they dressed, the language they spoke (Ottoman Turkish), the carriages in which they rode, and the rest of the paraphernalia associated with their authority.

This nucleus of state apparatus gradually became what we can call a full-

<hr />

[15] For the Sait–ʿAbbas affair and the gun-control policy, see Toledano, *State and Society*, 45–46, 164–66.

[16] *Ibid.*, 77–83.

fledged state bureaucracy. During the nineteenth century, the government increasingly assumed new roles and functions in promoting economic and social development. A hierarchical structure influenced by both western and Ottoman models evolved, so that by the 1870s the "old concessionary system, in which administration was carried out by autonomous social groups," was replaced by a "centralized bureaucracy." The new administrative elite consisted of technocrats with European training and an Ottoman–Egyptian outlook, but it still offered opportunities only to elite members and those on the relatively narrow mobility-affording social boundaries, while keeping out and down the rest of society.[17]

One of the main factors that bonded the ruler and his dependent elite – hence also one of the foundations of state power – stemmed from agricultural land, the main resource of Ottoman Egypt. From the late 1820s, land grants to members of the Ottoman–Egyptian elite became one of the main devices in binding that group to the house of Muhammad 'Ali. Concomitantly, land ownership became a major source of elite power, especially from the third quarter of the nineteenth century onward. Since we shall discuss further below the controversy over private land ownership and elite formation, it is only necessary here to note that land ownership played an important role in the emergence of state power, in the rise of the rural notability as a propertied class, and ultimately in the rise of Egyptian nationalism. This process is often described in the nationalist narrative as emanating from the dynastic rule of the house of Muhammad 'Ali, whose rulers gradually extended property rights in land.[18]

The issue of the emergence of a strong state is inevitably linked to control. However, in order again to avoid presenting the state as standing outside society and somehow imposing upon it "its" will, we use the notion of actual control together with that of the invisible, implicit permeation of patterns of state authority. Generally speaking, the dynastic rule of the house of Muhammad 'Ali is associated with a marked increase in central authority, which manifested itself in the two categories of control. This came at the expense of alternative foci of power, mostly on the local level, in both the urban and the rural settings. Thus, for example, Muhammad 'Ali's "unprecedented degree of control" in the countryside is seen to have reduced "traditional village autonomy," as state officials joined village shaykhs in wielding authority, especially with regard to land redistribution.[19] Similarly, neighborhood, guild, and Sufi-order shaykhs – not to mention the 'ulama' of

---

[17] Some of the views in this paragraph are drawn from Hunter, *Egypt under the Khedives*, 230.

[18] Kenneth M. Cuno, *The Pasha's Peasants: Land, Society, and Economy in Lower Egypt, 1740–1858* (Cambridge, 1992), 206.

[19] *Ibid.*, 201.

al-Azhar – were subjected to increasing supervision and inspection by state officials.

The emergence of a strong, centralized state in nineteenth-century Egypt was greatly facilitated by the availability of European technologies and models of authority. Western transport and communication technologies were introduced into Egypt earlier, faster, and on a larger scale than in most non-European countries. The first railway line, between Alexandria and Cairo, was constructed under ʿAbbas Pasha in 1852–54, while Ismaʿil Pasha expanded the network from 500 to 1,100 miles. By 1914, there were over 1,700 miles of railway in Egypt, and the Egyptian State Railways was the largest single employer in the country, with 12,000 workers. Roads were paved by European methods, linking the provinces to the capital and to the coastal and Suez Canal ports. Boat transportation was dramatically expanded with the enlargement of the irrigation system, and in Ismaʿil's time alone 112 canals, totaling 8,400 miles, were dug.[20]

With 5,000 miles of telegraph lines and a cross-country postal service, Egypt had evolved into a fairly unified territory toward the last quarter of the nineteenth century. This served to promote the expansion of the state within Egyptian society, enhancing actual, explicit control. The other side of the coin was, however, that within that dynamic and expanding network of communication, political ideas could now move with much greater ease. The expansion of literacy – from about 1 percent at the beginning of our "long nineteenth century" to about 3 percent in the middle of the period, and to about 4–5 percent in the 1880s – and the proliferation of printing and the press, served as the main vehicles for the transmission of ideas.[21] In other words, the expansion of the state contained within itself the seeds of resistance and opposition to its growing power.

Another manifestation of the state's "explicit control" was its extensive project of registration and documentation, which was inextricably intertwined with a vast legislative program.[22] The power of the state in nineteenth-century Egypt was embedded in legal projects that made it necessary to use documents to authenticate transactions, establish qualifications, and facilitate the working of the economy. Thus, for example, the land laws that were introduced from mid-century onward required documentation for transactions in land, deployed the tools with which private land ownership would later be created, and further privileged the wealthier and stronger

---

[20] Data in this paragraph is drawn from Toledano, *State and Society*, 6–15; Juan R. I. Cole, *Colonialism and Revolution in the Middle East: Social and Cultural Origins of Egypt's ʿUrabi Movement* (Princeton, 1993), 110–12; and Joel Beinin and Zachary Lockman, *Workers on the Nile: Nationalism, Communism, Islam and the Egyptian Working Class, 1882–1954* (Princeton, 1987), 72.

[21] Cole, *Colonialism*, 111–18; Toledano, *State and Society*, 12.

[22] For a theoretical view on this, see Cohn and Dirks, "Beyond the Fringe," 227.

segments in the population (rural notables, merchants, and Europeans). It protected ownership from claims by contestants but not from the ruler.[23]

Using the enormous facilities and effective tools that the state had acquired during the period under consideration, government officials tried to maximize income by harnessing the peasantry and the urban workers to its growing and oppressive appropriation machinery. The result was a rural and urban squeeze.[24] That squeeze was manifested in coercive conscription to the army for long years of service and wars, mainly during the reign of Muhammad 'Ali, the forced appropriation of peasant labor under the corvée for public works, such as irrigation and construction projects, an increased tax burden, and exploitation of urban laborers by the government through low pay and poor working conditions.

The overwhelming power of the state made resistance to abuse and exploitation quite difficult. One of the main features of the "long nineteenth century" is a marked decline in rural and urban revolts.[25] Many of the peasant revolts in the first two-thirds of the nineteenth century occurred in Upper Egypt against excessive taxation, conscription, and the corvée. They were fought by masses of armed fallahin, not by guerrilla tactics, and were almost immediately crushed by the government. Only two such revolts, in 1880 and 1882 in Lower Egypt, achieved their goal, owing mainly to the extreme weakness of the government at the time of the 'Urabi crisis.[26]

But not all resistance was organized and collective. Not infrequently, individuals resorted to evasion, flight, and sabotage at the workplace. Others yet wrote individual or group petitions, and entered into negotiations with their employers.[27] As we shall see, during the last decade of the nineteenth century, trade union activity began to be felt in the Egyptian labor market, mainly among transportation and textile workers. Another subversive form of resistance was the gradual penetration of the bureaucracy by groups alienated from the main processes of elite formation and the rise of the state, such as the 'ulama', who had been deprived of their teaching and judicial positions as a result of legal, educational, and administrative reforms.[28]

Only in recent years, scholars have become sensitized to the working of the other form of control, the one defined above as "invisible." Here we refer mainly to the crucial power of the state to define and categorize, mainly through the imposition of legal categories, and the deployment of a

[23] Cuno, The Pasha's Peasants, 203–04.
[24] See in detail, Toledano, State and Society, 181–220.
[25] See Gabriel Baer, Fellah and Townsman in the Middle East: Studies in Social History (London, 1982), 223–323.
[26] Ibid., 308–11.
[27] Toledano, State and Society, 181–95, 213–16; Cole, Colonialism, 174–89.
[28] See, for example, Hunter, Egypt under the Khedives, 230.

system of meaning and representation dominated by sovereign and elite symbolism. By restricting the vocabulary and concepts of the person, the body, the family, and gender, and then relegating them to the private sphere,[29] the state shaped public discourse and subjected it to the interests of the ruling elite. To this we might add yet another means of "invisible control," namely the introduction of an all-encompassing system of discipline designed to harness the bodies and minds of the people and instill in them "implicit obedience." This was embodied in the *nizam-i cedit* (Arabic *al-nizam al-jadid*), or New Order along European lines, which began in the new army, but was especially evident in the new schooling system introduced in Egypt in the nineteenth century.[30]

These invisible means of control were inseparably attached to the explicit ones. Explicit, naked control would not have been possible without covert deployment of the defining and inculcating mechanisms of implicit control. Only through the latter could the state produce the cultural legitimization that enabled it to rule without constantly resorting to coercion by force of arms. Thus, in a way, the state secured its legitimization through the use of technologies that enabled both control and self-constitution, as some theorists have suggested.[31] The emergence of the strong and centralized state in nineteenth-century Egypt was made possible through effective manipulation – albeit not necessarily in a conscious way – of the two aspects of control, which fed on each other and produced social and cultural legitimacy.

Social forces and elite formation

The notion of "social forces" implies some level of group action, rudimentary organization, common purpose, and leadership. Even when group, or class, consciousness is eliminated as a necessary condition, most available analyses end up with a heavy concentration on elites. At least in the case of Egypt, almost all attempts to rectify that bias by materialist class analysis – especially with regard to the eighteenth century – have been quite unsatisfactory.[32] As we move into the "long nineteenth century," the available interpretations of Egyptian social history become considerably more inclusive, and the role of non-elite groups is given its appropriate place. This has been done by combining socio-cultural explanations with insights from political economy.

At the beginning of our period, the overwhelming majority of Egyptians existed outside politics. An Ottoman–Egyptian ruling elite, estimated at about 10,000 men and women, monopolized all political, economic, and

[29] Cohn and Dirks, "Beyond the Fringe," 227 (quoting O'Hanlon, p.c.).
[30] Timothy Mitchell, *Colonising Egypt* (Cambridge, 1988), 175.
[31] Cohn and Dirks, "Beyond the Fringe," 228.
[32] See, for example, Peter Gran, *Islamic Roots of Capitalism* (Austin, 1978).

cultural resources of the country. The rest of the population made occasional forays into political history when pushed to revolt against unusual exploitation or oppression. Even then, their group actions were short lived and not very effective. At the end of our period, an Egyptian nationalist elite – made up mainly of the remnants of the old Ottoman–Egyptian elite and a strong rural notability – and rapidly growing urban middle class and proletariat were all active in a much more expanded political, economic, and cultural arena.

With this framework in mind, we can now chart the rise of the Ottoman–Egyptian elite under dynastic order in the nineteenth century. The Ottoman–Egyptian elite continued to be essentially an office-holding elite, and its members served in the most senior positions of the governor-general's household government (and later state bureaucracy), in the governor-general's household itself, in the agencies administering the governor-general's estates, and in the top ranks of the army. The elite (known as *zevat* in Turkish, *al-dhawat* in Arabic) included wives, children, and freed slaves. Their rank (pasha, bey, effendi) marked their elite status and gave them access to positions that enabled many of them to acquire financial means, and later in the century also landed property.

They spoke Ottoman Turkish, their outlook was formed in an Ottoman administrative and military tradition, they dressed and behaved as their counterparts in Istanbul, identified with the empire, but were totally loyal to the house of Muhammad ʿAli, and committed permanently to serving and living in Egypt, unless political circumstances made this impossible. The ruling elite was predominantly, though not exclusively, Muslim, but it was ethnically quite diverse, making the once-prevailing categories of "Turco-Circassian" and "Turkish" obsolete. The Ottoman Christians in the elite were mainly Armenian, with some Copts and later Syrians, but a sizable group of European experts also served in the upper echelons of the administration from the time of Muhammad ʿAli.[33]

Under the dynastic rule of the house of Muhammad ʿAli, we can detect three generations of high bureaucrats. The first was recruited by Muhammad ʿAli himself from among his family members, associates from Kavalla, his home town, and some skilled Armenian bureaucrats. That group served in his administration and in that of his eldest son, Ibrahim. The general outlook of this group was pro-reform and pro-Europe, but it also contained a small ideological opposition, which was critical of the pace and scale of reform. The latter group centered around ʿAbbas Pasha, who came to power in 1848, after the death of Ibrahim.

Because ʿAbbas mistrusted the personally loyal and reformist elite re-

---

[33] For a detailed explanation of the makeup and character of the Ottoman–Egyptian elite, see Toledano, *State and Society*, 16–18, 68–93.

cruited by his grandfather, his ascent to power also signaled a generational change within the Ottoman–Egyptian elite. Hence, the second generation emerged after the struggle for power between 'Abbas and Ibrahim's sons in the early 1850s, reached its peak during the reign of Isma'il, and had disappeared by the early 1890s. The third generation consisted of second-generation sons, who had received a different, much more Europeanized education; it lasted well into the twentieth century and played a role in the rise of the nationalist movement and the modern nation state of Egypt.[34]

The second generation of the Ottoman–Egyptian elite began to amass large landed property, as a result of land grants by the rulers. The latter were interested in regenerating income from estates that had fallen into tax arrears, but they later used land grants as a means of bonding elite members to them. However, with the dramatic intensification of European penetration during the mid-1870s, which saw the introduction of the Dual Control system, the direct links now forged between the land-owning elite and foreign economic interests enabled the Ottoman–Egyptian elite to trade its dependence upon the ruler, Isma'il, for dependence on the European powers. It has been argued that the loss of elite support since 1875 was one of the major factors that ultimately facilitated the deposition of Isma'il by Anglo-Ottoman consent in 1879.[35]

Before we look more closely at the changes that occurred during the third quarter of the nineteenth century, let us describe the socio-cultural process that took place within Egyptian society during that period. The main groups concerned in this context were the peasantry, the rural notability, the urban commercial, intellectual, and administrative elites, and the urban workers, artisans, small traders, and the poor. Each of these subcultures had a distinct core, but their peripheries overlapped in varying degrees. Thus, for example, core members of the Ottoman–Egyptian elite spoke Turkish and were literate, shared the values and heritage of Ottoman elite culture, were mostly, though not exclusively, Muslim, and came from various ethnic origins. As the century progressed, more elite members were born and raised in Egypt. Further from that core, lower-level bureaucrats and army officers had lower income, small or no land holdings, and a more restricted access to power. But they, too, were considered Ottoman gentlemen, and their wives were classified as Ottoman ladies, with all that these notions implied in dress and etiquette. Ottoman–Egyptian elite culture was imperial, universal, and Istanbul oriented, but Cairo–Alexandria based.[36]

Despite the internal differentiation between its core and periphery, the

---

[34] The last two paragraphs are based on Hunter, *Egypt under the Khedives*, 82–83, and Toledano, *State and Society*, 41–49.

[35] This view is elaborated in Hunter, *Egypt under the Khedives*, 179–226. Cf. Cuno, *The Pasha's Peasants*, 203–04.

[36] This and the following paragraphs draw mainly on Toledano, *State and Society*, 16–18.

Ottoman–Egyptian elite was fairly homogeneous. The cores of the other elites were also fairly well defined, with rich merchants and high 'ulama' almost exclusively Arabophone and oriented toward Egypt itself. The non-elite subcultures encompassed over 95 percent of the population, and – almost by definition – were much more diffuse, and the core's common denominator was broad, though still quite meaningful and distinguishable. All core members of the non-elite subcultures spoke Arabic and, with the exception of the low 'ulama', were mostly illiterate, and their culture was immersed in the local setting, replete with themes and images of both rural and urban life in the Nile valley. Most core members of non-elite groups were born in Egypt, and were either Muslim or Copt. Within the Egyptian-Arab culture, the distinction between the various elite and non-elite groups was mainly material, though elite groups were more culturally affected by Ottoman–Egyptian elite culture as a result of frequent interaction.

The most significant and dynamic socio-cultural process in nineteenth-century Egypt occurred along the boundaries between the Ottoman–Egyptian elite and those groups most closely bordering on them. It was there that negotiation was taking place, offering a real dynamic of change and mobility. From the 1840s onward, but perhaps most dramatically in the third quarter of the century, a dual process was in motion: members of the Egyptian-Arab elites, especially the rural notability, were allowed to enter the officer ranks of the army and receive appointments in the rural, and gradually also in the central, administration. With time, they rose to be provincial governors, heads of bureaus and ministries, and army colonels, becoming full members of the Ottoman–Egyptian elite. Simultaneously, and while elite ranks were being broadened, a "dilution" of the core components occurred, with the incorporation of more elements from Egyptian-Arab culture at the expense of Ottoman ones.

This dual process – inclusivist by its very nature according to Ottoman tradition – transformed the Ottoman–Egyptian elite toward the last part of the "long nineteenth century." At the turn of the century, the ruling elite was an Egyptian one, with a strong Ottoman–Egyptian heritage nevertheless, but now fully embroiled in the production of an Egyptian nation state. Many of its core members spoke Turkish and felt a close affinity to Istanbul, but Arabic predominated even in the administration, and certainly in intellectual and economic life. The failure, in early 1881, of core Ottoman–Egyptian officers to stage a coup against the rising power of the 'Urabists removed the last obstacle on the way to equality in both the army and the bureaucracy between the native Egyptian notable sons and core Ottoman–Egyptians.[37] Interaction between the political elite and the commercial and intellectual ones, with full social mingling and exchange, became easier and

[37] On this, see Cole, *Colonialism*, 276.

quite common; it finally produced the monarchical elite of the interwar period.

The leading figures in the old Ottoman–Egyptian elite gradually disappeared: Sultan Pasha died in 1884, and Sharif Pasha in 1887; ʿAli Pasha Mubarak retired in 1891, and Nubar Pasha left the government in 1894. In the administration, the British promoted and further recruited members of minorities, such as Syrians and Copts, and English advisors from British universities.[38] But, at the same time, non-elite groups were gradually using the new educational system deployed by Ismaʿil to gain access to resources and junior positions in the army and administration. Early in the twentieth century, this would be the basis for an emerging *effendiyya* middle class.

In retrospect, there can hardly be any doubt that the 1860s and 1870s qualitatively transformed Egyptian society in a way that launched it into the twentieth century and the age of colonialism and nationalism. Historical explanations of the processes that took place during that period have led most scholars to tie them to the events of 1881–82, the ʿUrabi movement, and the British occupation. Broadly speaking, most writers on the topic have concentrated on the last phase of Ismaʿil's rule – the second half of the 1870s – as precursor to the events leading to the British occupation in 1882.[39] Their explanations are largely socio-economic, grounded in both class analysis and dependency theories. A recent contribution to that debate has taken a long-term approach, seeking the roots of the ʿUrabi movement in the processes that had taken place not merely in the preceding half decade, but rather in the preceding quarter of a century.[40]

In that approach, economic, social, and cultural processes during the period 1858–82 created within Egyptian society "challenger strata" that were ripening toward a revolution. The weakening of the state security apparatus, perceived interests, a fairly high degree of social organization, means of communication, and a uniting discourse were the conditions those strata needed in order to act. When they did, in the early 1880s, they tried to change the existing distribution of power within society. European penetration, as already mentioned, created the conditions that enabled a community of discourse to emerge through which political ideas, revolutionary in this case, were carried. Population growth and an ensuing pressure on land, and an acceleration in Egypt's incorporation into the world economy, provided a fertile background to the development of opposition to khedival rule, even among members of the Ottoman–Egyptian elite.

[38] Hunter, *Egypt under the Khedives*, 229.
[39] See, for example: Alexander Schölch, "The Formation of a Peripheral State: Egypt 1854–1882," *L'Egypte au XIXᵉ Siècle*, 176–85; Abd El-Azim Ramadan, "Social Significance of the ʿUrabi Revolution," *ibid.*, 187–94; and Hunter, *Egypt under the Khedives*, 227–30.
[40] Cole, *Colonialism*, esp. 273–82.

These factors affected the various groups in the following manner, as some reacted against the Ottoman–Egyptians and others against the Europeans: the middle management in the bureaucracy was anti-European more for fear of losing jobs to European experts and Syrian Christians than for begrudging the Ottoman–Egyptians their hold on the highest state offices; junior army officers from a smallholding background resented the privileges of the Ottoman–Egyptians more than they did those of the Europeans; merchants and merchant guilds appear mainly to have directed their energies against their European competitors, and were anti-Ottoman–Egyptian not because of land-tax privileges, but because of the alliance between Ottoman–Egyptians and European merchants, financiers, importers, and speculators; artisans were more anti-European, because they resented low-priced foreign goods and an influx of European traders and workers more than Ottoman–Egyptian-imposed taxation; and in some instances, rural notables opposed the large Ottoman–Egyptian land owners, but village opposition to European land owners was no less intense.[41]

One view of the confrontation is that the Ottoman–Egyptians caved in before the challenge, while the Europeans reacted rather strongly, which ultimately resulted in the British occupation of 1882. The European community wanted the British to occupy Egypt not merely to restore order, but mainly to prevent the process of state formation that was in the making – embodied, as it was, in the ʿUrabist government in Cairo. This process was accompanied by the emergence of a new political discourse, centering around the nation, which excluded Europeans.[42]

An alternative view sees the same events as generated by a somewhat different socio-economic engine. Egyptian elites consisted of a ruling class,[43] the autochthonous section of the agrarian bourgeoisie, and the commercial and financial bourgeoisie. There was a "common economic basis of interest" among the commercial, financial, and the whole (indigenous and "foreign") agrarian bourgeoisies. However, one of the essential factors in the events of 1881–82 was the significant difference within the agrarian bourgeoisie, as the non-autochthonous circles were much more involved in "central power functions" than autochthonous circles.

This view posits all these elites as collaborators with the European powers, as "facilitators of dependency," and "guarantors of integration into the world market." Thus the collapse of the political order in the late 1870s occurred as a result of European "direct financial, economic, and political

---

[41] *Ibid.*, 273–74.

[42] *Ibid.*, 281–82.

[43] This includes Turco-Circassians, members of some minorities, especially Armenians, Europeans in the ruler's service, indigenous experts and technicians, and a few provincial notables serving as provincial governors (Schölch, "Formation," 180–81). The rest of this paragraph draws on pp. 182–83.

interference," not because of "a quasi-mechanical breakdown," which made interest-free direct control somehow necessary. Direct European control (first the Dual Control, then the Nubar government) deprived the ruling elite of its power bases, and deposed the ruler himself. This internal power vacuum made it possible for an anti-interventionist coalition to move in and later resist attempts by a new pro-European coalition to replace the old ruling elite of Isma'il. The coalition, hoisting "the banners of self-determination and patriotism," held together from the autumn of 1881 until May 1882. It disintegrated because class interests reemerged from "behind these banners," owing to the threat of British military intervention.[44]

This anti-interventionist coalition – or "challenger strata" – consisted of three groups: the 'Urabist officers (embodying "autochthonous Egypt") and the indigenous intellectuals (who supported social reforms to improve the lot of the peasants, but never talked of "social or political revolution"); members of the former chamber of delegates (who represented the indigenous agrarian bourgeoisie and the Egyptian merchants, opposed European domination, and demanded constitutional rights and power sharing); and intellectuals of various persuasions, including Muslim reformers and fundamentalists, Syrian Christian journalists, and "indigenous technicians" (who propagated various ideas, some of them clearly conflicting, such as constitutionalism, parliamentarism, nationalism, and Islamic social and political reform of all kinds). This coalition formed the political elite of Egypt for five months (January–May 1882).

When it became clear that the Europeans would defend their interests by force, the coalition disintegrated, with only the officers and the Muslim reformers and fundamentalists remaining in open opposition to the British and the collaborating elite. That elite consisted of the former ruling class and indigenous land owners, i.e. the agrarian bourgeoisie, the commercial and financial bourgeoisies, and the indigenous technicians. The non-autochthonous and indigenous components of the agrarian bourgeoisie were no longer in real conflict among themselves, due to the discrimination practiced by the British occupation. After the First World War, these elements would merge and form the politically dominant class of modern Egypt.

Yet a third understanding of the same events and processes begins where xenophobia, patriotism, and nationalism mix together in a bewildering cocktail. In this view the events of the early 1880s are a "wider-dimensioned class revolution," rather than a mere military revolt. The 'Urabi revolution was the result of cooperation between two groups: the leaders of the agricultural bourgeoisie (demanding economic, constitutional, and national liberation) and the military group around 'Urabi (a petty bourgeois movement). Thus during the late 1870s, a national liberation movement emerged

---

[44] This and the following two paragraphs refer to *ibid.*, 177, 182–85.

that dominated Egyptian history until 1952, through its struggle against the monarchy and European presence. The 'Urabi revolution failed because the Egyptian bourgeoisie was not willing to trade the khedive's despotism for that of the army.[45]

It thus appears that there are two lines of demarcation along which the socio-economic and political conflict evolved: one split the Ottoman–Egyptian elite internally between its Ottoman–Egyptian component and its incorporated Egyptian one; the other separated Egyptians and Europeans. A cross-section of these lines occurred in 1881–82, which made it possible for anti-European Egyptians to drive a wedge within the Ottoman–Egyptian elite, and enlist its indigenous component in the service of an anti-European, patriotic cause. The most obvious weakness of this analysis is the fact that alliances and disintegrations seem to have occurred overnight, rather than to stem from longer, sustained, and more profound social processes.

In addition, the inclusivist processes that occurred within the Ottoman–Egyptian elite in the second and third quarters of the nineteenth century should not have made it so easy for an autochthonous agrarian elite to fall out with the rest of the Ottoman–Egyptian elite. That this was not a result of failed integration can be seen from the fact that the indigenous notability was quick to join the Ottoman–Egyptian elite in the face of an external threat to its socio-economic position.

In any event, what is needed to complete this rather complex socio-political picture is a reminder that the second Ottoman period is characterized by hegemonic rule, only temporarily interrupted during the last phase of Qazdagli ascendancy late in the eighteenth century and during the first decade of the nineteenth century (until 1811). What surely happened in the period 1876–82 was again the temporary loss of hegemonic (and by then also dynastic) rule, as no group or coalition could hold together for long, or take into its hands the reins of power.[46] In 1881–82, central authority broke down, dynastic order was challenged, and the loyal elite temporarily disintegrated. When it was restored, it was only at the mercy of the British, who had made it captive of their own imperial ambitions.

Egypt and the world economy

The main economic process that took place during the "long nineteenth century" was the incorporation of Egypt into the European-dominated world economy. This process was closely intertwined with social processes and had far-reaching consequences for the whole of Egyptian society. It is by now beyond dispute that Egypt's peripheralization had profound social,

[45] Ramadan, "Social Significance," 187–88, 194.
[46] For a similar view, see Hunter, *Egypt under the Khedives*, 227–30.

political, and cultural implications that have lasted well into the twentieth century, shaping much of the history of the modern state.

The process of Egypt's integration into the world economy was gradual and long, but its intensity varied during the period reviewed here.[47] Having recovered from its eighteenth-century crisis, Egypt formed new links with European traders, and began to produce agricultural goods for European markets. However, meaningful trade relations flourished only in the first half of the nineteenth century. The process was dramatically accelerated in the second half of the century, creating full dependence during the last quarter, especially under British rule. In that sense, the "rupture," or break with the previous pattern, clearly occurred in the third quarter, leaving the previous period very much on the other side of the continuum.

A first landmark in the intensification of economic relations with Europe was the reluctant application, in the mid-1840s, by a weakened Muhammad 'Ali, of the 1838 Anglo-Ottoman commercial treaty of Balta Liman. The second stage occurred from the late 1850s onward, in which European penetration included investments in infrastructure, especially in the Suez Canal, in the public (viceregal) debt, in the financing of foreign trade (export of cotton and import of machinery and luxury goods), and in direct investment by land companies in agriculture. The period 1740–1858 has been viewed as one unit, which ended with the 1858 land law – the embodiment of state regulatory power.[48] The reorganization and reorientation of agriculture took place under a strong state, which provided security and regulated land tenure procedures. It was also accompanied by an elaborate legal project that regulated and undergirded the commoditization of land and the restructuring of the entire agricultural economy.

Changes in agriculture and the emergence of a strong state were closely related to the rise of private land ownership in nineteenth-century Egypt. One view is that a major transformation occurred in agricultural production and land ownership in Egypt from the eighteenth century to the nineteenth.[49] Agriculture in late eighteenth-century Egypt produced essentially for subsistence, was neither commoditized nor monetized, and involved no

---

[47] Economic processes are among the best-researched aspects of nineteenth-century Egyptian history, owing largely to the work of Charles Issawi, Roger Owen, and others. The following survey and analysis are based mainly on Issawi, *The Economic History of the Middle East 1800–1914* (Chicago, 1966), and his many articles on the Egyptian economy; E. R. J. Owen, *The Middle East in the World Economy 1800–1914* (London and New York, 1981); E. R. J. Owen, *Cotton and the Egyptian Economy, 1820–1914: A Study in Trade and Development* (Oxford, 1969); Schölch, "Formation," 178ff.; and Cuno, *The Pasha's Peasants*, 198–207.

[48] Cuno, *The Pasha's Peasants*, 207.

[49] See, for example, Gabriel Baer, *Studies in the Social History of Modern Egypt* (Chicago and London, 1969), 62–78, and Issawi, *Economic History*, 359–74. This line was formulated earlier by Silvestre de Sacy and Yacoub Artin.

ownership rights in usufruct. The land laws of 1847, 1855, and 1858, in this view, introduced a major change by laying the ground for private land ownership. Finally, the "brutal but successful" introduction of cotton by Muhammad 'Ali (to reach 75 percent of the total value of exports in 1880–84, 92 percent in 1910–13),[50] and other cash crops, firmly linked Egypt to the European-dominated world economy.

An alternative interpretation argues that there was no change in land ownership in Egypt between the eighteenth century and the middle of the nineteenth, because the peasants' right to inherit and alienate usufruct rights existed well before 1800. The land laws of 1847, 1855, and 1858 did not create a new situation, but only codified existing practice. The market responsiveness of nineteenth-century peasants was the same as it had been in the eighteenth century; it did not constitute a "recent transition from subsistence to cash-crop farming, but rather the persistence of a pattern of mixed subsistence- and market-oriented production, a familiarity with money exchange, and as before a willingness or else a need to borrow in order to make it from one harvest to the next." Thus, realities in the period 1740–1858 were more complex, consisting of "a substantial development of agricultural production and exports, and proportionately an even greater growth in the European share of Egypt's external trade."[51]

What is not in much dispute is that the agricultural policies of Muhammad 'Ali helped create a landed rural notability, as he reassigned deserted land and land over which taxes fell into considerable arrears – causing the ranks of the landless peasantry to swell further. Many others who managed to cling to their smallholdings were driven into debt and arrears by tax increases, which the governor-general imposed to resolve his revenue-generating problems. There is also agreement among scholars that formal, documented, full-fledged private land ownership was created in the early 1870s, as a result of the *muqabala* (Ottoman *mukabele*) law, introduced by Isma'il to bring much-needed cash into his bankrupt treasury. The khedive granted full ownership in return for advance payment of six years of land taxes, to be cut in half later.

This process was enhanced under the British, so that by 1907, 75 percent of the land was owned by 147,000 large and medium holders, while the remaining 25 percent was held in small, often fragmented, plots by 1,120,000 land owners. At the same time, 21 percent of rural Egyptian families were landless, 70 percent of them held some property, but less than the five faddans required for subsistence, while only 9 percent owned more than five faddans, including here very large, medium, and small holders. Among the landowning class, there was a growing number of European companies.[52]

[50] Owen, *The Middle East*, 68, 219.
[51] Cuno, *The Pasha's Peasants*, 198–201.
[52] Owen, *The Middle East*, 218.

The other type of economic activity that deserves mention is the attempts to introduce industry into Egypt. Muhammad 'Ali's industrial experiment has received a great deal of attention that has often been blown out of proportion. Here we can only mention that in the 1830s, there were thirty state-owned and operated cotton spinning and weaving factories, and a number of wool, silk, and linen factories throughout Egypt, several plants producing military equipment (guns, cannons, swords, munitions, gun-powder, and saltpeter), and a few factories engaged in the processing of agricultural products (sugar refineries, indigo works, rice mills, and tanneries). These aimed mainly at import substitution, and to an extent managed at least partially to achieve that goal. Owing to a shrinking military market following the loss of Muhammad 'Ali's regional empire, and due to technical problems with production-equipment maintenance, many of these were falling into disrepair by the last phase of the Pasha's reign (1840–48).[53]

Although Isma'il tried in the early 1870s to reintroduce state industries, the project was not very successful. Save for a number of arms-producing plants, and his own network of sugar refineries, there were several privately owned industrial enterprises that processed cotton and other agricultural products or produced household equipment and food for the European communities. An important point to note, however, in this context, is that despite the abundance of European goods available in Egypt from the third quarter of the nineteenth century onward, and contrary to dependency-model expectations, local manufacturing was not destroyed, but rather adapted to the new realities and managed to survive, produce, and play an important role in the Egyptian economy.[54]

The last phase of the "long nineteenth century" did not witness a major change in industrial deployment in Egypt, leaving the "rupture" in this process to the post-war period. Not surprisingly, the British colonial regime was mainly concerned with developing the agricultural sector of the Egyptian economy. Industrial development was slow and unimpressive, with only twenty-three companies active in the field in 1901, twenty of which were established in the 1890s. The number of industrial companies increased only to thirty-seven by 1911. The British administration intervened in few cases, mainly cotton factories and sugar plants, to prevent collapse of the companies, because they wished not to be seen by nationalist circles as allowing a large-scale loss of jobs to occur without stepping in to help. At the same time, the British acted to prevent the development of a local textile industry that would compete with manufacturers in Britain itself.[55]

[53] *Ibid.*, 69–73.
[54] *Ibid.*, 148–52.
[55] *Ibid.*, 19–26.

In any event, in 1909 Britain was importing 50 percent of all Egyptian exports and supplying 30 percent of all Egyptian imports.[56] A large and growing foreign community was sustaining and further promoting this state of economic and political dependence. As already mentioned, the number of Europeans increased dramatically in the second half of the nineteenth century. Owing to the need for their technical skills and their desire to profit economically, Europeans flocked to Egypt, and their number increased from 6,000 in 1840 to about 68,000 in 1870, to 90,000 in 1882, and to 111,000 in 1897. Railway construction, digging of the Suez Canal, the cotton boom, and the large projects initiated by Isma'il were the main attractions that lured Europeans to Egypt in those years. The size of the British community tripled as a result of the occupation. Some 90 percent of the Europeans lived in the cities (where they comprised about 10 percent of the population).[57]

Earlier models of modernization and westernization depicted the process as a positive one, in which a rather backward and stagnant Ottoman province was liberated from its shackles to join the civilized, modern world. Later models of dependency have looked at the same phenomenon differently, describing a rather negative process of aggressive, self-interested peripheralization that relegated a wealthy and fairly independent country to a pitiful state of dependence on and exploitation by the European powers.

The force of one such analysis is, *inter alia*, that it does not seek to allocate blame for what happened, but rather to understand the very complex processes that occurred. What took place in Egypt during the nineteenth century does not conform to a simplistic model of dependency, but has to be studied carefully in its historical setting.[58] In general, this view stresses the activities and input of local actors in the economy, without denying the role of external, European forces. Thus, the picture that emerges is much more balanced than the one of classical dependency theorists, depicting a European actor pillaging a passive, helpless Egyptian victim. Egypt's incorporation into the world economy is characterized by six elements, which also apply – *mutatis mutandis* – to the incorporation of other Middle Eastern regions. These are:

1. The value of exports clearly increased more rapidly than population, suggesting that Egyptian income grew during the period discussed here. The impact of this growth was only marginally affected by the payment of interest on European loans or by an unfavorable balance of trade.

---

[56] Robert L. Tignor, *State, Private Enterprise, and Economic Change in Egypt, 1918–1952* (Princeton, 1984), appendix, table A.11.

[57] Panzac, "Population of Egypt," 26–29.

[58] Owen, *The Middle East*, 287–93.

However, this does not mean that the rise in income was evenly distributed through society, since benefits accrued only to a small number of elite families who owned large tracts of cultivated land.

2. Much of the agricultural surplus was appropriated via taxation and rent, and only little of it was reinvested in agricultural improvement or capital works. Most of the appropriated surplus was simply spent on consumption and a European-style standard of living for the Ottoman–Egyptian and other elites, but also on exerting influence over local politics in cooperation with the European powers, and later the colonial state. It was mainly the government and foreign enterprises that invested in agriculture.

3. The dramatically increased seaborne trade with Europe induced significant changes in the structure of commerce, particularly in the ports, especially Alexandria and Port Said. Credit arrangements, improved means of transportation and irrigation, intensification of monetary relations among producers, landowners, and traders, increased agricultural specialization, and the consequent emergence of foreign commercial communities are the main features of the process. Muslim merchants also played an important role, and a purely ethnic or religious division of labor did not exist.

4. The impact of European forces on the Egyptian economy can be seen as occurring in three stages: a purely commercial phase during the early decades of the nineteenth century, in which trade expanded and political influence was used to facilitate that expansion; the financial–commercial phase from the 1840s on, in which the government of Egypt could no longer finance its reform project by taxation, while European capital was becoming available for foreign investment and earnestly seeking opportunities abroad (this increased the dependence of the Egyptian government on the European lenders, made it easier for European companies to demand further concessions, and expanded trade with Europe even more); and finally, from the last quarter of the nineteenth century, the political–financial–commercial phase, in which direct involvement in the Egyptian economy created full dependence, as export prices, availability of credit, and the distribution of public revenues were determined by European forces.

5. The khedival government played an important role in the economic processes that were taking place. Efforts at reform, centralization, and building military capabilities stemmed from fear of European penetration, but ultimately exposed the regime to further European pressures, because those attempts to modernize required European expertise and reliance on European finance.

6. Growing economic dependence was perceived as government weakness, giving rise to nationalist sentiments during the first decade of the twentieth century. In Egypt, these feelings were increasingly expressed by Egyptian entrepreneurs and professionals, pointing at the combined political and economic weakness of the country vis-à-vis the British colonial state and the European powers, who formed the "structure of dependence." A program of creating a national economic policy was forged, only to be frustrated after the First World War by the British.

Individual and society

We have so far dealt with groups – their formation, evolution, action, disintegration – rather than with individuals. We now turn to the effects the processes described above had on individuals of all strata of Egyptian society. The major project of social and economic history, undertaken from the 1950s on, diverted attention from elites to "the masses," but the subjects of most studies remained nameless and rather faceless. Problems of suitable sources, and preferences for certain methodological approaches, have produced studies of large formations, structures, institutions, and classes, with little attention to how individuals fit into these frameworks, and what those frameworks did to their lives.

The advent of social anthropology and its fruitful interaction with history have in recent years produced studies of microhistory that seek to examine social, economic, political, and cultural processes from the individual's point of view.[59] This project has not yet been fully developed, but many scholars working on Muslim societies have committed themselves to it, and their joint efforts are expected to appear in the coming decade.[60] This means that the following survey is not a definitive statement, but rather an analysis based on recent work and work still in progress.

Individuals join groups, or are initiated into them, by processes of socialization and acculturation. The family, the household, the education system, and various other communal organs provided individuals in nineteenth-century Egypt with the code that enabled them to belong to various groups throughout life. They would then participate in the processes that initiated the next generation into the same patterns, thereby reproducing the

---

[59] In Middle Eastern history, the best example is Edmund Burke, III (ed.), *Struggle and Survival in the Modern Middle East* (Berkeley and Los Angeles, 1993).

[60] For the main effort currently in progress, see Robert Ilbert and Paul Dumont, "Individual and Society in the Mediterranean Muslim World," submitted to the *European Science Foundation (ESF)* as framework for a five-year research program. The *ESF* Programme involves some one hundred scholars, and is expected to run until 1999. There are also various international projects dealing with civil society in the modern Middle East.

social order that prevailed in their time, and incorporating the changes that occurred in society during their lifetime. Social reproduction obviously involved the perpetuation of privileges enjoyed by certain groups in Egyptian society, and the exploitation that was the lot of the disprivileged groups.

The family is certainly one of the most important agents of socialization and social reproduction. It is both noteworthy and indicative that the family, the roles of individual family members, and role relations among them changed very little during the "long nineteenth century." The central position of the father, the dependent position of women, gender segregation, the extended family's standing as both the unit of dwelling and property owning (whose property, labor, and income were controlled by the father), the role of age in determining status, and the practice of arranged marriages (with preference to clan endogamy and cousin marriage) all continued to predominate at the beginning of the twentieth century in both rural and urban Egypt.[61]

This may create the impression that the social and economic processes discussed above were rather superficial if they failed to affect the basic socioeconomic unit of Egyptian society. However, this was certainly not the case, as the study of non-elite women clearly shows.[62] This demonstrates how the rise of the state and Egypt's incorporation into the world economy impacted on the family and the status of women. These economic processes changed the power relations within the family, usually to the disadvantage of women. In the family, the women's position vis-à-vis that of the men was determined by their ability to generate income and hold property; these, in turn, were affected by changes in the Egyptian economy.

Thus the demand put on rural families by the state, and the commercialization of agriculture, weakened prevailing cooperative arrangements within which women could negotiate a better deal from a position of greater strength. In the urban setting, Muhammad 'Ali's attempt to industrialize, and the difficulties experienced by local crafts because of European competition, impaired women's ability to earn a living, thereby weakening their position within the family. Consequently, village women saw their property rights eroded, and townswomen were pushed from production to services; this only reinforced women's traditional reproductive and caring roles. In the tougher economic realities of late nineteenth-century Egypt under the colonial state, women were assigned the weaker and less attractive share of the labor market, and were further barred from education and career opportunities.

According to this line of reasoning, market forces, rather than the state or

---

[61] Baer, *Studies*, 210–12.
[62] Judith Tucker, *Women in Nineteenth-century Egypt* (Cambridge, 1985), chaps. 1–4, summarized in the conclusion. For a critique of some of Tucker's views, see my review in *Middle Eastern Studies*, 25/1 (January 1989), 113–19.

the value system, determined the status of women in nineteenth-century Egypt. While this might be more true for the second half of the century, the actions of the Ottoman–Egyptian state had played an important role in the first half. Conscription and the corvée gave women a greater role in managing family resources while men were away, and higher taxation forced women to take on an additional workload in the fields. One should also look at how the belief system – in which Islamic and local traditions intermingled – accommodated new economic realities brought about by Egypt's incorporation into the European-dominated world economy.

The impact of social and economic processes on the individual is perhaps most noticeable in the realm of state-initiated reforms. Until recently, both Egyptian and western narratives hailed the reforms of Muhammad ʿAli and Ismaʿil almost as manna from heaven. A more critical approach has now entered the literature, which brings up the other side of the balance sheet, namely the enormous cost in human lives, dislocation, and suffering.[63] The rural and urban squeeze ravaged the lives of many Egyptians in the huge mass of non-elite groups. At that level, individuals seem to have stood almost alone vis-à-vis the ruthless determination of rulers and their loyal officials, as the communal organs deployed to protect them caved in, collapsed, and miserably failed them.

A major component of elite formation under the house of Muhammad ʿAli was the deployment of a school system that trained future officers and bureaucrats for government service. The system was built from the top down, beginning with professional schools for army officers, engineers, doctors, veterinarians, and translators, and only during the reign of Ismaʿil were reforms introduced that addressed the primary and secondary systems. But even then, there were elite "primary" schools and old-style "elementary" ones, i.e. *kuttabs*. The latter led either to the old Azharite curriculum, a few mediocre trade schools, or back to the village, where students would revert to illiteracy and hard work in the cotton fields.[64]

Although there was no intention to open up the Ottoman–Egyptian elite for the entire population, from the moment the schools were established pressure mounted to allow access to members of the groups closest to the boundaries of the ruling elite, mainly the rural notability. The precedent was, of course, inclusion of such young men in student missions sent by

---

[63] This view is reflected in the following evaluations of the reforms of Muhammad ʿAli: Khaled M. Fahmy, "All the Pasa's Men: The Performance of the Egyptian Army during the Reign of Mehmed Ali Pasha," D.Phil. thesis, University of Oxford, 1993, 350–51; Ehud R. Toledano, "Muhammad ʿAli Basha or Mehmet Ali Pasa?" *Middle Eastern Studies*, 21/4 (1985), 141–59; Encyclopedia of Islam, 2nd ed., s.v. "Muhammad ʿAli Pasha," by Ehud R. Toledano. For a similar approach to Ismaʿil's policies, see Cole, *Colonialism*, 85.

[64] Donald Malcolm Reid, *Cairo University and the Making of Modern Egypt* (Cambridge, 1990), 14–15.

Muhammad ʿAli to study in Europe. Once those channels of mobility were in place, the only questions remaining were when they would be used first by non-Ottoman–Egyptians, and how wide the channel would be. It was during the formative and dynamic 1860s and 1870s that access became routinized, and by the 1880s employment prospects were far better for state-school graduates. Certification, in general, tended to restrict access to employment and increased the importance of accreditation by the new schools.[65]

In other words, in education, as in public health, a spill-over occurred to benefit broader segments of the population, mostly affecting other elites and those closest to the Ottoman–Egyptian one. But if in 1882 it seemed, for a moment, that access to the ruling elite would become easier for certain other elite groups, the colonial state acted quickly to close some avenues. Cromer's policy discouraged development of a solid education system in Egypt, and before he left there were only three state secondary schools, graduating in 1902 fewer than a hundred students altogether. Cromer never rescinded his avowed opposition to the establishment of an Egyptian university, which had to wait for his successors. Some twenty years into the occupation, education received less than 1 percent of the Egyptian state budget, rising to 3.4 percent before the First World War. A change would occur only when Egyptians assumed control of the ministry in 1922.[66]

In any event, at the close of our "long nineteenth century," education was becoming a major asset in Egyptian society, a much-coveted commodity for socially mobile groups. On December 21, 1908 the Egyptian University was opened in Cairo, with the future king, Ahmad Fuʾad, serving as its first rector. But despite the inroads that education made in Egyptian society, the rate of illiteracy in Egypt stood at 93 percent.[67]

The main "losers" from the spread of state-sponsored modern education, it seems, were the ʿulamaʾ. Reforms in education and the legal system restricted the access of religiously trained men to jobs they had previously virtually monopolized. Lawyers, judges, codes, documents, and scribes replaced the old Shariʿa system, and the introduction to the new schools of teachers who were not ʿulamaʾ threatened the previous order.[68] Gradually, as the century wore on, ʿulamaʾ were confined to the old-style school system, which was less attractive to ambitious young men. At the same time, ever-growing areas of law and social activity were being removed from the

[65] A. Chris Eccel, *Egypt, Islam and Social Change: Al-Azhar in Conflict and Accommodation* (Berlin, 1984), 114. It was in the 1880s that a friend told Ahmad Lutfi al-Sayyid's family, when he was ten, that state professional schools should be preferred to an al-Azhar education, which the family intended him to have (Reid, *Cairo University*, 15). For ʿAli Mubarak's decision to become a bureaucrat rather than a Sharʿi jurist, see Baer, *Studies*, 24.

[66] Reid, *Cairo University*, 18.

[67] *Ibid.*, 20, 31.

[68] Eccel, *Social Change*, 114.

jurisdiction of the Shariʿa court system, which reduced the number of judiciary positions available to ʿulamaʾ.

If the public space of ʿulamaʾ activity and influence was gradually restricted, there were other groups whose ability to act was enhanced by the social and economic processes described in this chapter. Such groups also afforded individuals greater freedom of action, gradually empowering them within the groups to which they belonged, and vis-à-vis the state. Without getting into the question of state versus civil society, we can still observe that the emergence of the individual as peasant, worker, student, bureaucrat, merchant, artisan, reader, consumer, performer, and the like gave rise to new solidarities, replacing those that had dissolved as a result of these processes.

Migration from villages to towns, but mainly to the large cities of Cairo and Alexandria, and also to the Canal towns, affected the absorbing communities no less than it did individual migrants and their families. Residential neighborhoods and guilds, for example, had traditionally favored "the known faces" in their milieu, while treating with great suspicion the unfamiliar outsider (the *gharib*).[69] As long as rural migration was fairly limited, there was no change in that urban attitude toward migrants. But in Alexandria and Cairo from the middle of the century, and elsewhere from the late 1870s onward, as each year brought in thousands of migrants needing food, shelter, and employment, greater openness and flexibility became the norm. Hence, most rural migrants were absorbed into urban society rather smoothly, via existing neighborhood, guild, and other networks.

Until the middle of the "long nineteenth century," such networks formed part of the state's urban control mechanism, intended to keep individuals at bay and manage their labor, income, and dwelling-space. However, even then, and especially with regard to guilds, headmen were also attentive to the needs of the membership, and their loyalty was often divided between the state and their guild members. The general trend in the second half of the period was toward an increase in the commitment between guild headmen and members, with guilds emerging less as tools in the service of the state, more as supporters of members' interests. Conflict over the right of members to choose their guild leadership also indicates a rise in individual input and a movement to greater representation.[70]

However, actual union activity had to wait for the end of the nineteenth century and the first decades of the twentieth. A proper Egyptian "working class" was formed only at the turn of the century, with the consolidation of a new group of urban wage workers, who were employed in relatively large,

---

[69] On this, see Toledano, *State and Society*, 196–205.
[70] On this, see Cole, *Colonialism*, 164–89.

modern industrial and transport enterprises, owned no means of production, and earned their livelihood solely from the sale of their labor. These were not the only people who belonged to the working class, but they were relatively more self-aware and better organized for action.[71]

The actual emergence of labor activism occurred between 1899 and 1914. Although there had been strikes as early as 1882, organized union action did not take place before that period. As wages lagged behind prices, causing a decline in standard of living, workers felt a need to organize and seek some protection in united action and mutual aid. Those years saw the "first sustained, large-scale collective action" by industry and transport workers, including major crises, such as the strike and clashes at the 'Anabir railway in Cairo in 1910. However, the "real birth" of the labor movement in Egypt coincided with the nationalist uprising of 1919.[72]

Cooperation between the unions and nationalist groups predated the events of 1919, and joint activity with the National Party served both sides, as it combined a political nationalist campaign with a social one. The nationalist lawyers acted as spokesmen for the workers and helped them to improve their negotiations with employers, but at the end of the day the two agendas only partially overlapped: the nationalists sought an independent Egypt ruled by its elite, though cracks in the alliance appeared only after the First World War. At the time, union membership was still small, about 4,600 in Cairo in 1911. Soon after 1910, it dwindled and lost much of its force, owing to the repressive measures against both the nationalist and the labor movements taken by the government. In late 1914, a general clampdown on nationalist activities brought the whole movement to a halt.[73]

As we have seen thus far, dissent began to manifest itself in the 1870s–1880s in guild and later union activity, as well as among the intelligentsia and the Ottoman–Egyptian elite. The ranks of the educated and socio-culturally aware and active people – officers, bureaucrats, teachers, and educated merchants – grew considerably during that period, and newspapers and journals began to appear and attracted large audiences. At the same time, social clubs and cultural societies proliferated, the best known being the Free Masons, Young Egypt, the Young Officers, the Islamic Philanthropic Society, the Helwan Society, and the various cultural salons of Ya'qub Sanu'.[74]

---

[71] Beinin and Lockman, *Workers on the Nile*, 5–7. The authors define another group as the "urban petty bourgeoisie," which differed from the "working class" in their possession of "some means of production, capital, or education." There was, however, a "low level of social differentiation between the lowest of the urban middle strata and the working class."

[72] *Ibid.*, 48–49, 72–76, 80, 82.

[73] *Ibid.*, 76–80.

[74] For details, see Cole, *Colonialism*, 118–26, 133–63.

These were funded mostly by the members themselves, in order to avoid the political strings that came with large donations from wealthy patrons. Much of their activity was in opposition to the ruler, who usually had no great difficulty in suppressing it. But the very process served as important experience in political activity and alliance forming. Another experiment in the working of consultative politics took place in the chamber of delegates, established by Isma'il in 1866. One view is that the chamber was not a focus of opposition to Isma'il and his ruinous financial policies, since the indigenous part of the agrarian bourgeoisie, too, collaborated with the ruling class and the khedive, whose policies enabled them to increase their privileges and wealth. Thus the chamber was actually a dependent, consultative body, and – contrary to the nationalist narrative – never really demanded more constitutional rights, nor did it oppose the policy of Europeanization.[75]

While this is probably true, things had changed during the crisis of 1879–80, following the deposition of Isma'il. The chamber had actually turned into one of the most relevant arenas for the political confrontation between the various contending forces. None of the attempts to achieve control during that chaotic period was more significant than "the stunning but short-lived triumph" of the Ottoman–Egyptians in the chamber, who carried out an interesting experiment in constitutionalism, backed by the majority of the Egyptian people.[76]

Another group that gradually emerged toward the latter part of our period as benefiting from and contributing to the process of individual advancement was urban elite women. Education and socialization for elite women was restricted to the harems, where women were taught to read and supervise home activities. It was there, too, that they socialized and became aware of the developments in the male world outside. During the middle years of the century, state primary-school education became available to girls in restricted numbers, and by the late 1870s these schools had some 400 female students. During the last decade of the nineteenth century, and more intensely during the early twentieth century, women became active in publishing periodicals and books and forming societies and clubs of their own. Women's position in Egyptian society and other political and social issues of the day were discussed, and demands for reform voiced. But like the trade union movement, the women's movement came of age only with the intensification of the nationalist struggle after the First World War.[77]

---

[75] Schölch, "Formation," 182.

[76] Hunter, *Egypt under the Khedives*, 227–30.

[77] For a recent study on the women's press and readership, see Beth Baron, "Readers and the Women's Press in Egypt," in Israel Gershoni and Ehud R. Toledano (eds.), *Cultural Processes in Muslim and Arab Societies*, special issue of *Poetics Today*: 15/2 (Summer 1994), 217–40. There was a midwifery school, established by Muhammad 'Ali and Dr.

Under the British-dominated colonial state, dissent became open opposition, though about a decade had to elapse before it was channeled into political parties. For the elites, such dissent and opposition were expressed mainly in the various clubs and societies, the rapidly growing newspapers and journals, the newly printed books, the chamber of delegates, and the parties; the other strata had the guilds, the budding trade union movement, and the nationalist parties. These prospered owing to individual drive and a sense that individual action could be effective. In this, they differed from earlier formations, which essentially submerged individuals and disempowered them.

Some segments of the population did not benefit from these processes. These fall into two categories, quite different from each other: peasants and urban marginals. Peasants bore the brunt of the commoditization of land and the incorporation of Egypt into the world economy. Not so much during the first half of our period, but certainly from the 1860s onward, landlessness and destitution in Egypt's agricultural estates increased, while protective mechanisms, such as cooperative arrangements and even the village community under a strong 'umda, failed to stop the tide.

The urban marginals are a different case, since they had, in a way, acted as individuals all along, and certainly well before the processes that enabled individual active participation in the political, economic, and cultural life of Egypt. These processes had little or no impact on the many street performers and entertainers who inhabited the city centers of Cairo, Alexandria, and Port Said. Female and male dancers, snake charmers, fortune-tellers, singers, musicians, fast trickers, jokers, magicians, acrobats, monkey-trainers, actors, and shadow-puppet-show performers were all a familiar sight in the urban setting of the Ottoman Middle East. And there were others who set rules of behavior for themselves, existing on the margins of a society that was undergoing profound change: prostitutes, the mad, the criminal.[78]

Conclusion

The social and economic processes described here have only been separated for analytic purposes. In nineteenth-century Egypt they were inseparable. The three most significant processes in that period were the emergence of hegemonic and dynastic rule, Egypt's incorporation into the world economy, and the rise of groups that enabled individual action and expression. The undergirding process was the emergence of hegemonic rule under the

Clot Bey, but its students were recruited from the lower strata, not the elite. For female health officers, see Kuhnke, *Lives at Risk*, 122–33. For a survey of the women's movement, see Soha Abdel Kader, *Egyptian Women in a Changing Society, 1899–1987* (Boulder, 1987).

[78] Toledano, *State and Society*, 231–40, 243–48.

Qazdagli household in the eighteenth century and the creation of dynastic order under the house of Muhammad 'Ali in the nineteenth century. Centralized state power clearly affected the market, as the leading household tried to mobilize all resources to entrench its rule and support the ambitions of its leading figures, which now were directed toward regional expansion, with the home front fairly pacified and secure.

While change throughout the period was incremental and sustained, the third quarter of the nineteenth century was a period of more concentrated, intensive change that produced a real turning point within the "long nineteenth century." After that point, Egypt was placed under direct foreign domination, which was *exclusivist* in its approach to the local elites and exploitative economically, in contrast to the *inclusivist* rule of the Ottomans, which also allowed a greater share of the surplus to be spent in Egypt itself. After that point, too, Egypt was more closely integrated into the world economy in a dependent status. During the last phase of our period, clubs, societies, newspapers, books, parties, and unions began to create a public sphere, in which, at the beginning of the twentieth century, individuals formulated an anti-colonial, nationalist discourse that led to the post-war intelligentsia- and elite-led nationalist movement.

12

The liberal age, 1923–1952

SELMA BOTMAN

>‹

During Egypt's liberal age, between 1923 and 1952, European-style constitutionalism and political pluralism were incorporated into the country's
political landscape. The period witnessed genuine, though irregular, electoral competition among individuals and groups, cross-class participation in
the process, and an operative, if imperfect, system of political and civil
liberties. While elites controlled democratic practice, people from humble
social classes also engaged in political activity.

Eager for independence from British control and for social and economic
reform, the population considered competing ideologies for Egypt's political
and economic development including western-style liberalism, monarchy,
Islamic fundamentalism, Marxism, feminism, and secular nationalism.
Nonetheless, the excessive powers of the monarchy, the lack of an indigenous bourgeoisie with political strength, and the absence of a developed
proletariat able to defend the liberal experiment combined to impede
pluralistic democratic development.

Political parties during the liberal age

In 1922, Britain granted Egypt formal independence, limited by four British-
imposed conditions: the security of imperial communications, defense of
Egypt against aggression, protection of foreign interests and minorities, and
continued British administration of the Sudan. The colonial authorities
changed the title of Egypt's head of state from sultan to king, and within a
year sanctioned promulgation of a democratic constitution. With Egyptians
assuming increasing control over their state, the age of liberal politics
began.[1]

The liberal era, which spanned the years between 1923 and 1952, featured

---

[1] The classic account of the liberal era is Marcel Colombe, *L'évolution de l'Egypte,
1924–1950* (Paris, 1951).

a political system characterized by western-style constitutionalism and parliamentary government.[2] Egypt's constitution was patterned on western liberal documents, and drawn up by Egyptian legal experts sympathetic to the king and the British. The framers of the constitution intended to limit the strength of the nascent Wafd party,[3] constrain the mass popular movement that had emerged during the 1919 nationalist revolution, and introduce a limited form of self-government into the country. They created a parliament consisting of a senate and a chamber of deputies elected by male suffrage, except for two-fifths of the senate which was appointed by the king. Bills enacted by the parliament did not acquire the status of law until signed by the monarch. If the king rejected a piece of legislation and sent it back for amendment, the deputies, in turn, could pass the original bill with a two-thirds majority; the king was then obliged to sign it into law.[4] In this way, legislative authority was to be shared by the king, the senate, and the chamber of deputies.

From the outset, King Ahmad Fu'ad disdained the constitution and intensely resented sharing power. Regrettably for the new democratic state, the constitution gave excessive powers to the monarch, who was granted the authority to dismiss ministers, suspend parliament, and install or remove prime ministers. For thirty years, King Ahmad Fu'ad and his son Faruq subverted the constitutional process and opposed the nationalist movement. As a result, while Egypt exhibited the structure of western-style constitutionalism, its practice was regularly compromised by the palace and its appointed ministers. Although designed as a semi-liberal political document, the constitution could not fully sustain liberalism's democratic content. Despite a multiplicity of political parties, elections, parliamentary sessions, and freedom of the press and associations, the constitution was repeatedly ignored, suspended, and even at times altered. In essence democratic practice was periodically paralyzed because neither the Wafd – the main nationalist party in Egypt – nor any other political organization successfully exercised a brake on the dominance of the king.

During this era, four groups alternately managed political life in the country: the palace, the British, the Wafd, and the so-called minority parties, in particular the Liberal Constitutionalist Party, the Saʿdist Party, the

[2] For different views on the liberal age see Jacques Berque, *Egypt: Imperialism and Revolution*, trans. Jean Stewart (New York, 1972); Leonard Binder, *In a Moment of Enthusiasm: Political Power and the Second Stratum in Egypt* (Chicago, 1978); Afaf Lutfi al-Sayyid Marsot, *Egypt's Liberal Experiment* (Berkeley, 1977); Muhammad Husayn Haykal, *Mudhakkirat fi'l siyasa al-misriyya*, 3 vols. (Cairo, 1977–78); Nadav Safran, *Egypt in Search of Political Community* (Cambridge, MA, 1961).

[3] For an institutional history of the period see Marius Deeb, *Party Politics in Egypt: The Wafd and its Rivals, 1919–1939* (London, 1979).

[4] Hassan Youssef, "The Democratic Experience in Egypt, 1923–1952," in Ali Hillal Dessouki (ed.), *Democracy in Egypt*, Cairo Papers in Social Science (Cairo, 1978), 26.

People's Party (*Hizb al-Sha'b*) and the Unity (*Ittihad*) Party. In contrast to the Wafd, which regularly could depend on the support of the entire nation at polling stations and at protests and marches, the minority groups were little more than the expression of the personalities who monopolized and manipulated them. Organizations outside the political mainstream such as the Muslim Brotherhood,[5] Young Egypt,[6] communist groups,[7] and women's associations[8] also contributed to the shaping of Egypt's political culture. But these groups were intentionally excluded from systematic parliamentary life in the country.

The Wafd was the foremost nationalist party and dominated the political landscape in Egypt. A tenacious political organization, at least for the first two decades of its existence, it defended the constitution as the sole guarantee against anti-democratic behavior. The Wafd saw itself, and was seen by others, as the embodiment of liberal democracy in Egypt. It represented a new Egyptian political elite in contrast to the Turco-Circassian leadership that had previously dominated. Wafdist leaders were indigenous Egyptians who came from the rural landed middle class as well as from the commercial and professional urban elites. The party claimed to represent people of all social classes and from all geographical areas. It attracted Muslims and Copts into its ranks,[9] which was a notable accomplishment at the time.

With a bourgeois-democratic ideology, the Wafd was secularist on the issue of church–state relations, and generally hostile to the king and his allies. Although the party held power for only about seven years between 1923 and 1952, it was invincible whenever free elections were held. Founded in November 1918, the Wafd at first was simply a national delegation claiming to represent Egypt on the issue of independence. In a short time, it became the center of an anti-British movement that spanned Egypt and won support from all sectors of the population, from the poor peasant to the big land owner, and from the urban worker to the intellectual and merchant. The party was led by Sa'd Zaghlul, whose towering political

---

[5] The standard work on the Muslim Brotherhood is Richard P. Mitchell, *The Society of the Muslim Brothers* (London, 1969); see also Sayyid Kotb, *Social Justice in Islam*, trans. John B. Hardie (Washington, DC, 1953).

[6] For a detailed study on Young Egypt see James P. Jankowski, *Egypt's Young Rebels, "Young Egypt": 1932–1952* (Stanford, 1975).

[7] On the communist movement in this period see Selma Botman, *The Rise of Egyptian Communism* (Syracuse, 1988).

[8] For more information on the women's movement in Egypt see Akram Khater and Cynthia Nelson, "Al-Harakah al-nissa'iya: The Women's Movement and Political Participation in Modern Egypt," *Women's Studies International Forum*, 11 (1988), 465–83; Margot Badran, *Feminists, Islam, and Nation: Gender and the Making of Modern Egypt* (Princeton, 1995).

[9] On the Copts see B. L. Carter, *The Copts in Egyptian Politics* (London, 1986).

stature and uncompromising nationalist credentials gave hope to those eager for self-rule.

The Wafd operated as a coalition of the rural middle class and high-status urban groups such as lawyers, doctors, financiers, industrialists, intellectuals, and students.[10] The Wafd was able to mobilize support in the countryside through its association with landlords, schoolteachers, and village *'umdas* who encouraged peasant loyalty in elections. But it was also endorsed by the *effendiyya*, professionals and civil servants, and by sections of the petty bourgeoisie and groups of workers in cities and towns.

The party favored moderate ideological and socio-economic positions that were held by the majority of the Egyptian elite. Accordingly, while leaders acknowledged the need to improve the conditions of life for the country's impoverished majority, this was always a distantly secondary priority. On the issue of full national independence from Britain,[11] however, the Wafd was more aggressive. In its early years, the party was so uncompromising in its anti-colonialist stand that the British government considered it intemperate. Eventually, however, the British discerned the Wafd's inherent moderation, and accordingly recognized it as the primary Egyptian proponent of full independence.

Despite its liberal image, because of the non-democratic internal structure of the Wafd and the nature of limited constitutional rule in Egypt, the party did not impart lasting democratic features to the political system. The Wafd's political ideas and strategies were handed down from above after consultation among only its most prominent members. Although the Wafd mobilized the Egyptian citizenry, gave people occasional opportunities to participate in the political process through elections, marches, and meetings, and helped shape the values and opinions of the population, the party was not committed to deepening the process of regularized democratic activity in Egypt by encouraging independent political thought in the population. In particular, it looked with disfavor upon any autonomous political activity from below, whether it came from women's organizations, the left, or the religious right.

In contrast to the Wafd, other elite political parties that stood as its rivals were often called minority parties, since they customarily had little support among the people and were essentially founded as vehicles through which leading politicians could be elected to parliament. Often little more than splinter groups of the Wafd, they were typically set up after important

[10] Blinder, *Moment of Enthusiasm*, 39.
[11] On British policy in Egypt see Lord Lloyd, *Egypt since Cromer*, 2 vols. (London, 1933–34); W. Roger Louis, *The British Empire in the Middle East, 1945–1951* (New York, 1984); Peter Mansfield, *The British in Egypt* (London, 1971); *Great Britain and Egypt 1914–1951* (London: Royal Institute of International Affairs, 1951).

members were expelled or chose to leave because of personal or ideological conflicts.

The Liberal Constitutionalist Party was founded in 1922 and run by distinguished intellectuals, large landlords, and notable political figures who left the Wafd because of basic disagreements with Saʿd Zaghlul. The Liberal Constitutionalists were nationalists, but only moderately so. The party's plan was to engage in gradual and low-key negotiations with the British for complete national independence in contrast to the aggressive strategies of Zaghlul's Wafd.

Essentially acting in the interests of large land owners and marked by an aristocratic image, the Liberal Constitutionalists had little connection to the masses. Although they believed that the people would gain from their paternalistic approach, they did little, when in office, to improve socio-economic conditions. Despite their respect for the constitution of 1923, the Liberal Constitutionalists were no more tolerant of opposing political trends than the Wafdists they criticized. Ahmad Lutfi al-Sayyid, ʿAdli Yakan, Ismaʿil Sidqi, and Muhammad Husayn Haykal were some of its most important leaders.

Another political formation, the Unity (*Ittihad*) Party, was established in 1925 as the king's own conservative vehicle. As a reward for those who joined the monarch's side, he elevated party leaders – there were not many of them – to high political positions through royal decrees. Monarchists, notables, government functionaries, and high-ranking army officers joined the new political organization in exchange for political patronage. In this way, the king undermined the nascent parliamentary system and kept a decisive hand in the operation of government.

Ismaʿil Sidqi, one of Egypt's most ambitious politicians, set up the People's Party (*Hizb al-Shaʾb*) in 1930. More a clique than a political party, it supported Sidqi's own political aspirations and undermined the interests of the Unity and Wafd parties. Those who associated with Sidqi benefited from the appointments and jobs he was able to distribute. Throughout the liberal age, Sidqi was a force to be reckoned with.

The Saʿdist Party, which came into being in 1937, was another splinter group of the Wafd. It gained prominence among urban financial and industrial interests and was strongest among members of the indigenous bourgeoisie who were tied economically and ideologically to the Federation of Industries and Bank Misr.[12] Having inherited the liberal nationalist ideas of the Wafd, its few members supported constitutionalism, democracy, civil liberties, and a measure of social justice.

[12] See Eric Davis, *Challenging Colonialism: Bank Misr and Egyptian Industrialization 1920–1941* (Princeton, 1983); Robert L. Tignor, *State, Private Enterprise, and Economic Change in Egypt, 1918–1952* (Princeton, 1984); Robert Vitalis, *When Capitalists Collide: Business Conflict and the End of Empire in Egypt* (Berkeley, 1995).

These political parties dominated parliamentary life during the constitutional period. Their leaders often used the parties as platforms to express their own positions and as vehicles to advance their own careers. None encouraged independent popular participation in the political process or succeeded in achieving national independence.

From the close of the First World War until the Free Officers' accession to power in 1952, the struggle for political preeminence was often fought in an anti-democratic fashion. A typical pattern emerged in Egyptian politics: whenever a free election was held, the Wafd would be guaranteed a sweeping victory, but a conflict with the British or the palace led inevitably to the Wafd's resignation or dismissal, the dissolution of parliament, and the suspension or modification of the constitution. The Wafd would remain in opposition until a disagreement between the palace and a minority party, or a decision by the British, caused the Wafd's return to office.

Throughout this period, the national question dominated Egypt's political culture. This reflected Britain's stubborn refusal to leave the country, and the conservative ideologies that indigenous parliamentary leaders represented. In particular, no party in Egypt made issues of social and economic reform an essential part of its platform. Even the Wafd, which was the most socially responsible party, did not concentrate on advancing the country's impoverished popular classes. In effect, since Britain maintained a degree of control over the country's military, political, and economic status despite Egypt's nominal independence, national liberation was the predominant issue. Indeed, in reaction against the British, a vibrant movement of national liberation, led by the Wafd Party, emerged. Crossing class, geographic, and gender lines, the Egyptian population joined together periodically to struggle against colonial interference in local issues.

Despite the fact that during the militant nationalist struggle of 1919 feminist women fought alongside men, after independence and the declaration of the constitution, women were deprived of the formal political rights of citizenship. They could not vote, stand for office, or influence national policy. They were not allowed to attend the opening of parliament, except as wives of ministers or other high officials. In this nascent democratic order, men granted themselves the exclusive authority to enact and enforce laws pertaining to both the public arena and the private domain of the family. In an effort to protest against and moderate male dominance, Huda Sha'rawi and other upper-class and well-connected women established the Egyptian Feminist Union (EFU) in 1923, through which they pursued nationalist and feminist goals.[13] By the end of the 1920s, the founders had recruited some 250 women into the organization and began focusing on how to ameliorate conditions of life for poor women. The EFU also became

---

[13] Badran, *Feminists, Islam, and Nation*, 13, 86, 207.

involved in regional and international issues. At home, however, the idea of female emancipation touched only a small minority of the Egyptian population – male or female – and the activists could not depend on government support.

Nationalism, constitutionalism, and inchoate democracy

In 1923, martial law was lifted. Sa'd Zaghlul and other nationalists who had been exiled by the colonial power for their anti-British activities were permitted to return to Egypt and allowed to enter the first parliamentary elections in January 1924. After the Wafd won 90 percent of the seats in the chamber of deputies, the king asked it to form the first government, and appointed Zaghlul prime minister in March. The first parliamentary government served only nine months. Zaghlul's position was weakened by his tight-fisted control of the chamber, the king's strong opposition to legislative initiatives, and by secret terrorist organizations which had carried over from the 1919 revolution.[14]

Zaghlul and the new democratic system were thrown into disarray when a political crisis occurred in November 1924. Sir Lee Stack, the British commander-in-chief of the Egyptian army and governor-general of the Sudan, was assassinated in Cairo by disgruntled nationalists. The British high commissioner in Egypt, Lord Allenby, acting without authorization from London, issued an ultimatum to the Egyptians, the most important points of which were the withdrawal of the Egyptian army from the Sudan, payment of a huge indemnity, and a prohibition of political demonstrations. Allenby attributed the crime to Zaghlul who, however, apparently knew nothing about it. Zaghlul refused to accept the ultimatum except for the payment of the indemnity. The British government supported Allenby, forcing Zaghlul's resignation on November 23 and effectively ending his political career. He was never again allowed to serve as prime minister.

Allenby's swift reaction to Stack's assassination demonstrated that the British were still inclined to treat Egypt like a traditional protectorate. When the high commissioner intervened in Egyptian affairs without regard for the country's new sovereign status or democratic structure, he continued the process of British intervention that would last until the revolution of 1952.

Not only did Allenby topple Zaghlul's government, he also ensured that the next prime minister, Ahmad Ziwar Pasha, first president of the senate from the Unity party, would weaken the Wafd Party and the national movement through the promotion of anti-democratic and restrictive legislation. After Ziwar agreed unconditionally to the British ultimatum, the

---

[14] Arthur Goldschmidt, *Modern Egypt: The Formation of a Nation-State* (Boulder, 1988), 61.

military authority arrested assumed terrorists and removed all Egyptian army units from the Sudan.[15] Ziwar also amended the electoral laws so that multistage rather than direct elections would take place, and gerrymandered electoral districts. In addition, he campaigned to increase the voting age and to impose educational and property requirements on the voters. The intent was to cripple the Wafd and to contain its supporters. Very early in the life of this semi-liberal state, the rule of democracy was tested. Unfortunately, Egypt was not yet ready to meet the challenge of an imperial power, a hostile king, and a group of undemocratic politicians. Only a year after the Wafdist victory had occurred, the hopes of Egyptian democrats were dashed, and the pattern of interventionist, non-democratic politics was set.

This pattern was repeated in March 1925 when, following the Wafd's victory in new parliamentary elections, winning 54 percent of the vote, the king dismissed the chamber nine hours after it had assembled, and reappointed his ally Ahmad Ziwar to office. Under Ahmad Ziwar, the emphasis changed from the conflict between the Wafd and the British to that between the Wafd and the palace. Isma'il Sidqi, a former Wafdist, joined Ziwar's government as minister of the interior. He prevented civil servants from engaging in political activities and sought the electoral support of provincial governors and district officers, thus guaranteeing the success of government-sponsored candidates.[16] In protest against the blatantly anti-democratic behavior of the monarch, the Liberal Constitutionalist Party – once an ally of the king – later left the government.

Anti-democratic and obtrusive behavior repeated itself in May 1926 when the new British high commissioner, Lord (George) Lloyd, refused to allow Zaghlul to take power after the Wafd had again won an overwhelming electoral victory. Lloyd, a staunch defender of imperial interests in Egypt, let it be known that he had asked the British government to station a gunboat outside Alexandria to convince Zaghlul of the seriousness of Britain's position. In June, Zaghlul agreed to a coalition government with the Liberal Constitutionalists to be led by 'Adli Yakan as prime minister. Zaghlul held the presidency of the chamber of deputies. Yakan, who came into conflict with the palace in April 1927, resigned from office. He was succeeded by a member of his party, 'Abd al-Khaliq Tharwat, who negotiated a draft treaty with the British. Since it was not approved by the Wafd, the treaty never became law.

At the age of sixty-seven, on August 23, 1927, Sa'd Zaghlul died; but he would not be forgotten. Zaghlul was acclaimed as an exemplary leader of the nationalist movement and a statesman. He was admired posthumously

---

[15] P. J. Vatikiotis, *The Modern History of Egypt: From Muhammad Ali to Mubarak*, 4th ed. (Baltimore, 1991), 283.

[16] See J. C. B. Richmond, *Egypt: 1789–1952* (New York, 1977), 193; and Vatikiotis, *Modern Egypt*, 284–85.

by both his supporters and his adversaries; his prodigious reputation set a high standard for political activism and commitment to principle. In reality, however, in his determination to win national independence for Egypt, Zaghlul introduced a system of patronage into public life and used violence and public demonstrations as weapons against the opposition.[17] He was domineering in style and personality and asserted absolutist control over party politics, which has been a hallmark of Egyptian political life ever since.

Egypt's political culture suffered from the consequences of restricted democratic practice, and constitutionalism was undermined by politicians who ruled according to their own arbitrary standards. Tharwat resigned in March 1928 after failing to win a treaty with Britain; he was followed by Mustafa al-Nahhas, Zaghlul's successor in the Wafd party. Serving only until June 1928, al-Nahhas was dismissed by the king, who simultaneously dissolved parliament. The constitution was canceled and Egypt was ruled by decree under Muhammad Mahmud of the Liberal Constitutionalist party until his resignation in October 1929. As prime minister, Muhammad Mahmud dissolved parliament and initiated a period of undemocratic rule that, though punctuated by a caretaker government of ʿAdli Yakan and a Wafdist victory in December 1929 that temporarily elevated Mustafa al-Nahhas to premier, culminated in the appointment of the dictatorial Ismaʿil Sidqi to office only months later.

In the 1929 election, the Wafd gained its largest majority to date, capturing 90 percent of the seats in the chamber. On January 1, 1930, the Wafd formed its third government since independence and its second under al-Nahhas. The Wafd hoped to negotiate a new treaty with the British, as well as to reestablish the legitimacy of the constitution. As prime minister al-Nahhas failed on both counts.[18] Treaty negotiation faltered over administration of the Sudan, from which Egypt had been all but ousted in 1924. Al-Nahhas also struggled with the king over the latter's influence in political life, seriously straining relations between the palace and the Wafd. In June when al-Nahhas was implicated in a corruption scandal (and later exonerated) in which he and two associates were accused of influence-peddling, the palace capitalized on the event to force the Wafd out of office in disgrace. Al-Nahhas could neither establish the primacy of the constitution nor come to terms with the British.

Consequently, the late 1920s and early 1930s constituted a decidedly bleak period for constitutionalism in Egypt. After Ismaʿil Sidqi took power in 1930 to head a pro-palace government, he dissolved parliament, deferred elections, abolished the constitution of 1923, and created a new one that gave even more authority to the king. Sidqi ruled Egypt with dictatorial

---

[17] Afaf Lutfi al-Sayyid Marsot, *A Short History of Modern Egypt* (Cambridge, 1985), 85.
[18] Vatikiotis, *Modern Egypt*, 287.

firmness in what is considered one of the harshest periods in Egypt's modern political history. His appointment to the premiership marked the third palace coup in seven years and represented the longest period of rule by decree in the country. Egypt's liberal democracy would never recover from the shock Sidqi sent throughout the political system. Violence became a regular feature of the political culture, Wafdists and Liberals were irrevocably estranged from the monarchy, and, from the perspective of the public, parliamentary politics was irreversibly compromised. It was Sidqi's intention to rule without interference from the Wafd, and he did so until January 1933 when, after a disagreement with the king, he resigned from office. The king reappointed him almost two months later to form a new government which lasted only until September. Palace-appointed governments ruled Egypt for nearly two years, led first by 'Abd al-Fattah Yahya and then by Tawfiq Nasim. For a time, the king even assumed all powers himself. Then, in 1935, the demands of a national front of major political parties, in addition to the advice of the new high commissioner, Sir Miles Lampson, convinced the king to reestablish the constitution of 1923.

With the resumption of constitutional life, Egyptian politicians were eager to renew negotiations with the British. A coalition of politicians created a list of demands to raise in upcoming talks: the end of the occupation, elimination of restrictions on the strength of the Egyptian army, transfer of the army's command from British to Egyptian hands, local control over Egypt's minority communities, and full Egyptian authority over the Sudan. Although the record of Anglo-Egyptian negotiations was discouraging, since attempts in 1924, 1927, and 1929–30 had failed to produce results, by the mid-1930s expectations had improved. In fact, it was an international crisis, the Italian invasion of Ethiopia in 1936, that prompted the British and the Egyptians to come to terms.

Fascist Italy had gained control of both Libya and Ethiopia and had become a threat to the British position in the region. The British wanted the Egyptians on the side of the European democracies in any future crisis.[19] While all Egyptians resented the wartime costs of food, clothing, and housing and the imposition of British, Canadian, Indian, Australian, New Zealand, and South African troops on their soil, the population was divided on the issue of which side to support in the war. There were those who hoped for a Nazi victory to free them from British control and those who feared that the fascists would be harsher overlords than the British.[20] The Allied authorities, however, suspected King Ahmad Fu'ad and his associates of pro-Italian sympathies. In recognition of the growing international

[19] For more information on the Second World War see George Kirk, *The Middle East in the War* (London, 1952); and Martin W. Wilmington, *The Middle East Supply Centre* (Albany, 1971).

[20] Goldschmidt, *Modern Egypt*, 74.

tensions and their implications for the Middle East, the British decided that this was an auspicious time to solidify local anti-fascist sentiment. Consequently, they were prepared to grant the Egyptians increased national autonomy.

After Nasim resigned on January 22, 1936, a caretaker government led by 'Ali Mahir assumed control on January 30 and held power until elections were held in May. Meanwhile, King Ahmad Fu'ad died in April, and was succeeded by his son Faruq who was initially seen as ambitious, bright, and patriotic.[21] The Wafd formed the next government in May after gaining a majority of seats in parliament. With al-Nahhas in command and the new king on the throne, there was renewed expectation that an accord could be reached with Britain. A multiparty delegation, made up of representatives of all the political parties except the National Party of Mustafa Kamil, was charged with negotiating with the imperial authority. On August 26, 1936, it reached a historic compromise and the Anglo-Egyptian treaty was signed into law. That al-Nahhas stood at the head of the government was important because the British recognized that only the Wafd party could convince the Egyptians of the legitimacy of a new agreement.

All the participants believed the twenty-year agreement to be advantageous. The Egyptian leadership was satisfied with Britain's recognition of Egypt as an independent and sovereign state and confident that the country was moving toward full national independence. The British, on the other hand, favored the treaty because it stipulated that Britain could come to Egypt's aid in the event of an emergency, and that Egypt would grant Britain the military facilities required to protect its lines of communication.

Primarily a defense pact which included specific strategic and military provisions, the agreement restricted Britain's 10,000 troops to the area of the Suez Canal Zone during peacetime, and maintained the status quo in the Sudan. In order to moderate the controversial defense aspects of the agreement, Britain pledged to support Egypt's membership of the League of Nations and committed itself to abolition of the Capitulations.

As anticipated, in 1937 the Montreux Convention ended the system of Capitulations. Foreigners and minorities became the responsibility of the Egyptian government and the mixed courts were abolished, though this was to be accomplished over a thirteen-year period. After Egypt was permitted to apply for membership of the League of Nations, it established embassies and consulates around the world. Thus, for the first time since the British occupied the country in 1882, Egyptians were free to create their own foreign policy and determine their own national interest.

---

[21] On Faruq see Miles Lampson's diaries, ed. Trefor Evans as *The Killearn Diaries, 1934–1946: The Diplomatic and Personal Record of Lord Killearn* (London, 1972). A second volume, ed. M. E. Yapp, is forthcoming.

Although the Anglo-Egyptian treaty was accepted by a wide range of the public, there was opposition to its military provisions. Dissatisfaction came from both ends of the political spectrum. For the left, the treaty was inadequate because British troops were to remain in Egypt for another twenty years and because promises of unobstructed democracy and self-determination were absent. For the right, notably the Muslim Brotherhood and Young Egypt, the treaty was incomplete; any compromise with the occupying authorities was branded unacceptable.

Those who opposed the treaty perceived the Wafd, the palace, and the minority parties as unable to answer three basic questions of the time: the national issue, socio-economic reform, and political representation. Their objections not only signaled a growing popular impatience with the political center and an increasing disaffection with the Wafd, but also an emerging interest in the Muslim Brotherhood, Young Egypt, the women's movement, and the anti-fascist groups that eventually developed into the communist movement of the 1940s.

Marxism emerged in Egypt along with the nationalist sentiment generated during the 1919 revolution. At that time, ideas of socialism and trade unionism were slowly gaining prominence among small circles of intellectuals and workers of both Egyptian and European origin. In order to take advantage of workers' militancy, radical activists founded the eclectic Socialist Party in 1920–21. The party was legal and open to all shades of the Egyptian left, which included Fabians, social democrats, and Marxists.[22] Having as its goal the radicalization of the trade union movement, the party entered a second stage of development when it was transformed into the Egyptian Communist Party in 1922.

Sa'd Zaghlul was well aware of the Communist Party's activities among workers and its influence over some nationalist intellectuals. Although the left was not a major force in Egyptian society at this time, its presence proved menacing to the government. As a result, Zaghlul crushed the movement in 1924. When the party was outlawed the following year, it had already been rendered impotent; as an organized political movement, communism temporarily ceased to exist in Egypt. Left-wing oppositional activity resumed in the mid- and late 1930s when anti-fascist sentiments began to be expressed, initially by members of Egypt's Jewish community.[23] This group, together with Muslim and Coptic dissidents, revived Marxist thinking in the country.

Like the radical left, the Islamic right rejected Wafdist-style liberalism, viewed Egyptian constitutionalism as too conciliatory to the British, and

[22] For more information on the Fabians see Vernon Egger, *A Fabian in Egypt: Salamah Musa and the Rise of the Professional Classes in Egypt, 1909–1939* (Lanham, 1986).

[23] An important work on the Jewish community in Egypt is Gudrun Kramer, *The Jews of Modern Egypt, 1914–1952* (Seattle, 1989).

resolved to topple the country's mainstream political leaders and free the country from foreign control. But while left-wing and anti-fascist movements were committed to the Allied efforts to defeat Nazism, the Muslim Brotherhood with its theocratic beliefs and Young Egypt with its blend of pharaonic and chauvinistic attitudes supported Germany and Italy during the Second World War. Their defense of the Axis countries not only mirrored the views of important sectors of the intelligentsia, for whom fascism was a militant form of nationalism, but it was also attractive to members of the lower and middle classes, who found liberalism ineffective in its failure to address continuing social and economic crises.

Young Egypt (*Misr al-Fatat*) was established in 1933 as a patriotic, militaristic, and socially conservative organization. In keeping with its Islamic orientation, Young Egypt stressed religion and morality as the guiding principles of life, and was actively and philosophically opposed to the European-style democracy practiced by the Wafd. It recruited among secondary-school and university students in urban areas at a time when dissatisfaction with the Wafd and with liberal, secular democratic politics was growing.

Its competitor, the Muslim Brotherhood, was the most important Islamic group in the 1930s, 1940s, and early 1950s. Founded in 1928 by Hasan al-Banna', the Muslim Brotherhood initially took the form of an Islamic revivalist movement. Soon afterwards, it began to oppose the secular parties and European-style government and culture. Hasan al-Banna', whose goal was to infuse Islam into every aspect of life in Egypt, promoted a simple and absolute message: struggle to rid Egypt of foreign occupation; defend and obey Islam.

In addition to activity in the field of education, the Brotherhood generated urban projects that provided jobs for the poor and set up industrial and commercial enterprises that concurrently helped the indigent and added economic strength to the organization. In the 1930s, as it became more pan-Islamic and more visible, its numbers increased. Although the newest members of the Brotherhood were particularly receptive to its missionary activity, the general economic distress caused by the 1929 depression contributed to the group's increasing popularity.

In essence, as the Wafd and the practice of European-style liberalism were weakening in Egypt, competing trends began appearing. Fascism had its adherents, a left-wing intellectual movement emerged, and increasing alienation found expression in religious fundamentalism. That the Muslim Brotherhood, Young Egypt, and the communist organizations could emerge in Egypt and flourish was testament to the novelty of pluralism. Although democracy was constantly obstructed, popular activism was tenacious despite both structural and social obstacles.

Although al-Nahhas had successfully extended Egypt's independence through the treaty of 1936 and stood at the height of his power, conflict with King Faruq led to the dismissal of his government in December the next year. Muhammad Mahmud of the Liberal Party formed his second government, and called for new elections in April. The number of parliamentary seats was increased and redistricting took place in an effort to weaken the Wafd. This was facilitated by an internal split in the party which led to the formation of the Sa'dists. In the election of April 1938, the Wafd won only twelve seats.

Governmental stability was short lived. Mahmud's government was dismissed by the king in August 1939, and 'Ali Mahir assumed the position of prime minister which he held until June 1940. The Sa'dists participated in the government; the Liberals stayed out. By this time, war was raging in Europe. British wartime security interests and the continuing conflicts between the Wafd and the palace, and between the Wafd and all other political parties, further subverted constitutional life in Egypt. During the first eight years of constitutional life, parliament had been dissolved four times. In the fifteen-year period 1923–38, there had been seven general elections. No parliament lasted its allotted term of four years.[24]

Britain's interest in Egypt's internal politics increased during the war, provoking the nationalist and other opposition movements. In keeping with its treaty obligations, Egypt was placed under martial law in 1939, censorship was instituted, and diplomatic relations with Germany and Italy were broken. Egypt was considered strategically vital to Britain's wartime operations and the Egyptian government's cooperation was deemed essential to the stationing and supplying of the Allied forces. The country was asked to put its resources at the disposal of the Allied war effort and to accept some half-million Allied troops during the course of the conflict. Although the treaty stipulated that the number of British troops would be limited to 10,000 in peacetime, no limits had been placed on wartime numbers.

At the outset of the conflict, most Egyptians wished to keep out of what they perceived as a war of the western powers. They expected, at least initially, that the Allies would defeat the Germans during the early months of battle. But the fall of France changed people's perceptions. As the Germans began to look stronger, local support for them increased. Seeing Germany as a potential counterbalance to the British in Egypt, some in the population began to advocate the fascist cause as a protest against British occupation.

The Egyptians had been exposed to Axis propaganda before the war through German staff officers, diplomats, and Nazi dignitaries who visited the country in the hope of attracting nationalists to their cause. Italian and German propaganda was also heard on the radio in Egypt, touting the

[24] Vatikiotis, *Modern Egypt*, 296–97.

successes of Mussolini and Hitler. A number of Egyptian political officials initiated secret talks with the Nazis. Some military personnel, including the arch-nationalist General 'Aziz 'Ali al-Misri and Colonel Anwar al-Sadat, made preliminary efforts to join Marshal Rommel and the Nazi war campaign. As the pro-Axis current grew, some nationalists applauded Rommel after he landed in Egypt's western desert and engaged the British at al-Alamayn. Expecting the battle to be a decisive first step in the liberation of Egypt from British control, this group was disappointed by the British victory and subsequent destruction of the German army.

Because the Allies were fearful that their position might be undermined in Egypt in the early 1940s, the British demanded the dismissal of General 'Aziz 'Ali al-Misri and the prime minister, 'Ali Mahir, in June 1940; their acknowledged fascist sympathies were intolerable during wartime. General al-Misri was first placed on leave and then retired from active duty. After a meeting at the palace of all party leaders, 'Ali Mahir resigned and the independent Hasan Sabri formed a coalition government which lasted only months. Hasan Sabri died unexpectedly while delivering a speech in parliament; he was succeeded by Husayn Sirri, another independent, in November 1940. Sirri led two successive governments until his resignation, on February 2, 1942, after the king expressed displeasure with the government for having broken diplomatic ties with Vichy France without consultation with the palace.

Britain's intrusion into Egypt's political life peaked two days later when the British, through their emissary Lampson, demanded that the king appoint the Wafdist leader al-Nahhas as prime minister in an entirely Wafdist government.[25] Since al-Nahhas was recognized as an anti-fascist, he was trusted by the British. Although he could not match Zaghlul's popularity or influence, he was the Allies' best choice to advance their cause.

The king and Lampson negotiated for two days, during which time Faruq argued for an interim coalition government under al-Nahhas, rather than an exclusively Wafdist one. Owing to the Allies' alarm at the situation in the western desert, Lampson sent an ultimatum to Faruq: comply with the Allied request, or abdicate. When Faruq failed to yield, Lampson surrounded the palace with troops. Having no choice, the king capitulated to British pressure.

Faruq viewed the ultimatum as an abrogation of the Anglo-Egyptian treaty and an insult to the independence of the country. From the Allied perspective, however, Lampson's ultimatum was a wartime measure justified by military emergency. The British supported al-Nahhas because of his

---

[25] For more information on the events of this period see Gabriel Warburg, "The 'Three-Legged Stool': Lampson, Faruq, and Nahhas, 1936–1944," in Gabriel Warburg, *Egypt and the Sudan* (London, 1985) and Charles Smith, "4 February 1942: Its Causes and its Influences on Egyptian Politics," *International Journal of Middle East Studies* 10/4 (November 1979), 453–79.

acknowledged antipathy toward the fascists and because they expected him to resist palace interference. As for al-Nahhas, he probably accepted the leadership in the hope of extracting for Egypt material assistance from Britain; he may also have wanted to undermine the minority parties' alliance with the king.

The events of February 1942 proved disastrous for all involved. The palace and the Wafd were irrevocably distanced. The king was disgraced. A wide breach separated the Wafd from the non-parliamentary parties. All recognized that the Wafd accepted power through the strength of British bayonets, not as the result of an electoral victory. As such, its patriotic and nationalist standing in the country was greatly diminished. Wafdist leaders might have thought they were manipulating the British and the king, but the party's younger members, organized as a pressure group and called the Wafdist Vanguard, were disappointed by their leaders' obeisance and never forgave al-Nahhas for the national humiliation in which he acquiesced.

The Vanguard, made up of students and other youth associated with the Wafd, analyzed the national question in world terms, identified the economic bases of imperialism, and looked with favor upon the Soviet Union and national liberation movements. In Egypt, the group defended the rights of workers and peasants by criticizing what it saw as the excesses of capitalist exploitation. Influenced by liberal and socialist thought, the Wafdist Vanguard revealed some communality with the Marxist forces that were simultaneously coming into their own in Egypt.

After 1942, the Wafd no longer stood as the hegemonic nationalist power in the country. Although it could still win a majority of votes in electoral competitions, as it did in March 1942 when the Liberal and Sa'dist parties abstained from the campaign, it was not the radical party of its youth. Its leaders had become more moderate, its attitude toward the British less aggressive, and its ability to capture the masses diminished by its complicity with the colonial power.

From this time onward, unofficial and underground political movements began to appeal to significant numbers of people below the upper echelons of the political elites. Sectors of the urban bourgeoisie, the petty bourgeoisie, and the working class entered the political process. Middle-class women also joined the political discourse through advocacy of voting rights, improved female education, and reform of personal status laws.

The growth of the Muslim Brotherhood, Young Egypt, and the communist underground pointed to the decline of the secular and gradualist approach that characterized the Wafd. As the leadership of the nationalist movement gradually shifted from the Wafd to these non-parliamentary parties, their organizing efforts and journalistic activities began to influence the content of social and political discourse in the post-war period.

Ahmad Husayn, the leader of Young Egypt, for instance, made efforts to broaden the organization's appeal in 1940. Not only did he change the group's name to the National Islamic Party but he also expressed its ideology in radically religious and chauvinist terms. The organization, however, was constantly overshadowed by the Muslim Brotherhood, and its appeal was comparatively diminished. Even after it became the Socialist Party before the 1952 revolution and stressed the twin themes of anti-imperialism and social reform, its activity was limited to that of a small opposition group. Still, the existence of Young Egypt and its successor parties signified the escalating disenchantment that sections of the population felt toward the established secular parties.

The Muslim Brotherhood counted among its members civil servants, students, workers, policemen, lawyers, soldiers, and peasants, and the movement's strength was variously estimated at hundreds of thousands to a million or more activists by the outbreak of the Second World War. An extraparliamentary organization, the Brotherhood exerted a considerable influence on lower- and middle-class Egyptians. This influence was especially evident in the countless demonstrations, marches, and protests the Brotherhood staged between 1945 and 1948, the period when the movement was strongest. Opposed both to the secular bases of communist and Wafdist ideologies and to the democratic, constitutional, and cosmopolitan society they envisioned, the Brotherhood sabotaged meetings, precipitated clashes at public gatherings, and damaged property. The movement was forced underground after members committed terrorist acts, including political assassinations, in the 1940s.

Of all the causes embraced by the Brotherhood in the 1940s, the struggle in Palestine was among the most passionate.[26] The organization collected money and arms, trained volunteers, and sent a battalion of troops to Palestine in 1948 to join the Arab forces already stationed there. Engaged in the Palestine conflict abroad and committed to revolution at home, the movement posed a radical threat to domestic politics until the murder of its charismatic leader, Hasan al-Banna', in late November 1948, a murder carried out by the political police, and probably inspired by the government.[27] Underground until 1951, the Brotherhood temporarily reemerged as primarily a social, cultural, and spiritual organization until banned by 'Abd al-Nasir in 1954.

On the political left, the experience of Egyptian communism after the Second World War was one of factionalism and dissension. No single,

---

[26] For Egypt's involvement in the Palestine war see Israel Gershoni, *The Emergence of Pan-Arabism in Egypt* (Tel Aviv, 1981); James Jankowski, "Egyptian Responses to the Palestine Problem in the Interwar Period," *International Journal of Middle East Studies* 12/1 (August 1980), 1–38; Yehoshua Porath, *In Search of Arab Unity, 1930–1945* (London, 1986).

[27] Mitchell, *Muslim Brothers*, 71.

recognized communist party existed. Instead, when Marxist militants launched their formal activity in the early 1940s, they established a number of different, sometimes mutually hostile, organizations. The most important groups were the Egyptian Movement for National Liberation (EMNL), Iskra, and the New Dawn. After the nationalist movement gained momentum in 1947, a partial, but only temporary, unification in the Marxist movement occurred and produced the Democratic Movement for National Liberation (DMNL). This organization was then challenged by a newly established Egyptian Communist Party (1949).

The communist organizations were highly nationalist and critical of Egypt's traditional political culture. Formal activity took place in small, autonomous, clandestine groups. Insecurity and skepticism divided the leftists and shaped the content of the clandestine organizations. The movement was weakened by dissension, personality clashes, and police campaigns against it. The communists were isolated from the people they hoped to represent.

In the end, the communists never managed to disseminate their ideas widely. They were unable to move out of the political center of Cairo and outside the social strata of urban students, professionals, and skilled workers. Despite some efforts, communists with few exceptions could not penetrate the rural villages or the poor urban neighborhoods. They did not transform their message of popular participation in the political process into concrete activity.

But despite the movement's difficulties, Egyptian communism had a surprisingly enduring presence. In the 1940s and 1950s, it influenced intellectual and political life through journalism, poetry, fiction, and philosophical and political publications, and through demonstrations and strikes. The communists were active at key moments of nationalist, student, and trade union militancy and they helped lay the ideological basis – social justice, planned economic development, and distrust of the west – that became a central component of the political, social, intellectual, and artistic life of Egypt under Jamal 'Abd al-Nasir.

The non-parliamentary organizations contributed to the ultimate destabilization of the constitutional monarchy in Egypt. By criticizing the Wafd and questioning its commitment to independence and modernization and by charging that the king and his political associates acted as obstacles to change, the opposition helped create an ideological climate in which Nasir's Free Officers could organize and operate. Indeed, the campaign to discredit the mainstream parties helped pave the way for the emergence of Nasir and his military partners.

The Second World War also brought to the fore increasingly varied feminist perspectives and a new phase of gender-oriented politics undertaken by a generation of younger women disillusioned by the purpose and tactics of the Egyptian Feminist Union. In the years before the war, during the first phase of women's activity, social homogeneity and ideological cohesion existed in the Egyptian feminist community. However, by the late 1930s, the broadening of political activity generally in Egypt resulted in an organizational fracture within the EFU and the launching of the second phase of feminist activity. In particular, as a result of the EFU's disinclination to recruit a more socially diverse membership, for the first time, Huda Sha'rawi and her associate Saiza Nabarawi confronted factionalism within the secular feminist community as activists raised concerns about the class-based character of the movement and about the goals of feminism. The upper-class women of the group, whose world-view was largely secular and foreign, spoke French, wore western dress, and looked to Europe for cultural enrichment. Challenging them were the more recently organized middle-class women who spoke Arabic and were rooted in local culture and traditions.

Tension between upper-class feminists and middle-class female political activists could not be avoided and ideological differences could not be bridged. Some women, such as Zaynab al-Ghazali, for example, leaned toward Islamic fundamentalism. Other women, for example Duriyya Shafiq, Inji Aflatun, and Latifa al-Zayat, embraced more radical ideas and were prepared to engage in more aggressive strategies for change. Their tactics were more populist, their goals more comprehensive, and their tone more strident and forceful. In this era of feminist politics new organizations and dynamic younger leaders demanded that women gain the right to vote and that the socio-economic system underlying the oppression of women be changed.[28]

Among new associations was the Egyptian Feminist Party founded by Fatma Nimat Rashid in 1944 – the first distinctly women's political party. Its platform supported social and economic reforms, and it was the first feminist group to advocate birth control and abortion. Duriyya Shafiq undertook more vigorous action when she founded *Bint al-Nil* (Daughter of the Nile) in 1948. She called for equal political rights for women, including female suffrage, and women's representation in parliament, and a woman's right to an identity outside the boundaries of home and marriage. She supported an agenda of social reform, emphasizing the importance of health and social services, literacy, and job creation for poor women.

Leftist feminists also emerged from the communist underground. Although the Egyptian communist movement was largely male in membership, women were involved in small numbers. Rejecting the social conservatism of the family and the conventions of society, they criticized women's

---

[28] Khater and Nelson, "Al-Haraka al-nissa'iyah," 468.

limited involvement in government, education, business, and professional life.

The end of liberalism in Egypt

The king dismissed the Wafd and al-Nahhas in October 1944, and Ahmad Mahir of the Sa'dist party formed a new government.[29] The Wafd boycotted the next set of elections held in January 1945 and the Sa'dists won a majority of parliamentary seats. Ahmad Mahir was assassinated in February 1945, after his government secured parliamentary approval for a declaration of war against the Axis powers. His successor, Mahmud Fahmi al-Nuqrashi, formally declared war on February 26, 1945;[30] until that time the country remained neutral.

Egypt participated in the post-war conference in San Francisco where the Great Powers prepared for the establishment of the United Nations. Egyptians hoped for a British declaration of complete Egyptian independence at the war's end, upheld by the United Nations, as a reward for the country's support for the Allies. But since the new British Labour government decided to move cautiously on the colonial front, British troops remained in the Canal Zone and Egypt was disappointed once again.

Throughout the liberal age it was the national question that provoked discontent in Egyptian society. But the painfully slow movement toward social and economic reform, the outrageous behavior of the king, and publication of the so-called *Black Book* implicating al-Nahhas and his wife in corruption were among the factors that brought the political center into disrepute.

Frequent demonstrations after the war reflected the sentiments of a people impatient with the continued British presence and disappointed by the lack of responsiveness of mainstream politicians. In particular, workers and students signaled their discontent when for three turbulent weeks between February 9 and March 4, 1946 they demonstrated, protested, and marched. While they did not constitute a disciplined political opposition, their protests attested to deep distress within the population, a distress expressed through the more radical social and political ideologies that had emerged during the Second World War.

The demonstrations and political chaos that ensued led to a crisis in the government. To quell impassioned nationalist activity and restrain the opposition, the king brought Isma'il Sidqi back as prime minister in February 1946. His government included independents and Liberals. By the following

[29] A very good account of this period is Tariq al-Bishri, *al-haraka al-siyasiyya fi misr, 1945–1952* (Cairo, 1972).
[30] Vatikiotis, *Modern Egypt*, 355–56.

summer, in accordance with the king's orders, Sidqi had arrested hundreds of journalists, intellectuals, political and labor leaders, students, and professionals on charges of seditious activity. He ordered dissolution of political, cultural, and labor organizations, and also closed down left-wing and Wafdist journals.

After silencing the opposition, Sidqi thought it an auspicious time to resume withdrawal negotiations with the British. To that end, he flew to London expecting to come to terms with the British foreign secretary, Ernest Bevin. After hard bargaining, the negotiators indeed drew up a new protocol: Britain would leave Egypt within three years, Egyptian sovereignty in the Sudan would be recognized, and the two states would conclude a mutual defense pact. But Egyptian and British opposition to provisions of the protocol prevented its implementation, and Sidqi was obliged to resign from office. A chapter in Anglo-Egyptian relations had ended; the British could never again find an Egyptian leader capable of resolving the two sides' differences over evacuation of Egypt and sovereignty in the Sudan.

Sidqi's departure led to al-Nuqrashi's return as prime minister in December 1946. Although he resumed the crusade to gain complete independence for Egypt by bringing the case before the Security Council of the United Nations in 1947, he was ultimately unsuccessful. Despite persistent Egyptian efforts to convince the international community of the principle of national sovereignty, the Security Council did not recognize Egyptian appeals and recommended only the resumption of negotiations with the British. Egyptian public opinion was convinced that the traditional political parties, however well intentioned, would not solve the national question.

In September 1947, one month after al-Nuqrashi returned from the Security Council, the United Nations recommended the partition of Palestine. In response, the Egyptian government pledged its support to the Palestinians to prevent the United Nations from realizing its plan. The Muslim Brotherhood encouraged mass demonstrations, whipped up anti-Jewish sentiment in the country, and began a campaign of political violence and assassinations. On December 8, 1948, al-Nuqrashi dissolved the Brotherhood, banned its activities, and confiscated its property. Less than three weeks later, he was assassinated by a member of the organization. On February 12, 1949, Hasan al-Banna', Supreme Guide of the Ikhwan, was murdered.

In order to stabilize the country and the government, the palace decided to form a coalition government led by the Independent Husayn Sirri in July 1949. Sirri held power until the next general election in January 1950 when the Wafd was returned to power and Mustafa al-Nahhas once again assumed the premiership.[31] This proved to be al-Nahhas's last term in office

---

[31] On this period see Joel Gordon, "The False Hopes of 1950: The Wafd's Last Hurrah

and the Wafd's final government during the liberal age. Eager to remain in power, the Wafd allowed political openness to return and responded to the pressure exerted from below by addressing some of the glaring inequities in Egyptian society. Al-Nahhas appointed the famed writer Taha Husayn as minister of education and elevated Ahmad Husayn to minister of health. Both these figures brought improvement to Egypt's indigent population: Taha Husayn abolished tuition payments in state secondary and technical institutions, and Ahmad Husayn designed a social insurance system for widows, orphans, the old, and the infirm. A sense of optimism reemerged and there was renewed hope for political recovery.

The pace of change encouraged many activists to renew anti-colonialist militancy. The university campuses came to life with political vibrancy, workers' strikes multiplied throughout the country, the peace movement rallied, and opposition forces began to rebuild their strength. Capping nineteen months of negotiations with the British on October 8, 1951, al-Nahhas declared the 1936 treaty and the 1899 Sudan Conventions null and void. By this action he unleashed the nationalist opposition that dominated the political scene for the next three months. The focus of nationalist activity was the Suez Canal Zone, the last physical vestige of the occupation. Organized loosely as a united front, communists, feminists, Muslim Brothers, Socialist Party adherents, and the left wing of the Wafd waged guerrilla war against the British. In addition, Egyptian workers and office employees walked out of their British-affiliated factories and agencies, and railway workers, customs officials, airline employees, and longshoremen refused to handle British supplies.

In January 1952, Egyptian commandos struck at Tall al-Kabir, the largest British garrison for materials and munitions in the Middle East. A violent battle ensued and there were casualties on both sides. Days later, when the British attacked the police station in the city of Isma'iliyya, more Egyptian lives were lost. When the news reached Cairo, demonstrations erupted, a general strike closed all factories in the country, and students from the universities and al-Azhar marched on the center of the city, joining forces with workers who had gathered from the suburbs. The crowds were incited to riot, and eventually Cairo was set ablaze.[32] Although no definitive evidence exists to this day, there is much speculation about who was responsible for the torching of Cairo.[33] There is strong suspicion that it was initially the work of members of the Socialist Party (formerly (*Misr al-Fatat*), and that the palace sent in agents to further weaken the Wafd's ability to

and the Demise of Egypt's Old Order," *International Journal of Middle East Studies* 21 (May 1989), 193–214.

[32] See Muhammad Anis, *Hariq al-qahira fi 26 yanayir 1952 ala dawi wathaiq tunshar li-awwal marra* (Cairo, 1982).

[33] For another view of the event see Marsot, *Modern Egypt*, 104–05.

govern;[34] crowds were also involved.[35] By all accounts, the old order was breaking down.

The political and social chaos that followed ultimately drove the Wafd from power. The king dismissed al-Nahhas on January 27; he was succeeded by 'Ali Mahir who formed an independent government which lasted until March 1952. His successor, Najib Hilali, survived only until the end of June. Husayn Sirri became prime minister on July 2; he was replaced by Najib Hilali again on July 22. Four cabinets succeeded one another, providing clear evidence that no individual or party could maintain control or address the twin issues of independence and reform. The old regime was at its end. When the Free Officers staged a bloodless coup d'état on July 23, 1952, they overthrew the king and dismantled the liberal state. The coup's leaders, all military men, abolished the monarchy, limited the power of the landlords, eventually brought independence to Egypt, and charted a new course in economic development and international alignment. Led by Jamal 'Abd al-Nasir, the Free Officers replaced the semi-liberal civil society with a closed and politically uniform system. Because the new regime secured national independence, achieved a measure of economic reform, and brought a sense of dignity and self-esteem to the country, most Egyptians were, at least initially, supportive.

With the consolidation of Nasir's rule came the end of liberal democracy in Egypt. The political diversity so characteristic of the 1920s, 1930s, and 1940s was crushed and the pluralism, as exemplified by the independent activism of the population, rejected.

Conclusion

In 1923 the Egyptian political elite created a political culture based on European parliamentarianism in the hope that the progress achieved in the west could similarly be attained in Egypt. The framers of this new era introduced the principles of constitutionalism, individual civil rights (for men), and democracy. But they did not adequately fit the system to the realities of Egyptian social and political life. As a result, the newly constituted democratic system faced major, and ultimately insuperable, challenges: constitutionalism was undermined by a European power that periodically interfered in the country's domestic policies, a monarchy that enjoyed disproportionate power, parliamentary leaders who deliberately compromised the democratic structure, and a system that denied women the rights and privileges inherent in liberalism.

Experimentation with liberalism in Egypt came at a time when the

[34] Goldschmidt, *Modern Egypt*, 88.
[35] See Berque, *Imperialism and Revolution*, 670–74, for one account of the crisis.

country was just beginning to develop a conscious working class active in
labor unions, able to articulate political demands and to insist upon
governmental accountability. Democratic practice was adopted when Egyptian entrepreneurs were still dominated by foreign and minority capitalists
and were only beginning to embark on their own struggle for economic
independence. Because Egypt lacked an influential and indeed broad-based
movement committed to defending constitutional concepts, democracy in
Egypt could be, and regularly was, subverted by absolutist political leaders
or by the anti-democratic tendencies of the monarchs and their clients.
Inevitably, liberal parliamentary government could not be sustained.

Many of liberalism's so-called practitioners were not committed to
allowing the system to become truly democratic. Even the Wafd, which
could have expanded its base, educated the population, and involved more
people in the political process, refrained from so doing. In consequence,
Egyptian liberal democracy developed in a fragmented and uneven manner,
with most political leaders jealous of their positions and uneasy about
potential popular activity.

That Egyptians from the non-elite sectors of society participated in the
political arena is in fact a testament to the will of the people to become
involved in politics. By voting in general elections or by associating with the
Muslim Brotherhood, Young Egypt, the communist movement, and
women's organizations, they made themselves part of Egypt's political
culture. In this way, Egyptians insisted that political experience not be
reserved only for the politically entrenched and powerful.

As liberalism began to lose its attractiveness during the 1930s and 1940s,
non-parliamentary forces argued more convincingly for nationalism, Islamic
fundamentalism, communism, and to a lesser extent fascism. By the end of
the Second World War, liberalism had failed to achieve political freedom,
civil rights, true independence, or economic development. The students,
workers, young professionals, and intellectuals who denounced the old
order through non-parliamentary organizations, strikes, street protests, and
the oppositional press demonstrated increasing political sophistication and
rising aspirations. While their movements were not successful and their
demands went largely unsatisfied, they managed to destablilize the government and create an environment where the basic tenets of liberalism were
called into question. Finally, on July 23, 1952, a small, secretive, politically
diverse military group carried out a coup d'état that put an end to liberal
democracy in Egypt.

13

Egypt: society and economy, 1923–1952

JOEL BEININ

⇥⇤

The constitution of 1923 consolidated a new legal and institutional frame-work for the Egyptian state. Yet this political moment is an inadequate marker of the economic and social developments inextricably bound up with it. Changes in a society and its political economy are best analyzed in terms of long-term historical and structural tendencies that cannot be dated with precision.

The years between the accession of Khedive ʿAbbas Hilmi (r. 1892–1914) and the election of the first Wafd government in 1924 in many ways delimit a single era. This conjuncture was formed by stabilization and subsequent frustration of British colonial rule; increased capital investment in agricul-ture, transport, commerce, and industry; and dramatic expansion, followed by sharp decline, in agricultural productivity. From this perspective, the popular reaction to the Dinshawai incident of June 1906 was not a spontaneous originary moment of nationalist mobilization, but a response to the developments that preceded it and informed its meaning. A reconfigured market; a reactivated political movement featuring a mélange of Egyptianist, Ottomanist, and Islamist discourses; new social groups; revised ideals of gender relations; and new forms of culture and politics elaborated and legitimized one another. After the First World War, the moral, economic, and political crisis of Anglo-French colonialism created an environment conducive to a new political order in Egypt.

The nationalist movement was an effect of urban middle strata educated in modern, western-style, schools – the *effendiyya* – and circles of large landholders simultaneously articulating and responding to collective anti-colonialist sentiment and action. This dynamic process reorganized the structural and discursive limits governing nearly every major question in Egypt until well after the military coup of July 23, 1952. During these years, foreigners and Egyptians formulated a new set of prospects and problems for Egypt. These were, in turn, continually modified by struggles over the terms for their resolution. The failure of the 1956 Suez war to reverse the nationalization of the Suez Canal; the massive expropriation of the assets of foreign nationals as well as permanently resident Greeks, Italians, Armenians, Syrian Christians, and Jews (the *mutamassirun*) after the war; and the emergence of a new political discourse of pan-Arab nationalism and, by 1961, of Arab socialism mark the end of the social formation consolidated in the 1892–1924 period.

A central element of the political economy of the 1892–1924 era was a multifaceted rural ecological crisis. After expanding rapidly in the 1890s, crop yields and cultivated areas reached a plateau, as agriculture attained the economic limits of the environment, deployed technology, and the social relations of production. Inadequate drainage of the irrigation system degraded the soil, cotton pests multiplied, and epidemic bilharzia afflicted the peasantry. Consequently, agricultural yields declined by about 15 percent from 1900 to 1920 and recovered only in 1930.[1]

The security of British colonial rule and the climate for capital investment were enhanced by the conquest of the Sudan in 1899 and the Entente Cordiale in 1904. Thus, when cotton prices collapsed during the international economic crisis of 1907, some businessmen concluded that a mono-crop cotton-export economy was no longer the most lucrative investment strategy. During the First World War, economic and social hardships swelled popular dissatisfaction with British rule and quickened the impulse to economic diversification. In 1918 the report of the government-appointed Commission on Commerce and Industry advanced a program of limited import-substitution industrialization financed by Egyptian and foreign capital, gradual Egyptianization of skilled labor and management, and a coordinated response to the first expressions of workers' collective action.[2] The entire business community embraced this strategy despite tactical differences about its implementation.

The establishment of Bank Misr, the Egyptian Federation of Industry (EFI), and the Agricultural Syndicate marked the emergence of an ethnically and nationally diverse Egyptian business class with interlocking interests in agriculture, commerce, and industry. Muhammad Tal'at Harb Pasha (1867–1941), a leading advocate of economic nationalism, had promoted establishing an Egyptian industrial bank since at least 1911.[3] In May 1920 he persuaded a group preponderantly composed of large cotton growers to establish Bank Misr – "an Egyptian bank for Egyptians only," with the

[1] Bent Hansen, *The Political Economy of Poverty, Equity, and Growth: Egypt and Turkey* (Oxford, 1991), 39, 104–05.
[2] Commission du Commerce et de l'Industrie, *Rapport* (Cairo, 1918); Robert Vitalis, *When Capitalists Collide: Business Conflict and the End of Empire in Egypt* (Berkeley, 1995), 43.
[3] Tal 'at Harb, *'Ilaj misr al-iqtisadi wa-mashru' bank al-misriyyin aw bank al-umma* (Cairo, 1911).

objective of financing industrial development.[4] In 1922 a group of resident European and *mutamassir* industrialists – Isaac G. Lévi, Henri Naus, Mikés Salvagos, and S. Sornaga – established the Association of Industries, later renamed the Egyptian Federation of Industry. Agrarian interests assumed an organizational form about the same time. In 1921 large cotton growers led by Yusuf Nahhas, angered by the fluctuation in cotton prices during 1920–21, established the General Egyptian Agricultural Syndicate. Egyptian growers attributed these price fluctuations to the machinations of foreign-dominated banking and export firms.

Two social groups participated in the early efforts to promote Egyptian industrialization: Muslim (and a few Coptic) land owners seeking to diversify their investments, and *mutamassirun*. The ideological pronouncements of Tal'at Harb's Misr group and the *mutamassirun* of the EFI differed, but their business activities were similar. Both groups collaborated and overlapped with large landholders. The structural pressures of the market and the requirements of capital reproduction proved more compelling in the business world than political commitments, no matter how deeply felt. Yet most businessmen whose field of activity was primarily Egypt (as opposed to multinational firms such as the Suez Canal Company and the Shell Oil Company) framed their economic projects as beneficial to the national interest, even if they eschewed the discourse of nationalism.

After the Dinshawai incident, the newly organized political parties recruited a popular constituency for nationalist politics, confirming the legitimacy of mass urban political action. The intersection of Khedive 'Abbas Hilmi's personal ambitions, the growing realization that British rule was not to be a brief venture, increased foreign investment, rapid economic development, the growth of the urban *effendiyya*, and the increased production and consumption of newspapers, novels, and printed colloquial poetry articulated the existence of an Egyptian nation and its collective demands.[5]

By the end of the nineteenth century, urban working people began to pose demands and engage in collective actions with social and political content. The nationalist *effendiyya* embraced this activity, transforming those formerly regarded by the educated and powerful as an uncivilized rabble into noble citizens of the Egyptian nation.[6] Trade union leaders and their political supporters adopted this understanding, which offered an interpretation of the social relations of production that provided political legitimacy and social allies for the industrial struggles of urban wage-workers. The

---

[4] Tal 'at Harb, "An Egyptian Bank for Egyptians Only," in Anouar Abdel-Malek (ed.) *Contemporary Arab Political Thought* (London, 1983), 55–57.

[5] On colloquial poetry see Joel Beinin, "Writing Class: Workers and Modern Egyptian Colloquial Poetry (*Zajal*)," *Poetics Today* 15/2 (Summer 1994), 191–215.

[6] Zachary Lockman, "Imagining the Working Class: Culture, Nationalism and Class Formation in Egypt, 1899–1914," *Poetics Today* 15/2 (Summer 1994), 157–90.

outlook of the incipient trade union movement was indelibly shaped by the fact that its most active sectors were employed in new, large-scale enterprises owned and managed by foreigners or *mutamassirun*.

The Cairo Tramway Company workers – employees of a concessionary monopoly established in 1894 by the Belgian financier Baron Edouard Empain – exemplified this condition. They struck in 1908 and 1911. Prominent among their grievances was the claim that foreign inspectors and managers abused Egyptian workers. *Al-Liwa'*, the newspaper of the National Party, actively supported the tramway workers' strikes and other workers' collective actions. Organizing urban craftspeople and wage workers became an element of the National Party's strategy, and the reciprocal relations between the nationalist movement and the labor movement became a defining feature of Egyptian trade unionism. Workers and their unions were prominent activists in the popular uprising that followed the arrest and deportation of Sa'd Zaghlul Pasha and his Wafd colleagues in March 1919. Although the Wafd initially had no contacts with trade unions, some of its leaders soon came to regard them as an important component of the party's urban social base.

Women, too, demanded recognition as citizens with public rights. The first women's newspaper in Egypt, *al-Fatah* (The Young Woman) was established by Hind Nawfal in 1892. The women's press of the 1890s posed questions about women's status in the new modern Egypt while training a cohort of activists to articulate these concerns.[7] Thus Qasim Amin's *The Liberation of Women*, published in 1899, was not an original statement. His text reveals the strong influence of colonialist cultural stereotypes about Muslims and urban, elite prejudices against peasants and the urban lower classes.[8] Nonetheless, *The Liberation of Women* gained recognition as the first call for women's emancipation and became the hub of a lively public debate, perhaps because Amin represented a current among the men of the landed gentry and urban upper middle class who were anxious to cultivate proper bourgeois housewives. Elite men and women began to encourage the "women's awakening" – education of women and their entry into white-collar professions (at least until marriage or after widowhood), and the formation of women's social and political organizations – as expressions of a national revival.[9]

Internationally, the Egyptian insurgency of March 1919, followed a month later by the Amritsar massacre and its aftermath in India, challenged

---

[7] See Beth Baron, *The Women's Awakening in Egypt: Culture, Society, and the Press* (New Haven, 1994).

[8] Leila Ahmed, *Women and Gender in Islam: Historical Roots of a Modern Debate* (New Haven, 1992), 144–68.

[9] Juan R. I. Cole, "Feminism, Class and Islam in Turn-of-the-Century Egypt," *International Journal of Middle East Studies*, 13 (1981), 387–407.

the stability of the British empire. Both Woodrow Wilson's Fourteen Points and the foreign policy of the Russian Bolshevik regime endorsed the right of nations to self-determination. Increasing international acceptance of this principle during the following decades contributed to the undermining of the ideology and practice of colonial empire.

The population question

According to census returns, Egypt's population increased from 9.7 million in 1897 to 19 million in 1947, an annual average rate of growth of about 1.4 percent. But technological capacity to utilize the waters of the Nile has historically limited the extent of cultivated land. So despite two extensions of the first Aswan dam (constructed in 1902) and considerable expansion of perennial irrigation, by 1914 the rural population began to increase faster than the cropped area.[10] Indeed, for most of the twentieth century agricultural production lagged behind population growth, and per capita output of major field crops declined by some 40 percent.[11]

There has been a broad consensus throughout the twentieth century that Egypt was overpopulated in relation to its arable land.[12] This neo-Malthusian understanding has tended to direct attention toward the apparently scientific and apolitical question of numbers. Its conservative assumptions about the social, economic, and political arrangements have, it is possible to imagine, been largely unexamined.[13]

Population pressure on agricultural land induced steady migration from the countryside to the cities. The combined population of Cairo and Alexandria, 1.24 million in 1917, rose to over 3 million by 1947 – growth over three times more rapid than that of the overall population. Only a small fraction of new urban dwellers found work in manufacturing.

Social construction of a national political field[14]

The institution of a modern national state – whether the indigenous, autocratic, Europeanizing project of Khedive Isma'il, British colonial rule, or

[10] Robert L. Tignor, *State, Private Enterprise, and Economic Change in Egypt, 1918–1952* (Princeton, 1984), 16.

[11] Roger Owen, "Large Landowners, Agricultural Progress and the State in Egypt, 1800–1970: An Overview with Many Questions," in Alan Richards (ed.), *Food, States, and Peasants: Analyses of the Agrarian Question in the Middle East* (Boulder, 1986), 91.

[12] An early and influential expression of this view is Wendell Cleland, *The Population Problem in Egypt: A Study of Population Trends and Conditions in Modern Egypt* (Lancaster, PA, 1936).

[13] Timothy Mitchell, "America's Egypt: Discourse of the Development Industry," *Middle East Report*, 169 (March/April 1991), 18–34.

[14] The term is Sami Zubaida's. See *Islam, the People, and the State: Essays on Political Ideas and Movements in the Middle East* (London, 1989), 155.

the hybrid model of the constitutional monarchy – entailed creation of new political subjects – citizens – and new political entitlements – rights. Western-style education concurrently expanded the ranks of the *effendiyya* and provided a vocabulary for imagining Egypt as a political space comparable to European nation states. Thus empowered, the *effendiyya* presented themselves as bearers of a national mission and sought to forge new relations with both foreigners and lower-class Egyptians.

Political journalism became a prominent feature of the post-Dinshawai era. While transmitting the vocabulary of the modern social and physical sciences and reforming the Arabic language, the press provided business opportunities for Syrian Christian emigré intellectuals and their local rivals. Important elements of the *effendiyya* embraced this genre as a medium of expression, acquiring at the same time an audience and a conceptual framework.

Consequently, well before 1923 a nationalist discourse elaborating concern about the negative effects of foreign capital, the need for industrial development, the authentic Egyptianness of workers and peasants, the proper behavior and status of enlightened women, and the desire to end the British military occupation and achieve national independence was a prominent feature of the public culture of the *effendiyya*. Nationalist ideologues embraced different strategies for realizing the program implicit in these themes. But the structural limits they faced and the struggles over the "true" meaning of these concepts defined the era of the constitutional monarchy.

The participation of women in street demonstrations during the 1919 nationalist uprising irrevocably endowed the women's awakening with nationalist legitimacy. In 1923 Huda Sha'rawi (1879–1947) was elected president of the Wafdist Women's Central Committee and also became the founding president of the Egyptian Feminist Union (EFU). Sha'rawi embodied the complementary social and political relations of the two movements.[15] In May 1923 she and Saiza Nabarawi (1897–1985) removed their face veils (*niqab*) at the Cairo railway station upon returning from a meeting of the International Alliance of Women in Rome. This highly self-conscious gesture has become reified as the emblem of Egyptian feminism. However, the identities of those who undertook and embraced it delineate the class and cultural orientation and contingent character of the movement. Most of the eleven charter members of the EFU were from wealthy, landed families living in Cairo; it was primarily the Francophone wives and daughters of the

---

[15] Translating *nisa'iyya* as "feminist" is problematic. A case could be made for designating Huda Sha'rawi's organization as the Egyptian Women's Union. See Baron, *Women's Awakening*, 6–7.

elite who first became interested in becoming citizens with rights, although others later joined them. The EFU journal, *L'Egyptienne*, edited by Saiza Nabarawi, did not appear in Arabic until 1937.

The three Egyptian delegates to the International Alliance of Women were single women without living fathers or husbands. Huda Sha'rawi – the daughter of Muhammad Sultan Pasha, one of the wealthiest land owners in Egypt, and the wife of 'Ali Sha'rawi, a large land owner, a major investor in Bank Misr, and a leader of the Wafd – was independently wealthy and a founding investor in Bank Misr in her own right. Only after the death of her husband in 1922 did she unveil publicly, though she had considered this step for several years. Saiza Nabarawi, her younger comrade in this action, had been raised in Paris. Her father had died in 1922. Nabawiyya Musa (1886–1951), the first Egyptian women to obtain a secondary education certificate, had neither a father nor a husband when she first removed her *niqab* around 1909 when she was serving as principal of the girls' school in Fayyum, where face-veiling was uncommon. Musa remained in Alexandria after returning from Rome with Sha'rawi and Nabarawi, and did not participate in their demonstration. She was from a more modest, middle-class background, and her consistent stand against making an issue of veiling suggests that she might not have been comfortable with their intentionally provocative action.[16]

Sa'd Zaghlul's wife, Safiyya, had removed her *niqab* in London in 1921, but continued to wear it in Egypt. In the summer of 1923 she wished to disembark bare-faced from a boat carrying her and Huda Sha'rawi to Egypt. Her wish was vetoed by male leaders of the Wafd as too provocative for the wife of the national leader.

These details indicate both the combination of personal initiative, class privilege, European culture, and nationalist politics that enabled elite, urban women to appear in public with their faces uncovered and the restraints on this practice. Public sanction for what had by then become the prevailing style came only in 1927, when the Fatwa Committee of al-Azhar ruled that the Hanafi and Maliki schools of Islamic jurisprudence did not require women to cover their faces.[17]

After the death of her husband, Huda Sha'rawi continued to exercise her considerable political skills. In 1924 she publicly demanded that Sa'd Zaghlul resign after his government accepted parts of the British ultimatum that followed the assassination of the governor-general of the Sudan, Sir Lee Stack. Several times Sha'rawi adopted more militant nationalist positions than the Wafd under Mustafa al-Nahhas Pasha, whom she disliked. She was

[16] Margot Badran, *Feminists, Islam, and Nation: Gender and the Making of Modern Egypt* (Princeton, 1995), 38–45, 92–93, 98–99.
[17] *Ibid.*, 93.

a pioneer of pan-Arab political action among the Egyptian elite. In response to an appeal from Palestinian women, the EFU initiated an Arab women's conference on the Palestine question in 1938, and in 1944 Sha'rawi became president of the Arab Women's Union.

By then, the Egyptian women's movement had grown beyond the limits of its original class and political base. Nonetheless, under and long after the monarchy the activities and vision of the leading current in the movement were contained within a discourse about public rights, citizenship, and economic development. Participation of women in the public sphere altered its configuration. New concepts of family life and gender-role models appealed especially to sectors of the educated, urban middle strata, whose daughters began to attend secondary school in 1925 and university in 1929 thanks to successful campaigning by the EFU. The material and social status of these women, who were enabled to pursue professional careers, improved markedly.

In the private sphere, however, gender relations changed more slowly and unevenly. The EFU was unable to achieve legal reform in the areas of divorce and polygamy. Upper- and upper-middle-class families adopted bourgeois forms of sociability that required women to be literate and conversant about topics of the day, appear at receptions and parties, and dress fashionably. *Mutamassir* families were typically more adventurous than Muslims and Copts in this regard. But class culture was usually a more significant determinant of social mores than religious affiliation or ethnic identity. Many elite and middle-class families came to regard social behavior patterned on what they imagined to be the European model as a requisite of a modern, nationalist Egypt.

The formation of a national political field bestowed on women, peasants, and urban working people the status of citizens with nominal rights. But the substantive content of those rights rarely included active political participation or the exercise of power in the institutions of the newly reconstituted national state. The (predominantly male) *effendiyya* served as the publicists and activists of all the contending political currents; and the business elite – primarily large land owners and, secondarily, industrial, financial, and commercial entrepreneurs – dominated the leadership of all the major political parties. The interests of the political class were not unified. Yet, despite personal and sectoral rivalries, all sectors of the business elite shared an interest in preserving the existing social order and minimizing the social power of peasants and working people. This was most unequivocally expressed by the inability of any government of the era to legislate land reform or an industrial minimum wage.

The common dependency-theory and nationalist interpretations of the social base of politics under the monarchy as a struggle between "feudal" agrarian elements and "progressive" industrial elements, or between "comprador" and "national" capital, cannot be sustained.[18] Although the Wafd had the broadest popular appeal and adopted the most consistently populist rhetoric, the social bases of the various parties were not sharply differentiated. Characterizing the Wafd and the Liberal Constitutionalists as representatives of agrarian interests and the Saʿdists as spokespersons for industry is misleading because important individuals and salient political moments do not fit this scheme. These political parties were shaped as much by relations of kinship, clientage, and *shilla* (clique), regional interests, and personal rivalries as by public proclamations of ideology and program. Landed elements were the preponderant force in both the Wafd and its major rivals, and landlords and industrialists were often the same people or members of the same family. Only a few foreign or *mutamassir* businessmen had no agricultural interests. Sectoral diversification was a common investment strategy.

The preponderant power of landed wealth was amplified by the lack of any organized social or political movement of the peasantry. The Socialist Peasant Party, established in 1938, had no significant following.[19] The Wafd had strong rural electoral support, but never felt obliged to take the side of peasants against their ʿumdas, landlords, or local notables, the backbone of its rural base.

Only months after the formation of the first Wafd government in 1924, ʿAbd al-Rahman Fahmi Pasha, one of Zaghlul's lieutenants, became president of the General Union of Workers. This was the first of many attempts by the Wafd to exercise tutelage over the labor movement by sponsoring a national trade union federation. Wafd patronage of unions was common and especially strong when the party was in power during 1942–44. But it was often contested by non-Wafd effendis and workers.

Muhammad Kamil Husayn, a lawyer identified with the Nationalist Party, emerged as a leader of the Cairo Tramway Workers' Union during the high tide of the nationalist uprising in August 1919. In February 1924, misjudging the popularity of the newly installed Wafd government and the mood of public confidence and optimism it inspired, Husayn and several tramway workers attempted to foment a strike. They were arrested for violating public order and insulting the prime minister. Saʿd Zaghlul was unwilling to countenance anything that might discredit the Wafd government or his claim to lead the nation.[20]

[18] Tignor, *State, Private Enterprise, and Economic Change*; Vitalis, *When Capitalists Collide*.

[19] Nathan J. Brown, *Peasant Politics in Modern Egypt: The Struggle against the State* (New Haven, 1990), 160–61.

[20] Joel Beinin and Zachary Lockman, *Workers on the Nile: Nationalism, Communism, Islam and the Egyptian Working Class, 1882–1954* (Princeton, 1987), 110, 113–15, 128–35.

The Wafd similarly smashed the Communist Party of Egypt when its supporters miscalculated their strength. The communist-led Confédération Générale du Travail, formed in 1921, had become the leading force among the trade unions of Alexandria, particularly those with large contingents of foreigners and *mutamassirun*, as its French name suggests. In February–March 1924 the confederation led a series of strikes and sit-ins in Alexandria. The Wafd took the occasion to crush the communists' organization and their influence in the labor movement, just as they destroyed Muhammad Kamil Husayn and his supporters in the Cairo Tramway Workers' Union.

The formation of a national political field thus both enabled and constrained the political expression of hitherto marginalized social groups. Nationalist discourse acknowledged subaltern groups as components of the nation, though only as functionally differentiated subordinate parts of an organic whole. But it limited their political participation to domains and issues authorized by the leaders of the nationalist movement. There was a constant contest over these boundaries and the "true" understanding of the national interest.

In the late 1930s the image of the nation formulated by the previous two generations was sharply disputed by populist political and social visions that gave priority to Egypt's Arab-Islamic cultural heritage. Struggles over criteria of inclusion and exclusion, inherent in the constitution of nationalist politics, became acute. Young Egypt and, more importantly, the Society of the Muslim Brothers came to represent those sections of the *effendiyya* who were economically and culturally alienated from the project of a secular, liberal, European-style society. The Muslim Brothers' message had a particular appeal among members of pious families, migrants from provincial towns to Cairo and Alexandria, and those employed by large foreign firms where they suffered from wage discrimination and cultural exclusion.

Colonial capitalism

Under the monarchy, the cultivation and export of cotton remained the largest sector of the economy despite substantial industrial growth, especially in textile spinning and weaving, during the 1930s and 1940s. Large land owners dominated society and politics, comprising 43 percent of parliamentary deputies and 58 percent of cabinet members between 1923 and 1952.[21] Shipping, railways, and urban services in the Europeanized parts of Cairo and Alexandria were developed to market cotton and other crops and to provide an acceptable standard of living for Europeans and their agents. Especially in the early part of the period, the dominant fraction

---

[21] 'Asim al-Disuqi, *Kibar mullak al-aradi al-zira'iyya wa-dawruhum fi al-mujtama' al-misri, 1914–1952* (Cairo, 1975), 212, 220.

of capital was controlled by foreigners residing in Europe (the Suez Canal Company, the National Bank of Egypt, Shell Oil Company), foreigners residing primarily in Egypt (Baron Edouard Empain, Henri Naus), and *mutamassirun* holding either foreign or Egyptian citizenship.

The stability of the social order of the monarchy, including the privileged status of foreigners and *mutamassirun*, ultimately depended on the British military occupation. Soldiers were garrisoned in downtown Cairo until 1947, and the British base in the Suez Canal Zone quartered as many as 100,000 troops in the late 1940s – far more than the maximum stipulated in the 1936 Anglo-Egyptian treaty. The Anglo-French–Israeli invasion of October 1956 manifested, among other things, British ambivalence about abandoning an imperial role in Egypt.

This social formation can be characterized as "colonial capitalism" – a formulation that privileges the categories of political economy, social class, and the state and is informed by a particular current within the modern European tradition of social theory.[22] Egypt's modern trajectory is similar enough to that of other localities with which it shares few cultural similarities to justify an analytical approach that does not focus on its cultural specificity. Moreover, the usual alternatives – "feudal," "semi-feudal," "traditional," and "pre-modern" – are too vague, Eurocentric, or teleological to be useful. They suggest a lack of social dynamism or an ontological otherness dividing Egypt from a modern, progressive Europe.

"Colonial capitalism" encompasses both British colonial rule and Egypt's subordinate integration into the world capitalist market, while linking many salient features of the social order. The economy was characterized by private ownership of the means of production, production of commodities for a market, commodification of labor, rational calculation of profits, a tendency toward capital accumulation, and the emergence of bureaucratically administered, large-scale agricultural, industrial, and commercial enterprises. However, family production units and urban crafts did not persist simply as vestiges of a "pre-capitalist" economy or markers of difference between "true" European capitalism and a weak colonial variant. Their activities were reorganized and redefined to provide critical linkages integrating the modern economy.[23] "Colonial capitalism" also suggests a radically stratified society, an extroverted economy, and a state with limited

---

[22] Anouar Abdel-Malek, *Idéologie et renaissance nationale* (Paris, 1969), 112; Roger Own, "The Development of Agricultural Production in Nineteenth Century Egypt: Capitalism of What Type?" in A. L. Udovitch (ed.), *The Islamic Middle East, 700–1900: Studies in Economic and Social History* (Princeton, 1981), 521–46.

[23] Judith E. Tucker, *Women in Nineteenth Century Egypt* (Cambridge, 1985); Kristin Koptiuch, "Other Workers: A Critical Reading of Representations of Egyptian Petty Commodity Production at the Turn of the Twentieth Century," in Zachary Lockman (ed.), *Workers and Working Classes in the Middle East: Struggles, Histories, Historiographies* (Albany, 1994), 41–70.

capacity to regulate markets and social relations. Nominally independent Egypt was legally constrained by lack of tariff independence until 1930, the Capitulations until 1937, and the mixed courts until 1949. The infamous four "Reserved Points" of the 1922 British unilateral declaration of independence imposed additional constraints on state capacity. Finally, "colonial capitalism" indicates the complex of political and social issues that engaged political elites and popular social movements from the mid-1930s until the fall of the monarchy.

Colonial capitalism was not a static social formation. Technological developments in agriculture and urban migration altered crop patterns, market relations, and the social character of village communities. The depression of the 1930s stimulated consolidation of a new economic vision and increased opportunities for import-substitution industrialization. The depression also impelled British imperial proconsuls, bureaucrats, and business managers to negotiate new political and economic arrangements with politicians and businessmen in the colonies or the formally independent semi-colonies, such as Egypt. The abolition of the Capitulations encouraged Egyptian business elites to aspire to a larger share of power relative to foreign capital. Their intimate ties to the newly reorganized state facilitated, to a considerable degree, realization of these aspirations. By the 1940s a clear tendency toward Egyptianization of capital and the skilled labor force was evident. Nonetheless, with the exception of the cotton manufacturing and export sectors, Muslims and Copts were significantly underrepresented at the commanding heights of the economy, especially its financial sector.

As modern transport and industry expanded the ranks of urban wage laborers, the Wafd and its rivals regarded trade unions as an important base for mobilizing a concentrated urban constituency. Workers, Wafdist effendis, and the idiosyncratic Prince 'Abbas Halim – sometime ally and sometime rival of the Wafd – engaged in a complex tug-of-war in which each side attempted to use the others to establish its legitimacy and achieve its own ends. In the process, the trade union movement became a permanent fixture of urban life; the "labor question" was inscribed on the public political agenda; and the existence of a social collectivity commonly identified as workers or the working class was affirmed.

In 1937–38, Muhammad Yusuf al-Mudarrik and trade union leaders associated with the Commission to Organize the Workers' Movement began to advocate a trade union movement independent of the political parties. This marked the beginning of a radicalization of a sector of the working class geographically centered on Cairo's industrial suburb of Shubra al-Khayma and concentrated in the textile industry. Although small in number, they and their allies, mainly supporters of the various Marxist circles that reorganized in the late 1930s, imparted a radical social content to the nationalist movement after the Second World War.

Stagnation and crisis in agriculture

Agriculture comprised about two-thirds of the gross domestic product under the monarchy. Its poor performance for much of the period was a major constraint on economic development. The protracted agrarian crisis had three elements: technological challenges such as poor drainage, soil depletion, and cotton pests; the collapse of international market prices during the depression of the 1930s and the 1951–52 recession; and social oppression – the poverty, illiteracy, and disease of the peasantry and the increasingly unequal distribution of agricultural land.

The cultivated area stabilized at 5.5–5.8 million faddans from 1900 to 1940 and then expanded about 10 percent from 1940 to 1959.[24] Extensive government investment in irrigation and drainage in the 1930s raised crop yields above the 1900 level for the first time. Shortages of fertilizer and other inputs lowered agricultural productivity again during the Second World War, and crop yields did not recover until after the 1952 military coup.

The cotton crop lost about two-thirds of its nominal value in 1931–33 compared to the late 1920s.[25] As a consequence of the depression, the total value of agricultural production declined 32 percent; agricultural wages declined 40 percent; and rents declined 35 percent from 1928 t9 1938.[26] Heavily indebted land owners could not pay mortgages and taxes. Landless peasants migrated to the cities hoping to find work in new enterprises established after the Tariff Reform Act of 1930.

From the beginning of the twentieth century until the 1952 land reform, the royal family perched at the peak of a privileged, agrarian elite of about two thousand large estate-holders. This elite and a second stratum of agrarian notables comprised some 12,000 families holding fifty faddans or more, equivalent to about 40 percent of the cultivated land. During the same period, the number of smallholders of five faddans or less increased from 760,000 to 2.64 million, while the area of their holdings only doubled. The average size of a small peasant-holding declined from 1.46 faddans to 0.8 faddans between 1900 and 1952, while the landless rural population increased.[27] The poor rural majority lived in appalling poverty, disease, squalor, and illiteracy. Nonetheless, concentration of land ownership and absentee management of farms were not necessarily economically inefficient, as some Egyptian social reformers claimed.[28] They may even have facilitated capital accumulation.

Investment in manufacturing did not increase dramatically until after the

---

[24] Hansen, *Political Economy*, 91.
[25] *Ibid.*, 94.
[26] *Ibid.*, 75.
[27] Owen, "Large Landowners," 69–71, 92.
[28] *Ibid.*, 75–78.

expiration of the Capitulations in 1937, and manufacturing employment actually declined from 1927 to 1937.[29] Industrial development did not rapidly expand employment opportunities or dramatically increase the national income. Hence, reformers of the late 1930s turned their attention to rural economic and social conditions.

By 1939 over 90 percent of rural families were landless or owned less than three faddans, the minimum required to support a household of four.[30] Many peasants lived as sharecroppers on estates (*'izbas*) where, in exchange for cultivating the landlords' cotton and other cash crops, they were permitted to grow food. Official statistics document the pauperization of the rural majority and the social structure of rural life. But illiterate and politically marginalized peasants can leave few records documenting their experience or consciousness. Peasants are often subjected to considerable violence, and the culture of fear regulating their lives further distorts the validity of whatever historical evidence may exist.[31] Landlords and state officials often portray peasants as unchanging, irrational, ignorant, and criminal. In the absence of direct contradictory testimony from peasants themselves, literary works may offer the best representation of rural life from a perspective sympathetic to the peasantry. 'Abd al-Rahman al-Sharqawi's 1954 novel *Egyptian Earth* (*al-Ard*), set in the early 1930s, graphically portrays the rural notables' domination of the peasantry in a struggle over water rights. This text became a cultural icon of the Nasirist regime, as it determined to break the social and political power of landed wealth.

In 1935, as part of its campaign to organize mass support to restore a democratically elected Wafdist government, the Wafd formulated an agrarian program. 'A'isha 'Abd al-Rahman, the first woman from a peasant background to attend Cairo University, worked with the Wafd on rural questions for a time and wrote two books bitterly protesting about the misery of the peasants.[32] In 1938 Mirrit Ghali and Dr. Hafiz 'Afifi, representing the views of "enlightened" land owners and industrialists respectively, published widely acclaimed calls for social reform.[33] All these manifestos ignored or opposed the redistribution of agricultural land. By the middle of the Second World War, however, rapid population growth and urbanization, limited expansion of the cultivated area, high rates of unem-

[29] Hansen, *Political Economy*, 116.
[30] Brown, *Peasant Politics*, 30–31.
[31] Timothy Mitchell, "The Representation of Rural Violence in Writings on Political Developments in Nasserist Egypt," in Farhad Kazemi and John Waterbury (eds.) *Peasants and Politics in the Modern Middle East* (Miami, 1991), 222–51.
[32] Bint al-Shati' ('A'isha 'Abd al-Rahman), *al-Rif al-misri* (Cairo, 1936); Bint al-Shati', *Qadiyyat al-fallah* (Cairo, [1938 or later]).
[33] Mirrit Ghali, *Siyasat al-ghad* (Cairo, 1938); Hafiz 'Afifi, *'Ala hamish al-siyasa* (Cairo, 1938).

ployment, disruption of the urban food supply, and perhaps a degree of social and moral embarrassment forced land redistribution onto the public agenda.

In 1944 Muhammad Khattab, a Sa'dist Party senator, launched the first political initiative for land reform: a private bill limiting new purchases of land to fifty faddans in one lot. His proposal was so vehemently attacked that the Sa'dist leader, Mahmud Fahmi al-Nuqrashi Pasha, expelled him from the party.[34] In 1945 Mirrit Ghali altered his stand and appealed for agrarian reform as a means to direct resources from agriculture to manufacturing and commerce, deepen the domestic market, and ensure "economic independence and social dignity."[35] Ahmad Sadiq Sa'd, a leader of the New Dawn communist group, advocated agrarian reform from a Marxist perspective.[36]

The large landholders' predominance in the political system prevented any of these proposals from receiving serious consideration by any party in parliament except the Socialists (formerly Young Egypt). The Wafd's own minister of social affairs in the cabinet of 1950–52, Dr. Ahmad Husayn, reported "unmistakable signs of revolution" after a trip to the countryside.[37] But the leading tendency in the party, represented by the minister of the interior, Fu'ad Siraj al-Din Pasha, one of the largest land owners in Egypt, would not discuss land redistribution. Industrial firms and the urban economy more generally might have benefited from land reform. But most elite families with manufacturing and commercial interests were themselves economically and socially intertwined with landed privilege and were unwilling to advocate measures challenging the sanctity of private property.

Industrialization and its discontents

Who promoted industrial development in Egypt, and why? What were the relations among the industrialists, the Egyptian nationalist movement, and its leading organized expression, the Wafd? Who benefited from industrialization? To what extent did it succeed? These controversial questions may be addressed by tracing the personal, business, and political relations among the businessmen who were members of the Commission on Commerce and Industry appointed by the government in 1916 – Isma'il Sidqi, Yusuf 'Aslan Qattawi, Henri Naus, Tal'at Harb, Amin Yahya, and M. F. Bourgeois. These pioneers of Egyptian industrialization represent the constituent ele-

---

34 Owen, "Large Landowners," 80; Tariq al-Bishri, *al-Harka al-siyasiyya fi misr, 1945–1952* (Cairo, 1972), 195.
35 Mirrit Ghali, *al-Islah al-zira'i: al-milkiyya, al-ijar, al-'amal* (Cairo, 1945), quotation from p. 9.
36 Sadiq Sa'd, *Mushkilat al-fallah* (Cairo, 1945).
37 Quoted in Brown, *Peasant Politics*, 108.

ments of capital under the monarchy: economic nationalists associated with Bank Misr, resident foreigners and *mutamassir* minorities associated with the EFI, Muslim Egyptians seeking alliances with foreign capital, and foreign holding companies. Three other commission members – two British citizens employed by the Egyptian government, and the French commercial attaché – provided international technical and political supervision, an expression of the subordinate status of the Egyptian state and economy.[38]

The chairman of the commission was Isma'il Sidqi Pasha (1875–1950), an advocate of balanced development of agriculture and industry and of cooperation among the indigenous Egyptian business class, resident foreigners, and foreign capital. An early supporter of the Wafd, he was arrested and deported to Malta with Sa'd Zaghlul in March 1919. At the Paris peace conference that spring he split with Zaghlul. In 1921 he joined the anti-Wafdist government of 'Adli Yakan as minister of finance.[39] As prime minister in 1930–33 and again in 1946–47, his rule was autocratic and criticized as anti-nationalist by the Wafd and its supporters. Sidqi was the most prominent Muslim Egyptian identified with the EFI. The protectionist import duties his government enacted after 1930 were supported by a broad coalition of industrial interests. In addition to their importance as a revenue-generating measure, tariffs were critical to the viability of local industry, especially textiles, the largest modern industrial sector by the end of the decade. Only a minority of politically aware trade unionists and their supporters, concerned about equity for the urban poor, opposed the tariff reforms.[40] Sidqi also appointed several prominent industrialists as members of the senate, including Ahmad 'Abbud, Tal'at Harb, and Yusuf 'Aslan Qattawi. Their designation signaled Sidqi's commitment to industry and acknowledged the interlocking economic interests of rival political camps. But whenever Sidqi had to choose between conflicting urban and agrarian interests – over tariff rates on cotton and flour and creation of a local sugar monopoly – he, like every other prime minister under the monarchy, favored the large land owners.[41]

The Belgian sugar expert Henri Naus was managing director of the Sugar Company (La Société Générale des Sucreries et de la Raffinerie d'Egypte) – the largest industrial enterprise in Egypt until the late 1920s. Established in the 1880s by the Jewish Suarès family on the ruins of the state-owned sugar industry, the Sugar Company was reorganized with an infusion of French capital in 1897. A German-English financier with other investments in Egypt, Sir Ernest Cassel, rescued the firm from bankruptcy in 1905. Cassel employed Naus and Sir Victor Harari, a Jew of Lebanese ancestry holding

[38] Vitalis, *When Capitalists Collide*, 42–43.
[39] Isma'il Sidqi, *Mudhakkirati* (Cairo, 1950), 21–22.
[40] Hansen, *Political Economy*, 87–88.
[41] Owen, "Large Landowners," 73–74.

British citizenship who had been a high official in the ministry of finance, to manage his investment.

Yusuf 'Aslan Qattawi Pasha (1861–1942) belonged to a family claiming residence in Egypt since the Fatimids and with close connections to the house of Muhammad 'Ali. His grandfather, Ya'qub Qattawi, had directed the state mint under 'Abbas Pasha (r. 1854–63). The Qattawis operated a family bank and collaborated with the Suarèses in several enterprises including the Sugar Company and the Kom Ombo Company (La Société Anonyme de Wadi Kom Ombo) which developed and cultivated some 70,000 faddans of sugar and other crops in Aswan province. The Kom Ombo Company took over the Sugar Company in 1905 in collaboration with Cassel and became the lynchpin of the Qattawis' extensive business interests and political influence. The Qattawis considered themselves patriotic Egyptians of Jewish faith, though they were not Wafdists. Yusuf 'Aslan was president of the Cairo Jewish community from 1924 to 1942. He and his two sons were vocal anti-Zionists.[42]

Tal'at Harb, already a leading publicist for economic nationalism when he joined the Commission on Commerce and Industry, began his career in business as an employee of the Suarèses and Qattawis in the Kom Ombo Company and freely acknowledged his debt to them. On the basis of their longstanding and fruitful relations, Harb asked Yusuf 'Aslan Qattawi to serve as vice-chairman of the board of Bank Misr in 1920. Harb served as managing director of Bank Misr until 1939, when he was ousted after a run on the bank. By then, the Misr group comprised twenty-seven industrial, commercial, and financial firms.[43] Of Misr's industrial ventures only the textile firms were consistently profitable. The emblem of Bank Misr's industrial development project, the Misr Spinning and Weaving Company founded in Mahalla al-Kubra in 1927, became the largest industrial enterprise in the Middle East by the end of the Second World War.

Tal'at Harb staged his business career as a nationalist drama, portraying himself as the promoter of national economic development.[44] He touted Bank Misr as a "genuinely Egyptian bank," and Egyptian citizenship was a condition of membership on its board of directors. Misr enterprises generally employed more Muslims in the ranks of skilled labor and management than other firms. Hence, Harb's claim that Bank Misr was an Egyptian national institution was widely accepted.

Amin Yahya Pasha became a major competitor of the Misr group. He and later his son, 'Ali, controlled firms engaged in exporting produce, cotton pressing, insurance, and shipping. The Yahyas also undertook several joint

[42] Gudrun Kramer, *The Jews of Modern Egypt, 1914–1952* (Seattle, 1989), 40–42, 88–90.
[43] Eric Davis, *Challenging Colonialism: Bank Misr and Egyptian Industrialization, 1920–1941* (Princeton, 1983), 145.
[44] *Ibid.*

ventures with foreign capital: the Egyptian Salt and Soda Company, La Filature Nationale d'Alexandrie, and La Banque Belge et Internationale en Egypte.

The last business-member of the Commission on Commerce and Industry was M. F. Bourgeois, a director of the Alexandria Gas Company. Representing a French firm operating a monopoly concession that disproportionately served foreigners and *mutamassirun*, Bourgeois embodied the stereotypical image of foreign capital in Egypt.

Relations among sectors of the business class – associates of Bank Misr, the EFI, and others – were regulated by common investment and management strategies, common views on economic and social policy, and sharp personal, economic, and political rivalries.[45] Alignments and coalitions fluctuated, and the balance of forces among individuals and groups of businessmen was dynamic throughout the period. This underscores a vital but often overlooked point: nationalism was a lucrative enterprise for Tal'at Harb and Bank Misr; and accumulation is, above all, the motive force of capitalism.

When Sa'd Zaghlul was exiled to the Seychelles in 1921–22, the Wafd called on Egyptians to boycott British firms, to buy only from "national stores," and to withdraw their funds from British banks and deposit them in Bank Misr.[46] In 1925 provincial and town councils withdrew their funds from the National Bank of Egypt and opened accounts with Bank Misr. Nonetheless, Tal'at Harb did not identify Bank Misr closely with the Wafd. Harb's view that economic development was a requirement for effective political independence placed him closer to the Liberal Constitutionalist Party, the Wafd's leading rival. The bank's industrial projects were a major beneficiary of the industrial policy of Isma'il Sidqi, who was a director of Misr Spinning and Weaving's biggest local competitor, La Filature Nationale. Sidqi's protective tariffs benefited both enterprises. Bank Misr supported the Wafd government of 1936–37. But after King Faruq removed Mustafa al-Nahhas as prime minister, the Wafdist press attacked the bank for being too friendly to the new Liberal Constitutionalist–Sa'dist government.

Not only was Tal'at Harb an inconsistent supporter of the Wafd, but his business activities indicate far less aversion to collaborating with foreign capital than his public pronouncements suggested. In 1924 he joined the board of the Crédit Foncier Egyptian, one of the most powerful foreign-controlled financial institutions in Egypt. The next year he joined the board of the EFI, the bastion of foreign and *mutamassir* capital. In 1927 foreigners were admitted as directors of four new enterprises established by Bank Misr.

[45] Vitalis, *When Capitalists Collide*.
[46] Davis, *Challenging Colonialism*, 116.

In 1929 Bank Misr and the German cotton magnate Hugo Lindemann jointly established the Misr Cotton Export Company – Misr's first collaboration with a foreign enterprise. A more conspicuous departure from Misr's nationalist image was the negotiation of several joint ventures with British firms in the 1930s: Misr Air and Air Work, Ltd. in 1931; Misr Insurance Company and C. T. Bowring & Company of Lloyd's in 1933; Misr Travel and Cox & Kings Ltd. in 1935. The most substantial Misr–British joint venture established two new textile mills – Misr Fine Spinning and Weaving Company and Misr Bayda Dyers Company – at Kafr al-Dawwar in 1938.[47] Bradford Dyers, a large but declining firm, sought an Egyptian partner to avoid the tariff enacted by the Sidqi government, while Misr was anxious to offset the advantage of La Filature Nationale, which had established a joint venture with the British firm Calico Printers in 1934.[48]

The Misr group's most powerful competitor was Muhammad Ahmad 'Abbud Pasha (1899–1963), a maverick of humble origins who established a construction firm in the early 1920s and built it into the most successful business group of the era. 'Abbud was a Wafdist parliamentary deputy in 1926 and a major financial backer of the party until Mustafa al-Nahhas became leader in 1927. By the 1940s 'Abbud controlled the Sugar Company (continuing collaboration with the Qattawi interests), the Khedival Mail Line (a shipping company), and the Egyptian General Omnibus Company (Cairo's municipal bus fleet). He was also the largest shareholder of Bank Misr and battled his way to a seat on the board of directors in 1950. In the same year he also became the first Egyptian to serve as a director of the Suez Canal Company, the most powerful foreign firm operating in Egypt. 'Abbud resumed support of the Wafd during its final years in power in close collaboration with Fu'ad Siraj al-Din, the party strongman. The preponderant influence of 'Abbud, Siraj al-Din, and their cronies in the Wafd did not prevent some from taking seriously Siraj al-Din's pronouncement that the Wafd was "a socialist party."[49]

'Abbud's career is distinguished from that of other Egyptian entrepreneurs of his era chiefly by his exceptional flamboyance and success. He was reputed to be one of the ten richest men in the world when he died in London. 'Abbud's checkered career, the interlocking and diversified interests of most of the business members of the Commission on Commerce and Industry, and their collaboration with *mutamassir* and foreign firms demonstrate the limited usefulness of the categories of nationalist political economy: "national bourgeoisie," "comprador bourgeoisie," and "feudalist." As in many former colonies and semi-colonies, economic development in

[47] Robert Tignor, "Bank Misr and Foreign Capitalism," *International Journal of Middle East Studies* 8/2 (1977), 170–74, 177–78.
[48] Robert Tignor, *Egyptian Textiles and British Capital, 1930–1956* (Cairo, 1989), 23–42.
[49] Quoted in Vitalis, *When Capitalists Collide*, 176.

Egypt was neither a function of nationalist political rhetoric nor directed toward serving the interests of any broad sector of the subaltern strata.

Working conditions in industrial manufacturing were unsafe, unhealthy, and personally degrading. Wages, though certainly higher than those of landless migrant workers ('*ummal al-tarahil*), were usually too low to sustain an adequate standard of nutrition. Even when supplied by employers, housing was filthy and overcrowded. Firms employed far more workers than the technical relations of production required to compensate for frequent absenteeism, a practice which lowered both wages and productivity. Though nationalist politics recognized workers and their rights, they were expected to be humbly grateful for their jobs and to cooperate with their employers' definition of national economic development. Those impelled to oppose their employers by dire necessity or an alternative vision of the national interest were often severely chastised by their employers or the state apparatus. The court that convicted fifty-five workers for striking on July 18, 1938 to demand a higher piece rate expressed

its strongest regret and astonishment at this foolish action on the part of the weaving workers of the Misr Spinning and Weaving Company at Mahalla ... they have departed from fulfilling their duty toward a company which helped them, supported them, and opened a door for them which they might enter while they were still ignorant ... The workers must ... cooperate with the company for production and sacrifice every personal interest in order to serve the fatherland, develop its commerce, and not lose the fruits of that gigantic effort because of the influence of dangerous opinions which we do not like to see among the workers, whatever the reason ... strikes and destruction have nothing to do with Egyptians. These acts are completely repulsive to them by virtue of their education, their circumstances, and their religion, which is based on forgiveness, cooperation, and nobility of character. This young company, one of the pillars of our current renaissance, did not overwork the workers and did not ask more than their capacity, wages being determined in accordance with output.[50]

The limits of the old regime, 1942–1952

During the 1930s the urban economy expanded too slowly to provide employment for all graduates – the aspiring *effendiyya* – thus contributing to their social radicalization. The world-wide crisis of liberal capitalism provided attractive new social and political ideals with an international network of allies against British imperialism. The massive allied buildup in Egypt during the Second World War stimulated rapid industrial development, a spurt in manufacturing employment, and deepening of the local market, with planning and technical assistance provided by the Middle East

[50] Quoted in André Eman, *L'Industrie du coton en Egypte: étude d'économie politique* (Cairo, 1943), 183–84. My translation from the French.

Supply Centre. Expansion of the stable industrial wage labor force enhanced the potential for a workers' movement contesting the limits of the paternalism and corporatism of the Wafdist *effendiyya* and its competitors for leadership of the trade unions. In 1942 the Wafd government recognized and tried to regulate this development by legalizing trade unions, but it was unable to maintain its hegemony over the labor movement.

Toward the end of the Second World War, some 250,000 workers were dismissed from war-related jobs, and in subsequent years sharp fluctuations in production and a drive to intensify mechanization in the textile industry resulted in recurrent unemployment. Industrial growth and trade union activity had increased wage levels during the 1930s. But the cost-of-living index soared from 100 in 1939 to 331 in 1952, and real wages did not keep pace.[51] These circumstances were the immediate impetus for a wave of strikes and radical working-class political organizing in 1945–46, notably of the Shubra al-Khayma textile workers' union led by Taha Sa'd 'Uthman (b. 1916) and Mahmud al-'Askari (1916–87), who soon joined the New Dawn communist group. The suburban Cairo textile workers continued to form the center of gravity of the radical current in the workers' movement under the leadership of Muhammad 'Ali 'Amr and Muhammad Shatta of the Democratic Movement for National Liberation, the largest of the Egyptian communist organizations.

Radicalization of the *effendiyya* and sectors of the trade union movement, intensifying demands for full British military evacuation, growing perception of agrarian crisis, and the personal disgrace of King Faruq infused the nationalist movement with a quasi-Marxist social content. The salient expression of a new social direction in the nationalist movement and the emergence of an alternative leadership was the general strike and demonstration called on February 21, 1946 by the National Committee of Workers and Students – a coalition of student organizations and trade unions supported by several rival Marxist groups and the radical youth of the Wafdist Vanguard led by Dr. Muhammad Mandur and Dr. 'Aziz Fahmi. Between December 1945 and July 1946, autumn 1947 and the outbreak of the Palestine war in May 1948, and for a third time from the abrogation of the Anglo-Egyptian treaty on October 8, 1951 until the Cairo fire of January 26, 1952, a social movement of urban wage workers, students, and recent graduates mounted strikes and demonstrations demanding social reforms and an end to the British occupation. This movement, though radically challenging the monarchy and its social bases, remained within the boundaries of the secular, liberal, nationalist discourse. Even the Society of Muslim Brothers, the main political force contesting the notion that Egypt should be

---

[51] Beinin and Lockman, *Workers on the Nile*, 267, based on statistics from the *Annuaire Statistique*, 1951–54.

a secular, liberal nation state modeled on Europe, operated within the national political field, thereby reinforcing its legitimacy even as the Brothers sought to reconfigure it.

In the late 1940s the growing number of women in universities and institutes of higher education broadened and radicalized the feminist movement. Inji Aflatun (1924–89), a student activist at Cairo University and member of the Iskra communist organization, founded the League of University and Institutes' Women in 1945. She and Saiza Nabarawi were the leading spokeswomen for the Marxist–progressive–nationalist–feminist current in the late 1940s and 1950s.

Duriyya Shafiq (1908–75), the daughter of an engineer, grew up in Delta towns. After she was placed second in the country in the 1925 French baccalauréat examination, Huda Sha'rawi helped her obtain a scholarship from the ministry of education to attend the Sorbonne. While in France, Shafiq wrote for *L'Egyptienne*. She then edited her own journal for several years before establishing the Daughter of the Nile (*Bint al-Nil*) Union in 1948. Its name emphasized the new organization's indigenous and popular character in contrast to the Turco-Circassian elite image of the EFU. Shafiq emphasized direct political action for women's suffrage, literacy programs, and reform of the personal status laws. Campaigning on these issues extended the feminist movement into the urban middle strata. In February 1951, Shafiq led a women's sit-in at the parliament to demand the vote for women. Later that year she transformed *Bint al-Nil* into a political party with a largely student membership. Duriyya Shafiq's persistent feminist campaigning and her liberal critique of the new regime after 1952 represented the first expression of a women's political agenda independent of the nationalist movement. Consequently, she came to be seen as an antinationalist. In 1957 Saiza Nabarawi, Inji Aflatun, and other prominent women publicly denounced her, and she was forced to resign from *Bint al-Nil*.[52]

Despite the continuing rural crisis, peasant resistance to landed power was less potent than contemporary movements in China, Malaysia, and Vietnam. From 1944 to 1952 there were some thirty-five recorded incidents of peasant collective action against landlords or state authorities. The most substantial was the anti-landlord uprising at Buhut in June 1951 on the estate of the Badrawi-'Ashur family – the largest land owners outside the royal family and relatives by marriage of Fu'ad Siraj al-Din.[53] While nationalist discourse often romanticized the authenticity of peasant life, the

---

[52] Cynthia Nelson, "Biography and Women's History: Interpreting Doria Shafik," in Nikkie R. Keddie and Beth Baron (eds.), *Women in Middle Eastern History: Shifting Boundaries in Sex and Gender* (New Haven, 1991), 310–33; Badran, *Feminism, Islam, and Nation*, 153–54, 217–18.

[53] Brown, *Peasant Politics*, 108–09, 141–47.

long tradition of Cairo-centered politics relegated peasants to the role of rural reserves for contending urban forces. The social movements after the Second World War were too disparate and too isolated from the peasant majority to dislodge the structure of landed power, and, on their own, peasants were too remote from the centers of power to challenge the old regime. Nonetheless, the persistent presence of the peasantry contributed substantially to destabilizing it.

One aspect of the social radicalization of the nationalist movement after the Second World War and the generational challenge to existing political leaderships posed by the young urban *effendiyya* was the persistent call to Egyptianize the economy. Its proponents argued that political independence was incomplete without economic independence. Egyptianization also provided investment opportunities for businessmen and positions and promotions for engineering and professional graduates among the *effendiyya*, who often found themselves excluded from foreign- and *mutamassir*-owned businesses where fluency in European languages and ethnic or family connections were prerequisites for employment.

The Sa'dist governments of 1944–49 undertook several nationalist economic measures: excavation for a new hydropower plant at Aswan that eventually developed into the high-dam project; a parastatal industrial development bank; negotiations that culminated in the construction of the Helwan iron and steel complex in 1954; and support for the demands of the Shell Oil Company and Suez Canal Company workers to increase the number of permanent Egyptian workers and supervisors and equalize their wages with those of foreign nationals.

The most comprehensive of these measures was the company law of 1947, which required 75 percent of all salaried employees, 90 percent of all workers, and 51 percent of paid-up capital of joint stock companies to be Egyptian. Firms were required to report their employees' nationalities and salaries and were thus forced to answer the vexed question: "Who is an Egyptian?" There is no unequivocal, transhistorical answer to such a question. Indeed, it could be posed only after the historically and socially formed categories of "nation" and "citizen" had become naturalized, as the fate of the department-store chain of Les Grands Magasins Cicurel et Oreco illustrates.

When the Wafd called on Egyptians to purchase only at "national stores" in 1921–22, the Cicurel department store near Cairo's Opera Square was specified as an approved shop.[54] Its founder, Moreno Cicurel, had migrated to Cairo from Izmir in the mid-nineteenth century. The Cicurel family held Italian citizenship at the time. Moreno's son, Yusuf, was born in Cairo in 1887. He and his brothers built the family store into the largest and most

---

[54] Davis, *Challenging Colonialism*, 116.

fashionable retail chain in Egypt. Yusuf Cicurel Bey was a member of the Cairo Chamber of Commerce, a leading forum for nationalist economic opinion, and one of the ten original members of the board of directors of Bank Misr in 1920. His younger brother, Salvator, was captain of Egypt's 1928 Olympic fencing team and president of the Cairo Jewish community from 1946 to 1957.

The Cicurel store in Cairo was firebombed during the 1948 Palestine war, probably by supporters of the Muslim Brothers, and it was burned a second time as a symbol of European influence during the Cairo fire of January 26, 1952. Both times the store was rebuilt with the support of the government. A memorandum submitted to the ministry of commerce in 1948 described the Cicurel firm as "one of the pillars of our economic independence."[55] Nonetheless, the Cicurel store had a European cultural character because of its largely Jewish staff, its expensive and largely imported merchandise, and the use of French by employees and customers on the shop floor. Even many of the Egyptian-born Jewish members of the Cicurel staff did not hold citizenship papers and were classified as "stateless." Cicurel's contradictions could not be balanced indefinitely. At the outbreak of the 1956 Suez war, unlike in 1948, the Cicurel firm was placed under sequestration. The Cicurel family soon ceded its majority holding to a new group headed by Muslims, and in 1957 Salvator Cicurel left Egypt for France.

The fate of the Cicurel family and its firm suggests that the business classes of the *mutamassir* communities in Egypt underwent two contradictory processes during the first half of the twentieth century. Until the mid-1930s there was a strong tendency toward assimilation and the formation of a multi-ethnic, culturally cosmopolitan haute-bourgeoisie. After 1936, the limits of economic development; growing realization that tax laws, cultural custom, and entrenched positions tended to favor urban foreign and *mutamassir* businesses; competition for the limited number of white-collar positions in the urban economy; radicalization of the *effendiyya*; exacerbation of the Arab–Zionist conflict; the British governments' refusals to recognize that their days in Egypt were over; and, finally, the Anglo-French–Israeli invasion of 1956 resulted in the social and political isolation and economic expropriation of the *mutamassirun*.

Despite the acceleration of industrial development induced by the depression and the Second World War and the consequent self-assertion of indigenous businessmen as against foreign capital, the development of Egyptian society and the political economy were ultimately constrained by the economic interests and social customs embedded in the dominance of landed wealth and by the historical role of foreign capital. The indecisive

[55] Quoted in Nabil 'Abd al-Hamid Sayyid Ahmad, *al-Hayat al-iqtisadiyya wa'l-ijtima'iyya li'l-yahud fi misr, 1947–1956* (Cairo, 1991), 39.

struggle between the new social radicalism of the nationalist movement and the old order was reflected in the policies of the Wafd government of 1950–52, which oscillated between the populism of its youthful wing and the moderate pro-business reform and social conservatism of Siraj al-Din and his supporters. If the disastrous performance of the army in Palestine had not provoked a cohort of junior officers to organize themselves around a vague, authoritarian vision of national unity and economic development, the Wafd or a similar political formation might have muddled through indefinitely. But the configuration of capital, culture, and political power embodied in Egyptian colonial capitalism is unlikely to have had more success serving the needs of the majority than similar social formations in other former colonies of Asia and Africa.

14

Republican Egypt interpreted:
revolution and beyond

ALAIN ROUSSILLON

><

> Egypt is one of a restricted group of developing countries whose politics have assumed a special significance as test cases of opposing models of development. Egypt shares with India, China, Algeria, Yugoslavia and Cuba the analytical interest of partisan and academic observers for the light its experience may shed upon the competing theories of development and for the possibility that its history may reveal a unique and unanticipated model
>
> Leonard Binder, *In a Moment of Enthusiasm*, p. 1.

Introduction

Towards the end of the 1970s, as the opening up (*infitah*) toward the west and the liberalization of the economy were sharply criticized as "betrayal" of the 1952 revolution's goals, as return of the exploitative bourgeoisie, and as abandonment of the Palestinian cause, certain observers, Egyptian and foreign, began to lay out a new "model" for the reading of contemporary Egyptian history. This model attempted to view Egypt's various "experiments," before and after the revolution, from a common perspective; it also made it possible to explain the "cycles" through which Egypt has ultimately failed to "modernize" and regain the place among nations that its millenia of history allows it to demand. Muhammad 'Ali and Nasir, breaking with a past of national humiliation, both incarnated Egypt's "will to power" by basing restoration of its regional and international role on a state economy heavily reliant on industry and the construction of a national armed force: the failure of both projects was brought about by conjunction of the "perverse" consequences of their own options and methods, and by the hostility from coalitions of external interests, alarmed by the regional role to which Egypt aspired. The successors of Muhammad 'Ali and Nasir, Isma'il and Sadat, both betrayed or distorted their predecessors' "developmentalist" aims and sacrificed the public good and Egypt's independence to the mercantile interests of a class of speculators and unscrupulous businessmen that served as a wedge for foreign penetration. The crucial point here is *the repetition itself* and the way these successive "cycles" may be articulated: Nasir "repeats" Muhammad 'Ali, precisely because, under Isma'il, the work of his grandfather had been swayed from its objectives; in the same way, if Sadat "repeats" Isma'il, it is because the conditions that had led to Muhammad 'Ali's failure were still in force, producing the same effects, and enabling the articulation of something that may appear as a "law" pertaining to the specific history of Egypt.

By stretching the logic of this model to its most contemporary limit, one may state that if Muhammad 'Ali and Nasir, Isma'il and Sadat seem to correspond, from one century to another, Hosni Mubarak has not yet found his destiny, nor, by the same token, have the figures who anticipated him: Ahmad Fu'ad I, the autocratic modernizer who established a number of institutions under which Egypt continues to live today; or Faruq, the tyrannical libertine and friend of unscrupulous businessmen, during whose reign the "national bourgeoisie" failed to assume its historic role, and who was ousted by a revolution. Having failed yet to acquire its own identity, Hosni Mubarak's regime is presented as having inherited a situation characterized by the determinations – and contradictions – of the two preceding regimes – "a complex inheritance of the Nasser and Sadat eras."[1] For another observer, Mubarak's Egypt is "the hybrid result of the opening up of an economy, dominated by the state under Nasser, to the international capitalist market," and thereby submitted to the "cumulative constraints of the eras of Nasser and Sadat."[2] A third view reflects uncertainties supposedly expressed by Egyptians themselves about the "real" identity and intentions of their president: "A crypto-Nasserist waiting to leap forward with a capital N on his chest" (for those who fear that Sadat's *infitah* will be questioned); "a Sadatist in every way except by name"[3] (for those who fear that the "gains" of the 1952 revolution will continue to be dismantled at the same, or an even more rapid, pace).

This "model," the simplistic and overly mechanical nature of which has been elsewhere discerned,[4] does not serve here simply as a rhetorical device or a straw man: one may see in it the most contemporary realization of a more general and comprehensive paradigm that aims at nothing less than Egyptian permanence, virtually from pharaonic antiquity to the present day.

---

[1] Nazih Ayubi, "Government and the State in Egypt Today," in Charles Tripp and Roger Owen (eds.), *Egypt under Mubarak* (London and New York, 1989), 1.

[2] Raymond Hinnebusch, "The Formation of the Contemporary Egyptian State from Nasser and Sadat to Mubarak," in Ibrahim M. Oweiss (ed.), *The Political Economy of Contemporary Egypt* (Georgetown, 1990).

[3] Robert Springborg, *Mubarak's Egypt: Fragmentation of the Political Order* (Boulder and London, 1989), v.

[4] Robert Ilbert, "La cohérence et l'informel: essai pour servir à une histoire de l'Egypte contemporaine," in *Itinéraires d'Egypte. Mélanges offerts au Père Martin* (Cairo, 1992).

Within the logic of this paradigm, "understanding Egypt" – writing its history, describing its social or political systems, and decoding present ideologies – involves highlighting long-term, quasi-ecological continuities linked to the relation between river and desert, while showing how the breaks, apparent or effective, that create the rhythm of this long history – changes in language, religion, foreign masters – recompose the meaning of continuity while confirming it.

From the vantage point of Egypt's most contemporary history, which may be said to have begun on July 23, 1952, the question posed by this dialectic concerns the inaugural status of the Free Officers' movement. The official writing of the Egyptian republic, as well as that of most observers, scientists and journalists, and even of its most resolute opponents, who see in this movement the cause of all the country's present ills, all concur on this point. On the one hand, what is at question is the impact of breaks caused by the Free Officers' movement in the underlying continuities of Egyptian society with respect to the *ancien régime*; on the other, a question is posed about the relation Nasir's heirs have to this inaugural moment: do they pursue the revolution by other means or betray the hopes inspired and that it brought, as Muhammad 'Ali had to the middle of the last century, to the beginnings of fulfillment.

Moreover, the continuity-break paradigm raises the main questions that every attempt to write Egypt's contemporary history must pose. More than any other period, post-revolutionary Egypt has been the object of abundant literature, especially in English, renewed at each of the "breaks" – here, changes in regime – that create the rhythm of this history. Considering the three regimes that have successively taken command of Egyptian social formation since 1952 in terms of "continuities" and "breaks" consists, in most works, in answering three questions.

The question of relations between the elite and the masses is double-barreled. On the one hand, it concerns relations between the state and what is today commonly designated "civil society"; and, on the other, the way social forces may exert control on the state and transform that control into economic benefit, whether by maintaining the status quo or redividing the spoils. How has the evolution in modes of power distribution taken place? What were the conditions for exercising power, from the *ancien régime* to the revolution, from Nasir to Sadat and Mubarak? How have resources been distributed and mobilized, both those of scarcity (land and water, capital), and those of surplus (labor)? What are the "class bases" and interest systems that preside over the periodic reorientations of public economic, social, and educational policies?

A second question concerns the relations between internal and external constraints. Several factors tend to make the "balance" between these one of the "structuring" questions in approaches to contemporary Egyptian history. The starting-point here is the contrast between Egypt's status as former "colony" and its determination, never denied, to act in its regional environment in the name of Egyptian "centrality," of Arab or Islamic solidarity, or of non-aligned third worldism. On the one hand, the role of exterior constraints – access to arms, foreign assistance (especially food aid) – are examined in relation to the recomposition of the Egyptian political system and/or the economic strategies applied. On the other, the question concerns internal conditions, especially the increasing difficulties faced by the authorities in satisfying the demands of a country undergoing a demographic explosion.

The third basic question observers pose deals with the relation between "identity" and "modernity." Here a "theoretical" reinterpretation of the two preceding relations is posed, whereby it is necessary to show how they are articulated and interact to outline the field of the "possible" in the framework of Egyptian continuity, an almost mandatory exercise in every attempt to enunciate the meaning of contemporary Egyptian history. According to one's point of view, the question addresses either capacity of elites to induce change in society with the imported apparatus of modernity under conditions of unequal exchange, or society's capacity for resistance or effective reappropriation in the face of authoritarian modernization. The purpose here is to evaluate the real impact of profound breaks – sociological, cultural, spiritual – brought about by reconstructions of the political system (renewal of elites, of action systems) and of economic management strategies (redistribution, reallocation of resources). Were the relations between elites and masses, between Egypt and the west, significantly transformed by political independence and the modernization of management systems? In many studies, the dialectic between "identity" and "modernity" takes the form of a constantly renewed confrontation between "Islam," as both the most demanding and the most active component of Egyptian identity, and the state, as the only possible promoter and vector of modernizing rationality. The relative failure of pan-Arabism as a possible realization of the Egyptian identity actually seems to have convinced most observers that the religious dimension of this identity – the almost exclusive source of legitimacy, mode and model for mobilization, utopia, and reality of social relations – is indeed, in the final analysis, the main "challenge" confronting those who aspire to the modernization of this society, and that its future depends on the outcome of this confrontation: continuation of an "authentic" backwardness or construction of a modernity imbued with identity.

From coup d'état to revolution

When the Free Officers took power in Cairo on July 23, 1952, under General Muhammad Najib, the conspirators' "true" identity, but also that of the movement bringing them to power, was problematic. It has often been said that the second-rank officers forming the Revolutionary Command Council (RCC) had no program, almost no ideology, and barely any "philosophy." The military may have constituted the "armed hand" of the movement, but its militant base and its links to society were made up of two trends that could not be reconciled and that the new regime immediately repressed: the Muslim Brotherhood and the Marxist left, to both of which certain officers were linked.

In terms of how it presented itself and was received by observers, diplomats, and journalists, the Free Officers movement, approved at first by all Egyptian political parties, appeared as an expected, necessary reaction to the "anomie" of which the 1948 disaster in Palestine, the proliferation of peasant revolts, and the burning of Cairo on January 26, 1952 constituted obvious symptoms. Faruq's forced abdication and exile on July 26, like the dissolution of political parties on January 16, 1953, could still be presented as public safety measures – "a painless lancet blow on a stinking abscess," according to one colorful expression.[5]

The first agrarian reform,[6] promulgated on September 9, 1952, one of the first actually "revolutionary" measures of the new government, shed very little light on its identity and its options: at the time of its promulgation, the agrarian reform could also appear as a public safety measure, and one advocated before 1952 at that by certain wealthy land owners among others. Limiting land ownership to 300 faddans per family, creating a cooperative system for the beneficiaries of redistribution, and regulating relations between land owners and renters, the law of September 1952 applied to fewer than 2,000 land owners – including the royal family, whose possessions were confiscated – and only 450,000 faddans. Those who owned excess land were authorized to sell it at a price fixed at seventy times the land tax within a time limit of a month and a half starting from the law's promulgation, unsold land being requisitioned by the state in return for indemnities fixed at ten times the rent value of the land increased by the value of equipment and machinery, including even the price of trees. Clearly, nothing overly threatening to property rights was implied, especially in light of the fact that the new regime had not hesitated, on August 13, 1952, to order troops to open fire on workers who had occupied the textile factory of Kafr al-Dawwar, belonging to the Misr group, in order to obtain salary raises; nor had it hesitated to hang two "leaders" of the strike, who were accused of counter-revolutionary activities.

---

[5] J. and S. Lacouture, *L'Egypte en mouvement* (Paris, 1956), 146.
[6] See Mahmoud Abdel-Fadil, *Development, Income Distribution and Social Change in Rural Egypt, 1952–1970* (London, 1975); and Hamied Ansari, *Egypt, the Stalled Society* (Albany, 1986).

The episode of the "tripartite aggression" of 1956,[7] where some of the options with the heaviest consequences for the Officers' regime were sketched out, did no more to shed light on its identity. The episode began in September 1955, with the purchase of Czech weapons by Egypt, in retaliation for the west's refusal to arm a regime whose precise political identity remained vague and which stubbornly refused to enter into military alliances that the USA and Europe were attempting to establish in a bid to contain the "Soviet threat." Despite the new rulers' repeated anti-communist declarations, the role played by Egypt in the foundation of the "non-aligned" movement at the Bandung conference, in April 1955, contributed to convincing the American administration to withdraw the support it had granted the movement by announcing, on July 18, its refusal to participate as arranged in financing the construction of the Aswan high dam. The announcement on July 26, 1956 of the nationalization of the Suez Canal, the revenue from which, according to Nasir, would finance this construction, certainly had "revolutionary" consequences as a precedent and by virtue of the blow it struck against post-colonial interests; it remained, nonetheless, a "retaliation" that testified to the continued vigor of Egyptian nationalism, but without giving explicit content and identity to the regime that incarnated it. Nasir's capacity to transform the military defeat of the Egyptian troops at Suez into a political and diplomatic victory did not force Egypt to "choose sides": the retreat of the French, British, and Israeli troops, in fact, was imposed by the combined pressure of the USA and the USSR.

Even the first nationalizations of 1956–57, which struck French and British interests in return for the tripartite aggression, then those directed against Jewish, Armenian, or Syrian–Lebanese interests, did not in themselves constitute a break with respect to the logic of Egyptianizing the state and the economy, already begun in the 1920s with the foundation of Bank Misr: what was especially "revolutionary" about a decision to make the boards of directors and the capital of all commercial banks and insurance companies operating in Egypt Egyptian?[8] Granted, the property seized during this first wave of nationalizations was maintained in the public domain under the control of an "economic organism" created in January 1957; confiscated wealth was not returned to the private sector. But most of the directors of the "Egyptianized" banks kept their positions, and the first five-year plan – a revolutionary innovation indeed – still reserved 79 percent of projected investments for the private sector. The constitution of this public-sector embryo, on the basis of economic assets which the tripartite invasion provided the opportunity of seizing, may appear as the outcome of

---

[7] See P. J. Vatikiotis, *Nasser and his Generation* (London, 1978); and Muhammad Hasanayn Haykal, *Les documents du Caire* (Paris, 1972).

[8] Charles Issawi, *Egypt in Revolution: An Economic Analysis* (London, 1963); Robert Mabro, *The Egyptian Economy, 1952–1982* (Oxford, 1974).

the struggle begun by the 1919 revolution, leading as it did to the decisive liquidation of the appropriation of Egypt and its resources by foreign interests after political independence.

Emergence of the Nasirist state

If there is indeed a break, one must seek it no doubt in the way that the conflict between General Najib – who fulfilled the functions of president of the Republic (proclaimed on June 18, 1953) and of prime minister – and Nasir, at the head of the RCC where the regime's decisions were made – was settled in February–March 1954. What was at stake in this conflict was henceforth phrased in polemical terms: the "return of the military to their barracks"; the return to a parliamentary system (demanded by the elements making up the "United Front" – the representatives of the dissolved parties, but also certain "leftist" Officers) versus the return of the ancien régime and the exploitative pashas under the cover of corrupt and corrupting parties, especially the Wafd, the Officers' *bête noire* and the party sure of winning any election. The support of the army and the decisive backing of the trade unions would allow Nasir to wrestle General Najib to the ground, leading to the latter's arrest and the assumption by Nasir of the presidency and the functions of prime minister.

This stabilization of the balance of power within the military hierarchy allowed the regime to turn against the only two forces still capable of contesting the autonomy of the military apparatus-made-government after the liquidation of the Wafd: the Egyptian communists, who had broken with the Free Officers' movement after the leaders of the strike at Kafr al-Dawwar were hanged, and the Muslim Brotherhood, guilty of having taken Najib's side in his showdown with Nasir. The repression of these two groups could be described as "symmetrical" in that it reflected the double weakness inherent in the Free Officers' ascendancy system. Between 1952 and 1958, the repression of the communists was sporadic: it struck trade unionists, teachers, or militant peasants whose action could endanger the revolutionary order by radicalizing the demands of the masses; simultaneously, the regime encouraged the structuring of a "legal left," and of which the daily publication of *al-Misa*, established in October 1956 by Nasir himself, with Khalid Muhi al-Din as editor-in-chief, became the main rostrum. The (apparent) paradox is that the "great trial" of the Egyptian communists began the very day after the "historic" visit of the Egyptian head of state to Moscow, in April 1958, reflecting the reversal of Egypt's alliances and its entrance into the "anti-imperialist" camp. It is precisely because Egypt was entering the Soviet orbit (for arms supplies, financing, and carrying out its industrialization, by welcoming a constantly increasing number of experts and "advisors") that the activity of groups of a communist persuasion became unacceptable. The refusal of the Egyptian Communist Party – created on February 28, 1958 by the fusion of different factions of this persuasion – to dissolve itself so that its members might rally individually to the National Union provided the pretext for sending hundreds of communist cadres and militants to the camps, accused of taking orders from Moscow just when the USSR and the socialist bloc had been designated as Egypt's strategic allies. With the communists, what provoked the regime "preventively," as it were, was the risk that professional militants, making up a vanguard and equipped with a "globalizing" ideology, would put pressure on the state by using its capacity to organize the demands of the masses. That the regime would later use "repentant" communist militants, after the self-dissolution in January 1956 of the ECP, shows that it was this "globalizing" ideology that the regime rejected while preparing itself to establish new means and methods of social and economic control directly borrowed from the political systems produced by that same ideology.

The first confrontation between the regime and the Muslim Brotherhood[9] began when the association was dissolved in January 1954, and with the revenge-assassination attempt on Nasir in Alexandria by a Brother, which provided the pretext for violent repression – the hanging of six leaders and hundreds of arrests. Officially, the society still pursued the goals that its founder ascribed to it: it was an association for mutual help and spiritual consciousness-raising and solidarity, a youth movement – anything but a political party, even if the "secret apparatus" created in the 1930s did not balk at political assassinations. It thus managed to evade the dissolution that struck others in January 1953 in this way; it leaders also aspired to impose their "guidance" on the Free Officers – indeed, to impose on all their policies, notably in matters of education, sexual morality and culture. With the communists, the regime had to deal with relatively marginal groups, "cut off from the masses" despite their pinpointed organizational capacities; the Muslim Brothers constituted, after the liquidation of the Wafd, the only structured, hierarchical political force on a national scale, disposing of an organizational culture directly rooted in its social environment. More than a party or a secret organization, the Muslim Brothers, who recruited among the effendis and the workers much more than in religious circles, tended to gather under their jurisdiction the functions of mobilization and infra-political practices, formerly the province of craft guilds, Sufi brotherhoods, and self-help associations. This was a *sociological opposition*, as it were, as shown by the number of Brothers the regime found it safer to detain between 1954 and the end of the 1970s, not to mention those executed after summary trials or simply eliminated in the camps. Among these was Sayyid

---

[9] Richard Mitchell, *The Society of the Muslim Brothers* (London, 1969); Olivier Carré and Gérard Michaud, *Les frères musulmans, 1928–82* (Paris, 1983).

Qutb, the association's main ideologue, hanged on August 29, 1966, under the pretext of plotting against the state but in fact because he was the first to coin a phrase that was to have extremely serious consequences. By denouncing the "jahiliyya of the 20th century" – unbelief and those who serve it, justifying the launching of a new internal jihad – Sayyid Qutb laid down the framework of the recurring competition between the modern authoritarian state and the radical militant fringe of the Islamic trend for the control of values tied to religion. This very violence of the repression of the Brotherhood by the Nasirist regime demonstrated that this regime continued to consider these the central values of Egyptian society.[10]

The crucial point is that the cadres of the Brotherhood and the communists, and the officers controlling the state, encompassed the same social determining factors – education, social mobility, and reformist trends. To paraphrase Mahmoud Hussein,[11] a faction of the petty bourgeoisie in the process of constituting itself as state power liquidates its direct competitors; yet the objectives of the Officers and those of the Brotherhood, or the way they represented society, did not differ radically, apart from the way they were phrased and systems of legitimization on which they rested.

A philosophy for the revolution?

Hence the importance for Nasir's regime to articulate a "world vision" justifying the army's retention of power, while allowing it to stand up to the competing ideologies of the Marxists and the Brotherhood by retrieving socially effective values. The two main "options" – Arabism and confrontation with Israel – upon which this world vision was constructed may be analyzed as the product of "circumstances," i.e., of political conjunctions, but they may just as well be the necessary results of history or geo-politics.

Taking a "diffused" Arabism as harking back to the Great Arab Revolt, which in any case took place in the Fertile Crescent rather than in Egypt itself, the first Arabist expressions in Egyptian discourse accompanied Nasir's efforts in 1955 to create obstacles to the signing of the Baghdad pact, whereby Great Britain attempted to counterbalance its evacuation of the Canal Zone. But the "unitarian" Arabist argument put forward to isolate the Iraqi monarchy, which was tempted to place itself under British protection, was clearly not conclusive since the Iraqi revolution that overthrew Faysal in 1958 adopted a violently anti-Egyptian position. The union Egypt concluded with Syria in February 1958, which gave birth to the United Arab Republic (UAR – the name by which Egypt was officially designated until

---

[10] For Sayyid Qutb, see Olivier Carré, *Mystique et politique, lecture révolutionnaire du Coran, Frère musulman radical, 1906–1966* (Paris, 1984).

[11] Mahmoud Hussein, *La lutte des classes en Égypt, 1945–1970* (Paris, 1971).

July 1971, when it became the Arab Republic of Egypt) seems to have been not so much the result of "conscious" Arabist aims of the Egyptian leadership as the starting-point for reelaboration of Egyptian nationalism, the "positive" ideology Nasir's regime needed to face the liberals, Muslim Brothers, and Marxists. To support this reading, we may cite the fact that the very initiative for union came from the Syrian Ba'thists, who were anxious to consolidate their position vis-à-vis the "bourgeois parties" and who applied strong pressure on the hesitant, if not outright skeptical, Nasir. Further, it is clear that the Egyptian project in Syria was limited to attempts to organize Egypt's grip on the "northern province" – and achieved the unanimity of the Syrian parties, headed by the Ba'th, in opposition. A military coup d'état, supported by Syrian business circles opposed to the application in Syria of "socialist measures" adopted in Egypt (see below) put an end to the union in September 1961. "Arab socialism" was thus the product, not so much of the experience of unity with Syria, but of the very failure of this experience: priority was given to defending and deepening the revolution in Egypt itself, both center and vanguard of the Arab nation, while conditions were awaited for its generalization in other Arab states, classified, according to their attitude toward the Egyptian leadership as "progressive" or "reactionary," with King Faysal's Arabia leading the latter.[12]

As for the second "option" upon which the world vision of the Nasirist leadership was based – confrontation with the "Zionist entity" – its analysis runs the risk of being anachronistic, all the more so since the subsequent evolution of the Israeli–Arab conflict has tended to confer upon it a certain fatality or ineluctability which was not necessarily acquired at the time of the 1952 revolution.[13] Much more than the rapid consolidation of the Zionist state created in 1948, the main issue for Egyptian diplomacy, until the signing of the December 1954 accords on the evacuation of the last British troops, was the Sudanese question (Egypt, as a matter of tactics, had assumed that the majority of Sudanese would vote for joining Egypt in an independence referendum of 1956). The 1948 defeat obviously played an important role in the genesis of the Free Officers' movement, but it is not equally clear that the Egyptian army's perception of the Zionist *"fait accompli"* was the same as that imposed after 1956. If, in *Philosophy of the Revolution*, Nasir was particularly forthcoming about the humiliation felt by the Egyptian military forces, he emphasized mainly the Egyptian, internal factors of this defeat – corruption, the elites' betrayal. In contrast, the tone adopted with respect to Israel was remarkably "neutral": it was Great

---

[12] See Malcolm Kerr, *The Arab Cold War, 1958–1964: A Study of Ideology in Politics* (London, 1965); Samir Amin, *La nation arabe: nationalisme et luttes de classe* (Paris, 1976).

[13] See Henry Laurens, *Le grand jeu: Orient arabe et rivalités internationales* (Paris, 1991).

Britain's maneuvering, much more than the Jews' ambition to acquire a state, that was denounced. There was still room, it seems, for negotiated cohabitation between Arabs and Jewish colonizers, if only the latter had broken with the colonial logic that had created the "Jewish homeland," allowing Zionism and Israel itself to be depicted as *"progressive elements, in contrast with the rotten Arab regimes of the Middle East."*[14] The participation of Israel in the "tripartite aggression" of 1956 posed, not the question of Israel's existence, but that of the Nasir regime's capacity for regional leadership. Only at the time of the break with Syria did confrontation with the "Zionist entity" acquire its definitive status in the production, by the Egyptian regime, of the meaning of history in the making and in its management of the system of external and internal constraints to which it linked its survival. On the internal front, the role of vanguard assigned to the armed forces in the country's preparation for the inevitable battle was confirmed; on the regional front, Arab unity, under Egyptian leadership, would guarantee victory over the Zionist enemy and the liberation of Arab land; on the international front, battling Israel was only the local facet of the struggle that set the Arabs in general, and particularly Egypt, against imperialism and its agents – "imperialism, Zionism, and Arab reaction," in the vocabulary of the time – and through which the connection with the third world was established after the signing of its "birth certificate" in Bandung by Nasir, Chou En Lai, Tito, and Nehru.[15]

Revolution within the revolution

The relaunching and radicalization of the agrarian reform program, in July 1961, was an implicit admission of the first phase's failure. At the beginning of the 1960s, redistributed land accounted for around 10 percent of the total cultivated, and benefited fewer than 250,000 families. Proprietors of under five faddans may well have risen from 35 percent of landholdings to 49 percent at the end of the 1950s – notably because large land owners sold off surplus lands to the peasants who worked them – but this implied that the number of micro-proprietors, the size of whose landholdings did not allow them to wrench themselves out of misery, had grown. Further, land redistributions having benefited mainly those who owned or rented small holdings, landless peasants and seasonal laborers seem to have been those most neglected by the 1952 reform. One of the most significant consequences of this first phase of agrarian reform was the decline of absenteeism in rural areas, which tended to strengthen, between micro-holdings and what remained of the large holdings, a layer of intermediate proprietors (five

---

[14] Vatikiotis, *Nasser*, 249.
[15] See Hassan Riad, *L'Egypte nassérienne* (Paris, 1964).

to fifty faddans): "Egyptian kulaks, which the regime [was] intent on consolidating, and which it [would] surround by an increasingly large layer of small landowners."[16] With the "socialist measures" of July 1961, the maximum limit of ownership was reduced to 100 faddans per proprietor (against 200 previously, or 300 per family), with prohibition on renting more than 50 faddans. Almost 250,000 extra faddans were thus redistributed, to which were added, between 1962 and 1964, the lands belonging to sequestrated individuals (around 45,000 faddans), and those confiscated by the Higher Council for the Liquidation of Feudalism (HCLF), created in 1966 (see below). In total, the amount of land redistributed between 1952 and 1969 is estimated at a little under 1 million faddans, benefiting approximately 320,000 families.

The agrarian reform had been well received by industrial and banking circles; the wave of nationalizations that made up the second part of the July 1961 "socialist measures," and the increasingly widespread recourse to sequestration and expropriation as means of political control, did as much to alienate from the revolution those designated as "national capitalists" by posing in radically different terms the question of the officers' economic identity: "socialism" or "state capitalism" in the jargon of the time. With the promulgation of laws 117, 118, and 119 of 1961, the essential financial apparatus and non-agricultural means of production in fact passed under the state's direct control: the entire banking sector was nationalized, as were insurance and transport; heavy or "strategic" (especially chemical and pharmaceutical) industries, textiles, sugar refineries, and the production of basic foodstuffs were nationalized; public works and construction, hotels, department stores, cinemas, theaters, newspapers, and publishing houses all underwent the same process. Around a hundred enterprises not directly affected by the nationalization law were forced to convert 50 percent of their shares to public property, while individuals holding portfolios – almost 44,000 stockholders – had to hand over to the state their shares above a ceiling of LE10,000. Income over LE10,000 per annum was subjected to a tax rate of 90 percent. "Few developing nations, other than those explicitly professing Marxism, have cut so deeply as Egypt into their private sector."[17]

In 1956 a ministry of industry had been created, headed by 'Aziz Sidqi and guaranteeing, through an economic development organ, the management of nationalized economic and commercial establishments and the setting up of major infrastructural projects. After the creation, in 1957, of a national planning council, transformed into a ministry in its own right in

---

[16] Anouar Abdel-Malek, *Egypte, société militaire* (Paris, 1962), 77.
[17] John Waterbury, *The Egypt of Nasser and Sadat: The Political Economy of Two Regimes* (Princeton, 1983), 76.

1960, the "socialist measures" of 1961 gave the signal for complete reorganization of the productive apparatus: 438 public enterprises – but also those enterprises of which 50 percent belonged to the state – were divided among thirty-nine "General Organizations" operating on a sectoral basis, placed under the supervision of relevant ministries, with activities coordinated by the plan; the main nationalized banks were also assigned specialized sectors in which to intervene; external trade was placed entirely under state control and subjected to the priorities of the plan.

Arab socialism or Arab application of socialism?

The National Action Charter (al-Mithaq), adopted by a "National Congress of Popular Forces," in May–June 1962, asserted the meaning of the "socialist measures" and the objectives they pursued by providing them with both a doctrinal translation – "scientific socialism" and/or its "Arab application" – and a political interpretation, through the creation of the Arab Socialist Union (ASU). For all the vigorous slogans, what was tentatively elaborated through the 1962 charter appears as essentially "reactive." In the history of the revolution's genesis as presented by the charter, the succession of failures undergone by the national movement made military intervention necessary, and demanded the "socialist solution" since the capitalist path "could not but reinforce the political power of the class which owns and monopolizes resources."[18] The ideology crystallized in the charter was, again, "reactive" in that the notion of socialism it elaborated was primarily explained in negative terms: exclusion of communism or Marxism, presented as "symmetrical" to capitalism insofar as they imply, as it does, one class's absolute domination in society; negation of the class struggle, not so much as reality but as a modality for resolving social conflict, which it is precisely the state's role to arbitrate; and exclusion of even the doctrinal dimension of this socialism. Nazih Ayubi has identified its character: essentially "technical," "instrumental" within both official and intellectual circles, which prefer to call the Egyptian doctrine "Arab socialism," thus avoiding all suspicion of theoretical or practical connection with Marxism, while authorizing, at the same time, the introduction of spiritual, nationalist, or religious elements in the formulating of this doctrine."[19] In this logic, "socialism" could be summed up as the refusal of exploitation – "creating a sort of economic equilibrium among citizens which allows justice to be achieved" – provision of equal opportunities for all and the preservation of national unity, identified as "democratic interaction among the forces of the working population: *fallahin*, workers, soldiers,

[18] Abdel-Malek, *Egypte*, 316.
[19] Nazih Ayubi, *Bureaucracy and Politics in Contemporary Egypt* (London, 1980), 117.

intellectuals and national capital,"[20] of which the Arab Socialist Union presented itself as the guarantor. As for the "scientific" nature of that socialism, it placed the priority of industrial development within a strategy of import substitution, centralized management of agriculture with respect to "hydraulic" imperatives, and the urgency of making the management of public affairs more rational and moral. Finally, the Officers' regime did not succeed in controlling fully the values that a posteriori, appear as much more central and loaded than Arab socialist stances, especially those linked to religion, those actors that were not completely integrated into the official political scene – or were even hostile to the revolution – still exerting a firmer grip over these than did the revolution's ideologues.

During debates of the National Congress of Popular Forces, held in May 1962, and preceding adoption of the Charter of National Action, a challenge came from within the regime's ideological apparatus: Shaykh Muhammad al-Ghazali of al-Azhar virulently denounced the "secular" nature of the charter. The relay baton was taken up in al-Azhar's higher echelons, through a communique demanding that "Islam, the official religion of the State, permeate the laws of the State, educational curricula, social mores, the orientation of the media, family ties, and all assistance provided by the State to society and individuals," and that "the paragraph of the Charter relating to equality between men and women be completed by the words: within the limits of Islamic religious law."[21] Numerous "conservative" claims tumbled into the breach opened by the 'ulama', challenging especially the stand of the charter relating to "workers'" and "peasants'" representation, fixed at half the seats in all elections. Kamal al-Din Husayn, at the forefront of the Free Officers and, like Muhammad al-Ghazali, close to the Muslim Brothers, took the initiative in mediating between Nasir and challengers within the congress, by proposing that a commission be created to study possible amendments. The text of the charter put forth by Nasir was finally adopted unanimously and without amendment after the decks had been stacked with "Nasirist" delegates, but the ten-point report of the commission was to be "annexed" to the charter. One of the most significant aspects of this report was the distinction it established between "Arab socialism" and "the Arab application of socialism," which was to fuel future discussions. It was much more than just a Byzantine debate: it revealed the problem posed by a distinction between modernity, whose principal "effects" were recognized as imported, and "identity" or "authenticity," which some always feel are threatened. *Arab socialism*, i.e., the realization in Egypt and the Arab world of a universal which would allow a Hegelian-type vanguard to remodel heritage and give it access to modernity itself, was opposed to an *Arab* – or

[20] Quoted in Abdel-Malek, *Egypte*, 315.
[21] *Al-Ahram*, June 14, 1962, quoted in Abdel-Malek, *Egypte*, 324.

rather, Muslim – *application of socialism,* i.e., the borrowing system effected in another thought form through a filter of demands of loyalty to the Self. In the interval between these two "readings" is the nexus of the two symmetrical imperatives of ideological construction: to show that the socialism applied by Egypt was already anticipated or germinated in Revelation, which it has simply made concrete – this, for instance, is the method employed by Shaykh Hasan al-Bakri, former leader of the Muslim Brothers who passed into the service of the revolution in his capacity as minister of Waqfs, and of Mustafa al-Siba'i, the Syrian Muslim Brother who, in his *Socialism of Islam,* published in 1959, provided the regime with one of its rare "breviaries," to show that none of the policies adopted by the revolution contradicted divine command by explicitly setting out the terms of their compatibility – for example, within this logic al-Sanhuri, at the beginning of the 1960s, set himself the task of producing a synthesis of reformed Shari'a inherited from Muhammad 'Abduh and his school, and the positive legislation in force.[22]

It is in this context that the second wave of repression that struck the Muslim Brothers from 1965 on may be understood. After the 1954–55 offensive, which had led to the dissolution of the Brotherhood, the regime had placed less pressure on the Brothers and encouraged a few of them, such as the above-mentioned Hasan al-Bakri, to rally to the National Union. It tolerated the activities of Zaynab al-Ghazali, of the Muslim Women's Association who, while assisting the families of prisoners or released members of the Brotherhood, was working to reconstitute clandestine networks linking Brothers inside and outside the country, especially those who had taken refuge in Saudi Arabia. Further, the regime authorized the creation, in 1958, of Dar al-'Uraba, which published the writings of the Islamic trend's main theoreticians, among them Muhammad al-Ghazali, 'Abd al-Qadir 'Awda, and Sayyid Qutb. In 1964 Nasir himself ordered that Sayyid Qutb's *Ma'alim fil-tariq* be published – after it had been banned by the censors – the author himself having been released for health reasons. Several hypotheses have been suggested to explain the Nasir regime's position on the Muslim Brotherhood issue, an example of which was the trap Nasir laid for the association: the systematic discovery of Sayyid Qutb's "manifesto" during searches of August 1964 confirmed, in the eyes of the authorities, the existence of a "conspiracy," denounced by Nasir in a speech given in Moscow on May 30, where he threw suspicion on the Brothers' links with the American secret service, CENTO, and reactionary Arab regimes – to wit, the Saudi monarchy, with which Egypt's relations were at their lowest point within the context created by the Yemeni civil war – giving the signal for a new wave of repression. One wonders,

---

[22] See Bernard Botiveau, *Loi islamique et droit dans les sociétés* (Paris, 1994).

however, whether the opening given the Brotherhood between 1959 and 1965, a time when the regime hoped that it had definitely pulled the organization to pieces, reflected a temptation within Nasirist circles to retrieve not so much the Brotherhood's ideology, but their capacity to manage politically those values associated with religion, for the great benefit, it was predicted, of the regime's internal control system and regional influence. According to this hypothesis, it was only when it became obvious that the Brotherhood was in the process of reconstituting its organization clandestinely and, further, that this reconstitution was taking place with the blessings of the Nasirist project's greatest competitor – oil-rich Saudi Wahhabism – that the repression of this ideology again became inevitable in 1965. Hence the necessary hanging of Sayyid Qutb himself – both the most committed ideologue among the Brotherhood leaders and previously the closest to the Free Officers and Nasir, to the extent that he had occupied an office in the RCC headquarters – despite the widespread condemnation that the execution aroused throughout the Muslim world.

Egypt: military society?

Relations between Nasir and Field-Marshal 'Abd al-Hakim 'Amir, frequently stormy, pose the question of the regime's evolution, from the RCC's collective authority to the extreme "personalization" of Nasir's power starting from the beginning of the 1960s: schematically, Nasir, in order to rid himself of his rivals within the RCC – 'Abd al-Latif al-Baghdadi and Khalid Muhi al-Din, advocates of more liberalism in the economy and in political life, Kamal al-Din Husayn, who was close to the Brotherhood – was forced to seek support not from the army itself, through which these rivalries ran, but from the type of control that Field-Marshal 'Amir exerted on the armed forces. In this he provided the latter with the possibility of organizing the military as his personal fief. His behavior as commander of the "northern province," during the union with Syria, and the way the war in Yemen was conducted, give an idea of the extent of autonomy 'Amir's "loyalty" to Nasir won him – an authority that Nasir tried in vain to restrict in May 1962 with the creation of a "presidential council" responsible for examining promotions to superior ranks in the army and with the field-marshal's "promotion" to the rank of vice-president. Faced with 'Amir's refusal to relinquish his control over promotions, which was the cornerstone of his patronage network, Nasir had no choice but to give up his project, no doubt as much because 'Amir's clients would have remained loyal to him as because his eviction threatened to reinforce the networks of Nasir's potential rivals in the inner circle of the Free Officers and the former RCC.

Within the logic of this system of relations, Nasir's reply was to turn to the ASU, conceived as "a civilian counterpart to the military"[23] or a structure whose vocation was to integrate, in competitive positions and within a framework allowing their control, the personal networks of the regime's main figures. On one hand, ASU membership – almost 6 million in 1964 – and access to various positions of responsibility within it were organized on both professional and "sociological" bases: 50 percent of all ASU offices, like seats in parliament, were reserved for "peasants" and "workers," while the rest were shared among various socio-professional categories: liberal professions, cadres, intellectuals. The stakes of the political power balance from then on became the definition of what was to be understood by "peasant" or "worker" – a power balance that tended to play itself out to the benefit of medium property owners, a'yan or "new kulaks"[24] in the case of the former, whose posts in local ASU branches allowed them to ensure their control over cooperatives and mechanization units, and to that of union elites, in the case of the latter, encouraging what Nazih Ayubi describes as a "bureaucratisation of labour."[25] The ASU's task was to control unions and professional organizations, as well as access to certain professions – especially journalism – or to certain functions – for example, those of university rectors or faculty deans.

The counterpart of the corporatist organization of ASU membership was the system of exclusions it applied to "the enemies of the people's socialist revolution": all those, that is, who were affected by the agrarian reforms of 1952 and 1961, the nationalization measures of 1960 and 1961, or those whose property had been sequestrated or who had been detained for corruption or abuse of power. At the beginning of the 1960s, some even suggested extending to the male relatives of former large land owners the "political isolation" that was also, in the nationalized Egypt of the 1960s, economic and social isolation – a suggestion that was in fact applied by the HCLF, created in May 1966 under Field-Marshal 'Amir's presidency. It is this isolation, far more than the revolution itself, that explains the emigration of an important part of the old economic elites, especially members of the Syrian–Lebanese community, who had played a major part in the establishment of the banking sector, industry, and the press.

Corporate-style integration of citizens on one hand, exclusion of the "enemies of the revolution" on the other: between the two, the ASU pursued a series of objectives, contradictory at first glance but reflecting the system of internal constraints to which the Nasirist regime was subjected – to mobilize, at the local level, through neighborhood, village, and factory

---

[23] Waterbury, *Nasser and Sadat*, 216.
[24] Ansari, *Stalled Society*, 97ff.
[25] Ayubi, *Bureaucracy*, 451.

committees, the living forces of the nation. In other words, it set out to organize the reception and implementation of the regime's directives, while avoiding the constitution of new "feudalities" at the intermediary levels of the party and trade unions, capable of taking private benefits from its intermediary position and its connections with the "center of power"; to transform society "from above" in the name of socialist construction, and simultaneously depoliticize the class alliance on which the regime was based – "workers" and "peasants" – in order to avoid claims that could undermine "national unity."

Hence a permanent tension existed, "structural" one might say, a pendulum movement between the options and slogans of the more "radical" components (grouped around ʿAli Sabri and Shaʿrawi Jumʿa) and those of the more "moderate" groups (around Anwar al-Sadat and Zakariya Muhi al-Din) within the ASU. The creation in 1964 of the "political apparatus" (*al-jihaz al-siyasi*), also known as the "Socialist Vanguard" (*al-taliʿa al-ishtirakiyya*), a true party within the party, dramatized the stakes of this tension. It is precisely because Nasir had given the ASU, directed by the "radical" ʿAli Sabri, the mission of controlling the government, the administration, the media, and the public sector, and, through them, society as a whole, that it was necessary to establish the means of controlling the ASU itself – the mission the Vanguard was assigned. The list of its members was kept secret, as was the scope of its prerogatives; everyone knew only that, through its main figures – ʿAli Sabri, Shaʿrawi Jumʿa, Sami Sharaf – it had control over the police and the main non-military information services. It also controlled the Youth Organization (*munazzamat al-shabab*), an important "reservoir" of militants, the ASU Committee on Ideological Questions, and the High Institute of Socialist Studies, the party's school for cadres.

The activities of the HCLF in 1967–67 illustrate, by pushing it to its paroxysm, the way this control system functioned. Created in May 1966, after the assassination of Salah Maqlad, a former Muslim Brother who had become secretary of the ASU committee in Kamshish (Minufiya), by the hitmen of a "feudal" family whose interests were threatened by his activism at the head of the peasants, the HCLF, presided over by ʿAbd al-Hakim ʿAmir and with members including the principal patrons of the "centers of power" (no doubt in order to implicate some of them in the repression of their own clients), was assigned by Nasir the task of uncovering all the cases in which the agrarian reform laws had been contravened by former or current "feudalists." Several hundred families were subjected to investigation throughout the country, almost 60,000 faddans were seized, and thousands of people related to the incriminated "feudalists" were divested of their functions in local administration, the party, the magistrature, and the security forces before Nasir himself, after the June 1967 defeat, admitted that grave abuses had been committed and ordered that over 60 percent of these procedures be canceled.[26]

The paradoxes resulting from this control system have been studied and described elsewhere. The implementation of the most radical projects was systematically assigned to the most conservative "patrons": Husayn Shafi'i, the first secretary-general of the ASU, belonged to the right wing of the regime and was linked to the Muslim Brothers; Sadat, president of parliament, was expected to pass the most radical items of legislation; 'Abd al-Hakim 'Amir, placed by Nasir at the head of the HCLF, himself came from a large, land-owning family; while not a single representative of the Marxists with which the regime had concluded an alliance from 1965 onward was a member of the committee. In much the same way, the method different patrons used to manage their clients tended to encourage alliances "against nature": for instance, that of 'Ali Sabri, the main middleman between the regime and the Soviet leaders and one of the government's most radical elements, with 'Abd al-Hakim 'Amir, concerned with guaranteeing a flow of weapons, and whose conservative tendencies have been mentioned. The most paradoxical aspect remains the role played by the Marxists in the ideological and organizational orchestration of Nasirist socialism: less than six months after their release from the prison camps of the western desert, where communist militants and Muslim Brothers rubbed shoulders, and while Krushchev, visiting Aswan in May 1964 for the inauguration of the first phase of the high dam, was declaring that Egypt was indeed "building socialism," it was the Marxists (the Egyptian Communist Party was to announce its self-dissolution and the adherence of its individual members to the ASU in January 1965) who would provide Nasir with the personnel he needed to frame the radicalization of the revolution – precisely when anti-communism was on the agenda more than ever in Egypt. The ultimate paradox lies in the fact that the radicalization of the revolution as Nasir envisaged it – that is, as the way of breaking the "centers of power" that threatened his own – would contribute decisively to strengthening them. Ultimately, it aggravated the regime's isolation from society until the collision with the "reality principle" – the repeated financial crises, starting in 1962, that reflected the regime's inability to fund both industrialization and redistribution, and which inaugurated the difficult relations between Egypt and the IMF; and especially the disaster of June 1967, which laid bare the illusions of recaptured glory couched in the rhetoric of Arab socialism.

Return to the principle of reality

"After 1967, Egypt no longer had an economic plan or a political organization with clear objectives – Egypt's socialist experiment in terms of economy

[26] On these investigations, see Ansari, *Stalled Society*, 110ff.

had not lasted more than five years, and that of the socialist vanguard on political terrain, not more than two."[27] Two contradictory hypotheses explain the political and economic failure of Nasirism and the genesis of the "counter-revolution" initiated by Sadat after his accession to power in autumn 1970.

For advocates of the internalist hypothesis, the reasons for this failure lie within the internal logic of the Nasirist project and the conditions of its authoritarian implementation, supported by the Soviet Union. While certain authors[28] underline the remarkably favorable terms of socialist-bloc aid to the Egyptian economy – almost 600 million Egyptian pounds between 1958 and 1977, not counting arms supplies – and the decisive role played by this aid in the country's transition from an almost exclusively agricultural base to an industrial one, the sharpest criticism is directed toward the project of "industrialization through import substitution" itself, encouraged by the Soviet Union for "ideological" reasons: the creation of an industrial proletariat; priority placed on heavy industry; lack of financial realism, which made the country increasingly dependent on external sources of finance, in a context within which the regime did not intend – or could not afford – to sacrifice the improvement in the standard of living of its social base to the financial requirements of industrialization; lack of economic realism in a context within which, while funding the establishment of "outsized" industries, the socialist bloc imported only agricultural primary products (with a few exceptions); and the perverse effects of protectionist logic on labor productivity and the emergence of what Clement Moore designates as an "anomic division of labor,"[29] where middlemen received the lion's share. In other words, the "Arab socialism" implemented in Egypt in the 1960s was destined to fail from the outset, because of inherent contradictions that condemned its champions to a sort of "forward flight." The announced radicalism of policies is here seen only as the counterpart of the regime's "objective" failures in the country's economic development.

For the advocates – Nasirists and neo-Nasirists, Marxists, third worldists, and other Arab nationalists – of the externalist hypothesis, the failure of Nasirist development policies may be attributed to the explicit hostility of "imperialism, Zionism and Arab reaction," the adversaries designated by the Egyptian leadership.[30] Within this logic, the possibility that the "Egyptian experience" would succeed, with the support of the Soviet Union, justified the "holy alliance" concluded to prevent the Nasirist regime from

---

[27] Waterbury, *Nasser and Sadat*, 332.
[28] For instance *ibid.*, 391ff.
[29] C. Moore, *Images of Development: Egyptian Engineers in Search of Industry* (Cambridge, 1980), 73.
[30] For instance, Muhammad Hasanayn Haykal, *Le sphinx et le commissaire*, Paris, 1978; Mahmoud Hussein, *L'Egypte II, 1967–73* (Paris, 1975).

"exporting the revolution" and achieving the unity of the Arab peoples as enshrined in the charter of the Arab League, based in Egypt since its foundation in March 1945. In another scenario, from the point of view of those less sympathetic to the Nasirist experience, the Egyptian leadership's will to regional hegemony in the context of the cold war could only confront the imperatives of *realpolitik* followed by the two superpowers, concerned above all else with preventing the conflicts between their respective "clients" from escalating into direct confrontation.[31]

It is not our purpose here to favor one hypothesis or the other. Rather, we attempt to show how both may be articulated to reveal the stakes, both external and internal, of the options that constituted "Nasirism." We may start with the evolution of relations between the Nasirist regime and "imperialism," denounced as "enemy no. 1" of the Egyptian revolution. The question posed here is not so much that of whether the hostility of successive American administrations toward Nasir's regime was real – nor, on the contrary, whether Nasir "really" stood up to the American superpower – as it is the way in which these antagonistic relations evolved and were expressed in discourse and reality. The USA's initially favorable stance toward the Free Officers has been mentioned above: not only were the Americans the first to be notified that the coup was imminent, but, taking into account the discreet contacts made with the officers through their representatives, in July 1952 they had many reasons to think that "their men" had seized power on the banks of the Nile – an opinion shared by many of the new regime's opponents, particularly among the left. Aid to Egypt within the framework of Point Four (the ancestor of today's USAID) shot from less than $6 million before 1952 to $40 million only a few weeks after the coup, and Dean Acheson, the US secretary of state, asserted that Egypt could henceforth count on the USA's "active friendship." The withdrawal of this sympathy in 1955, when Nasir purchased weapons from Czechoslovakia after the American authorities had repeatedly refused to sell arms to Egypt as long as it was not a member of a regional military alliance under American leadership – a step that was evidently unacceptable to Egypt, so recently removed from British tutelage – has also been mentioned. The American reaction to the tripartite aggression and the terms of the ultimatum addressed to the French, the Israelis, and the British – exceptionally violent for a text involving "allies," and which was further cosigned by the "Soviet enemy" – makes it possible to measure the stakes of this "sympathy" and the limits of the "antagonism," brought about by the Czech arms affair, toward the new Egyptian leaders. For the USA, the main "merit" of Nasir's regime was that it had just put a credible end to colonial rule, and America's main "message" to its allies, in agreement with the

[31] See Nissim Rejwan, *Nasserist Ideology: Its Exponents and Critics* (New York, 1974).

Soviets on this point, was that there was no question of restoring it in any form – in Egypt, but especially as far as British disengagement from the Arabian peninsula was concerned. At the very instant when the American administration was adopting measures of undisguised hostility toward Nasir's regime – particularly the retraction of proposals to finance the high dam – it began a food aid program to Egypt that constituted significant support for the internal stability of Nasirist power: between 1954 and 1966, Egypt thus received American wheat shipments valued at $643 million, largely subsidized by the US treasury and paid for in Egyptian pounds. The shipments were not interrupted by the "socialist measures" of 1961–62, nor by the increasing penetration of Soviet cooperation in the Egyptian economy, which allowed one writer to observe that "the USSR helped Egypt industrialize while the US was helping feed its labor force."[32] The same author stresses that for the same period, and if Soviet military supplies are not taken into account, American aid to Egypt outweighed Soviet aid. One might add that it was qualitatively equally decisive – at least in that it allowed the Americans to have their say in the country's evolution.

The reasons for which and the way that the American administration interrupted food aid to Egypt in 1965, in retaliation for the increasingly massive intervention – up to 40,000 men – in the Yemeni civil war, illustrate both the ambiguity in American perceptions of the Nasir regime and the way the internal and external stakes in the regime's options were articulated. While the Americans had at first recognized the pro-Egyptian republican regime established in Sana'a by Brigadier-General 'Abdallah al-Sallal in November 1962 – which leads us to think that it was not the eventual emergence of "Nasirist-type" forces they had feared – aggravation of the Egyptian–Saudi conflict, which soon appeared as the foremost aspect of the Yemeni crisis, was the factor that convinced them, almost three years after the beginning of the crisis, to suspend food aid to Egypt. The cessation of wheat shipments considerably aggravated the Egyptian financial crisis: in 1965–66 the value of wheat and flour imports was greater than that of Egyptian exports to western markets. Behind the conflict with Saudi Arabia, beyond the competition of two states vying for the leadership of the Arab world, was Nasir's questioning of the way Arab petroleum wealth was distributed and used. The "theory of the three circles," which made of Egypt both center and vanguard of the Arab, African, and Islamic worlds, was, as has been mentioned, significantly radicalized by the failure of the union with Syria, which the Egyptians attributed, among other causes, to Saudi maneuvering. Within the new Egyptian strategic vision, Arab unity could only be realized through the generalization of Arab socialism, which implied the

---

[32] Waterbury, *Nasser and Sadat*, 404. See also W. J. Burns, *Economic Aid and American Policy toward Egypt, 1955–1981* (New York, 1984).

overthrow of reactionary monarchies. Hence the tone of the new Egyptian activism, which tended to oppose Nasir's regime to America's allies in the region.

This viewpoint is also useful in attempts to understand the evolution of the conflict between Egypt and the Arab states on one hand, and the "Zionist entity" on the other – a conflict that resulted, on June 6, 1967, in defeat of the Arab armies. If we discount the supposedly axiomatic, ineluctable character of the "battle for destiny" between Israel and its Arab neighbors, linked to the very "survival" of the Arab nation, which provided the main part of Arab war propaganda, Egypt's management of this conflict may be seen in two contradictory yet complementary ways. By maximizing the Israeli threat and setting the stage for Egyptian preparations for the final confrontation – meant to free Jerusalem and return their land to the Palestinians – Nasir could justify his active hostility toward the Arab regimes dubbed reactionary by playing the "peoples-against-dynasties" card. Egyptian propaganda in fact aimed primarily at standing up to the ideological competition represented by Ba'thist propaganda in its Syrian and Iraqi variants. This strategy was not entirely unsuccessful both with Arab masses, among whom the Egyptian za'im was immensely popular, and on the inter-state level, thanks to Egypt's control of the Arab League. As far as Egypt's autonomous strategy was concerned, before 1967 Nasir seems to have been mainly preoccupied with avoiding the risk of a generalized confrontation with Israel at any cost, seeing that a war could only have been extremely costly for Egypt given American support for the Jewish state and the division of Arab ranks.

Between 1960 and 1965 there was a relative "detente" in relations between Egypt and Israel: the "moderates" were in power in Tel Aviv and a sort of complicity seems to have been established between Nasir and Levi Eshkol, the Israeli prime minister, similar to that before the "tripartite aggression," between Nasir and Moshe Sharett.[33] From 1965 on, however, Palestinian operations based in Jordan and supported by Syria, Iraq, and Algeria caused tensions to rise once again, brought about conditions favorable to the return of "hardliners" in the Israeli cabinet, and forced Egypt itself to harden its position in order to avoid being "outstripped." While recognizing the PLO as the vanguard of "Arab revolutionary action" during the Second Palestinian National Congress in Cairo in May 1965, Nasir saw no reason why he, too, should not encourage Palestinian guerrilla actions. While attempting to find a reply to both radical Arab "provocations" and to Israeli retaliatory operations against Jordan and Syria, Nasir gave the Israelis the pretext they needed to destroy the Egyptian armed forces: on May 20, 1967 he ordered that the United Nations forces stationed in Gaza and Sinai

---

[33] Olivier Carré, *L'Orient arabe aujourd'hui* (Paris, 1991), 78ff.

since 1957 be removed two days later, and decreed the closing of the Gulf of Aqaba to all Israeli ships and a blockade of the Tiran straits. Between June 5 and 10, 1967, the Israeli army destroyed most of the infrastructure of the Egyptian armed forces, especially the grounded air force, and occupied the West Bank and Gaza, the Golan Heights, and all of Sinai.

The question of who started the war remains, as posed, undecidable. If Nasir's gesticulations appeared as a *casus belli*, the unbelievable lack of preparation of the Egyptian armed forces suffices to show that he had no intention of taking the initiative in military operations. A number of observers agree today that Nasir was relying, "thanks to a concert of Soviet and American assurances, on avoiding armed confrontation and negotiating definitively the two basic questions left hanging since 1949, the question of frontiers and that of refugees."[34] In other words, 1967 may have been an anticipation of 1973, when a "substitute for war,"[35] or rather a "substitute for victory," finally allowed President Sadat to begin settling the Egyptian aspect of the conflict. Instead, the humiliation of 1948 was repeated, with the aggravating circumstance that the army, which held power directly, could not back down by citing the corruption and incompetence of the palace or the political parties.

Maintained in power by gigantic demonstrations through which Egypt almost unanimously refused his resignation while demanding that he shoulder his responsibilities in defeat, Nasir saw his room for maneuver drastically reduced both internally and externally. On one hand, the absolute priority placed on rebuilding the armed forces, not only justified by "external" constraints – liberating Palestine, destroying the Zionist entity – but also by occupation of national territory, was reflected in a considerable increase in military spending. Austerity measures and shortages on a daily basis were the only option for seven long years, during which

the economic contraction (*inkimash*) had as its counterpart economic and military firmness (*sumud*), which meant: asking the Egyptian people to bear the enormous military expenditures necessary if capitulation to Israel was to be avoided. All measures of social and economic policy were in a way suspended, frozen; the public sector apparatus was barely kept alive, as were the government service programme and the very infrastructure of the country. In per capita percentage, if not in absolute terms, the level of production, the quantity and quality of available services, began to decline.[36]

On the other hand, and for the same reasons, Egypt's dependence on the Soviet Union and the latter's direct intervention in the management of Egyptian affairs increased considerably and acquired an everyday visibility

[34] *Ibid.*, 82.
[35] Ghali Shoukri, *Egypte, contre-révolution* (Paris, 1979), 179ff.
[36] Waterbury, *Nasser and Sadat*, 112. See also 407ff.

all the more difficult to bear when part of Egyptian public opinion placed the blame for the scale of defeat on the poor quality of Soviet arms: when Sadat expelled them, in 1972, there were almost 12,000 military advisors in Egypt, capable of controlling every cog of the Egyptian armed forces, and several thousand advisors criss-crossing the public sector and government apparatus.

On the internal scene, the 1967 disaster provided the opportunity for the first public demonstrations of opposition in Egypt since 1965. First, in February 1968, after extremely lenient sentences had been handed down against officers on trial, students of Cairo and Alexandria universities, joined by workers of the arms factories in Helwan, demanded that those responsible for the Six Day defeat be punished, and insisted above all on reestablishment of political freedoms. The manifesto, made public by students of the Polytechnic Faculty in Cairo, also demanded, among other measures, "that freedom of expression be re-established, as well as that of the press; the restoration of a truly representative parliament; the removal of secret police from university campuses; the promulgation of laws establishing or reinforcing political freedoms."[37] The regime responded first by giving in a little, in an attempt to confine student mobilization to the campuses. It announced that responsible officers would be re-tried, freedom of expression restored on campus, an independent student union allowed. When demonstrations started again in November 1968, the authorities turned to the stick, arresting hundreds of students, putting "leaders" on trial, and justifying this repression by citing the necessity of preserving the unity of the internal front in the struggle against the Zionist enemy. But the 1967 defeat had transformed the theme of struggle against Israel – or, rather, support for the Palestinian struggle – into a theme of opposition that provided students and intellectuals with one of their main calls for mobilization against the regime. The "war of attrition" launched by Nasir on the Canal front, in the last months of 1968, in an attempt to improve the Egyptian position in planned negotiations, was no doubt, in large part, a reply to internal pressures exerted by students in particular. The June 1967 defeat, followed by the inevitable retreat from economic and social objectives trumpeted by the regime, paradoxically marked the beginning of the transformation of Nasirism itself, from the "hard-core" version of the early 1960s into an opposition resource, making defense of "socialist gains" and continuation of the process of unifying the Arab nation the main arguments of the ASU's left wing and of the intellectual left, a trend that Sadat would confront as soon as he took power.

[37] Quoted by Ahmad Abdalla, *The Student Movement and National Politics in Egypt* (London, 1985), 152.

From socialism to an open-door policy: counter-revolution or realization of the revolution's objectives by other means?

Nasir's death, on September 28, 1970, brought to power Anwar al-Sadat, who had been named vice-president less than a year before.[38] Although he had accumulated a series of important functions within the Nasirist control system – secretary-general of the Liberation Rally, then of the National Union, editor-in-chief of *al-Gumhuriyya*, the Free Officers' unofficial organ, president of the parliament – he appeared, to most outside observers, if not a new face at least an unknown and, to say the least, not a very significant one. Those with more insight saw his advance as a compromise or transitional solution, masking a power struggle until a new strongman could impose himself. The question here is that of the "true beginnings" of Sadat's regime. He himself placed them on May 15, 1971, with the "corrective revolution" (*thawrat al-tashih*) and the liquidation of "power centers" (*marakiz al-quwa*) inherited from the 1960s; taking the initiative in the confrontation, Sadat had the "barons" of the Nasirist left arrested: 'Ali Sabri, secretary-general of the ASU and vice-president of the Republic; Sha'rawi Jum'a, minister of the interior; Muhammad Fa'iq, minister of information; Sami Sharaf, minister for presidential affairs; Muhammad Fawzi, minister of war – in all almost ninety individuals who had intended to impose, as in the first days of the revolution, a collective leadership of the state and who, unable to obtain his consent regarding restriction of presidential prerogatives, had begun to plot against him. But most observers place the true beginnings of the Sadat era in October 1973, with the new legitimacy the "hero of the crossing" obtained through the "victory" over Israel of the Egyptian armed forces who recaptured the eastern bank of the Canal, occupied since 1967. This legitimacy enabled him to impose his own options and dismantle his predecessor's policies. "Hero of the crossing, [Sadat] really became the *rais*: he no longer owed anything to Nasser and the October war founded his regime. Sketched out on May 15, 1970, Sadat's Egypt took shape by breaking with the past."[39] He now imposed his own options regarding the open-door policy (*infitah*), the west, political parties, and peace with Israel.

---

[38] On the Sadat period in general, see Raymond Hinnebusch, *Egyptian Politics under Sadat: The Post-Populist Development of an Authoritarian-Modernizing State* (Cambridge, 1985); Shoukri, *Egypte*; David Hirst and Irene Beeson, *Sadat* (London, 1981).

[39] Pierre Mirel, *L'Egypte des ruptures* (Paris, 1982), 31.

Liberalization or de-Nasirization?

The situation inherited by Nasir's successor and the options open to the new Egyptian leadership may be summed up in three ways:

1 A political system that, we may assume, functioned relatively well with the army no longer constituting a political threat, and an ASU purged of "radical" Nasirist elements and more docile than ever with regard to the executive's desires enjoyed absolute political hegemony except in the universities, where Marxists and Nasirists preserved solid bases. The new regime asserted a system of "sacred" goals, with respect to which unanimity was required, even if differences as to how they would be achieved were allowed: freeing the national territory occupied by the Israeli enemy and preserving the "gains" of the July revolution.

2 The system of external alliances with the Soviet bloc had shown its limits in 1967: on one hand, the poor performance of Soviet arms and the qualitative and quantitative inadequacy of weaponry delivered to Egypt were blamed in part for the Six Day disaster; on the other, the Soviets had clearly shown unwillingness to risk an open confrontation with the USA in the Near East. We may add that Moscow had no particular reason to encourage a man who had consolidated power through distancing and imprisoning the Soviet Union's most important "friends" within the Egyptian state apparatus.

3 Sadat inherited a particularly bad financial situation, increasing budget deficits, a chronic currency shortage, and the "classic" consequences of this sort of situation: factories operating at a third of their capacity owing to a shortage of raw materials, assembly lines grinding to a halt because of lack of spare parts, neglect of equipment, and other problems.

After the tergiversations of 1972, the year announced by the new president as "decisive" in the Arab–Israeli conflict and which ended without any "decisive" developments, the October 1973 war and "psychological" victory of Egyptian troops allowed Sadat to silence his critics and escape from cyclical resource shortages. The way he had prepared for the war speaks volumes about the goals it would allow him to pursue. On the one hand, the war would have to be fought with Soviet weapons since the west had not been prepared to arm Egypt; in May 1971, just as Sadat was launching the corrective revolution, he signed a "friendship and cooperation treaty" with the Soviet Union, which would contribute to reconstruction of the Egyptian armed forces. On the other hand, the war itself had to be fought without the Soviets in order to make possible a renewal of relations with the United States; Sadat expressed a conviction that the USA held "100 percent of the cards" in the resolution of the conflict. Hence the expulsion in

July 1972 of Soviet military experts who, incidentally, had advised him against this particular adventure.[40]

It is conventional to consider that the October war made *infitah* possible by rupturing the main Nasirist options: alliance with the Soviet bloc; primacy of the public sector; one-party government. But the October war itself only acquired meaning from the *infitah*: it allowed the regime to transform what was, in reality, a military defeat of sorts – for the first time Israeli troops had acquired a foothold on the African bank of the Canal and the third army, surrounded at Suez, only escaped capitulation because of American pressure on Israel – into a political victory. The regime then transformed this victory into a "government program," with objectives set down in the "October Document" presented by Sadat in March 1974: opening up to the market and to the west, which would allow association of Arab capital, western technology, and Egyptian know-how in the pacified Near East.

Law 43 on Arab and foreign investment, voted by parliament in June 1974, constituted the cornerstone of the *infitah*. It established an organism for investment and a list of activities and sectors designated as priorities, and offered considerable guarantees and privileges to foreign investors: repatriation of capital and profits, tax exemptions for five to eight years, and customs exemptions for equipment and raw materials necessary for production. Law 43 also put an end to public-sector monopoly on banking activities, by allowing intervention in Egypt of foreign banks operating in foreign currency. Above all, the law allowed that any joint venture established between foreign partners and a public-sector firm would automatically be considered as belonging to the private sector, even if the public sector held the majority shares. This was a strong incentive for managers of public enterprises to seek this type of association to guarantee substantial increases in revenue and an improvement in work conditions and to open up vistas of rationalized production, especially by allowing these enterprises to dodge the labor legislation (minimum wage, hiring of university graduates, worker representation) in force in the public sector. Anxious to please and to demonstrate that the nationalization page had been turned, Sadat himself took the initiative and had files of individuals placed under sequestration in the 1960s reopened, allowing considerable amounts of property – buildings, factories, lands – to be returned to their original owners.

We shall return later to the social consequences of *infitah* and the reallocation of available resources it brought about. Here we may stress what appears the essential aspect in the first phase of implementation of the open-door policy: the fact that *it did not work* – or at least not the way the regime

[40] See Muhammad Hasanayn Haykal, *The Road to Ramadan* (London, 1975).

had hoped it would.[41] Despite the incentives and guarantees offered to foreign investors, only sixty-six projects had been registered by the end of 1976 under Law 43, with a total capital amounting to LE36 million and only 3,450 employees. Far from engaging in productive activities, most of these projects were concentrated in tourism, banking, and investment companies, transforming Law 43 into a powerful drain on the remittances in hard currency of Egyptian workers who had migrated to the oil states (see below). If the October war had made *infitah* possible, the policy's success still required the true economic and political participation of the west, and especially of America, in supporting a regime that constantly trumpeted its membership of the western camp. In order to obtain this support, Sadat took two closely related steps: on the economic side, negotiations with the IMF began in 1976 and were virtually uninterrupted from letter of intent to structural adjustment program; on the political side, peace with Israel, if possible general but if not then separate, which was seen as the main incentive for western powers to reinforce the stability of the Egyptian regime.

With regard to the IMF, the goal of 'Abd al-Mun'im al-Qaysuni, supreme manager of the *infitah*, was to obtain the fund's support in a context where the increase of subsidies on consumer goods – a reaction to the inflation brought on by the *infitah* itself – had led the budget deficit to explode, dragging Egypt into the spiral of short-term debt. Subsidies on consumer goods for the poor reached 33.6 percent of current spending, LE433.5 million in a budget whose deficit approached LE700 million; service on debt alone reached 40 percent of total revenue from exports. To "appease" the IMF, the authorities announced, on January 17, 1977, removal of subsidies from a certain number of basic commodities: butane, flour, rice, sugar, oil, a measure presented as a first step toward diminishing the deficit and returning to "real pricing." Much has been written about the "perverse effects" of the subsidy system, especially about the "unjustified" increase in consumption that it encouraged, the waste it entailed, the black market and the fact that, designed to help the poor, it also benefited the rich.[42] The fact remains that these measures, announced without the slightest preparation, could only result in yet another decline in the standard of living of the population, since they led, overnight, to increases ranging from 15 to 45 percent in the prices of the affected goods.

Revolt was immediate and spontaneous, even if the security services and Sadat himself denounced the activities of "communist saboteurs"; it swept across the entire country and lasted for three days, pitting demonstrators,

---

[41] See, among others, John Waterbury, *Egypt: Burdens of the Past, Options for the Future* (Bloomington, 1978).

[42] On this debate see Alain Roussillon, "Développement et justice sociale dans une économie sous perfusion: les enjeux des subventions en Egypte," *Annuaire de l'Afrique du Nord*, 23 (1984).

who attacked all the symbols of *infitah* (shop windows, travel agencies, nightclubs), against an impotent police force, then against the army, which rolled out the tanks several times, clamping down in Cairo and Alexandria. The result was many more dead than the hundred or so officially announced, thousands of wounded, and mass arrests. On January 20, the government backtracked suddenly, simply canceling the measures announced three days earlier and promising, while they were at it, 10 percent increases in salaries and pensions. Even if later the government was able to enact most of the price increases demanded by the IMF – doing so more tactfully and progressively, avoiding the shock effect that had done much to unleash people's anger – "hunger revolts" remain today the greatest fear of the Egyptian government, indicating the social limits beyond which "de-regulation," "structural adjustment," and other economic "liberalization" measures cannot go. For the first time since 1952, the army had intervened against the people, reflecting the limits of the consensus Sadat's regime had hoped for in its project to dismantle the system of redistribution set up by the Nasirist state. But the uprising of January 1977 also remains today the main "scarecrow" the Egyptian government uses to resist, with consummate agility, the more insistent "recommendations" of the IMF and Egypt's international creditors, by highlighting the potential damage to the country's stability of a too-hasty return to real pricing and market forces. Above all, the January uprising bore witness to the need for the *infitah* to keep the promises of a return to prosperity that Sadat had made after the October war: it would provide the ultimate justification for the riskiest bet placed by the Sadat regime – far more than the *infitah* itself: the signing of a separate peace with Israel, which Sadat hoped would lead to the launching of an American "Marshall Plan" to Egypt's benefit.

Although it was by far the costliest of the Israeli–Arab wars in terms of human lives, the October 1973 war held the keys, as it were, to its own "peaceful" interpretation. Barely a month after the Egyptian offensive had been launched, diplomatic relations were restored between Cairo and Washington. A few days later, at "kilometer 101," negotiations described as "technical," relating to supplies for the third army blocked at Suez and the exchange of POWs, constituted the first diplomatic contact between Egyptians and Israelis. In all Arab forums, especially at the sixth summit meeting in Algiers in November 1973, Egypt pleaded the case for the Arabs' need to take advantage of the new situation created by the October "victory" and the oil embargo to obtain a "peace of the brave." Above all, as soon as the first agreement on withdrawal had been signed, under American auspices, Egypt threw itself into clearing the Suez Canal and rebuilding Suez, Isma'iliyya, and Port Said. On June 5, the eve of the anniversary of its closing in 1967, Sadat "reinaugurated" the waterway with full ceremonies, an irrefutable proof of Egypt's desire that this war be the last. Moreover, with the signing of the second withdrawal accord, in September 1975, whereby Egypt regained control of Sinai (up to the strategic passes) and the Gulf of Suez oil wells, it agreed – with American guarantees that satisfied almost every Israeli demand, especially as far as arms were concerned – to renounce force in managing the two sides' disagreements.

The sticking-point of Sadat's position was that every concession deepened the gulf between Egypt and its Arab allies, was accompanied by a hardening of Israeli positions, and increased the intransigence of Syria and the Palestinians. In the Israeli elections of May 1977, while the Egyptian government was beginning to take stock of the January uprising, Menachem Begin's Likud was borne to power on a program that entailed nothing less than the creation of a "Greater Israel" and brushed aside negotiations for the evacuation of Gaza and the West Bank. Sadat's famous "bluff" – his announcement in November 1977 that he was ready to go anywhere, including the Knesset, to advance the peace process – was aimed at making the west realize the literally dramatic nature, for Egypt, of the situation in Geneva where talks, begun in December 1974, were deadlocked owing to Israeli and Arab intransigence. The next step was predictable, despite Sadat's denial in his speech to the Knesset that Egypt could sign a separate peace. Israeli refusal to budge and American pressure on the one hand, the Arab front created at a summit in Tripoli in December 1977 which had decided to freeze relations with Egypt, on the other, left Sadat nowhere to go but forward: on September 17, 1978 two frameworks for a treaty were sketched out at Camp David, after twelve days of negotiations, one concerning Israel's evacuation of the Sinai over a three-year period and the other the future of negotiations on other occupied territories, especially the West Bank and Gaza. A peace treaty was signed on March 26, 1979, by Sadat and Begin, in the presence of President Carter, who was its principal craftsman. The result was Egypt's expulsion from all Arab organizations, including the League itself, on March 31, 1979, and termination of diplomatic relations between Cairo and the other Arab capitals (except Khartoum and Musqat).

We shall return to the stakes of the separate peace with regard to the Egyptian political scene. What were the consequences of peace for implementation of the open-door policy? There is no doubt that the peace treaty opened the dikes of American aid to a country that had become crucial to its "national interest": from 1979 on, Egypt received annually between $1 billion and $1.5 billion in civilian aid from the USA, virtually the same as Israel, and considerable military credit, handed out all the more generously since Sadat, in order to compensate for Egypt's "neutralization" on the Arab scene, posed as the new "policeman" of the Red Sea and the Horn of Africa, confronting the Soviet and Cuban menace from Ethiopia and the gesticulations of the "Libyan madman."[43] Sadat conceded important naval facilities to the American fleet and participated in the maneuvers of the "Rapid Deployment Force" created by Carter after the Tehran hostage crisis. Nor is there any doubt that this aid, managed by a permanent USAID mission in Cairo with a plethora of experts and advisors, directly and massively contributed to setting up the country's basic infrastructure – telephones, transport, energy – which had barely been maintained since the late 1960s. In the early 1980s, American wheat shipments to Egypt made up 27 percent of the country's annual consumption, and this percentage increased thereafter. But at the same time, the breach created by the Camp David agreement in relations between Egypt and the Arab states defeated the purpose of the *infitah* itself: there was no longer any question of massive injections of surplus petrodollars that the October war had helped to create; if western or Japanese technology was brought into Egypt, it was not in the form of equipment that would develop the country's productive capacities, but as electronic gadgets to satisfy long-repressed consumer desires. The Egyptian labor force, whose education, low wages, and docility were intended to facilitate the "marriage" of Arab capital and western technology – to the great benefit of employment rates in Egypt – migrated to the Gulf in increasing numbers to seek work and social promotion. In other words, what was intended to be the first of its kind in North–South cooperation models increasingly appeared as a new form of Egyptian dependence, no longer on the eastern bloc but this time on the economics of the industrialized west.

Liberalization vs. democratization?

By appropriating the power conferred upon him by election to the presidency of the Republic on October 7, 1970 and confirmed by referendum on October 10 (90.1 percent voted yes) and by getting rid of rivals within the ASU Sadat justified strong-arm tactics – dubbed "corrective revolution" and celebrated every year with at least as much pomp and circumstance as the revolution itself – by a need to restore or establish the "state of institutions" (*dawlat al-mu'assasat*), as he put it, and the effective rule of law. Until the October war, this commitment was limited to a few cosmetic measures: questioning the most visible repressive aspects of Nasirism; reversal of sequestration measures and relieving the political "isolation" in which certain individuals with the reputation of right wingers were living. The "permanent" constitution of the Arab Republic of Egypt (no longer the United Arab Republic), solemnly promulgated in September 1971, was new

---

[43] This was how Sadat referred to Colonel Gaddafi after Libya broke diplomatic relations following the first Egypt–Israel disengagement in November 1973.

only in terms of its "permanence"; Sadat amended it as often as he deemed necessary, resorting to plebiscites on topics as varied as the confirmation of Egypt's democratic socialist identity; its membership of the Arab nation; the 50 percent "quota" of electoral positions reserved for workers and peasants and the social gains of the revolution; whether or not Islam was the state religion – Shari'a being at the time one of the main sources of the law; and confirmation of the president's designation by the people's assembly. The ASU itself was reined in and handed over to Sayyid Mar'i, for support he had given the president during the "corrective revolution," and the state of emergency was maintained under the pretext that lifting it could appear as a sign of weakness in the confrontation with Israel. The most revealing indicator of the regime's evolution on the ideological level was the progressive release of the Muslim Brothers, whose supporters on university campuses were allowed to create *jama 'at islamiyya* (Islamic associations), whereby the regime hoped they would be able to get rid of the Nasirist and Marxist left.

Adopted by referendum on May 15, 1974, the "October document" that fired the starter's gun for economic opening up of the country and political liberalization was doubly linked to the 1973 "victory": Sadat was no longer only the country's "legal" president but also the "hero of the crossing." The legitimacy acquired during the October war allowed Sadat to take the risk of weakening his legal hold on the system. Meanwhile, radical transformation of the regional and international situations allowed the regime to hope that a fruitful collaboration could be undertaken with the west and the Arab "moderates" and demanded an ideological *aggiornamento* that itself rendered necessary the transformation of the political framework. The ASU was invited to consider possible means of introducing pluralism in political structures that would not threaten the "gains" of the July revolution, whose main merit, despite the errors made, was to have opened the path for "peaceful social and political transformations sparing the country violent class conflicts, if not a civil war." In fact, the way in which the ASU was dismantled and replaced by a pluralist political structure between 1974 and 1979 allowed the president to maintain, and even strengthen, his grip on the main tools of control, while deploying these tools in other institutions.

The first episode in this process of political liberalization "from above" concerned the constitution of "platforms" (*manabir*) within the ASU, after extremely heated debates about the country's political future, to which were invited all "organic" components of the Egyptian nation: workers and peasants, intellectuals, businessmen and unions, students, women. At the end of these debates, almost 140 projects for creating such "platforms" were registered with the general secretariat of the ASU. It accepted only four – right, center, left, and Nasirist – which Sadat reduced to the first three, under the pretext that no organization could claim the sole right to represent the Nasirist heritage (nor, for that matter, Islam – which was the common property of all Egyptians). This argument was used to oppose attempts to create a Nasirist party until one was finally authorized after recourse to legal channels in April 1991. The legislative elections of October 1976, in which candidates of each platform were authorized to participate, were characterized by two main features. The overwhelming and predictable victory of the "central platform," that of the president and henceforth designated as the "Egyptian Arab Socialist Organization" or, more simply, as the "Egypt party" – 280 seats against 12 for the right and 2 for the left – was in a sense tainted by the surprising success of "independent" candidates of every persuasion, who took 48 seats and whose presence proved that true opposition took place outside the system. These independents participated so vigorously that some were expelled from parliament for having "insulted the head of state." The second feature of these first pluralist elections was the low level of popular participation: less than half of the electorate – 3.8 million voters out of 9.5 million – took part in the exercise, thus establishing a constant characteristic of Egyptian political life.

The May 1977 law that transformed the three platforms into political parties in the full sense of the word and dissolved all the organizations of the ASU – except for its secretariat and the Women's Union – and the constitutional reform submitted to referendum on May 21, 1979 completed the new "formal" political scene. The law stipulated that no party could be authorized if its principles and objectives were not clearly distinct from those of existing parties; it forbade creation of any party on religious, ethnic, or class bases, which would threaten the principle of national unity. A committee made up of the secretary-general of the ASU – henceforth his only function – the ministers of justice and the interior, the president of the state council, and two magistrates appointed by the president was given the task of determining how "original" proposed parties were as well as the compatibility of their programs with the 1962 charter, the 1971 constitution and, last but not least, the October Document, promoted to the status of an intangible national consensus. The committee followed an extremely restrictive interpretation of these clauses: out of twelve active parties at the end of 1992, seven had obtained their status through judicial means after the committee itself had refused their applications.

A consultative council (*majlis al-shura*) conceived to represent all categories in the population, and which reaffirmed the principles of reserving electoral positions for workers and peasants and protecting national unity, was created through the constitutional reform of May 1979. The ideal of complete social representation, previously attributed to what was only a political organization – the ASU – was now inscribed in the very heart of the constitution, which authorized the president to appoint to parliament and the consultative council members of categories "underrepresented" by universal suffrage – mostly Copts, women, and leaders of political parties who had failed to win parliamentary representation by election; he was also authorized to reject as illegitimate any political expression from outside the system. In fact, the political institutions set up by Sadat tended to organize perpetuation of a power balance between a majority, "by definition" in a sense, and an opposition also "by definition"; this was a case of the president choosing his majority rather than the majority choosing the president, thus determining both his "centrality" on the political scene and the fact that the president's party could be only "from the center." A significant illustration of this phenomenon was the restructuring of the majority in September 1978, when Sadat created the National Democratic Party (NDP) to "orchestrate" a new ideology – "democratic socialism" – and to improve the performance and credibility of his parliamentary base. The program of the new presidential party was, in essence, the constitution itself: building a modern state founded on science and faith; affirming that Shari'a was one of the main sources of legislation; preserving national unity and social peace; reconciling individual and collective interests. Attempts of "right" and "left" to reach power – or even to share it – and their confinement in the role of "constructive," "respectful" opposition to the opinion of the majority as embodied by the president were branded as illegitimate. For instance, the Egyptian–Israeli peace agreement, adopted by referendum in April 1977 (99 percent voting "yes") stood no more chance of being opposed than did the principle of the *infitah* itself, inscribed in the October Document.

The reconstitution of the Wafd Party in February 1978, and the creation of the Socialist Labor Party in the same year, illustrate the "opposition problem" that immediately faced Sadat's regime. The Wafd was external to the system in two ways: it did not emerge from the defunct ASU, which constituted the common matrix of existing parties; and it claimed legitimacy inherited directly from Sa'd Zaghlul and the anti-colonial struggle and denounced the betrayal of the Free Officers' "putsch." Having succeeded in "leading astray" the twenty deputies required to form a party from among the "independents" or from within the government party, the Wafd, to the president's great displeasure, was allowed to relaunch itself and, most importantly, to publish a newspaper that rapidly became a podium for virulent opposition, notably with regard to negotiations with Israel – a podium where not only liberals, but also many left-wing writers, found an opportunity to express themselves. Now came proof that opposition from outside the system was unacceptable; Sadat dedicated himself to eliminating the Wafd from the political scene: by referendum (98.29 percent voted "yes") he had a series of measures adopted on May 21, 1978 regarding "the protection of the internal front and social peace" which barred from political activity all those – former ministers, party leaders – who had contributed to "corrupting political life" before the revolution. Some 200 individuals were expelled by the parliament from political parties, the administration, and the press. The measure was clearly aimed at Fu'ad Siraj al-Din, president of the new Wafd, who had been the party's last secretary-general before Nasir ordered it to be dissolved in 1953. At the beginning of June 1978, the Wafd announced the freezing of its activities, which began again only after 1981, when Sadat himself was dead.

Creation of the Socialist Labor party presents a sort of reverse image of the way the opposition problem was posed. Sadat himself took the initiative in suggesting to Ibrahim Shukri, minister of agrarian reform and former leader of Young Egypt – the only party, with the National Party, not to have been dissolved in 1953 – the creation of a new party to constitute the "opposition wing" of his own NDP. The government went so far as to provide the new party with the deputies it needed to obtain authorization, including the president's own brother-in-law, Mahmud Abu Wafiya. In principle, no ideological differences were supposed to mar relations between the two wings, both of which claimed to honor the July revolution while affirming the need to correct its excesses and errors. But "the policies effectively implemented by Sadat put him on the right of his party's official line, while, behind the smoke-screen of official conformity, the conceptions of a number of Labour party leaders were on the left of the official program."[44] In practice this meant: yes to a just peace with Israel, no to the separate peace of Camp David; yes to opening up the west, no to a privileged alliance with America; yes to free enterprise, no to corruption. The opposition went so far as to challenge the prime minister, Mustafa Khalil, accused in the party press of having accepted bribes.

In May 1980 Sadat had a series of measures adopted by referendum to control both the democratic process and the opposition's activities. The constitutional limit on the number of consecutive terms the president could serve was abrogated. While this might have revealed Sadat's wish to maintain himself in power indefinitely, the main aim of the measure was probably to sacralize the exercise of supreme power: if the president could be reelected indefinitely – Sadat resisted the suggestion of some supporters that the "hero of the crossing" be named president for life – then opposition to his person was illegitimate and could only be perceived in terms of insult, morally unacceptable, and politically insignificant. Several deputies, expelled from parliament for having dared to attack the president personally, understood this. The second part of this policy was adoption by parliament on April 29, 1980 of an "ethics law," called the "law of shame" by its opponents, and creation of a "tribunal of values," made up exclusively of magistrates and public figures appointed by the president and charged with

44 R. Hinnebusch, *Egyptian Politics*, 168.

the mission of punishing any action, opinion, or stand opposed to "society's superior values." The first to be threatened were exiled Egyptian intellectuals who dared to criticize the regime in the Arab press, especially for having signed the treaty of resignation with Israel and having aligned itself with America. A third aspect of this system of control became clear after the referendum of May 1980, when the Shari'a was no longer noted as *one* of the principal sources of legislation, but as *the* principal source. This measure has usually been seen as one of numerous concessions made by Sadat to the most conservative trends in Egyptian society, and it certainly was. But again the consequences of this measure, and the double edge it came to reveal may be seen elsewhere, in the illegitimacy it imputed to the act of opposing a state and a power founded on the Shari'a: negation of the idea that there could be a legitimate alternative on which to base critiques of the regime. By presuming to base his exercise of power on the *Shari'a* and on it alone, without taking into account all of its dispositions, Sadat ran the risk of being accused of hypocrisy, if not of impiety. In this way he himself staked out the territory from which the most radical opposition to his regime would spring.

Islam vs. secularism?

There is no doubt that Sadat's policies, and those of his successor, allowed the Islamic trend in all its manifestations to rebound from the marginality to which it had been reduced under Nasir to occupy the central position that most observers grant by the mid 1990s. The Muslim Brothers retained their influence, thanks in no small part to their connections in Saudi Arabia and Germany, but their increasing freedom from 1971 onwards, and the authorization of their publications *al-Da'wa* and *al-'Itisam* – although the Brotherhood itself remained illegal – could be seen as a calculated risk. Sadat himself might well have thought that he had created the *jama'at islamiyya*, part and parcel, that had been unleashed on the left and the Nasirists in the universities. This is, incidentally, precisely the accusation that they leveled at him: the first "Islamic youth camps" were organized under university auspices, and the "apparatus" provided the Islamist militants with resources for their propaganda; many facilities were provided for the *jama'at* to take over the student unions in March 1976, against a left identified by the regime as its main adversary. The first "warnings" may well have been cause for worry as symptoms of underground processes, but they tended to confirm marginality: the attack on the military academy in May 1974, by a group led by a Palestinian, Salih Sirriya, was more adventurism than anything else, and the plot was subverted with minimum effort; the kidnapping and assassination, in July 1977, of Shaykh al-Dhahabi, former minister of waqfs, by the group dubbed *al-Takfir wa'l-Hijra* by the police and the media, was carried out by people who felt targeted and had placed themselves on the margin of society. Above all, there was as yet no "complicity" between the Azharite religious establishment and traditionalist opinion, on the one hand, and the *jama'at*, which were in a process of radicalization, on the other, in a context where the Islamic nature of society was not yet posed as a problem. Only "morality" was at issue and 'Umar al-Tilmisani, Supreme Guide of the Muslim Brothers, could still state that Egyptian legislation was "95 percent in conformity" with Shari'a.[45]

Last but not least, the state itself took the initiative in launching the Islamization debate, in order to please its new fundamentalist allies, and face the "atheist" left, at the risk of inciting opposition from the Coptic community, led since 1971 by the very energetic Pope Shenouda III. Meanwhile the law of apostasy, which stipulates that renouncing Islam is punishable by death, was adopted in 1977 – a measure especially threatening to Christians who had converted to Islam in order to marry Muslim women, and who sought to return to their original faith after divorcing or finding themselves widowers. A program aiming to Islamize legislation in general was set up by Sufi Abu Talib, speaker of the people's assembly. During this period the media, especially television, began to air various religious programs and censor "illicit" scenes – kisses, alcohol, adulterous situations, and to interrupt programs for the call to prayer; "Islamic garb" – head-veil and flowing garments – became widespread among women, and men began to grow longer beards.

What brought the Islamist movement from the margins in the regime's concerns, and in public opinion, was the fact that Islamic elements – Muslim Brothers, university *jama'at* – with which Sadat had sought to ally himself, or at least to curry favor, began to oppose the regime. The break between Sadat and the Islamist trend was played out by rejection of the Camp David accords, which the Islamists stressed far more effectively than did the left, in the name of the need to liberate Jerusalem. The regime's attitude to the Islamic revolution in Iran, and the warm welcome given the deposed shah in Egypt, represented in their eyes a direct provocation. Renewed repression encouraged reiteration of Sayyid Qutb's analysis of the regime's *jahiliyya* among the movement's more radical elements. The counterpart was the systematic, specifically Islamist demand that Shari'a be immediately and completely implemented, a demand that came to structure the Islamist trend into "radical" and "moderate" camps, a distinction that had more to do with the means than with the end itself. When "Jihan's law"[46] was promulgated in 1971, tension between the regime and the Islamist trend as a whole, including the Azharite apparatus, reached its peak.

[45] On the early manifestations of these groups, see H. Dekmejian, *Islam in Revolution* (Syracuse, 1985); John Esposito, *Voices of Resurgent Islam* (Oxford, 1983).
[46] Reform of the personal status law (*al-ahwal al-shakhsiya*), actively promoted by President Sadat's wife, would have allowed the wife the right to ask for divorce if her

The "re-Islamization" project launched by the regime itself threatened to turn against it: "In 1965, they put up scaffolds for those who said 'there is no god but God'," thundered Shaykh Kishk in April 1981. "Then, we got rid of personal status altogether; now, we are submitting Shariʿa to the People's Assembly. Will you be satisfied, Assembly of the People, or will you reject it? Here we are submitting God's Shariʿa to a handful of his faithful, that they may approve or reject God! What is this farce?"[47]

By passing over to the opposition, the Islamists – whether "radical" or "moderate" – ceased to be marginal: those impressed by their mobilization skills emphasized the services they provided in neighborhoods and villages, the photocopying services they provided to underprivileged students, the buses for female students wanting to escape the promiscuity of public transport, or the Islamic health-care centers they set up around the mosques;[48] those worried by their potential as a threat stressed the threat of "confessional violence" they presented to the country, pointing out the drastic increase in confrontations between Muslims and Christians in Upper Egypt, culminating in the riots of al-Zawiya al-Hamra in Cairo itself that gave Sadat the pretext for putting an end to his liberalization schemes.[49]

The way Sadat went about trying to tame an increasingly "chaotic" political and social situation has most often been analyzed in terms of "crisis of authority," the president's "loss of control" over his own nerves as well as of a process he himself had started. Over a thousand people representing all the supposed opposition forces in the country – right and left wing, radicals and moderates, civilians and religious figures, politicians and intellectuals – were thrown in jail on September 5, 1981, accused by Sadat of plotting to overthrow him. The communists along with the Muslim extremists were accused of incitement, aided and abetted by the Soviet ambassador, who was expelled a week later. This wave of repression, it has been said, was a sort of attack of madness, a diagnosis that would explain the indifference, if not the visible relief, of Egyptian public opinion following the "podium event." One may wonder whether a direct causal link exists between these arrests and Sadat's assassination: on one hand, numerous Islamists – Muslim Brothers and jamaʿat members – were on the lists of those arrested, including the brother of one of the main suspects; on the other, Sadat's decision to imprison the main representatives of the movement that he himself had set up appeared to most observers as the clearest sign

     husband took a second wife without her consent, and to stay in the familial home until
     the children came of age.
[47] Quoted by G. Kepel, Le prophète et Pharaon: les mouvements islamistes dans l'Egypte
     contemporaine (Paris, 1984), 198.
[48] See, for instance, Bruno Etienne, L'islamisme radical (Paris, 1987).
[49] For example, Emmanuel Sivan, Radical Islam, Medieval Theology and Modern Politics
     (New Haven and London, 1985).

that it had fulfilled its historic "mission" and should now leave things to him – which it clearly did not intend to do. The pivotal issue here is the army's attitude: as even if "these assassins [were] religious extremists, their attack was clearly a military operation,"[50] which begs the question of high-level conspiracy within the armed forces, a question still open today. Whatever the case may be, the sequence of events that began with the September 1981 arrests and ended with "Pharaoh's" assassination presents a paradoxical illustration of how stable the Egyptian system was, and how well it functioned, as well as the limits of the steps taken toward liberalization. While the head of state had just been assassinated, just as he was celebrating that which provided the basis of his personal legitimacy – the October 1973 victory – the transition of power was carried out almost automatically: the fact that Hosni Mubarak is himself a military man had much to do with his entirely constitutional accession to power, but it is that accession, under the circumstances, that should appear noteworthy. At the same time, when the people's assembly, and then a referendum on October 13 (98.4 percent voted "yes"), confirmed his accession to power, the click could be heard as the political system locked.

Mubarak's synthesis or a fragmented political order?[51]

Hosni Mubarak began his third presidential mandate on October 4, 1994 (approved by 96.28 percent of voters) and it is therefore impossible to reach definite conclusions about his regime. At most we may attempt to determine how his regime has dealt with the internal and external constraints that pose the conditions for its stability, and whether his options conform to, or diverge from, those of his predecessors.

Deregulation of the *infitah*: debt as the motor of reform

Ensuring the stability of the regime has amounted to maintaining the open door, which implies the pursuit of western, especially American, aid and guaranteeing the loyalty of those sectors of the political and economic establishment for which channels of communication with the west are the main source of accumulation of wealth and influence. The military is a case in point; a forced march was undertaken to reequip the Egyptian army with American supplies, thanks to the generous credit lines opened up by the Reagan administration: five years after the Camp David agreements had been signed, Egyptian military debt skyrocketed to $4.5 billion, as opposed

---

[50] Mirel, *L'Egypte des ruptures*, 237.
[51] Title borrowed from Robert Springborg, *Mubarak's Egypt: Fragmentation of the Political Order*.

to $2 billion borrowed from the Soviet Union over two decades, during which Egypt had gone to war three times.[52] That *infitah*, though, had to be "rationalized" and "justified" Mubarak was careful to note in one of his first speeches: rationalized in that the last years of the Sadat era, marked by shady dealings, speculation and consumerism had to give way to a "productive *infitah*"; justified in that a few scapegoats from among the late president's entourage, notably his brother 'Ismat, would be brought before the ethics tribunal for illicit gains.

Ensuring stability has meant maintaining the state's redistributive role, especially through subsidies on consumer goods and government employment, in order to avoid a too-brutal degradation in the standard of living of those who had benefited least from the *infitah* – notably salaried employees, who had been struck by an inflation rate of about 20 percent throughout the 1980s. From 1974/75 to 1985/86 direct and indirect subsidies on essential goods, electricity, and petrol rose from LE661 million to LE2.2 billion, or 7 percent of GNP and 28 percent of the state's current expenditures in a budget that itself ran a deficit of 22 percent of GNP. Almost 60 percent of these subsidies maintained the price of the flour and bread that constitutes, with beans – also heavily subsidized – the staple diet of the vast majority of Egyptians. Efforts made with respect to public-sector employment were as great, as expensive, and no more productive: between 1977 and 1981, the volume of manpower employed by the state rose by 29.6 percent, four times the population growth rate. In other words state recruitment was accelerating at precisely the time that the state was attempting to "disinvest" in the public sector, when the capital injected into the state economy reached its lowest level, and when the regime decided to stake its future on the private sector and foreign investment.

The accumulation of budget deficits (15–20 percent on average throughout the 1980s), which was rendered more acute by collapse of petrol prices in 1986 and by regional developments (the Lebanese war, the Iran–Iraq war) and "convulsions" of the internal scene (rebellion of the internal security forces in 1986, Islamist agitation), was mechanically reflected in a geometric progression of Egyptian indebtedness. This resembled Khedive Isma'il's situation, in the 1870s, with the role of the *caisse de la dette* now played by the International Monetary Fund; the total debt reached $10 billion in 1976, $17 billion in 1981, $40 billion in 1987, and over $53 billion by the end of the decade. This massive accumulation of debt appeared, paradoxically, as the motor accelerating the process of economic "liberalization." In 1987 the IMF granted Egypt drawing rights of $325 million, but with conditions similar to those of 1977 – elimination of

---

[52] See Heba Handoussa, "Fifteen years of US Aid to Egypt: A Critical Review," in Oweiss (ed.), *The Political Economy of Contemporary Egypt*, 114.

subsidies, liberalization of agricultural prices, increase in the prices of electricity and petroleum-derived products, a rise in interest rates. Reforms announced in the "letter of intent" signed by the Egyptian leadership were not implemented; the budget deficit and debt yawned ever wider. Between 1987 and 1991 relations between Egypt and the IMF were marked by Egyptian government dodging and stalling and by the IMF's intransigence, but conclusion of any new agreement – a necessary condition for rescheduling the debt – depended on implementation of IMF recommendations. In this respect, 1989 appeared as a watershed. Unable to pay an installment of $600 million due on the military debt to the USA, Egypt was slapped back with the Brooke Amendment, which stipulates the suspension of all civilian aid to defaulters on payment for American weapons. Unable to obtain new credit, Egypt had to pay for food imports in cash. The debt hit $50 billion, on which annual service alone was more than $2 billion, and arrears approached $5 billion.

At the moment when the Egyptian government was resigned to submitting to the IMF, having devalued the pound yet again, freed prices of most agricultural products, and announced a list of public-sector firms subject to privatization, the Gulf war exploded following Iraq's occupation of Kuwait in August 1990. The government's support for the UN and its capacity to mobilize a "club of friends"[53] devoted to the country's stability were reflected in cancelation of a substantial tranche of the Egyptian debt after the signing of a new letter of intent and the conclusion, in May 1991, of a new stand-by agreement with the IMF. This does not imply that the IMF had lowered its expectations; the government was encouraged to implement the measures it had agreed to – reduction of the budgetary deficit to less than 5 percent, reduction of tariffs and liberalization of foreign trade, unification of the exchange rate, "price reality" – conditions for canceling a second 20 percent tranche and rescheduling the remaining 50 percent. Implementation of these measures, after more procrastination excused by Islamist agitation and the earthquake of October 1992, led to the signing, in September 1993, of a third accord with the IMF, and the opening up of increased credit facilities ($596 million) and reduction of external debt to around $20 billion, as against more than $50 billion before the Gulf crisis.[54] The paradoxical result was the appearance, after 1991, of a comfortable margin in current accounts ($4 billion in 1993) and accumulation of

---

[53] Expression taken from Waterbury, *Nasser and Sadat*, 407.
[54] On the relations between Egypt and the IMF since 1987 see Timothy Niblock, "The Egyptian Experience in Regional Perspective: Internal Factors and Economic Liberalisation in the Arab World," in Louis Blin (ed.), *L'économie égyptienne: libéralisation et insertion dans le marché mondial* (Paris, 1993). On the September 1993 agreement see Louis Blin, "Le renouvellement de l'accord entre l'Egypte et le fonds monétaire et ses conséquences," *Egypte/monde arabe*, 15–16, 3–4 (1993).

considerable hard currency reserves ($14 billion in the same year), while the economy's growth rate stagnated at under 0.5 percent, in large part because of reduction in public investment, a drop in imports, and a collapse in tourist revenue owing to Islamist agitation.

The reforms to which the government committed itself in this last agreement with the IMF – especially fiscal reform and privatization of public firms – was the more difficult since such measures exacerbate conflicts between interests involved in "deregulating" the Egyptian economy. External pressures were the main impetus for implementation, and opposition in the people's assembly came ironically from members of the governing NDP.[55] By the mid-1990s Egypt remained poor and indebted, but some Egyptians were very rich; private funds abroad were rumored at $40 billion to $50 billion. It became increasingly difficult for the Egyptian authorities to convince those most affected by unemployment (over 25 percent of the active population), and those who watched already-meager purchasing power halve because of price increases and the reduction of subsidies, that their impoverishment was not the counterpart of the extreme affluence of a few: those able to turn the logic of "deregulation" to their immense benefit, and whose ostentatious behavior made acute inequality ever more visible.[56]

What were the sources of, and paths to, accumulation of wealth in Egypt throughout the 1980s, and how did structural adjustment programs shape them? Two processes allow us to characterize the way distribution and mobilization of resources operated during this period: the transformation of Egypt into a *rentier* economy and the reorientation of activities induced by the injection of massive external financial resources.

Rent itself is not a new element in the Egyptian economy. The use of revenues from the Canal, American wheat shipments, and even Soviet economic assistance allowed Nasir to finance simultaneously – albeit insufficiently – industrialization through import substitution and the social progress made during the "socialist" decade.[57] From the mid-1970s and especially in the 1980s both the origin and composition of this rent changed, as did the terms of the contest to appropriate it. A considerable portion remained under direct control of the state bourgeoisie-bureaucracy: the Suez Canal and oil revenues are the main cases in point. The Canal's annual revenue fluctuated, after its reopening in 1975, between $800 million and $1.2 billion, while petrol revenue shot from $187 million in 1977, when Egypt retrieved its wells in the Gulf of Suez, to $3.3 billiion in 1981–82, at the time of the second petroleum shock. The bulk of revenues from petrol and the Canal was poured into the state budget to finance the ever-growing

[55] Niblock, "Egyptian Experience," 46.
[56] See Heba A. Nassar, "Quelques conséquences sociales des programmes d'ajustement structurel," *Egypte/monde arabe*, 12–13, 4 (1992)–1 (1993).
[57] Waterbury, *Nasser and Sadat*, 37ff.

burden of subsidies on consumer goods and to serve the debt. Another fraction of the rent, no less considerable, tended increasingly to escape state control and serve a flourishing black market and finance the imports. The impact of tourism, from which revenues fluctuated between $1 billion and $2 billion a year after 1970, and the remittances of millions of migrant laborers in the oil states in the 1980s, are difficult to evaluate since these were outside the control of official banking. In 1986, the ministry of emigration estimated remittances at about $10 billiion: $2 billion through official routes, the rest through informal networks. It is estimated that, in 1980–81, a quarter of global investment in Egypt, and 81 percent of private-sector investment, had been made possible by these remittances. Establishment in 1974 of the system known as "import without cash transfer" allowed "informal" appropriation of rent through the currency black market, fed by remittances of migrant workers and currency changed by tourists and foreign residents. Importers were no longer required to obtain currency through official banking channels. In the late 1970s, imports through this system may have represented a quarter to a third of total imports, and consumer goods only a sixth.[58] We have noted that under Law 43 every joint venture made up of a public-sector firm and a foreign or Egyptian private-sector enterprise would be considered to belong to the private sector, even if the former held the majority of shares. Even if this formula was neglected by foreign investors, it paved the way for "public–private symbiosis," one of the most influential processes operating in the recomposition of the *infitah* economy. The "state bourgeoisie," which occupied the higher echelons of the administration and public sector, managed to benefit from the comparative advantage offered by their mastery of administrative codes and procedures and their access to the "informal" decision-making networks within ministries and government-service sectors. In a context where almost everything was subject to authorization, license, or exemption, where obtaining these involved a veritable obstacle course, and where administrative and fiscal controls did not simply verify that an activity conformed to legal norms, the presence of former ministers, governors, or retired officers on the boards of private-sector firms had something in common with the role played by the military in the 1960s. The difference was that with privatization the logic of intervention was reversed: instead of representing, almost personally, the Nasirist leadership in the cogs of the economy and guaranteeing the application of its directives, their role by the mid-1990s was to protect their private patrons from the administrative or fiscal services' excess of zeal. A public–private symbiosis also meant "recapitalizing" public property for the benefit of private interests: land, equipment, raw materials, public finances, the state having partially or totally given up

[58] *Ibid.*, 171ff.

the dividends of these resources in order to "encourage" the private sector to exploit them and increase their value on a basis dubbed more "rational" than state management. This was indeed the logic of the choice of tourism as the first sector opened to privatization: with tourism – including major hotels and air transport – public property was not handed over to weak private interests, but to one of the most dynamic sectors of the Egyptian economy, one which, furthermore, controlled one of the country's main sources of hard currency. The same was true of the large public enterprises that manufactured foodstuffs for local consumption, which were among the most profitable businesses in the public sector, were designated as early candidates for privatization, and – taking account of the high prices of imported foodstuffs – seemed likely to hold on to their share of the market.[59] In attacking the very logic of privatization, its enemies used the theme of insufficient evaluation of privatized assets and denounced the fact that public-sector firms were sold off for next to nothing, a policy that threatened to place the country at the mercy of foreign capital. Keeping in mind the very low rates of household savings in the Egyptian economy and the salary levels in force in public sector, the announcement that employees would be allowed to purchase shares in public-sector companies undergoing privatization did not reassure detractors of this policy.

"Islamic savings societies" turned finances upside down in the 1980s by directly addressing Egyptians, especially migrant workers, and proposing to put their savings to work in any one of a host of projects – commercial, industrial, agricultural. The so-called Islamic contract model whereby lender and borrower share in the profits and losses incurred by these projects, illustrated in truly emblematic fashion "rent" and "informality." Justifying their call for the public's savings in the name of Islam's rejection of the interest rates imposed by banks – termed "usurious" – and by promising 20 to 25 percent return on savings (as against a maximum of 13 percent, below the inflation rate, on the official circuits), these societies managed to attract from $10 billion to $35 billion from hundreds of thousands of small nest-eggs in less than five years.[60] At first, creation of these companies appeared as the reaction of certain currency black marketeers to the attack by the minister of the economy, Mustafa al-Saʿid, an attack that resulted in the creation, in 1987, of the currency "free market," in a context where the devaluation of the pound made it particularly urgent for large parts of the population to find channels for preserving their savings. In 1986–87, the peak of activity for Islamic savings societies, the authorities noticed a 45

[59] Significatively enough the very first firms to be nationalized were the local representatives of Coca-Cola and Pepsi Cola.

[60] On these companies, see A. Roussillon, *Sociétés islamiques de placements de fonds et "ouverture économique": les voies islamiques du néolibéralisme en Egypte*, Dossiers du CEDEJ, 3 (1988).

percent decrease in savings in pounds deposited in banks, a decrease which reached 65 percent of foreign currency savings. But large investment projects intended to provide revenue with which these companies were meant to pay depositors back, and in the name of which they went so far as to tout themselves as the "Islamic alternative" to the public sector, were most often mere facades: in the best of cases, real estate activities or contracts for importing electrical appliances or vehicles, more often playing against the Egyptian pound on the international money market or the stock exchange; in the worst, simple thuggery, with the savings of new depositors going to pay off their predecessors. These companies continued to operate, however, for almost eight years in the case of the longest-running examples, on the margins of, if not in direct contradiction with, the law. They technically retained a familial or individual character – meaning that they avoided all control, whether of the minister of economy over stockholders' companies or of the Central Bank over banking activities. When the government took the offensive in spring 1988 to limit the competition that these companies represented to official banks most of them were forced to submit their accounts for inspection and thousands of small depositors lost their savings. There is little chance that the lawsuits that continue to this day will allow them to retrieve their property.

Democratization or new political division of labor?

Since Muhammad Najib had been superseded by Nasir, an unwritten rule of Egyptian politics seemed to stipulate that claims to supreme power were illegitimate and that access to the head of state's functions could not be the object of competition, however "democratic." In other words, his designation constituted a sort of necessity, characterized essentially by relations between the regime and the army and "managed" in practice by the president through his designation – optional according to the constitution – of a vice-president, both as eventual successor and appointed heir. But at the same time, a second unwritten rule, the constitutional legitimacy of the head of state, derived from the modalities of his designation, seemed to require a personal, charismatic legitimacy, which allowed him not only to take control of the political system – of which he formed the axis – but also to impose his own options. Nasir with the nationalization of the Suez Canal and his victory against the tripartite aggression, Sadat with the October war, each knew, in his day, how to acquire that personal legitimacy, "supra-constitutional" one might say, that Hosni Mubarak faced. For want of this trait, his "popularity," more than his legitimacy and the margin for maneuver available to him, depended on the consensus that different aspects of his policy might create. The fact that Hosni Mubarak did not have this "additional" legitimacy made possible an irrefutable "pluralization" of the

Egyptian political scene and a considerable extension of the field of public freedoms. At the same time, the absence of this "additional" legitimacy designated a "normal" mode for the Egyptian political system and the limits of its liberalization.

At the very time Hosni Mubarak's third mandate began, and while several components of the "legal" opposition had refused the renewal of their "pledge of allegiance" (*mubaya'a*) to the president, the Egyptian regime was once more involved in a violent confrontation with the so-called "radical" wing of the Islamist trend, while "moderate" groups within this movement were still denied the right to form autonomous political organizations. If Hosni Mubarak never questioned the pluralism established by his predecessor, and if he considerably enlarged the scope of freedom of expression, the majority of the population seemed less interested than ever in "formal" political participation – whether by exercising their right to vote or by adhering to political parties. The very process of return to a multiparty system, in fact, manifested both the limits and the problems of the "democratization" begun by Sadat and pursued by his successor: the problem of delegating and exercising political power and the problem of the political division of labor among various actors.

Taking into account the role of the deputies in designating the president and renewing his mandate, the political system demanded a parliament that was simply an extension of the ruling party, whose members were united principally by allegiance to the president. As was the case within the late Arab Socialist Union, the president's control of the political system passed first through that of his own party which, more than an instrument of power, constituted the closed arena where the struggle for power and the resources it generates took place between different factions. After Hosni Mubarak came to power, it was through the electoral law itself that the ruling party's deputies were controlled. A system introduced in 1984 guaranteed the possibility for the ruling party to "punish" deputies who did not demonstrate sufficient respect for the party line or voting orders; a rule setting a limit of 8 percent of total votes beneath which a party was not represented allowed the regime to reduce to its simplest expression the presence of an opposition in parliament. Another condition for the system to function properly was that the prime minister should not be a "politician" and that he should not appear as the "head of the majority" but as a simple executive. Hence there was recourse more and more systematically to technocrats or university figures such as 'Ali Lutfi or 'Atif Sidqi, whose main merit was lack of connections with the effective networks of influence within the political establishment.

The modalities for the third consecutive renewal of Hosni Mubarak's mandate, in July 1993, hinted at the integration by the Egyptian opposition of the unwritten rule prohibiting any struggle over access to power: even if the presidential candidate was unbeatable once he decided to run, no party leader or public figure ever declared himself to be a candidate, even "in principle," for succession. The limits of the system were reached when the main opposition parties – Wafd, Labor (Islamist), Tagammu', Nasirists – refused to renew their "allegiance" (*mubaya'a*) to Hosni Mubarak without putting forth alternatives to his reelection by presenting their own candidates and program. The question here is that of the political parties' "status" – including that of the government party – and that of the very nature of the role they played in a system where power was not likely to be an object for competition, or more precisely in a system where "formal" political competition was not likely to threaten the control of state and government in any way.

Another question concerns the widening of the party scene after the legalization, in April 1990, of the Green Party, the Arab and Socialist Egypt Party, the Democratic Unionist Party, and Young Egypt, and in April 1991 of the Nasirist Party. While the proliferation of parties tended to fragment the opposition, the Egyptian regime constantly opposed creation of new parties through restrictive interpretation of the law. Paradox lies in the fact that the Nasirist Party, although the regime had been particularly keen to prevent its legalization, was able to organize its activities openly. With the exception of the Nasirists, none of these parties engaged in any serious activity, to the extent that one wonders about the meaning of their very creation. The most common hypothesis, applied to the Umma Party as well as to the Liberals, holds that these are clientist, even family-type, structures, created to guarantee the "visibility" of leaders with charismatic aspirations while managing local interest groups. Approaches that focus on the patronage or the extent of representation of these parties, however, seem to obscure the very terms of the political division of labor as it was reconstituted after the dissolution of the ASU and the way in which certain trends were excluded from the "formal" political scene. The hypothesis is that the main "functions" of political life – to represent different components of opinion, to organize and mobilize various sectors of society – formerly carried out by the ASU have been farmed out among organizations of varying status, competence, and legitimacy: political parties; unions; and what could be called social groupings at the local levels – clubs, mutual assistance associations, and so forth. The object was to detach the masses from political parties by making the exercise of politics a professional prerogative. A peasant party or a Muslim party could not exist any more than could one gathering engineers, women, or the inhabitants of Upper Egypt. In return, professional organizations, unions, and other corporate groups could legitimately take charge of defending and promoting their members' professional and material interests, but it would be illegitimate for them to express an opinion regarding questions of major national importance, even if they were called upon to express solidarity. One of the main mistakes made by the leaders of the new Wafd, at the time of the first attempt to reconstitute the party in 1978, was to let it be understood that it had "specific" client networks: jurists, the liberal professions, even the Copts. Along the same lines, Egyptian political humor suggests that the regime only allowed the creation of a Nasirist party when the destruction of the public sector had gone so far that the party could not hope to find a clientele therein. One can form an idea of the regime's "tolerance" for Muslim Brother candidates on the Wafd Party lists, in 1984, then on those of the Labor Party in 1987: by running under these banners, the Brotherhood was accepting the new political division of labor dissociating their political existence as deputies from their aspiration to encircle society at the base – an aspiration the regime could tolerate only if it did not take on an explicitly political dimension. With the help of the state of emergency, which prohibited demonstrations and public gatherings at any other time than during elections, any attempt at contact between the opposition parties and the masses was slapped down by a true structural prohibition. This was the case in 1987 during the railway workers' strikes, to which the Tagammu' party tried to contribute organizational assistance, and to which the regime immediately responded by arresting the activists on the ground and a number of national leaders, accused of subversive agitation. Under these conditions, party activity tended to be restricted to the publication of a newspaper. Relations between opposition parties and their "sympathizers" were not necessarily translated into electoral terms in a system where the logic of election was often summed up, as far as the low proportion of voters is concerned, in choosing an intermediary between the local community and central power.

Given political parties structurally "isolated from the masses," the non-governmental arena may appear as the true locus of political life in Egypt, but of a political life that may be designated as "informal." Unions, professional associations, charity or service-type organizations all define the field where the "objective" material interests of various sectors of society interact with state management, and through which considerable resources pass.[61] Trade unions and professional associations in Egypt are in fact far more than simple organizations defending members' interests; among the services they offer are retirement funds, credit, mutual assistance; they play an important role in access to housing, health services, leisure activities, and offer loans to young couples, and even a place in a cemetery to members after death. In the same way, belonging to a sporting or leisure club or membership of various associations plays an important role in social

---

[61] See Robert Bianchi, *Unruly Corporatism: Associational Life in Twentieth-Century Egypt* (New York, 1990).

strategies and provides privileged ground for contact with the regime or those who hold power. Associations, particularly professional ones – doctors, engineers, lawyers or pharmacists, the journalists' syndicate – are, far more than parliament, an arena of interaction and power sharing between the ruling party and the opposition, on the one hand, and among the latter's various components, on the other: elected on a proportional basis, the administrative councils of these organizations are *de facto* the only concrete manifestation of political pluralism. Above all, the syndicates have provided the field where the principal actors excluded from the "formal" political scene could be reinserted starting from the early 1980s, with the Islamist trend conquering the administrative council of the most prestigious syndicates, mainly in competition with the Nasirists: the doctors' syndicate, that of the engineers – formerly under Nasirist control – and, since 1992, the lawyers' syndicate, formerly the bastion of the liberal trend.

An *informal* political scene?[62] One can use this term first because the terminology of these groupings is more corporatist than political, or, more precisely, because within them political discourse is converted into one of corporatist tendencies: when Sadat dissolved the lawyers' syndicate council in June 1981, it had posed a grave challenge to his policies, especially the peace accords with Israel; but on one hand, the lawyers' criticism was formulated in "legal" terms – constitutionality of the treaties, human rights – and Sadat condemned them for having stepped outside the bounds of strictly corporatist logic and delving into politics. The syndicate scene is informal also because the stakes are not the conquest of power but social reform from the perspective of each profession's "specialty." This is the case with the doctors' syndicate, the first to have been taken over by the Islamist trend as early as 1984: the Islamization of medicine as preached by this trend is presented as its members' specific contribution to the moral reform of society, within the perspective of health, hygiene, prevention. It should be emphasized that the few "digressions" that the Islamist leaders of the syndicate allowed themselves outside the medical field have mainly focused on overarching "humanitarian" causes, not on the Egyptian scene: supporting the Afghan jihad against the communist occupation, solidarity with the Palestinian *Intifada*, calling for mobilization in support of the Muslims in Bosnia. These professional organizations, furthermore, especially those controlled by the Islamists, are not necessarily foci of opposition, as is generally thought; it might even be suggested that the unions controlled by the Islamist trend – doctors, engineers, pharmacists – are those that in past years enjoyed the most "relaxed" relations with power, as opposed to those

[62] See Alain Roussillon, "Islam, islamisme et démocratie: recomposition du champ politique en Egypte," *Peuples méditerranéens*, 41–42 (October 1987–March 1988).

of the influence of "legal" opposition parties – the Tagammu' in the journalists' syndicate, the Wafd among the lawyers until 1992 – which may be explained by the prudence this trend has employed in managing its relations with the state. In the syndicates that they control, the Islamists have thus taken over all the strategic posts: general secretariat, treasury, management of the professional publications, while leaving leadership to personalities most likely to guarantee, through their connections and experience, contact between the profession and the authorities: 'Uthman 'Ahmad 'Uthman, president of Arab Contractors, Hasab Allah al-Kafrawi, minister of housing in the engineers' syndicate, Mamduh Jabr, former minister of health, in the doctors' syndicate, Ahmad al-Khawaja, prominent lawyer, in that of the lawyers.

Most observers attribute the success of the Islamist trend in the professional unions to their members' indifference toward union-type activities. Participation in the election of their administrative councils has rarely risen beyond 20 percent of registered voters, a phenomenon that the Islamists – clearly the most organized and motivated among the actors on the scene – have skillfully exploited. This also seems to have been the opinion of the Egyptian government which, in the context of open confrontation, attempted to reduce Islamist influence in these organizations by reforming the law governing the election of the administrative councils in September 1993, setting the minimum rate of participation at 50 percent of those registered in the first round, 30 percent in the second. If these conditions were not met, the union was placed under the tutelage of a provisional administrative council made up of magistrates until the necessary quorum was met. These measures entailed the risk of bringing the Islamist trend and the totality of Egyptian opposition forces together in their common refusal of the state's intrusion in the affairs of the professional syndicates. The promulgation of this law was met with such an outcry that its implementation remained doubtful. One can nevertheless wonder as to the meaning of this supposed indifference: how was it that the pharmacists' syndicate, for instance, 60 percent of which was Coptic, accepted unflinchingly the Islamist takeover? Again, how was it that the engineers' syndicate, where military engineers weighed heavily in the balance, was one of the first to have an Islamist-dominated administrative council? Surely the indifference of the various professions' members did not go so far as to allow union management to go against their corporatist interests; the "tolerance" accorded to the Islamists by most non-voters must signify, at the very least, that their management was compatible with these interests, or again just as efficient as any other. One is then led to question the central position of the Islamist trend on the Egyptian political and social scene as a whole.

Centralization of the Islamic question

Between 1970 and 1981, the Islamists ceased to be marginal, but the "Islamic question" had not yet become central, as the assassination of Sadat, and the conditions under which power was transmitted to his successor, paradoxically demonstrated. The Islamists had proved their capacity to penetrate the army: Khalid al-Islambuli and 'Abbud al-Zumur, Sadat's assassins, were no marginals, excluded by society, but high-ranking officers who both belonged to families of notables. But al-Jihad, the organization to which they belonged, remained a tiny grouping which the security services easily dismantled – at least temporarily: twenty-four were found guilty, five death sentences pronounced. As for the Asyut uprising, even if it succeeded at first in upsetting the local garrison, it remained localized, did not spread to other parts of the country, and was easily strangled by the army albeit at the cost of many dead and hundreds of arrests: 302 were prosecuted.

What seemed to make up the crux of the Islamic question was not so much the threat the militant Islamists posed to the regime and its stability, nor the influence they may have had in society, especially among young people – both of which were indisputable – but, rather, the way in which this threat and this influence were dealt with by the regime. It was precisely the trials of Sadat's assassins and the Asyut rebels that marked the turning-point in the regime's approach. These trials provided the opportunity for the regime to send a clear message of appeasement to the Islamists, of both "radical" and "moderate" persuasion: the death sentences of Sadat's direct assassins were carried out, but 'Umar 'Abd al-Rahman, the defendants' spiritual guide, suspected of having pronounced the *fatwa* that made the president's blood "legitimate," was acquitted for lack of evidence. In the Asyut rebels' trial, 299 death sentences were requested out of 302 suspects, yet the verdict was clemency: no death sentence was pronounced, 16 were imprisoned for life, 176 were acquitted.

For Sadat, the Islamization of legislation was mere gesturing, the means of quelling the left and the Islamists, and, or so he hoped, of confirming his own legitimacy; what changed at the beginning of the 1980s was the fact that Islamizing the framework of Egyptians' daily lives was perceived by Hosni Mubarak's regime as the means of quelling Islamism itself – that is, its most radical exigencies: the establishment of an Islamic republic, renewal of the confrontation with Israel, implementation of the *hudud* (punishments laid down in the Qur'an), forced veiling of women, reestablishment of the status of *dhimmis* for Copts. One of the first results of this change in attitude was the implementation of the process of informal integration of "moderate" Islamists into the formal political scene through parties and the professional organizations mentioned above. The "deal" struck between the regime and these "moderates," especially the Muslim Brothers, may be summed up in the statement that they were allowed to exert pressure from within the system itself, no longer on its margins only, for the realization of their objectives – essentially, the application of Shariʿa and the Islamization of the social framework – against which they would take responsibility for bringing "radicals" back to the legal fold.[63]

The legislative elections of 1984 appeared to be the first "test," into which the Muslim Brothers ventured with only a few candidates on the Wafd party lists, without their own slogans; in the 1987 elections, the government ignored what was tantamount to a public takeover bid launched by the Brotherhood against the Labor Party, made possible by the alliance with the fraction of this party that descended from the pre-revolutionary Young Egypt Party. The takeover provided them with an organization and, especially, through the weekly al-Shaʿb, with a publication that allowed them to have some of their most visible leaders elected to the people's assembly: Maʾmun al-Hudaybi, official spokesman for an organization that remained illegal and the nephew of Hasan al-Banna"'s successor to its leadership; and Sayf al-Islam Hasan al-Bannaʾ, son of the founder of the Muslim Brotherhood. This time they could declaim their own "program": "Islam is the solution." Another aspect of this change in attitude in dealing with the Islamists was the tolerance shown by the government toward the activities of the so-called Islamic investment companies, also mentioned above. This tolerance acquired full meaning in the context of a strategy opening up spaces for "Islamic resocializing," organized mainly around the numerous mosques over which the Islamists managed to acquire control, and which the regime hoped would satisfy their aspirations toward conformity with the divine will. While the implementation of this strategy did not imply the government's official permission for the Islamists to constitute "explicit" political parties, as has been said, under the pretext that the authorization of a Muslim party would justify the symmetrical authorization of a Coptic party, it nevertheless required that a modus vivendi be established between the Islamists and some official personalities, among them governors, university deans, intermediate cadres in the government party, high-level functionaries. Asyut and Middle Egypt provided the "laboratory" where this modus vivendi was tested: de facto prohibition of the distribution and consumption of alcohol in the governorate, starting in April 1986 with the cancelation of all distribution licenses, although Asyut had one of the highest percentages of Copts in the country; de facto sexual segregation in university halls; Islamist takeover of sporting and youth clubs. This very logic led to the recruitment of numerous Islamists on university

---

[63] See A. Roussillon, "Entre al-Jihâd et al-Rayyân: bilan de l'islamisme égyptien," Maghreb-Machrek, 127 (January–March 1990).

campuses and especially in the ministry of education's primary and secondary schools, or, as social workers, by the ministry of social affairs. This wave of recruitment put them in direct contact with a public to which they could deliver their message under optimal circumstances.

While this strategy was aimed at relieving tension by clearing out a space in society for the Islamists – the "moderates" among them and, it was hoped, the "radicals" as well – the terms of a new confrontation were in fact being put in place: on the one hand, the absence of any significant steps in the application of Shari'a tended to compromise the "participatory" stance of the "moderate" Islamists, placing the Muslim Brotherhood in the front line of more "radical" criticism; on the other, through tension-creating strategies, the state was challenged to accomplish its commitments to the Islamization of society. When repression was renewed, it became possible to demonstrate the leaders' "hypocrisy" and the futility of any attempt at compromise with the regime. In this respect, the "green march" which Shaykh Hafiz Salama intended to organize in June 1985, during the month of Ramadan, may be seen as a crucial turning-point. On his own initiative, Shaykh Salama, imam of al-Nur mosque, close to the *jama'at*, and the leader, in 1973, of the Suez resistance when the city was briefly occupied by the Israelis, made himself the spokesman for Muslims exasperated with the government. The march was to take peaceful demonstrators, armed only with their Qur'ans, from al-Nur mosque to 'Abdin square, the official headquarters of the presidency, and they were to occupy the square until the government decided to accept the immediate and integral application of the Shari'a. The march was, of course, banned, and Shaykh Salama briefly imprisoned, but the event's significance was derived first and foremost from the reactions it received from the opponents of the Islamist trend.

By calling for creation of a "patriotic front" (*jabha wataniyya*) to confront Islamism, designated as the main threat to Egyptian society, the novelist 'Abd al-Rahman al-Sharqawi made a decisive and paradoxical contribution to the "centralization" of the Islamist question in Egyptian political life: through the debates it sparked and the realignments it signaled, the front – which, like the march, never saw the light – contributed to establishing two "camps," "Islamists" and "secularists" (*'ilmaniyin*, the contours of which cut across the usual dichotomies of the political scene, "left" and "right," "opposition" and "government," "progressive" and "reactionary"). The question could then be explicitly debated within the opposition, especially the Wafd and the Tagammu', but also among the Nasirists, whose newspaper called for historic reconciliation between Nasirists and Muslim Brothers.

Since the "green march" was banned, the Mubarak regime had to face different sorts of action through which the "radical" Islamists successfully attempted to drag it into a spiral of violence which repression never managed to break. In 1986–87 a group dubbed "those saved from hell" (*al-najun min al-nar*) by the media attempted to assassinate former ministers of the interior responsible for anti-Islamist repression under Sadat; during the same period, repeated attacks were made on video clubs, places where alcohol was served, and theaters, as an application of the principle of "commanding the good and forbidding the evil" (*al-ʿamr bi'l-maʿruf wa'l-nahi ʿan al-munkar*). Above all, religious strife proliferated, especially in Upper Egypt. Copts tended to be the first victims of the escalating confrontation between state and Islamists: to attack the Coptic community, within the logic of the Islamist strategy, was tantamount to a "metaphoric" designation of the regime's illegitimacy without a direct attack on the government itself. Copts could all the more easily be represented as the symbolic incarnation of infidel power in that their social status tended to be more elevated. Hence the legitimization by certain groups of their attacks on Copt-owned stores, the booty from which was meant to finance the pursuit of jihad. Hence, also, the proliferation of attacks on the symbols of Christian superiority, doctors or pharmacists whose establishments were often the Islamists' prime targets.[64]

The assassination on June 8, 1992 of Faraj Fuda, one of the principal spokesmen of the secularist trend and a virulent opponent of Islamist fanaticism, cast doubts on the way the regime was managing the Islamist question, while it dramatized the stakes of the confrontation. On one hand, the government launched a large-scale offensive during the summer of 1992 against the "radical" Islamists in an explicit attempt to put an end to "extremism" (*tatarruf*) and "terrorism" (*irhab*) once and for all. The confrontation was especially violent since the Islamists responded with a series of attacks on tourist sites and on the security forces themselves, while the explosion of several bombs in Cairo, attributed by the regime to the Islamists although no proof was adduced, caused tension to rise further. The death sentences passed by military tribunals – the most numerous since 1954, and immediately carried out – confirmed, if any doubts remained, the regime's determination to put an end to the "radicals'" activities. Simultaneously, the regime sent a barrage of messages to the "moderates," who were commanded to renounce any solidarity with the "terrorists": Ibrahim Shukri, head of the Labor Party, and ʿAdil Husayn, editor-in-chief of its newspaper, were brought before the prosecutor after Husayn published an article in which he wondered whether tourism was licit (*halal*) or illicit

---

[64] See A. Roussillon, "Changer la société par le *jihâd*: 'sédition confessionnelle' et attentats contre le tourisme: rhétoriques de la violence qualifiée d'islamique en Égypte," in Ricardo Bocco and Mohammad Reza Djalili (eds.), *Moyen-Orient fin de siècle: migrations, démocratisations, médiations: enjeux locaux et internationaux, à paraître aux PUF*, September 1994.

(*haram*)[65] – a way of suggesting that they could be designated as "instigators" of attacks on tourists. At the same time, the authorities launched a series of "skirmishes" aiming at second-rank Brotherhood leaders accused of cooperating with forces outside the country – Iran, the Sudan, and the Afghan *Hizb-i Islami* – and of working to reconstitute the association and even, in the case of a computer firm named Salsabil, close to the Brotherhood, of plotting to overthrow the regime.

One of the first results of confrontation was the renewed solidarity with the regime of the secular opposition front, still reeling from Faraj Fuda's assassination: from the Wafd to the Tagammuʿ, the opposition fell in step with the government on the issue of putting an end to terrorism, ending criticism of repression, and the maintenance of the state of emergency, with only a few reservations expressed regarding the fact that the accused were tried in military courts. The regime's capacity to separate the "radical" and "moderate" components of the Islamist trend, on the other hand, was far more problematic, and a few indices tend to confirm that both "radical" strategies and the repression launched against them resulted in the radicalization of the Islamist trend as a whole. Al-Azhar was first on the list: invited in April 1993 by the people's assembly to participate in a debate on violence, Shaykh Gad al-Haqq, the rector of the al-Azhar, was obliged to refrain from intervening, revealing divergences among the ʿulamaʾ themselves regarding the "definition" of events: anti-terrorist campaign or war on Muslim youth? The statement made by Shaykh al-Ghazali, the eminent Azharite theologian close to the Muslim Brothers, cited by the defense at the trial of Faraj Fuda's assassins, in June 1993, gives an interesting indication as to the state of mind of certain "moderate" Islamists: questioned about the status of the Muslim who calls for the Shariʿa not to be applied, the shaykh defined him unhesitatingly as an apostate against whom a death sentence must be pronounced; questioned about the status of the individual who, following the state's abstention from passing this sentence, takes the initiative of executing the apostate himself, the shaykh declared that he would only be transgressing his prerogatives as an individual, an attitude Islam does not sanction. The attempt to mediate between the government and rebellious Islamist militants, suggested to the minister of interior in April 1993 by a "clerical committee for reform," presided over by the celebrated Shaykh al-Shaʿrawi, the most popular preacher in Egypt, grouping all the trends of "moderate" Islamism and presented as the "third force" between the protagonists, is even more significant: "Dear brothers in God," we read in the letter addressed by the committee to the "prison leadership," "may His peace and compassion be with you. We pray to God that He delivers you from your torment and puts an end to the suffering of Muslims throughout

[65] *Ibid.*

the world. Our country is today in the throes of a wave of violence which has caused people fear and affliction, fearing for themselves and for their property, which has allowed the enemies of Islam to raise their heads everywhere to calumniate our religion and cause it to appear as a creed of violence and terror, while it is in fact a religion of compassion and tolerance." In the "working programme" annexed to this letter, the 'ulama' lay out their analysis of the situation and what seem to be the stakes of the confrontation:

We are living today at a time of utmost disorder (*fitna ma ba'daha fitna*) ... A believer who may choose to grow his beard, thus conforming with the orders of the Prophet, is accused of being a hooligan, a madman or a terrorist ... Every believer who decides to wear the head veil (*hijab*) or the full veil (*niqab*) becomes the symbol of reaction and backwardness ... A merciless campaign has targeted Shari'a and its implementation while an equally merciless war is being waged against Islam, which fails to distinguish between the faithful 'ulama', who follow the path of the Book of God and the Sunna of his Prophet, and those who have let themselves be led astray by the Devil, who has paralyzed their capacity to choose.

'Abd al-Halim Musa, the minister of interior, appointed in 1986, was condemned because he had seemed to be on the verge of accepting mediation formulated along the same lines, officially on his own initiative and without having consulted the president and the government. The fact remains that, in the 'ulama''s terms, although they distanced themselves from the "few individuals led astray by the Devil," they explicitly affirmed their solidarity with the Muslims persecuted for having tried to live in conformity with divine rule.

But the almost cyclical evolution of relations between the state and the various components of Islamist movement, throughout the past half-century, begs the immediate question of the modalities for relaying and exercising political power in Egypt. The remarks accumulated throughout the present chapter suggest the hypothesis that the stability and proper functioning of the system are played out at the level of articulation between the central state – government, central administration, planning and control bodies – as the locus of political decision making and global management, and the urban and rural "peripheries" as the locus of effective social control and regulation of objective interests. In brief, the Egyptian state, despite the heavy, all-powerful "hydraulic" apparatus and the multitude of its agents, controls only the "main axes" of the country – the avenues and squares in the towns, the checkpoints between governorates and the course of the river; as to the Egypt of the villages, *harat* and urban quarters, and still more that of the "spontaneous communities," *'ashwa'iyat*, mushrooming on the urban peripheries, it lives largely under a regime of self-management, within a logic that could be called that of the micro-community, where human groupings with very strong local "sub-identities" – to live in this area, to be from that village – collectively set about promoting their interests, that is to say limiting the incursions and control of the state and capturing, for the benefit of the group, part of the resources distributed by the state, such as dealing with the (unequal) distribution of wealth. The Egyptian state's recurrent problem as a central/centralized state is that of identifying the *intermediaries* through which it may preserve global control over these collectivities, maintain public order and impose the social items regarding which the regime refuses to negotiate. Under the old regime, the role of intermediary between central power and the local level was played, in the countryside, by the owners of latifundiae enjoying absolute authority over their villages and peasants, through an army of foremen, managers, lenders, right-hand men, and, in the city, by the notability system and the *futuwwa* network. In revolutionary Egypt, the Nassirist regime "coopted" the stratum of "new kulaks" in the countryside which the agrarian reform had helped to put in place, and, in the city, was supported by the new workers' elite. Both categories were carefully encompassed, as has been seen, by the organizations of the Arab Socialist Union. Under Sadat, and more clearly still under Mubarak until the end of the 1980s, the regime attempted to coopt the Islamist trend for this role; the failure of this attempt is what constitutes the framework of confrontation while it determines the differentiation between "moderates" and "radicals" within this trend. The point is to know to what extent this redistribution of roles, beyond the divergences in policy through which it operates and the differences in ideological "climates" it determines, will transform fundamentally the ways in which effective power is exercised in Egypt: paternalism as a way of exercising authority, clientelism as a register for expressing loyalties and partisan positions; further, neo-patrimonialism as the logical framework for the management and distribution of available resources; all seem to function equally well within a "dirigist" and a "liberal" context. From this perspective, the arrival of the Islamists, if not directly in power, then at least in the position of intermediaries between the regime and "real" society, would only strengthen the logic of the system itself by achieving Durkheim's ideal of sacralization of social norms.

At a second level, the pursuit of the liberalization of the Egyptian economy, in the context marked by renewed confrontation between the regime and the Islamists, poses the question of the modes of mobilization and distribution of available resources. The centralization and appropriation of the major part of available surplus resources, whether at the hands of a "feudal" oligarchy, self-proclaimedly "socialist" state bourgeoisie, or the "parasitic" new bourgeoisie spawned by *infitah*, counterposes another problem: the modalities of a necessary redistribution, at least to enable the simple reproduction of the labor force and to ensure the minimal conditions of a stable social order, if not to allow the cause of social justice to advance. Because it could not understand this, by refusing to limit the concentration of agricultural land, reducing larger and larger sectors of the peasantry and the poorer inhabitants of the cities to despair, the old regime's landed oligarchy had to make way for the military technocracy. In turn, the latter forced through the considerable levies carried out in the name of "socialism," especially in the rural areas, but only by setting up channels for social mobility with egalitarian pretensions – schools, the army, government service, one party – and by improving considerably the Egyptian people's "basic" conditions of life – education, health, infrastructure. In the same way, the subsidies on consumer goods and the expenditures lowering the cost of necessary services, which exploded at the end of the 1970s and during the 1980s, appeared as the counterpart of a system where inflation and the existence of a dual market and a dual pricing system constituted the main mechanism of quick gain for certain sectors of the new bourgeoisie. One of the seemingly most characteristic traits of the composition of Egyptian social elites is their "cumulativity," in the sense that successive newcomers do not replace the already constituted strata but add to them, not without imposing new rules to the game, which allows them to arrive in positions of socio-economic dominance. The point is, again, to know to what extent the conquest of power by the Islamists or the further "Islamization" of the Egyptian economic scene would modify significantly the conditions for distribution and utilization of available resources. Yet again, the emergence of a self-proclaimed Islamic economic sector or economic actors does not constitute a break with the logic of *infitah*, the opening up to the west, but could on the contrary reflect the strengthening and deepening of this logic to the extent that they contribute to legitimizing with the seal of Islamic authenticity the modes of consumption, exchange, or investment that objectively participate in the "globalization" process of world economies.

Finally, at a third level, the question is that of the stakes in the reemergence of a form of Islamic activism and its confrontation with the state from the perspective of Egypt's insertion in regional geo-politics. On one hand, the general Islamization of political and social idioms (in which the role of the state, even before that of the Islamists, has been shown) constitutes one of the modalities for Egypt's redefinition of its regional role after the Camp David peace, and especially after the end of its quarantine and reintegration into Arab ranks in the context of the Iran–Iraq war. The Egyptian regime's reliance on an Islamic identification allowed the terms of a "cold peace" with the Zionist state, which continues to occupy the holy places of Jerusalem, to be outlined. The same identification allowed the regime to distance itself from Arabist stances and to highlight Egypt's renunciation of Nasirist projects of hegemony over the Arab nation. On the

Arab scene itself, the implementation of the Islamic referential is instrumental in Egypt's alignment with the petro-monarchies against the last
advocates of Arab progressivism: a confrontation that was dramatized
further in the crisis opened up by Iraq's occupation of Kuwait. Last but not
least, the promotion of Egypt's Muslim identity was particularly adapted to
the expansion of migrant labor in the markets of the peninsula; in return,
these emigrants were one of the main vectors for the "Wahhabization" of
Egyptian society. But on the other hand, by refusing the denomination of
"Islamic state" and by choosing the option of confrontation with the
Egyptian Islamist trend, Mubarak's regime has taken the side of conservatism in the confrontation – presented as axial – that is working its way
through the Arab, and in general the Muslim, world; a confrontation that
opposes not "secular" and "religious" camps, but the partisans of preserving
the social status quo – as legitimized by the Islamic referential, if need be –
and those who have become convinced that the overthrow of the existing
regimes, and the construction of just societies, constitute the only hope for a
place in the sun.

15

Modern Egyptian culture in the Arab world

PAUL STARKEY

❧

From Napoleon to Sa'd Zaghlul (1798–1919)

The beginning of modern Egyptian cultural development has traditionally been set at 1798, the date of Napoleon's invasion. Although the significance of this date for the socio-economic development of Egypt has in recent years become the focal point for some of the liveliest debates in Middle Eastern history,[1] its status as a cultural turning-point is difficult to ignore; as one recent commentator has noted, "the postulation of the French occupation ... as the original event that stirs modern Arabic literature [and, by implication, other branches of modern Arab culture] to life ... is heavily documented and cannot easily be gainsaid."[2] Essentially an episode in the history of Anglo-French imperialist rivalry, the French invasion has generally been judged a military failure, but the three-year occupation that followed saw developments that were radically to change the cultural and educational development of the country. The teams of scholars and scientists Napoleon brought with him undertook a comprehensive survey of the country, subsequently published as *Description de l'Egypte*; a scientific Institut de l'Egypte was founded; a printing-press was introduced to Egypt, used not only for printing proclamations for the local people but also for production of a newspaper, *Le courier de l'Egypte*, and a scientific and educational journal, *La décade égyptienne*. To win support Napoleon also set up an administrative council and a series of provincial councils, by means of which the Egyptians were involved in western representative institutions for the first time.[3]

---

[1] On this, see chaps. 3, 4, 5, and 11 above. For a recent discussion of some aspects of the debate, see Kenneth M. Cuno, *The Pasha's Peasants: Land, Society, and Economy in Lower Egypt, 1740–1858* (Cambridge, 1992).

[2] Muhammad Siddiq, review of M. M. Badawi (ed.), *Modern Arabic Literature* (Cambridge, 1992), in *Journal of Arabic Literature*, 26 (1995), 270 (my insertion).

[3] For a convenient summary of these developments, see M. M. Badawi, "Introduction: The Background," in Badawi (ed.), *Modern Arabic Literature*, 1ff.

It is not surprising that the reaction of educated Egyptians to these developments was ambivalent. Al-Jabarti's account of the year of the invasion describes it as "the beginning of a reversal of the natural order and the corruption or destruction of all things." Elsewhere, however, he makes clear his admiration for the scientific and cultural achievements of the French, while sounding a warning-note about the dangers to traditional Muslim morality inherent in the mingling of the two cultures.[4]

A crucial place in any account of the Egyptian *nahda* ("renaissance") belongs to Muhammad Ali who, in the wake of the confusion surrounding the departure of the French, had by 1805 been able to establish himself as ruler of Egypt. Modeling himself to some extent on the Ottoman sultan Salim, Muhammad 'Ali embarked on a program of military and political reform, the principal aim of which was to consolidate his own position: in so doing, however, he laid the foundations for the development of modern Egyptian culture.

The principal cultural innovations of Muhammad 'Ali's reign lay in the sphere of education. This was a two-way process. On the one hand, foreign teachers (at first Italian, later mainly French) were imported to train the administrators and officers needed to run his new Egypt. At the same time, Egyptian students were dispatched to study in France and Italy. On their return, they were often required to translate the textbooks they had studied. In 1828 the Egyptian official newspaper, *al-Waqa'i' al-Misriyya*, was founded, and in 1835 new impetus was given to the translation movement with the founding of the school of languages under Rifa'a Rafi' al-Tahtawi. The gradual replacement of Turkish by Arabic as the language of administration and education toward the end of Muhammad 'Ali's reign was also an important factor in the rise of a specifically Egyptian consciousness.

Although it was this period that arguably saw the beginning of an educated Egyptian middle class, these cultural developments rested on a precarious basis and were closely dependent on the personality and military fortunes of the governor himself. The reigns of Ibrahim, 'Abbas I (1849–54), and Sa'id (1854–63) saw fewer cultural innovations; indeed, 'Abbas's policies at times amounted to a deliberate reversal of changes initiated by Muhammad 'Ali. With the reign of Isma'il, however (1863–82), developments instigated by Muhammad 'Ali again began to gather pace. The number of European-run schools increased; Catholic missions set up orders in Egypt; the state school system was revitalized, to incorporate for the first time a clear distinction between "civil" and "military" establishments. Al-Tahtawi's school of languages, originally founded in 1835, was reopened in

---

[4] 'Abd al-Rahman Al-Jabarti, *'Aja'ib al-athar fi'l-tarajim wa'l-akhbar*, 7 vols. (Cairo, 1322 [1904/5]), III, 2ff. (quoted in Albert Hourani, *Arabic Thought in the Liberal Age* [London, 1962], 51).

1868; the Khedival (now the National) Library (Dar al-Kutub) was established in 1870; and the following two years saw the foundation of the first higher training college (1872) and the first Egyptian state girls' schools (1873).[5]

The impetus toward formation of an educated middle class provided by these developments was further enhanced by émigrés from greater Syria. The history of the *nahda* in Syria had taken a somewhat different course from that in Egypt. Although during the nineteenth century greater Syria remained integrated into the Ottoman empire to a far greater extent than Egypt, its contacts with the west were of longer standing, largely as a result of the large Syrian Maronite community, which had had its own school in Rome since the sixteenth century. When religious differences erupted into civil strife in 1860, many Christians fled Syria to Egypt, and this wave of immigrants provided a fresh stimulus for the development of a modern Egyptian culture. This phenomenon – the enrichment of Egyptian cultural life through the absorption of immigrants from other parts of the Arab world (particularly, but not exclusively, from greater Syria) – was to recur at several points in the next fifty years or so.

This influx of talent from Syria was particularly important in two fields: journalism and theater. Although Egypt had had an official newspaper since 1828, the first non-government journal, *Wadi al-nil*, had not been set up until 1866 and it was not until the 1870s that independent journalistic activity in Egypt began to flourish. In 1877 an Egyptian Jew, James Sanua (Yaʿqub Sanuʿ) founded a satirical magazine, *Abu naddara*, in colloquial Arabic, which ran for fifteen issues before it was banned. But it was the Syrians Salim al-Naqqash, Adib Ishaq, and the Taqla brothers Salim and Bashara who played the leading role in the establishment of the press in Egypt. Indeed, the Taqla brothers' *al-Ahram* (founded in 1876) went on to become the leading newspaper in the Arab world.[6] Although the chief importance of journalism during this period lay in its function as an organ for political opposition, it also served as a training-ground for new writers. The wider readership beginning to emerge as a result of developments in education moreover demanded a new, simpler prose style free from the artificialities of traditional Arabic *sajʿ* (rhymed prose), and the press played an important role in its evolution, helping to develop a language adaptable to new scientific and technological terminology from Europe.[7]

The evolution of the theater in modern Egypt again owes something to Sanuʿ, who staged a number of Arabic productions in colloquial Arabic in

---

[5] See J. Heyworth-Dunne, *An Introduction to the History of Education in Modern Egypt* (London, 1939; repr. 1968).

[6] See J. S. Meisami and Paul Starkey (eds.), *Encyclopedia of Arabic Literature* (London, 1998), s.v. "The Press."

[7] See Jaroslav Stetkevych, *The Modern Arabic Literary Language* (Chicago, 1970).

the early 1870s. Although an institution known as the "Comédie" had been established during the French occupation in 1800, and occasional European productions had been staged in Cairo and Alexandria, it was not until the opening of the Cairo opera house, built to mark the opening of the Suez Canal in 1869, that western plays and operas became widely available to the Egyptian public.[8]

The theatrical efforts of Sanuʿ himself were comparatively short lived, as it soon became clear that he was using the stage as a platform to ridicule the government, and his theater was closed. The next theatrical productions in Arabic were staged not by Egyptians but by the Syrian émigré Salim Khalil al-Naqqash, who with his fellow Syrian Adib Ishaq staged a number of plays, usually adapted from French originals, in Alexandria. They enjoyed little success, however, and al-Naqqash and Ishaq turned to journalism, leaving their leading actor Yusuf al-Khayyat to continue the theatrical experiment. Unfortunately, for his first production in the Cairo opera house he unwisely chose to stage al-Naqqash's *The Tyrant*, which Ismaʿil not unnaturally interpreted as an attack on his own court; al-Khayyat was banished and returned to Syria, and for a second time in a decade promising theatrical activity was brought to a close for political reasons.[9]

The varying fortunes of the theater during this period illustrate the precarious relations between literature and politics that have continued to this day. The political and intellectual climate of Egypt changed radically, however, in 1881–82, when the failure of the ʿUrabi rebellion led to the British occupation of Egypt that lasted, in one form or another, until 1956. Further isolated from Turkey and from her Arab and Islamic neighbors, Egypt entered a period in which increased political awareness, manifested in the increase in the number of newspapers and magazines, was accompanied by a more urgent reexamination of the relationship between Islam and the west and by increasing preoccupation with religious and social reform.[10] In this process a leading role was played by Muhammad ʿAbduh (1849–1905) who, influenced by the earlier preaching of Jamal al-Din al-Afghani, sought to reconcile the seemingly conflicting demands of Islam and modern scientific rationalism – an aim that in turn implied reform of the traditional curriculum of al-Azhar; among his other objectives were reform of the writing of Arabic itself, combining the strength of traditional Arabic style with modern flexibility. In the social field, Qasim Amin signaled the beginning of Egyptian feminism with his books *Tahrir al-marʾa* (1899) and *al-Marʾa al-jadida* (1900); the feminist movement later found its first leader

[8] See Jacob M. Landau, *Studies in the Arab Theater and Cinema* (Philadelphia, 1958).
[9] See M. M. Badawi, *Early Arabic Drama* (Cambridge, 1988), esp. chaps. 2, 3.
[10] See Hourani, *Arabic Thought*.

in Huda Sha'rawi, who in 1923 founded a union to press for women's rights.

In journalism, a leading role continued to be played by Syrians: Ya'qub Sarruf founded *al-Muqtataf* in 1876, and 1892 saw the start of Jurji Zaydan's monthly *al-Hilal*. Women's magazines appeared for the first time in the 1890s, and party political newspapers made a first appearance with Mustafa Kamil's *al-Liwa'*, founded in 1900; this was followed by Lutfi al-Sayyid's *al-Jarida*, with which the new school of Egyptian modernists may be said really to begin. These developments in the press continued not only to reflect the growth of a wider reading public and a development of social and political consciousness, but also to provide opportunities for younger writers to refine their skills.

With the rise of the press, the short essay and article had emerged as the dominant prose forms in the literature of this period. Economic considerations undoubtedly played a part in this development, for the reading public – though expanding – remained too small to support the independent publication of many large-scale works, and even full-length compositions such as al-Muwaylihi's *Hadith 'Isa ibn Hisham* were usually published first in serial form. Despite (or perhaps because of) the British occupation, translations from other languages continued to be dominated by French novels and short stories, often worthless stories of romantic love. Traditional Arabic narrative forms continued to be used by a few writers: al-Muwaylihi's *Hadith 'Isa ibn Hisham*, for example, published in book form in 1907, attempted to use the traditional *maqama*[11] form as a vehicle for social criticism, relating the story of a pasha from Muhammad 'Ali's time who is resurrected to find himself in a new, Europeanized Cairo; by this means, the author is enabled to compare present Egypt with the past, and to comment on the influence of Europe on Egyptian society. Despite al-Muwaylihi's own skill, however, the attempt to revitalize the *maqama* form in this way proved something of a dead end, as writers opted instead to produce original Arabic compositions based on western models. From the 1890s, Jurji Zaydan – another Syrian émigré – had produced a series of some twenty-two historical novels each of which treated some incident in Islamic history. The first novel with a genuinely modern Egyptian setting and a plot developed on western lines, however, was Muhammad Husayn Haykal's *Zaynab*, which appeared in 1913; the work is a landmark in the development of the modern Egyptian novel, despite being marred by overlong descriptive passages and by weakness of plot and characterization.[12]

---

[11] A classical Arabic literary form, usually involving the use of *saj'* (rhymed prose), in which a narrator relates the exploits of his companion. Many *maqamat* are characterized by a concentration on linguistic virtuosity at the expense of narrative structure.

[12] For al-Muwaylihi (including a translation of *Hadith 'Isa ibn Hisham*), see Roger Allen,

Meanwhile, the theater in Egypt had continued to depend largely on the efforts of Syrian émigrés. From 1882 onward Sulayman al-Qardahi staged a series of productions in Alexandria and Cairo (including adaptations of *Télémaque* and *Hamlet*); increased economic stability was leading to an increase in the number of theatrical troupes, and the tradition of Syrian involvement was continued by a number of actors including al-Qabbani, Iskandar Farah, and Jurj Abyad (the last of whom did much to awaken the educated public to the idea of a classical theater in the western tradition). Local Egyptian involvement in the theater, by comparison, was slow to gather momentum: the first Egyptian Muslim of importance to appear on the stage was Salama Hijazi, who joined Iskandar Farah in 1891; his productions elevated music to the center of attention, and his subsequent success owed much to his legendary voice.

In poetry the movement for "renewal" through the importation of western techniques had begun somewhat later. Traditionally the most prestigious of Arabic literary forms, poetry in Arabic had behind it a continuous tradition of some fourteen centuries, representing what many regarded as one of the pinnacles of Arab civilization. It is, therefore, perhaps not surprising that the influence of western forms, attitudes, and modes of expression that found such a ready route into Arabic prose literature through the translation movement should have had few parallels in poetry. At the same time, the growth of new, rival forms of literary expression – together with the wider availability of classical Arabic poetic *diwans* made possible by the printing-press – were undoubtedly helping to foster a feeling that Arabic poetry in its turn needed reinvigorating. As with the theater, the first stirrings of this revival were apparent in greater Syria; but it was in Egypt rather than Syria that what was subsequently known as the "neo-classical" movement came to fruition in the person of Mahmud Sami al-Barudi (1839–1904). Soldier and statesman as well as poet (a combination reflected in his description as *sha'ir al-sayf wa-al-qalam*, "poet of sword and pen"), al-Barudi's eventful life included a seventeen-year exile for his part in the 'Urabi revolt. His work combines a new attempt at a poetic expression of his experience and personality with a generally traditional use of language, meter, and *aghrad* (thematic types), the conscious return to the poetic style of an earlier age reflecting the need to reassert an Arab cultural identity in a world of rapidly changing political realities.

Al-Barudi's example was followed and developed in Egypt by Ahmad Shawqi (1868–1932) and Muhammad Hafiz Ibrahim (1871–1932) – known respectively as "the prince of poets" (*amir al-shu'ara*) and "the poet of the people" – whose rival merits split the younger generation of Egyptian writers into two camps. Despite the continuing predominance of panegyrics and other "official" verse in their output, the *diwans* of both men also provide evidence of increasing concern with social and political questions. At the same time, the first stirrings of a new trend of romanticism were apparent in the poetry of Khalil Mutran (1872–1949), a Syrian who had settled in Egypt in 1892 after fleeing the persecution of the sultan 'Abd al-Hamid. Unlike the neo-classical poets, the new trend sought deliberately to break away from the poetic diction of the classical Arabic heritage, seeking inspiration in western European rather than in pre-Islamic or 'Abbasid models.[13]

Although the main trends of Egyptian cultural development during the nineteenth century – as indeed, during the twentieth – can most easily be illustrated through the development of formal literature, the period (like those that followed it) is characterized by an underlying tension between three distinct traditions of cultural activity: the Arabic-Islamic "elite" tradition, primarily associated with literature in *fusha* (classical, or formal, Arabic); a parallel, though less well-documented, tradition of "popular" culture, frequently involving the use of *'ammiyya* (colloquial Arabic); and new influences and literary forms derived from the west. In the case of drama, an "elite" Arabic form was largely lacking; but new western models continued to be heavily influenced by the native tradition of farces performed by itinerant actors known as *muhabbazun* or *awlad Rabiya* (after the actor Abu Rabiya) and described by E. W. Lane and other European travelers at various times during the nineteenth century. Such performances continued well after the introduction of western-based theatrical forms in Syria and Egypt toward the middle of the century.[14] In poetry, the tradition of *zajal* (colloquial poetry, usually in strophic form) was used by 'Abdallah Nadim and Ya'qub Sanu' for political purposes, with newspapers such as *al-Arghul*, *al-Ustadh*, and others publishing *zajals* composed by readers, thus harnessing popular poetry to the nationalist cause.[15] Meanwhile, the traditional reciters of romances, with their "attractive and rational entertainments" described by Lane,[16] continued to live on in the cafes of Cairo and other urban centers; effectively extinct today, their functions have to some extent been assumed by the modern mass media of radio and television.

[13] For a general account of the neo-classical movement in poetry, see S. Somekh, "The Neo-Classical Arabic Poets," in Badawi (ed.), *Modern Arabic Literature*, 36ff. For Mutran, see R. C. Ostle, "The Romantic Poets," in *ibid.*, 86ff.

[14] On this, see Shmuel Moreh, *Live Theatre and Dramatic Literature in the Medieval Arab World* (Edinburgh, 1992), esp. 152ff.

[15] See Marilyn Booth, "Poetry in the Vernacular," in Badawi (ed.), *Modern Arabic Literature*, 463ff.

[16] Edward William Lane, *The Manners and Customs of the Modern Egyptians* (London, 1908; new ed., 1954) 397ff.

From Zaghlul to the Second World War (1919–45)

The period between the 1919 uprising and the Free Officers' coup of 1952 saw the coming to maturity of the modern Egyptian novel, short story, and drama, and the rise and fall of romanticism in poetry, against a political background dominated by instability in Anglo-Egyptian relations. In this respect, Egypt's experience paralleled that of other parts of the Arab world, most of which were preoccupied with the attempt to emerge from western domination and to achieve statehood. The Egyptian modernist movement gained further impetus at the start of this period with reorganization of the Egyptian University under Lutfi al-Sayyid and the founding in 1922 of the Liberal Constitutional Party, whose journal, *al-Siyasa*, was edited by Muhammad Husayn Haykal. In the same year, the discovery of Tutankhamun's tomb both inspired national pride and encouraged the view that the greatness of Egypt – and, by implication, its potential for future development – was independent of the rest of the Arab and Islamic world. This "pharaonic" interpretation of Egypt's role in the modern world soon found expression in a number of significant literary works, including Tawfiq al-Hakim's *'Awdat al-ruh* (Return of the Spirit, 1933) (see p. 403). On another level, the search for accommodation between traditional institutions and modern realities continued to be manifested in debate about reform of al-Azhar and its relations with the emerging secular institutions of higher education.

The ferment in Egyptian intellectual life following the First World War manifested itself in two *causes célèbres*. The first, in 1925, centered around publication of a work by 'Ali 'Abd al-Raziq, *al-Islam wa-usul al-hukm*, in which he argued that the caliphate was not an integral part of Islam; the book led to a government crisis and expulsion of 'Abd al-Raziq from the body of the 'ulama'.

The second case, in 1926, turned on a work of literary criticism by the blind author Taha Husayn, *Fi al-shi'r al-jahili*. Although Zaydan[17] and others had made some attempt to evaluate the classical Arabic literary heritage, serious literary criticism in Egypt had been slow to emerge. An increasing trend not only toward methodical criticism but also toward iconoclasm was heralded in 1921, when 'Abbas al-'Aqqad and Ibrahim al-Mazini collaborated on the critical work known as *al-Diwan*, in which they mercilessly attacked conservatives such as Shawqi and al-Manfaluti. Taha Husayn's book occasioned a far greater outcry, however, since his work struck not only at the heart of the literary establishment but also at traditional Islamic belief, by arguing that religious motives had contributed to the forging of pre-Islamic poetry and by referring to certain Qur'anic

---

[17] On this, see Pierre Cachia, "The Critics," in Badawi (ed.), *Modern Arabic Literature*, 424–25.

stories as myths. The conservative 'ulama' demanded his dismissal from his university post, but the affair merely served to increase his popularity with students and liberals, and the book, which the author had been forced to withdraw, was reissued in revised form the following year (1927) under the new title *Fi al-adab al-jahili*.[18]

By this stage, a number of literary groupings had begun to emerge, distinguishable by the predominant literary influences on their work. One group, of whom the most prominent members at this stage were Haykal and Taha Husayn, was mainly influenced by French romantic literature; a second group, led by 'Abbas al-'Aqqad and Ibrahim al-Mazini, drew mainly on the English tradition. This dichotomy often reflected differing educational patterns: both Haykal and Taha Husayn, for example, had studied in Paris, while 'Aqqad and al-Mazini (the leaders of the so-called "Diwan Group") were graduates of the teachers' training college in Cairo; another member of the same group, 'Abd al-Rahman Shukri (1886–1958), had studied in England, at Sheffield University. A third group – more radical than either of these, and heavily influenced by the writings of the Syrian Christian Shibli al-Shumayyil – was represented by Salama Musa, Isma'il Mazhar, and others; drawing on the theories of Darwin and Freud, these writers adopted a rationalist position, exalting western culture and rejecting Islamic values. This extremism is also apparent in Salama Musa's attitude to traditional Arabic style, which he held to be inferior to English or French.[19]

Whether because writers were preoccupied with political questions, or because they lacked the skills necessary to master the novel, over a decade passed before Haykal's *Zaynab* found a successor in Muhammad Farid Abu Hadid's first historical novel, *Ibnat al-mamluk* (1926). This represented a significant advance on the less sophisticated efforts of Zaydan, although it was not until the later 1930s that the historical novel began to achieve maturity. The year 1926 saw also the beginning of an autobiographical tradition with the publication of one of the best-loved works of modern Egyptian literature: the first part of Taha Husayn's *al-Ayyam* (published serially in 1926–27 and in book form in 1929), which offered novelists not only psychological insight into an Egyptian country childhood but also a prose style of exemplary clarity. Two further parts of *al-Ayyam* followed, and Taha Husayn also produced a series of novels, beginning with *Du'a' al-karawan* (1934), but his importance lies rather in his contribution to the intellectual and educational development of twentieth-century Egypt than in his fiction *per se*.[20]

---

[18] See P. J. Vatikiotis, *The Modern History of Egypt: From Muhammad Ali to Mubarak* (Baltimore and London, 1969), 300ff.; Pierre Cachia, *Taha Husayn* (London, 1956), 59–60.

[19] See Hourani, *Arabic Thought*, 248ff.; Vatikiotis, *Modern Egypt*, 302ff., etc.

[20] For Taha Husayn, see Cachia, *Taha Husayn*.

The increasing popularity of the novel at the beginning of the 1930s is reflected in the institution of a novel-writing competition, won by Ibrahim al-Mazini's *Ibrahim al-katib* (1931). Despite the author's protestations, the title is an obvious pointer to its partly autobiographical content, and in this respect the work set a precedent followed by many Egyptian writers during the following decade. The work revolves around the writer Ibrahim's relations with three women – a Syrian nurse, his cousin Shushu, and the more westernized Layla – and may be seen as exemplifying the social plight of the contemporary Egyptian intellectual, caught between tradition and modernity; unfortunately, although the work is marked by some nice touches of humor, it is also marred by weaknesses both of characterization and of plot, and by an excessively egotistic outlook – to the extent that it has been described as a novel of self-praise (*fakhr*).[21]

Although al-Mazini went on to produce further novels, including a sequel to *Ibrahim al-katib* entitled *Ibrahim al-thani* (1943), the most significant novel of the early 1930s was probably Tawfiq al-Hakim's *'Awdat al-ruh*, published in two parts in 1933. Begun in French during the author's period of study in Paris, this work marked the beginning of a new realistic trend in Egyptian literature, and was closely modeled on the author's own experiences in Cairo during the period of the First World War. The work depicts the life and frustrated loves of an Egyptian family of the period, culminating in the 1919 popular revolt that for al-Hakim represented the "Return of the Spirit." It is this ending that has been responsible for the novel's "nationalist" reputation, attracting the admiration of, among others, the Egyptian president 'Abd al-Nasir. Like many of the author's works, however, the novel may be read on several levels: long sections in the second part are devoted to a debate about the nature of the Egyptian fallah, whom al-Hakim regarded as directly descended from the builders of the pyramids; but the work may also be read as a novel of adolescent love, or simply for the picture it gives of life in contemporary Egypt. Despite its many faults – most notably the tendency to rambling digression that marks many of al-Hakim's works – the work epitomized the new spirit of Egyptian patriotism and continues to strike a chord in the hearts of many Egyptians to this day.[22]

Al-Hakim's *'Awdat al-ruh* was followed by three further novels, in all of which the autobiographical element plays a significant part. The most successful of these, *Yawmiyyat na'ib fi al-aryaf* (Diary of a Country Attorney, 1937) derives from the author's experiences in the Egyptian Delta and presents a damning picture of conditions in the countryside and of the legal system based on the Napoleonic Code with few concessions to the

[21] See Hilary Kilpatrick, "The Egyptian Novel from *Zaynab* to 1980," in Badawi (ed.), *Modern Arabic Literature*, 223ff.

[22] See Paul Starkey, *From the Ivory Tower: A Critical Study of Tawfiq al-Hakim* (London, 1987) esp. 84–92.

mentality of the fallahin to whom it was being applied; the novel's particular combination of well-directed social criticism and assured literary technique has seldom been surpassed in modern Arabic literature.[23] Inferior from a literary point of view but of more significance in terms of general trends, is 'Usfur min al-sharq (Bird of the East, 1938). Although published later, this derives from an earlier period of al-Hakim's life, and explores conflicts between east and west through the eyes of Muhsin, an Egyptian student in Paris who is clearly closely modeled on al-Hakim himself. Although artistically flawed, the work marks an important step in the development of the east–west theme, anticipated in the nineteenth century in such works as al-Tahtawi's Takhlis al-ibriz ila talkhis Bariz (1834–35), and subsequently developed in a series of novels by writers not only from Egypt but also from other parts of the Arab world. Despite the importance of al-Hakim's novels for development of the genre, however, his main interest lay in the theater rather than the novel, and after al-Ribat al-muqaddas (The Sacred Bond, 1945), which paints a picture of an "ivory tower" intellectual, he produced no more full-scale works of this kind.[24]

To this stage in the development of the Egyptian novel belong also the efforts of Mahmud Tahir Lashin, whose one novel, Hawwa' bila adam (Eve without Adam, 1934), touches on themes of class conflict and the emancipated woman's search for new forms of relations with men; and 'Abbas Mahmud al-'Aqqad's Sara (Sarah, 1938), the sole contribution to the genre of one of the leading literary figures of the first half of the twentieth century. By the beginning of the 1940s the novel was both beginning to claim for itself a new status (reflected in the institution of a novel-writing competition in 1941) and to be marked by a number of new directions. A new generation of novelists, taking its cue from the corruption of Egyptian politics in the inter-war period rather than from the optimism of the 1919 revolution, was beginning to produce works characterized by a new realism.[25] Paradoxically, this trend was accompanied by a new enthusiasm for historical subjects, set either in the pharaonic or in the pre-Islamic or early Islamic historical period. At the same time. the period saw a rise in a type of "popular" novel, exemplified most obviously in the works of Ihsan 'Abd al-Quddus, in which romantic love – not untouched by sensationalism – plays a major part; although despised by more serious writers, works of this type have accounted for a large proportion of the output of Egyptian fiction in this and succeeding periods, as well as providing ready material for the growing Egyptian film industry.

[23] Ibid., 140–53. The novel is available in an English translation by Abba Eban, The Maze of Justice (London, 1947; new ed., with foreword by P. H. Newby, London, 1989).

[24] See Starkey, Ivory Tower, 53–56, 108–18, etc. 'Usfur min al-sharq is available in an English translation by R. Bayly Winder, Bird of the East (Beirut, 1967).

[25] See Kilpatrick, "Egyptian Novel," 232ff.

Among the writers who produced historical novels set in ancient Egypt was the future Nobel prize winner, Najib Mahfuz [Naguib Mahfouz]; but although he had planned to embark on a series of historical novels, he soon redirected his attention to contemporary Egypt, producing a series of works set in various quarters of Cairo which explore the search for new values in the changing society of contemporary Egypt. This series of novels culminated in the monumental *Thulathiyya* (Trilogy, published in 1956–57, but written before the 1952 revolution), which lovingly chronicles the life of a lower-middle-class Egyptian family and the transition from a traditional to a more modern way of life, in the period between the two world wars. A hint of the turbulent period on which Egypt was about to embark is given at the end of the novel, when the two brothers Ahmad and ʿAbd al-Munʿim go their separate ways, one to the left wing of the Wafd, the other to the Muslim Brothers.[26]

In the meantime, the short story – whose length gave it advantages over the novel in terms of ease of publication in newspapers and journals – had also been developing rapidly. As in the nineteenth century, Egyptian literature continued to benefit from the exodus of Syrians from their native country. A crucial role in developing the genre was played by the Syro-Lebanese brothers ʿIsa (d. 1922) and Shihata (d. 1961) ʿUbayd, who called for a new Egyptian literature that would depict the social and national life of contemporary Egypt in a realistic fashion.

The key role in the maturation of the Egyptian short story was, however, played by the Egyptians Muhammad Taymur (1892–1921) and Mahmud Tahir Lashin, and by Mahmud Taymur, the brother of Muhammad. Muhammad, who also played an important role in the development of Egyptian drama, had studied in France, where he had read widely in European literature. Like the ʿUbayd brothers, his view of the course that Egyptian literature should take was influenced by contemporary political developments, but although he played a key role in helping to shape the emerging genre, his influence was cut short by his early death, and it was left to others to bring the Egyptian short story to full maturity.

Muhammad's works were edited after his premature death by his brother Mahmud (1894–1973), who went on to become one of the most prolific writers in modern Egyptian literature, with more than twenty collections of short stories to his name. His name, like that of Lashin (1894–1954), is associated with the "Modern School" (*al-madrasa al-haditha*), a group of writers whose literary weekly *al-Fajr*, founded in 1925, played a key role both in widening the potential reading public for the short story and in developing a new literary sensibility appropriate for the period. Like other

---

[26] For Mahfuz, including details of the extensive secondary literature on his writing, see Rasheed El-Enany, *The Pursuit of Meaning* (London, 1993).

members of the school, he was influenced not only by the short stories of de Maupassant but also by Russian writers such as Chekhov and Turgenev, and his short stories were consciously rooted in the lives of "ordinary" Egyptians. Despite this, both his themes and his characterization remained somewhat limited, and it is to Lashin's stories (particularly his *Hadith al-qarya*, published in 1929) rather than Taymur's that the credit must be given for moving the Egyptian – and indeed, the Arabic – short story forward into a new, mature, phase of development. The importance of this story, which revolves around an educated narrator's visit to the countryside, lies not only in the assurance with which Lashin manipulates the narrative form (which incorporates a "story within a story"), but also in its perfect mirroring of the social and political dilemmas facing contemporary Egypt, caught in an unresolved conflict between traditional and modern values. Discouraged by the reception given to his work, Lashin abandoned writing at the end of the 1930s, but his short stories provided the starting-point for a new, realistic mode of narrative (brought to perfection in the works of Yahya Haqqi [1905–92]) that provided a counterweight to the growing number of light-weight, "sentimental" works in the genre.[27]

Meanwhile, the theater in Egypt had continued to revolve until the 1920s mainly around melodramatic productions, which often relied heavily on music for their effect. The presence of foreign troops during the First World War had introduced new varieties of western comic techniques to the Egyptian public, and a new kind of popular theater known as the "Franco-Arab revue" had been created by the Syrian-born 'Aziz 'Id. This style of theater had been further developed by the Egyptian Najib al-Rihani, much of whose material was adapted from the French vaudeville, but whose principal character, a village headman ('umda) named Kish-Kish Bey, was archetypically Egyptian. Serious critics scoffed at his technique, but his popularity remained immense.[28]

Despite the growing popularity of these forms of theater, and despite the large number of western plays translated by such men as Najib Haddad and Tanyus 'Abduh, few original plays of literary value had yet been written in Egypt, and the question of whether to use classical or colloquial Arabic for serious drama remained unresolved. Significant contributions to the development of the genre were, however, being made by Farah Antun, Antun Yazbak, and especially Muhammad Taymur, already mentioned in the discussion of the short story. Taymur's four comedies in colloquial Egyptian, written between 1918 and 1921, derived inspiration from a belief that to raise standards it was necessary to "Egyptianize" the theater, and to this end

---

[27] See Sabry Hafez, "The modern Arabic short story," in Badawi (ed.), *Modern Arabic Literature*, 270ff. For Lashin, see Sabry Hafez, *The Genesis of Arabic Narrative Discourse* (London, 1993), esp. 215ff.

[28] See Landau, *Theater and Cinema*, 86ff.

his dramas attempted to treat social and domestic themes of relevance to the Egyptian public, but they were unable to compete with the more popular entertainment provided by al-Rihani and others, and Taymur, discouraged, turned his attention from the theater to the short story.[29]

The next phase in the development of Egyptian theater was dominated by the figure of Tawfiq al-Hakim, who between 1921 and 1926 produced some six plays in colloquial Arabic for the popular theater of the 'Ukasha brothers. (An indication of the low status enjoyed by the theater at the time is the fact that al-Hakim was forced to write under the name "Husayn Tawfiq" to escape the attention of his family.) The plays were largely based on the traditional form known as the "operette," with music and songs playing a significant part, and in most of them al-Hakim followed the common practice of giving his play an Egyptian setting, even when adapting the work from a western original. The themes of two of the plays, however – *al-Dayf al-thaqil* and *al-Mar'a al-jadida* – combined the elements of comedy and melodrama with serious political and social comment, and as such point forward to the author's subsequent career.[30]

The social and financial base of the Egyptian theater in the 1920s remained a precarious one, and when al-Hakim returned in 1928 from studying in Paris he found many of his previous theatrical associates bankrupt. During the following six years, he produced some half-dozen plays in both colloquial and classical Arabic on a variety of themes, some of which suggest the influence of Pirandello and other contemporary western writers. The decisive date, both in al-Hakim's career as a writer and in the history of modern Arabic drama, was the publication of *Ahl al-kahf* in 1933. The play (based on the Qur'anic story known in Christian tradition as the sleepers of Ephesus) represented the first in a series of "intellectual" dramas of a type unprecedented in the Egyptian theater; clearly intended to refer to the contemporary situation of Egypt as it awakened from centuries of stagnation to face the challenge of the twentieth century, the work enjoyed a spectacular success, going through two editions in its year of publication. When the government-sponsored National Troupe was established in 1935, the company opened with al-Hakim's play. *Ahl al-kahf* was followed in 1934 by *Shahrazad* and a series of other "philosophical" plays in the same mold, and al-Hakim continued to dominate the Egyptian theatrical scene until well after the fall of the monarchy. Indeed, to him belongs the chief credit for making prose drama an accepted form of literature in modern Egypt. His eclectic approach to his art, and his willingness to draw on a variety of sources (Islamic, "popular," western, or classical), make classification of his work difficult; many of his plays were designed to be read rather than acted,

[29] For Muhammad Taymur, see Ed de Moor, *Un oiseau en cage* (Amsterdam, 1991).
[30] See Starkey, *Ivory Tower*, 22.

but despite his popular image as an "ivory tower" intellectual, his works often provide a mirror on developments in contemporary Egypt.[31]

The period between the two world wars that saw the coming to maturity of new narrative and dramatic forms was, in poetry, above all the period of Romanticism. It is impossible to consider the phenomenon of Romanticism in Egypt in isolation from other parts of the Middle East (or indeed, the Mahjar[32]), since developments spread rapidly throughout the Arabic-speaking world. A key figure in sowing the seeds of the new trend, however, was the Syrian-born Egyptian poet Khalil Mutran (1872–1949), whose first published volume of verse (*Diwan al-khalil*, 1908) included a preface in which he sought to distance himself from traditional Arab concepts of poetry by laying a new emphasis on the structural unity of the poem. Although Mutran's work is characterized by a new belief in the primacy of the individual artist, however, his subsequent poetry failed to develop the new trend to any significant degree, and it was left to the members of the Diwan Group – al-ʿAqqad, al-Mazini, and ʿAbd al-Rahman Shukri (1886–1958) – to bring the influence of the neo-classical poets to an end.[33]

The main influence on the poets of the Diwan Group (so-called after the critical work entitled *al-Diwan* by al-ʿAqqad and al-Mazini published in two volumes in 1921) was English lyrical poetry of the eighteenth and nineteenth centuries. However, it was probably less through their poetry itself than through their criticism that al-ʿAqqad and al-Mazini played a significant part in changing the current of literary taste. Continuing Mutran's stress on the importance of the unity of a poem, they added a new emphasis on the importance of emotion and the need to write poetry that was the direct result of the poet's own experience. This trend was continued by the members of the Apollo Society founded in 1932, which centered around the periodical *Apollo*, founded and edited by Ahmad Zaki Abu Shadi (1892–1955). A loose association of poets whose membership stretched beyond the borders of Egypt, the Apollo Society was subsequently to form the core of the Romantic movement in Egypt, including ʿAli Mahmud Taha (1902–49), whose poetry (much of it set to music) achieved enormous popularity in the 1930s and 1940s, and Ibrahim Naji (1898–1953), whose

---

[31] See *ibid.*, 36ff., etc. In this respect, the series of plays on social themes originally published in the newspaper *Akhbar al-yawm* and subsequently reprinted in the collection *Masrah al-mujtamaʿ* (1950) is particularly interesting. Unlike many Egyptian writers of his generation, Tawfiq al-Hakim had consistently refused to identify himself with any political party, arguing that a writer must maintain his independence to preserve his moral authority; his articles in the 1930s and 1940s took as their targets Egyptian politicians of all persuasions, and the plays of *Masrah al-mujtamaʿ* echo this spirit in the context of Egypt after the Second World War – a time when, as the author points out in his preface, the country was again in a state of social turmoil.

[32] "Mahjar" is the name given to Arab émigré communities in North and South America.

[33] See Ostle, "Romantic Poets," 88ff.

love poetry represents a unique fusion of the classical Arabic and western romantic traditions. A particularly intriguing feature of Abu Shadi's own work is the number of poems inspired by paintings – an indication, as has recently been observed,[34] "of how universal the author intended the cultural mission of the Apollo Society to be." Similar manifestations of this liberal vision of Egyptian culture can be seen in the sculpture of Mahmud Mukhtar and the painting of Muhammad Naji.

Despite the desire of the Romantic literary critics to break away from classical Arabic poetic traditions, much romantic poetry continued to adhere fairly closely to traditional norms of meter and rhyme. In language and imagery, however, a revolution was under way. In the hands of the most gifted poets, the new trend produced a number of works in which a new lyricism and simplicity of language is deployed to considerable effect. At the same time, in the hands of less gifted poets, the introspection associated with the new style led to a host of publications in which the poet's isolation, feelings of nostalgia, and concepts such as *al-majhul* (the unknown) produce a sense rather of literary escapism.

To what extent the phenomenon of Arab Romanticism was a direct imitation of western Romanticism and to what extent it arose as a result of the political and cultural changes occurring in the Middle East in the period following the First World War is a question much debated. What is not at issue, however, is that Romanticism in a general sense perfectly mirrored the political realities of the age. The First World War had resulted in the dissolution of the Ottoman empire, and in Egypt (declared a British protectorate in 1914) nationalist sentiments had spilled over into widespread revolt in 1919. The search for new means of expressing an Egyptian identity provided a natural stimulus for authors to seek new means of expression, and the literature of European Romanticism – itself a product of the tension between the individual and the society around him – provided a natural focus for writers anxious to cast off the literary conventions that the neo-classicists had largely maintained. As the idealism of 1919 gave way to disillusion with increasing corruption as the various political parties maneuvered for power, the more escapist facets of Romanticism again must have mirrored the mood of many in the country.

The same factors responsible for the attractiveness of Romanticism in poetry and in other arts manifested themselves in a number of other intellectual debates during this period. The growth of political activity and awareness following the 1919 revolt had led to a continued increase in the importance of journalism, with individual parties trying to recruit distinguished authors to their daily or weekly papers. The "pharaonic" trend in

---

[34] See Robin Ostle, "Modern Egyptian Renaissance Man," *Bulletin of the School of Oriental and African Studies*, 57 (1944), 184ff.

Egyptian thought found perhaps its most eloquent exposition in Tawfiq al-Hakim's 'Awdat al-ruh and Ahl al-kahf, but the Egyptian heritage, and the position of Egypt in the contemporary world, was more complicated than to yield to such simplistic, and potentially isolationist, theories, and a number of other important – and often contradictory – intellectual trends can be identified during this period. In his book Mustaqbal al-thaqafa fi misr (1938), for instance, Taha Husayn (who had been a professor of classical civilization) sought to demonstrate that Egypt had always belonged to a wider, Mediterranean civilization – in effect arguing that the future of Egypt lay with Europe rather than with Islam or the Arab world.[35] Equally important, perhaps, was the restatement of the Islamic heritage undertaken by such leading writers as Muhammad Husayn Haykal (in Hayat Muhammad), Ahmad Amin (in Fajr al-Islam, 1929–52), and indeed Taha Husayn himself ('Ala hamish al-sira). The process of intellectual rediscovery and reappraisal represented by these works had a more sinister counterpart in a number of social and political groupings that shared a belief in violence as a legitimate means for achieving their aims: these included not only groups such as Misr al-fatat (Young Egypt), whose popularity was comparatively short lived, but also the Muslim Brethren (al-Ikhwan al-muslimun), founded by Hasan al-Banna' in 1928, whose influence has continued into the post-1952 period.

Alongside these developments in "elite" culture, the inter-war period witnessed a parallel development in more popular forms of literary expression. Popular zajal-type[36] verse forms had served during the 1919 revolt to articulate nationalist sentiment, and a number of newspapers had been founded by zajjals, or employed "resident" zajjals as resident columnists. A curious, and particularly Egyptian, phenomenon was the appearance during the 1930s of some scores of spurious autobiographies, many in the colloquial and many purporting to be written by lower-class characters – thieves, prostitutes, and the like. The interplay of vernacular literature with contemporary social and political developments is nowhere better illustrated, however, than in the career of Mahmud Bayram al-Tunisi (1893–1961). Born in Alexandria into a family of Tunisian extraction, Bayram al-Tunisi began by composing poetry in the classical idiom for the Alexandrian press, but soon became aware of the advantages of more colloquial forms of expression as a medium for the development of political consciousness. Though banished from Egypt for most of the inter-war period for his political activities, he published much material in the popular-satirical press and popular arts reviews of urban Egypt during this period, as well as

---

[35] See Cachia, Taha Husayn, 77ff.
[36] Zajal: a term applied to a type of popular verse in strophic form. Zajjal: a composer of zajals.

contributing to the by now well-established Egyptian popular theater. From the early 1940s he was also engaged in production for newer forms of mass media which had begun to gain popularity in the country. From 1942 he collaborated with Zakariyya Ahmad in composing lyrics for the popular singer Umm Kulthum (d. 1975), whose songs – which married a subtle eroticism with a careful respect for Islamic propriety – represented a unique cultural phenomenon. Her concerts, records, and other activities made her immensely wealthy, but despite this she continued to hold the affection both of ordinary Egyptians and of Egypt's rulers, and her songs – which seemed to express the heart of the Arabs – became a rallying-point for Egyptian and Arab sentiment, especially at times of crisis and defeat. Like Bayram himself, Umm Kulthum also used the radio as a vehicle by which to reach a mass audience, as well as contributing to the burgeoning Egyptian film industry; the first films had been seen in Egypt as long ago as 1905, and the country had had a film recording studio since 1919. Although most films had been made with a view to financial reward rather than artistic merit, the industry was already beginning to play an important part in reinforcing the cultural hegemony of Egypt over other parts of the Arab world.[37]

Egypt after the Second World War (1945–95)

The course of Egyptian cultural life in the second half of the twentieth century again well illustrates the close relations between intellectual and political trends. The Second World War and succeeding events – in particular the creation of Israel in 1948 – heightened Egyptian awareness of the failure of the democratic experiment, and both intellectuals and the people generally began to turn to alternative philosophies to provide a way forward from the corruption of the current regime. Though the mass appeal of Marxism was limited by its atheistic foundations, the critic Luwis 'Awad (1914–90) had already published Marxist interpretations of English literature in Taha Husayn's review *al-Katib al-misri* and, more generally, radical thinkers such as Salama Musa had begun to stress the need for literature to promote socialist values in a language ordinary Egyptians could understand. These ideas found a ready response, not only among the emerging generation of writers including Najib Mahfuz, but also among established writers such as Taha Husayn himself. At the other end of the political spectrum, the Muslim Brotherhood was proving more attractive as a mass movement, combining a reputation for ruthlessness and violence with a wide-ranging program of schools, clinics, and welfare institutions that could not fail to attract increasing numbers of the Egyptian poor. The movement reached its high point during the Palestine war of 1948, when members distinguished

---

[37] For Bayram al-Tunisi, see Marilyn Booth, *Bayram al-Tunisi's Egypt* (Exeter, 1990).

themselves as volunteers and auxiliaries; banned in 1954 but later allowed to reemerge under Sadat, its presence (and that of other fundamentalist groups) has provided a somber backdrop to the cultural and intellectual life of Egypt in the subsequent period.[38]

To these overtly political influences must be added a third, more philo-sophical, trend whose effect on the course of intellectual life in post-war Egypt was considerable. This was the existentialist philosophy of Jean-Paul Sartre and others, with its concept of *engagement* (translated into Arabic as *iltizam*), which was thrust into prominence in the Arab world in January 1953 with the publication in Beirut of the first issue of the literary journal *al-Adab*, whose editor Suhayl Idris loudly proclaimed its advocacy of "com-mitted literature." Idris's call for commitment was followed by a series of debates in the Egyptian press and elsewhere about the meaning and implica-tions of this concept, in some of which a "generation gap" began to emerge – al-ʿAqqad and others defending a position that might crudely be described as "art for art's sake" – against a younger generation of "committed" writer and critics. Nor was the younger generation itself united: various shades of "commitment" are apparent, mingling the influences of Marxism, existen-tialism, and Arab nationalism, not to speak of other, more esoteric "isms" of one kind and another. From this point, however, the concept of *"iltizam"* was one that no Egyptian, or Arab, writer could ignore: "commitment" took over from Romanticism as the dominant mood of the period.[39]

The attractiveness of the concept of *iltizam* to Egyptian intellectuals was undoubtedly rooted in the particular combination of social and political factors prevailing at the time. In the same way as Sartre's *engagement* came to prominence in Europe largely as a result of the experience of the Second World War, *iltizam* struck a chord with an Egypt that appeared to have found a political way forward with the Free Officers' revolt of 1952 but that continued to suffer from seemingly intractable economic and social pro-blems. In poetry, the change of mood had already been accompanied by major changes in form, as the first generation of post-Second World War poets began to experiment with various forms of "free verse" (in which the foot rather than the line is used as the basis of meter), under the influence of western poets such as Eliot and others. Although the first experiments along these lines took place mainly in Iraq, the new style quickly spread to Egypt and other parts of the Arab world.[40]

To the immediate post-war period belong some of the best-known novels of Najib Mahfuz (b. 1911), whose Nobel prize for literature in 1988 not

[38] See Vatikiotis, *Modern Egypt*, 329–30, etc.
[39] See Badawi, "Introduction," 21ff.
[40] On these developments, see Shmuel Moreh, *Modern Arabic Poetry 1830–1970* (Leiden, 1976); and esp. Salma Khadra al-Jayyusi, *Trends and Movements in Modern Arabic Poetry*, 2 vols. (Leiden, 1977).

only capped a literary career of astonishing length and variety, but also served to awaken many in the west and elsewhere to the achievements (indeed, to the existence) of modern Arabic literature. Like most Egyptian writers, Mahfuz was unable to support himself by writing alone for most of his career, and until his retirement in 1971 he served in a variety of government departments, including the General Organization for Film Industry, Broadcasting, and Television, the ministry of national guidance, and (ironically) the film censorship office. His first works were on historical themes, but he soon turned to contemporary Egyptian society for inspiration, and a series of "realistic" novels ensued, set in the quarters of Old Cairo: the novels (published between 1945 and 1949) are peopled with the colorful inhabitants of the Cairo backstreets and reflect the search for new moral values in a society whose foundations were looking increasingly shaky. This series of novels reached its highest level of achievement in *al-Thulathiyya*, whose characters reflect the changes in Egyptian society in the period between the two world wars: as in Mahfuz's earlier novels, a prominent theme is the search for meaning and moral certainty. Both in scale and in maturity, the work remains unique in Egyptian literature as a faithful mirror of this eventful period in the nation's life.[41]

Mahfuz's own reaction to the 1952 Free Officers' revolt was a curious one. Apparently feeling that the social problems that had earlier preoccupied him would be solved by the new regime, he stopped writing for five years until – his disillusion with 'Abd al-Nasir already apparent – he began writing *Awlad haratina*.[42] But his reaction of silence to contemporary events was not shared by the majority of Egyptian authors, and it was not long before the change of regime began to be reflected in Egypt's literary production. If one had to select a single work epitomizing the new mood of commitment and realism following the Free Officers' revolt of 1952, the most likely candidate would probably be 'Abd al-Rahman al-Sharqawi's (1920–87) *al-Ard*, first published in 1954 and recently described as "arguably the most widely known work of modern Arabic fiction both inside and beyond the Near and Middle East."[43] (The work is in fact probably better known to the average Egyptian through Yusuf Shahin's popular film version than through the book itself.) In the course of the novel, which is set in the early 1930s during the dictatorship of Isma'il Sidqi, two main struggles are acted out between the oppressed inhabitants of a Delta village and the authorities: in the first, an attempt is made to deprive the villagers of the water needed for irrigation; the second revolves around the local land owner's scheme to build a new road to his estate across their land. In the

---

[41] See El-Enany, *Pursuit of Meaning*, 70ff.
[42] Trans. as *Children of Gebelawi* by Philip Stewart (London, 1981).
[43] Robin Ostle, introduction to *Egyptian Earth*, trans. Desmond Stewart (London, 1992).

course of the narrative al-Sharqawi gives us a vivid picture of a number of village "types" – schoolteacher, smallholder, 'umda, imam; the realism of the description is considerably enhanced by the use of dialogue in vigorous colloquial. From a formal point of view also, the novel is of considerable interest, for while the first and third sections are narrated by a schoolboy returning from Cairo to the countryside for his summer holidays, the central section reverts to a more conventional third-person narrative. Although writing of events during the 1930s, al-Sharqawi was almost certainly expressing an unspoken fear about the future course of developments under the Free Officers' regime – the use of historical analogies to comment on contemporary developments being observed also in writers belonging to the so-called "generation of the sixties."[44] This technique represents an obvious but often effective device for evading the attentions of the censor – a factor that has had to be taken into account by Egyptian intellectuals at almost every point during the period under discussion.

Although al-Sharqawi went on to write three further novels, he never repeated the success of al-Ard in articulating the brief period of optimism that followed the Free Officers' revolt of 1952. The trend toward "realism," however, was not confined to the full-scale novel. Among short-story writers, even members of the older generation such as Muhammad Taymur and Yahya Haqqi felt compelled to reflect the new political reality in their published work. At the same time, a new generation of writers was emerging whose work – often spanning more than one literary genre – seemed at times almost to have been written with the intention of providing the new regime with an agenda for action.

Among this generation, Yusuf Idris (1927–91) is perhaps the outstanding figure. Widely acknowledged as one of the most talented of modern Arabic short-story writers, Idris – who originally trained as a doctor – also wrote several novels and made important contributions to the development of the drama. His first collection of short stories, Arkhas layali (The Cheapest Nights, 1954), was an immediate success, and four more collections followed over the next few years, each marked by the same concern for the underprivileged (particularly the peasants of the countryside), by a keen eye for the foibles of human behavior across a wide social spectrum, and by a unique blend of colloquial and standard Arabic.[45]

In drama, the mood of optimism and need for social reconciliation following the 1952 revolution found an early echo in Tawfiq al-Hakim's al-Aydi al-na'ima (1954), an essentially light-hearted play that nonetheless contains a strong element of social criticism in its repeated emphasis on work rather than wealth as the basis for social order. Al-Aydi al-na'ima was

[44] For these see below, pp. 418ff.
[45] See P. M. Kurpershoek, The Short Stories of Yusuf Idris (Leiden, 1981).

followed by other works whose relevance to contemporary Egypt could not be doubted. In *Izis* (1955), for example, al-Hakim discusses the age-old philosophical question of means and ends against the background of the Ancient Egyptian myth of Isis and Osiris, concluding (in a phrase well suited to the political mood of the moment) that judgment in such matters belongs to the people alone. The setting of *al-Safqa* (1956), by contrast, is a contemporary one, revolving around the attempt of a group of peasants to secure a land deal in the face of almost unsurmountable difficulties; the language of the play represents an attempt to solve the dilemma of classical vs. colloquial Arabic by employing a simplified "third language" which can be read either way.[46]

Although these linguistic experiments and gestures toward "commitment" on the part of Egypt's foremost dramatist undoubtedly reflected the spirit of the age, the tone of al-Hakim's plays remained generally conciliatory. During the same period, however, a more impassioned, even angry, generation of playwrights was beginning to make its mark. The new mood was heralded by the appearance in 1956 of Nu'man 'Ashur's *al-Nas illi taht* (The People Downstairs), which combined social criticism with a strong element of popular comedy. The play, which enjoyed a considerable success, was followed by *al-Nas illi foq* (The People at the Top, 1957), representing a powerful and almost wholesale condemnation of the old Egyptian aristocracy, and by *'A'ilat al-dughri* (1962), in which the author uses the break-up of a middle-class Egyptian family to symbolize the disintegration of society in post-revolutionary Egypt. Written only ten years after the Free Officers' revolt of 1952, the play provides a vivid illustration of how quickly the optimism engendered by the change of regime had given place to disillusionment.[47]

Nu'man 'Ashur's plays are among the first manifestations of what has sometimes been called the "new wave" of Egyptian dramatists – a group that also includes, among others, Lutfi al-Khuli, Alfred Faraj, Sa'd al-Din Wahba, and Yusuf Idris (already mentioned as a short-story writer). Although each of these playwrights retained his own particular literary stamp, they shared a number of characteristics that spanned both the political and literary spheres. Almost universally "committed" politically (to the extent, in some cases, of having been imprisoned for their views), they had no hesitation in using colloquial Arabic for their plays. Taking their cue from the more general nationalistic mood, a number of them (including even the conservative al-Hakim, in *Qalabuna al-masrahi*, 1967) were consciously attempting to mold a specifically Egyptian drama, and to relate their work to older forms of Egyptian theatrical activity, for example by introducing the

---

[46] See Starkey, *Ivory Tower*, 34, 174–75, etc.
[47] See Badawi, *Modern Arabic Drama in Egypt* (Cambridge, 1987), 140–48.

traditional Arab story-teller into their plays. At the same time, they were acutely aware of theatrical developments in the west, including not only the "committed" theater of Sartre, Brecht, and others, but also the dramatists of the so-called "theater of the absurd," whose principal exponents were Beckett, Ionesco, and Artaud.[48] In this respect the eclectic Tawfiq al-Hakim – despite belonging to a previous generation – again provides a convenient barometer of contemporary trends: *Ya tali' al-shajara* (1962), for example, despite the derivation of the play's title from an old Egyptian peasant song, employs the dramatic techniques of Beckett and Ionesco; by contrast, *al-Ta'am li-kull fam* (1963) is characterized by a didactic, Brechtian tone.[49]

The development of Egyptian drama during this period was undoubtedly helped by the new regime's recognition of the theater's potential as a vehicle of propaganda. Indeed, the late 1950s and early 1960s have been widely seen as one of the most creative periods in Egyptian theatrical history. The establishment of the General Foundation for Theater, Arts, and Music in 1960 was followed by the setting up of several new theaters and theatrical troupes; increasingly, theatrical activity was linked to the comparatively new mass medium of television, which was not only producing its own plays but also screening the works of new dramatists originally written for the theater. At the same time, the regime was making conscious efforts in other ways to bridge the gap between the "elite" culture of the Europeanized theater and the ordinary Egyptian – for example, by arranging provincial tours of contemporary dramatic productions.[50]

If Nu'man 'Ashur's plays *al-Nas illi taht* and *al-Nas illi foq* deserve the credit for launching the "new wave" of the 1950s, the mood of the following decade is perhaps best epitomized by Yusuf Idris's *al-Farafir* (1964), which the author claimed represented an example of a truly Egyptian drama. In a series of articles in the literary periodical *al-Katib* Idris had stressed the need to break down the barriers between actors and audience and to forge links between the modern theater and traditional Arab forms of dramatic entertainment, including the shadow theater (*karagöz*)[51] and the social gathering known as the *samir*. Despite this theorizing, the play itself probably owes more to contemporary western dramatic techniques than to traditional Arab forms of entertainment. It begins with the author addressing the audience to introduce his main character Farfur (a made-up name, translated as "Flipflap," and intended to symbolize the average Egyptian), and the action revolves around the relation between Farfur and his master, whose actions become increasingly arbitrary as the play proceeds. The play

---

[48] *Ibid.*
[49] See Starkey, *Ivory Tower*, 34ff.
[50] Badawi, *Modern Arabic Drama*, 140ff.
[51] The principal character in the Turkish shadow-play, and also the shadow theater itself. See *Encyclopaedia of Islam*, 2nd ed., s.v. "*Karagöz*," by P. N. Boratov.

raises fundamental questions about the nature of power and the structure of society, implying that the division between rulers and ruled is an unalterable one; it ends with Farfur spinning dizzily around his master, as he desperately tries to make sense of his own situation. Whatever one's views on Idris's theorizing, *al-Farafir* remains an important landmark in the Egyptian theater, for its combination of dramatic qualities (not least its typically Egyptian humor), its social and political commitment, and its ability at the same time to raise wider questions of the meaning of human existence; although Idris went on to write several more plays, many with political and social overtones, he never surpassed the dramatic achievement of *al-Farafir*.[52]

As a broad generalization, it may be said that although Egypt has been in the vanguard of most cultural developments in the Arab world since the Second World War (including not only the novel, short story and drama – literary forms of largely western inspiration – but also the newer media such as film and television), in poetry other parts of the Arab world have been more innovative. As already noted, the main formal poetic developments of the late 1940s and early 1950s took place in Iraq; while more recently, much of the most original poetry in Arabic has been produced by poets of Lebanese or Syrian origin. That is not to say, however, that Egyptian poetry has been isolated from trends either in other literary genres or in other parts of the Arab world. The early poetry of Salah 'Abd al-Sabur (1931–81), in particular, not only owes much to the formal experiments of the Iraqis al-Sayyab, al-Mala'ika, and the like, but also epitomizes in verse the social commitment so much in vogue in the mid-1950s not only in Egypt but also in other parts of the Arab world. In *al-Nas fi biladi* (1954), for example, he presents a picture of a collection of simple villagers listening to a tale told by his uncle Mustafa; the tale starts the villagers wondering about the meaning of life, and about the Angel of Death who sends the soul of the rich man tumbling down to the depths of hell; but when the narrator returns to the village, he finds that it is Mustafa who has died in the year of hunger. Written in a language that deliberately aimed to bridge the gap between classical diction and the more everyday language of the people, 'Abd al-Sabur's poetry encountered fierce resistance from some critics, but he continues to be regarded by many as the foremost poet of post-war Egypt.[53]

Although the 1952 revolution had engendered a brief mood of optimism widely reflected in the cultural productions of the Arab world, the Arab defeat in the 1967 war with Israel set the seal on a mood of disillusion that was already becoming widespread, as it became clear that the ideals of the

---

[52] Badawi, *Modern Arabic Drama*, 153ff.
[53] See Salma Khadra al-Jayyusi, "Modern Poetry in Arabic," in Badawi (ed.), *Modern Arabic Literature*, 158ff.

revolution were not being realized. The growth of bureaucracy, the increasing involvement of the state in all areas of life, and the imposition of state censorship on the press and other publications had all had the effect of curtailing creative experimentation. For much of the 1950s and 1960s, most Egyptian intellectuals were either employed by the ministry of culture or worked for one of the state-controlled newspapers and were thus, in effect, state employees – an arrangement that suited the authorities, since it enabled them to neutralize those with "awkward" views. The state's recognition of the value of the arts as a propaganda tool had indeed had some positive effects (e.g., the creation of new theaters); but other contemporary developments, including the increasing standardization of education and the rewriting of school textbooks, were leading to a culturally impoverished generation regarded by Egyptian intellectuals such as Taha Husayn as practically illiterate.

As before, although political events were to give birth to a distinctive new group of literary voices, the mood of the moment was already reflected in the works of established writers such as Najib Mahfuz, whose novels from *al-Liss wa-al-kilab* (1961) to *Miramar* (1967) may be seen as an increasingly pointed series of protests at the direction the new regime was taking. As befits a novelist of Mahfuz's stature, none of the novels is *solely* a work of political protest: most also contain elements of wider metaphysical and existential concern, and *Miramar* in particular is technically innovative. Nonetheless, read in a purely Egyptian context, the novels provide a graphic literary counterpart to the more prosaic account of the loss of faith in 'Abd al-Nasir's regime provided by Tawfiq al-Hakim in his *'Awdat al-wa'y* (1974). Significantly, perhaps, Mahfuz (who had earlier stopped writing altogether for a period following the 1952 revolution) wrote no more novels after the Six Day War until 1972, though he continued to produce short stories.[54]

If the 1950s and early 1960s belonged to the dramatists, the period following the 1967 defeat is perhaps most obviously associated – at least so far as "elite" culture is concerned – with a group of writers (predominantly novelists and short-story writers) generally known as the "generation of the sixties." Like the "new wave" dramatists, these writers shared a number of characteristics, both of attitude and experience. Politically committed and more outspoken than their predecessors, many had already been imprisoned for their views. In contrast to the positive commitment of al-Sharqawi's generation, however, the characteristic mood of the new writers is one of rejection, disillusionment, and self-doubt. Consciously searching to redefine the role of the writer in society, their works are characterized by a rejection of the past and a desire for a new beginning; at the same time, while drawing

[54] See El-Enany, *Pursuit of Meaning*, 99ff.

freely on western modernist techniques, many have also been aware of the creative possibilities of folklore, and of forms derived from the Arabic literary tradition. The group of intellectuals associated with this new movement gathered around a literary and cultural magazine, *Gallery 68*, which appeared in eight issues between 1968 and 1971 under the editorship of, among others, Idwar al-Kharrat (b. 1926), himself one of the most innovative writers of his generation, as well as a prolific translator.[55]

The credit for producing the first work of the new trend is usually given to Sunʿ Allah Ibrahim, whose novella *Tilka al-raʾiha* appeared in 1966; banned in Egypt, it reappeared two years later in an edition from which passages containing political criticism or sexually explicit material had been removed. (The complete text was only published in 1986, in Morocco.) The work, which is autobiographically based (the author had been released from jail in 1964) is an early example of so-called *adab al-sujun* ("prison literature"), in which the sense of alienation is at times almost overpowering: the narrator, who has been released from prison on parole, leads a humdrum existence, restlessly moving from place to place in Cairo as he visits friends and relations, recording the minutiae of his daily round and sexual encounters in a language stripped of all but the barest essentials. When he learns of his mother's death, he betrays no emotion.[56]

Tilka al-raʾiha, which attracted considerable criticism not only for its political outspokenness but also for what Yahya Haqqi described as its "flawed sensibility,"[57] was followed in 1974 by a full-length novel, *Najmat aghustus* (a satirical account of the construction of the Aswan high dam), and in 1981 by his most successful novel, *al-Lajna*. Here again, Ibrahim uses irony to considerable effect. The narrator in *al-Lajna* receives an order from the Committee to write an account of the most eminent contemporary Arab personality, but before he can record his findings, he is condemned to terminate his own life by eating himself. The work, which continually juxtaposes the narrator's straitjacketed situation with the Committee's assurances that he is free, represents one of the most powerful attacks on dictatorship published in the modern Arab world. *Bayrut, Bayrut* (1984), on the Lebanese civil war, though less successful, is of interest as one of relatively few examples of an Egyptian novel set elsewhere in the Arab world. Ibrahim's later novel, *Dhat* (1992), returns to the environment of Cairo, treating the commercialization of the 1980s and 1990s in a satirical manner; the title of the novel ("self" in Arabic, but also containing an allusion to the princess Dhat al-Himma[58]) is itself enigmatic, and the author

---

[55] See Kilpatrick, "Egyptian Novel," 258ff.
[56] See Samia Mehrez, *Egyptian Writers between History and Fiction* (Cairo, 1994), 39ff.
[57] *Ibid.*, 44.
[58] A mythical princess and heroine of a popular Arabic romance, which relates her exploits in the Byzantine wars of the early ʿAbbasid period.

makes frequent use of newspaper clippings and other "external" documents as a means of organizing his story – a technique that can also be found in other authors of this group.[59]

Space forbids discussion of all but two of the other more interesting authors of this generation. In Yusuf al-Qaʿid (b. 1944), we see clearly an evolution of technique and theme from a first novel, *al-Hidad* (1969), which revolves around the comparatively conventional subject of the conflict between the requirements of official justice and patterns of family retribution prevalent in the Egyptian countryside. The same setting forms the background for *Akhbar ʿizbat al-manisi* (1971), which again centers on a murder and the investigation that follows it – a murder, in this case, of a young girl, Sabirin, who has been ravished and made pregnant by her master's son. It is probably no accident that the date of the fictional Sabirin's murder and subsequent investigation (April–May 1967) is a mere month or two before the Middle East war, and indeed, in the novel's closing chapter the affairs of the outside world impinge on the Egyptian village for a brief moment, as the characters learn from radio and newspaper of the Egyptian army's losses in Sinai and withdrawal across the Suez Canal.

The publishing history of al-Qaʿid's next novel, *Yahduth fi misr al-an* (1977), well illustrates the difficulties facing "progressive" writers in the intellectual climate of the time. Written in 1974–75, it was not passed by the censor until 1977 when, having been rejected by several houses, it was published in Cairo at the author's own expense; further editions appeared in Beirut and Acre, but it was not until 1986 that the novel was brought out by an Egyptian house, Dar al-Mustaqbal al-ʿArabi which has also published many other works by the new generation of writers. The work itself, which is strongly anti-American in tone, is an attempt to expose the hypocrisy of the Egyptian government in its new-found friendship with the USA; its anti-establishment tone is continued in the more successful *al-Harb fi barr misr* (1978), set at the time of the 1973 war, which revolves around an impersonation devised by a village ʿumda to avoid his son being drafted into the army. Most ambitious, however, is his *Shakawa al-misri al-fasih* (three volumes, 1981–85), which relates the journey undertaken by an impoverished Cairene family from the City of the Dead, where they have been living, to Maydan al-Tahrir, where they attempt to put themselves up for sale; a disturbance follows, arrests are made, and there is a subsequent investigation. The novel describes the background to these events (set on Friday November 19, 1976), and their aftermath, ending with Sadat's return to Egypt in November 1977, following his visit to Jerusalem in an attempt to initiate the Middle East peace process – a visit viewed with distaste by many members of this generation of writers. In the course of his account, al-Qaʿid

[59] See Mehrez, *Egyptian Writers*, 119–46.

not only indulges in some biting social and political criticism of Sadat's policies, both domestic and foreign, but also attempts to explore the creative process in a way that extends the author's previous experiments in this field. Thus, al-Qaʿid provides the reader with not one but three possible ways to begin the story, from which the reader is invited to choose the most appropriate; there are also three endings, and at various stages the reader is addressed directly, invited to choose titles, to stop reading, and so on. Unfortunately, although the work represents a *tour de force* of experimentation, the author's technique is inadequate for the task he has set himself, and the result is at times little more than a sprawling mess.[60]

More accomplished than the journalistic Yusuf al-Qaʿid is Jamal al-Ghitani (b. 1945), whose first novel, *al-Zayni barakat*, was published in Damascus in 1974, having been written in 1970–71 immediately after the death of President ʿAbd al-Nasir. The book illustrates a device already mentioned to avoid the attention of the censor – the use of a historical period as an analogy for the present. Set in early sixteenth-century Cairo during the reign of the Mamluk sultan al-Ghawri, just before the Ottoman invasion of Egypt in 1517, the work takes as its "hero" al-Zayni Barakat ibn Musa, a historical figure who served as *muhtasib* of Cairo for some twenty years from AD 1505, surviving in office after the military collapse of the Mamluks into the first years of Ottoman rule. The picture that emerges of al-Zayni is an ambiguous one: we never decisively establish whether he is working in the interests of the people or manipulating both the people and the Mamluks themselves. He is, however, both an opportunist and a survivor, and in this, as in his almost puritanical obsession with reform, he is a clear metaphor for Jamal ʿAbd al-Nasir, whose survival of the defeat of 1967 parallels al-Zayni's survival of the Mamluk defeat of 1517. Al-Ghitani's Mamluk Egypt, with its interlocking networks of spies and informers, is indeed the perfect symbol for the police state of contemporary Nasirist Egypt; while in Saʿid al-Juhayni we can see al-Ghitani's own generation of disillusioned Egyptians, brought up under the ideology of Jamal ʿAbd al-Nasir but progressively destroyed by the system.[61]

The use al-Ghitani makes of Ibn Iyas's medieval text in *al-Zayni barakat* to construct his own "hypertext" is paralleled by his use of newspapers and official reports in his second novel, *Waqaʾiʿ harat al-zaʿfarani* (1976), which, like its predecessor, deals with themes of power and coercion, this time in the setting of a working-class Cairo quarter. As the alley succumbs to an epidemic of impotence, the mysterious Shaykh ʿAtiyya uses his position to assert his control. The work is as replete as its predecessor with contem-

<hr />

[60] See Paul Starkey, "From the City of the Dead to Liberation Square," *Journal of Arabic Literature*, 24 (1993), 62–74. For *Yahduth fi misr al-an* see also Elad, *Village Novel*, 113ff.

[61] See Mehrez, *Egyptian Writers*, 96–118.

porary political allusion, the author giving us in Hasan Anwar – a frustrated government employee who sees his entire life in terms of newspaper headlines – a cruel, but prophetic, caricature of Anwar al-Sadat. Through the course of the novel, he withdraws deeper into his illusions, until he becomes insane; his last actions are a series of demented commands, which parallel (so it has been suggested) al-Sadat's own increasingly desperate moves, culminating in the arrest of several thousand intellectuals in 1981, a short time before his assassination.[62]

In his later novels al-Ghitani has continued to use the classical Arabic literary tradition as a source of inspiration. In *Khitat al-ghitani*, he returns to the medieval historiographical tradition, parodying the classical literary form of the *khitat* in order to create, as it were, a fictional *khitat* of modern Egypt. It does not take much imagination, however, to equate al-Ustadh with Jamal ʿAbd al-Nasir; and the relations to contemporary political events become still more explicit when al-Ustadh disappears, to be replaced by al-Tanukhi, under whose authority corruption becomes still more rife as he is caught up in a war with "al-Aʿda" (enemies). Al-Ghitani's most ambitious work to date, *Kitab al-tajalliyat* (3 volumes, 1983–86), uses Ibn ʿArabi's *al-Futuhat al-makkiyya* as a source text for a work that mingles personal and mystical elements with social and political criticism of contemporary Egypt.

We have dwelt at some length on the "generation of the sixties" in order, first, to show the sort of political attitudes expressed by an important group of Egyptian writers, and secondly, to give an idea of the obstacles to free expression encountered in contemporary Egypt and the means intellectuals have adopted to circumvent them. Although the rigor with which censorship has been applied in Egypt in recent years has varied with the scope allowed for political expression more generally, it would be no exaggeration to say that Egyptian writers have at times played almost the role of a political "opposition" – a role aided by the existence of a number of powerful men (of whom Muhammad Hasanayn Haykal and Yusuf al-Sibaʿi are the two most obvious examples) who have bridged the divide between the worlds of politics and culture. It would, however, probably be naive to pretend that "elite" contemporary literature of the sort written by Jamal al-Ghitani has much appeal for the average Egyptian "man in the street." In order to provide a fuller account of contemporary Egyptian culture, it is therefore necessary to look at alternative levels of discourse, and to consider the part played by the modern mass media in the diffusion of attitudes and ideas.

First, as already noted, the post-1952 regime was quick to recognize the potential of culture as a means of harnessing popular support. Folklore

---

[62] See Kilpatrick, "Egyptian Novel," 264ff. *Al-Zayni barakat* is available in an English translation under the title *Zayni Barakat* by Farouk Abdel Wahab (London, 1988). *Waqaʾiʿ harat al-zaʿfarani* is available in a translation by Peter O'Daniel as *Incidents in Zafrani Alley* (Cairo, 1986).

studies and the theater probably benefited most from this recognition; but colloquial poetry – whose potential as an instrument of political change had already been recognized by Bayram al-Tunisi and others – was also acknowledged as a valuable "populist" medium. Led by Fu'ad Haddad and Salah Jahin, a new generation of colloquial poets came to the fore, reflecting both the optimism of the post-1952 period and the despair of the 1967 defeat in a language that consciously strove to demonstrate that the colloquial was fully as expressive as the classical *fusha*. A number of these poets came together in 1959 to form the Ibn 'Arus League (named after an eighteenth-century predecessor) and the scope of vernacular poetry has been further extended in recent years by the publication of collections (notably by 'Abd al-Rahman al-Abnudi) in Upper Egyptian (Sa'idi) dialect, and by a number of female poets who have been consciously trying to erase the boundary between *fusha* and *'ammiyya* poetry.[63]

On another level, account must be taken of the "popular romantic" fiction of such writers as Muhammad 'Abd al-Halim 'Abdallah (1913–70), Ihsan 'Abd al-Quddus (1919–93), and Yusuf al-Siba'i (1917–78), who seldom receive much attention in the standard accounts of modern Egyptian literature but whose works, many times reprinted, undoubtedly form the staple fictional fare of a large proportion of the Arab reading public, not only in Egypt itself but elsewhere in the Arab world; indeed, Ihsan 'Abd al-Quddus was voted "most popular living writer in Arabic" in a poll conducted by the American University in Cairo in 1954.[64] Although each of these writers has his own favored milieu in terms of class and setting, they are united by their concentration on romantic love, which not infrequently tends to sentimentality or sensationalism. (Parallels in the English-language reading publics are of course not hard to find.) Despite this, some at least of these authors have seen their literary work as "socially committed": both Yusuf al-Siba'i and Ihsan 'Abd al-Quddus, for example, have dealt with the struggle of Egyptian girls to escape traditional constraints on the choice of marriage partners, and Yusuf al-Siba'i (who served as minister of culture, as well as holding other important state offices) also used important national events – e.g., the Palestine war of 1948 – as a setting for some of his novels.[65]

More important than such purely literary developments (though closely linked to them) has been the growth since the Second World War of the modern mass media: newspapers, radio and television, and the cinema. The close relations between the press, the growth of a wider reading public, and the development of new literary forms have been observed at several stages

[63] See Booth, "Poetry in the Vernacular," 474ff.
[64] See Trevor Le Gassick, introduction to translation of Ihsan 'Abd al-Quddus, *I Am Free and Other Stories* (Cairo, 1978).
[65] See Kilpatrick, "Egyptian Novel," 246–47.

of this survey, and the best-known Egyptian daily, *al-Ahram*, founded in 1876, continues to be one of the most respected newspapers in the Arab world. Effectively nationalized together with other print media in 1960, it fulfilled for a time a unique role because of the close relations that its then editor, Muhammad Hasanayn Haykal, enjoyed with President ʿAbd al-Nasir. More recently, in line with general government policy, some tentative moves toward a more pluralistic approach to the press have been evident: a law of 1977 permitted the new political parties to publish their own newspapers, but the new papers encountered serious financial difficulties, as well as political ones, in competing with the large publishing houses. In the political environment of contemporary Egypt, relations between the government and the press remain somewhat fluid, dependent not only on policies but also on personalities.[66]

The first radio broadcasts in Egypt date from the 1920s, but did not begin to be appreciated as a medium for communication on a national scale until 1934, when a contract was signed with the Marconi Company of the UK to provide a non-commercial broadcast service.[67] At first decidedly "British" in tone, the service became Egyptian owned and operated in 1947, providing ʿAbd al-Nasir with a ready-made instrument of propaganda following the Free Officers' revolt of 1952. The influence of the new medium was far greater than the number of sets might suggest, as many were installed in cafes, where they were heard by large audiences, particularly in the evening. From the 1950s private radio ownership became common, however, and the Main Program (usually known as "Radio Cairo") has continued to attract large audiences not only in Egypt but also in other parts of the Middle East, even in periods when Egypt has been effectively outlawed in the Arab world. Since 1952 the Main Program has been supplemented by a number of other programs, some aimed at domestic audiences, others directed to listeners in other parts of the Middle East (including Israel) and beyond, both in Arabic and in other languages. The best known of these, the "Voice of the Arabs" (*Sawt al-ʿArab*) – a name that itself implies an Egyptian claim to leadership of Arab public opinion – was started in 1953 and rapidly became a vehicle for ʿAbd al-Nasir's revolutionary propaganda. The station lost credibility during the 1967 war, however, when it repeatedly claimed victory for the Arabs long after it had become clear that the opposite was the case, and it has since then had to cope with increasing competition both from television and from radio services based in other Arab countries more attuned to the needs of local audiences.[68]

Television broadcasts in Egypt began in 1960.[69] From the start, the

---

[66] See William A. Rugh, *The Arab Press* (London, 1979).
[67] See Douglas A. Boyd, *Broadcasting in the Arab World* (Philadelphia, 1982), 13ff.
[68] *Ibid.*, 253ff.
[69] *Ibid.*, 33ff.

service made use of Egyptian-produced film material, which already had a history dating back to 1922. Although the "propaganda" potential of the new medium was quickly appreciated by the regime, in practice much transmission time has been accounted for by light entertainment of various kinds, which has also proved a valuable source of income for the country; as any suitable satellite system will reveal, Egyptian television productions form a high percentage of many Arab countries' transmissions, and are an important factor in maintaining Egypt's cultural dominance over the Arab world.

Although the first films had been seen in Egypt in 1905, it was not until 1923 that the first Egyptian film (*al-Bash-Katib*, by Muhammad Bayyumi) was produced, and it was not until the founding of the Misr Studio in 1935 that the Egyptian film industry can be said to have started as a serious venture. From early times, there has been a close link between the Egyptian cinema and Egyptian literature, whether the novel or drama: the first Egyptian silent film of importance, *Zaynab* (1930) was adapted from Muhammad Husayn Haykal's novel of the same name, and a number of important personalities in the development of the Egyptian theater, including Jurj Abyad, Yusuf Wahbi, and Najib al-Rihani, were also involved in the Egyptian cinema. Many early Egyptian films, like their counterparts in the Egyptian theater, relied heavily on singing and dancing for their effect – a trend that has continued to the present day. At the same time, however, a number of directors have risen to prominence whose productions have achieved world-class standards: they include Salah Abu Sayf (b. 1915), sometimes known as the "father of Egyptian realism," and particularly Yusuf Shahin [Yusuf Chahine] (b. 1925), whose productions include the film version of 'Abd al-Rahman al-Sharqawi's seminal novel *al-Ard* (1969).[70] The close connection between development of the Arabic novel and the cinema in modern Egypt is further demonstrated by the fact that many novels both of Najb Mahfuz and of the popular "romantic" novelist Ihsan 'Abd al-Quddus have themselves been adapted for the cinema.

Conclusion

It is difficult to summarize the state of Egyptian culture. On the one hand, there is no doubt that the country has to a considerable extent retained the position it has held since the beginning of the *nahda* as a leader in most fields of modern Arab culture. Egyptian culture, in its widest sense, remains at the forefront of Arab culture, with Egyptian films, radio, and television programs exported to most Arab countries even during periods when Egypt

[70] See Lizbeth Malkmus and Roy Armes, *Arab and African Film Making* (London, 1991), esp. 28ff.

has been "odd man out" in the Middle East – a process that has contributed both to the country's economy and to the leading place the Egyptian colloquial dialect continues to occupy in the Arab world. The appeal of Egyptian singers such as Umm Kulthum and Muhammad ʿAbd al-Wahhab has spread far beyond their native country to the Arab world generally. Most obviously, in the global context, the award of the Nobel prize for literature in 1988 to the Egyptian novelist Najib Mahfuz may be seen as recognition not only for the author himself but also for the development of a modern Arab literary tradition that has "come of age" in comparison with world literature generally. At the same time, Egyptian cultural life clearly continues to be characterized by a number of unresolved tensions. Of these, some simply echo the divide between "serious" and "popular" culture in the west: the average Egyptian reader may admire Najib Mahfuz, but he (or she?) probably reads Ihsan ʿAbd al-Quddus in preference. These tensions are both reflected in, and exaggerated by, unresolved arguments about the merits of *fusha* and *ʿammiyya* in particular cultural contexts. Other tensions have a certain "third world" flavor arising from the particular stage of political development at which Egypt, like most Middle Eastern countries, finds itself: from a cultural point of view, these most obviously include the fluctuating demands of state censorship. More insidious, however, is growing evidence of a part covert, part overt religious censorship. Although religious censorship itself is not a new phenomenon (Najib Mahfuz's *Awlad haratina* (1959) has for religious reasons never been published in book form in Egypt), the assassination of the liberal writer Faraj Fuda in 1992, the subsequent attack on Najib Mahfuz himself, and other difficulties placed in the way of writers, publishers, and booksellers dealing in "unorthodox" material has cast a shadow over Egyptian cultural development in recent years. The development of modern Egyptian culture over the last two centuries, however, suggests that the cultural base, together with the traditional Egyptian virtues of stoicism and good humor, is now solid enough to withstand such attacks.

SELECT BIBLIOGRAPHY

✦

PRIMARY SOURCES

Afandi, Husayn, *Ottoman Egypt in the Age of the French Revolution*, ed. and trans. Stanford J. Shaw (Cambridge, 1964)

Akhbar al-nuwwab min dawlat al-'uthman min hin istawla 'alayha al-sultan salim khan, Istanbul, Topkapi Palace Library, MS Hazine 1623

Bowring, Sir John, "Report on Egypt and Candia," *Parliamentary Papers: Reports from Commissioners*, 21 (1840)

Cezzar Ahmad Pasha, *Ottoman Egypt in the Eighteenth Century: The Nizam-name-i Misir of Cezzar Ahmed Pasha*, ed. and trans. Stanford J. Shaw (Cambridge, 1962)

Commission des Monuments d'Egypte, *Description de l'Egypte* 1st ed., (Paris, 1810–29)

Copies of Original Letters from the Army of General Bonaparte in Egypt: Intercepted by the Fleet under the Command of Admiral Lord Nelson (London, 1798)

Coppin, Jean, *Les voyages en Egypte de Jean Coppin 1638–1646* (Cairo, 1971)

Correspondance de Napoléon I: publiée par ordre de l'empereur Napoléon III, 32 vols. (Paris, 1858–70)

al-Damurdashi, Ahmad Katkhuda 'Azaban, *al-Damurdashi's Chronicle of Egypt: 1688–1755*, ed. and trans. Daniel Crecelius and Abd al-Wahhab Bakr (Leiden, 1991)

al-Durra al-musana fi akhbar al-kinana, British Museum, MS Or. 1073–74

Evans, Trefor (ed.), *The Killearn Diaries, 1934–1946: The Diplomatic and Personal Record of Lord Killearn* (London, 1972)

Evliya Çelebi, *Evliya Çelebi seyahatnamesi*, ed. Ahmed Cevdet, 10 vols. (Istanbul, 1888–1938)

Ghiselin de Busbecq, Ogier, *The Turkish Letters of Ogier Ghiselin de Busbecq*, ed. and trans. E. S. Forster (Oxford and London, 1968)

al-Hallaq, Muhammad ibn Yusuf, *Tarih-i misir-i kahire*, Istanbul University Library, ty628

Hamont, Pierre, *L'Egypte sous Mehemet-Ali*, 2 vols. (Paris, 1843)

Hurewitz, J. C. (ed.), *The Middle East and North Africa in World Politics: A Documentary Record*, 2nd ed., 2 vols. (New Haven, 1975)

Ibn Abi l-Surur al-Bakri al-Siddiqi, Muhammad, *al-Tuhfa al-bahiyya fi tamalluk al- 'uthman al-diyar al-misriyya*, MS HO 35, Vienna

   al-Qawl al-muqtadab fima wafaq lughat ahl misr min lughat al-'arab, ed. al-Sayyid Ibrahim Salim; intro. Ibrahim al-Ibiari (Cairo, 1962)

   "Kashf al-kurba fi raf al-tulba," ed. 'Abd al-Rahman 'Abd al-Rahim 'Abd al-Rahim, in *al-Majalla al-tarikhiyya al-misriyya*, 23 (1976), 291–384

Ibn Iyas, Muhammad ibn Ahmad, *An Account of the Ottoman Conquest of Egypt in the Year AH 922 (AD 1516)*, trans. W. H. Salmon (London, 1921)

al-Jabarti, 'Abd al-Rahman ibn Hasan, *'Aja'ib al-athar fi'l-tarajim wa'l-akhbar*, 7 vols. (Cairo, 1322 [1904/05]; later ed. 1958–67)

   al-Jabarti's Chronicle of the First Seven Months of the French Occupation of Egypt, trans J. S. Moreh (Leiden, 1975)

   'Abd al-Rahman al-Jabarti's History of Egypt, ed. and trans. Thomas Philipp and Moshe Perlman, 4 vols. and guide (Stuttgart, 1994)

al-Jaziri, 'Abd al-Qadir ibn Muhammad, *Durar al-fawa id al-munazzama fi akhbar al-hajj wa-tariq makka al-muazzama* (Cairo, 1964)

al-Kashshab, Isma'il, *Khulasat ma yurad min akhbar al-amir murad*, ed. and trans. Hamza 'Abd al-'Aziz Badr and Daniel Crecelius (Cairo, 1992)

Laurens, Henry (ed.), *Correspondance: Kleber en Egypte, 1798–1800: Kleber et Bonaparte, 1798–1799*, 2 vols. (Cairo, 1988)

al-Makki, Qutb al-Din Muhammad ibn Ahmad al-Nahrawali, *al-Barq al-yamani fi l-fath al-'uthmani*, ed. Hamad al-Jasir (Riyadh, 1967)

al-Muhibbi, *Khulasat al-athar fi a'yan al-qarn al-hadi 'ashir*, 4 vols. (Cairo, 1248 AH)

Muhimme Defterleri, Basbakanlik Arsivi (the archive of the Prime Minister's Bureau), Istanbul

Mustafa Ali's Description of Cairo of 1599, ed. and trans. A. Tietze (Vienna, 1957)

al-Nadim, Abdullah, *Mudhakkirat al-siyasiyya li abdullah al-nadim*, ed. M. Ahmad Khalafallah (Cairo, 1956)

Ninet, Jean, *Lettres d'Egypte 1879–1882*, ed. Anouar Louca (Paris, 1979)

Planat, Jules, *Histoire de la régénération de l'Egypte* (Paris, 1830)

Pococke, Richard, *A Description of the East and Some Other Countries*, 2 vols. (London, 1743)

Raymond, André and Wiet, Gaston, *Les marchés du Caire: traduction annotée du texte de Maqrizi* (Cairo, 1979)

Sambari, Yosef ben Yitzhak, *Sefer divre Yosef*, ed. S. Shtober (Jerusalem, 1994)

Shalabi [Celebi], Ahmad ibn 'Abd al-Ghani, *Awdah al-isahrat fi man tawalla misr al-qahira min al-wuzara wa al-bashat*, ed. 'Abd al-Rahim 'Abd al-Rahman 'Abd al-Rahim (Cairo, 1978)

Shaw, Stanford J., *The Budget of Ottoman Egypt 1005–1006/1596–1597* (The Hague and Paris, 1968)

Turk, Niqula, *Chronique d'Egypte: 1798–1804*, ed. and trans. Gaston Wiet (Cairo, 1950)

'Urabi, Ahmad, *The Defense Statement of Ahmad 'Urabi the Egyptian*, trans.
    Trevor Le Gassick (Cairo, 1982)
Walsh, Thomas, *Journal of the Late Campaign in Egypt* (London, 1803)
Wild, Johann, *Voyages en Egypte 1601–1610*, ed. and trans. O. V. Volkoff
    (Cairo, 1973)
Wittman, William, *Travels in Turkey, Asia-Minor, Syria, and Egypt, 1801*
    (London, 1803)

SECONDARY SOURCES

Abdallah, Ahmad, *The Student Movement and National Politics in Egypt*
    (London, 1985)
'Abd al-Karim, Ahmad Izzat (ed.), *'Abd al-rahman al-jabarti, dirasat wa buhuth*
    (Cairo, 1976)
'Abd al-Rahim, 'Abd al-Rahman 'Abd al-Rahim, *al-Rif al-misri fi al-qarn al-
    thamin ashar* (Cairo, 1974)
    "Land Tenure in Egypt and its Social Effects on Egyptian Society:
    1798–1813," in Tarif Khalidi (ed.), *Land Tenure and Social
    Transformation in the Middle East* (Beirut, 1984)
    "Yusuf al-Mallawani's *Tuhfat al-ahbab* and Ahmad Shalabi ibn 'Abd al-
    Ghani's *Awdah al-isharat*," in Crecelius (ed.), *Eighteenth-century Egypt*
    "The Documents of the Egyptian Religious Courts (*al-mahakim al-shar'iyya*)
    as a Source for the Study of Ottoman Provincial Administration in Egypt,"
    Journal of the Economic and Social History of the Orient, 34 (1991)
Abdel-Malek, Anouar, *Egypte, société militaire* (Paris, 1962)
Abir, Mordechai, "Relations between the Government of India and the Shariff
    of Mecca during the French Invasion of Egypt, 1798–1801," *Journal of the
    Royal Asiatic Society* (1965)
    "The Arab Rebellion of Amir Ghalib of Mecca (1788–1813), *Middle Eastern
    Studies*, 7 (1971)
Abu Lughod, Ibrahim, "The Transformation of the Egyptian Elite: Prelude to the
    Urabi Revolt," *Middle East Journal*, 21 (1967)
Abu Sulayman, 'Abu al-Hamid A., *Crisis in the Muslim Mind* (Herndon, 1993)
'Afifi, Hafiz, *'Ala hamish al-siyasa* (Cairo, 1938)
Ahmad Abd al-Latif, Layla, *Tarikh mu'arrikhu misr wa al-sha* (Cairo, 1979)
Ahmed, Leila, *Women and Gender in Islam: Historical Roots of a Modern
    Debate* (New Haven, 1992)
Akdag, Mustafa, *Celali iyanlari (1550–1603)* (Ankara, 1963)
Aksan, Virginia, "Choiseul-Gouffier at the Porte, 1784–1792," *Studies in
    Ottoman Diplomatic History*, 4 (1990)
Albin, Michael, "Napoleon's *Description de l'Egypte*: Problems of Corporate
    Authorship," *Publishing History*, 8 (1980)
Allen, Roger, *A Period of Time* (London, 1992)
Amin, Samir, *La nation arabe: nationalisme et luttes de classe* (Paris, 1976)
Anderson, Robert and Fawzy, Ibrahim (eds.), *Egypt in 1800: Scenes from
    Napoleon's* Description de l'Egypte (London, 1988)

Anis, Muhammad, *Madrasat al-ta'rikh al-misri fi al-asr al-'uthmani* (Cairo, 1962)

al-Antaqi, Da'ud, *Tadhkarat awla al-albab* (Beirut, n.d.)

The Arabian Nights, trans. Husain Haddawy (London, 1990)

Arthur, George, *Life of Lord Kitchener* (London, 1920)

Ayalon, David, *L'esclavage du mamelouk* (Jerusalem, 1951)

    "Studies on the Structure of the Mamluk Army," *Bulletin of the School of Oriental and African Studies*, 15 (1953)

    "Furusiyya Exercises and Games in the Mamluk Sultanate," *Scripta Hierosolymitana*, 9 (1961)

    "Studies in al-Jabarti I: Notes on the Transformation of Mamluk Society in Egypt under the Ottomans," *Journal of the Economic and Social History of the Orient*, 3/2, 3/3 (1960)

Ayubi, Nazih, *Bureaucracy and Politics in Contemporary Egypt* (London, 1980)

    "Government and the State in Egypt Today," in Charles Tripp and Roger Owen (eds.), *Egypt under Mubarak* (London and New York, 1989)

Bacque-Grammont, Jean-Louis, *Les Ottomans, les Safavides et leurs voisins* (Istanbul, 1987)

Badawi, M. M., *Modern Arabic Drama in Egypt* (Cambridge, 1987)

    Early Arabic Drama (Cambridge, 1988)

Badawi, M. M. (ed.), *Modern Arabic Literature* (Cambridge, 1992)

Badran, Margot, *Feminists, Islam and Nation: Gender and the Making of Modern Egypt* (Princeton, 1995)

Baer, Gabriel, *Studies in the Social History of Modern Egypt* (Chicago and London, 1969)

    "Fellah and Townsman in Ottoman Egypt: A Study of Shirbini's *Hazz al-Quhuf*," *Asian and African Studies*, 8 (1972)

    Fellah and Townsman in the Middle East: Studies in Social History (London, 1982)

Baghat, Ali, "Acte de mariage du General Abdallah Menou avec la dame Zobaidah," *Bulletin de l'Institut Egyptien*, 3rd series, 9 (1899)

    "La famille musulmane du General Abdallah Menou," *Bulletin de l'Institut Egyptien*, 4th series, 1 (1900)

Bannerth, Ernst, "La Khalwatiyya en Egypte: quelques aspects de la vie d'une confrérie," *Mélanges de l'Institut Dominicain des Etudes Orientales*, 8 (1964–66)

Barkan, Omer Lutfi, *Osmanli imparatorlugunda zirai ekonominin hukuki ve mali esaslari* (Istanbul, 1943)

    "The Price Revolution of the Sixteenth Century: A Turning Point in the Economic History of the Near East," *International Journal of Middle East Studies*, 6 (1975)

Baron, Beth, *The Women's Awakening in Egypt: Culture, Society and the Press* (New Haven, 1994)

al-Batrik, Abdel Hamid, "Egyptian Yemeni Relations 1819–1840," in Holt (ed.), *Political and Social Change*

Beaucour, Fernand, et al., *The Discovery of Egypt*, trans. B. Ballard (Paris, 1990)

Behrens-Abouseif, Doris, *Azbakiyya and its Environs, from Azbak to Isma'il, 1476–1879* (Cairo, 1985)
  Egypt's Adjustment to Ottoman Rule: Institutions, Waqf, and Architecture in Cairo (Sixteenth and Seventeenth Centuries) (Leiden, 1994)
Beinin, Joel, "Writing Class: Workers and Modern Egyptian Colloquial Poetry (*Zajal*)," *Poetics Today*, 15/2 (Summer 1994)
Beinin, Joel and Lockman, Zachary, *Workers on the Nile: Nationalism, Communism, Islam and the Egyptian Working Class, 1882–1954* (Princeton, 1987)
Berque, Jacques, *Egypt: Imperialism and Revolution*, trans. Jean Stewart (New York, 1972)
Berthier, Louis-Alexandre, *Relation des campagnes du General Bonaparte en Egypte et en Syrie* (Paris, 1800)
Beshir, M. O., *The Southern Sudan* (London, 1975)
Bianchi, Robert, *Unruly Corporatism: Associational Life in Twentieth-century Egypt* (New York, 1990)
Binder, Leonard, *In a Moment of Enthusiasm: Political Power and the Second Stratum in Egypt* (Chicago, 1978)
Bint al-Shati' ('A'isha 'Abd al-Rahman), *al-Rif al-misri* (Cairo, 1936)
  Qadiyyat al-fallah (Cairo, 1938[?])
al-Bishri, Tariq, *al-Harka al-siyasiyya fi misr, 1945–1952* (Cairo, 1972)
Blackburn, J. R., "The Collapse of Ottoman Authority in Yemen, 968/1560–976/1568," *Die Welt des Islams*, n.s., 19, 1, 4 (1979)
Blunt, Wilfrid Scawen, *Secret History of the English Occupation of Egypt: Being a Personal Narrative of Events* (New York, 1922)
Booth, Marilyn, *Bayram al-Tunisi's Egypt* (Exeter, 1990)
  "Poetry in the Vernacular," in Badawi (ed.), *Modern Arabic Literature*
Botiveau, Bernard, *Loi islamique et droit dans les sociétés arabes* (Paris, 1994)
Botman, Selma, *The Rise of Egyptian Communism* (Syracuse, 1988)
Bouley de la Meurthe, Alfred, *La directoire et l'expédition d'Egypte: étude sur les tentatives du directoire pour communiquer avec Bonaparte* (Paris, 1885)
Boyd, Douglas A., *Broadcasting in the Arab World* (Philadelphia, 1982)
Broadley, A. M., *How we Defended Arabi and his Friends* (London, 1884; repr. Cairo, 1980)
Brown, Nathan J., *Peasant Politics in Modern Egypt: The Struggle against the State* (New Haven, 1990)
Burke, Edmund III (ed.), *Struggle and Survival in the Modern Middle East* (Berkeley and Los Angeles, 1993)
Burns, W. J., *Economic Aid and American Policy toward Egypt, 1955–1981* (New York, 1984)
Cachia, Pierre, *Taha Husayn* (London, 1956)
  "The Critics," in Badawi (ed.), *Modern Arabic Literature*
Carré, Jean-Marie, *Voyageurs et écrivains français en Egypte* (Cairo, 1956)
Carré, Olivier, *L'orient arabe aujourd'hui* (Paris, 1991)
Carré, Olivier and Michaud, Gérard, *Les frères musulmans, 1928–1982* (Paris, 1983)
Carter, B. L., *The Copts in Egyptian Politics* (London, 1986)

Chabrol, "Essai sur les moeurs des habitants modernes de l'Egypte," *Description de l'Egypte, état moderne*, vol. II (Paris, 1822)

Chamberlain, M. E., "The Alexandria Massacre of 11 June 1882 and the British Occupation of Egypt," *Middle Eastern Studies*, 13 (1977)

Charles-Roux, François, *Les origines de l'expédition de l'Egypte*, 2nd ed. (Paris, 1910)

   Autour d'une route. L'Angleterre, l'isthme de Suez et l'Egypte au XVIIIᵉ siècle (Paris, 1922)

   "Une négociation pour l'évacuation de l'Egypte: la convention d'el Arich (1800)," *Revue d'histoire diplomatique*, 37 (1923)

   "Le projet français de conquête de l'Egypte sous le règne de Louis XVI," *Mémoires de l'Institut d'Egypte*, 14 (Cairo, 1929)

   Bonaparte, gouverneur d'Egypte (Paris, 1936; trans. E. W. Dickes as *Bonaparte, governor of Egypt* [London, 1937])

   "France, Egypte et Mer Rouge de 1715 à 1798," *Cahiers d'histoire égyptienne*, 3 (1951)

Chevalier, M., "La politique financière de l'expédition d'Egypte, 1798–1801," *Cahiers d'histoire égyptienne*, 7 (1955), 8 (1956)

Cleland, Wendell, *The Population Problem in Egypt: A Study of Population Trends and Conditions in Modern Egypt* (Lancaster, PA, 1936)

Clement, R., *Les Français d'Egypte aux XVIIᵉ et XVIIIᵉ siècles* (Cairo, 1960)

Cohn, Bernard S. and Dirks, Nicholas B., "Beyond the Fringe: The Nation State, Colonialism, and the Technologies of Power," *Journal of Historical Sociology*, 1/2 (1988)

Cole, Juan R. I., "Feminism, Class and Islam in Turn-of-the Century Egypt," *International Journal of Middle East Studies*, 13 (1981)

   Colonialism and Revolution in the Middle East: Social and Cultural Origins of Egypt's 'Urabi Movement (Princeton, 1993)

Collins, R. O., *The Southern Sudan in Historical Perspective* (Tel Aviv, 1975)

Colombe, Marcel, *L'évolution de l'Egypte, 1924–1950* (Paris, 1951)

Cook, M. A., *Population Pressure in Rural Anatolia, 1450–1600* (London, New York, and Oxford, 1972)

Crecelius, Daniel, "The Emergence of the Shaykh al-Azhar as the Pre-eminent Religious Leader in Egypt," in Andrée Assabgui et al. (eds.), *Colloque international sur l'histoire du Caire* (Cairo, 1969)

   The Roots of Modern Egypt: A Study in the Regimes of Ali Bey al-Kabir and Muhammad Bey al-Dhahab, 1760–1775 (Minneapolis and Chicago, 1980)

   "Unratified Commercial Treaties between Egypt and England and France, 1773–1794," *Revue d'histoire maghrebine*, 12 (1985)

   "Ahmad Shalabi ibn 'Abd al-Ghani and Ahmad Katkhuda 'Azaban al-Damurdashi: Two Sources for al-Jabarti's '*Aja'ib al-athar fi'l tarajim wa'l akhbar*," in Crecelius (ed.), *Eighteenth-century Egypt*

Crecelius, Daniel (ed.), *Eighteenth-century Egypt: The Arabic Manuscript Sources* (Claremont, 1990)

Cromer, Lord, *Modern Egypt*, 2 vols. (London, 1908)

Cuno, Kenneth M., *The Pasha's Peasants: Land, Society, and Economy in Lower Egypt, 1740–1858* (Cambridge, 1992)

Daly, M. W., *The Sirdar* (Philadelphia, 1997)

Davis, Eric, *Challenging Colonialism: Bank Misr and Egyptian Industrialization, 1920–1941* (Princeton, 1983)

Deeb, Marius, "The Socioeconomic Role of the Local Foreign Minorities in Modern Egypt, 1805–1961," *International Journal of Middle East Studies*, 9 (1978)

   Party Politics in Egypt: The Wafd and its Rivals, 1919–1939 (London, 1979)

Deringil, Selim, "The Ottoman Response to the Egyptian Crisis of 1881–82," *Middle Eastern Studies*, 24 (1988)

al-Disuqi, 'Asim, *Kibar mullak al-aradi al-zira'iyya wa dawruhum fi al-mujtama' al-misri, 1914–1952* (Cairo, 1975)

Dodge, Bayard, *Al-Azhar: A Millennium of Muslim Learning* (Washington, DC, 1974)

Dodwell, Henry, *The Founder of Modern Egypt* (Cambridge, 1931)

Doss, Madiha, "Military Chronicles of Seventeenth-century Egypt as an Aspect of Popular Culture," paper presented to the Colloquium on Logos, Ethos and Mythos in the Middle East and North Africa, Budapest, September 18–22, 1995

   "Some Remarks on the Oral Factor in Arabic Linguistics," *Dialectologia Arabica: A Collection of Articles in Honour of the Sixtieth Birthday of Professor Heikki Palva* (Helsinki, 1995)

Douin, Georges, *L'Egypte de 1802 à 1804* (Cairo, 1925)

Douin, Georges (ed.), *La mission du Baron de Boislecomte, l'Egypte et la Syrie en 1833* (Cairo, 1927)

Douin, Georges and Fawtier-Jones, E. (eds.), *L'Angleterre et l'Egypte*, 3 vols. (Cairo, 1928–30)

Dresch, Paul, *Tribes, Government, and History in Yemen* (Oxford, 1989)

Dunya, 'Abd al-'Aziz Hafiz, *al-Shahid muhammad kurayyim* (Cairo, n.d.)

Eccel, A. Chris, *Egypt, Islam and Social Change: al-Azhar in Conflict and Accommodation* (Berlin, 1984)

Egger, Vernon, *A Fabian in Egypt: Salamah Musa and the Rise of the Professional Classes in Egypt, 1909–1939* (Lanham, 1986)

Elad, Ami, *The Village Novel in Egypt* (Berlin, 1992)

El-Enany, Rasheed, *The Pursuit of Meaning* (London, 1993)

Elgood, Percival S., *Bonaparte's Adventure in Egypt* (London, 1931)

Eman, André, *L'industrie du coton en Egypte: étude d'économie politique* (Cairo, 1943)

Encyclopaedia of Islam, 2nd ed. (Leiden, 1960–)

En-Nahal, Galal, *The Judicial Administration of Ottoman Egypt* (Minneapolis and Chicago, 1979)

Etienne, Bruno, *L'islamisme radical* (Paris, 1987)

Faraj, Muhammad, *al-Nidal al-sha'bi didd al-hamla al-faransiyya* (Cairo, 1963)

Fargette, Guy, *Mehemet Ali: le fondateur de l'Egypte moderne* (Paris, 1996)

Faroqhi, Suraiya, "Rural Society in Anatolia and the Balkans during the Sixteenth Century," *Turkica*, 9 (1977), 11 (1979)
  Pilgrims and Sultans: The Hajj under the Ottomans (London and New York, 1994)
Faroqhi, Suraiya, with Erder, Leila, "Population Rise and Fall in Anatolia, 1550–1620," *Middle Eastern Studies*, 15 (1979)
Fedorak, Charles John, "The French Capitulation in Egypt and the Preliminary Anglo-French Treaty of Peace in October 1801: A Note," *International History Review*, 15 (1993)
Fernandes, Leonor, "Some Aspects of the *Zawiya* in Egypt at the Eve of the Ottoman Conquest," *Annales islamologiques*, 19 (1983)
Garcin, Jean-Claude, "Le Proche Orient à l'époque mamluke," in Jean-Claude Garcin (ed.) et al., *Etats, sociétés et cultures du monde Musulman médiéval Xᵉ–XVᵉ siècles* (Paris, 1995)
Gershoni, Israel, *The Emergence of Pan-Arabism in Egypt* (Tel Aviv, 1981)
Ghali, Mirrit, *Siyasat al-ghad* (Cairo, 1938)
  al-Islah al-ziraʿi: al-milkiyya, al-ijar, al-ʿamal (Cairo, 1945)
Ghali, Wajdi Rizq, *al-Muʾajamat al-ʿarabiyya, biblighrafiyya shamila mashruha*, intro. Husayn Nassar (Cairo, 1971)
al-Ghannam, Sulayman M., *Qiraʾa jaddidah li siyyasat muhammad ʿali al-tawasuʿaiyyah* (Jidda, 1980)
al-Ghitani, Jamal, *Incidents in Zafrani Alley*, trans. Peter O'Daniel (Cairo, 1986)
  Zayni barakat, trans. Farouk Abdel Wahab (London, 1988)
Ghorbal, Shafik, *Beginnings of the Egyptian Question and the Rise of Mehemet-Ali* (London, 1928)
Gillespie, Charles C., "Scientific Aspects of the French Egyptian Expedition 1798–1801," *Proceedings of the American Philosophical Society*, 133 (1989)
Gillespie, Charles C. and Dewachter, Michael (eds.), *Monuments of Egypt. The Napoleonic Edition: The Complete Plates of Antiquity from the Napoleonic Description de l'Egypte* (Princeton, 1987)
Girgis, Samir, *The Predominance of the Islamic Tradition of Leadership in Egypt during Bonaparte's Expedition* (Frankfurt, 1975)
Goby, Jean-Edouard, "Contribution à l'inventaire des sources manuscrites et à l'étude bibliographique de l'histoire de l'expédition française en Egypte," *Bulletin de l'Institut d'Egypte*, 33 (1952)
  "Les quarante éditions, traductions, et adaptations du 'Voyage dans la Basse et la Haute Egypte' de Vivant Denon," *Cahiers d'histoire égyptienne*, 4 (1952)
Goitein, S. D., "Townsman and Fellah: A Geniza Text from the Seventeen Century," *Asian and African Studies*, 8 (1972)
Goldman, I. M., *The Life and Times of Rabbi David Ibn Abi Zimra* (New York, 1970)
Goldschmidt, Arthur, *Modern Egypt: The Formation of a Nation-State* (Boulder, 1988)
Gordon, Joel, "The False Hopes of 1950: The Wafd's Last Hurrah and the Demise of Egypt's Old Order," *International Journal of Middle East Studies*, 21 (May 1989)

Gran, Peter, *Islamic Roots of Capitalism* (Austin, 1978)
   "Late Eighteenth–Early Nineteenth-century Egypt: Merchant Capitalism or
   Modern Capitalism?" *L'Egypte au XIXe siècle*
Gray, Richard, *A History of the Southern Sudan 1839–1889* (London, 1961)
Groupe de recherches et d'études sur le Proche-Orient, *L'Egypte au XIXe siècle*
   (Paris, 1982)
Guemard, Gabriel, "Les auxiliaries de l'armée de Bonaparte en Egypte
   (1798–1801)," *Bulletin de l'Institut d'Egypte*, 9 (1927)
Haddad, George A., "A Project for the Independence of Egypt, 1801," *Journal
   of the American Oriental Society*, 90 (1970)
Hafez, Sabry, *The Genesis of Arabic Narrative Discourse* (London, 1993)
   "The Modern Arabic Short Story," in Badawi (ed.), *Modern Arabic Literature*
al-Hakim, Tawfiq, *The Maze of Justice*, trans. Abba Eban (London, 1947)
   Bird of the East, trans. R. Bayly Winder (Beirut, 1967)
Halls, J. J., *The Life and Correspondence of Henry Salt*, 2 vols. (London, 1834)
Hamawi, Ahmad Muhammad, *Fada'il salatin bani 'uthman*, ed. Muhsin
   Muhammad Hasan Salim (Cairo, 1993)
Hanna, Nelly, *An Urban History of Bulaq in the Mamluk and Ottoman Periods*
   (Cairo, 1983)
   Habiter au Caire aux XVIIe et XVIIIe siècles (Cairo, 1991)
   "The Administration of Courts in Ottoman Cairo," in Nelly Hanna (ed.), *The
   State and its Servants: Administration in Egypt from Ottoman Times to the
   Present* (Cairo, 1995)
   "Cultural Life in Mamluk Households (Late Ottoman Period)," paper
   presented to the international conference on The Mamluks in Egyptian
   Politics and Society, Bad Homburg, December 1994 (forthcoming)
Hansen, Bent, *The Political Economy of Poverty, Equity, and Growth: Egypt
   and Turkey* (Oxford, 1991)
Hathaway, Jane, "Sultans, Pashas, *Taqwims*, and Muhimmes: A
   Reconsideration of Chonicle-writing in Eighteenth-century Ottoman
   Egypt," in Crecelius (ed.), *Eighteenth-century Egypt*
   "The Role of the Kizlar Agasi in Seventeenth–Eighteenth-century Egypt,"
   Studia Islamica, 75 (1992)
   "The Wealth and Influence of an Exiled Ottoman Eunuch in Egypt: The Waqf
   Inventory of 'Abbas Agha," *Journal of the Economic and Social History of
   the Orient*, 37 (1994)
   "The Military Household in Ottoman Egypt," *International Journal of
   Middle East Studies*, 27 (1995)
   The Politics of Households in Ottoman Egypt: The Rise of the Qazdaglis
   (Cambridge, 1997)
Hattox, Ralph S., *Coffee and Coffeehouses: The Origins of a Social Beverage in
   the Medieval Near East* (Seattle and London, 1985)
Haykal, Muhammad Hasanayn, *Les documents du Caire* (Paris, 1972)
   The Road to Ramadan (London, 1975)
   Le sphinx et le commissaire (Paris, 1978)
Haykal, Muhammad Husayn, *Mudhakkirat fi'l siyasa al-misriyya*, 3 vols. (Cairo,
   1977–78)

Herold, J. Christopher, *Bonaparte in Egypt* (New York, 1962)

Heyworth-Dunne, J., *An Introduction to the History of Education in Modern Egypt* (London, 1938; repr. 1968)

Hill, Richard, "The Gordon Literature," *Durham University Journal*, n.s., 16/3 (1955)
  Slatin Pasha (London, 1965)

Hill, Richard and Hogg, Peter, *A Black Corps d'Elite* (East Lansing, 1995)

Hinnebusch, Raymond, *Egyptian Politics under Sadat: The Post-populist Development of an Authoritarian-Modernizing State* (Cambridge, 1985)
  "The Formation of the Contemporary Egyptian State from Nasser and Sadat to Mubarak," in Ibrahim M. Oweiss (ed.), *The Political Economy of Contemporary Egypt* (Georgetown, 1990)

Hirst, David and Beeson, Irene, *Sadat* (London, 1981)

Holt, P. M., "The Exalted Lineage of Ridwan Bey: Some Observations on a Seventeenth-century Mamluk Genealogy," *Bulletin of the School of Oriental and African Studies*, 22 (1959)
  "The Beylicate in Egypt during the Seventeenth Century," *Bulletin of the School of Oriental and African Studies*, 24 (1961)
  "al-Jabarti's Introduction to the History of Ottoman Egypt," *Bulletin of the School of Oriental and African Studies*, 25 (1962)
  "The Career of Kuchuk Muhammad (1676–94)," *Bulletin of the School of Oriental and African Studies*, 26 (1963)
  Egypt and the Fertile Crescent, 1516–1922 (Ithaca, 1966; 2nd ed. London, 1980)
  "Ottoman Egypt (1517–1798): An Account of Arabic Historical Sources," in Holt (ed.), *Political and Social Change*
  The Mahdist State in the Sudan, 2nd ed. (Oxford, 1970)
  "The Islamization of the Nilotic Sudan," in Michael Brett (ed.), *Northern Africa: Islam and Modernization* (London, 1973)
  Studies in the History of the Near East (London, 1973)

Holt, P. M. (ed.), *Political and Social Change in Modern Egypt* (London, 1968)

Holt, P. M. and Daly, M. W., *A History of the Sudan*, 4th ed. (London, 1988)

Hopkins, A. G., "The Victorians and Africa: A Reconsideration of the Occupation of Egypt, 1882," *Journal of African History*, 27 (1986)

Horn, Michael Serge, "The 'Urabi Revolution: Convergent Crises in Nineteenth-century Egypt," Ph.D. thesis, Harvard University, 1973

Hourani, Albert, *Arabic Thought in the Liberal Age* (London, 1962)
  "Conclusions," *L'Egypte au XIXᵉ siècle*

Howard, Douglas A., "Ottoman Historiography and the Literature of 'Decline' of the Sixteenth and Seventeenth Centuries," *Journal of Asian History*, 22 (1988)

Humaydah, B. K., *Malamih min ta'rikh al-sudan fi ad al-khidawi isma'il* (Khartoum, n.d.)

Hunter, F. Robert, *Egypt under the Khedives, 1805–1879: From Household Government to Modern Bureaucracy* (Pittsburgh, 1984)

Hussein, Mahmoud, *La lutte des classes en Egypte, 1945–1970* (Paris, 1971)

Ibrahim, H. A., *Muhammad 'ali fi'l sudan*, 2nd ed. (Khartoum, 1991)

Ilbert, Robert, "La cohérence et l'informel: essai pour servir à une histoire de l'Egypte contemporaine," in *Itinéraires d'Egypt: Mélanges offerts au Père Martin* (Cairo, 1992)

Inalcik, Halil, "The Ottoman Decline and its Effects upon the Reaya," in Henrik Birnbaum and Speros Vryonis, Jr. (eds.), *Aspects of the Balkans, Continuity and Change: Contributions to the International Balkan Conference Held at UCLA, October 23–28 1969* (The Hague, 1972)

    The Ottoman Empire: The Classical Age, 1300–1600 (London, 1973)

    "The Socio-political Effects of the Diffusion of Firearms in the Middle East," in V. J. Parry and Malcolm Yapp (eds.), *War, Technology and Society in the Middle East* (London, 1975)

    "Military and Fiscal Transformation in the Ottoman Empire, 1600–1700," *Archivum Ottomanicum*, 6 (1980)

Inalcik, Halil and Quataert, Donald (eds.), *An Economic and Social History of the Ottoman Empire, 1300–1914* (Cambridge and New York, 1994)

Index of Mohamedan Monuments, Cairo Survey Department (Cairo, 1951)

Ingram, Edward, "The Failure of British Sea Power in the War of the Second Coalition, 1798–1801," in Edward Ingram, *In Defence of British India: Great Britain in the Middle East, 1774–1842* (London, 1984)

Issawi, Charles, *Egypt in Revolution: An Economic Analysis* (London, 1963)

    The Economic History of the Middle East 1800–1914 (Chicago, 1966)

al-Jabri, M. A., *Fi sha'n allah* (Cairo, n.d.)

Jallad, Filib (ed.), *Qamus al-idara wa'l qada*, 4 vols. (Alexandria, 1890–92)

al-Jami'i, 'Abd al-Mun'im Ibrahim al-Disuqi, *'Abdallah al-nadim wa dawruhu fi al-haraka al-siyasiyya wa l-ijtima'iyya* (Cairo, 1980)

    al-Thawra al-'urabiyya: buhuth wa dirasat watha'iqiyya (Cairo, 1982)

al-Jami'i, 'Abd al-Mun'im Ibrahim al-Disuqi (ed.), *al-Thawra al-'urabiyya fi dar al-watha'iq al-misriyya* (Cairo, 1982)

Jankowski, James P., *Egypt's Young Rebels: "Young Egypt," 1932–1952* (Stanford, 1975)

    "Egyptian Responses to the Palestine Problem in the Interwar Period," *International Journal of Middle East Studies*, 12/1 (August 1980)

Johansen, Baber, "Legal Literature and the Problem of Change: The Case of the Land Rent," in Chibli Mallat (ed.), *Islam and Public Law* (London, 1993)

La Jonquière, Clément Etienne de, *L'expédition d'Egypte*, 5 vols. (Paris, 1899–1907)

Kazemi, Farhad and Waterbury, John (eds.), *Peasants and Politics in the Modern Middle East* (Miami, 1991)

Kedourie, Elie, "Sa'ad Zaghlul and the British," *St. Antony's Papers*, 11, *Middle Eastern Affairs*, 2 (Oxford, 1961)

    Afghani and Abduh (London, 1966)

Kelly, J. B., *Britain and the Persian Gulf, 1795–1880* (Oxford, 1968)

Kepel, G., *Le prophète et Pharaon: les mouvements islamistes dans l'Egypte contemporaine* (Paris, 1984)

Kerr, Malcolm, *The Arab Cold War, 1958–1964: A Study of Ideology in Politics* (London, 1965)

Khadra al-Jayyusi, Salma, *Trends and Movements in Modern Arabic Poetry*, 2 vols. (Leiden, 1977)

"Modernist Poetry in Arabic," in Badawi (ed.), *Modern Arabic Literature*

Khater, Akram and Nelson, Cynthia, "al-Harakh al-nissa'iyah: The Women's Movement and Political Participation in Modern Egypt," *Women's Studies International Forum*, 11 (1988)

Khury, Fuad Ishaq, *Imams and Emirs: State, Religion, and Sects in Islam* (London, 1990)

Kilani, Muhammad Sayyid, *al-Adab al-misri fi dhill al-hukm al-'uthmani 922–1220/1517–1805* (Cairo, 1984)

Kilpatrick, Hilary, "The Egyptian Novel from *Zaynab* to 1980," in Badawi (ed.), *Modern Arabic Literature*

Kimche, David, "The Opening of the Red Sea to European Ships in the Late Eighteenth Century," *Middle Eastern Studies*, 8 (1972)

King, David, *A Catalogue of the Scientific Manuscripts in the Egyptian National Library*, part 2 (Cairo, 1986)

Kirk, George, *The Middle East in the War* (London, 1952)

Kramer, Gudrun, *The Jews of Modern Egypt, 1914–1952* (Seattle, 1989)

Kuhnke, LaVerne, *Lives at Risk: Public Health in Nineteenth-century Egypt* (Berkeley, 1990)

Kunt, Metin, *The Sultan's Servants: The Transformation of Ottoman Provincial Government, 1550–1650* (New York, 1983)

Kurpershoek, P. M., *The Short Stories of Yusuf Idris* (Leiden, 1981)

Kurtoglu, Fevzi, *Turk bayragi ve ay yildiz* (Ankara, 1938)

Lacouture, J. and Lacouture, S., *L'Egypte en mouvement* (Paris, 1956)

Landau, J. M., *Parliaments and Parties in Egypt* (Tel Aviv, 1953)
Studies in the Arab Theater and Cinema (Philadelphia, 1958)

Landau, J. M. (ed.), *The Jews in Ottoman Egypt (1517–1914)* (Jerusalem, 1988) (in Hebrew)

Landes, David, *Bankers and Pashas: International Finance and Economic Imperialism in Egypt* (Cambridge, MA, 1958)

Lane, Edward William, *The Manners and Customs of the Modern Egyptians* (London, 1836; new ed., London, 1954; repr. 1989)
The Thousand and One Nights, 3 vols. (London, 1859; repr. 1980)

Laurens, Henry, *Les origines intellectuelles de l'expédition e'Egypte: l'orientalisme islamisant en France (1698–1798)* (Istanbul and Paris, 1987)
"L'Egypte en 1802: un rapport inédit de Sabastiani," *Annales islamologiques*, 23 (1987)
L'expédition d'Egypte: Bonaparte et l'Islam: le choc des cultures (Paris, 1989)
Le grand jeu: Orient arabe et rivalités internationales (Paris, 1991)

Laurens, Henry et al., *L'expédition d'Egypte: 1798–1801* (Paris, 1989)

League of Arab States, Institute of Arabic Manuscripts, *Catalogue of Microfilmed Manuscripts* (Cairo, 1970)

Lewis, Bernard, *The Emergence of Modern Turkey*, 2nd ed. (London and New York, 1968)

The Middle East and the West (London, 1968)

Livingston, John W., "Shaykh Bakri and Bonaparte," *Studia Islamica*, 80 (1994)

Lloyd, Lord, *Egypt since Cromer*, 2 vols. (London, 1933–34)

Lockman, Zachary, "Imagining the Working Class: Culture, Nationalism and Class Formation in Egypt, 1899–1914," *Poetics Today*, 15/2 (Summer 1994)

Louca, Anouar, "La renaissance égyptienne et les limites de l'œuvre de Bonaparte," *Cahiers d'histoire égyptienne*, 7 (1955)

Louis, W. Roger, *The British Empire in the Middle East, 1945–1951* (Oxford, 1984)

Mabro, Robert, *The Egyptian Economy, 1952–1982* (Oxford, 1974)

Macksey, Piers, *British Victory in Egypt, 1801: The End of Napoleon's Conquest* (London and New York, 1995)

al-Maghrabi, Yusuf, *Daf' al-isar'an kalam ahl misr*, ed. with intro. 'Abdul-Salam Ahmad Awwad (Moscow, 1968)

Magnus, Philip, *Kitchener: Portrait of an Imperialist* (London, 1958)

Mahfuz, Najib, *Children of Gebelawi*, trans. Philip Stewart (London, 1981)

Maksudoglu, Mehmet, *Osmanli History* (Kuala Lumpur, forthcoming [1998])

Malet, Edward, *Egypt, 1879–1883* (London, 1909)

Malkmus, Lizbeth and Armes, Roy, *Arab and African Film Making* (London, 1991)

Manaf, 'Abd al-Azim (ed.), *al-Thawra al-'urabiyya, mi'at amm, 1881–1981* (Cairo, 1981)

Mansfield, Peter, *The British in Egypt* (London, 1971)

Mantran, Robert, "Avant-propos," *L'Egypte au XIXe siècle*

Maqar, Nasim, *al-Bikbashi al-masri salim qabudan wa al-kashfan manabia al-nil al-abyad* (Cairo, n.d.)

    Misr wa bina al-sudan al-hadith (Cairo, 1993)

Marlowe, John, *Anglo-Egyptian Relations 1800–1953* (New York, 1970)

    Cromer in Egypt (London, 1970)

Marsot, Afaf Lutfi al-Sayyid, *Egypt and Cromer* (New York, 1969)

    "The Role of the Ulama in Egypt during the Early Nineteenth Century," in Holt (ed.), *Political and Social Change*

    "The 'Ulama' of Cairo in the Eighteenth and Nineteenth Century," in Nikki R. Keddie (ed.), *Scholars, Saints and Sufis: Muslim Religious Institutions since 1500* (Berkeley, Los Angeles, and London, 1972)

    "The Political and Economic Functions of the Ulama in the Eighteenth Century," *Journal of the Economic and Social History of the Orient*, 16 (1973)

    Egypt in the Reign of Muhammad Ali (Cambridge, 1984)

    A Short History of Modern Egypt (Cambridge, 1985)

    "A Comparative Study of 'Abd al-Rahman al-Jabarti and Niqila al-Turk," in Crecelius (ed.), *Eighteenth-century Egypt*

Martin, B. G., "A Short History of the Khalwati Order of Dervishes," in Nikkie R. Keddie (ed.), *Scholars, Saints and Sufis: Muslim Religious Institutions since 1500* (Berkeley, Los Angeles, and London, 1972)

Maury, B., Raymond, A., Revault, J., and Zakariya, M., *Palais et maisons du Caire, II, époque ottomane* (Paris, 1983)

Mayer, Thomas, *The Changing Past: Egyptian Historiography of the Urabi Revolt, 1882–1983* (Gainesville, 1988)

Mayeur-Joouen, C., *al-Sayyid al-Badawi: un grand saint de l'Islam égyptien* (Cairo, 1994)

McNeill, William H., *Europe's Steppe Frontier, 1500–1800* (Chicago and London, 1964)

Mehrez, Samia, *Egyptian Writers between History and Fiction* (Cairo, 1994)

Mellini, Peter, *Sir Eldon Gorst: The Overshadowed Proconsul* (Stanford, 1977)

Mengin, Felix, *Histoire de l'Egypte sous le gouvernement de Mohammed-Aly*, 2 vols. (Paris, 1823)

Mingana, A., *Catalogue of the Arabic Manuscripts in the John Rylands Library, Manchester* (Manchester, 1934)

Mirel, Pierre, *L'Egypte des ruptures* (Paris, 1982)

Misr lil misriyyin: mi'at amm ala al-thawra al-'urabiyyin (Cairo, 1981)

Mitchell, Richard, *The Society of the Muslim Brothers* (London, 1969)

Mitchell, Timothy, *Colonising Egypt* (Cambridge, 1988)

"The Invention and Reinvention of the Egyptian Peasant," *International Journal of Middle East Studies*, 22 (1990)

Mohammed Ahmed, Jamal, *The Intellectual Origins of Egyptian Nationalism* (London, 1960)

Moor, Ed de, *Un oiseau de cage* (Amsterdam, 1991)

Moore, C., *Images of Development: Egyptian Engineers in Search of Industry* (Cambridge, 1980)

Moreh, Shmuel, "Reputed Autographs of 'Abd al-Rahman al-Jabarti and Related Problems," *Bulletin of the School of Oriental and African Studies*, 28 (1965)

Modern Arabic Poetry 1830–1970 (Leiden, 1976)

Live Theatre and Dramatic Literature in the Medieval Arab World (Edinburgh, 1992)

Munier, Henri, *Tables de la description de l'Egypte, suivies d'une bibliographie sur l'expédition française de Bonaparte* (Cairo, 1943)

A-Nabulsi, 'Abdul Ghani, *al-Haqiqa wal majaz fi al-rihla ila bilad al-sham wa misr wal-hijaz* (Cairo, 1986)

al-Nahel, Galal H., *The Judicial Administration of Ottoman Egypt in the Seventeenth Century* (Minneapolis and Chicago, 1979)

al-Naqqash, Salim, *Misr lil-misriyyin*, vols. IV–IX (Alexandria, 1884)

Niblock, Timothy, "The Egyptian Experience in Regional Perspective: Internal Factors and Economic Liberalisation in the Arab World," in Louis Blin (ed.), *L'économie égyptienne: libéralisation et insertion dans le marché mondial* (Paris, 1993)

Nour, Riza, "L'histoire du croissant," *Revue de turcologie*, 1 (1933)

Nusus yamaniyah 'an al-hamlah al-faransiya ala misr: nusus mukhtarah min al-makhtutah al-yamaniyah (Sana'a, 1975)

Ostle, Robin, introduction to *Egyptian Earth*, trans. Desmond Stewart (London, 1992)

"The Romantic Poets," in Badawi (ed.), *Modern Arabic Literature*

"Modern Egyptian Renaissance Man," *Bulletin of the School of Oriental and African Studies*, 57 (1994)

Owen, E. R. J., *Cotton and the Egyptian Economy, 1820–1914: A Study in Trade and Development* (Oxford, 1969)

The Middle East in the World Economy 1800–1914 (London and New York, 1981)

"Large Landowners, Agricultural Progress and the State in Egypt, 1800–1970: An Overview with Many Questions," in Alan Richards (ed.), *Food, States, and Peasants: Analyses of the Agrarian Question in the Middle East* (Boulder, 1986)

State, Power and Politics in the Making of the Modern Middle East (London and New York, 1992)

Panzac, Daniel, "The Population of Egypt in the Nineteenth Century," *Asian and African Studies*, 21/1 (March 1987)

Peirce, Leslie P., *The Imperial Harem: Gender and Sovereignty in the Ottoman Empire* (New York and Oxford, 1993)

Penzer, N. M., *The Harem* (London, 1936)

Peres, Henri, "L'Institut d'Egypte et l'œuvre de Bonaparte jugés par deux historiens arabes contemporains," *Arabica*, 4 (1957)

Peters, Rudolph, "The Battered Dervishes of Bab Zuwayla: A Religious Riot in Eighteenth-century Cairo," in Nehemia Levtzion and John O. Voll (eds.), *Eighteenth-century Renewal and Reform in Islam* (Syracuse, 1987)

Petry, Carl, *Twilight of Majesty: The Reigns of the Mamluk Sultans al-Ashraf Qaytbay and Qansuh al-Ghawri in Egypt* (Seattle and London, 1993)

Phelps, William, "Political Journalism in the 'Urabi Revolt," Ph.D. thesis, University of Michigan, 1978

Philipp, Thomas, *The Syrians in Egypt, 1725–1795* (Stuttgart, 1985)

"The French and the French Revolution in the Works of al-Jabarti," in Crecelius (ed.), *Eighteenth-century Egypt*

Piterberg, Gabriel, "The Formation of an Ottoman Egyptian Elite in the Eighteenth Century," *International Journal of Middle East Studies*, 22 (1990)

Poliak, A. N., "Some Notes on the Feudal System of the Mamluks," *Journal of the Royal Asiatic Society* (1937)

Poonawala, Ismail I., "The Evolution of al-Gabarti's Historical Thinking as Reflected in the *Muzhir* and the *'Aja'ib*," *Arabica*, 15 (1968)

Porath, Yehoshua, *In Search of Arab Unity 1930–1945* (London, 1986)

al-Qaddal, Muhammad Said, *al-Mahdiyya wa al-habasha* (Beirut, 1992)

Qindil al-Baqli, Muhammad, *Abtal al-muqawamah al-sha'abiyah li'l-hamla al-faransiya fi misr* (Cairo, n.d.)

Rabie, Hasanayn, "The Size and Value of the Iqta' in Egypt, 564–741/1169–1341," in Michael Cook (ed.), *Studies in the Economic History of the Middle East* (Oxford, 1970)

Rafi'i, 'Abd al-Rahman, *Asr isma'il*, 2nd ed., 2 vols. (Cairo, 1948)

al-Za'im ahmad 'urabi, 2nd ed. (Cairo, 1952)

al-Thawra al-'urabiyya wa al-ihtilal al-injlizi, 3rd ed. (Cairo, 1966)

Asr muhammad ʿali (Cairo, 1989)
Rafiq, ʿAbd al-Karim, *Bilad al-sham wa misr: 1516–1798* (Damascus, 1968)
Ramadan, ʿAbd al-ʿAziz, "Social Significance of the ʿUrabi Revolution," Groupe
    de recherches et d'études sur le Proche-Orient, *L'Egypte du XIXᵉ siècle*
    (Paris, 1982)
Raymond, André, "Quartiers et mouvements populaires au Caire au XVIIIᵉ
    siècle," in Holt (ed.), *Political and Social Change*
    Artisans et commerçants au Caire au XVIIIᵉ siècle (Damascus, 1974)
    "The Ottoman Conquest and the Development of the Great Arab Towns,"
    International Journal of Turkish Studies, 1/1 (1979–80)
    "The Economic Crisis of Egypt in the Eighteenth Century," in A. L. Udovich
    (ed.), *The Islamic Middle East 700–1900* (Princeton, 1981)
    "L'impact de la pénétration européenne sur l'économie de l'Egypte au XVIIIᵉ
    siècle," *Annales islamologiques*, 18 (1982)
    "L'architecture dans les pays arabes à l'époque ottomane," in Robert Mantran
    (ed.), *Histoire de l'empire ottoman* (Paris, 1989)
    "L'activité architecturale au Caire à l'époque ottomane (1517–1798),"
    Annales islamologiques, 25 (1990)
    "The Opuscule of Shaykh ʿAli al-Shadhili: A Source for the History of the
    1711 Crisis in Cairo," in Crecelius (ed.), *Eighteenth-century Egypt*
    Le Caire (Paris, 1993)
    *Le Caire des Janissaires: L'apogée de la ville ottomane sous ʿAbd al-Rahman
    Katkhuda* (Paris, 1995)
Reid, Donald Malcolm, *Cairo University and the Making of Modern Egypt*
    (Cambridge, 1990)
Reimer, Michael J., "Social Change in Alexandria, 1850–1882," *International
    Journal of Middle East Studies*, 20 (1988)
Rejwan, Nissim, *Nasserist Ideology: Its Exponents and Critics* (New York,
    1974)
Riad, Hassan, *L'Egypte nassérine* (Paris, 1964)
Richmond, J. C. B., *Egypt: 1789–1952* (New York, 1977)
Rida, Muhammad Rashid, *Ta'rikh al-ustadh al-imam al-shaykh muhammad
    ʿabduh*, vol. I (Cairo, 1931)
Rivlin, Helen B., *The Agricultural Policy of Muhammad Ali in Egypt*
    (Cambridge, MA, 1961)
Robinson, Ronald and Gallagher, John, *Africa and the Victorians* (London,
    1961; 2nd ed. 1981)
Roussillon, Alain, "Développement et justice social dans une économie sous
    perfusion: les enjeux des subventions en Egypte," *Annuaire de l'Afrique du
    Nord*, 23 (1984)
    "Islam, islamisme et démocratie: recomposition du champ politique en
    Egypte," *Peuples méditerranéens*, 41–42 (October 1987–March 1988)
    *Sociétés islamiques de placements de fonds et "ouverture économique": les
    voies islamiques du néolibéralisme en Egypte*, Dossiers du CEDEJ 3 (1988)
    "Entre al-jihâd et al-Rayyân: bilan de l'islamisme égyptien," *Maghreb-
    Machrek*, 127 (January–March 1990)
    "Changer la société par le *jihâd*: 'sédition confessionnelle' et attentats contre le

tourisme: rhétoriques de la violence qualifiée d'islamique en Egypte," in Ricardo Bocco and Mohammad Reza Djalili (eds.), *Moyen-Orient fin de siècle: migrations, démocratisations, médiations: enjeux locaux et internationaux, à paraître aux PUF* (September 1994)

Royal Institute of International Affairs, *Great Britain and Egypt 1914–1951* (London, 1952)

Rugh, William A., *The Arab Press* (London, 1979)

Sabry, Muhammad, *La genèse de l'esprit national égyptien, 1863–1882* (Paris, 1924)

Sa'd, Sadiq, *Mushkilat al-fallah* (Cairo, 1945)

Safran, Nadav, *Egypt in Search of Political Community* (Cambridge, MA, 1961)

Said, Edward, *Orientalism* (New York, 1979)

al-Sa'id, Rif'at, *al-Asas al-ijtima'i li l-thawra al-'urabiyya* (Cairo, 1967)

Salim, Muhammad Latifa, *al-Quwwa al-ijtima'iyya fi al-thawra al-'urabiyya* (Cairo, 1981)

Sami, Amin, *Taqwim al-nil wa asr muhammad 'ali* (Cairo, 1928)

Sayyid Ahmad, Nabil 'Abd al-Hamid, *al-Nashat al-iqtisadi li'l-ajanib wa athruhu fi al-mujtama al-misri, min sanat 1922 ila sanat 1952* (Cairo, 1982)

Schölch, Alexander, *Ägypten den Ägyptern! Die politische und gesellschaftliche Krise der Jahre 1878–1882 in Ägypten* (Zurich, 1972), trans. as *Egypt for the Egyptians! The Sociopolitical Crisis in Egypt, 1878–1882* (London, 1981)

"The Formation of a Peripheral State: Egypt 1854–1882," *L'Egypte au XIXe siècle*

Schweitzer, G., *Emin Pasha, his Life and Work* (London, 1898)

Serjeant, R. B., "The Coastal Population of Socotra," in Brian Doe (ed. and comp.), *Socotra: Island of Tranquility* (London, 1992)

Shaw, Stanford J., *The Financial and Administrative Organization and Development of Ottoman Egypt, 1517–1798* (Princeton, 1962)

Between Old and New: The Ottoman Empire under Sultan Selim III, 1789–1807 (Cambridge, MA, 1971)

The History of the Ottoman Empire and Modern Turkey, vol. II, *Reform, Revolution and Republic, 1808–1975* (Cambridge, 1977)

Shaw, Stanford J. (ed.), *Ottoman Egypt in the Age of the French Revolution* (Cambridge, MA, 1964)

al-Shayyal, Jamal al-Din, *Tarikh al-tarjama wa'l haraka al-thaqafiyya fi asr muhammad 'ali* (Cairo, 1951)

"Some Aspects of Intellectual and Social Life in Eighteenth-century Egypt," in Holt (ed.), *Political and Social Change*

Shibayka, Mekki, *al-Sudan fi qarn* (Cairo, 1957)

"The Expansionist Movement of Khedive Isma'il to the Lakes," in Yusuf Fadl Hasan (ed.), *Sudan in Africa* (Khartoum, 1971)

al-Shinawi, 'Abd al-'Aziz, *'Umar makram: al-muqawamah al-sha'biyya* (Cairo, 1967)

al-Shirbini, Yusuf, *Hazz al-quhuf* (Bulaq, 1274 AH)

Shukri, M. F., *al-Hukm al-misri fil sudan 1820–1885* (Cairo, 1948)

Misr wa al-sudan (Cairo, 1958)

Shuqayr, N., *Gughrafiat wa ta'rikh al-sudan*, 2nd ed. (Beirut, 1967)

Siddiq, Muhammad, review of Badawi, *Modern Arabic Literature* in *Journal of Arabic Literature*, 26 (1995)

Silvera, Alain, "Bonaparte and Talleyrand. The Origins of the French Expedition to Egypt in 1798," *American Journal of Arabic Studies*, 3 (1975)

Smith, Charles, "4 February 1942: Its Causes and its Influences in Egyptian Politics," *International Journal of Middle East Studies*, 10/4 (November 1979)

Smith, I. R., *The Emin Pasha Relief Expedition 1886–1890* (Oxford, 1972)

Somekh, S., "The Neo-classical Arabic Poets," in Badawi (ed.), *Modern Arabic Literature*

Sorby, Karol, "The Struggle between Great Britain and France to Influence the Character of Government in Egypt, 1801–1803," *Asian and African Studies* (Bratislava), 22 (1986)

"Decline of Mamluks' Power in Egypt (1803–1804)," *Asian and African Studies* (Bratislava), 23 (1988)

"Egypt – The Last Phase of Political Anarchy, 1804–1805," *Asian and African Studies* (Bratislava) 24 (1989)

el-Soroughy, M. M., "Egyptian Historiography of Napoleon Bonaparte in the Twentieth Century," *al-Majallah al-tarikhiyya al-misriyyah*, 20 (1973)

Springborg, Robert, *Mubarak's Egypt: Fragmentation of the Political Order* (Boulder and London, 1989)

Starkey, Paul, *From the Ivory Tower: A Critical Study of Tawfiq al-Hakim* (London, 1987)

"From the City of the Dead to Liberation Square," *Journal of Arabic Literature*, 24 (1993)

Stetkevych, Jaroslav, *The Modern Arabic Literary Language* (Chicago, 1970)

Stripling, G. W. F., *The Ottoman Turks and the Arabs, 1511–1574* (Urbana, 1942)

Sureyya, Mehmet, *Sijill-i 'osmani*, 4 vols. (Istanbul, 1308 AH)

al-Suruji, Muhammad Mahmud, *al-Jaysh al-misri fi al-qarn al-tasi 'ashar* (Cairo, 1967)

Taha, Samir Muhammad, *Ahmad 'urabi wa dawruhu fi al-hayah al-siyasiyya al-misriyya* (Cairo, 1986)

al-Tawil, Tawfiq, *al-Tasawwuf fi misr ibban al-asr al-'uthmani*, 2 vols. (Cairo, 1938, 1988)

Temperley, H. W. V., *England and the Near East* (London, 1964)

Terry, Janice, *The Wafd 1919–1952* (London, 1982)

The Thousand and One Nights, ed. and trans. Muhsin Mahdi (Leiden, 1984)

Tignor, Robert L., *Modernization and British Colonial Rule in Egypt, 1882–1914* (Princeton, 1966)

"Bank Misr and Foreign Capitalism," *International Journal of Middle East Studies*, 8/2 (1977)

"The Economic Activities of Foreigners in Egypt: 1920–1950: From Millet to Haute Bourgeoisie," *Comparative Studies in Society and History*, 22 (1980)

State, Private Enterprise, and Economic Change in Egypt, 1918–1952 (Princeton, 1984)

Egyptian Textiles and British Capital, 1930–1956 (Cairo, 1989)

Toledano, Ehud R., *State and Society in Mid-nineteenth-century Egypt* (Cambridge, 1990)

"The Emergence of Ottoman-Local Elites in the Middle East and North Africa, 17th–19th Centuries," in I Pappé and M. Ma'oz (eds.), *Essays in Honour of Albert Hourani* (Oxford and London, 1996)

Tuchscherer, Michel, "Le pèlerinage de l'émir Sulayman Gawis al-Qazdugli, sirdar de la caravane de al Mekke en 1739," *Annales islamologiques*, 24 (1988)

Tucker, Judith, *Women in Nineteenth-century Egypt* (Cambridge, 1985)

Tusun, Umar, *Butulah al-urtah al-sudaniyyah al-misriyyah fi harb al-maksik* (Alexandria, 1933)

al-Ba'athat al-'ilmiyya fi ahd muhammad 'ali thumma fi ahdayy 'abbas al-awwal wa sa'id (Alexandria, 1934)

'Urabi, Ahmad, *Mudhakkirat 'urabi: kashf al-sitar an sirr al-asrar fi al-nahda al-misriyya al-mashhura bi l-thawrah al-'urabiyya*, 2 vols. (Cairo, 1953)

Uzuncarsili, I. H., *Mekke-i mukerreme emirleri* (Ankara, 1972)

Vatikiotis, P. J., *The Modern History of Egypt: From Muhammad Ali to Mubarak* (Baltimore and London, 1969; 4th ed. Baltimore 1991)

Nasser and his Generation (London, 1978)

Vitalis, Robert, *When Capitalists Collide: Business Conflict and the End of Empire in Egypt* (Berkeley, 1995)

Wafi, Muhammad 'Abd al-Karim, *Yusuf basha al-qaramanli wa al-hamlah al-faransiya ala misr* (Tripoli, 1984)

Walz, Terrence, *Trade between Egypt and Bilad as-Sudan: 1700–1820* (Cairo, 1978)

Waqf 'abdul rahman katkhuda, no. 940, archives of the ministry of waqfs, Cairo (dated 1157 AH and 1190 AH)

Warburg, Gabriel, "The 'three-legged stool': Lampson, Faruq, and Nahhas, 1936–1944," in Gabriel Warburg, *Egypt and the Sudan* (London, 1985)

Waterbury, John, *Egypt: Burdens of the Past, Options for the Future* (Bloomington, 1978)

The Egypt of Nasser and Sadat: The Political Economy of Two Regimes (Princeton, 1983)

Wavell, Viscount, *Allenby in Egypt* (London, 1943)

Wilkinson, John G., *Modern Egypt and Thebes*, 2 vols. (London, 1843)

Williams, John Alden, "The Monuments of Ottoman Cairo," in *Colloque international sur l'histoire du Caire* (Grafenhainichen, 1972)

Wilmington, Martin W., *The Middle East Supply Centre* (Albany, 1971)

Winter, Michael, "The Writings of Abd al-Wahhab Ash Sha'rani: A Sufi Source for the Social and Intellectual Life of Sixteenth-century Egypt," Ph.D. thesis, University of California, 1972

"Turks, Arabs, and Mamluks in the Army of Ottoman Egypt," *Wiener Zeitschrift für die Kunde des Morgenlandes*, 72 (1980)

Society and Religion in Early Ottoman Egypt: Studies in the Writings of Abd al-Wahhab al-Sharani (New Brunswick, 1982)

Egyptian Society under Ottoman Rule, 1517–1798 (London and New York, 1992)

Youssef, Hassan, "The Democratic Experience in Egypt, 1923–1952," in Ali Hillal Dessouki (ed.), *Democracy in Egypt*, Cairo Papers in Social Science (Cairo, 1978)

Yunus, ʿAbdul Hamid, *Khiyal al-Dhill* (Cairo, 1994)

Yusuf, Muhammad Sabri, *Dur al-mutassawifa fi tarikh misr fil ʿasr al-ʿuthmani* (Cairo, 1994)

Zayid, Mahmud, *Egypt's Struggle for Independence* (Beirut, 1965)

Zetland, Marquess of, *Lord Cromer* (London, 1932)

Zidan, Jurji, *Tarikh adab al-lugha al-ʿarabiyya*, 4 vols. (Cairo, n.d.)

Zilfi, Madeline C., *The Politics of Piety: The Ottoman Ulema in the Post-classical Age, 1500–1800* (Minneapolis and Chicago, 1988)

Zygulski, Zdzislaw, Jr., *Ottoman Art in the Service of the Empire* (New York, 1992)

INDEX

>-<

447